S0-BHE-211

Death Sentences in Missouri, 1803–2005

ALSO BY HARRIET C. FRAZIER

*Runaway and Freed Missouri Slaves and
Those Who Helped Them, 1763–1865*
(McFarland, 2004)

Slavery and Crime in Missouri, 1773–1865
(McFarland, 2001)

Death Sentences in Missouri, 1803–2005

A History and Comprehensive Registry of Legal Executions, Pardons, and Commutations

HARRIET C. FRAZIER

HV
8694
.F73
2006
West

McFarland & Company, Inc., Publishers
Jefferson, North Carolina, and London

LIBRARY OF CONGRESS CATALOGUING-IN-PUBLICATION DATA

Frazier, Harriet C.
Death sentences in Missouri, 1803–2005 :
a history and comprehensive registry of legal executions,
pardons, and commutations / Harriet C. Frazier.
p.   cm.
Includes bibliographical references and index.

ISBN-13: 978-0-7864-2719-2
ISBN-10: 0-7864-2719-1 (softcover : 50# alkaline paper) ∞

1. Capital punishment — Missouri — History.
I. Title.
HV8694.F73   2006   364.6609778 — dc22   2006017638

British Library cataloguing data are available

©2006 Harriet C. Frazier. All rights reserved

*No part of this book may be reproduced or transmitted in any form
or by any means, electronic or mechanical, including photocopying
or recording, or by any information storage and retrieval system,
without permission in writing from the publisher.*

Cover photograph: Triple hanging, Jefferson City jail, June 27, 1907
(*St. Louis Globe-Democrat* Archives, St. Louis Mercantile Library,
University of Missouri–St. Louis)

Manufactured in the United States of America

McFarland & Company, Inc., Publishers
Box 611, Jefferson, North Carolina 28640
www.mcfarlandpub.com

To the memory of
Justice Harry Blackmun,
who got it right

Acknowledgments

My thanks begin with remembering two decisions which the Central Missouri State University (CMSU) Library made at my request. In 1989 it purchased the Missouri files of Watt Espy, Headland, AL. In 1993 it bought a multi-reeled microfilm edition of the *Register of Inmates, Missouri State Penitentiary, 1836–1931.* To Nancy Littlejohn goes the credit for these purchases. Without these aids, it is unlikely this book would exist. Among the other past and present librarians at CMSU who aided me on numerous occasions are Doris Brookshier, Pat Downing, Lori Fitterling, Joyce Larson, Linda Medaris, Wanda Moore, Patty Morrison, and Naomi Williamson.

The Western Missouri Manuscript Collection at the University of Missouri, Columbia, and the University of Missouri, Kansas City, are thanked for the use of documents such as various Missouri governors' pardon papers.

At the Missouri State Historical Society, Columbia, Laurel Boechman has assisted me over the longest period of time. She has always been there when I needed her. I made a number of trips to Columbia to read stories about executions in this organization's superb newspaper collection. For the last newspaper stories I needed Laurel Boechman gave me Laura Crane's name, and Mrs. Crane found the remaining accounts of hangings in Missouri I had not earlier obtained.

Janice Schultz, manager of the Genealogy and Local History Branch of Mid-Continent Public Library, Independence, Missouri, has helped me on numerous occasions. Among her other admirable qualities, she is persistent. Her staff is also thanked for its help.

At the Kansas City Public Library, Kansas City, Missouri, I thank Dennis Halbin, Judy Klamm, and Bill Osment for answering numerous reference questions. Mary Beveridge, Missouri Valley Room, located the dates and places of the jails of Kansas City; this was not an easy task. Theresa Pacheco and Linda Wilson are thanked for their assistance with this library's extensive newspaper collection, including both paper and microfilm. At the Johnson County Public Library, Overland Park, Kansas, Linda Riehle insured that I had the numerous newspaper stories I needed in late stages of researching and writing this book.

Shelly Croteau and Patricia Luebbert, archivists at the Missouri State Archives, Jefferson City, are due my profound thanks. This office was especially important in helping me confirm the specifics of various Missouri governors' commutations and pardons of persons earlier sentenced to death.

The library at the law school from which I graduated, University of Missouri–Kansas

City, was a constant source of information for me during the years in which I researched and wrote this book. Three reference librarians are especially thanked for their assistance: Kathleen Hall, Lawrence MacLachlan, and Nancy Morgan. Lawrence MacLachlan assisted me over the longest period of time.

Alice Evans researched relevant military records for me at the National Archives, Washington, D.C. She did a wonderful job. My chapter on "Union Army Executions, 1861–1865" would be skimpy without her able assistance.

The staff of the Family History Center, Church of Jesus Christ of Latter-Day Saints, Independence, obtained microfilm for me of all the extant transcripts of capital cases which arose from Union Army courts-martial in Missouri.

Janet Wray, public information officer, U.S. Army, Fort Leavenworth, Kansas, made inquiries of experts any time I had a question she could not immediately answer. She always answered my e-mails; I owe her a huge debt of gratitude.

The following persons are thanked: John Fougere, public information officer, Missouri Department of Corrections, for answering many of my e-mail questions regarding prison inmates throughout Missouri; Stephanie Schmidt, Records, Fulton Reception and Diagnostic Center, for locating information about those whose death sentences were commuted between the 1930s and the late 1950s, Sandra Bender, St. Louis City Vital Records, for answering numerous e-mail questions regarding the race and age of the executed and their victims, and Daniel Hearn for date-checking Appendix I.

Jeff Blackman was my constant source of assistance regarding the use of the computer. Without his help, I cannot imagine writing this book on it and doing the research I did on such a piece of equipment.

Dorothy McKinley, Susan Ray, and John and Rosemary Schmiedeler are also thanked. Among much else, they often listened as I talked about what I was then working on.

Finally, I thank Tom Fairclough, Sioux City, Iowa, for reading this book, and doing so with amazing accuracy, knowledge, wit, and wisdom. The mistakes that remain are mine alone.

Contents

List of Illustrations

Preface

My research for this book began after I met Watt Espy in the late 1980s. At that time and from a ramshackle house in the town of Headland, Alabama, he was the premier collector of the specifics of the death penalty in America. I did all my early work with his help. His co-authorship of *Executions in the United States, 1608–1987: The Espy File* is regularly cited in books and on websites about the death penalty in America. Espy has vigorously disavowed that book because of its inaccuracies. For example, its Appendix B states that 285 executions took place in Missouri between 1800 and 1987. This figure is at least 178 fewer than I eventually confirmed between these dates. Some of the 285 counted as executions in Missouri in *The Espy File* took place in other states.

Because there are no statewide collected records of the executed in Missouri until 1938, it was essential that someone begin the collection process. The ravages of the Civil War, fires, floods, tornadoes, and general neglect have long since obliterated any chance that information can be collected in its entirety by going to the courthouse of the counties wherein execution(s) occurred. Among other approaches Espy used to amass information about the death penalty, he wrote to the librarian in the county seat of the approximately 4,000 counties in the United States, asking if there had been any executions in the county. If so, would the librarian send him any available information on those put to death pursuant to a court order in that specific county. Many librarians took the time and energy to send him information, but a number of others did not.

Espy neither assembled nor analyzed the death penalty laws of Spain, the United States, the state of Missouri, the Civil War–era Union Army, or the U.S. Army. All these authorities obtained death sentences here. Likewise, he never collected information about commutations and pardons of those sentenced to death. He also excluded from his files courts' reversals of convictions which prevented executions. I discuss the numerous laws of capital punishment, commutations and pardons of those condemned to death, and many appellate courts' reversals of death sentences in Missouri. Without this additional information, all one is left with is a list of those who died pursuant to court order. A list is not an account of what happened. I include all known death sentences obtained in Missouri which resulted in executions through 2005, including three carried out in Kansas.

In September 1989 and at my request, the library at my school, Central Missouri State University, bought Espy's individual files of the executed in Missouri, in so far as he had located this information. Without any exceptions, I checked every name. I fleshed out Espy's Missouri files by adding information to almost all of them and also collected approximately 100 Missouri executions he had missed. In the process I was able to establish or correct many demographics, primarily pertaining to race and age. I discarded some hangings which probably occurred, but not in this state. I worked on the project for a number of years before I began writing about it.

Chapter 1, "Indians and Whites, 1803–1864," recounts French, Spanish, United States, and state of Missouri capital punishment laws. It discusses Indians in Spanish and American courts when charged with death penalty offenses. Its focus is the white men executed here under *civil* authority from the earliest extant record through the Civil War years.

Chapter 2, "Slaves and Free Blacks, 1826–1863," assumes that the earliest records of Negroes being put to death are lost. In 1720, slaves were brought here, and there were many more death penalty statutes for them than whites. No reliable record of the execution of a slave survives until 1826. Between 1826 and 1863, approximately 50 executions of persons of color, mostly those in bondage, can be and are documented.

Chapter 3, "Union Army Executions, 1861–1865," discusses 89 death sentences carried out by military authority here. The first took place on July 14, 1861, and the last on June 2, 1865. At least four times, the Union military attempted to put 10 or more men and boys to death on the same day. In Kirksville and for the offense of parole violation, 15 died simultaneous firing squad deaths in 1862.

Chapter 4, "Black and White, 1866–1889," recounts the initial slowness of court-ordered death sentences; mostly those put to death were lynched. By the 1880s both lynchings and executions reached numbers never previously attained.

Chapter 5, "The Nineties and Beyond, 1890–1907," discusses the most violent time in Missouri, the 1890s. During it there were more executions than at any time in the state's history. There were many hangings here in the early twentieth century.

Chapter 6, "Reform Attempts and the Continuation of Hangings, 1907–1937," explains that in March 1907, the jury was finally allowed to find the accused was guilty of first degree murder and assess his punishment as life in prison; earlier its only option with a finding of first degree murder was a death sentence. The Missouri General Assembly abolished capital punishment effective April 13, 1917, and then reinstated it effective July 9, 1919. Clearly, capital punishment lost favor. Approximately three times as many persons were executed between the years 1866 and 1906 than between 1907 and 1937.

Chapter 7, "The Gas Chamber, 1938–1965," concerns the first officially kept records on this state's executions. They began when the gas chamber at the prison in Jefferson City replaced the gallows in the county seat of the conviction of the crime. In all 39 persons were gassed to death in this prison facility.

Chapter 8, "Juveniles, 1838–1993," discusses those persons put to death who were less than 18 years of age at the time of the crime(s). The first known in Missouri was Slave Mary, aged 13 or 14 when she committed murder; she was hanged in 1838. The last was Frederick Lashley, aged 17 at the time of his crime; he was executed in 1993. Because slave births were usually not recorded, it is difficult to know any slave's exact age. As a result, I have confirmed that somewhere between 14 and 18 juveniles have been executed in Missouri. In 2003, the Missouri Supreme Court held in the case of death-sentenced Christopher Simmons, aged 17 at the time of his crime, that the execution of juveniles violates the 8th and the 14th Amendments' prohibition against cruel and unusual punishments. In 2005, the U.S. Supreme Court upheld the Missouri court.

Chapter 9, "Rape, 1891–1964," begins by noting that Missouri was the only slave state on the eve of the Civil War that did not execute a black male found guilty of the rape of a white female. This state first enacted a death penalty for rape in 1879, and it executed its first convicted rapist, in a case that was never appealed, in 1891. It put to death its last man convicted of rape in 1964.

Chapter 10, "Women, 1834–1953," deals with the paucity of females put to death in Missouri. Though the state hanged at least four slave females, perhaps six, its execution of free women, white or black, includes only two, both white. One of the two was a federal case wherein the U.S. borrowed Missouri's gas chamber. A number of women have been sentenced to death in Missouri, but only two can be confirmed as executed.

Chapter 11, "Pardons and Commutations, 1803–1999," begins with the Spanish in 1803 pardoning four death-sentenced Indians, and ends in 1999 when at the request of Pope John Paul, then visiting the state, Governor Mel Carnahan commuted Darrell Mease's death sentence to life imprisonment. Historically, one governor commuted a death sentence and a successor-governor pardoned a death-sentenced individual. Approximately 129 known death-sentenced persons have not been executed here as the result of executive clemency of a Spanish governor-general, a U.S. president, and a Missouri governor.

Chapter 12, "Appellate Court Reversals, 1818–2005," begins with the Superior Court of Missouri Territory reversing the death sentence of Slave Elijah. It ends with the Supreme Court of Missouri, on July 28, 2003, ordering the immediate release from prison of Joe Amrine, sentenced to death in 1986 for a crime he did not commit. Printed copies of all of this state's appellate reversals of death sentences are to be found in any accredited law school in the United States. As a result of their ready availability, many are not discussed.

Chapter 13, "Lethal Injection, 1989–2005," describes Missouri's increasing pace of executions. Because information is accessible both on the web and in any accredited law school library regarding those whom the state of Missouri has lethally injected, not all are discussed, but all are included in Appendix 1. Multiple efforts to end capital punishment here continue, but Missouri, as of this writing, remains a capital punishment state. It is fourth in the country in the numbers executed in modern times (1989 to 2005).

Map of Missouri Counties

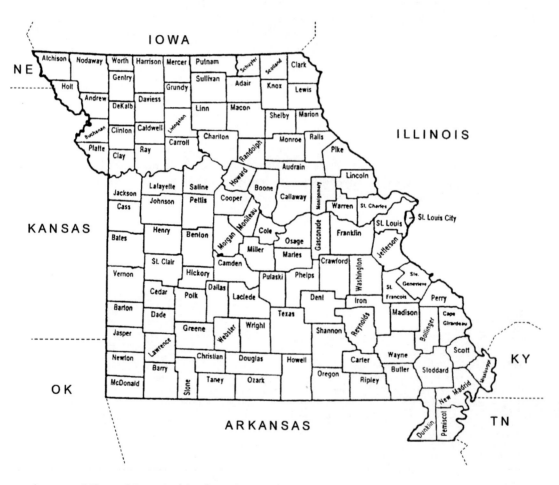

(courtesy Missouri State Archives).

Executions and Commutations
or Pardons in
Missouri, 1803–2005

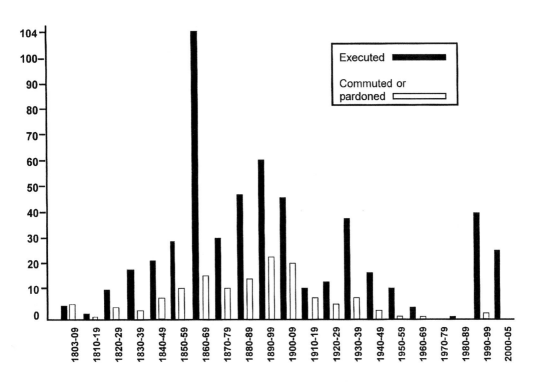

Decade by decade chart of capital punishment in Missouri.

1

Indians and Whites, 1803–1864

One would assume from looking at the law books that what is now Missouri was a hotbed of capital punishment. The apparent enthusiasm for the death penalty here can be found in numerous statutes which its rulers enacted for the governance of the region. The French, this state's first white inhabitants, adopted "Edict Concerning Negro Slaves in Louisiana," a 55-article document, in 1724 in the city of New Orleans. It was often termed "Le Code Noir" or "The Black Code." Five of its articles allowed or required a death sentence for offending blacks. Article 13 prohibited the assemblage of slaves belonging to different masters, and it permitted capital punishment for repeat offenders. Article 27 mandated it the first time any slave struck her owner, her owner's spouse, or their children either on the victim's face or so as to bruise or draw blood. Both articles 28 and 29 contain a death penalty provision. The former allowed it to punish "the abuse and violence which shall be offered by slaves to free persons," and the latter permitted its imposition when slaves or free Negroes stole certain livestock, such as "horses, mares, mules, oxen, or cows." Article 32 dealt with the crime of *marronnage*, i.e. slaves running from the service of their owners, and it imposed a death sentence the third time any unsuccessful runaway was captured.[1] The French also punished attempted poisonings, murders, and rapes with death. Likewise, counterfeiting notes of the Royal Treasury was a capital offense.

When Spain began its ownership of Louisiana in the 1760s the first Spanish governor-general, Alejandro O'Reilly, required that the 1724 "Edict Concerning the Negro Slaves in Louisiana" be translated into Spanish and strictly enforced. None of O'Reilly's successor governor-generals repealed it, and theoretically it remained in effect for the first seven months of American ownership of the Purchase. O'Reilly also put in place his own Ordinances and Instructions, and they contained some stunning death penalty crimes. Section V (9) "Of Punishments," required that "he who shall be guilty of fornication ... with a professed nun ... shall be punished with death," and (15) provided that "He who shall steal the sacred vessels in a holy place shall suffer death." Less exotic offenses under Spanish governance of Louisiana are also contained in O'Reilly's Ordinances and Instructions. Section V (1) required that "insurrection against the King or the state ... shall be punished with death"; (4) "he who shall ravish [rape] a girl, a married woman, or a widow of reputable character, shall suffer death"; and (5) "he who shall commit willful murder ... shall suffer death."[2]

When the United States bought Louisiana, in due course, American law replaced French and Spanish. The statutes governing Missouri derived from two sources. "The Law Respecting Slaves" came from Virginia. Its sections 14 (slave conspiracy to rebel, make insurrection, or murder; 15 (slave preparation, exhibition, or administration of any medicine); 21 (stealing or selling a free person for a slave); and 22 (stealing a slave) all mandated a death sentence.[3] The law for the general population, including slaves, came from the Northwest Territory. Its capital crimes included treason, murder, arson, and if an innocent person died, burglary and robbery.[4] Both the Virginia and Northwest Territory statutes were signed into Missouri law in 1804. Had not these specific laws been adopted here, the Federal Crimes Act of 1790 would have supplied a jurisdictional basis for the United States to prosecute murder in territorial Missouri. It provided, among much else, that any person or person who shall commit "willful murder ... in any ... place or district ... under the sole and exclusive jurisdiction of the United States ... being thereof convicted shall suffer death."[5]

When we look to the actual use of the death penalty, the record is far less detailed. Probably the French executed some persons in what is now Missouri, but there are no extant records of any use this colonial nation made of capital punishment here.

Some record, much of it meager, survives of four investigated homicides from Spanish rule of Missouri. It should be noted that there was no authority in any one of Upper Louisiana's five districts either to try a capital case or to sentence any person to death. The potentially capital cases which have survived from Spanish control of Missouri were sent to New Orleans for disposition. In this city, the governor-general made his decision, but only after he secured the permission of the captain-general in Cuba could any execution be carried out. The Spanish colonial authorities kept a tight rein on their use of the death penalty.

The earlier known potentially capital case arose in St. Genevieve District in 1779 when the soldier-perpetrator, Pedro Armand Riault, artillery gunner, stabbed Slave Quierry after his victim, who had been offered a puff of the perpetrator's pipe, happened to break it. The stabber was probably drunk because, as Derek Kerr explains, the incident took place "at a seemingly friendly riverside gathering."[6] Nothing more is known of the incident because this soldier's case would have been tried in the governor's military court, and these records were returned to Spain. The second arose when Jean-Baptiste Lacroix, an overseer of Jean Datchurut (one of the wealthiest slaveholders in Missouri), struck Slave Tacouä in the head with a pickax at the work site after the slave continued to answer a question that the overseer had asked him about the salt furnace not already being lit. When the perpetrator told the victim to keep silent and the victim resumed his explanation, the white man felled the black with a single blow to his head. An eyewitness to this event, Slave Jacob, testified at the inquest regarding what he had witnessed the previous day, November 15, 1783. The town surgeon's inspection of the victim's head injury corroborated Jacob's account of this killing, and the surgeon ruled that the slave came to his death as a result of Lacroix's blow to his head.[7] Though Spanish law made the murder of a slave a criminal offense, there is no record of any punishment. The overseer who struck and killed Slave Tacouä was still a member of the owner's household four years later.[8]

The third surviving record of a homicide from Spanish rule of Missouri also arose in St. Genevieve District when Slave Philippe, owned by one prominent resident, killed a slave belonging to another prominent resident, Jean-Baptiste Valle. The lieutenant governor of Upper Louisiana, Don Zenon Trudeau, conducted the investigation of this crime, and the evidence of the perpetrator's guilt was strong. His owner testified against him, and the accused admitted his guilt. Early in 1795 both the prisoner, Slave Philippe, and a detailed record of the evidence against him were sent to Governor-General Carondelet in New Orleans for trial and sentencing. As time passed, reports began reaching Ste. Genevieve from New Orleans that the prisoner, Philippe, was conducting himself as a free man. In the spring of 1798 Louis Caron, Philippe's owner, received a bill from the New Orleans jailer asking that he remit the cost of living expenses for his supposedly imprisoned slave. On behalf of the slaveholder, the St. Genevieve post commandant and other prominent persons wrote an indignant letter to the governor-general of Louisiana, explaining that the miscarriage of justice in Philippe's case would, in the future, discourage owners from reporting any criminal violations by their slaves.[9] Though the outcome of this case is unknown, Derek Kerr's research of Spanish Louisiana judicial records leads him to conclude that "slaves convicted of murdering their masters always received the death penalty, but the murder of another slave often secured a milder sentence."[10]

The fourth known intentional killing under Spanish rule of Missouri survives from New Madrid District. It involves another demographic mix of crime and punishment, and its record is the most detailed. It is also the best known example of Spain's disposition of a criminal case here; several histories of Missouri mention it.[11] The most complete account is a compilation of documents by a descendant of the victim, David Trotter, a white man born in Augusta County, Virginia c. 1755 and a veteran of the American Revolutionary War. In 1790 he was listed in the census of Bourbon County, Kentucky, and by 1801 he, his wife, about eight children, and five or six slaves had migrated to New Madrid District. By 1802 Trotter was living in Grand Prairie, and he was permitted to sell liquor to Indians. He died in January 1802 at the hands of at least five Mascoutens to whom he refused to supply intoxicants. The perpetrators shot, hacked, scalped, and stabbed Trotter and burned his house and its contents.

Unlike the known murders in Ste. Genevieve District, wherein all the victims were slaves, in the Trotter case the perpetrators were Indians and the victim a white man. The former commandant of New Madrid District, Charles Delassus, had been appointed lieutenant governor of Upper Louisiana in 1799, and he occupied the position through the remainder of Spanish rule of Missouri. He ordered a large number of militia, the main group of which came from New Orleans, to search for the perpetrators of this crime. After a six week expedition to New Madrid, the troops captured five of the Indian suspects, and the defendants were sent to New Orleans for trial and sentencing. In this city, the governor-general found Tewanaye, the prime culprit, guilty of David Trotter's murder and condemned him to death by firing squad. Spanish troops returned the convicted Indian from New Orleans to New Madrid by boat. In preparation for his execution, the Spanish assembled a formidable show of force in the event of an Indian uprising. Lieutenant Governor Delassus's troops were joined in New Madrid by 184 trained militia from Cape Girardeau District. These men had been promised grants of land if they agreed to act as guards during Tewanaye's execution. Amidst this impressive assemblage of Spanish military might, the first known execution in Missouri under the authority of white men took place on January 3, 1803, in New Madrid District when a firing squad shot to death the Mascouten Indian Tewanaye. It is significant that only one of the Trotter murderers was executed. In accord with the Spanish policy of keeping the peace with various Indian tribes, the other four Indian prisoners were released to their chiefs; in effect, they were pardoned. White men's lenient treatment of Indian offenders in their courts is a recurrent theme in these early cases. Their nations might need one Indian tribe or another as allies in their wars against various belligerent European powers.

Though there would be no further use of the firing squad in any execution in Missouri until the Union army employed it during the Civil War, the four known homicides in Missouri which Spanish authorities at least investigated set the pattern for what would most likely result in an execution and what would not under American rule. If the perpetrator was an Indian, the authorities were unlikely to carry out a death sentence. If the perpetrator was not an Indian, then the race of the victim(s), not that of the perpetrator(s), was key to whether or not the county sheriff would officiate at a hanging. A white victim of a crime most likely resulted in an executed perpetrator.

Just as the Spanish took considerable care when it came to the actual use of the death penalty, so likewise did the American governing authority. From the first uses of American rule here until 1821, the year the state of Missouri was admitted to the Union, all crimes were offenses against the United States of America. The rules governing these cases were a combination of the criminal provisions contained in the first ten amendments to the U.S. Constitution, i.e. the Bill of Rights, and statutes passed by the federal congresses and the territorial legislatures. In 1790 the first U.S. Congress enacted and President Washington signed major legislation dealing with crime and punishment. Among other features, the law specified that "The manner of inflicting the punishment of death shall be by hanging the person convicted by the neck until dead," and it also allowed the judge to add an additional sentence of dissection after death as punishment for condemned murderers.[12] In 1808 the Missouri territorial legislation enacted an identical provision for executed felons: "The court ... may at their [sic] discretion add to the judgement, that the body of such offender [after death by hanging] shall be delivered to a surgeon for dissection."[13] The state of Missouri continued these practices. In 1835 the Missouri General Assembly permitted dissection under three circumstances. The next-of-kin of the deceased might give permission; those donors were few. Otherwise the only legal source of cadavers was "the body of the criminal executed for crime, or the body of a slave with the consent of his owner."[14]

However, before there could be a cadaver as a result of an execution, the governing authority had to obtain a conviction which carried a death sentence. The first Congress did not make this an easy task for the prosecution. It specified that in capital cases upon the request of the accused, the judge was "authorized and required immediately ... to assign such person counsel, not exceeding two ... to whom such counsel shall have free access at all seasonable hours."[15] As a further restriction on the meting out of death sentences in Missouri, between 1804 and 1807 and after 1810 until statehood, capital cases were heard only by the Superior Court, also known as the General Court. The only way any attorney in the territory became a judge on the Superior Court was by his appointment to it by the president of the United States. During the years 1808 and 1810, another court heard all potentially capital cases. Its chief judge was the presiding judge of the Superior or General Court, and he assigned himself and justices of the Court of Common Pleas to sit as judges on courts known as oyer and terminer. All such courts had two judges at a minimum. They could be convened in any of the districts which then made up the territory of Upper Louisiana: Cape Girardeau, New Madrid, St. Charles, St. Louis, and Ste. Genevieve.[16] These many restrictions on the implementation of the death penalty during Missouri's territorial years help explain the paucity of executions.

At the start of American rule here, the law provided that any person convicted of arson receive a death sentence. However, the only extant mention of a person arrested for this crime was a slave. In 1805 the prominent St. Louis resident, Pierre Chouteau, wrote Henry Dearborn, President Jefferson's secretary of war, that one of his slaves, an unnamed female, had "lighted the fire with her own hands which devoured my property and that of the United States which I had." He assured Dearborn that he had not mistreated the accused slave, but because of her vengeance, the major part of his wealth was destroyed. The Frenchman continued his letter with this ominous comment, "She is now in prison and the first general court will decide her fate."[17] Because neither court records are extant from this early time period nor was there a single newspaper in Missouri until 1808, there is no way to confirm that she was found guilty of arson, sentenced to death, and executed in St. Louis in 1805. Probably, she was.

Other early capital cases concern Indians as defendants; only two, both in 1806, are known to have been executed. Most likely they were the Kickapoos, Quabesca and Ouifumcaka, found guilty in June 1806 in St. Louis of killing a white man on December 30, 1805, near the Osage River. They were hanged on June 10, 1806, in St. Louis; Lewis and Clark heard the news of this then recent execution on September 3, 1806, from a Scotch trader, James Aird, whom they met as they were traveling downriver to St. Louis, he upriver. Aird had left St. Louis earlier that summer. Their journal records, "2 Indians had been hung in St. Louis and several others in jale [jail]."[18] A third Kickapoo, Hononquise, was also implicated in this 1805 murder, but President Jefferson's policy toward Indians disallowed the execution of any more than two for the killing of one white man. As a result, James Wilkinson, the governor of the territory, pardoned Hononquise.[19]

In May 1808 two Ioway Indians, White Cloud and Mera Naute, returned the fire of two French traders, Joseph Thibault and Joseph Marchal, and the white men died in the gun battle. The trial of the Indians for murder in a St. Louis court in August 1808 ended when the judges decided that they had no jurisdiction in the case because the crime, if it were a crime, was committed beyond the boundary line, as established by treaty between the United States and the Indians. The defendants were sent back to jail, and the governor, Meriwether Lewis, decided to keep them there until the advice of the president might be obtained.[20] According to Foley, in July 1809 and after languishing in jail many months, the two Ioway prisoners managed to escape. They rejoined their tribe, and no further effort to recapture them was undertaken. The new acting governor, Frederick Bates, believed that "the transgression ought to be forgotten as silently as possible."[21] Meanwhile another fatal encounter in 1807 between a Sac warrior, Little Crow, and a white trader, Antoine Le Page, in St. Charles County had resulted in the death of the white man, and this Indian's trial was also held in St. Louis in July 1809. During the proceedings, the Sac was tried, found guilty, and sentenced to hang. However, Governor Lewis granted Little Crow a reprieve in order to avoid favoring one Indian tribe over another since the case involving the Ioway defendants was then unsettled. Once the other Indians escaped, the U.S. Indian agent, William Clark, recommended that President Madison pardon Little Crow. On February 25, 1810, the president granted him a "full, free and entire pardon ... in consideration of the promises of the said Sac tribe to behave well in the future."[22]

Missouri's then only newspaper mentions that three other Indians, members of the important Osage tribe, were brought to St. Louis in May 1814 by Pierre Chouteau, Indian Agent, and charged with the murder of Elijah Eastwood at the headwaters of the Gasconade River. As the party made its way to St. Louis, it was accompanied by 12 or 15 warriors and a chief. The Indians' account of the victim being shot and killed suggests that his death was accidental. The white men were dressed "like the southern Indians (their enemies)," and they only discovered the deceased was a white man after his death. As a result they did not scalp him.[23] A subsequent newspaper story confirms that the three Osage prisoners were committed to jail to wait their trial, but the editor predicted that their fate would be the same as that of the Ioways and the Sac Indians, that is, they would avoid punishment.[24] There is no record of precisely what happened to them, but it is not credible that, if they were hanged in St. Louis the newspaper chose not to cover their gallows death. Therefore, they were gotten out of the criminal justice system by some event other than their execution.

Expectedly, no white man was hanged for the murder of an Indian. At the time of intense conflict between native tribes and soldiers and settlers in Missouri, both grand and petit juries were composed entirely of white men. They would neither indict an accused white nor find him guilty when an Indian died at his hands. Routinely, Indians came to their deaths because white men gunned them down in the wilderness. However, so important was it to American interests to keep the peace with various tribes that Jefferson's Secretary of War, Henry Dearborn, established a payment ranging from $100 to $200 for the wrongful death of each Indian, and this sum was standard payment to each tribe which lost a member at the hands of Americans.[25]

When an Indian committed a crime against another Indian, as Prucha notes, "offenses among Indians within the tribe or nation were tribal matters that were to be handled by the tribe and were of no concern to the United States government."[26] An Indian was apprehended for a crime against a white either because his own tribal members turned him over to civil authorities or a search party of American soldiers found, transported, and deposited him in a jail. Once the accused was in custody, as Prucha clarifies, "Indians who committed crimes against whites in peace time received scrupulously fair treatment from the United States government."[27] When he was put on trial — and extant documentation suggests that at least nine Indians were tried for the murder of white men in St. Louis prior to statehood years — only two, both on June 10, 1806, were executed. Foley explains the matter in these terms: "Although sporadic Indian outbursts would continue in the territory, ... a steady influx of new settlers ... accomplished what inadequate military forces had been unable to achieve. After 1815 the Indian threat steadily declined in Missouri."[28] No Indian appears to have been sentenced to death in Missouri once it became a state in 1821, or if he or she were tried, no known record of the case exists.

What happened to persons of color, principally slaves, who committed capital offenses will be discussed in the next chapter. An examination of the known executions of white persons under civil authority in Missouri from the earliest records through the Civil War years makes clear that all committed crimes against white persons. When a white committed a potentially capital crime against a Negro, either slave or free, the perpetrator went unpunished. Joseph Leblond was an exception. He was arrested and briefly detained when the dead body of a free black woman, "Negress Sylvia," was found in his house in St. Louis shortly before November 16, 1813. The coroner conducted an inquest, and his jurors determined that "the said Sylvia came to her death from mortification caused by irons placed on her legs by said Joseph Leblond." Although death by gangrene of the legs that results from another's chaining could never arise without the perpetrator's immense malice aforethought toward his helpless victim, four of Leblond's friends, relatives, or business associates were permitted to post a $4,000 recognizance bond to guarantee his court appearance. On November 20, 1813, and on the order of John B.C. Lucas, an appointee of President Jefferson as a judge of the General Court, Leblond was released on bail. When his case was heard, the General Court fined him $500 and sentenced him to two months in jail. This extraordinarily light punishment was the most severe that could be located in any antebellum Missouri record when a white committed a crime against a person of color.[29]

During the territorial period, or prior to 1821, four cases are known of the arrest, trial, and execution of a perpetrator of murder under the authority of the United States. One arose in St. Louis, two in Ste. Genevieve, and one in New Madrid. Some contemporary documentation, much of it slight, exists regarding three of these four cases. The earliest, *U.S.* v. *John Long Jr.*, contains the most complete detail.

We pick up Long's legal difficulties as early as June 5, 1809, when his stepfather, George

Gordon, gave testimony before a Justice of the Peace for Bonhomme Township, St. Louis District, "that from threats and menaces ... he the said deponent is afraid that John Long will take his life or do him other injury."[30] Slightly over two weeks later on June 26, 1809, John Long Jr. shot and killed his stepfather on the victim's doorstep after lying in wait for him. Among other motives for the murder, the stepson resented the transfer of his father's property after his father's death, as the law required, to his mother's second husband, George Gordon. On August 14 the grand jury indicted Long for murder, and on August 21 he went on trial for his life before a jury at a special term of the court of oyer and terminer. He was tried before Chief Judge John B.C. Lucas, Silas Bent, and August Chouteau. The jury found him guilty, and the judges sentenced him to death by hanging. The stepson was hanged for the murder of his stepfather in the town of St. Louis on September 16, 1809. The newspaper covered his death in considerable detail:

> John Long, the younger, was executed here last Saturday, pursuant to his sentence, for the murder of George Gordon. The unfortunate criminal was attended by clergymen of several denominations; he appeared much interested in his eternal welfare; his supplications to the throne of grace was [*sic*] earnest and sincere; his fortitude and intrepidity was [*sic*] deserving a better fate; on the way to the gallows he sang several psalms with his spiritual attendants; he mounted the cart and examined the rope very unconcerned, and asked the sheriff if he did not think it necessary to tie his hands, and requested him to give him a cap, having it on, he placed his hands behind to be tied exclaiming, "well I hope Jesus Christ will have mercy on me." A chair was placed on the cart to raise him to the rope; he assisted the executioner to adjust it, and without waiting for the cart's being drawn off he kicked the chair from him and launched him into eternity.[31]

Long's hanging was the first execution in Missouri for which a contemporary newspaper account exists. As a result, writers of Missouri history assume it was the first gallows death here under American authority. This is inaccurate. We know that two Indians were hanged in 1806, and most likely one or more persons, probably slaves, were hanged pursuant to court order in St. Louis District or another of Upper Louisiana's four other districts in the slightly less than five years which elapsed between the first implementation of American law in October 1804 and John Long Jr.'s execution in September 1809.

Three additional hangings, all of white men for the murder, in all probability, of other white persons, also took place during Missouri's territorial period. We know about the race of the perpetrator (s) and the victim(s) in these homicides because persons of color, including those that were free, were invariably identified throughout most of Missouri's history with reference to their race in both court documents and newspaper accounts, i.e. victims such as "Negress Sylvia." Therefore, any person identified by both Christian and surname without any reference to race can reasonably be assumed to have been white.

On May 25, 1810, in Ste. Genevieve District, Peter Johnson murdered a John Spear or a John Space. Thanks to the survival of an advertisement of "100 dollars Reward" which ran in the territory's only newspaper in June 1810, we know that the perpetrator was a native of Holland, served some time in the British Navy, was 5'5" or 6", spoke broken English, had tattoos on his arms, including the picture of a ship, was much "pock marked and very liable to get drunk."[32] When Peter Johnson was taken into custody and tried, he was represented as federal law required by two attorneys. A court of oyer and terminer was convened on July 9, 1810, at which sat five judges. The jury found him guilty, and the judges sentenced him both to hang on August 3, 1810, and his body to be dissected after death. A Dr. Walter Fenwick obtained Johnson's cadaver to carry out the second part of the sentence.[33] Dissection following sentence of death was one of few ways medical men of the time in the Midwest managed to study human anatomy first hand.

A second capital case arose in Ste. Genevieve District when Charles Heath stabbed Hugh Jones with a knife in the left side, and he died from his injury two days later on December 23, 1811. A jury at a court of oyer and terminer, at which Chief Judge John B.C. Lucas and his associate, Joseph Pratt, presided, found the perpetrator guilty on January 11, 1812, and the next day the judges sentenced him to be hanged on March 9, 1812 between the hours of 10:00 a.m. and 2:00 p.m. Judge Lucas concluded his remarks to the condemned, Charles Heath, "Your country has so far done you justice: I leave it to other ministers to offer you other comforts. I mean those that are to be found in religion."[34] According to the county history, the sentence of death by hanging was carried out on March 9, 1812, in a section of Ste. Genevieve known as Academy Hill.[35]

No contemporary documentation exists for what was probably the last hanging pursuant to court order during the territorial period. It took place in New Madrid County, and apart from the names of the condemned, William Gordon, the sheriff John H. Walker, the circuit attorney Greer W. Davis, and the prosecuting authority the United States, the county history contains only this detail: "The circumstances of the murder have been forgotten, and the papers relating to the case destroyed."[36] Because as early as 1804 Missouri law required that any applicant to practice law have attained the age of 21 years and according to the county history, Greer W. Davis (1799–1878) moved from Mercer County, Kentucky to Missouri in 1818,[37] he probably prosecuted the case in behalf of the United States in 1820. Its date cannot be fixed with any greater certainty.

Despite the fact that Missouri was not officially admitted to the Union until August 1821, the first death sentence under state authority was carried out in April 1821. The Missouri Constitution, written in St. Louis by 41 elected delegates from 15 counties between June 12 and July 19, 1820, among many other grants of authority, gave the circuit court of each county jurisdiction in all criminal cases. Madison County tried its first capital case the next year. It arose on December 13, 1820, when 19-year-old John Duncan, a Virginia native raised in Tennessee, went to the home of John B. Stephens in Madison County on the pretext of purchasing a tract of land from him. The would-be buyer lured his victim into the woods where he first shot him and then finished him off by cutting his throat. Duncan then returned to the Stephens residence where he killed three additional persons: the wife and mother, Elizabeth Stephens, and two of the couple's sons, an infant and a 10-year-old. The motive for Duncan's mass killing was robbery. He took from his victims $68. Thanks to the survival of two Stephens daughters and a son, the murders were quickly known, the perpetrator was immediately pursued, and soon captured, and when taken into custody, he confessed. He was then placed in the Madison County jail in Fredericktown.

The grand jury returned four indictments for murder against Duncan; he was arraigned and tried by a jury at the March 1821 term of court. It found him guilty on all counts and assessed his punishment at death. The circuit court judge sentenced him to be hanged by the neck until dead on April 5, 1821, between 11:00 a.m. and 2:00 p.m. The day before his death, Duncan gave a lengthy account of his crimes from his jail cell. The persons who recorded his detailed explanation of his wicked deeds, probably county officials, subsequently made it available to the public. It survives in both a St. Charles and a St. Louis newspaper published shortly after Duncan's death.[38] Another St. Louis newspaper identifies Duncan as "the first person who has suffered the punishment of death under the laws of the state government, and it is on that account particularly that we mention the fact."[39] Unlike John Long Jr.'s execution, no contemporary account of which identifies it as the first under the authority of the United States, the hanging of John Duncan on April 5, 1821 *was* the first under Missouri law.

In addition to the first execution under state law, there are 11 known additional capital cases between 1824 and 1834 involving white perpetrators which resulted in the execution of the accused. Federal and territorial law had mandated hanging as the only allowable means of executing under the authority of the United States, and the state of Missouri continued the use of the county seat gallows until the gas chamber replaced the noose in 1938. The state also followed federal law when it provided the accused two attorneys in any capital case. We turn now to an examination of these earliest statehood cases which followed Duncan's.

All but one involved white male perpetrators. The exception was a woman, and she will be discussed in Chapter 10, "Women." Three involved a change of venue. The crimes took place in Ralls County (tried in Boone), Randolph (tried in Howard), and Scott (tried in Cape Girardeau). All additional proceedings took place in the county of the crime: Howard, Lafayette, and St. Louis. This last mentioned locale was the scene of four executions during this early period. Because of the large population of the city of St. Louis, this county remained the scene of more hangings than any other.

Only two of these early cases were appealed to the Supreme Court of Missouri, a three-member appellate body which the Missouri Constitutional Convention established in 1820. Until the General Assembly changed the law by allowing the election of judges to this court in 1851,[40] the governor appointed its members. Its first death penalty decision is a brief pedestrian piece of writing. It upholds two contested rulings of the trial judge: (1) his allowing a substitute juror to be discharged because of the illness of his wife (the juror's absence never affected the number of the original panel) and (2) his refusal to sequester the witnesses so they could not hear the testimony of other witnesses. Though the reported case contains mention that the charge was murder, one must read carefully in order to realize it upholds a death sentence: "The judgment of the Circuit Court is affirmed, ... and it is remanded to the Circuit Court to be carried into effect."[41] The second appellate decision in a capital case contains no more facts of the crime than the first; its issues, among others, deal with juror summons. On appeal, the Court affirmed the murder conviction, and it contains this specific detail, "Sentence of death was pronounced."[42]

All but one of these cases, wife murder, involve solo adult perpetrators of solo adult white male victims; robbery is a motive in some and quarreling brought on by liquor in others. Most have contemporary newspaper coverage, but were there none in one of them, the sheriff's appeal in a civil suit against Howard County for its inadequate reimbursements for his hanging expenses provides the documentation for Sheriff Ford's execution of two persons, one of them Jacob Stuart in 1830.[43]

Soldiers figure in three of these early hangings. James Jenkins, a discharged British soldier, murdered his wife, Sinah Jenkins, an adulteress living with an American soldier at Jefferson Barracks in St. Louis. The outraged husband attempted to end his own life after he killed his wife, but he lived to be tried August 23, 1830, and executed September 29, 1830.[44] Two U.S. soldiers stationed at Jefferson Barracks in St. Louis were hanged for the murder of another U.S. soldier in separate and unrelated cases in 1827 and 1829. Despite newspaper mention that Hugh King, whose victim was a sergeant, was guarded by U.S. troops en route to the gallows,[45] his trial and punishment and that of Michael Cogland for the murder of a corporal, were civil, not military matters. The state of Missouri, not the U.S. Army, tried the accused in St. Louis Circuit Court, and the sheriff of St. Louis County officiated at their hangings. Soldier King's appeal was the first capital case decided by the Supreme Court of Missouri.[46]

The authority of the state to prosecute military personnel derived from the Ninth

Congress in 1806 adopting Articles of War for the governance of the armies of the United States. Among many other provisions, these articles mandated that "when any soldier shall be accused of a capital crime," his commanding officer was required" upon application duly made ... to deliver over such accused person ... to the Civil Magistrate." Until their modification during the Civil War, the army's 1806 military code remained in effect until its revision in 1873.[47]

The Laws of the Northwest Territory, first adopted in 1788, prohibited only two types of killing: murder and manslaughter, and this classification continued in Missouri's criminal code in 1804. As a result, all homicide prosecutions here between 1809 and 1834 were for the crime of murder, with no distinction of degree. When a jury could not reach a unanimous verdict on this charge, it might settle for a manslaughter conviction. In one early St. Louis case, this subjected the accused to a fine of $300 and a two year sentence in the county jail.[48]

In 1835 the law concerning homicide underwent a dramatic change. For the first time in its tenure, the General Assembly decreed:

Every murder which shall be committed by means of poison, or by lying in wait, or by any other kind of wilful, deliberate and premeditated killing or which shall be committed in the perpetration or attempt to perpetrate any arson, rape, robbery, burglary, or other felony shall be deemed murder in the first degree.

All other kinds of murder at common law, not herein declared to be manslaughter, or justifiable or excusable homicide, shall be deemed murder in the second degree.[49]

The division of murder into two degrees became an enduring part of Missouri law. Once enacted, it continues at the present time.

The 1835 statutes specified that the punishment for first degree murder was death and that of second degree, confinement in the penitentiary for not less than 10 years. The legislature could only pass this sweeping revision of the law once plans were well underway for the building of this prison. As early as 1830, the Ways and Means Committee of the Missouri General Assembly was issuing reports on a penitentiary, and by 1833, an act for establishing the prison in Jefferson City had become law. In anticipation that the work would be completed in October 1834 and the building(s) ready soon thereafter to begin receiving inmates,[50] in 1835, the legislature, among much else, split what had previously been the crime of murder into first and second degree. The prison received its first inmates in 1836, and it continued to be a depository for murderers that those in charged wished to punish, but not capitally. For the first years of the penitentiary's existence no known white person was executed in this state. It seems, if ever so briefly, to have become a kinder and gentler place for white offenders, but after slightly more than five years without any executions of free persons (April 4, 1834–May 10, 1839), the court-ordered hanging of Caucasians resumed. However, there are no known white juveniles, i.e. persons less than 18 years of age at the time of their crime(s), capitally punished by civil authority during the antebellum years. The first known executions of white children here were carried out by the Union Army during the Civil War. The state of Missouri began executing Caucasian youth after the surrender at Appomattox.

Between 1838 and 1864, 39 white males were executed under civil authority here; 37 were state cases, two were federal. There would have been a 40th court-ordered execution had a lynch mob not taken over the sheriff's hanging duties.[51] Ten cases involved changes of venue: Boone (tried in Howard), Cass (tried in Lafayette), Clark (tried in Lewis), Henry (tried in Johnson), Perry (tried in St. Francois), Ripley (tried in Oregon), Shannon (tried in Crawford), Taney (tried in Greene), Warren (tried in Franklin), and the most peripatetic of any death penalty case in this book, Lafayette (tried in Jackson and after a reversal of the first hanging sentence by the Missouri Supreme Court, a second change of venue from Lafayette to Henry). All other trials and punishments occurred in the counties of the crime: Bates, Cole, Jackson, Montgomery, Ray, and St. Louis. This last named place accounted for 18 of these hangings. Between 1857 and 1878, no change of venue out of St. Louis County was possible. The legislature passed a special law, applicable only in St. Louis County, which allowed a person charged with a criminal offense a removal of his case only from Criminal to Circuit Court.[52] In other counties, changes of venue continued. Those who got their cases moved out of the county of the crime were overwhelmingly white. This nicety of due process in their behalf was one of several ways they received better treatment than black offenders.

No bright line separates these cases from those decided before the legislature divided homicide into first and second degree. In several, insufficient facts are known about the crime to judge whether or not it contained the necessary elements of first degree murder. For example, in Dodge, alias Vanzandt and Schoen, alias Shawnee, we do not have so much as the names of their victim(s). All we know is that they were hanged in St. Louis July 22, 1853.[53] Most likely they were not partners in a single crime. Likewise, the city of St. Louis was also the scene of Hugh Gallagher's execution. All that we know about his case is that he murdered Mary Ann Cosby on July 4, and he was hanged December 13, 1850 in St. Louis.[54] In other cases, the facts are equally sketchy. A man named Howard was hanged in Boonville (Cooper County), August 13, 1841. The extant newspaper reported only that the first time the cord broke, "and after some delay he was taken up and swung off the second time."[55] Joel Elliott obtained a change of venue when he was charged with the murder of William Smith in Cass County; he was hanged September 10, 1852 in Lexington, Lafayette County.[56] Likewise James M. Nichols' trial for the murder of Lewis Farrel in Henry County in May 1853 resulted in a change of venue to Johnson County. Nichols was hanged in Warrensburg, the seat of Johnson County, June 5, 1857.[57]

In other of these cases, especially those in which the Supreme Court of Missouri wrote lengthy decisions, we know that premeditation was an unlikely factor. In a Ray County case, a shoemaker, Ben White, stabbed a farmer, Martin Adams, with a butcher knife 17 times on Main Street in Richmond in the presence of many witnesses in 1841. In an 1853 Buchanan County case, the death-sentenced man, August Otis Jennings, and three accomplices whipped Edward E. Willard to death over a bad debt. In 1856 in St. Louis, Jacob Neuslein beat his wife, Mary Ann, to death when she refused to cook his breakfast. In all three prosecutions, the accused was found guilty of murder in the first degree. Surely it could be argued in all these cases that once enraged persons commence stabbing, whipping, or beating their victims, it is hard to stop. These cases suggest murder in the second degree or even manslaughter might have been appropriate verdicts. Most likely all three perpetrators were repulsive human beings, and their juries found them guilty of the highest allowable degree of homicide. White's case was not appealed, but the Supreme Court of Missouri affirmed death sentences for Jennings and Neuslein.[58]

In a Montgomery County case, the crime occurred on June 16, 1852, and the perpetrator, John Huting, spent more than three years in the county jail between his trials, his appeal, and the issuance of a court order that he be hanged by the neck until dead. Huting, an emotionally unstable suitor, used a shotgun to fire multiple pellets into the face of his beloved, Caroline Schoten, killing her instantly, because she refused to marry him. The defense was insanity, and at his first trial in April 1853, the jury was hung. Clearly, one or more jurors believed that Huting was of unsound mind at the time of his crime. The

German-speaking defendant was provided an interpreter and two capable attorneys, one of whom, the Honorable John Jameson, attorney for two slaves in unrelated capital cases in Callaway County, was a dogged defender of the accused. Despite a spirited defense, at his second trial in April 1854, the jury found Huting guilty of murder in the first degree. On appeal, Jameson and his co-counsel, argued, among other points, that the lower court gave improper jury instructions concerning the defense of insanity. The Supreme Court of Missouri upheld the refusal of the trial judge to instruct the jury that it must acquit if it has a reasonable doubt as to the insanity of the defendant. The Court cited the rule in an English case, *Regina* v. *McNaghten* (1843): "Where insanity is interposed as a defence to an indictment for an alleged crime, the inquiry is always brought down to the single question of capacity to distinguish between right and wrong, *at the time when the act was done.*[59] The sheriff of Montgomery County hanged Huting in Danville on August 31, 1855. Though governors pardoned several death-sentenced murderers in the antebellum period because they believed them non compos mentis, the Missouri Supreme Court then and later gave little or no relief to those whose defense to a criminal act was insanity.

Another group of offenders whose crimes put them at considerable risk of a death sentence were those who killed law enforcement officers and prison guards. In this inquiry the wholly unexpected is the first Missouri hanging wherein the crime scene was the state penitentiary. The *perpetrator* was a prison guard, Henry Lane, and the *victim*, a 21 or 22-year-old named Henry Coatmire, a German inmate from St. Louis, convicted of grand larceny and sentenced to three years. Coatmire was received at the prison on October 8, 1838, and Lane shot him in the head without provocation some ten months into his sentence on August 12, 1839. This murder is confirmed by both a contemporary newspaper and the Register of Inmates, Missouri State Prison.[60] Lane was tried September 5, 1839, and hanged October 14, 1839, on a public gallows in Jefferson City, county seat of Cole County. Lane's execution did not take place within the prison; nor for almost another century did any other death sentence in this state.

The other prison killing which resulted in a hanging during the antebellum period is the expected. An inmate, William H. Berry, beat an overseer, i.e. a guard, William Bullard, to death with a hammer in June 1841 while he and others were making their getaway from a work detail outside the prison. One newspaper used the escape of the prisoners to criticize the penitentiary for allowing inmates to work outside the physical structure of the prison "in digging cellars, in farming, and in such labors as honest men may be engaged in."[61] However, in due course, Berry and five other escaped prisoners were arrested many miles east of the place of the crime in St. Charles County. The trial and death sentence took place in Jefferson City. Berry was hanged February 10, 1842, and among those who noted his gallows death without ever naming him was George Thompson, the most famous of Missouri's many abolitionist prison inmates. Thompson wrote "one of our number was hung, outside the wall."[62]

Two crime scenes involved murdered law enforcement officers and the subsequent execution of their slayers pursuant to court order before the conclusion of the Civil War. In the first case, Conrad Myers was found guilty of the April 1844 murder of Samuel B. Wingo, sheriff of Shannon County, on a change of venue to Crawford County, and he was put to death in Steelville on May 24, 1844.[63] The second was a burglary in St. Louis the night of December 10, 1861; a policeman, John C. Gilmore, attempted to arrest two men, William Wilson and Joseph Burns. The officer was shot in the process and died of his injuries two weeks later on Christmas Eve. The perpetrators were eventually arrested in Pennsylvania, returned to St. Louis, and tried separately. Wilson was found guilty of first degree murder and executed June 27, 1862. Joseph Burns was found guilty of the same crime in another trial; an appeal was taken from it, and the Missouri Supreme Court affirmed his sentence. Burns was hanged in the city of St. Louis nearly a year after his "confederate," as the newspaper termed Wilson, on May 8, 1863.[64]

This city was also the trial and execution scene of a crime which took place in what was then "Indian Country" or "Unorganized Territory," present-day Rice County, a locale now in the middle of the state of Kansas, approximately 50 miles southwest of Salina and 400 miles west of St. Louis. In 1834 the 23rd Congress passed "An Act to regulate trade and intercourse with the Indian tribes, and to preserve peace on the frontiers." Late in a law concerned almost exclusively with Indians, it assigns "the judicial district of Missouri" to carry the act into effect in lands which now comprise the state of Kansas (sec. 24). Excluding Indian-on-Indian offenses, it used language lifted from the 1790 Federal Crimes Act to establish a statutory basis to prosecute wrongdoing: "That so much of the laws of the United States as provide for the punishment of crimes committed within any place within *the sole and exclusive jurisdiction of the United States* shall be in force in Indian country" (sec. 25). It also allowed the apprehension and transportation of any person or persons who are found within the United States and charged with a violation of the act "to the ... judicial district having jurisdiction" (sec. 26).[65]

Almost nine years later, these provisions were applied to white men from Liberty (Clay County), Missouri. Their involvement in criminal activity began in the early 1840s when the Republic of Texas, then an independent nation, recruited several guerrilla fighters to assist it in its ongoing war with Mexico. Among those who answered the call were John McDaniel and his young brother, David, both of Clay County, Missouri. On or about April 10, 1843, the McDaniels and approximately 13 other gang members were on a trail between Santa Fe and the United States when their paths crossed that of Antonio Jose Chavez, a Santa Fe, Mexico businessman, and five of his employees. The Texas guerrillas informed the Mexicans that they were prisoners of the Republic of Texas. In order to avoid any other persons on the main Santa Fe Trail, John McDaniel detoured the party to present-day Rice County, Kansas. In this place Chavez was shot to death, and the Missourians shared the money found on his body. For reasons never fully explained, John McDaniel permitted the five employees of the murdered Chavez to return to Santa Fe at the same time he and his associates came back to Missouri. By May 1843 they were arrested in Liberty, Clay County; shortly they were turned over to federal authorities.

In September 1843 proceedings against this guerrilla band began in Jefferson City when a federal district court judge, Robert B. Wells, convened a special session to try the case. The lesser figures in it were indicted for crimes such as larceny and illegally organizing a military expedition in the United States. On the more serious charge of murder, Wells set new trial dates in order to give the defendants sufficient time to prepare. On April 1, 1844, Wells and Supreme Court Justice John Catron, who then rode circuit, both presided in St. Louis at a session of the federal court for the District of Missouri. The prosecutor was William M. McPherson, and Edward Bates (later President Lincoln's attorney general), assisted by Uriel Wright, was the lead defense attorney. Three of Chavez's employees were prosecution witnesses and a member of the American party, William Mason, in exchange for charges being dropped against him, also testified for the prosecution that John McDaniel and others murdered Chavez. On April 11, 1844, the jury returned a verdict of murder against John McDaniel, and other juries hearing the evidence against his co-defendants, Thomas Towson, David McDaniel, and Joseph Brown, also came in with murder verdicts against them.

Edward Bates argued for a new trial on grounds that the U.S. Court for the District of Missouri lacked jurisdiction to try a case which occurred in Indian country. However, the judges cobbled together the 1790 Federal Crimes Act and relevant portions of the 1834 Act to Regulate Trade and Intercourse with the Indian Tribes, and they determined that they had jurisdiction and denied Bates' motion for a new trial. On April 27, 1844, Justice Catron sentenced John McDaniel, David McDaniel, and Joseph Brown to hang on June 14, 1844. He spared a fourth member of the guerrilla gang, Thomas Towson, whom the jury had found guilty of murder, on grounds of his mental deficiencies. Soon appeals for executive clemency began to John Tyler, then the tenth U.S. president, who gave a series of reprieves to John McDaniel and Joseph Brown, beginning with his staying the pair's initial death sentence of June 14, 1844. Finally on August 16, 1845, the U.S. Marshall hanged John McDaniel and Joseph Brown in St. Louis on the same county gallows upon which felons condemned to death under state law in St. Louis County were executed. On October 22, 1845, Tyler granted several pardons in the Chavez case, including the death-sentenced younger brother of John, David McDaniel.[66]

Though this Indian country case was not a first degree murder prosecution, the government could have proven it by showing that robbery of the victim was the gang's reason for the homicide in Rice County, Kansas. For good reason, the prosecution is never required to prove motive. Whatever compelled the accused to act as he/she did may not be susceptible to proof. However, the state may be able to prove the reason(s) for the perpetrator's criminal act(s). When it does, it typically puts on evidence of the defendant's motivation in order to strengthen its showing of his/her malice aforethought or premeditation. Perhaps the most frequent motive the prosecution proves in any homicide case is the personal gain of the defendant. Among the 37 hangings of white men which took place under the authority of the state of Missouri between 1835 and 1864, the elements of first degree murder can often be found in either or both the means which the perpetrators used to end the lives of their victims or the material advantage which accrued to the perpetrator as a result of the killing.

George Goster was the hit man in a murder-for-hire of Williamson Hawkins, a wife beater. Rebecca Hawkins, the abused spouse, recruited him for $150. Goster's receipt of this sum together with the manner of this killing, pushing the barrel of his gun through the chinks of a log cabin and shooting his victim to death as he sat by his fireplace, made this a first degree murder prosecution. Goster was hanged in Independence, Jackson County, on May 10, 1839.[67] The fate of Rebecca Hawkins is discussed in Chapter 10.

A man named Johnson was rightly or wrongly identified by the wife of the murdered victim, Major Gabriel Floyd, as one of five men who came to their St. Louis County home at midnight in order to rob them on August 26, 1842. Johnson was found guilty of first degree murder and hanged March 3, 1843, in St. Louis.[68] John C. Lester killed his brother-in-law, King B. Scott, by decoying his 20-year-old victim into the woods and crushing his skull in Lafayette County in June 1845. Lester was married to Scott's sister, and the victim and perpetrator were the only heirs of Scott's mother-in-law, a woman possessing considerable property. After several changes of venue and an appeal to the Missouri Supreme Court, Lester was hanged in Clinton, Henry County, on July 31, 1846.[69] When John Thomas killed Michael Stephen or Stevens, a retired soldier who lived near Jefferson Barracks, the perpetrator's motive was robbery. He was hanged on Duncan Island, city of St. Louis, February 14, 1851.[70]

Edward D. Worrell, a U.S. Army deserter and native of Delaware, murdered Basil H. Gordon, an engineer, some time after January 13, 1856, in Warren County. On a change of venue to Franklin County, the accused was found guilty of first degree murder. His motive was robbery, and his defense was partial insanity. As noted on appeal, his father, a Delaware physician, testified in his son's behalf at trial: "He has been subject to deliria during his whole life; this is not insanity but near kin of it."[71] However, the more compelling evidence was the robbed condition of the dead victim, Gordon. As the Court noted, "His pockets were turned inside out. His watch, his gloves, his horse, saddle-bags, saddle, and bridle were taking by the prisoner. The taking in this case was from the dead body; the murder was committed first."[72] Despite the pleas of his sorrowful father and mother to the governor, Worrell was hanged in Union, Franklin County on June 27, 1857.[73]

The personal gain of the perpetrator may have been more imagined than real. Robert Shehane killed John Merrill on a fishing trip in Ripley County because the murderer believed his victim, a well-dressed man, was wealthy. That the proceeds of the robbery totaled ten cents was irrelevant. On a change of venue to Oregon County, Shehane was tried for first degree murder, sentenced to death, and on appeal, the Supreme Court of Missouri affirmed.[74] He was hanged August 7, 1858.

The prosecution put on evidence of other motives in other murder cases. John Freeman, an ill-tempered drinker whose nose and upper lip were eaten by cancer, killed his father-in-law when the perpetrator's wife left him and returned to her parents. Freeman was tried and hanged in Montgomery County in 1844.[75] Joseph Thorton murdered Joseph Charless, the president of a St. Louis bank, in 1859. Earlier his victim had testified against him on a charge of bank robbery. Though the defendant was acquitted on the bank robbery charge, he revenged himself on a witness against him, Charless. Thorton was tried, found guilty of first degree murder, and hanged in St. Louis on November 11, 1859.[76]

Since the 1835 homicide statute specified that any intentional murder by poisoning was first degree murder, this means of death made the prosecutor's job a relatively easy one when the perpetrator confessed. Dedimus Burr murdered his wife by poisoning her, and he was hanged by the sheriff in Cole County July 8, 1842.[77] George Lamb murdered his wife by drowning her in the Mississippi River; however, twice earlier he had given her strychnine, a highly poisonous, colorless substance. The Missouri Supreme Court affirmed Lamb's death sentence, and he was hanged in St. Louis, June 17, 1859.[78]

During the 1850s the dead bodies of two known executed white men were dissected. Almost certainly there were others. When Willis Washam, killer of his stepson, was hanged in Springfield August 25, 1854, he gave his cadaver to a local physician "for scientific purposes."[79] Shortly before Robert Shehane mounted the gallows in Oregon County on August 7, 1858, the condemned specified in writing, among other matters: "I give my body to Dr. Lewis Griffith of Howell County, Missouri to be dissected this August the 7th, 1858." In return for the favor of Shehane's corpse, the physician supplied the prisoner with a gallon of corn whiskey, and he drank it before his hanging.[80]

The next to last crime tried under civil authority during the Civil War involved 19-year-old William Linville. In July 1863, he and a gang of guerrilla fighters entered the home of the victim's father-in-law, named Burns, in Andrew County. In the process, the homeowner's young son-in-law, a Union Army soldier, Thomas Henry, was shot and killed. Shortly, President Lincoln's troops, then in control of northwest Missouri, took Linville into custody and brought him to St. Joseph, the county seat of Buchanan County. This case did not involve a change of venue from Andrew to Buchanan County. By 1863 and throughout most of the state, no civil courts were functioning; most likely there was no circuit court in Andrew County at this time.

The Union Army commanding officer might have denied his prisoner, William Linville, a civil court hearing at which the legality of his custody could be tested. Nonetheless the Andrew County killer was tried in a civilian court. Judge Silas Woodson, later governor of Missouri, presided at Linville trial in St. Joseph in September 1863. The defendant was found guilty of first degree murder, and the judge sentenced him to death by hanging November 6, 1863. As in Soldier Hugh King's cortege in 1827, a military procession escorted Linville to the gallows. However, the sheriff of Buchanan County was in charge of the next to last execution in Missouri under civil authority during the Civil War years.

The last was that of a Union Army soldier, Valentine Hansen, a German, who had a quarrelsome wife. His landlord, a fellow German and a gunsmith, John Ellig, raised the rent on the Hansens in order to rid himself of the couple. After this falling out, Hansen reported to those in charge that Ellig was a secessionist. Shortly, Hansen shot and killed the gunsmith by, as the newspaper reported, "firing his musket through a window at Ellig,"[81] on a Tuesday evening, April 14, 1863. The victim died the next day. The perpetrator was tried in circuit court in St. Louis, where he was found guilty of first degree murder. His attorney filed an appeal with the Supreme Court of Missouri, but it denied any review. James R. Lackland, judge of the St. Louis Criminal Court, refused the motion to order a new trial, and in March 1864, he sentenced Hansen to be hanged in the city jail in St. Louis on April 16, 1864. This execution was not watched by an overflowing crowd.

The newspaper covering young Linville's 1863 hanging in St. Joseph described it as witnessed by "about 600 persons, including Negroes, boys, girls, women and men."[82] More than 30 years earlier at the day appointed for Samuel Earl's hanging in Columbia, the newspaper reported that "an immense collection of people, of all sexes and of all colors, assembled in the course of the day"[83] to witness the execution of the condemned. Excluding the city of St. Louis, large gallows crowds remained a feature of executions in Missouri until the 1890s. At the St. Louis hanging of Hugh Gallagher in 1850 the newspaper reported the crowd in attendance at between 8,000 and 10,000 persons.[84] Likewise, 10,000 persons attended the 1851 St. Louis hanging of John Thomas.[85] However, by the 1853 execution of Schoen, the St. Louis crowds of witnesses were no more. The newspaper reported that his hanging "was performed privately in the jail yard with comparatively few present. The gallows was erected in the space between the Criminal Court room and the Jail, so that none could see it, but those within the walls of the jail yard."[86] The last hanging in St. Louis under civilian authority during the Civil War years was Valentine Hansen's. The newspaper reported of it that "Not more than a hundred persons were admitted inside the jail-yard to witness the execution. This independent of the guard. Some of the most respectable citizens, including a number of physicians and army officers—invited by the Marshal—were among the spectators."[87] The limitation on witnesses to St. Louis hangings remained a feature of future executions in this city, but privacy at the actual moments of the carrying out of death sentences was not the order of the day elsewhere in the state.

In the course of hearing death penalty appeals from white persons between its first in 1827 and its last prior to the conclusion of the Civil War in 1863, the Supreme Court of Missouri upheld three death sentences prior to 1850, seven in the 1850s, and one in the 1860s. It affirmed and reversed an almost equal number. Its refusals to uphold death sentences will be discussed in Chapter 12, "Appellate Court Reversals, 1818–2005." As the next chapter clarifies, most appeals of death sentences during the antebellum period were not the lot of blacks, slave or free, charged with the commission of a capital offense.

2

Slaves and Free Blacks, 1826–1863

The early records of the execution of slaves and free blacks in what is now Missouri are either lost or badly misplaced. In 1720, a Frenchman, Philip Francois Renault, stopped in San Domingo (Haiti), then a French colony, where he purchased African slaves and brought them to work in the lead mines of the southeastern part of the state.[1] Even had all the new black arrivals been male, and this is unlikely, their co-habitation with the girls and women of various indigenous Indian tribes soon exponentially increased the numbers of those in bondage here. The French and Spanish initially enslaved Indians. Eventually Spain determined that human bondage as it pertained to Indians was not in accord with the pious laws of Spain, and the earlier colonial policy of enslaving Native Americans fell into desuetude.

The General Census of 1800 of Upper Louisiana, which the Spanish enumerated, included 1,191 slaves and 77 free persons of color.[2] In the first American census which included Missouri, that of 1810, Missouri's bondpersons were numbered at 3,011 and free blacks at 607. In the 1820 federal census, slaves had increased to 10,222 and free persons of color decreased to 347. In the 1830 federal census, there were 25,091 bondpersons and 569 free blacks here.[3]

We know that the Spanish, and probably before them the French, compensated slave owners when their human property was executed. There are extant records of the payments which the Spanish made to the owners of hanged slaves in what is now the state of Louisiana,[4] but whether or not Spain's governor-general paid the owners of condemned bondpersons here is unknown. The records, if there were any, are missing. That the earliest slave owners experienced no financial loss when their human properties were executed increases the likelihood that Spain, and before this nation, France, shipped some troublesome properties to New Orleans for purposes of executing them. Unlike Ste. Genevieve District's Slave Philippe, these unknown bondpersons were found guilty of capital crimes and put to death in this capital city prior to the Purchase.

Given the likelihood of owner compensation for executed slaves under colonial powers prior to American ownership of Missouri, the sizeable numbers of African-Americans here, and the abundance of crimes which made persons of color death-eligible under the French, the Spanish, and the Americans, it is not possible that no slaves or free blacks were capitally punished in Missouri prior to 1826. Since the state was settled as was the country from east to west, it is not believable that Boonville (Cooper County), a locale 145 miles west of St. Louis, was the site of the *first* execution of a slave. It is the place of the first *known* execution of a slave. It is equally unlikely that Liberty (Clay County), 247 miles west of St. Louis, was the site of the second court-ordered hanging of a slave. There must have been earlier executions of slaves in Missouri many miles east of Clay and Cooper counties.

The first extant record of any Missouri slave being tried on capital charges arose in St. Louis in 1818. Slave Elijah, together with Gabriel, a Negro boy, was indicted for conspiracy to commit murder. Elijah admitted that he put a large quantity of arsenic in the sausage which Rebecca, a slave woman, prepared for their mistress, Mrs. Mary N. Smith. The indictment handed up charged:

> Elijah, a negro man ... not having the fear of God before his eyes, but being moved and seduced by the instigation of the devil [on February 15, 1818] ... together with one Gabriel a negro ... and others whose names are to the jurors unknown did plot and conspire feloniously, willfully, and of their malice aforethought to kill and murder one Mary N. Smith.[5]

The arsenic-laced sausage did not kill Mrs. Smith, because she appeared as a prosecution witness against Elijah both before the grand jury that indicted him and at his trial in August 1818.

The judges of the Superior Court, as the law required, appointed Elijah's lawyers. They were Horatio Cozens and David Barton. Cozens (1795–1826) was the lesser known; he arrived in St. Louis in 1817, and he died in 1826. The famous man was Barton (1793–1837), a Tennessee native who by 1812 was a practicing attorney in St. Louis. Prior to his defending Elijah on capital charges, different territorial governors had already appointed him attorney general of Missouri Territory (1813–1814) and the first judge of the Northern Circuit of the territory (1815–1817).

As expected and despite the expertise of Elijah's defense team, an undated verdict in his case survives, "We the jury do find the prisoner Elijah, a Black man, Guilty as in the manner and form stated in this indictment." However, on September 7, 1818, the Superior Court heard the defense attorneys' arguments to stay the jury's guilty verdict and give Elijah a new trial. Among a number of other reasons advanced, Barton argued that a plurality of persons was necessary for the commission of conspiracy and Elijah acted alone. He convinced the three members of the Superior Court (John B.C. Lucas, President Jefferson's appointee; Silas Bent, President Madison's; and Alexander Stuart, President Monroe's) that Elijah deserved a new trial. The circuit attorney stated he would not further prosecute the case. As a result, Elijah was released from the St. Louis County jail on or shortly after September 7, 1818.

At the time of Elijah's and Gabriel's indictment, there were no territorial statutes in Missouri applicable to white defendants who committed the same act as did the slave(s). If the victim of a white poisoner survived, no capital charges could be brought against the perpetrator. We can be certain that David Barton thought the law was unfair. Two years after getting a death sentence against his slave client reversed, he had an opportunity to level the playing field for other persons of color when they were charged with capital crimes. It occurred when Barton became a delegate to the Missouri Constitutional Convention which met in St. Louis the summer of 1820. Shoemaker wrote of then 36-year-old Barton, "His vote on a constitutional measure was practically identical with the adoption or rejection of that measure.[6] This Tennessee native was not only one of St. Louis County's eight delegates; he was also chosen president of the convention. When Missouri was admitted to the Union as the 24th state, the General Assembly chose him as one of this state's first U.S. senators.

We can only guess what experiences Barton and other delegates such as Edward Bates had of slavery and capital punishment to compel them to include a detailed enumeration of slave rights in criminal cases in the 1820 Missouri Constitution. Most slave-state constitutions were silent on the subject. Expectedly, Missouri guaranteed those in bondage the same rights in criminal cases that the federal government required: the right to a jury trial in any criminal case and the assistance of counsel in one that was capital. The 1820 Constitution also decreed, "a slave convicted of a capital offense shall suffer the same degree of punishment and no other, that would be inflicted on a free white person for a like offence."[7] If state law permitted slaves to hang for conspiring to murder, it must also require the execution of white persons convicted of the same offense.

The language of the prohibition was clear. There could be no distinction between slave and free white in capital cases. Likewise, those in bondage could not be sentenced to be burned to death as they had been earlier in places such as Illinois and Virginia. Just two months before Missouri's 41 delegates met in St. Louis to write this state's first constitution, at least two Missouri newspapers, one in St. Louis County and the other in Cape Girardeau County, carried front-page reprints of an out-of-state news item about the execution of Slave Ephraim and Slave Sam for the murder of their master in Edgefield District, South Carolina. As the account made clear, these slaves' separate death warrants required Sam's death by fire and Ephraim's hanging and decapitation so that his head could be publicly displayed. The newspapers explained: "It must be a horrid ... sight to see a human being in the flames.... From some of the spectators we learned that it was a scene which transfixed in breathless horror almost everyone who witnessed it."[8] Almost certainly, most of the delegates read this newspaper account. They had all lived under the civility of federal statutory and constitutional law during Missouri's territorial period, and they showed their disdain for cruel slave capital punishment when they prohibited any distinction in the method of executing slave and free white.

Under Barton's leadership, the 1820 Missouri Constitution also required that within five years after its adoption the General Assembly eliminate capital offense distinctions between slave and free white and that it continue to revise, digest, and promulgate both civil and criminal statutes every 10 years. In marked contrast and as late as the mid–1850s, the Commonwealth of Virginia had 73 capital offenses for slaves, and only one of them, first degree murder, was also a capital offense for a free white. No such egregious denial of the equal protection of the law existed in Missouri. The legislature systematically eliminated capital offense distinctions between slave and white in 1825 and 1835 largely by phrasing the various laws as prohibitions affecting "every person." What the framers of Missouri's constitution earlier saw and heard about the capital punishment of slaves in what later became the state of Missouri is a mystery. We have no idea, but we know that it must have been considerably more than their acquaintance with Slave Elijah's brush with the law. We do know that they saw to it, at least in theory, that slaves received the same treatment as whites in capital cases. Equally important, the constitution these men wrote in 1820 lasted as long as did the peculiar institution here.

This document also created the circuit courts of the state, and it gave its judges the power to hear all civil and criminal cases, including those that were capital. No longer did presidential appointees serve as the only judges in death penalty cases. Under these circumstances, one would expect the number of those sentenced to hang to rise, especially when the defendants were blacks. After 1830, all trial or circuit judges were elected, and the franchise throughout slavery was limited to white males. Likewise, this demographic group was the only one eligible for jury service. Blacks on juries here were rare in the late

19th and early 20th centuries. As for women, white or black, none was permitted to sit on any jury in Missouri until a new constitution gave them that right in 1945.

The approximate number of bondpersons and free blacks put to death pursuant to court order during slavery is 50. This represents about 3% of the 1,500 slaves executed in the Commonwealth of Virginia, a place which began importing bondpersons more than a century before Missouri began this practice, compensated owners of slaves when their human property was executed, and eventually had 73 capital offenses for those in bondage. When we limit our comparison to a place such as Virginia, Missouri's criminal justice system for slaves seems quite attractive. There is no question that a bondperson had a much better chance of avoiding a death sentence here than in Virginia. However, when we look at the ways blacks and whites actually became dead persons walking in Missouri, the legal machinery was conspicuously less fair for persons of color than for whites.

Take the age of the accused as a starter. No known white aged less than 18 years at the time of the crime was executed under the authority of Missouri until after the Civil War. The penitentiary was the proper institution for Caucasian children convicted of first degree murder. Slaves could not be imprisoned; as a result, there are three known cases of slave children being sentenced to death. The first was that of Slave Mary whose case arose in Crawford County on May 14, 1837, when she drowned Vienna Jane Brinker, a child just shy of her second birthday. The victim was the granddaughter of Mary's initial owner, Abraham Brinker, a man who had not written a will when he was murdered by Indians southwest of Potosi (Washington County) in the spring of 1833. Shortly, his widow, Fanny, and his son, John, posted an $8,000 bond in order to serve as administrators of his estate; it was not probated until 1850. John Brinker appropriated Mary and did so despite a statute which forbade the private hiring of any slave by any administrator and subjected the private hirer to a fine of up to $500. The use John Brinker made of is Mary is clear. The young slave girl became Vienna Jane's babysitter, perhaps her almost constant attendant. As for why Mary drowned a small child, we have no coherent explanation. Suffice it to say that she did. Two out-of-state newspapers reprinted a St. Louis newspaper's story that gave Mary's age as "about 13"[9] at the time of her crime. Another in-state paper described her as being "about 14."[10]

Mary admitted that she killed Vienna Jane Brinker. When she was tried, the judge instructed the jury of 12 white men that her admission of guilt could only be received if it was made of "her own free will and not under the influence of hope or fear, torture or pain." He also gave this instruction:

> If the Jury shall find from the evidence that Mary, the accused person was under the age of fourteen years when she committed the offense alleged in the indictment, then, unless, they shall also find from the evidence that at the time when said offense was committed the said Mary had sufficient mind to know what act would be a crime or otherwise, they shall find for the defendant.[11]

As expected, the jury found her guilty of first degree murder and sentenced her to death. Her lawyers took an appeal to the Supreme Court of Missouri, and it accepted her case. There is no mention in its decision of Mary's age; it was not an issue. Though the appellate court granted Mary a new trial, the circuit court judge, popularly elected by white male voters, refused to grant her a requested change of venue from Crawford to Gasconade County. At her second trial Mary was again found guilty; no appeal was taken from it, and the sheriff of Crawford County hanged her on August 11, 1838. In a fanciful account of her case, the 1888 Crawford County History made her age 16 at the time of her crime, thereby aging her two or three years. The fact is that nearly 170 years later, Mary remains the youngest known person ever put to death by the authority of the state of Missouri. It is no accident that she was a female and a slave.

However, she was not the youngest known person sentenced to death in Missouri. That distinction belongs to Slave Mat. Because the exact age of any person held in bondage tended to be unknown, we cannot be certain of his precise age. He was possibly as young as 10, but he was certainly no older than 12 when he struck Allan Womack, the three-year-old son of a neighbor, in the head with a rock on July 9, 1855, in Callaway County. The child died from his injury on August 11, 1855. Mat's trial on charges of first degree murder began in Fulton on October 14, 1855, before the usual 12-white-male jury, and at the request of the prosecution, the trial judge admitted the child's confession, a statement against interest which white neighbors of the victim had extracted from this very young man. Before his case went to the jury, the judge refused to give it this instruction which required it to disregard the defendant's confession: "If the jury believe the prisoner was induced by fear, or terrified by threats of punishment, or that the confession was extracted by ACTUAL TORTURE." Likewise, the judge also refused to instruct the jury that if Mat "was under the age of sixteen years, when he committed the offense, they cannot assess and declare in their verdict that he shall suffer the penalty of death."[12] This would not be the law in Missouri for another 133 years, and when the change first occurred it would be imposed by a decision of the United States Supreme Court.[13] In 1855 enlightened opinion on the execution of black juveniles was very much in the future.

Mat's jury found him guilty of first degree murder, and the judge probably sentenced him to hang on November 16, 1855. A contemporary newspaper reported that this was the date selected for his gallows death. Shortly after the jury returned with its verdict, Mat's lawyers filed an appeal with the Supreme Court of Missouri, and it accepted his case. The issues it probably would have decided, had it reviewed his death sentence, include the admissibility of his confession and the legality of executing someone who was aged either 10 or 11 at the time of his crime. By this time in Missouri's history, the members of the state's highest court were no longer appointed; they were elected, and in their elective capacity they had already overruled more than 30 years of their own precedents when they wrongly decided the Dred Scott decision in 1852. One of Mat's attorneys, the Honorable John Jameson, was formerly both Speaker of the Missouri House and three times a member of the U.S. Congress. The other, Thomas R. Ansell, was not a slave owner; rather he was an Englishman who came to America in 1828 as an actor, eventually left the stage, and taught school until he began practicing law in Fulton, Missouri, in 1839. Both Jameson and Ansell were knowledgeable about the ways of slaveholding Missouri, especially how its courts decided life and death matters pertaining to slaves.

The night before Mat was sentenced to hang, he and his cellmate Celia, another death-sentenced slave, escaped from the Callaway County jail in Fulton. The newspaper specified that he was brought back by an unnamed gentleman at whose house he stayed. The paper speculated that "they were most likely assisted in their effort to escape from the outside."[14] The pair made their getaway a second time, and unlike Celia who was captured and returned to jail, Mat was neither taken into custody a second time nor does any contemporary newspaper mention his death. It is not believable that a child aged between 10 and 12 managed to reach safe haven during an especially brutal winter (1855–1856) without considerable assistance. Mat's lawyers were the most likely persons to have helped him make his getaway. They were in the best position to judge his chances before the Supreme Court of Missouri, and they rightly feared the worst. Nothing in English, federal, or Missouri law at that time prohibited the execution of a person who had attained the age of seven. It goes without saying that no white child of Mat's years was ever sentenced to death in Missouri.[15] As for the Callaway County history published in 1884, it contains no mention of Mat's case.

The last juvenile slave hanged was 16-year-old Henry. He shot and killed his master after his owner, 63-year-old Alfred N. Norman, whipped him for vandalizing a nearby school. The black retaliated by shooting the white while the latter sat in his dining room on the night of July 9, 1863. Soon thereafter, Henry confessed and gave those who questioned him the full details of the crime. In less than three weeks he was put on trial for his life at a special term of the Circuit Court of Moniteau County. He was found guilty and hanged August 28, 1863.[16] If Henry was not the last slave executed in the United States, he was one of the last. Six months before he committed his crime, Lincoln's Emancipation Proclamation freed all the slaves in the Confederacy. However, since Missouri never left the Union, slavery remained an institution here until January 1865. A Moniteau County history, published in 1936, aged Henry four years at the time of his crime, making him 20 years old.[17]

It should be noted that no birth certificates were issued in Missouri during the antebellum period; families, not the state, kept records about such matters. For the most part, slaveholders did not write down the birth dates of their bondpersons. It was to the owners' advantage if slaves did not know how old they were; if they were sold they could be passed off as younger than their actual years, and they could never lie about their age if they never knew it. As a result, it is possible that at least two additional slaves, 18-year-old Isaac who shot and killed his mistress, Mrs. Beston Callahan, in Warren County and 18-year-old Joe who axed and killed his leasor, James T. Points, in Boone County were in their 18th year rather than having actually attained the age of 18 on the dates when they committed their crimes. Both were subsequently tried, found guilty of first degree murder, and sentenced to death. The sheriff of Warren County hanged Isaac on November 14, 1851,[18] and the sheriff of Boone hanged Joe six years later on November 13, 1857.[19] No whites sentenced to death in the antebellum period were as young as at least three bondpersons, perhaps four or five.

Granting changes of venue and appellate review in capital cases were yet other ways that slaves and free blacks received less due process than whites. Since there are only two known capital cases involving free blacks during the antebellum period, it is of no significance that in neither did the defendant(s) get either a change of venue or an appeal. Though it cannot be said that no slave received a change of venue, they were rare. One male, Slave Jim, a co-defendant of another slave, Hampton, who murdered Hampton's master, William B. Johnson, received one, probably at the instigation of his owner, the Honorable David Todd, a circuit court judge. Though Jim and Hampton were found guilty at their trial on first degree murder charges in Howard County, we know that Jim was not hanged, as was Hampton, on March 23, 1832.[20] On appeal, the Supreme Court of Missouri reversed Jim's death sentence on grounds that the trial judge should have granted his requested change of venue. It ordered that the circuit court remove his case to another county. We have no knowledge about the final outcome of his case, but Jim had at least another year of life that his co-defendant Hampton did not have. Jim's appeal was the only death sentence of a male slave which the Supreme Court of Missouri reviewed.

In only two other known cases did a male slave get a change of venue. One arose in Callaway County when two bondmen murdered the master of one on December 29, 1835. The victim, Israel G. Grant, a Callaway County judge, owned Jake and he was leasing the other, Conway. Jake, tried and convicted in Callaway, was hanged June 20, 1836. Conway obtained a change of venue to Boone County where he was tried and convicted on capital charges. He too was hanged in Fulton on April 8, 1836.[21] In the second case, Slave Simon Anderson was tried three times as one of two bondmen responsible for the murder of their master, Benjamin Bruce. The first two trials resulted in a hung jury. The third time the state tried him, he received a change of venue from Randolph to Howard County where he was found not guilty.[22] The more solid evidence in the murder of Benjamin Bruce was against Simon Anderson's fellow bondman, Slave George. At his first trial, George was found guilty of first degree murder in Bruce's death on December 3, 1858, and he was hanged January 7, 1859.[23]

In the fourth and last slave case involving a change of venue, the Supreme Court of Missouri held that granting it from the county of the crime, Lincoln, to nearby Warren was improper. The Court so ruled in order to overturn the wrongful convictions of Slave Fanny and her son Ellick for the murder of two white children, William and Thomas Florence, aged approximately 8 and 10 years of age, on September 1, 1838, in Lincoln County. When these slaves were first tried in Warren County, the prosecution's theory of the crime was that both clubbed the children to death in Prewitt's orchard. Next they carried their two dead victims, the combined weight of which would have been at least 150 pounds, the enormous distance of 4,400 yards from this orchard to a creek where their bodies were found weighed down with stones. This body of water was 100 yards from the Jefferson Road, probably a public highway that led from Lincoln County to the state capital in Jefferson City. The sheriff coerced a confession from Ellick that this preposterous version of events was what had occurred. However, the remains of the boys were not found for at least 72 hours after they were first missed. The children's murders seem best explained as the act of a white stranger who had three days of lead time to depart the area before anyone found his victims. The prosecution never put on any evidence that the murdered children were ever in Prewitt's orchard the day they disappeared. Nonetheless, when Fanny was first tried in Warren County, the jury found her guilty of first degree murder.

On appeal, the Supreme Court of Missouri reversed these convictions. It ruled that the original change of venue from Lincoln to Warren County was improper; rather, Fanny and her son should have been tried in Lincoln County. The Court's reasoning had little to do with the venue of this case; rather it involved the manner of obtaining a confession from Fanny's son, probably a teenager. Missouri Constitution provided "that the accused cannot be compelled to give evidence against himself,"[24] and Fanny's attorney, Edward Bates, knew better than anyone present at these oral arguments the original intent of its framers. He was not only one of them, he was one of the most important. The decision of the judge who wrote for the court stated, "Abstracting from the evidence on the record the declarations extorted from the boy Ellick, there does not in my opinion remain any evidence to justify a jury finding the prisoner guilty."[25] When the Supreme Court of Missouri found fault with the granting of the change of venue, it did so to achieve the right result. Fanny was retried and acquitted in Lincoln County, and most likely the prosecutor dropped charges against her son Ellick. This appellate court ruled that his confession, which implicated both him and his mother, was coerced and could not be used. No other evidence connected these slaves or any others to the murder of the Florence boys.

The Missouri Supreme Court reviewed only four slave death sentences: Jim's from Howard County (1832), Mary's from Crawford County (1837), Fanny's from Lincoln County (1839), and one other, its first, Slave Jane's death sentence (1831). On December 9, 1830, in Callaway County, she smothered her daughter, Angeline, to death in bed clothes. The child died on December 11. Three days earlier on December 8, she gave her child laudanum, an opium derivative, and depending on the size of the ingestor and the amount ingested, a poison. Though it made her infant ill, it did not kill her. After the smothering incident, Jane was tried for murder, found guilty, and sentenced to hang. On appeal the Missouri Supreme Court reversed because it found error in the indictment.[26] We have no idea whether or not Jane was eventually hanged. The Supreme Court of Missouri granted only one additional review in a slave death penalty case, Slave Mat's in 1855, but this child prisoner's escape mooted his appeal. As a result, there are no reported slave capital cases in Missouri after 1839.

In contrast, appeals began early for white capital defendants and they remained a part of this state's jurisprudence throughout. Likewise, changes of venue were standard for whites from the start, and no appellate court need be involved to secure one.

Did an all-white male jury ever find any slave tried as the sole perpetrator on capital charges not guilty? No, not if he/she killed or was believed to have killed a white person. For example, in Montgomery County Slave Moses shot and killed his owner, John Tanner. According to the county history, the slave did so after Tanner "acted disgracefully towards Moses' wife, who was herself a slave, and told her husband of the fact." In the language of the 21st century, Tanner was sleeping black. As the county history continued, though there was some sympathy for the slave who sought to revenge his wife, "there were a few who thought he richly deserved death, because a slave, they held, ought not to have sympathies , affections, or sensibilities, which could not be interfered with by his master in any way, and to any extent." Not surprisingly, Moses was tried, found guilty of murder, and hanged in Lewiston (a village that no longer exists) in 1829.[27] Likewise when Slave Archie was tried in Boone County about 1835 for the murder of his master, a wealthy unnamed bachelor, notorious for cruelty to his slaves, he was found guilty and hanged. Afterwards, belief lingered that Archie was innocent and that other slaves of this cruel master had murdered him.[28]

If the demographics differed and a slave perpetrator killed the bondman of another owner, the usual penalty after 1835 was second degree murder. The circumstances of the victim-slave's death were irrelevant. Twice, first in 1837 and again in 1850, the Missouri Supreme Court ruled that no master of a slave whose human property killed the bondman of another master was civilly liable for the acts of his aggressive human property. The Court held that the owner is not responsible for "such remote consequences as [his slave]'s murder of another slave."[29] That Missouri's highest court revisited this issue indicates the frequency with which male slaves of different owners quarreled, often enough with deadly effects. Prior to 1836, the typical punishment for such a crime was a whipping of no more than 39 lashes. In 1836 the General Assembly provided an additional remedy for disposing of bondpersons convicted of violent felonies. The law required that the owner post a bond to insure his convicted–felon slave was taken from the state within 60 days and not returned to Missouri for at least 20 years "if [the felony] be of such a nature, in the opinion of the court, that it is not safe that such slave should stay in the State."[30]

It should also be noted that there are no known cases in Missouri of one adult slave killing another adult slave, either male or female, when both were owned by the same master. It is not possible that in the entire tenure of human bondage here one grownup slave did not kill another grownup slave when the perpetrator and victim shared the same owner. Equally unlikely is that all records with such a factual situation were lost. The matter was surely handled in-house; most probably, violent bondpersons were sold down the Mississippi River and the owner realized some profit rather than the total loss which inevitably resulted when a bondperson was hanged.

The victim need not be black for a homicidal slave to be sold. An undated account from Warren County concerns a wounded master who took the law into his own hands. When one of Mr. Bevins' slaves deliberately shot him and the owner's neighbors captured the culprit, the dying victim persuaded one of his slave's captors, Mr. Kountze, to take the killer to New Orleans. There he sold him for $1,000 and gave the money to the murdered white man's family. The sold slave was never indicted, and Mr. Bevins was buried before any law enforcement officers knew a crime had occurred.[31]

If the victim-slave was a young child, then the matter may not have been handled in-house. The second extant murder prosecution, solidly documented with hand-written court records, concerns a slave woman named Annice. On July 27, 1828, the grand jury in Clay County indicted her for the drowning deaths of five slave youngsters, all the property of her owner, Jeremiah Prior. Neither the parentage nor the ages of Ann, Phebe, and Nancy are specified; Bill, aged five years, and Nelly, aged two years, are identified as the perpetrator's children. Annice was found guilty of "the several counts" of murder in that on each count, probably in June 1828, she did push "One Ann a negro child slave ... into a certain collection of water of the depth of five feet and there choaked, suffocated, and drowned of which ... the said Ann [Phebe, Nancy, Bill and Nelly] instantly died." Annice was tried, found guilty of murder, and Sheriff Shubael Allen hanged her on a public gallows in Liberty on August 23, 1828.[32]

Though juries, judges, appellate courts, and governors almost never allowed a white female to be put to death, these same authorities had no such scruples when it came to slaves. We can confirm the execution of four female slaves, and two others are likely additions to this list. The unnamed bondwoman slave who set fire to Pierre Chouteau's property in St. Louis in 1805 was probably hanged pursuant to court order. The odds are that Slave Susan also died on a public gallows. On July 7, 1844, in Callaway County, she struck her mistress, Rosa Ann King, in the neck with an ax and killed her as her victim took a nap. Susan readily admitted her guilt and stated that her only motive was a desire to return to her former owner, the family of Mrs. King's father-in-law, and she thought by murdering her new mistress she could achieve her wish. Susan came to be owned by Rosa Ann King because the white woman received the slave as a wedding gift. In October 1844 the bondwoman was indicted, tried in Callaway County Circuit Court, found guilty of first-degree murder, and sentenced to be hanged on November 23. She was not executed on that date; rather a jail fee showed that she was boarded from July 8 to November 30, 1844, or 145 days at 25 cents per day.[33] There the records break off. She is not mentioned in the Callaway County history, and no extant newspaper confirms her execution. There is a slim chance that she escaped, but the greater likelihood is that she was hanged by the neck until dead in December 1844.

The biggest gap in our knowledge of slaves killing each other and whites concerns the weapon owners most feared in the hands of their human properties: poison. During the territorial period, any slave convicted of the preparation, exhibition, or administration of any medicine was judged guilty of a capital felony. The medicine the statute writers had in mind was arsenic. Unlike lye, whose caustic taste immediately alerted the ingestor to its toxicity, the taste of arsenic could easily be masked by putting it in coffee or tea. White persons were rightly afraid that their seemingly contented slaves would poison them with this household commodity. It was believed to be efficacious to combat paralysis, epilepsy, rickets, heart disease, cancer, parasites, headaches, colds, influenza, and general debility. The theory of its use was that the human body and its pathogen(s) were poisoned together; the arsenic killed the disease-causing agent(s), and the larger and strong host survived unharmed. There was no easier way for the slave to kill her owner than to increase the dose of arsenic that either the physician–apothecary prescribed or the self-medicating slave-holder used for many maladies. Though the autopsy was sufficiently perfected in America by the mid-eighteenth century to determine that the cause of demise was arsenical poi-soning, autopsies did not become routine practice of the coroner or medical examiner in questionable deaths until the end of the nineteenth century, that is, long after slavery had run its course. Moreover, its sale was unregulated here as late as the early 20th century.

Contemporary newspapers from Cooper and Boone counties contain stories about a Callaway County slave woman who in 1845 poisoned five children, four of them her own and the fifth a white child. She confessed her crimes, and almost certainly, had she lived, she would have been tried, found guilty, and hanged, but she committed suicide while in jail by taking the same arsenic she had earlier used to kill five children.[34] In 1855 in Boone County, Ann, owned by George Lytekliter, was indicted for attempting to poison her owner's daughter, found guilty, sentenced to a whipping of 39 lashes,[35] and probably she was also transported out of state for 20 years. However, and this is the point, all prosecutions involv-ing arsenic or bluestone, both deadly poisons, were for *attempted* murder, not murder. These products were stored in pantries and kitchens where slave women worked, and these substances became and basically remained women's weapons. Is it credible that all slave women who used arsenic as a weapon to kill another adult bungled their crimes? Some unde-tected slave women no doubt successfully poisoned their victims to death. Dying leasors and owners of bondwomen were clueless about the cause of both the sudden decline in their health (a large dose of arsenic) or the gradual decline (many small doses) and finally their untimely end. The deaths of such victims of slave stealth were mistakenly attributed to cholera or some other dreaded disease, never to the criminal designs of their seeming faithful bondwomen. There could be no death more premeditated than one by poisoning, but all slaves who *successfully* administered arsenic to white adults here got away with first degree murder.

When a slave killed a free black, neither a death sentence nor court-ordered trans-portation was ever imposed, so far as we know. In a case which arose in Jefferson County in 1852, John , a slave, killed "Free Jack," was brought into court in Hillsboro, pled guilty, and the judge assessed a penalty of 39 lashes. The county history commented: "Jack, the free Negro, represented no value, while John, the slave, did represent value, and his exe-cution for the crime would have been the destruction of so much property — hence the apparent reason for his being allowed to plead guilty and to escape with a whipping which ... did not materially injure the property."[36]

In yet another area, the law in capital cases was not equally applied to blacks and whites during the antebellum period. The largest number of persons arrested prior to the Civil War in a single case on charges of first degree murder was in one involving slave per-petrators. It arose in Boone County on March 20, 1843, when five bondpersons, three men and two women, took their owner, Hiram Beasley, by surprise and ended his life with an ax about sunset in a clearing three-quarters of a mile from home. By the next day all five were arrested, confessed their guilt before a justice of the peace, and were committed for further trial. Despite the fact that all accounts indicate that a Slave Mary participated in the murder of her master, she was not publicly punished. She appears to have taken up the ax, struck her master two licks in the head, and afterward thrown keys into a fire, presum-ably some piece of evidence connected with the crime. The full reasons that the system spared this woman are unknown. Unlike free white persons who could be fined and impris-oned, slaves could not. As a result, the criminal justice system of a slave state never had the flexibility in dealing with bondperson defendants that it did with whites. For example, in the federal government's prosecution of approximately 13 white men in the Rice County, Kansas case, the defendants received punishments ranging from fines through death sentences. During this same time period, the state of Missouri hauled Hiram Beasley's killers into court.

Although four slaves who participated in his murder were penalized, two males, David and Simon, were found guilty of second-degree murder and sentenced to 30 lashes and transportation out of state for 20 years. In no capital case in Missouri were more than two slaves ever hanged for the same crime. It should be remember that neither the U.S. government nor the state of Missouri paid slaveholders when their slaves were executed. As a result, the estate of any murdered slaveholder was out quite a princely sum if the victim owned, as Hiram Beasley did, all the co-conspirators and each was found guilty of first degree murder. Had all five been hanged, his estate would have suffered a mighty diminution, perhaps as much as $100,000 in today's money. Therefore, it was important to restrict the numbers on the county gallows for any individual crime. In Beasley's axing, two "married" slaves, Hiram and his wife, America, were tried for first degree murder, found guilty, and died on a public scaffold in Columbia on June 10, 1843, about 2:00 p.m., in the presence of nearly 2,000 witnesses.[37]

In contrast, when only one of the black co-defendants was a slave, and he was owned out-of-state by a Louisiana man, there was no restriction on the numbers that were death-eligible. Such a case did not touch the pocketbook of a single slaveholder in Missouri. One arose in the city of St. Louis on April 17, 1841, when four black men broke into a bank for purposes of taking sizeable sums of money from it. In the course of their attempted robbery, they were interrupted by the return of two white male clerks, both aged 22 years, Jesse Baker and Jacob Weaver. The perpetrators killed both, set fire to the bank building to cover their murders, and fled the scene without the anticipated cash proceeds of their crime.

The next day, the mayor of a horrified city offered a $5,000 reward for information leading to the criminals' arrest and conviction. No other slave crime in Missouri's history approaches this remuneration for its solution. This early TIPS hotline soon produced results. A free black barber, Edward Ennis, told a friend who went to the police that he, Ennis, knew the identities of those responsible. Soon the authorities had the names of the four suspects and their intended destinations. Slave Madison, 34 or 35 years old, was arrested sleeping on a steamboat's deck in St. Louis. His co-defendants were all free blacks in their late twenties: Charles Brown, James W. Seward, and Amos Alfred Warrick. Brown was arrested in Cincinnati, Ohio; Seward on a steamboat south of Cairo, Illinois; and Warrick on one docked at the central Missouri town of Arrow Rock, Saline County. By May 11, all four suspects were returned to St. Louis and incarcerated in its jail. Each was ably represented by counsel: Hamilton Gamble, a future governor of Missouri; John Darby, a former mayor of St. Louis; Wilson Primm, a former state legislator; and Joseph Spalding, a former city of St. Louis alderman and school board member. Their trial began May 24, and since each of the accused black men had made damaging admissions about the culpability of his own or his co-defendants' role in the crime, it was not difficult for the usual all-white-male jury to find all four guilty of first-degree murder. On June 1, the judge sentenced them to hang on July 9.

Crowd estimates of those who wished to watch them die range as high as 20,000 persons, half of whom were women, in a city whose population was then less than 30,000. On the appointed date, July 9, 1841, all four were hanged on Duncan's Island, an area approximately a mile south of the St. Louis Courthouse. A handbill for the steamboat *Eagle* survives. It advertises a round trip from Alton, Illinois, to Duncan's Island, St. Louis, Missouri, for passenger viewing of the hanging of the four. Its fare for the trip to St. Louis and return was only $1.50 to watch "FOUR NEGROES EXECUTED." It advises, "The Negroes are to be hung on the point of Duncan's Island, just below St. Louis. The Boat will drop alongside, so that ALL CAN SEE WITHOUT DIFFICULTY." After the bodies were taken down their severed heads were displayed in the showcase window of a St. Louis drugstore; later its proprietor made plastic casts of their heads for the then budding pseudoscience of phrenology, the study of character by examining the bumps on the head.[38] The simultaneous execution of four persons is a record number under Missouri statutes; it still stands nearly 170 years later. It is no surprise that the four hanged persons were black, a most unpopular color at that time.

Were there slave perpetrators who qualify as the worst of the worst, those whose crime(s) cannot be excused because they were bondpersons? Yes, Slave Ben is a splendid example. He first raped 12-year-old Susannah Bright and then killed her and her 10-year-old brother Thomas in order to cover up his sexual assault of the young girl. These murdered children left home in Marion County on a very gentle horse on October 30, 1849, for the purpose of gathering walnuts. Ben, owned by the Thomas W. Glascock family of nearby Shelby County, happened to be in the vicinity because Chancellor Brower had hired him to haul rock 50 to 100 yards from where the Bright children's bodies were found. Considerable physical evidence tied Ben to these murders. He was found guilty of first degree murder and hanged January 11, 1850.[39]

Among persons of color whose homicide(s) were less blameworthy than Ben's, there is neither a slave nor a free black sentenced to hang during the antebellum period who ever received either a commutation or a pardon for his crime. The only known pardon of a slave took place before she was tried for first degree murder; it is discussed in Chapter 11. No Missouri governor ever risked his political capital on such a rash act. In contrast, governors issued at least 10 known pardons for white persons convicted of capital offenses during slavery here. Several of these were for insane whites sentenced to hang, and no known slave homicide was ever defended on grounds of insanity. Though pardons are extant for two slaves after their trials, they were convicted of non-capital offenses. The first issued in 1849 in the Howard County conviction of Slave Bill for the attempted rape of an elderly woman who today would probably be diagnosed as suffering from Alzheimer's Disease. She mistakenly identified her attacker, if indeed a male of any race was even near her.[40] The second issued in 1854 for Slave John Anderson, convicted in St. Louis Circuit Court of the rape of Rebecca Ann Hewett, a white whore who consented to sex with the defendant when he paid her 50 cents.[41] In both cases, many influential citizens petitioned the governor for executive clemency. Clearly, the community approved the governors' actions. In the rape conviction, the governor issued his pardon only after the Missouri Supreme Court affirmed the only sentence available for a black man convicted of the rape of a white woman, that of castration.[42]

The dissection of hanged slaves was at least as common as that of hanged whites. We know that the dead bodies of at least three bondmen were given to doctors who attended their gallows deaths. The cadavers of Slave Moses in 1829 in Montgomery County, Slave Ben in 1850 in Marion County, and Slave Green in 1859 in Buchanan County were all carted away by physicians for their study of human anatomy. Probably there were more slave criminals than whites dissected after death. From 1835 until slavery perished here in 1865, the law allowed the dissection of any bondperson if his/her owner consented. If one who died in her sleep after a blameless life of services to her white owner and his family could be dissected, it is not difficult to imagine that more hanged bondpersons than we know about were anatomical specimens for the benefit of men of medicine and their apprentices.

When we look to the numbers of whites and blacks executed here during slavery under the authority of the state of Missouri there are approximately the same number, about 50. However, such figures in no way represent the equal protection of the law. If we look to the 1836 state of Missouri census, we find that bondpersons numbered 40, 540, free persons of color, 911, and white persons 202,757.[43] In 1856 there were 100,817 slaves and 784,699 white persons.[44] Since whites outnumbered persons of color in Missouri at nearly five to one in 1836 and by 1856 it was by nearly seven to one, it is a reasonable conclusion that a slave was four or more times as likely to be executed as a Caucasian. White girls and women were especially immune from death sentences. This was not true of black girls and women.

The contrast between the fate of a white man who killed a slave woman and the fate of a slave woman who killed a white man brings to vivid life what the abstractions of a lot of numbers cannot. William S. Harney, then a major in the United States Army, was posted to Jefferson Barracks, when in October 1833 he married Mary Mullanphy, a daughter of the wealthy and recently deceased St. Louis pioneer merchant, John Mullanphy; she brought a large dowry to her husband. Eight months later at the newlyweds' St. Louis home and over a period of three successive days, the major beat his slave woman, Hannah. He believed that she had hidden misplaced keys and if he whipped her with sufficient severity, she would reveal their location. She never did; she died. The coroner's jury viewed her body, heard the testimony of several physicians and other witnesses, and on June 28, 1834, it concluded that Hannah "came to her death by wounds inflicted by William S. Harney."[45]

Almost immediately, the major left town, and his wife, her sisters, their husbands, and his wife's attorney-brother, Brian Mullanphy, later mayor of St. Louis, knew his travel plans. Harney received four extant letters, dated July 4 through August 13, 1834, and they help chart his escape route. The earliest was sent to him to Wheeling, Virginia, and it informed him that the circuit court would be in session in August and a grand jury, "must find a bill against you. You cannot therefore return here until the excitement goes off, say two or three years." A second letter reached the runaway in Wheeling, it advised him, "I was confidentially informed the grand jury brought in murder. Do not go to New Orleans or on the Ohio River. If within reach, I fear they will get the governor to demand you." While in Washington, D.C. Major Harney received another letter from a family member who cautioned him "I repeat do not think of returning to this place unless I advise you to do so." Yet another letter informed Harney that a bond, presumably a recognizance bond, would be forwarded to him, "and in order that there be no doubt concerning it, the whole of the heirs of John Mullanphy have signed as your securities."[46]

In March 1835, approximately ten months after Slave Hannah's savage death, a St. Louis resident recorded in his diary, "Hear Maj. Harney is acquitted."[47] One must go to a small book which Reverend William G. Eliot, founder of Washington University, wrote and published approximately 50 years later, to discover the circumstances of the major's acquittal. Eliot moved to St. Louis in November 1834, and one of the "first things [he] heard was of a colored girl who had been whipped so severely by a 'gentleman' who lived not far from where I lodged that she died." He continues that the "Major_____" obtained a change of venue from St. Louis to St. Charles County, and there he was tried and found not guilty."[48] Eliot's discussion of the *never-named* defendant in the 1880s concerned a man who was still alive.

The Articles of War required that "when any soldier shall be accused of a capital crime," his commanding officer was required upon application duly made ... to deliver over such accused person ... to the civil magistrate." From the beginning of Harney's flight from St. Louis his commanding officer knew about and approved of his travel. Otherwise, this soldier would have been charged with desertion. Though the major was court-martialed four times between 1824 and 1847, there is no mention in his military record of his murder of Slave Hannah or any event surrounding it.[49] By the time the Mexican War began, the major had already received two promotions, and it was *Colonel* Harney who distinguished himself in April 1847 when he stormed an important mountain pass, Cerro Gordo, on the road between Veracruz and Jalapa, Mexico. As a result of his heroism and with the advice and consent of the Senate, President Polk chose him as one of three men whom the 29th Congress authorized the president to promote to brigadier general. At the end of his active military career in 1863 and with the advice and consent of the Senate, President Lincoln chose him as one of up to 40 men whom the 37th Congress authorized the president to promote to major general. Because his military file contains no mention of Hannah, it is virtually impossible that either Polk or Lincoln ever knew that their promoted general beat a slave woman to death over misplaced keys. It is equally unlikely that the city councils of Omaha, Nebraska, and St. Louis, Missouri, when naming thoroughfares *Harney*, were in full possession of the facts of his life.[50] Four years after Eliot's book was published, Major General William Selby Harney, whose first wife divorced him many years earlier, finally died with his second wife (his nurse) at his side in Florida in May 1889. Obituaries on him run in the *New York Times*, *Kansas City Globe*, and *St. Louis Globe* contain no mention of the murder he committed in 1834.

In contrast to the long life of General Harney (1800–1889) is the much shorter one of Celia, a slave girl whom Robert Newsom, then a widower aged more than 60 years, purchased at an action in Audrain County, when she was 13 or 14 years old. His reason for acquiring her was sexual; he enjoyed young black flesh. Court records suggest that he raped her on their journey back to his home in Callaway County the same day he bought her. Thus began his lengthy sexual relationship with his underage human property, a girl at least 50 years younger than her master. By the summer of 1855, two of Newsom's daughters, unmarried Mary Newsom and married Virginia Wainscott, and Virginia's children, including 11-year-old Coffee Wainscott, were living on his farm with Robert Newsom. By this time, Celia had been there four or more years, and she was the mother of at least two children. The older was probably fathered by a black man, and the younger, according to her statement in court records, was fathered by Newsom. Furthermore, she was pregnant with her third child. Perhaps the father of the begot but unborn child was George, a fellow slave who had begun spending nights with her. Equally likely is that her master Robert Newsom had inseminated her a second time. Her pregnancy was not healthy; she had not been well enough to work since February.

She had asked for help from various white members of the household in keeping her aged owner away from her. She got none. George, by now Celia's lover, was refusing to have anything more to do with her unless she "quit the old man." She asked the elderly rapist to stay away from her cabin, and she warned him that if he tried to force her, she would hurt him. Nonetheless he arrived at her door after 10:00 p.m. on a Saturday, June 23. The next morning, he was eventually missed. Initially when she was questioned she denied any knowledge of his whereabouts. When a neighbor told her she would have her children taken away from her and further he had a rope "provided for her if she did not tell," she admitted that she killed Robert Newsom the previous night.

Her confession never varied. She struck her owner with a board to avoid unwelcome and unwanted sexual intercourse, and she did so after she asked him to leave, and he refused. She struck him a second time because she feared that his hand would catch her. Once she ascertained that he was dead, her next thought was disposing of the body. She was afraid that if her role in his death became known, she would be hanged. She spent what remained of Saturday evening June 23 and most of the predawn hours of June 24 burning his corpse in a fireplace in her cabin. She enlisted the help of his 11-year grandson, Coffee Wainscott, to carry out the old man's ashes in the belief that they were "ordinary wood ashes." The dead man's remains were spread on the right hand side of the path between Celia's cabin and the stable. As we would expect, her fire did not consume all 206 of his bones. Once she confessed, searchers found what were almost certainly bits and pieces of his skeleton as well as a suspender buckle and buttons from his clothing. In October 1855, Celia was indicted on charges of first degree murder.

Some time before her trial began her judge appointed three attorneys to represent her: Chapman Kouns, the 22-year-old son of Fulton's most esteemed physician, Nathan Kouns; and Isaac M. Boulware, the 26-year-old son of Theodorick Boulware, a respected minister who founded the town's first Baptist church; and John Jameson. This last-named lawyer was simultaneously representing Slave Mat and he had earlier defended John Huting, the unbalanced suitor who killed his beloved in Montgomery County in 1852 and was hanged in 1855. In addition to an active life in politics and law, some time after 1840, Jameson became an ordained minister in the Christian Church.

His task of successfully defending Celia was almost impossible. The trial of any slave accused of killing his or her master who confessed to the deed, as had Celia, had a foregone conclusion. The all-white-male jury found the perpetrator guilty, and the judge sentenced the slave to hang by the neck until dead. Jameson and his young attorney assistants attempted to convince the trial judge that he should give the jury a number of instructions to guide it as this body decided her fate. Of the 13 refused instructions offered by the defense, nine concerned her right to use force "to protect herself against forced intercourse." The jury never received this instruction: "An attempt to compel a woman to be defiled by using force, menace, or duress is a felony within the meaning of the [law]," Likewise refused was this defense-proffered instruction: "The words any woman's [right to use deadly force to resist defilement] ... embraces slave women, as well as free white women." The judge's unwillingness to so advise Celia's jury meant that his interpretation of "any woman' excluded slave women when their rapists were their owners. As a result, the jury found Celia guilty of the only crime it was allowed to deliberate, first degree murder.

On October 13 the judge sentenced Celia to be hanged on November 16, 1855. A bill from a physician appears in the court costs that were allowed in this case. It was for Dr. Cotton's visits to Celia in the county jail. He saw "the prisoner" because of "sickness" and because he delivered her "dead child."[51] His services are undated, and as a result, we do not know precisely when Celia's pregnancy began, its length, or when it ended. She may have given birth almost any time after she was jailed on June 25. Perhaps she had her baby after October 13 but before November 16. During this same period, her attorneys appealed her case to the Supreme Court of Missouri, and it accepted her appeal. However, it refused to issue an order staying her execution until her case could be heard at its next scheduled session in January 1856. Automatically, the execution of the defendant cancels any decisions an appeals court might issue; its decision is mooted by death.

In the midst of all this legal maneuvering, Celia and her cellmate, 11- or 12-year-old death-sentenced Mat escaped. By November 25, Harvey Newsom, her master's son, had returned her to the jail. She had gone to his home to see her children, now assets of Robert Newsom's estate, and probably, in the case of one of them, a half-brother or half-sister of her dead owner's adult children. Soon after her return to the Callaway County jail, the judge set a new execution date for her of Friday, December 21. On December 14, one week before her scheduled hanging, the popularly elected members of the Supreme Court of Missouri refused to stay her execution. In its order the court noted that it had examined the record and proceedings in her case, and "it is thought proper to refuse the prayer of the petitioner; there being seen upon inspection of the record aforesaid no probable cause for such appeal." Accordingly, one week later and at 2:30 p.m. on Friday, December 21, 1855, the sheriff of Callaway County hanged Celia; she was approximately 19 years old. The *Fulton Telegraph* from this time period has not survived, but because its coverage of this teenager's death was carried in both the *New York Times* and the *Sun* (Baltimore), we know the local paper wrote, "Thus has closed one of the most horrible tragedies ever enacted in our county."[52] The Callaway County history, published in 1884, completely excludes any mention of *State* v. *Celia, a Slave*, presumably out of deference to the influential surviving descendants of Robert Newsom.

Just as Reverend Eliot protected General Harney's identity, so too did the first writer to extract the gruesome details about Celia's case which survive in Callaway County circuit court records. Judge Hugh P. Williamson, a longtime trial judge in Fulton, wrote, "Document: The State Against Celia, a Slave." It was published in 1956. In it Celia's owner is "Robert N. _____," his son is "Harvey N. _____," and his married daughter is "Virginia W. _____."[53] Today, Celia's story, including a book-length study of it,[54] has been told and retold with such frequency that she has become Missouri's equivalent of the guillotined French queen, Marie Antoinette, who died in 1793. The executed queen's son, Louis Charles, died June 8, 1795, at the age of ten, almost certainly of tuberculosis. Nonetheless, during the 19th century, at least 40 pretender Dauphins claimed descent from the queen.[55] Likewise, at least four unrelated families claim that they are direct descendants of the baby Celia gave birth to in jail. Her "dead child," as the delivering physician described him/her, has become the great-great-grandmother of a sizable number of persons. Such is the stuff of legend.

In contrast, the reality of the death penalty for slaves included the execution of juveniles, the execution of women, few appeals, few venue changes, few defenses, no commutations, one known pardon, and a lingering moral outrage that haunts us today. Consider the long happy life of Major-General Harney and the short sorrowful one of the teenage rape victim, Celia. To be sure, and in addition to Slave Ben, there were slaves in Missouri who committed despicable crimes, and their punishment was probably appropriate. A detailed account of such matters and more can be found in my book, *Slavery and Crime in Missouri, 1773–1865*. However, no one can study these matters—and I have—and not conclude that the death penalty was disproportionately and unfairly applied to persons of color in this state in most instances wherein it was used during slave days.

The next chapter recounts an especially effective killing machine, the Union Army. It executed more known persons in Missouri between 1861 and 1865 than surviving records indicate the combined jurisdictions of Spain, the federal government, and the state of Missouri put to death here in the entire antebellum period.

3

Union Army Executions,
1861–1865

In 1806 the Ninth Congress passed a detailed "Act for establishing Rules and Articles for the government of the Armies of the United States." Its Article 33 was referenced in both earlier chapters to explain that the state of Missouri prosecuted at least four members of the U.S. Army for homicides committed here in separate and unrelated cases in different years prior to and during the Civil War. Under this article, the commanding officer was required to turn over to the civil magistrate any officer or soldier "accused of a capital crime, or of having used violence, or committed any offence against the person or property of any citizen of any of the United States."[1] In other words, members of the military were also entitled to the privilege of the writ of habeas corpus, as the U.S. Constitution provides. They could only be put to death for crimes such as murder and rape after a civilian judge determined that their custody was legal. Military personnel were tried, as Article 33 explained, in state courts for offenses "punishable by the known laws of the land." Theoretically, every aspect of due process was afforded them, including the right to a public trial, that is, one at which the press was present.

Then the Civil War began, and military justice changed, among other places, in Missouri. On September 24, 1862, and by proclamation, President Lincoln suspended the privilege of the writ of habeas corpus for all persons "imprisoned ... by any military authority or by the sentence of any court-martial or military commission."[2] On March 3, 1863, the 37th Congress rubber-stamped the President's authority to abolish this writ. It decreed that during "the present rebellion" there was no required civil prosecution of crimes by members of the military. Further, the law specified that, "no military or other officer shall be compelled in answer to any writ of habeas corpus, to return the body of any person or persons detained by him by authority of the President."[3] In actual practice and on a routine basis, the U.S. Army began administering justice here well before either the presidential proclamation or the congressional enactment officially gave it the right to bypass local courts when trying both its own members and civilians. It did so swiftly with considerable shock and awe, and martial law continued here as late as July 1865.[4]

To be sure, the state of Missouri tried and executed eight known persons, including a Union Army soldier, during the Civil War. One hanging took place in Lewis County in 1861; another in St. Louis in 1862. Moniteau County executed a slave in 1863; other gallows deaths under state law occurred in 1863 in Buchanan, Jefferson, and St. Louis counties, and

St. Louis County in 1864. Not surprisingly, all three of these latter areas were inhabited primarily by Northern sympathizers. However, apart from these eight hangings between 1861 and 1864, the Union Army was the only entity here which executed civilians and soldiers during the war years. As far as we know, the Confederate Army never achieved sufficient strength in Missouri to carry out even one execution. The organized and dominant power here was the U.S. Army; the force was with it.

The documentation concerning the military's extensive use of capital punishment in this state during the war years is skimpy in many cases and surprisingly detailed in others. However, almost certainly there were even more Union Army executions in Missouri than extant records indicate. Many rural Missouri newspapers, which would have published these stark events that took place in their own locales, were no longer in business. Their editors and publishers were often Southern supporters, and the U.S. Army jailed them and destroyed their presses by throwing them into creeks, rivers, and the like.[5] The bulk of the newspapers which have survived from the war years were published primarily in areas solidly under Union control, in cities such as St. Joseph and St. Louis. Not surprisingly, they printed war news from the Union, not the Confederate, point of view. Given such gaps in newspaper coverage and other records, assuming these records even existed in the first place, it seems best to include as executions what would be disregarded as inadequately documented had not a Civil War engulfed most of the state during the reign of the Union Army.

The anomaly was that Missouri was both a slave jurisdiction and one which, officially at least, remained in the United States throughout the war years. Complicating matters and surely adding to the already great violence here was the mini–Civil War, which was fought on the Kansas-Missouri border in the years following passage of the Kansas-Nebraska Act in 1854.[6] Tempers were on the boil here, especially in western Missouri, long before the big Civil War began. In most of Missouri's counties, the citizenry was split into Confederate sympathizers, Union sympathizers, and those, perhaps the largest percentage, who devoutly wished to stay out of harm's way. Guerrilla warfare was the order of the day in most places here during the War of the Rebellion. Though the Union Army never went so far as to set the entire rural area of the state on fire in order to maintain control of it, its iron-fisted approach to law and order is splendidly revealed in its lavish use of the death penalty.

Its first execution in Missouri for which any record survives took place within two months after the April 14, 1861 surrender of Fort Sumter near Charleston, South Carolina. The last occurred almost two months after Lee surrendered to Grant at Appomattox Courthouse, Virginia, on April 9, 1865. Outside Springfield in Greene County, a Union Army firing squad shot to death its first known person in this state on July 25, 1861. His name was John Cole, and he was a Union Army private. He quarreled with a fellow soldier, and as a Lawrence, Kansas newspaper reported it, Cole "stabbed him in the back, killing him instantly."[7] Had he been tried in a civilian court, a jury might have come in with a manslaughter verdict, but the military tribunal found him guilty of murder.

Unlike the Confederate Army which ceased hostilities after Lee surrendered to Grant, Missouri's guerrillas continued to wage war. As a result, the Union Army used a firing squad to kill its last known capital offender here in Warrensburg, Johnson County, on June 2, 1865. He was a civilian, and he was executed for his secessionist activity. Shortly before his death he wrote his parents that he had been "sent to this place and ... sentenced to be shot." His brief note to them concluded, "I have to Die; there is no alternative. I am your affectionate son, G.P. Wright."[8] Between the federal army's shooting John Cole in July 1861 and G.P. Wright in June 1865, it sentenced to death at least 89 persons whose executions can be confirmed. It put many more civilians to death than members of its own army, but it condemned and killed both with a speed and efficiency never equaled before or since.

During the war years, crimes for officers and soldiers derived from two sources. One was the 1806 Rules and Articles. Among other offenses specified therein, desertion (Article 20) and quitting one's post or colors to plunder and pillage (Article 52) carried death sentences *or* another punishment ordered by the sentence of a court-martial. The other authority to execute members of the military and civilians for committing crimes such as murder, rape, and robbery was martial law. It comes into being when necessity requires it. Fairman expresses it this way:

> When an insurrection has ripened into war, and has been recognized as such by the constituted authorities, the inhabitants of the hostile territory become public enemies, beyond the pale of constitutional protection. In this situation the commander is the supreme law-giver, executive, and judge, subject only to the restraints imposed by the laws and customs of war, the orders of superior authorities, public opinion, and his own conscience. In this sense military government is the will of the general.[9]

Outside St. Louis, most of Missouri was under martial law during the war years. Civilians here could be and were executed for offenses that are unimaginable but for war. Overwhelmingly, those who died either before a firing squad or on a gallows were charged with some aspect or another of secessionist, guerrilla, or bushwhacking activity. The last term was a Civil War era synonym for guerrilla fighting, and the noun form of it, frequently in use during the war, was *bushwhacker*. From the Northern point of view, it was a term of derision equal to *terrorist* or member of *al-qaeda* (Arabic term meaning the base) in the United States in the early 21st century.

By July 1861 the 37th Congress had "by reason of unlawful obstructions, combinations, or assemblages of persons, or rebellion against the authority of the Government of the United States," given the President the power, among much else, "to suppress such rebellion in whatever State or Territory thereof the laws of the United States may be forcibly opposed, or the execution thereof forcibly obstructed."[10] These instructions and many others meant different things to different Union Army officers.

One group of rebels captured north of the Missouri River the summer of 1862 was fortunate. The provost marshal examined six of them in Carroll County, and he determined that they were, as the newspaper reported, "regularly sworn in the Confederate service by a commissioned officer, which exonerates them from a charge of bushwhacking." As a result, instead of dying at the hands of a Union Army firing squad, they were sent to St. Louis as prisoners of war.[11] Nichols clarifies that most captured Southerners were sent to Union Army prisons in the St. Louis area,[12] but most is not all.

During the same season of the same year, 1862, other captured Rebels were not so lucky. The first known attempt to use the infamous decimal system, that is 10 Rebels shot to death for every Northern soldier or supporter killed, took place about three miles from Lexington (Lafayette County) on June 8, 1862. Two marked for death managed to escape. As a result, a Union Army firing squad mowed down eight bushwhackers. There is no record of their names, but the extant St. Louis newspaper coverage of their deaths is laudatory. The story, headlined, "The Right Way and the Safe Way," concludes, "Colonel Huston ... has given the general order that all guerrillas taken lurking or ambushing with arms in their hands, be shot.... Under this very proper order the eight were shot."[13]

Following a battle in Kirksville (Adair County) between Confederate and Union forces, which the latter won, John McNeil, then a colonel in the Missouri State Militia, wrote in his official report on September 12, 1862:

Finding that fifteen of the persons captured had been prisoners before, and, upon their own admission, had been discharged on their solemn oath and parole of honor, not again to take arms against their country under penalty of death, I enforced the penalty of the bond by ordering them shot.[14]

Eight of the men executed at Kirksville were residents of Monroe County, four of Shelby, two of Marion, and one of Adair. The historian, E.M. Violette, when describing the August 7, 1862 firing squad deaths of these men, wrote "the day after the battle fifteen of the *Confederates* who had been captured in the fight were executed on the spot about two hundred yards southwest of the present Wabash depot."[15] No other known execution in Missouri's history equals or exceeds this one for the numbers put to death.

The next day, in the same town, and once more on the orders of Colonel John McNeil, Lt. Colonel Frisby McCullough was also shot to death by firing squad. Mudd quoted McNeil in a letter written in 1887 as stating that the deceased was tried by a military commission, a tribunal which might consist of as few as three jury-type officers. According to McNeil, it found McCullough guilty of "bushwhacking, or of being a guerrilla." However, despite a diligent search, Mudd could find no record of any such military commission. As for the man at whose command McCullough died, Mudd wrote, "with some personal knowledge of McNeil, before and after the war, I would not believe his word in anything."[16] Mudd's chapter on McCullough uses the condemned man's last words as its title, "May God Forgive you this Cold-Blooded Murder." In his column about this execution, James J. Fisher terms McCullough a "Confederate officer" and sums it up this way: "For the federals, it was an open and shut case. They'd executed a bunch the day before. Why not one more?"[17]

The Union Army put four additional men to death in this same section of the state between June and September 1862. Each died on a different date, in a different locale, for a different offense. In Monroe County on June 8, 1862, Colonel John Owens, "a notorious rebel" as the *Hannibal Herald* described him, was captured, and "preparations were made for his execution.... He was placed on a stump, in front of a file of soldiers, and at the word of command eight bullets pierced the body of the rebel, killing him instantly."[18] In Linn County on August 15, 1862, a Union Army General, Benjamin Loan, ordered the shooting of Calvin Sartain, a Lieutenant in Price's army, as the newspaper phrased it for "several crimes, ... among them the killing of the pilot of the *White Cloud*."[19] Sterling Price, a Virginia native, member of the U.S. Congress from Missouri (1845–46), and twice elected governor of Missouri (1853–57), officially joined the Confederate Army as a major general in March 1862.[20] The *White Cloud* steamboat, commandeered by the Union Army during the war years, transported Union troops on the Missouri River.[21] As such, from the Southern point of view, the death of its pilot was not murder; it was a casualty of war. On September 4, 1862, John Richardson was hanged in Liberty (Clay County) after being convicted of counterfeiting Confederate treasury notes.[22] This may seem an unlikely crime for the Union Army to prosecute, but if the funds of a nation are worth reproducing then the importance of that nation is advanced by such an act, or so someone in charge apparently reasoned. Two days after the hanging of Richardson in Liberty, the provost marshal in Richmond (Ray County) ordered the firing squad death of an unnamed slave charged with attempted rape. The local newspaper stated of the matter, "the guilt of the negro [was] established beyond doubt, not only by the negro's own voluntary admissions, by independent testimony. The negro was sentenced to be shot, which was accordingly done Saturday evening."[23]

Following the executions in Monroe, Linn, Clay, and Ray counties, another Union Army firing squad ended the lives of 10 additional Rebels/Confederates in Macon County on September 26, 1862. Mudd identified two of them, Drake and Riggs, as residents of Shelby County.[24] According to the county history, all were charged and found guilty of "capital crimes against the government."[25] Switzler listed the charges against them as "treason, perjury, and murder."[26] Mudd viewed their deaths in this light. He wrote, "It cannot now and here be stated why these men were shot," and he continued, "A convenient excuse was: He violated his parole, he robbed, he murdered."[27] General Lewis Merrill was in charge of their trials and deaths. On the morning of the date set for their deaths, he received a note from the youngest of the 10, J.A. Wysong, a 20 or 21-year-old:

> general for god sake spare my life for i am a boy I was perswaded do what i have done and forse i will go in service and figt for you and stay with you douring the war i wood been fighting for the union if it had been for others.[28]

On the same day, 10 died in the town of Macon, the Union Army executed another Rebel/Confederate, D.S. Washburne, in Huntsville (Randolph County), the county immediately south of Macon. Whatever might have been the capital charge or charges against him are now unknown.[29]

The next mass shooting of Confederate/Rebel men at the hands of the Union Army took place in Palmyra; five who died were residents of Lewis County, three of Ralls, one of Scotland, and one of Monroe. It is the best known and the most extensively documented of all military executions in Missouri. Colonel John McNeil had presided at the firing squad deaths of 15 men in Kirksville on August 7, 1862, and he implemented another use of the decimal system when now — General — John McNeil gave the order to kill 10 more men in an execution on October 18, 1862, an event that quickly became known as the Palmyra Massacre. Slightly over a month earlier, on September 14, 1862, he had bested the forces of the Confederate, Colonel Joseph C. Porter, in a battle in Palmyra, Marion County. Porter had taken prisoner a Union supporter, Andrew Allsman, aged approximately 60 years, who often snitched to federal authorities on his Southern sympathizing neighbors, and they in turn detested him. Members of Porter's command had almost certainly killed Allsman on either September 15 or 16, or approximately three weeks *before* William R. Strachan, Provost Marshal, Northeast District of Missouri, on orders of General McNeil, sent Joseph C. Porter a notice from Palmyra on October 8, 1862, which read in part:

> This is to notify you that, unless said Andrew Allsman is returned unharmed to his family within ten days from date, ten men, who have belonged to your band, and unlawfully sworn by you to carry arms against the government of the United States, and who are now in custody, will be shot as a meet reward for their crimes, among which is the illegal restraining of said Allsman of his liberty.[30]

Sadly, no trumpet sounded; the dead man, Andrew Allsman, was not raised incorruptible. The conditions set in Strachan's notice to Porter could not be met. As a result and at 1:00 p.m., October 18, 1862, and after Provost Marshal Strachan had shaken hands with them, ten more Rebels/Confederates died firing squad deaths at the fairgrounds near Palmyra. The place at which the eight unnamed guerrillas were shot in Lafayette County on June 8, the names of the 15 shot at Kirksville (Adair County) on August 7, the 10 at the city of Macon (Macon County) on September 26, and the 10 at Palmyra (Marion County) on October 18, 1862, are listed in Appendix 1, "Executions in Missouri, 1803–2005."

Unlike the Kirksville's mass shooting of 15 and Macon's 10, there is extant newspaper coverage of what happened in Palmyra.[31] An Illinois paper in nearby Quincy wrote in part of it, "The prisoners to be executed were chosen by lot, and among the ten selected was a man having a wife and seven children. Another prisoner having been sentenced to be shot

... voluntarily offered to take his place, which was agreed to by Col McNeil."[32] The *Palmyra Courier* story about the shooting was picked up, by among other papers,[33] the *New York Times*, and the New York newspaper also reprinted lengthy comments on this matter by the *London Star*. In part the English paper wrote, "What comment is needed upon a crime like this? Its stupidity is as astounding as its ferocity is terrible." It termed the death of the 10 who died at the Palmyra fairgrounds, "butchery."[34] Mudd reported that after the firing squad death of the 10, on one of his frequent trips to St. Louis, McNeil was introduced to a Union Army general. McNeil advanced to shake his hand, and "the officer turned his back on him saying, 'I do not shake the hand of a murderer.'"[35] Soon after October 18, 1862, the day 10 men were shot in Palmyra on McNeil's orders, he became known as "the butcher of Palmyra." The dirty name stuck with him. In 1891 at least one of his obituaries used the phrase in its headline about his death.[36]

The more publicized horror in Marion County's seat was the shooting of ten men. The monument to the Confederate dead in the Marion County Courtyard memorializes their deaths. The lesser known wrongdoing is the criminal activity of Provost Marshal Colonel William R. Strachan, General John McNeil's able assistant. On Sunday, October 19, 1862, and in Palmyra, Strachan had a visitor, Mrs. Mary Susan Humphrey, a 20-year-old with her two step-children and a two-week-old infant. She was the wife of Thomas Humphrey, a man originally scheduled to be shot but through his wife's efforts reprieved the previous day. She incorrectly believed, as the county history reported, that "Gen. McNeil intended to shoot ten men *every* Saturday until Mr. Allsman was returned. Her husband

Monument to the victims of the October 18, 1862, Palmyra Massacre, Marion County Courthouse Square. (Photographs by the author.)

had run one death gauntlet, and Mrs. Humphrey did not wish him to run another."[37] When Strachan told her that he had the power to have her husband shot or released, she believed him. When at his request, she agreed to make the beast with two backs with him in his office, this poontang was not consented-to sex; it was rape. The county history continued, "Two soldiers of McNeil's regiment saw Mrs. Humphrey's little step-daughter standing outside the building and crying. Investigating at once they saw enough to convince them that a fearful wrong had been committed, and they so reported throughout the camp, whereupon there was great indignation and denunciation."[38]

In September 1863, W.R. Strachan, by now a state representative from Shelby County in the Missouri General Assembly, was arrested in Quincy, Illinois, by order of the Provost Marshal General and taken from Quincy to St. Louis.[39] Early in 1864 the colonel was tried before a court-martial in St. Louis on 11 charges, all of which arose out of his conduct while Provost-Marshal at Palmyra. Among the alleged offenses were embezzlement, receiving bribes for the release of prisoners, extortion, willfully selling and disposing of the public property of the United States at private sale, and rape. The many witnesses against him included Mrs. Mary Susan Humphrey. Her testimony at Strachan's court-martial was clear:

Q. Did you know at the time you submitted to Strachan that your husband had been reprieved?
A. Yes sir, of course.
Q. By the Court. How long after this occurrence with Strachan was your husband released and allowed to go home?
A. It was on Wednesday or Thursday after the Sunday on which this occurred with Strachan.[40]

After a lengthy trial, the nine officers who acted as jury in Strachan's court-martial found him guilty of "extortion and oppression" and "prostituting his official power and position to the accomplishment of base and grossly immoral ends" and not guilty on the other charges, including rape. He was sentenced to pay the government $680 and to be imprisoned for one year. On appeal, that is on orders of Major General Rosecrans, the court-martial's findings and sentence were disapproved and the accused "honorably released from arrest."[41]

Despite wholly credible evidence, the officers who sat in judgment at Colonel Strachan's court-martial had insufficient courage to find him guilty of rape, a capital offense under martial law, at least for enlisted men, and we know that attempted rape was a capital offense under this same law if the accused was a slave. Even the relatively mild charges of which this high ranking officer was convicted disappeared when Rosecrans, then commander of the Department of Missouri, reviewed them. As a result, when John McNeil, no longer welcome in Palmyra or St. Louis, was transferred to the Union Army Post at Rolla, Missouri, he took Colonel Strachan with him. At Rolla, Strachan secured a confession from a Union Army private, which was an immense help to the judge advocate in securing the enlisted man's death sentence.

Following the killing of 10 in Marion County, the Union Army officiated at only one additional mass retaliatory execution of men here. The firing squad deaths of six Confederate prisoners of war took place in St. Louis, on the orders of General Rosecrans. As payback, he ordered the shooting of the men whose names appear in Appendix 1 on October 29, 1864. Somewhat earlier the bodies of James Wilson, a Union Army officer, and six of his men, captured in Iron County, were found 15 miles southwest of Washington, Franklin County, evidently shot in cold blood.[42] One of the prisoners selected to revenge the death of Wilson spoke immediately before his execution in St. Louis: "I have been a Confederate soldier for four years, and ... have served my country faithfully. And I am taken out now and shot ... for what I had nothing to do with. I never was a guerrilla, and I am ... to be shot ... for what I am not guilty of."[43] In this tit-for-tat environment, General Rosecrans intended to even the score for the murder of James Wilson, a major in the Union Army, with one of equivalent rank in the Southern Army. Shortly, Major Enoch O. Wolf, a Confederate officer, was captured, and the general ordered his execution for November 11, 1864. Some concerned residents of St. Louis secured a delay of 14 days in order for Wolf to ready himself for death. Soon afterwards, as Thomas Scharf related, "President Lincoln wired General Rosecrans: 'Suspend execution in case of Maj. Wolf until further orders, and meanwhile report to me in the case.' The execution of Maj. Wolf was never carried into effect."[44]

The adverse reaction of the out-of-state press to the most publicized employment of the 10-for-one system in Palmyra on October 18, 1862, appears to have ended the Northern Army's use of it. Instead of lining up large groups of Southern-sympathizing Missouri men and boys in order to shoot them to death, the policy changed. After examining extant records of military commissions held here, it is clear that the Union Army did not sentence to death all Missouri citizens convicted of bushwhacking, robbery, violating their oaths of allegiance, and the like. Instead, for Rebels captured here *after* 1862, the most common punishment these tribunals handed down was confinement at hard labor. A number were sent to the military prison at Alton, Illinois.[45] Their sentences might also combine imprisonment at Alton with a fine.[46] An 1863 St. Louis newspaper confirms that a military commission held at St. Louis sentenced 17 men, residents of the far-flung counties of Cass, Clark, Jackson, Johnson, Lewis, Monroe, and Texas, whom it found guilty of violating their oaths of allegiance, to the military prison at Alton "during the present rebellion."[47] In other cases, the Union Army sent bushwhackers to another correctional facility it then ran, the MSP (Missouri State Penitentiary) in Jefferson City.[48] According to the local newspaper, a military commission held in St. Joseph in 1864 sentenced five bushwhackers to MSP for the duration of the war. Accompanying them to Jefferson City was a Union Army private whom a general court-martial convicted of shooting with intent to murder a civilian; his sentence was one year at hard labor in the same prison.[49] Perhaps the most unexpected punishment a military commission handed down, to a resident of the southeast part of the state, was banishment from this state to a free state during the war, "not to return to Missouri under penalty of death." Specifically the prisoner was sentenced to live in Iowa.[50]

Though the *mass* execution of civilians here ended with the Palmyra Massacre, the execution of civilians did not. Those whom the Union Army put to death for their secessionist, rebel, guerrilla, or bushwhacking activity died either alone or with one other man or boy. They can be classified by the area of the state in which their lives were ended. At times the newspaper or county history report of the event mentions the proceeding which sentenced the accused to death; at others it does not. Likewise some accounts specific the method of death, whether a firing squad or a hanging, and others do not. A court-martial was usually convened for the trial of military personnel, and a military commission for the trial of civilians. Both proceedings typically allowed the condemned a minimum interval of one or more weeks between trial and death. On the other hand, a drumhead court-martial was held in the field, and its chief characteristic was speed; perhaps as brief a time span as 15 to 20 minutes for the arrest, trial and execution, or the condemned might live a few hours or days longer.

In the northeast section of the state, some record remains regarding five Confederate/ bushwhackers whom the Union Army shot or hanged between May 6, 1863, and March 3,

1865.[51] Documentation survives of nine persons executed in central Missouri by the same authority between August 1863 and June 2, 1865. Two men, Dr. Zimmerman and Frederick Hamilton, were charged with stealing horses; their defense was that they had taken the wrong animals, mistakenly believing them to be their own mounts. Union Army officer, Lt. Colonel Thomas T. Crittenden — later Governor Crittenden who pardoned Jesse James' killers—conducted a drumhead court-martial of which no written record appears ever to have been made, and at it he ordered that Zimmerman and Hamilton be shot to death two days later at 5:00 a.m. at Tipton, Moniteau County, on September 25, 1863.[52] We know about seven other central Missouri Union Army executions of Confederate/bushwhackers,[53] including 17-year-old Paddy Mullins, shot to death at Tipton (Moniteau County) on April 23, 1864, on orders of General Rosecrans.[54] Unlike many other persons dispatched by the Union Army here, John Nichols' case lays out a clear time span. He was tried by a military commission which convened on June 16; President Lincoln approved Nichols' death sentence on September 10, and he was hanged October 30, 1863, in Jefferson City, Cole County.[55] Before his death he confessed, "I have been a Confederate soldier and did all I could for the interests of the Confederacy.... I am not a guerrilla in its proper sense." Just before the drop fell, he spoke his last words, "See how a Confederate soldier can die."[56] Northwest Missouri accounts for five other Union Army executions of guerrillas between November 6, 1863 and September 9, 1864.[57] Finally, in the city of St. Louis, the military put to death six additional Confederate/bushwhackers between September 9, 1864 and March 25, 1865.[58]

Despite the fact that secessionist activities of the executed often occurred in remote areas, the military did not always end their lives in the sticks. We are able to confirm a number of death sentences of rebels because newspapers continued to be regularly published in places under Union control, especially St. Louis. In the 1860 election, this city's German and Irish residents gave Lincoln 17,028 of the 27,000 votes he received in all the slave states in the 1860 election.[59] There was no safer place in Missouri than the city of St. Louis for the North to hang and shoot those it sentenced to death. As a result we know what happened far more frequently than we would had the military ended the lives of all Confederate/bushwhackers in the Missouri counties where they had been at large.

Nonetheless, there are gaps in our knowledge. Two death sentences of civilians and one of a union soldier here *cannot be confirmed* as carried out. On August 27, 1863, in St. Joseph a military commission found William McDaniels guilty of being a military insurgent and sentenced him to be shot with musketry "by some United States forces, at such time and place as the General Command may designate."[60] Likewise in the city of Macon, a military commission which met on February 14, 1865, found Marion Erwin guilty of being a guerrilla in October 1864 and sentenced him to be hanged at Macon on March 17, 1865.[61] No county history or extant newspaper I discovered mentions him. Though President Lincoln on May 20, 1863 approved the death sentence which a military commission handed down to Private William Cox for violation of the laws of war, specifically for robbery and rape in Greene County on October 18, 1862,[62] nothing I could locate substantiates that Cox was executed.

We turn from the accounts of the Union Army putting primarily civilians to death to the proceedings in which Union soldiers were the defendants. Word-for-word transcripts of the trials, including Private William Cox's, which were held in Missouri are available in seven of the nine death penalty cases. In state court of the same time period, there is only a summary of the testimony. These handwritten records are in question and answer form; they provide an amazing look at the way the military dealt with its own.

For the most part we know these Union Army deaths took place because, in 1885 and after a number of requests, the Adjutant General reluctantly published "List of U.S. Soldiers Executed by United States Military Authorities during the Late War." It was "For Official Use Only," and handwritten on a copy at the National Archives is "Confidential." The list consists of 11 pages; in alphabetical order are the states which contributed volunteers to the Union Army, followed by categories such as U.S. Volunteers, Veteran Reserve Corp., U.S. Colored Troops, Regulars, and Miscellaneous. In the appropriate category are printed the Name, Rank, Company, Regiment, Date of Execution, Mode of Execution, (whether hanged or shot), Offense, and Authority (that is the number of the order, the department, and the date, usually the day before the execution), for each of the 268 members of the U.S. military put to death by the Union Army during the Civil War.[63] Of these, at least, 257 were privates, and the remainder corporals (two), sergeants (seven), and first sergeants (two). If there was even one U.S. officer shot or hanged by U. S. Military Authority, his name is not on the list nor is anything known about him. These who died these inglorious deaths were the lowest of the low. All executions which took place here involved white defendants.

Two without transcripts of the courts-martial which handed down the death sentence in Missouri can be confirmed from other information. In John Cole's case, some Union Army soldiers who were Kansas Volunteers published a newspaper, "Cosmopolite," and its July 23, 1861 issue recounts, "An unfortunate occurrence took place in our company, resulting in the death of a private name Stein, who was stabbed in the back.... The murderer's name was Jos. N. Cole.... A general court-martial being ordered, he was found guilty, and at sunset last evening was shot in presence of the whole regiment."[64] The shooting occurred by General Nathaniel Lyon's command in Greene County. The 1885 "List of U.S. soldiers executed by U.S. Military Authorities" contains Private John W. Cole's name under Kansas, his regiment was 1st Infantry, and the date of his execution July 14, 1861.

The service record of Private John Reily, Jr. clarifies that as punishment for the crime of murder, on April 29, 1864, this 21-year-old was shot to death by a 10-member-firing squad in Warrensburg (Johnson County). The quartermaster of the district provided the coffin and transportation and superintended the interment of the remains. A special order of April 25, 1864, laid out the order of the procession to the place of Reily's death: 1. Provost Marshal, 2. Brigade Band, 3. Firing Party, 4. Coffin borne by four men, 5. Hearse with prisoner and chaplain, 6. Provost Guard, and 7. troops.[65] The 1885 list contains John Reily, Jr.'s name under Missouri, his regiment was 2nd Artillery, and the date of his execution April 29, 1864.

For the remaining Union soldiers executed by the U.S. Army in Missouri, there are handwritten transcripts of the proceedings at which an odd number of officers decided that the accused must die. Usually, the carrying out of these shameful deaths of the enlisted men can be confirmed through their service records.

The crime most removed from any civilian experience which carried a death sentence was desertion. It was a capital offense for members of the U.S. military in war and peace until 1830 when the U.S. Congress decreed that in peace time desertion was no longer a capital offense.[66] The Civil War changed any thought that deserters would not be death-eligible. The 1885 Adjutant General's Report clarifies that approximately one-half of U.S. servicemen executed during the late war were found guilty of desertion. Those men who wished to avoid military service altogether were allowed under the Enrollment Act, which the 37th Congress passed in 1863, to pay no more than $300 to a substitute who would serve in place of the draftee.[67] Hence, sons of affluent persons could easily shun service in the Union Army. Poor persons were never able to buy their way out of their military obligations; $200 in 1863 is at least worth $10,000 in today's money. To add insult to injury, most Union Army executions for desertion took place after Congress passed the Enrollment Act in March 1863.

There is one known deserter arrested, prosecuted, and shot to death in Missouri. His name was Private Barney Gibbons, and he enlisted in the Union Army at or near San Augustine Spring, New Mexico Territory, in 1858. Eventually he joined Company A, 7th U.S. Infantry at Camp Floyd, Utah Territory, and he served with it approximately two years. While on a march from San Augustine to a U.S. Army post, named after President Millard Fillmore, Fort Fillmore, New Mexico Territory,[68] Union Major Lynde eventually surrendered his forces to the Confederates in July 1861. Instead of remaining a prisoner of war with his fellow soldiers, all of whom were finally paroled, Gibbons joined the Southern side and served under Confederate General Henry Sibley in New Mexico and Texas; when Gibbons left the Confederate Army he became a double deserter. After employments in New Orleans, Louisiana, and Knob Noster, Missouri, by chance he was standing on Broadway Street in St. Louis the summer of 1864, when former Union Army Sergeant Richard C. Day, with whom Gibbons had served two years in Company A, 7th U.S. Infantry, saw and arrested him. Day had previously last seen Gibbons in the Southwest, as he testified at Gibbon's court-martial, "riding out on a black horse with the rebels.... Yes, he was going out with the rebels to fight three companies of our regiment." Day further testified that approximately three years after their Southwest service together when Gibbons saw him on the St. Louis street, "He turned as white as a sheet." No, there could be no mistake in Day's identifying Gibbons because as Day stated of him, "He has a cut upon his lip and a peculiar manner of walking." Once the prosecution closed, Gibbons made a disastrous statement to the Court. He denied both that he had ever served in the Union Army and that his name was Barney Gibbons. That was his brother's name; he was Benjamin Gray. No one believed him. On July 15, 1864, two-thirds of the members of the Court concurred that Private Barney Gibbons was guilty of desertion, and the Court ordered him to be shot to death. General Rosecrans approved the death sentence; he ordered it to take place August 12, 1864, at St. Louis, Missouri.[69] On that date, Gibbons died before a six-member firing squad, as the newspaper reported in detail, "in the rear of Fort No. 4, in a southwestern suburb of the city [of St. Louis]"[70]

Had the Confederate Army managed the same control in Missouri as did its Union counterpart, Mark Twain might have been shot for desertion. In 1885 he wrote a whimsical piece about his brief service in the Confederate Army during the early summer of 1861, that is, when Union forces invaded his state. He and other young men "swore on the Bible to be faithful to the State of Missouri and drive all invaders from her soil."[71] After several weeks of soldiering with others from his home county of Marion (they called themselves Marion Rangers), he tired of military service and went home. About this same time, his brother, Orion Clemens, had secured an appointment as Secretary of Nevada Territory with the help of the St. Louis attorney, Edward Bates, now Lincoln's attorney general. As Twain's biographer, Margaret Sanborn, describes it, "to avoid being drafted to pilot a Union riverboat, or arrested as a possible spy," Sam Clemens accompanied his brother to Nevada Territory. They departed on July 18, 1861, and throughout the war years, Mark Twain remained in Nevada and California, far from the Civil War battlefields.[72]

Among those who chose a different path and became Missouri Volunteers in the Union Army was Private Edward Eastman. He enlisted at Springfield, Missouri, on May 31, 1864, when aged 19 years. Less than four months later he was tried by a five-member court-martial which convened in Rolla (Phelps County) on September 16, 1864. He was charged with leaving his colors to pillage and plunder, a violation of Article 52 of the 1806 "Act for ... the government of the armies of the United States." The allegations were that Eastman and Frank Jones, another private in the same company, went in the nighttime in civilian clothes to a farm where they robbed one Phillip Sommerlot, a citizen, of clothing and jewelry valued at $60 and Mrs. Nancy L. Davis of a revolver valued at $30. To these charges Eastman pled guilty.

Hence all proof in his case involved the additional charge that he and Frank Jones on September 12, 1864, went in the nighttime to the home of Thomas Cole, a citizen, and attempted by force of arms to possess some weapons belonging to him. The judge advocate's first witness was Thomas Cole, farmer. He testified that on September 12 about 10:00 p.m. two men knocked at his door and asked for water. He gave one man water, and the other asked if he had any firearms. Cole replied that he did, and when one said they wanted them, he replied they could not have them. One then cocked his revolver, and the farmer stepped around the door and shot him; both ran off. Cole knew the one he did not shoot at was the one of the two who wanted his arms, but he was unable to identify the prisoner, Private Edward Eastman.

The prosecutor then called his second witness, the man court-martialed in St. Louis early that same year, on rape and 10 other charges in connection with the Palmyra Massacre. In answer to the question, "State your name, occupation and residence," he replied, "My name is William R. Strachan. [I] am a Special Agent of the United States Secret Police, was ordered to report [here] to General McNeil [the butcher of Palmyra] on special service." Strachan testified about obtaining a confession from Eastman. He stated "the particulars of the transaction," namely that "this other man had importuned him to go out with him.... They stopped at this house for some water.... He asked the man of the house whether he was armed, when he asked him that question the man fired and shot his comrade." Strachan continued that Eastman had told him that "He went off with his comrade a piece, bandaged his wound, told his comrade he would leave him, and he started for his quarters; that is the substance of his statement." Through the further testimony of Strachan, the judge advocate got into evidence the dying declaration of Frank Jones, Eastman's companion whom Thomas Cole shot the night of September 12; Jones died the next day. General McNeil sent Strachan to take the testimony of the mortally wounded man. He testified of him, "I found him at the hospital very low. The Surgeon had announced to him that he could not live, and it was with difficulty that he could speak." To the judge advocate's question, "Was he [Frank Jones] aware that he was on the point of death?" he answered, "Yes he was." Through Special Agent Strachan, the prosecutor got into evidence Jones' dying statement that he and Eastman went to a farmer's house requesting water, next firearms, and the farmer shot him.

A third and final prosecution witness, 2nd Lt. Thomas Caris, testified that at 1:00 a.m. September 13 he was awakened, told a man of his battery was wounded, went three or four miles to a house where a squad of cavalry guarded the house. In it, he "found a man named Jones, lying on a bed on the floor mortally wounded." This officer "put him in the ambulance and brought him to the Post Hospital at Rolla," and Jones died at 10:00 a.m. the morning of September 13. With these three witnesses, the judge advocate closed the prosecution's case.

It was then Eastman's turn to put on his defense. It is unlikely that he was represented by his own attorney. If there were one present in his behalf, he conducted himself as a deaf mute. There were neither defense witnesses nor any cross examination of the prosecutor's three witnesses. Probably, the prosecutor was also the defense attorney. Article 69 of the

Rules of War contained this curious provision: "The judge advocate ... shall prosecute in the name of the United States, but shall [also] consider himself as counsel for the prisoner." Apparently this woebegone private relied on the prosecutor to act as his defense attorney. Clearly, the accused had not understood the grave implications of confessing the particulars of his crime to Special Agent Strachan; had he remained silent there is a slim chance that he might have been found not guilty. The first witness, Thomas Cole, could not identify him. Sadly, this young man's defense consisted of a brief and ungrammatical statement "that he was coaxed into it and never done anything of that sort until this time. This being my first break I hope the Court will be as easy with me as possible, and I will try to be a good soldier." He submitted his case without further comment; the jury panel found him guilty, and General Rosecrans signed the order that Eastman be shot to death with musketry on October 7, 1864.

From St. Louis, on September 24, 1864, Major General Rosecrans added to Eastman's death sentence for "leaving his colors to pillage and plunder in violation of the 52nd Article of War," this directive to General McNeil, now the Commanding Officer of the District of Rolla, Missouri, "The General Command may desire to warn all soldiers in his command of the stern punishment prescribed for offenses of this class of his determination to prevent their occurrence in future by vigorous enforcement of the rigors of law."[73] A newspaper carried a story that Eastman was to be shot on Oct. 1.[74] However, Private Edward Eastman's Service Record clarifies that he was executed on November 25, 1864 at Rolla, Missouri,[75] and the 1885 list also contains November 25, 1864 as the date of his execution.[76]

Additional courts-martial of Union Army soldiers include four for murder for which extant transcripts of the proceedings are available, one corporal and three privates. The earliest involves Corporal Paul Kingston, a 34-year-old married man. As his service record indicates, he had had prior difficulties. An order was out to apprehend him as a deserter by February 15, 1863, but apparently, nothing of consequence came of any desertion charge. Kingston's and Private George R. Sutton's leaving the Cape Girardeau Army Post for an evening of relaxation on August 29, 1863, at sundown appears to have been routine. According to Sutton, a prosecution witness, he and Kingston went to a saloon where the accused drank three glasses of beer, but the corporal did not become intoxicated. Sutton's testimony included mention that as he on horseback and Kingston on foot approached the Catholic Church near the tannery on Spanish Street in the town of Cape Girardeau, the defendant encountered John Charters on the sidewalk. All the witnesses agreed, Kingston fired three shots into him, and shortly the man died. Through Sutton, who had known the accused about two years, the judge advocate established that at the time Kingston shot Charters, he was not drunk, insane, or "subject to fits of insanity," but that he was, as Sutton testified, "of a quarrelsome disposition."

In addition to two other soldiers, the prosecution put on two women. The first was white, Mrs. Adelaide Harrison. She stated that the night of August 29, 1863, was a "clear bright moonlight night." On that evening, she stepped to a second-story window when she heard someone call "guard." Next, she saw and heard three shots fired into the victim, and immediately afterwards "ran downstairs and opened the door and found Mr. Charters lying at the door mortally wounded." The prosecutor's second woman witness was a person of color, Rachael Johnson; she was with Mrs. Harrison and babysitting a Mrs. Moon's children, when she too saw two men scuffling, heard three shots fired, and saw, as she testified, "the man that done the shooting then [run] down Spanish Street." Finally, she was asked whether or not the victim used any weapons. She answered, "He did not." Had the case been tried in any state court in Missouri at this time, no African-American was competent to testify against a white person, but this was not a civilian court. Expectedly, Rachael Jackson was illiterate; she signed her testimony with her mark, an X. (After all it was then a crime under Missouri law to teach a colored person, slave or free, to read and write.) She was the prosecutor's last witness, and the government then closed its case.

Kingston neither cross-examined any prosecution witness nor put on any defense witnesses. After the usual two-thirds of the court-martial panel found him guilty of murder, and the court sentenced him to hang, he wrote a self-serving confession about having consumed approximately 19 glasses of beer the night he staggered against a man who grabbed at his revolver, "and the pistol fired." The perpetrator fired again because the victim "was doing something with his hands and ... trying to get a weapon." His confession concluded, "In the eyes of the law I am a murderer but not in my heart. I did the deed while intoxicated. I ask your leniency.[77]

An extant newspaper story about the crime concludes, "Kingston was immediately arrested by the military and placed in confinement to await a trial by military court-martial. He unquestionably deserves to be hung."[78] His service record clarifies that at 11:00 a.m., November 27, 1863, Corporal Paul Kingston was hanged for murder at Cape Girardeau, Missouri.[79] The 1885 Adjutant General's Report correctly lists Kingston's crime as murder and the date of his execution as November 27, 1863.[80]

The youngest persons, both privates, whom the Union Army prosecuted here for murder and executed were Abraham Purvis and Ephraim Richardson. They were charged with the November 18, 1864 murder of a farmer, Dominick Patton, near Bridgeton in St. Louis County. At their court-martial held December 7, 1864, the judge advocate established through its witnesses, including a German speaker who required a translator, that the defendants stopped eight to ten wagons of travelers on the National Bridge Plank Road and asked each driver for half a dollar. In the process one of the young soldiers shot the victim. The crime occurred near dusk, and none of the witnesses could identify which of the boys fired the single shot, but it was established that Richardson's gun had recently discharged. The judge advocate's last witness was a physician. He testified that when he first saw the victim, he "was in a dying condition ... pulseless and cold.... A minnie ball passed directly through his lungs and liver and lodged in the vertebrae of his back." Dominick Patton, the doctor stated, bled to death.[81]

Neither Purvis nor Richardson, tried together, cross-examined any prosecution witnesses, put on any of their own witnesses, nor made any statements which are a part of the court-martial proceedings. They were apparently tried as the 1806 Articles of War permitted with the prosecuting attorney also serving as their defense lawyer. They were put to death in the city of St. Louis jail yard. The 1885 list is correct; it states that their crime was murder, and they were hanged on January 13, 1865.

No discovered document(s) contain their dates of birth, but all available records indicate that Abraham Purvis was the younger. Most likely, he was aged 16 years both when he committed his crime and when executed. The 1850 federal census, taken in January, lists him as aged one year and four months, living with his parents, the youngest of seven children, in Scotland County, Missouri. It suggests that he was born in September 1848. His service record establishes that he was illiterate; he put his mark to his volunteer enlistment. Also contained in his service record is the signature of his guardian, Patrick Chancellor, dated February 12, 1864, on a "Consent in Case of Minor Form," that his ward was aged 18 years. Chancellor committed perjury when he signed it[82]; most likely, Purvis was 15 years old when he enlisted in the Union Army. Ephraim Richardson, also from Scotland County, Missouri, was either aged 17 or 18 on the date of his crime. His service record contains his age as 16 on both November 16, 1862, and September 17, 1863, and 16 and 17 when paid on August 31, 1864.[83] One newspaper which covered their execution listed their ages: Purvis, 16, and Richardson, 17.[84] Another paper gave Purvis' age as 16 and Richardson's as 18.[85]

The previous spring, April 1864, and on orders of General Rosecrans, a Union Army firing squad shot to death Paddy Mullins, bushwhacker, aged 17 years. Prior to these two or three Union Army execution of boys aged under age 18 at the time of their crime, capital punishment for juveniles here had been reserved for African-Americans. The Civil War ushered in the death penalty in Missouri for white boys.

The remaining Union Army prosecution for murder took place in St. Joseph. It differs from the other military proceedings here in several respects. It is by far the longest, at least three times the length of other court-martial transcripts discussed herein. *U.S. v Jefferson Jackson* is approximately 58 handwritten pages. In addition, the accused was represented by his own attorney; he slightly cross-examined some of the judge advocate's witnesses, and he put on a few of his own. The most important difference between this case and the other homicide prosecutions is the inappropriateness of charging the accused with murder. The crime he committed was a textbook case of manslaughter. Going back centuries of English law and continuing in the American colonies and later the states, manslaughter was not a capital offense. Blackstone distinguishes it from murder in this way: "Manslaughter arises from the sudden heat of the passions, murder from the wickedness of the heart. ... [Manslaughter] must be done without premeditation."[86] Since the Union Army executed for murder, not a lesser degree of culpable killing of another human being, the accused was charged with a crime he never committed.

The offense took place outside a saloon in the town of St. Joseph on August 27, 1864. The defendant, Jefferson Jackson, a farmer from Sturgeon (Boone County), was an illiterate private, a Missouri Volunteer, who made his mark, an X, on his court-martial transcript. His service record indicates that he was aged 22 years when he enlisted; he had served under a Captain Adams about two years, making him approximately 24 years old when he went saloon-hopping with Private John Greene, Company K, First Cavalry Regiment, Iowa Volunteers, another member of the Union Army.[87]

The defense was well aware of the victim's earlier violation of the Rules of War when it put on its witnesses. Article 32 required that "every officer ... shall keep good order, and ... redress all abuses or disorders, which, may be committed by any ... soldier under his command; if upon complaint made to him of ... soldiers ... ill treating any person ... and reparations made to the party injured, as, far as part of the offender's pay shall enable him" Article 38 provided, "Every ... soldier, who shall be convicted before a court-martial, of having ... lost, through neglect his horse, arms, clothes ... shall undergo such weekly stoppages (not exceeding the half of his pay) as such court-martial shall judge sufficient for repairing the loss...; and shall suffer confinement."

The first defense witness, H.P. Lyon, a 47-year-old resident of St. Joseph, proprietor of a saloon and boarding house, testified to his personal knowledge of John Greene:

The first acquaintance I had with him he came into my saloon, drew his pistol and ordered some beer. When we gave him the beer he went out and told us to charge it to Uncle Sam. I told him I was not in the habit of doing that kind of business, and he had better come and pay for the beer or I would have him arrested. I reported the fact to a lieutenant of the First Iowa Cavalry, and he told me he was a desperate man and I ought not to fool with him. He came back about a couple days after that, and he had neither horse, hat, nor arms. He said they had been stolen, was very much in liquor and could hardly get along. I told him to go away. There was a captain and two lieutenants there of the First Iowa Calvary, and they told me his character; they said he had not done any service since he had been in the regiment.

Q. Did you learn this from these officers or was it his general reputation?

A. His general reputation among the officers was that he was worthless, good for nothing, rude and insulting to everybody. That when I ordered him out of the house it was a great wonder he did not draw his revolver and shoot me.

A second witness, the proprietor of the Waverly Hotel, also testified that a besotted Greene had lost his revolver. Had due diligence been at work, Jackson's victim would have spent some time in the guardhouse and forfeited part of his pay for the dual infractions of refusing to pay his bar bill and losing his horse, hat, and arms because he was drunk. No punishment appears to have been meted out to him for these offenses, and as a result, he was once more a patron of the saloons of St. Joseph with plenty of money to spend on beer on August 27, 1864.

Most of the witnesses at Jefferson's court-martial were customers at, employees of, and owners of drinking establishments. The judge advocate called 19-year-old John Roach, "by occupation a bar keeper" at John McGinley's saloon. Roach testified that Greene came in and "treated a lot of soldiers to beer," including the defendant. The witness heard the victim say that "he was down on bushwhackers." The word *bushwhacker* appears repeatedly throughout the transcript. Roach recalled that the prisoner said of himself that he was a bushwhacker, but it was unclear whether or not he said it in jest or in earnest. Another prosecution witness, T.K. McGuire, the proprietor of an eating establishment, Waverly House, testified: "My impression is that the prisoner used it, and it appeared that he used it as a repetition of a charge made by the deceased." McGuire recalled that the only difficulty between the deceased and the prisoner was "about that term bushwhacker." Another prosecution witness was Timothy Deasay, aged 27 years, occupation railroading, and a McGinty's Saloon patron on August 27. His testimony included mention that Greene had called "us all to have some beer" and "I heard something about Greene's accusing him [Jefferson Jackson] of being a bushwhacker. Jack said he was or something like that in a funny way." Deasay also remembered that Greene had addressed two other civilian men in this bar as "you damm butternuts," a derogatory term for soldiers or supporters of the Confederacy. The defense attorney asked the railroader, Timothy Deasay, "Did the prisoner appear to be much excited about being called a bushwhacker?" The judge advocate objected to the question, but Deasay had already answered, "Yes."

Another prosecution witness, Andrew Burns, a 23-year-old proprietor of the Cottage Home Saloon, also recalled Greene and Jackson being in his place of business and hearing "the term bushwhacker used." His memory was that Jackson had said it "in reference to someone having called him a bushwhacker." The judge advocate asked Burns if "the prisoner here was drunk at the time when you saw him. Burns answered, "I believe he was a little the worse of liquor." Yet another prosecution witness, John McGinty, a 22-year-old saloon keeper, recalled Jackson's reaction: "All I know is that Jack said he didn't allow any dammed man to call him a bushwhacker."

The witnesses who saw the killing agreed that it took place on the street immediately in front of the door of the Cottage Home Saloon. John Greene died within a few minutes after Jefferson Jackson struck him three times with a piece of wood, "a heavy hickory club," as it was termed in the charge against him. It was also agreed that the defendant was not carrying the stick as a concealed weapon. Rather he had picked it up, as one government witness testified, "from the wood yard in the street." The blows fell on the back of Greene's head, said one who testified; on the back of his neck, said another. The judge advocate's last witness was James T. Bruner, a physician, called to examine the body of the deceased.

He determined that the occipital bone, the bone that forms the back part of the skull, "had been mashed into fragments.... And the blood still flowed copiously, showing there had been a rupture of internal blood vessels." The victim had hemorrhaged to death.

Had Private Jackson struck his superior officer, or lifted up any weapon against him, regardless of the outcome, under Article 9 of the 1806 Rules, he would have been death-eligible. This was a case, however, of one private, who had been drinking. striking and probably accidentally killing another private who the perpetrator believed had called him a vile name, *bushwhacker*. Jackson, an illiterate young man, was ill-equipped to respond verbally to any remark, such as the defendant put his X to, which "bring[s] disgrace upon a party so charged." He could not riposte with a cutting comment of his own. He heard fighting words, and he struck the speaker of them in a heat of passion.

Jackson attempted to obtain a continuance in order to put on a character witness. He had been unable to subpoena an officer in his regiment because Captain Adams had left by train for St. Louis immediately before Jackson was notified that his court-martial was set for trial. Had the continuance been granted, and it was not, Adams, his superior officer would have testified that for a period of more than two years Private Jackson had conducted himself "in a manner highly satisfactory."

On September 9, 1864, and after a three-day proceeding, the requisite two-thirds of the jury-officers found him guilty of murder. The Court sentenced him to be shot to death. On September 9, the papers in the case were forwarded from St. Joseph to Union Headquarters in St. Louis. On September 23, Major General Rosecrans approved them and set October 24 as the date for Jackson's execution.[88]

Contemporary press coverage about Private Jefferson Jackson, which confused his first and last name, began on October 20 with mention that Jackson Jefferson [*sic*] was "to be shot."[89] A week later the paper reported, "A Murderer Reprieved. Execution of Jackson Jefferson [*sic*] Postponed for One Week."[90] A firing squad ended Private Jackson's life on October 28, 1864, as the 1885 list, his service record, and the local newspaper reported.[91] Nowhere in any coverage of this case, including a local newspaper, an 1881 history of Missouri, and a 1904 history of Buchanan County, is there any mention of the victim's character or of the defendant being called a terrible name, *bushwhacker*. It was the judge advocate's call, not the defendant's in the Civil War era, as to whether or not the press would be admitted to courts-martial proceedings. *U.S. v Jefferson Jackson* was not open to the public; had it been, there would be newspaper coverage of it, including mention of the constant use of the word *bushwhacker* throughout the trial.

Had the writ of habeas corpus not been suspended, among many other rights these civilians and enlisted men would have been entitled to before they were put to death was the right to a public trial, the right to a jury of their peers, the right to a unanimous verdict of their guilt by that jury, the right to their own attorney, and the list goes on. Desertion, attempted burglary, counterfeiting Confederate treasury notes, violation of parole, rape, manslaughter, being a guerrilla, and a host of other charges were not capital crimes under Missouri law. Had there not been a war raging all around the Union Army's many uses of gallows and firing squads, their prosecutors would have obtained very few, if any, death sentences. However, this was war, and the results would linger long after the shooting stopped.

4

Black and White, 1866–1889

The Union Army executed 81 identified, eight unidentified, and an unspecified number of unknown persons during the Civil War in Missouri. Additionally, the war involved the loss of nearly 13,000 men and boys from this state as a result of battlefield deaths, wounds, and the ravages of disease.[1] The civilian population here also suffered mightily. Two recent books deal exclusively with guerrilla fighting here during the conflict.[2] Outside St. Louis, scarcely a county was untouched by the killing, burning, looting, and destruction of crops and livestock. An earlier writer, Joseph P. Mudd, described the hostilities here in these vivid terms:

> The [Union Army] plan of conducting the war 'with great severity' seemed to multiply the number of rebels; the burning of their houses multiplied it, the killing of prisoners multiplied it, confiscations multiplied it…. We had orders to remain as still as death until the enemy [the Union Army] began to come up the hill and were fully abreast of our line. When the river was full of men and swimming with horses a murderous fire from the two companies was poured upon them at from twenty to one hundred and twenty yards. The effect was terrible. Not less, I think, than a hundred and twenty-five men must have fallen at the single volley from double-barreled shotguns and rifles. Nearly all who fell from any cause into the swift current were drowned amid the plunging horses.[3]

Persons who survive such chaos and confusion may carry undetected battle scars. A physician, Mendez Da Costa, treated Union Army troops at a military hospital in Philadelphia. He observed among the soldiers what he termed "irritable heart." He noted that otherwise healthy men developed cardiac problems when they were assigned "constant and heavy duty on the picket line or during active movements in the face of any enemy." He noted symptoms among these battle-weary troops such as "disturbed rest, … unpleasant character of the dreams, and inordinate sweating of the hands."[4] Today, this doctor's discovery of the psychosomatic difficulties of war veterans is a precursor of what was eventually termed post-traumatic stress disorder (hereinafter PTSD). It arises, as I.S. Parrish explains, "as a delayed and/or protracted response to a stressful event or situation (either short or long lasting) of an exceptionally threatening or catastrophic nature, which is likely to cause pervasive distress in almost anyone."[5]

It is my contention that the war in Missouri affected her entire society long after seemingly peaceful times returned. The concept of PTSD helps to explain why, 15 to 35 years after the War of the Rebellion ended, this state experienced more peacetime lynchings and executions than at any time in its history. Those at risk to develop this disease, as a diagnostic manual phrases it, include persons who "experienced, witnessed, or were confronted with an event or events that involved actual or threatened death or serious injury or a threat to the physical integrity of self or others."[6] This broad category includes virtually the entire population of rural Missouri old enough to remember the lootings, burnings, and killings of both bushwhackers and Union troops. When discussing President Truman's forbears, his biographer, David McCullough, writes of Civil War Missouri, "Neither then nor later did the rest of the country realize the extent of the horrors.... Atrocities were committed on both sides, and it was innocent civilians who suffered most."[7] The devastating effects of this bloodlust continued for years. Simply put, violence begot more violence. Expectedly, punishing wrongdoers under state authority resumed.

Immediately after the war, the pace of executions here was extremely slow. This was not because people here had had their fill of killing. Quite the contrary; throughout most of the state, lynch mobs roamed about and settled many a score. From 1866 until 1870, for every two known executions in Missouri, there were approximately nine known lynchings. The essence of any lynching is its lawlessness; no court issued a death warrant and no sheriff or other law enforcement officer puts a condemned person to death. However, as McGovern explains, this gang activity has "community approval."[8] No persons are so much as arrested, let alone tried for murder in the first degree and hanged. The extralegal deaths during the late 1860s appear to have been predominately white victims of white mobs.

Slowly the courts began functioning again. There were six known executions between 1866 and 1869; five involved white victims, one a black; four had white perpetrators, and two black. All were under state authority, and no appellate decision issued in any of these cases. One court-ordered hanging took place in each of four counties: Buchanan, Clinton, Monroe, and Morgan; the other two were in St. Louis. Because death penalty appeals did not become mandatory until the late 1970s and court records and newspapers continue to be missing from the second half of the 19th century, there may have been other legal hangings during the late 1860s. This is what we know about the six which can be confirmed.

The first two involved robber co-defendants. In the Buchanan County case, the jury deliberated five minutes before finding a black man, Green Willis, guilty of first degree murder in the November 9, 1865, ax murder and robbery of Jacob Kuhn. Willis' accomplice, a young black male, Charles Clark, confessed, and in the process cleared the murder of John Lohr, which had taken place a short time earlier; Clark was sent to the penitentiary. Willis was hanged in St. Joseph March 1, 1866.[9] In a similar case in early 1865, Zeke and Tom Hart, brothers, went to the home of a family named Murry, who lived six miles southeast of Versailles, the county seat of Morgan County. The Harts demanded money; the Murrys defended themselves, and in the process Mr. Murry was shot and killed. The would-be robbers were identified by surviving family members, and Tom, the younger brother, confessed. They were tried separately in September 1866. Zeke was sentenced to death and hanged October 19, 1866; Tom received a prison sentence.[10]

At first blush, the third case during this time period bears a strong resemblance to the first two. A black man, Thomas Blue, was charged and convicted of the December 26, 1866 murder in the course of robbing an elderly and much respected white couple, William and Sarah Vandeventer, in Florida, Missouri. The husband died the same day as the robbery, and his wife from her injuries May 6, 1867. She identified the 19- or 20-year-old black male as the person who picked her up and placed her on a bed after she was shot. He was tried for first degree murder at the May term of Monroe County Circuit Court, found guilty, and hanged in Paris, June 21, 1867.[11]

There the matter rested for a number of years, but in approximately 1883, an ex-convict, Perry Thrall, died in Macon City, Missouri. On his deathbed, he confessed that he, not Tom Blue, had murdered the Vandeventers. Though Blue had been at the crime scene, Thrall and others convinced him that they would rescue him if he maintained his silence. Blue believed them, kept quiet until it was too late, and he died protesting his innocence. More than 20 years after Blue's execution and under the headline, "Hanged the Wrong Man," a Missouri newspaper ran the story about Perry Thrall's acknowledged role in the murder of the Vandeventers. It observed, "Several of those who are said to have had a hand in the deed are still living."[12] MSP records show that Perry Thrall, a white man convicted of grand larceny in Monroe County Circuit Court, became an inmate in May 1868 and Governor McClurg, a thrifty Presbyterian, pardoned him in May 1870. Documents in his pardon file suggest that in return for his testimony against his co-defendant, the prosecutor permitted Thrall to plead to the lesser offense of stealing when he had committed one or more robberies.[13] Most likely, Thrall and perhaps his co-defendant, H.C. Price, murdered the Vandeventers. They died in their Monroe County home in the course of a robbery, and Thrall was a Monroe County robber. Like Slave Archie who was hanged for the murder of his cruel master when another slave may have killed the victim, Blue was probably executed for a murder someone else committed.

On June 6, 1867, 19- or 20-year-old Peter Christian, a German immigrant and a total orphan by 1861, murdered his employer, Edward Ross, and Moses, Ross's eight-year-old son, with an ax on a small farm nine miles from the city of St. Louis. His motive was retaliation for Ross's refusal to pay him owed wages. The wife and mother discovered the bodies on June 8. When apprehended, the perpetrator readily confessed, and he attempted to plead guilty before a judge, but the magistrate refused to accept his plea. Instead the judge appointed an attorney to represent him; at his trial, October 1 and 2, the defense was insanity. It did not succeed. However, his attorney's plea to the governor was signed by all the jurors. Governor Fletcher did not intervene, and Peter Christian was hanged in the St. Louis jail December 6, 1867.

A more appropriate defense than insanity for the wayward young man was mental retardation. He seems not have known his exact age. A newspaper reporter present in the courtroom when the judge sentenced Christian to death described the condemned: "he was chewing tobacco the whole time, and appeared more intent upon masticating his cud than listening to the sentence, and he bent his head frequently to eject the saliva from his mouth. His eyes were fixed upon the judge, but there was no expression in them."[14] Another reporter who either visited Christian in his jail cell or attended his hanging wrote of him: "In appearance [he] was repulsive, in intellect, dull and narrow, and in disposition surly and unamiable."[15]

Not until the French psychologist, Alfred Binet (1857–1911), began his pioneering work in testing intelligence and published *Mentally Defective Children* (English translation 1907) was the concept of retardation in minds of the experts, let alone in the public consciousness. Prior to America's entry into World War I, there was no widespread attempt to assess intelligence in the United States. Likewise, mental retardation was not even attempted as a defense in death penalty cases until well into the 20th century, and the execution of the retarded was not prohibited in Missouri until the 21st century. In 1989 the U.S. Supreme Court held in a Texas case that the 8th and 14th Amendments did not categorically prohibit the execution of mentally retarded capital murderers.[16] In 2002 the High Court revisited this issue, and it held that that the state putting to death a retarded person violations the cruel and unusual punishment clause of the 8th and 14th Amendments.[17] Following this ruling, the Missouri legislature enacted a law which bars a death penalty where it is shown by a preponderance of the evidence, that it is more likely than not, that the defendant is mentally retarded. He may be sentenced to life imprisonment without eligibility for parole or release except by act of the governor. This statute governs offenses committed on or after August 28, 2001.[18] Were a person such as Christian capitally charged today, his attorney's request for an evaluation of his client's intelligence would be routine. A number of executions of likely retarded persons in Missouri followed the 1867 hanging of Christian, but his was the first case wherein extant news stories suggest a mental defect other than insanity impaired the condemned criminal's ability to understand, process information, and reason logically.

The remaining cases from the late 1860s both involve former slaves. One was rural and the other urban. The rural case arose on November 12, 1867, when Alfred Hughes killed his employer, Daniel Jenkins, the white proprietor of Planter's House in Platte City, Platte County. Hughes received a change of venue to nearby Clinton County. The outcome of many other capital cases here was influenced by the threat of mob action, but Hughes' trial was the first known change of venue granted in order to avoid a lynching.[19] He was tried June 11, 1868, found guilty of first degree murder, and hanged in Plattsburg, July 24, 1868.[20]

The urban case arose in St. Louis on December 5, 1868, when William Edwards stabbed Louis Wilson to death at a Negro dance in an altercation involving Nancy Thompson, whom Edwards claimed as his wife. All participants in this matter were black. This killing was no higher degree of homicide than manslaughter, if even that level of culpability were present. The obvious defense was self-defense. A newspaper reporter asked the condemned if "he intended to kill Wilson when he stabbed him, and he replied that he did...; that he struck in self-defense, and believed if he had not killed Wilson, the latter would have killed him. He said Wilson was a large and powerful man, weighing 180 or 190 pounds, and was pressing him when stabbed."[21] Another contemporary newspaper wrote of Edwards' death sentence:

> If [Edwards] had been a wealthy white man, no jury in the land would have convicted him. Look at the circumstances. The wife of Edwards was grossly insulted at a ball. When she resented the insult by calling the man a liar, he struck her; knocked her down. Her husband, being present, as a matter of course went to her assistance. In the fight which ensued he slew the man who had insulted and struck his wife.[22]

Unfortunately, Edwards' court-appointed attorney was unable to convince the all-white-male jury that the stabbing was in self-defense, or manslaughter, or second degree murder. It found him guilty of a crime he did not commit, first degree murder. On April 17, 1869, this illiterate 22-year-old was sentenced to hang on June 12; however, the governor reprieved him until July 23, 1869, as the record noted, "on a petition of influential citizens, claiming there were mitigating circumstances connected with the killing, and to give time for the proper preparation and presentation of those circumstances."[23] Among those who sought a commutation of Edwards' death sentence to life imprisonment were the St. Louis chief of police, the St. Louis circuit attorney, and the St. Louis county marshal. (This last mentioned official was the county's public hangman.) Unfortunately for the condemned, Missouri's governor, Joseph W. McClurg, was a keeper of strict doctrine. His recent biographical entry stresses his devout Presbyterianism, and its corollaries, his abhorrence of alcoholic beverages, profanity, and immorality.[24] Had McClurg been a devoted congregant of a less austere religion, most likely he would have commuted Edwards' death sentence, but the governor was not. His later pardon of the prison inmate, Perry Thrall, suggests that thrift may have played a role in this Scotch-Irishman allowing Edwards to hang July 23, 1869. After all, the sheriff's fee was only $25. The cost to the state to imprison Edwards would have been far more than the compensation the sheriff of St. Louis County received for executing him. One account of this black man's execution concludes, "Governor McClurg was severely criticized for denying all executive mercy."[25]

During the 1870s there was one more confirmed execution than lynching here: 31 and 30. Of the extra-legal killings, the percentage of blacks significantly increased from the years 1866 to 1869. Executions took place in 22 counties with six hangings in St. Louis, as earlier, more than any other locale. Of these 31 cases, only five involved a change of venue, and all recipients of it were white. Likewise 16 of these capitally convicted defendants had their cases reviewed by an appellate court, and in two of them, the newly established court of appeals in St. Louis reviewed the death sentence before the Supreme Court of Missouri ruled on it. Just as all who received changes of venue were white, so also, with a single exception, were those whose cases were fully reviewed by an appellate court. Of equal interest, the names in all appeals were of men whose forbears came from Western Europe. Among those granted changes of venue, an actual appeal, or both, there is only one black person and their names are easy to pronounce.

Those surnamed Ables, Daniels, Hamilton, Orr, and Skaggs received a change of venue. Of these five, three were also reviewed by an appeals court. Because Hamilton was a juvenile on the date of his crime, his case is discussed in Chapter 8. Orr had one or more co-defendants, and Ables, Daniels, and Skaggs acted alone. However, in each of their crimes, there was only one murdered victim.

John H. Skaggs killed Robert V. Richardson in Clarkton, Dunklin County, on January 6, 1870. He was tried in Bloomfield, Stoddard County, and the jury found him guilty of first degree murder. Several prominent persons, including a judge, sought to obtain either a reprieve or a commutation, but the thrifty Presbyterian governor, McClurg, refused to intervene. On August 6, 1870, the sheriff of Stoddard County hanged Skaggs; he was inexperienced, and he did not manage to break his prisoner's neck. When the body was taken down, two physicians sought to revive the dead or dying man with a "galvanic battery." The reporter's story was headlined, "A Bungling [sic] Execution — Attempt to Resuscitate," and it concluded, "The result of the attempt at resuscitation is not yet known, but is supposed to have been a failure."[26]

Samuel Orr, aged 25, and Albert Cox murdered George Davis, a farmer, on December 11, 1873, in Christian County. Their motive, according to the newspaper, was money promised by one R.K. Hart, then a prison inmate but previously a major in the Missouri state militia during the Civil War. During his military service, Hart murdered a man for his cash; Davis was in the same regiment, knew of the killing, and threatened to go to the authorities because Hart refused to share the loot. Initially, Samuel Orr was jointly indicted with his father, James Orr, R.H. Hart, and Albert Cox in Christian County Circuit Court. On a change of venue to Lawrence County, the younger Orr was tried, and the jury found him guilty of the first degree murder of Davis. Among other evidence introduced at his trial was testimony that the defendant had said he would receive $400 or $500 if he killed a man. Equally important, Orr had little wealth previous to Davis' murder, and afterwards, as the Court phrased it, "flourished a roll of bills as large as a man's wrist, saying that he had blood money." On the night of the victim's murder, according to the Missouri Supreme Court decision affirming his death sentence, "Orr returned to the saloon in Springfield at which he was a bartender ... and when he took off his coat he pulled out three pistols."[27] Samuel Orr, aged 26, was hanged in Mount Vernon on May 18, 1877. [28]

The remaining venue changes from the 1870s involve solo perpetrators who killed solo victims. On April 16, 1874, John T. Ables, aged at least 60 years, murdered John L. Lane in McDonald County, believing his victim was a lover of the old man's young and faithless wife. The killing took place in a desolate area, and testimony that the defendant was riding the victim's horse and displaying his revolver was used at his first trial, which took place in Jasper County from March 13 through 18, 1875. An appeal was taken to the Missouri Supreme Court, and it reversed. Following his second trial, Ables received first a respite to a later date and then a postponement of the second execution date. On his second appeal, the Court affirmed[29]; however, his lawyers continued to fight for Ables' life. Immediately before his hanging, they argued that their client had become insane, but the sheriff was not satisfied of the truth of their assertions. Finally on February 15, 1878, three years and 10 months after the crime, John T. Ables was hanged in Carthage.[30]

The last change of venue during the 1870s concerned the prosecution of John William Daniels for the Pettis County murder of Jesse R. Miller on February 22, 1877, in Johnson County. The evidence against the accused showed that the perpetrator and victim, both white men, were traveling together, and Daniels returned home without Miller, but in possession of his team and wagon. An ax, missing from the wagon, was the weapon the accused used to crush Miller's skull. The defendant was found guilty, and after the Missouri Supreme Court upheld his sentence, he was hanged in Warrensburg on March 1, 1878.[31]

The huge demographic surprise was the first degree murder conviction of William Foster, a white man, for the killing on August 29, 1875, of an unknown black man in Warren County. The victim was found shot in the back of his head; an apple was in his hand, and a bite of apple in his mouth. Other evidence, such as the victim's watch and trousers in the possession of the perpetrator, tied the accused to the crime. The juries hearing the case did not believe that Foster acted in self-defense. He was convicted, and after his case was affirmed by the St. Louis Court of Appeals, the Supreme Court of Missouri reversed. At his second trial, he was again found guilty, and on June 19, 1876, in Warrenton, the sheriff put him to death. Among the headlines in a St. Louis newspaper's extensive coverage of his crime and punishment was, "First Execution of a White for the Slaughter of a Black."[32] The second and only other known execution in Missouri of a white man for murdering a black took place in 1995. This crime took place in prison; one inmate killed another.

Monroe Guy was the only black person whose death sentence was reviewed by the Missouri Supreme Court in the 1870s. He was a 21- or 22-year-old former slave who borrowed a revolver, and with it he went to a black Methodist church near De Soto, where a revival was being held Christmas night 1878. He sent a message to his rival for the attentions of Nancy Thompson,[33] Aaron McPete, who was in the church. McPete came outside, and Guy drew his gun and shot him dead. All participants and witnesses were African-Americans. The perpetrator applied for but was denied a change of venue. He was tried in Jefferson County Circuit Court, and the jury found him guilt of first degree murder. The Supreme Court of Missouri affirmed his case, and the sheriff of Jefferson County hanged 22-year-old Monroe Guy on June 6, 1879, just outside Hillsboro.[34]

The appealed cases of white men during the 1870s included three who murdered their in-laws: John Grable his brother-in-law, Joel Drake, in Buchanan County on January 2, 1870; he was executed in St. Joseph on September 9, 1870[35]; Harris Travis his father-in-law, Squire Masterson, in Scott County November 3, 1874, and was hanged in Commerce on April 16, 1875[36]; and John Blan his brother-in-law, Elijah Warren, in St. Charles County in September 1878, and was put to death in the town of St. Charles June 6, 1879.[37] John West eliminated his traveling companion, Frank Shinn, and took clothes and money from his corpse in early October 1878 in Cooper County; he died on the gallows May 16, 1879, in Boonville.[38] Richard Green slew Henry Hughes, a deputy marshal, in Jackson County on February 10, 1877, in order to avoid being arrested for assault. Green was executed on March 1, 1878, in Independence. The governor commuted the death sentence of his accomplice, Frank Miller.[39] On January 29, 1877, William Wiener(s), a six foot, 200–225 pound private watchman at the Theatre Comique Saloon in St. Louis killed his fellow employee, an assistant bartender, Americus Lawrence, five foot, 120 pounds, when the victim told him that his alcoholic wife, Mrs. Wiener(s), wished to speak with him. Wiener(s) was put to death on February 1, 1878, in St. Louis.[40] Frank Davidson quarreled with William Haggerty at a picnic in Johnson County on September 21, 1878, after he told Haggerty's wife that he intended to have sex with her. She repeated his boast to her husband, and in the ensuing argument Davidson pumped three bullets into Haggerty, thereby killing him, and he was hanged July 10, 1879 in Warrensburg.[41]

The documentation for two cases contains no motive for the crime. John Carlisle stabbed George Weker to death on July 4, 1872, in Saline County. The victim's body was found in a ditch with 13 wounds. Carlisle died on the gallows in Marshall on July 24, 1874.[42] Poindexter Edmundson lay in ambush for William Shaw while his victim was working at Kapp's sorghum mill in Stoddard County on October 2, 1876. The sheriff of Stoddard County put Edmundson to death on July 24, 1877.[43]

William Pints, aged 30 years, axed to death nine-year-old Catherine Burr (Burroughs) in the presence of her seven-year-old brother Eph Burr (Burroughs), while the three were picking wild grapes in Bolinger County, on November 6, 1875. The perpetrator, who later raped his dead victim, may have been retarded. A local retrospective about his case contains, "Pints seems to have been a capable farm hand and was sensible enough at times. Perhaps he was what is known as a moron, ... one who has the intelligence of a child of ... twelve years of age ... and the passions of an adult."[44] Although the Supreme Court of Missouri accepted Pints' appeal, a rarity in cases of this sort, its decision neither mentions the victim's age nor the circumstances of her death. It does little more than affirm his death sentence. He was executed in Marble Hill on April 27, 1877.[45]

Most of the decisions of the Missouri Supreme Court in these cases contain few facts of the crime; instead, they overflow with minute distinctions between first and second degree murder. Clearly, in most instances wherein one man killed another, the jury might have found the accused guilty of second degree murder. Its members did not, and their verdicts were all upheld on appeal. One unexpected feature of Travis Harris' Scott County case was his trial and appellate lawyer before the Supreme Court of Missouri. He was Louis Houck, a distinguished historian of Spanish and territorial Missouri. His three-volume *History of Missouri* (1908) and his two-volume *Spanish Regime in Missouri* (1909) remain standard reference works nearly a century after their publication.

Some of the unappealed cases from the 1870s resemble those that were reviewed by a high court. Jeremiah Bailey, aged 20 years, a total orphan by 12 or 13, and white, was initially indicted for second degree murder in a drunken brawl killing on March 25, 1868, of another white male, 24-year-old James Brock, in New Madrid County. While he was out on bail, he was implicated in the murder of a farmer, William Barton; the prosecutor decided his first charge of Bailey was a mistake and this "desperado character," as the newspaper termed him, now faced a first degree murder indictment for killing Brock. Bailey was tried, found guilty, and hanged in the town of New Madrid on December 13, 1870.[46] Similarly, a feckless young white farm hand, Richard Isaacs, killed a white farmer, Henderson B. Clark, on August 27, 1878, in Cass County, in order to obtain his cattle. The perpetrator sold the livestock, was soon arrested, confessed, was tried, convicted, and hanged in Harrisonville on October 25, 1878.[47]

There was no guarantee that a black who was sentenced to death for killing another black would have his case reviewed by the Supreme Court of Missouri. For example, neither Robert Champion, who killed his wife, Rachael, in Howard County in July 1872, nor Samuel Walker, who killed his wife, Katie, in Clay County in October 1873, had their cases reviewed. Juries found both men guilty of first degree murder, and without further court action, Champion was hanged near Fayette on February 21, 1873, and Walker in Liberty on May 15, 1874.[48]

However, if a black was convicted of the first degree murder of a white, the chances of an appellate court actually reviewing his case were slim to none. The jury of Henry Brown deliberated 15 minutes before finding him guilty of the May 25, 1875 first degree murder in St. Louis County of a white, a German farmer named Phillip Pfarr. Most probably Brown's jurors had earlier read the extensive newspaper coverage which described the accused prior to his trial in these terms: "The black fiend who murdered Phillip Pfarr and ravished [raped] his wife last Tuesday night at their home on the Skinker Road has been arrested and is now locked up in the county jail on a charge of first degree murder."[49] After Brown was sentenced to death, his attorneys attempted to appeal his case to the Missouri Supreme Court on grounds that the victim set his dog on the accused prior to the killing. As a result, the proper verdict was second degree murder. The court refused to hear Brown's case. The sheriff of St. Louis County put him to death on October 22, 1875. Five months *after* Brown's execution, the St. Louis Court of Appeals issued a brief non-decision in his case: "an appeal cannot be taken from a judgment sentencing the defendant to death, where the sentence has been executed."[50]

Likewise, Daniel Price, a black man who was sleeping white with the wife of his victim, was convicted of the June 19, 1876 first degree murder of Samuel Taylor in Warren County in a November 1876 trial. The Court of Appeals in St. Louis affirmed in a memorandum decision which omitted the crime, the sentence, the county, and the first name of the defendant. However, by it and the county history's account of the case including the prosecutor's name, W.L. Morsey, this brief piece of legal writing can be identified as pertaining to Daniel Price. It is with considerable latitude in the meaning of the word *appeal* that this death-sentenced black man can be said to have had one. The sheriff hanged Price on January 18, 1877.[51]

Another popular prejudice of these post–Civil War years helps explain the shortness of the time lapse between the crimes and the hangings in other 1870s cases. As John Higham describes the phenomenon, nativism was the belief that native born Protestants whose forbears multiple generations back were also born in the United States were more worthy than those who were Catholic and/or had recently arrived from a foreign country.[52] As such these outsiders were less deserving of appeals and venue changes than real Americans in capital cases.

Without benefit of an appeal, Patrick O'Shea, an Irishman, killed his wife and was hanged at the county jail in St. Louis on April 9, 1875.[53] In Gasconade County, Henry Hallenscheid, a German, killed his son-in-law, Christ Alband, in an argument about prohibiting Wilhelmina, Christ's wife and Henry's daughter, from wearing a particular dress. Both Henry and his wife, Anna, were charged with first degree murder. They requested but were denied a change of venue. The accused did not understand English; at his and his wife's trial, the circuit clerk was his interpreter. Both were sentenced to death. Though the governor commuted Anna Hallenscheid's punishment to life imprisonment, the sheriff hanged her husband in Hermann on December 17, 1875.[54]

Perhaps the prejudice against foreigners was at its most virulent in the first triple hanging for the same crime under state authority in Missouri's history. There would be three others, and two of the later ones were affirmed by the Supreme Court of Missouri. In the first case, three Sicilians killed Francisco Palermo, an Italian lemon seller, aged 25 years, in an ambush. The accused were Antonio Catalano, Dominico Damina, and Bastiano Lombardo. They were devout Catholics, were tried together, and hanged simultaneously on February 18, 1876. A contemporary newspaper described them as "The Doomed Sicilians,"[55] and in a story about the governor denying their request for commutation of their death sentences, the headline was "The Case of the Three Italian Murderers."[56] The newspaper story the day after their execution described the shrine in their cell to the Virgin Mary and Jesus, the three priests who attended their hanging, and the crucifix each wore suspended by his neck by a black ribbon at the moment of death.[57] One source about this massive instance of capital punishment states, "The case was carried to the Supreme Court upon appeal, but without changing the result."[58] The statement is misleading; it does not mean that the Supreme Court of Missouri accepted or decided their case. It did neither. These young Italian men died as did the Irishman and the German, without any appeal.

The final group of cases from the 1870s wherein neither a venue change nor an appeal exists are characterized by the enormities of the crimes. On November 19, 1870, in Washington County, two cousins, Charles Jolly and John Armstrong, shot, axed, raped, and severed the heads of five members of the Lapine family, and set their home on fire. The newspaper's headline of its account of the event reads as follows: "Horrible Murder and Butchery! Five Persons, Brutally Massacred, The Bodies Mutilated and Burned to Cinders!!! No Motive Apparent! Pursuit and Capture of the Inhuman Fiends."[59] The Lapine family members were their victims: the parents, their 18-month-old son, a sister-in-law, and her infant daughter. After the perpetrators were captured, they were indicted for first degree murder. The jury deliberated three minutes before its members returned with death sentences for both murderers. The condemned men were kept in the St. Louis jail after their trial to avoid their being lynched. The sheriff of Washington County hanged them in Potosi on January 27, 1871.[60] Earlier that same month and year, B. Gratz Brown was sworn in as Missouri's governor. His biographer, Norma Peterson, writes of him: "Capital punishment was repugnant to Brown, and no criminal was executed during his term of office."[61] She is mistaken. Even fierce opponents of the death penalty are unlikely to waste political capital in preventing the hanging of persons who murder children not yet old enough to talk. Though Governor Brown did commute other death sentences, he did not intervene in the dual execution of Armstrong and Jolly.

Similarly, when Charles Waller, a Civil War veteran, was finally captured for the 1867 Webster County murder of a family in order to rob them, he was quickly tried and sentenced to death. His victims were William Newlon, his wife, Hannah, and their 18-month-old child. Waller's wife and son received lesser sentences in this crime; expectedly, the sheriff hanged him in Marshfield on May 17, 1872.[62] The swift trial, sentencing, and execution of person(s) who committed horrendous crimes remained a feature of the death penalty here. Changes of venue were rarely if ever granted, and neither appellate courts nor governors spared the lives of these perpetrators.

This next decade, the 1880s, remains one of the most violent in Missouri's history. There are no figures on the number of persons who were homicide victims, but both lynchings and legal executions climbed to new highs. There were 49 known executions and 34 known lynchings in this state between January 23, 1880 and September 12, 1889, or one approximately every 44 days from the start of the decade to its finish. Death penalty cases arose in 25 counties; these were dispersed widely across the state, with the majority, as earlier, arising in St. Louis. Only two changes of venue were granted, and both occurred early in the decade. Both recipients were white men who murdered another white man in the course of robbing or attempting to rob him, and their separate cases were appealed to the Supreme Court of Missouri which affirmed their convictions.[63]

Another small group of perpetrators was blacks convicted of the murder of whites. Excluding the juvenile discussed in Chapter 8, there are three cases. The first arose in Audrain County when Joseph Muldrow and his half-brother, Nathan Faucett, both former slaves, killed a white man, Octave Inlow, on September 30, 1879, at the request of Emma Prilley, a white woman, in retaliation for Inlow, her lover, slapping her. The black males were tried and found guilty; their case was not appealed, and they were hanged together in Mexico, the county seat of Audrain County, on April 16, 1880. After their deaths, their former owner received their bodies and buried them.[64] On December 25, 1879, Noah Forrest, a young white man, and other whites terrorized a former slave, John Cropp, as the black man bought Christmas gifts for his family. Later that same day and with a double-barreled shot gun, Cropp killed Forrest. To no avail, the black pled self-defense to the killing. He was tried, found guilty, no appeal was taken, and he was hanged on June 11, 1880, in Keytesville, the county seat of Chariton County.[65] The third and last black killer of a white victim whose case resulted in a death sentence was Charles Wilson, a roustabout, or deckhand, who, on July 31, 1882, in St. Louis, murdered William David, the second mate on the steamboat *Fannie Tatum*, when they quarreled over the pay to which the black man was entitled. Wilson's case was appealed. The Missouri Supreme Court's decision in this case is little better than a joke; it is 17 lines in its entirety, and the death-sentenced black was not represented by an attorney on appeal. Charles Wilson was hanged in St. Louis on January 15, 1886.[66] Most other blacks who were alleged to have committed or attempted to commit violent crimes against whites in Missouri in the 1880s were lynched.

In contrast, most Negroes who were tried for killing another person of color and sentenced to death usually had their cases reviewed by the Supreme Court of Missouri. In nine unrelated cases, a black man killed one black victim, and there is an appeal in all but one of them. In none of these black-on-black murders is the motive robbery. When he killed another man, either the perpetrator quarreled with his victim over cards[67] or work,[68] or settled an old grudge after drinking all day.[69] When his victim was female, he murdered his wife,[70] his sweetheart,[71] or his mistress.[72] These domestic difficulties are nicely summed up by the Supreme Court of Missouri when quoting Jeff Wilson, the head cook at a Lexington hotel and killer of his mistress, Jennie Sanford. At his trial he took the stand in his own behalf and said of the deceased, "The dammed bitch didn't behave herself."[73] It affirmed Wilson's conviction, and he was hanged in Lexington, Lafayette County, on April 2, 1886.[74]

White murderers in this time period present variations which blacks do not. The most horrendous killing of this decade involved the son of one farming family as perpetrator and the daughters of another as victims. It arose in Andrew County on August 31, 1884, when seven-year-old Austie and her nine-year-old sister, Adella, children of the Bateman family's neighbor, John McLaughlin, visited a Miss Bateman at her home on a Sunday afternoon. Her brother, 22-year-old Oliver Bateman, enticed the little girls into a cornfield to find hazelnuts and see some baby rabbits. When he had gotten them out of sight and hearing of his family's farmhouse, he shot the older child in the head, killing her instantly, and he shortly cut the throat of the seven-year-old. He held the younger child until she died, and he then raped the dead body of the nine-year-old. Afterwards he split her body open in order to convince whoever found her that a deranged person had committed the crime. He then left their remains and returned home. Once the children were missed and their corpses discovered, an outraged community determined to find the perpetrator. After his brother, Newton Bateman, was suspected and cleared, on September 8, Oliver gave authorities a full confession of his crime. It contained details such as, "When I went back to the oldest one I enlarged her with my knife and had connection [sex] with her.... I never had sexual intercourse with a woman in my life."[75]

Extensive newspaper coverage regarding his case once more suggests that the perpetrator was retarded. One reporter wrote of him, "In appearance he looked what he was, an ignorant, narrow minded clodhopper, who was only 'good' because had neither sufficient brain nor character to be bad.... He looked too dumb to be dangerous."[76] Another described Bateman in these words, "talks disconnectedly, is forgetful, connecting sentences, places, incidents and circumstances rather badly. He comes of a respectable family."[77] A third interviewed one of young Oliver's teachers, who said of him, "He was a stupid student and learned but little. In arithmetic he was very dull, and even at the age of twenty had not progressed further than the multiplication table. In reading he never got out of the third reader, and his spelling was in the same proportion.... At play he was equally as dull."[78] His confession points to mental deficiency: "I never would have told it, but you described to me so nearly how I did it that I thought you must have seen me."[79]

Even had there been a trial, and there was not, these many indicia of retardation would never have been presented to a jury. One newspaper editor or reporter used the words "emotional insanity"[80] to describe the killer; perhaps the phrase was a first cousin of retardation, but it was not a correct label for Bateman's mental deficiency. None of this mattered to the community, or for that matter the perpetrator. After he confessed, he was secretly transported to jail in St. Joseph in order to avoid a lynching. There, according to the county history, he was visited by three physicians; they examined him "as to his mental condition ... [and] pronounced him sane." He refused an attorney, entered a guilty plea to two counts of first degree murder in an appearance in Andrew County Circuit Court, which began on October 6 at 2:05 p.m., and after 27 minutes, or at 2:22 p.m., the judge sentenced him to death. Bateman's only objection to the speed of his case was the court's death date for him was approximately six weeks *later* instead of the day of his guilty plea.[81] There was no appeal in his case; on the appointed day, November 21, 1884, Oliver Bateman was hanged in Savannah. His family buried his body on its farm because officials would not allow it to be interred in a public cemetery.[82] This case parallels others involving children as rape and homicide victims in the short time span between the crime, court proceedings, and execution. Typically, from their ghastly start until their finish less than two months elapse.

Far more common white-on-white murders of the 1880s are those in which the motive is the perpetrator's personal gain. More often than not, there was no appellate review in these cases. John Patterson's has already been mentioned as one involving a change of venue; excluding one discussed later in this chapter, the details of six other follow. Twice here in the 1880s two men together robbed another. On March 30, 1884, two ex-convicts who met in prison murdered a young German, Carl Steidle, for his $175 in cash as they traveled east from Sedalia by railroad. They dumped his body on the railroad tracks in Montserrat, Johnson County. The perpetrators, Charley Hamilton, alias Malsky, and Billy Hamilton, alias Ed Altman, then took a freight train to Kansas City, where they spent their ill-gotten gains. When they returned to Sedalia on April 2, they were arrested, and both confessed. They were tried separately in May in Johnson County Circuit Court, and they were hanged together in Warrensburg on July 11, 1884.[83] On December 29, 1885, in Daviess County, two men, Joe Jump and John Smith, murdered a fellow Rock Island Railroad employee, William C. Gladson, a resident of Monroe County, Iowa, for his wealth, over $100 in cash. The perpetrators drank and gambled most of Gladson's money, but Jump still had $20 of it in his hat when arrested. In due course, they confessed, were tried in May 1886 in Daviess County Circuit Court, and found guilty. Jump was hanged in Gallatin on July 23, 1886. His co-defendant, John Smith, went to his gallows death on the same scaffold, a few weeks later on August 6, 1886.[84] No appeals were made in either of these railroad murders. A third unappealed case concerns Charles Hardin's killing his fellow traveler, Robert Ferguson, on October 26/27, 1879, in St. Francois County for the victim's $350. The perpetrator was traced to Columbus, Kentucky, returned to Farmington, where he was tried in December, 1879, found guilty, and hanged in Farmington on January 23, 1880.[85]

Two other 1880s cases wherein robbery was the motive were appealed. One arose in the fall of 1879 when two men, Thomas Dickson and James McNabb, came to Stoddard County from Arkansas. Once arrived, they rented a farm, and in March 1880, McNabb was no longer seen. Dickson told neighbors that his companion had returned to Arkansas in order to arrest a man and had been killed in the arrest attempt. He took over McNabb's property, harvested a crop, and returned to Arkansas. In February 1882, a walnut timber buyer arrived, and the owner of the farm earlier rented by Dickson and McNabb unearthed a walnut log Dickson had buried. Under it was the remains of a body, which by clothing and other items was identified as McNabb's. The perpetrator was arrested, returned to Stoddard County, tried and convicted. The Supreme Court of Missouri affirmed, and Thomas Dickson was hanged in Bloomfield on May 2, 1884.[86] On August 5, 1885, Henry Stair, with the assistance of his common law wife, Nanneta Stair, killed two travelers, Jacob Sewell and his 16-year-old son, in Vernon County in order to take possession of their property. Two days later, the Stairs were arrested, soon tried, and found guilty. The Supreme Court of Missouri affirmed as to Henry Stair and reversed as to Nanneta. He was hanged in Nevada on January 15, 1886.[87]

Yet another variation of death penalty cases of this period which were strictly white-on-white crime was gang activity. Not only is this the era of Frank and Jesse James, Missouri's if not the entire country's most famous outlaws, it is also the time and place of other lesser-known desperados. On May 9, 1881, in New Madrid County, Jesse Meyers and Frank Brown, both members of the Meyers' gang, wounded a youth and killed a member of the sheriff's posse, Robert La Farge, as law enforcement officers pursued them. They and others were captured 10 days later and taken to St. Louis in order to avoid a lynching. Brown and Meyers were indicted June 10, 1881, on first degree murder charges, tried, and found guilty; no appeal was taken, and they were hanged in New Madrid on July 15, 1881. On the scaffold they confessed that they had organized with three others in order to imitate Jesse James' band.[88] Because the execution of other gang members of this decade involved a juvenile among the condemned, it is discussed in Chapter 8.

Other capital cases from this time period parallel the black-on-black homicides. White men quarreled over the disposal of corn fodder,[89] burnt wheat stacks,[90] and a debt.[91] Twice in the 1880s, one man killed another after many hours of drinking with him,[92] or because he believed the victim had spread false stories regarding the chastity of the perpetrator's wife.[93] Another murdered a workman against whom he had a grudge for about two years before he shot him to death.[94]

However, as with the black-on black executions of this decade the most frequent reason one white person killed another in the 1880s concerned domestic difficulties. Either habit, love, or lust turned the accused wrong side out, and he killed his wife,[95] his ex-wife,[96] his sweetheart,[97] his mistress and her mother,[98] his mother-in-law,[99] his real or imagined rival for his reputed wife,[100] or his would-be father-in-law.[101] The complicated relations of two cases require special mention.

The rural extravaganza began in upstate New York where Edward Clum and John White, born in 1844 and 1839 respectively, grew up together, joined the Union Army, served in the same company, and were present when Lee surrendered to Grant at Appomattox Courthouse on April 9, 1865. Following his Union Army service, in April 1869, Clum married Charlotte, then, a teenager; White had earlier wed Augusta during the war. By 1884, the Whites had three children when, on Memorial Day, then 40-year-old Mrs. Augusta White committed suicide. Her death was surely prompted in part by her husband's sexual liaison with his friend Clum's wife, Charlotte, also known as Lottie. This much of the story took place in rural New York.

By 1885 John White had purchased a farm in Barry County, five or six miles south of Pierce City, Lawrence County, Missouri. Soon Lottie Clum joined White in Pierce City, and on January 23, 1886, 35-year-old Lottie died at White's home of an unknown, if not suspicious, cause. Even before Lottie's death, 17-year-old Ella Bowe, a Monett community native, had become an occasional overnight guest at John White's farm. A volatile element was added when Ed Clum, now deceased Charlotte Clum's former husband, arrived on the White farm on March 4, 1886. Soon the bereft widower developed some interest in Ella Bowe, but she had none in him. On July 8, 1886, 41- or 42-year-old Edward Clum used a double-barreled shotgun to kill 47-year-old John White and 17-year-old Ella Bowe when he found them together on a creek bank on White's farm; the perpetrator then covered their bodies with straw. Ten days later their remains were found. Clum was arrested on July 20, and he was tried on two counts of first degree murder in Barry County Circuit Court. Following his conviction, an appeal was taken to the Supreme Court of Missouri, which affirmed; Edward Clum was hanged in Cassville on April 15, 1887.[102]

The urban case began a great distance from Missouri on the steamship *Cephalonia* en route from Liverpool, England, to Boston. One Englishman, Walter Maxwell, alias Hugh M. Brooks, among other names, met another, Charles Arthur Preller, at sea, and soon they became a gay couple, or as their love affair was described in an early twentieth century account, "The two men spent most of their time in Maxwell's room. The latter was very effeminate in his manner and a letter subsequently found, but which was not fit for publication, indicated that a peculiar relationship existed between them."[103] Brooks passed himself off to the wealthy Preller as a surgeon. Once landed in Boston, they discussed a trip to New Zealand, but cash-rich Preller had first to make a business trip to Canada and then one to Philadelphia. They agreed to meet in St. Louis, and on March 30, 1885, Brooks went to the Southern Hotel, Room 134. Shortly, Preller joined Brooks, and he was last seen alive after dinner in the hotel's dining room on Easter Sunday, April 5. A few days later Brooks checked out and left two trunks, one of them made of zinc, in his room. Afterwards, it was temporarily unoccupied. Eventually a pungent odor came from it, and when that odor became unbearable, the zinc trunk was opened. In it was the very dead body of Preller. He was clad only in undershorts; his chest had two gashes in the form of a cross. Written on a piece of paper found on the body was, "So Perish all Traitors to the Great Cause." Its handwriting matched Brooks' signature on the hotel's guest registration.

The police found prescription blanks from a Fernon's Drug Store in the other trunk. Upon checking with Mr. Fernon, they learned that he had sold Brooks, alias Maxwell, six ounces of chloroform on April 5. Shortly, an autopsy on Preller's body revealed that the cause of his death was chloroform poisoning. Through impressive detective work, the St.

Louis Police Department learned that Brooks had traveled to Denver, San Francisco, and was en route by freighter to New Zealand. He was arrested as his ship docked in Auckland. On May 25, 1885, President Grover Cleveland signed extradition papers for the return of Brooks to St. Louis. They were served by two St. Louis Police Department members, one of whom was Detective Tracy. After a delay of 77 days, during which Brooks' attorney unsuccessfully fought his extradition, the police had their man, and they returned him to St. Louis. Brooks was indicted, but before his trial began, the prosecutor arranged to have a St. Louis detective, posing as a check forger, placed in a jail cell with Brooks for the next 47 days.

Believing that his cellmate was a criminal, not a detective jailed on a fictitious charge, Brooks eventually told him that he became angry with Preller when he refused to pay his fare to New Zealand. When his companion complained of a pain in his side, Brooks told his intimate, who believed he was a surgeon, that he could cure his pain. He first injected his victim with a large amount of morphine. After he became unconscious, the perpetrator tied a cloth about Preller's face and kept it saturated with chloroform until his victim breathed his last. Next he stripped his body, stuffed it in the zinc trunk, and left town. Once the prosecutor conversed with Brooks' cellmate, he was ready to try his case. In May 1886, the state began its first degree murder case against Brooks. It put on 57 witnesses, including the putative check-forging detective who celled with the defendant and told the court and jury what Brooks told him about Preller's death. Brooks took the stand in his own behalf, and in the course of his defense, namely that he accidentally killed his fellow Englishman while administering chloroform for therapeutic reasons, he admitted that he took his good friend's money, clothing, and jewelry. On June 4, 1885, the jury found Brooks guilty of Preller's murder.

An appeal was taken to the Supreme Court of Missouri, and in a 23-issue decision, certainly one of the longest this court had written up to this time, on June 20, 1887, the appellate court upheld Brooks' conviction. From there, his attorneys took an appeal to the U.S. Supreme Court. As far as we know it was the first by any death-sentenced person in Missouri. On January 23, 1888, Chief Justice Waite granted the state's motion to dismiss Brooks' appeal.[104] The condemned had sought a new trial on grounds that the testimony of the detective posing as a check forger while Brooks' cellmate was inadmissible.[105] After a series of delays caused by queries from the British government and appeals for clemency to Missouri's governor, the diminutive Hugh Brooks, height 5'6" and weight 115 pounds, "the little chloroformer," as one St. Louis newspaper fondly termed him, was hanged at 6:30 a.m. in the St. Louis jail on August 10, 1888.[106] Even had most people who wished to watch him die been awake at this early hour, they would not have been admitted to the enclosed area in the jail yard where he was put to death.

In the antebellum period, massively-attended executions were a statewide feature of life; nonetheless, as early as the 1850s, the city of St. Louis limited the number of spectators at these events. As a result, excluding the state's only major city, the period 1866–1889 is the premier time in Missouri for public hangings as entertainment. There was no television, no motion pictures, no radio, and no electricity, and residents of rural areas craved amusements. One popular activity was watching the law take its course in capital cases. Both contemporary newspapers and county histories give crowd estimate at these events. The larger the number assembled for the gallows death, generally the greater the public indignation at the crime(s) of the condemned. Unlike St. Louis where the hangings took place in restricted areas of the jail early in the day, rural scaffold deaths occurred in the afternoon. The timing made it possible for men, their wives, and children to attend to the many morning chores of farming and still manage to get to their county's or an adjacent county's big event. Special seats up front were always reserved for the family of the victim(s). Some availed themselves of these seating privileges, and others did not.

The Clinton County hanging of Alfred Hughes in Plattsburg at 1:30 p.m. on September 30, 1868, took place in the presence of 8,000 witnesses, the largest crowd of people that ever assembled in Clinton's county seat according to the county history.[107] Samuel Orr's death in Mount Vernon at 2:46 p.m. on May 18, 1877, attracted between 5,000 and 8,000 witnesses. Three children of Orr's victim, as the newspaper noted, "occupied an allotted space immediately in front of the scaffold."[108] Monroe Guy's hanging near Hillsboro at approximately 2:15 p.m. on June 6, 1879, as the newspaper described it was attended by "fully 7,000 people, embracing all ages, sex, and sizes, and about equally divided as to blacks and whites.... Some came from St. Francois County, some from Franklin and Washington counties, and a few from Ste. Genevieve County."[109] When Oliver Bateman was put to death in Savannah at 12:51 p.m. on November 21, 1884, 20,000 assembled to witness his execution. A newspaper reporter wrote of it "Some had been traveling for the last two days in wagons.... Each wagon contained a complete family from father to baby in mother's arms."[110] Likewise, when Joe Jump died on the gallows in Gallatin at 2:45 p.m. on July 23, 1886, for the murder of a fellow railroad employee, a native of Iowa, the Rock Island Railroad ran a hangman's special from Iowa for the event. The newspaper also estimated the Jump crowd at 20,000 people.[111] No estimated number of viewers at any hanging in Missouri exceeded 20,000, including the mass execution of four Negroes in St. Louis in 1841.

As a spectator sport, watching the condemned die either because his neck was broken or he strangled to death was an exhilarating experience. Since Savannah and Gallatin were less than 60 miles apart, surely many who watched the sheriff of Daviess County hang Joe Jump were also on hand when the sheriff of Andrew put Oliver Batman to death.

In the eyes of the communities wherein these spectacular events occurred, justice was done in a way it had not been during the war. In the years since the Civil War had ended, both participants and bystanders old enough to remember the earlier conflict had lost their youth and perhaps their belief in good government. At least they had the opportunity to see people whom they believed evil breathe their last.

5

The Nineties and
Beyond, 1890–1907

Excluding the Civil War years, the most violent period in this state's history was the 1890s. Between March 6, 1891 and July 7, 1899, Missouri put to death 58 men and boys, and the number of known lynchings decreased by one from the 1880s, 32. This chapter excludes persons executed for rape, those aged less than 18 years at the time of their crime, and one adult accomplice in a juvenile hanging: in all, six cases. The remaining 52 capital cases are discussed herein. They arose in 36 counties, a greater geographical distribution than previous or later time periods. The number of appellate decisions in death penalty cases remained constant, but they usually contained more facts about the crime than heretofore. Capital defendants received more changes of venue than earlier. However, several of these were from the city of St. Louis to the county of St. Louis. Although the two became separate entities in 1876, no capital cases involving trials and hangings in Clayton took place until the 1890s. Likewise, hangings in Kansas City began during this decade. Earlier, all of Jackson County's legal executions had occurred in Independence. The 1890s also saw, and for the first time, a change of venue from an urban to a rural county: one from Jackson to Lafayette, and two from St. Louis City, one to Gasconade and the other to Franklin. A change in legislation, found in the 1879 revision of Missouri's statutes,[1] made possible the removal of a case not only from the city of St. Louis to Clayton but to another county. However, the last 20 trials of this decade which resulted in an execution took place in the county of the crime. Between June 1897 and December 1900, the accused frequently applied for, but was always denied, a change of venue.

Why was the 1890s the premier time for Missouri's use of capital punishment? The Civil War had ended almost 25 years before the decade began, and it would be almost 35 years in the past as the new century dawned. One would assume that the post–traumatic stress disorders of the earlier conflict had run their course, if not in the beginnings of the 1890s, then certainly by the end of it. Although at times we do not know the precise ages of the condemned, often we do. If those convicted of first degree murder and hanged in the 1890s were alive prior to April 1865, for the most part, they were not old enough to remember the reign of the Union Army here. The lingering effects of PTSD seem an uncomfortable stretch to explain the sheer volume of homicides at the tail end of the nineteenth century.

This much is clear. Though lynchings here were nothing new, they had an increased and lethal influence in capital cases in the 1890s, especially in rural counties. A pervasive fear existed that a mob would take the law into its own hands. Numerous death-sentenced prisoners were kept safe from its wrath in securely build and well-protected jails in the state's major cities, St. Louis, Kansas City, St. Joseph, and Springfield. Shortly before their scheduled hangings, they were returned to the county wherein their convictions were obtained, often under heavy guard, for a brief stay, if any, in the local jail and then transported to the local scaffold. In one capital case, the Missouri Supreme Court granted the defendant a second trial because the prosecutor told the jury at his first trial, "Escape of criminals at the hands of juries brings on lynch law."[2] Likewise, the threat of a lynching frequently compelled the perpetrator's confession to the crime. One man arrested for murder wrote his mother from Ava, Missouri, on May 26, 1896, "As I am liable to be lynched any minute I am going to tell you the truth."[3] In one capital case the jury instructions included: "If you believe any admission of the defendant ... was induced by fear on [his] part ... that he would be ... subjected to the perils of mob, then you will disregard such admissions, and all others made subsequent thereto."[4] In late 1896 or early 1897, Governor Stone went to the Cole County jail and promised those assembled, as the newspaper reported, "justice would take its course and ... the capital city of the state must not be disgraced with a lynching."[5] Eventually, the sheriff of Cole County hanged the jail inmate, Tobe Lanahan, whom the governor had earlier protected. In another capital case, the Missouri Supreme Court ruled that "some talk of mobbing [the defendant] and the sheriff removing him to another county for safe-keeping is not sufficient ground for [a] change of venue."[6]

The law and the lawless often went hand in hand, and this arrangement continued into the twentieth century. We have no precise knowledge that jury deliberations in Missouri during this time period were manipulated by the fear of mob violence, but it seems more likely than not. We know that the threat of a lynching in 1841 in Marion County influenced the jury to give three abolitionists an extremely harsh sentence, because one of them wrote a book. In it he described the atmosphere of his trial in these terms: "a mob had been organized, who had erected our gallows, provided ropes, blacked their faces, and were ready to take us at a moment's notice, in case we were acquitted and hang us on the spot."[7] No death-sentenced defendant in Missouri in the 1890s wrote a book about the circumstances under which a jury deliberated his fate, but the likelihood is great that mob violence was an omnipresent threat in rural Missouri in death penalty cases.[8] This danger in isolation is insufficient to explain the high number of legal executions in the 1890s in Missouri, but the fear of a lynching obviously contributed to the sheer numbers whom county sheriffs hanged.

The motivations of most murderers of the 1890s remained constant. They usually committed their crimes because of money, or rage, or love, or some combination thereof. Only four black men were tried and legally executed here during this time period because they murdered in order to rob. All of their victims were white. Two killed an employer; one murdered man owned a cigar store in St. Louis City,[9] and the other was a farmer struck down near Lohman, Cole County, when he returned from St. Louis with cattle money.[10] Two brothers killed a streetcar conductor in St. Louis County.[11] Otherwise, capital cases in Missouri of the 1890s wherein the motive for the robbery and death of the victim(s) was the perpetrator's personal gain were white-on-white crimes.

Nine white men were hanged in different locales in this era because they killed one or more white victims in a robbery or attempted robbery. The earliest case arose on October 22, 1886, in Franklin County,[12] and the last on July 31, 1897, in Jasper County.[13] The oldest of these 1890s white robber-murderers was 56-year-old Thomas Williamson, a Union

Army veteran. On May 25, 1890, this farmhand used an ax to murder his farmer-employer, 58-year-old Jefferson Moore and his 29-year-old son, Charles Moore, in Pettis County. The bodies of his victims were dug from an abandoned cellar, and items of theirs were found in the perpetrator's possession. In the course of the investigation and trial of his case, Williamson confessed to earlier killings, including his wife, a German man, and an entire family in Illinois. However he was prosecuted only for the murder of Jefferson Moore. The defense was insanity, and, as in similar cases, it did not succeed. He was convicted of first degree murder; the Missouri Supreme Court affirmed, and the sheriff of Pettis County hanged him in Sedalia on October 31, 1891.[14]

The youngest perpetrator aged more than 18 years at the time of his 1890s crime was 19-year-old Amos Avery. On September 22, 1891, he killed 21-year-old James Miles in Barton County. The victim was from Prairie County, Arkansas, and he with two others was canvassing for a family photograph album published in Chicago. Avery was arrested in Galena, Kansas, wearing Miles' coat, pants, and hat. After his trial and conviction on first degree murder charges in Lamar, it became known that his attorney had applied for a new trial. This necessitated the sheriff of Barton County and four of his deputies removing Avery from the local jail and bringing him to Kansas City in order to avoid his death at the hands of a 50- or 60-member mob. A Kansas City newspaper noted with obvious civic pride, "Amos Avery ... is in a cell in the Second Street jail. He is there because Barton County people will not let him stay in the Lamar jail where he belongs.... So Sheriff Ayers brought him to Kansas City, where men never get lynched."[15] Avery's judge denied him a new trial, and the Missouri Supreme Court affirmed. In due course the condemned was returned to Lamar, and the sheriff of Barton County hanged Amos Avery on May 24, 1893.[16]

Other first degree white-on-white murders in the course of attempted or completed robberies took place in Douglas,[17] Laclede,[18] and Mercer counties.[19] The most extensive newspaper reporting concerned one which arose in Jackson County. On September 9, 1893, Harry Jones and John Clark, alias William Ricksher, choked to death 56-year-old Madame Jane Wright, a woman who ran, among other businesses, an employment agency. She was known to carry money sewn in her clothing. Her body, minus a watch and $330, was found in her office in Kansas City. The perpetrators divided the proceeds of their crime, and Clark, a recently released inmate from the Kansas penitentiary, received his victim's watch. He soon gave it to a bartending friend, who had heard of the murder and gave the watch to a Kansas City police officer. Shortly, the men were arrested and confessed. They were tried separately; Clark in November and Jones in December 1893, and both were found guilty. An appeal was taken in Clark's case; Jones was too poor to afford an appeal. The men were kept in the Kansas City jail until their date with death. Jones was transported by train from Kansas City to Independence, where he was hanged at 9:06 a.m. on June 29, 1894. Clark died two hours and four minutes later at ll:10 a.m. in the jail yard in Kansas City on the same day. At the time of their crime, Kansas City, Missouri had a population of 150,000. Clark's hanging here was this city's first legal execution; it would not be its last.[20]

Black rage directed at another black explains a homicide in the Main Street pool room in Sedalia. On August 23, 1892, Charles Banks shot and killed Ike Palmer in a difficulty arising from crap shooting. The perpetrator, described by various witnesses as a bully, told the victim, "I have a notion to shoot you." He did, and on a change of venue, Banks was tried and found guilty; the Missouri Supreme Court affirmed, and the sheriff of Johnson County hanged him in Warrensburg on December 29, 1893.[21] Otherwise, independent of love relationships, angry blacks whose crimes resulted in death sentences killed white persons. One believed that a newsboy was cheating in a crap game.[22] Another occurred when the victim refused to tell the perpetrator where he lived,[23] and a third took place after the victim replaced the black church janitor with a white man.[24]

Two capital cases concerning a black defendant and a white victim involved, in one instance, a Missouri State Penitentiary (hereinafter MSP) guard, and in the other, a police officer. In the prison case, on August 3, 1892, a convict, Jacob Brown, alias John Coleman, stabbed to death Frank Macklin, a foreman in the Strauss saddle and harness shop at MSP, with a shoe knife. According to the Missouri Supreme Court, bad blood had existed between these men for some time. Violence erupted when the foreman required the inmate to report for a flogging. The issue was raised in Brown's case, as it had been in at least one earlier appeal brought by a death-sentenced black man, that the absence of any Negroes on the jury which heard Brown's capital case was a violation of the 14th Amendment. In its decision upholding the defendant's death sentence, the Missouri Supreme Court responded that a mixed jury was not required by the U.S. Constitution. Following his trial, conviction, and appeal, Brown was hanged in Jefferson City on May 4, 1894.[25]

The facts in the death of the police officer are far less clear. On October 6, 1890, two black barbers got into a fist fight in the city of St. Louis. Initially one policeman responded to the scene, which had moved into a nearby saloon; shortly, two other officers entered the bar. In the melee which followed, a fourth St. Louis policeman, James Brady, came into the premises and was shot and killed. The prosecution argued that the bullet came from a gun which Harry Duncan, alias William Harrison, a brother of one of the quarreling barbers, shot. Police officers testified that Duncan had confessed that he killed Officer Brady. The defendant denied that he had ever made any such confession. His theory of the case was that he did not kill Brady; rather the officer died because he was accidentally shot by another police officer or by the proprietor, Charles Stark, in the immense confusion then existing in the saloon. Today, the prosecution's witnesses would include both ballistics and fingerprint experts. This case took place too early for either. Only eyewitnesses placed the gun in the hand of the defendant and saw him fire the bullet which killed the officer. Such a presentation of evidence would never get to the jury today; it would be dismissed. This may be a case of factual innocence; a person other than the accused shot and killed the police officer.

Duncan was granted a change of venue from the city of St. Louis to St. Louis County. When he was found guilty of first degree murder, he was represented before the Missouri Supreme Court by Walter Farmer, a graduate of Lincoln University in Jefferson City and Washington University Law School in St. Louis, the first black attorney to argue before this body. When Farmer did not prevail before the appellate court in Missouri, he took Duncan's case to the United States Supreme Court. There he insisted that a federal question was involved in the defendant's wrongful conviction and death sentence. Expectedly, the high court determined that William Duncan's case did not involve a federal question, and he was hanged in Clayton on July 27, 1894.[26] In a rare instance of reporting, a small rural newspaper wrote, "The belief is strong among those who have watched [Duncan's] case closely that he did not kill the officer."[27] It is impossible at this date to determine that the accused was wrongly convicted, but doubt lingers. He may have been one more person executed for a crime he did not commit.

The other law enforcement officer victim in a 1890s capital case died at the hands of a white man. On June 14, 1890, John Turlington, alias William West, an ex-convict, killed the sheriff of Cooper County, Thomas Cranmer, in the process of escaping from the jail in Boonville. The perpetrator was incarcerated for the felony of assault with intent to kill because he had fired at a brakeman while getting off a train. In addition to the victim being an elected official at the time of his death, he had also represented Cooper County for two terms, 1880 and 1882, in the Missouri General Assembly. The defendant was prosecuted for a killing which occurred in the course of committing a felony, the crime of escape. He applied for but was denied a change of venue. The jury found him guilty of first degree murder. After his other escapes on October 31 and December 26, 1890, and subsequent recaptures, the Supreme Court of Missouri affirmed his conviction, and the new sheriff of Cooper County hanged John Turlington on March 6, 1891.[28]

A similar white-on-white capital crime took place in Mississippi County on January 12, 1897, when James Albright shot and killed the prosecuting attorney, George Elliott. The prosecutor was attempting to arrest the perpetrator as an accessory to his brother Joseph Albright's murder of their brother-in-law, Isaac Large; the in-law had earlier refused to stand their bond for other violent run-ins with the law. The defendant requested, but was denied, a change of venue. After he was tried, found guilty, and sentenced to hang, the trial judge ordered that he be moved to the Cape Girardeau jail for safekeeping, presumably from the wrath of a mob, during the pendency of his appeal. The Missouri Supreme Court affirmed; Albright was returned to Mississippi County, and the sheriff hanged him in Charleston on July 9, 1898.[29]

Seven other white-on-white homicides resulted in executions in the 1890s in seven different counties under these circumstances. Quarreling neighbors explained death penalty cases in Marion[30] and Harrison,[31] and contentious drinkers one in Lafayette;[32] a landlord-tenant dispute accounted for one in Holt;[33] a customer-storekeeper argument proved deadly in Mercer,[34] and a debtor-creditor first degree murder took place in Butler.[35] In Carroll County a prominent banker and lawyer was hanged after he killed an entire family because the husband and father intended to testify against him in a criminal proceeding; this will be discussed with other white-on-white multiple victim homicides of this decade.

During this time period three black men were hanged because they murdered their rivals for the affection of black women. These cases arose in the city of St. Louis,[36] Buchanan,[37] and Jackson County.[38] The defense of all three was self-defense; their juries rejected it. All were found guilty of first degree murder, and the Missouri Supreme Court affirmed their convictions.

Two 1890s capital cases arose because black men murdered their mistresses. In Kansas City on April 5, 1891, an illiterate ex-convict, William McCoy, bashed in the head of a black woman, Mollie McGruder, as she walked with washing. They had lived together and quarreled; he killed her in a jealous rage. He was linked to her murder by the fact that, among other pieces of evidence, as the newspaper explained, "the blood on his clothes was that of a human being."[39] This same paper also mentioned that there had been threats of lynching against him. Another news story stated that "a mob of Negroes stormed the jail ... with the intention of taking McCoy out and dealing summarily with him. The mob was repulsed by the jailers."[40] Perhaps for this reason or some other, McCoy's attorney requested and received a change of venue from Jackson to Lafayette County. Today, no urban defense attorney in a capital case would allow her client's case to be heard by a jury from a rural county. One made up of city dwellers is statistically far less likely to return a death sentence than one of country residents. McCoy was tried and found guilty; the Missouri Supreme Court affirmed, and the sheriff of Lafayette County hanged him on February 16, 1893.[41] The local newspaper's account of his execution begins, "The tenth official hanging in Lafayette County took place in Lexington; ... William McCoy, a Negro mistress-murderer, being the victim to suffer the penalty."[42] At this time, Jackson County had been the scene of three executions. Only one other change of venue out of Kansas City in a capital case would follow McCoy's, that of a woman's.

Artist sketch of the hanging of James Pollard on June 25, 1897, a black man who killed another black man, in the presence of nonchalant white men in St. Joseph, Buchanan County. Pollard killed Joseph Irwin, the brother of his intended victim. Pollard and David Irwin had quarreled about a young black woman teaching school. (*St. Joseph Weekly Herald*, July 1, 1897. Used by permission, State Historical Society of Missouri, Columbia. All rights reserved.)

The other black who killed his mistress during this decade was Dick Robinson. On October 24, 1892, this illiterate man stabbed to death Johanna Schollman, a white woman, then employed as a domestic by the family of the mayor of Sedalia. The Missouri Supreme Court decision affirming his death sentence mentioned that soon after Robinson's arrest, the sheriff of Pettis County became alarmed at the danger of mob violence and took the accused by a midnight train to the seat of Moniteau County, California. In a day or so, the perpetrator confessed to his crime. The case also detailed the desperate state of affairs between the lovers. According to the appellate decision, prior to her death at his hands, she said, "One of us has got to die. If you don't kill me, I will kill you. [He said] Hannah, if one of us has got to die I just as well be hung for you as you for me."[43] Robinson was tried and found guilty; while his case was on appeal to the Missouri Supreme Court, he was held in the Pettis County jail in Sedalia. One evening in early June 1893, five prisoners escaped from this facility by sawing through the iron bars of their cells. A newspaper reported, "The Negro, Robinson, who is under sentence of death for murder, refused to leave, although he had an equal chance with those who escaped."[44] Apparently he wished to be put to death for murdering the woman he loved, his mistress; on December 15, 1893, the sheriff of Pettis County hanged Dick Robinson in Sedalia.[45]

In two 1890s capital cases a solo perpetrator murdered one child. One was black-on-black and the other white-on-white. Both homicides aroused considerable anger in their respective communities. In Jefferson City on December 25, 1896, Tobe Lanahan, a black janitor and handyman at a furniture store, raped, murdered, and mutilated the body of Willie Gaines, a 12-year-old black girl. As mentioned earlier, Governor Stone managed to disperse an integrated lynch mob once Lanahan was in custody. The grand jury of Cole County indicted the defendant for one crime, first degree murder. His defense was that he was elsewhere at the time of the crime, but the jury believed the defendant's confession to the sheriff. Lanahan was found guilty; the Missouri Supreme Court affirmed, and he was hanged in Jefferson City on June 22, 1898.[46]

In Clay County on October 13, 1897, a widowed and remarried white man, William Carr, led three-year-old Belle Carr, his daughter by his first wife, to the Missouri River, tied her arms and legs with a stone, and threw her in the water. Her body was later found on a sandbar, and her neighbors, grandmother, and stepmother identified the dead child by her clothing. Although the second Mrs. Carr was never charged with any law-breaking, her husband committed the crime in order to please his wife; her child Allan and Belle had frequently quarreled. William Carr confessed on October 25; his trial began in mid–November, and the sheriff of Clay County hanged him in Liberty on December 17, 1897. As with other offenses which horrified the community, there was no appeal, and the time lapse between the crime and its punishment was short, just over two months.[47]

No death-sentenced black perpetrator during this time period killed more than one victim, and only one, Tobe Lanahan, murdered a child. The following white-on-white homicides are characterized by multiple victims, many of them small children. These cases arose in different locales, and the perpetrators' motives differed. The largest number of victims was amassed by Joseph Howell. In Linn County on January 19, 1890, this 24-year-old school teacher killed his first cousin, a widow, Mrs. Minnie Hall, and her four children, Roy, Nettie, May, and William, aged two, five, seven, and nine years, respectively. He then set their house on fire. An incinerated fetus was also found in the cellar of the burnt dwelling. At the time of her death, Minnie Hall had recently been five months pregnant by Joseph Howell, and Missouri law classified sexual relations between first cousins as incest and punished this activity with a prison term. In order to avoid the consequences of a known incestuous relation, he persuaded Mrs. Hall to have, in the language of the day, *a criminal operation*, but he apparently continued to fear detection, and to be on the safe side, he eliminated all five witnesses against him, four of them small children. Howell was specifically charged with one murder, that of five-year-old Nettie Hall. Although there was talk of lynching him, he received a great deal of due process. His first trial took place in Linneus, the county seat of Linn County, and the jury found him guilty. However, on appeal the Missouri Supreme Court reversed. He then received a change of venue to Grundy County, and his second trial resulted in a mistrial. In his third he was found guilty, and the Supreme Court of Missouri affirmed. According to the second appellate decision in this case, Howell confessed his crime to various cellmates, was overheard arguing with Mrs. Hall about her pregnancy, and had a "powerful motive" to wipe out an entire family. The sheriff of Grundy County hanged him in Trenton on August 4, 1893. The case received extensive press coverage statewide.[48]

The murder of the Meeks family also involved multiple victims. Its perpetrators were prominent: William Taylor, an attorney and banker in Browning, Linn County, had represented Sullivan County in the Missouri General Assembly in 1888.[49] His accomplice was his brother, George, a farmer, also sentenced to death, but he escaped from the jail in Carrollton and was never recaptured. On May 10, 1894, in Linn County, the Taylor brothers intended to kill Gus Meeks and his entire family; it consisted of Gus, his pregnant wife Delora, and their three children, 18-month-old Mamie, four-year-old Hattie, and six-year-old Nellie. Their motive was preventing the father and husband from testifying against William Taylor on charges of stealing cattle. Meeks had earlier been tried for this offense, found guilty, and was serving a prison term in MSP. He turned state's evidence, was pardoned, and allowed to return to his family on a promise of testifying against William Taylor at his forthcoming trial on cattle stealing charges in Milan, seat of Sullivan County.

For variously described sums of money, the perpetrators managed to persuade Gus to leave the area; his family went with him in a wagon. When they reached one of the Taylor farms, the brothers eliminated everyone, they thought, including a fetus which was aborted in the course of their multiple homicides. However, six-year-old Nellie survived, crawled out of a straw stack, and lived to tell the story of how her entire family came to be murdered on the Taylor farm. The brothers were arrested in Arkansas, and to avoid their being lynched, they were returned to Milan, under extraordinarily heavy guard. They were tried twice, first in Sullivan County, and after a mistrial in Milan, they received a change of venue to Carroll County. At their second trial in Carrollton, the jury found them guilty, and the Missouri Supreme Court affirmed. The sheriff of Carroll County hanged William Taylor on April 30, 1896. His escaped victim Nellie Meeks later took part in a show in St. Joseph. She had received a blow from an ax which left a slight but visible hollow in her head. As she sang various songs about her family's murder, she brushed her hair back so her audiences could see her dent. Nellie eventually ended her show days, married, and died in 1910 after giving birth to a daughter whom she named Hattie, in memory of her murdered four-year-old sister.[50]

Two white wife-murderers in the 1890s also killed their offspring. In Archie, Cass County, on April 21, 1891, Bates Soper bludgeoned to death with an ax his pregnant wife Delia and their two children, a three-year-old boy and a six-year-old girl. More than six years after his triple homicide in Missouri, a Kansas City police officer arrested him under the name of Homer Lee in Ashland, Oregon, on June 11, 1897. This perpetrator, an ex-convict, was a butcher by profession. In the course of Soper's incarceration and trial, he confessed to the murder of his Cass County family and various other killings, including his father and the child of his second marriage in Oregon. It seems that he was unable to resist the temptation to kill. His defense to his Missouri killings was insanity; it did not succeed. The jury found him guilty; the Missouri Supreme Court affirmed, and the sheriff of Cass County hanged Bates Soper in Harrisonville on March 30, 1899.[51]

Arthur Duestrow, the degenerate heir of his father, a deceased wealthy St. Louis businessman, Lewis Duestrow, also killed his wife and child. Among Arthur's addictions were

Photographs of the hanging of William Taylor on April 30, 1896, in Carrollton, Carroll County. He was sentenced to death for the murder of the Meeks family. (Retrospective, *Carrollton Democrat*, April 27, 1976. Used by permission, State Historical Society of Missouri, Coumbia. All rights reserved.) *Left:* Father Kennedy continues to pray for Taylor. *Right:* The hood is placed over Taylor's head. A sheriff stands ready to pull trapdoor lever."

drink and women. On February 13, 1894, he shot to death his wife, Albertine ("Tina"), and their two-year-old son, Louis, in their home in St. Louis. He was referred to in the extensive press coverage of his case as "the millionaire murderer" and the "millionaire criminal"; in today's money, this perpetrator was worth approximately 25 million dollars. His defense was insanity; among other personae, the defendant, aged mid–20s, pretended to be a cardinal in the Catholic Church, the surgeon general in the U.S. Army, and most frequently, an imaginary Union Army officer during the Civil War, *General Brandenburg*. He often referred to his dead wife as *Countess von Brandenburg*. Had he not had a side piece, his mistress Clara Howard, his defense might have succeeded. Just as attorneys in Jackson County removed McCoy's trial for the murder of his mistress from Jackson to Lafayette County, Duestrow's defense team got a change of venue out of the city of St. Louis to Franklin County. He was tried twice; his first resulted in a mistrial, but he was found guilty in his second trial. The Missouri Supreme Court wrote two decisions in his case; the first, issued by Division Two upon which sat three judges, affirmed his death sentence, and the second, by the entire court, determined that no federal question was involved and denied a motion to transfer his case to the court en banc. The sheriff of Franklin County hanged the only person of immense wealth ever executed in this state's history in Union on February 17, 1897.[52]

Other white-on-white capital cases of this decade involve a dismissed farmhand who killed his would-be father-in-law. His beloved had no interest in him.[53] Another concerned the victim's sister. The father objected to his daughter's romance with her suitor, but her brother did not. For reasons not susceptible to proof, the perpetrator fatally poisoned his dear one's brother.[54] The city of St. Louis was the locale of two first degree sweetheart murders; one suitor was hanged in the St. Louis jail in 1896,[55] and the other in this same facility in 1898.[56] A third St. Louis homicide involved a former mistress; she had won $5,000 in a lottery. Her ex-lover learned of her new wealth and returned from St. Paul, Minnesota. He wanted her money in order to purchase a saloon. She refused to give it to him, and he pumped five bullets into her, thereby causing her death. A policeman who responded to the scene took the stand at the perpetrator's trial and quoted him as saying, "I shot her, and they can take me out, and put a rope around my neck as soon as they want to." They did; on January 12, 1894, he was hanged in the St. Louis jail.[57]

The capital crime à la mode of the 1890s was wife-murder. In addition to their spouses, Bates Soper and Arthur Duestrow killed their little one(s). Soper was hanged in Cass County, and Duestrow, a St. Louis criminal, obtained a change of venue to Franklin County; he was put to death in Union. Other enraged husbands died on county gallows throughout the state. Andrew, Clark, Jackson, Macon, Oregon, St. Louis, Shannon, Scott, and Vernon counties were all scenes of the gallows death of a wife-murderer in the 1890s. Although more men were put to death during this time period because they killed their victims in a robbery or an attempted robbery, a homicide for personal gain is comprehensible in a way that one which arises from holy matrimony gone amok is not.

Three black husbands who killed their wives were executed in this decade. On June 29, 1895, William Wright axed Betty Wright to death in Vernon County because he believed that she had deliberately burned his dinner. Up to the time of Wright's trial, when a black committed a capital crime in Missouri the defense had never been insanity. This was probably so because no Missouri slave's defense to a homicide which was tried in a courtroom was ever insanity. Most likely, the belief existed that human property did not have the mental capacity to become crazy. In Wright's case, the insanity defense was used because he had earlier been an inmate in an insane asylum in Alabama. At his trial, experts testified for both the prosecution and the defense regarding the defendant's mental state at the time he killed his wife. The jury was probably persuaded by the testimony of witnesses for the state who quoted him as saying after his dinner was burned that "he had strapped her and that she (his wife) had run away. Defendant stated that he would never hit her again, but that the next time he would kill her.... While his wife screamed 'Murder! Murder'! The defendant said, 'G__ d__ you, I will kill you." The jury determined that Wright was sane and guilty; the Missouri Supreme Court affirmed, and the sheriff of Vernon County hanged him in Nevada on August 10, 1896.[58]

The other black wife-murderers followed a familiar pattern. She left him after years of abuse, and he retaliated by gunning her down. With a pistol that he used during his military service, Martin Reed, a 61-year-old former slave and Union Army soldier, shot his wife of 23 years, Hester Reed, in Kansas City in her mother's home on September 16, 1890. He attempted suicide, but he recovered, was tried and found guilty; the Supreme Court of Missouri affirmed. Martin Reed was hanged in the Kansas City jail on January 5, 1894.[59] Less than eight and one-half years later, his son, James Reed, an eight-year-old child playing in a nearby room when his father killed his mother, was hanged for the murder of his beloved from the same scaffold his father had died on. Since James Reed was aged 16 at the time of his crime, his case is discussed in Chapter 8. On July 24, 1897, in Scott County, Will Burns killed his wife, Mag Burns, who, tired of his abuse, left him. When she went to claim her clothes with a constable, her angry husband wounded the law enforcement officer with the same double-barreled shotgun the perpetrator used to murder his wife. He was tried, and the jury found him guilty; the appellate court affirmed his death sentence. The sheriff of Scott County hanged Will Burns in Benton on May 29, 1899.[60]

When the Supreme Court of Missouri upheld Burns' death sentence, the judge wrote for the court, "It is another case of wife murder—a class of crimes which has become very common. We have been called upon to consider three cases at this call of the docket, in which unoffending and helpless women have been shot down or butchered without the slightest provocation."[61] He was referring to the large number of white wife-murderers. On January 29, 1888, Louis Bulling killed his in St. Joseph. She had earlier left him, and according to the appellate decision, he disapproved when she attended a "disreputable ball" and at it she "wore a dress low in the neck and very short in the skirt." He murdered her the next day.[62] In the city of St. Louis on February 25, 1890, 300-pound Henry Henson killed his wife of three months, a widow with a 13-year-old son. The newlyweds ran a boarding house, and he accused Ida, his wife, of having an affair with one of their boarders, a crippled tailor. She vehemently denied the charge, and Henson shot and killed her and fired at but missed her terrified son.[63] On May 26, 1896, in Macon County, George Anderson, an upstanding farmer, stabbed his wife to death and attempted suicide by slashing his own throat. He wished to plead guilty, but the judge appointed counsel to represent him. There was no appeal in Anderson's case, and the sheriff of Macon County hanged him on August 21, 1896.[64]

The three wife-murders which the Supreme Court was probably referring to all occurred in 1898. On March 12, Fred Bronstine killed his wife, Amelia Jane, after she left him because of cruel mistreatment at their home in Lewis County and moved with their four children to the residence of her 78-year-old mother in Clark County. He went to his mother-in-law's home, and in her presence and two of their children, he shot and killed his spouse.[65] On March 22, 50-year-old Oscar Baker beat his 45-year-old wife, Annie, to death at Winona, Shannon County, after a night of his heavy drinking. In an attempt to defend herself, she hit her 240-pound ex-convict and drunken husband in the face with a wet rag; he was so outraged that he finished her off.[66] On June 27 in Oregon County Carroll Rice lay in wait for 20-year-old Mary Rice, his second wife; she had left him, and because she refused to return, he picked her off with a rifle.[67]

These many perpetrators of the 1890s were hanged by the sheriff of the county in which their death sentences were obtained. For the most part, they executed their death warrants in the county of the crime. However, the heyday of public hangings was over in Missouri. In 1887, the legislature restricted the number of spectators by requiring that the hanging take place "within the walls of the jail" or "in an enclosure surrounded by a wall ... or fence higher than the gallows ... to exclude the view of persons on the outside." The law also excluded persons aged less than 21 years who were unrelated to the convict from viewing the hanging.[68] In 1906, the state sheriffs' association adopted a resolution which requested that the legislature pass a law requiring executions at the prison. [69]

Even earlier, 11 other states had made more drastic changes in their execution practices. Beginning with Vermont (1864) and Maine (1864), and followed by New Hampshire (1869), Ohio (1885), Colorado (1890), New York (1890), California (1893), Connecticut (1894), Iowa (1894), Indiana (1897), and West Virginia (1899), the county sheriff was no longer in charge of carrying out death sentences.[70] In these jurisdictions, the warden of the state penitentiary officiated. By definition uninvited spectators were not admitted when a hanging took place within the high walls of a state prison, or beginning in 1890 in New York, when the condemned was electrocuted. It is not accidental that these above-named states were not, if ever, places of slavery on the eve of the Civil War. During slave days, owners often required their human property to attend the execution of one of their own, presumably for example-setting purposes. *Seeing* with one's own eyes what happened to the death-sentenced criminal was intended as a powerful reminder of the ill-advisedness of crime. Watching was supposed to keep the spectators on the paths of righteousness. As a result, Missouri and other former slave states were among the last places in the United States to abandon carrying out executions at the county of the conviction of the crime and finally transport the death-sentenced to the state penitentiary.

Despite a statute which limited the view of spectators to the hanging itself, the law said nothing about making sketches, taking photographs, or even producing a motion picture of the neck-breaking or strangling death of the condemned. Illustrations herein are possible because the law was silent. Many times the state's major newspapers did not run photographs, but the *Carrollton Democrat* did of William Taylor's in 1896. Though the movie is long lost or disintegrated, some enterprising film director made a 500-foot motion picture of Carr's hanging in 1897. In addition, a mob rushed the Clay County stockade and knocked it down while Carr's body dangled at the end of a rope. A viewer of Carr's hanging corpse also took a finger-ring from his dead body.[71] In Kansas City, a woman managed to obtain a ticket and got herself admitted to the jail to witness a hanging. Despite a statue which excluded children, she took her 12-year-old with her. This person ran a boarding house, and she told a reporter and her boarders, "I think it's wrong to hang people, but as long as they keep on doing it I might as well see it done."[72] The law was silent regarding the dead body of the convict. As a result, obtaining souvenirs of the event, such as cutting off the little finger of the hanged man and later having it mounted as a watch charm,[73] was not illegal.

To be sure, the law prohibited most persons who could not climb trees or gain access to rooftops from witnessing the actual hanging, but in no way did it prevent the multitude from viewing the dead body. After a reasonable interval during which the attending physicians ascertained that the hanged was actually now a stiff, the sheriff and his deputies placed the dead man in a coffin and transported him to a convenient viewing area. A church, a funeral home, a courthouse lawn, a corridor in a courthouse or one in a city hall were all locales at which hundreds and at times thousands of men, women, and children filed by and gazed upon the lifeless face of the wicked one. Such was not the practice in St. Louis, and the sheriff of Franklin County refused to display the dead body of the hanged millionaire, Arthur Duestrow. Although in general the sheriff followed the law when executing a death warrant, he also went out of his way to avoid disappointing the would-be attendees to his hanging duties. He made certain that all who wished to got an excellent view of the corpse. These arrangements continued here in the twentieth century.

Between 1900 and 1907, there were 42 executions and 19 known lynchings in Missouri. For the first time since the pre Civil War era, both the number of legal hangings and lynchings declined, and executions took place in significantly fewer counties than in the 1890–1899 decade. In all, including those executed for rape, 23 county seats were the locales where the sheriff, on one or more occasions, executed a death warrant. Counting only executions for murder, there were 19 counties. No change of venue was granted for any person whom the county sheriff hanged for first degree murder. The four executions for rape are discussed elsewhere; the 38 for murder are detailed herein.

The motives of most killers repeat familiar patterns. African-Americans hanged for the murder of other African-Americans between 1900 and 1907 include two men who murdered their wives, one in Jasper County[74] and the other in Cooper,[75] and three who stabbed or shot their beloved in a jealous mood when her attention turned to another man; two of these green-eyed killings took place in the city of St. Louis[76] and one in Kansas City.[77] One executed black helped another kill a rival for the beloved in Butler County.[78] Black neighbors had a deadly quarrel over a fence in New Madrid County[79] and black saloon patrons over cards in Kansas City.[80] In the city of St. Louis one African-American's debt to another proved deadly,[81] and for the first time as far as we know, one black who killed another in a robbery was put to death.[82]

Another first for any known executed African-American up to this time concerns a retarded person involved in a homicide which took place in St. Charles County on April 12, 1903. Three black males, including 40-year-old Price Edwards, the son-in-law of the elderly victim, participated in the shooting of Joseph Buckner and setting his house on fire to cover their crime. Their victim's body was burned beyond recognition. A year earlier Mrs. Price Edwards had her husband arrested for disturbing the peace, and he spent time in jail. At the time of the crime, she was not living with her husband, and Edwards blamed Joseph Buckner, his father-in-law, for his martial difficulties. Although the son-in-law masterminded the murder, he was not the trigger man. That lot fell to 18-year-old Allen Henderson, almost certainly a slow learner. According to the Missouri Supreme Court decision which upheld his death sentence, "Price was standing at [Henderson's] side, and [Henderson] hesitated about doing it, and Price nudged him and said, 'Shoot, shoot,' and then he shot."[83] Initially, Henderson, Edwards, and the third participant in the crime, Bruz Castlio, were all arrested and put on trial on first degree murder charges. However in the course of proceedings against them, both Edwards and Castlio died. This left only one person to hang for the crime. Once more, contemporary news coverage, not the Missouri Supreme Court decision, discusses Henderson's retardation. First, he readily confessed to the crime and talked freely of it. Equally important, a number of citizens, including the trial judge before whom Henderson appeared and 12 members of the St. Charles Bar Association, signed a petition to the governor urging him to commute Henderson's death sentence because, as the local newspaper reported, he "is not bright and no doubt Edwards' influence over him frightened him into doing the dirty work.... [He has a] weak mental condition."[84] Like other retarded criminals sentenced to death, as the newspaper reported, "Henderson does not seem to realize what it means.... Several times he has voiced his sentiments by saying why fool with the matter as he is ready to go out and be hung. He has a good appetite and sleeps well."[85] Almost certainly had another member of this killing party been alive to execute, the governor would have commuted the death sentence of this mentally deficient young man to a prison term. A local newspaper expressed it well, "The other two companions in crime died before they could satisfy the law and only Henderson remains to satisfy the gallows."[86] The governor did not intervene, and the sheriff of St. Charles County hanged Allen Henderson in St. Charles on June 15, 1905.[87]

The remaining five blacks hanged for their crime here between 1900 and 1907 killed white men. Three cases arose in the city of St. Louis. On July 4, 1899, James Nettles got into an argument with the conductor over a broken seat on a streetcar he had just boarded. First he tried to fix the seat, and when he could not, he demanded that his fare be returned. When he was refused, Nettles shot and killed Samuel Mann, the conductor. He was tried and found guilty; the Missouri Supreme Court affirmed, and James Nettles was hanged in the city of St. Louis on May 7, 1900.[88] On August 27, 1900, Henry Flutcher shot and killed Louis Roth on the street when the victim hurrahed for McKinley, then President of the United States. The black perpetrator appears to have perceived insult where none was intended. According to the Missouri Supreme Court decision which affirmed his death sentence, Fletcher told the President's supporter as he opened fire on him, "You white bastards. I'll make you respect my color ... I missed your brother last night, but you son of a bitch I'll not miss you." Flutcher was tried and found guilty; his sentence was upheld on appeal, and he was hanged in the city of St. Louis on April 11, 1902.[89] On June 23, 1900, Henry Wilson shot and killed the proprietor of a tavern, Thomas Mooney, during an attempted robbery. He was tried and convicted; the Missouri Supreme Court affirmed, and Wilson was hanged in St. Louis on May 8, 1903.[90]

Two other blacks were executed for the killing of a white man. In Cooper County on March 26, 1900, Ellsworth Evans shot and killed a deputized policeman, William Hennicke, who was attempting to arrest him on charges of robbing a cigar store. Evans was tried for first degree murder and found guilty; the Missouri Supreme Court affirmed. In its affirmation it noted that the defendant's innocence of the cigar store robbery was not a defense to the crime of killing the arresting officer. The sheriff of Cooper County hanged Evans in Boonville on April 12, 1901.[91] In Ralls County on April 28, 1902, in the town of Rensselaer, Jesse Johnson bludgeoned to death Marcus McRae, the postmaster and a merchant, in order to rob him. This illiterate man was captured and confessed to the crime. He was tried and found guilty of first degree murder; no appeal was taken, and the sheriff of Ralls County hanged him in New London on September 12, 1902.[92]

The remainder of the men executed for murder here between 1900 and 1907 were white, and all of their victims were white. Notably absent from the list of white-on-white capital crimes are men who killed their wives. Two blacks were hanged for this crime during this time period, but no white men. Most probably the all-white-male juries who heard the cases of white wife-murderers were unwilling to find them guilty of first degree murder; this crime then carried an automatic death sentence.

However, white men who killed either their beloved or a rival for her did not escape the gallows. On December 8, 1898, in Miltondale and at a school house while it was in use for religious services, Ernest Clevenger shot and killed George Allen and mortally wounded Della Clevenger. (Her father was the perpetrator's second cousin.) He intended to kill his rival, Allen, and Jennie Clevenger, the gunman's beloved. His aim was poor, and he shot her sister, Della, who was sitting beside Jennie. Della lingered over four months with a bullet in her brain before she finally died. The defense was twofold, insanity and drunkenness; they did not succeed. Clevenger was tried for the murder of George Allen and found guilty; the Missouri Supreme Court affirmed, and the sheriff of Clay County hanged Ernest Clevenger in Liberty on June 15, 1900.[93] In Kansas City, John Taylor, a married man in his twenties with a wife and child elsewhere, rented a room and lay in wait for three days with a rifle for 18-year-old Ruth Noland. She had earlier left him because he assaulted and choked her. On March 2, 1901, he gunned her down as she accompanied her sister who was going to work. According to the Missouri Supreme Court decision affirming his death sentence, Taylor told the arresting officer, "You would have done the same thing if she treated you that way." Taylor was tried and found guilty; the sheriff of Jackson County hanged him in Kansas City on April 17, 1903.[94] On June 25, 1901, in Butler County, Steve Clark stabbed to death Pearl Clark, a woman whom he had previously lived with but to whom he was not married. She had left him and was living with another man. He was tried and found guilty; the Missouri Supreme Court affirmed, and the sheriff of Butler County hanged this "jealous man," as a newspaper termed Steve Clark, in Poplar Bluff on February 6, 1903.[95]

Five white men were put to death between 1900 and 1907 for murder committed in the course of robbery or attempted robbery; two unrelated gallows deaths took place in

Bates,[96] one in Wayne,[97] one in Pulaski,[98] and one in Texas County. In this last-named place, the crime is discussed with others involving multiple victims.

In other death penalty cases of this era, the perpetrators' anger is their shared characteristic. In Dunklin County, an enraged customer shot and killed a storekeeper and lumberyard owner who wished to retain the purchaser's watch until he paid for an item.[99] In one Buchanan County case an ex-convict, recently released from MSP after serving a prison term for killing one man, murdered another whom he quarreled with at a dance.[100] In another from this same county, a man, intent on the destruction of either of two other men, shot and killed a brother of one of his intended victims.[101] In Osage County, an earlier dispute over the sale of land resulted in the perpetrator shooting and killing his victim on Christmas Eve in the presence of the victim's family as its members finished singing carols.[102]

In other crimes wherein the county sheriff hanged the defendant, an ill-humored family member killed his father-in-law or foster parents. These cases arose in the city of St. Louis[103] and Adair[104] and Warren counties. In Warren County, on August 31, 1903, 22-year-old William Church murdered Henry Yeater and his wife, who had raised him from age nine. He killed them because he believed that they did not intend to leave him any money. The perpetrator then left Warren County and enlisted in the U.S. Navy under an assumed name. He was finally arrested in Philadelphia, Pennsylvania, in March 1904. Church may have been retarded; according to the Missouri Supreme Court decision which affirmed his death sentence, the superintendent of the Boys Reform School at Boonville wherein the defendant had been an inmate testified that "the defendant was not a bright boy, and he never considered him strong mentally."[105] The defense in Church's case was not retardation; rather it was insanity, but it had a novel twist. His attorney sought to prove that his client's mental defect was brought on by his excessive masturbation. In the nineteenth and early twentieth centuries, the belief existed among both English and American physicians that masturbation, or onanism, or self-abuse, or self-pollution, or personal fornication— to cite a few of the names this vice was then known by—caused, among many other maladies, insanity.[106] As cited in the Missouri Supreme Court decision, among the witnesses the defense put on to prove Church's bad habits was the superintendent at Boonville. He testified that during his stay in reform school the "defendant was then addicted to the habit of self-abuse, and it became necessary to put night gloves on him for a time." Other defense witnesses included two guards from the St. Louis city jail who "saw him [Church] in the act of self-abuse.... They testified that they tried to persuade him to desist and tried to shame him, but without success."[107] The jury was not persuaded that the masturbatory habits of the accused caused him to become insane. It found him guilty, and after his sentence was upheld on appeal, the sheriff of Warren County hanged John Church on January 10, 1907.[108]

Other capital cases of this time include the killing of a Pinkerton detective, a member of a posse attempting to make an arrest, and prison guards. In all these cases the perpetrators had already committed other non-capital offenses, and they were either attempting to avoid arrest or were convicts breaking out of the Missouri State Penitentiary. The Pinkerton detective killing happened in Franklin County;[109] it resulted in the hanging of two men, and the prison-break cases took place in Cole. One resulted in a single hanging,[110] and the other was a triple execution.

The latter crime took place on November 24, 1905, when four MSP inmates, Charles Blake, Edward Raymond, George Ryan, and Harry Vaughan, all serving terms for robbery, shot and killed two guards, John Clay and Ephraim Allison, and tore open the prison's outer gate with nitroglycerin as they made their escape. The convicts commandeered a wagon, and in it they rode through the streets of Jefferson City until they were recaptured. The authorities' first concern was ascertaining how these men obtained guns and blasting material. The governor of Missouri, Joseph Folk, personally spent an hour pleading with Charles Blake, wounded in the escape attempt and dying, to reveal the source of his and his co-defendants' contraband. According to a newspaper account, Blake replied, " 'You don't know us Governor. When we stick to each other we stick.' [The Governor asked] 'Don't you know that if you do not confess you may be hanged.' ... [Blake replied] 'All right then go ahead and hang me.' These were his last words. A few minutes later he turned his face to the wall and died."[111]

On the newspaper's same front page, among other headlines, appeared, "Recaptured Men May Be Hanged Within Week."[112] Initially, the Cole County prosecutor's task of obtaining first degree murder convictions for all three seemed child's play. It proved otherwise. At their first trial, the jury was hung. At their second, the Missouri Supreme Court reversed because the trial judge did not give the defense-requested instruction that the members of the jury "are at liberty to find one or more of the defendants guilty and others not guilty."[113] At their third trial and with the proper instructions, the jury found all three guilty; the appellate court affirmed. Governor Folk offered Edward Raymond clemency if he would reveal the source of their guns and nitroglycerin. Like Blake before him, Raymond refused. On June 27, 1907, the sheriff of Cole County simultaneously put three men to death. Within the enclosure as either assistants or witnesses were the sheriffs of Adair, Boone, Cedar, Chariton, Howard, Moniteau, Osage, and Ralls counties.[114] It was the third time in Missouri's history that three men were hanged at the same time for the same crime.

A photographer captured the moment; his picture appeared in *St. Louis Globe-Democrat* the morning of their execution. Clearly visible in the photograph are two Catholic priests. They were Monsignor Joseph Selinger, pastor of St. Peter's Church in Jefferson City, and Father Henry Geisert, associate pastor. Both men were also assigned as chaplains at MSP.[115] One is wearing a linen garment called a surplice over his cassock, and the stole of the other is visible. Their clerical vestments are appropriate. On the scaffold they would have administered several of the sacraments, including that of penance and extreme unction, or the last rites of the Church, to the condemned. Later the bodies of these executed men were removed from the scaffold and interred in a Catholic service at the Missouri State Penitentiary's burial grounds.

We pick up the presence of a priest at the scaffold in St. Louis in the 1880s and again in the 1890s, but it is in Kansas City that two are of particular interest in their ministering to men sentenced to hang. One was Father John Glennon; he was present during an execution in 1895. The other, Father Thomas Lillis, was the parish priest at St. Patrick's; near his church was the Second Street jail, within its confines Kansas City's executions then took place. When Lillis attended the death of John Taylor in 1903, it was his sixth hanging. The priest convinced him that suicide was not the solution, and immediately before his scheduled death, Taylor gave his brother the packet of strychnine he would have used to end his life but for his conversion to Catholicism.[116] Both of these priests later became bishops of the diocese of Kansas City. Glennon's tenure as bishop was 1896–1903, and Lillis' was 1910–1938. In addition to the priests of Jackson County, several times the Sisters of Mercy visited death-sentenced inmates in Independence and Kansas City.

The appeal of Catholicism for the condemned was not based on the Catholic Church's opposition to capital punishment. In 1907, the same year three men were hanged in Jefferson City, the *Catholic Encyclopedia* began being published. It contains the statement, "The

Photograph of triple hanging at the Jefferson City, Cole County, jail on June 27, 1907. From left to right with nooses around their necks are Edward Raymond, Harry Vaughn, and George Ryan. They were inmates at the Missouri State Penitentiary, and while escaping on November 24, 1905, the prisoners killed two guards. On the scaffold with the condemned men are two Catholic priests, the officiating sheriff of Cole County, assisting sheriffs of Adair, Cedar, Chariton, Howard, Miller, Moniteau, Osage, and Ralls counties, and various other lawmen. A statute required that a fence higher than the gallows be built to exclude the view of persons on the outside. Nonetheless, surrounding hilltops and roofs overflow with men, women, and children spectators. (*St. Louis Globe-Democrat*, June 27, 1907. From the archives of the St. Louis Mercantile Library, University of Missouri–St. Louis.)

infliction of capital punishment is not contrary to the teaching of the Catholic Church."[117] However, any death-sentenced convert would have heard, among other prayers immediately before his death "May the Lord who frees you from sin save you and raise you up."[118] These were surely comforting words to men with nooses about their necks. These soon-to-die felons hoped to go straight to heaven. It would seem that the Catholic religion offered more solace than other systems of belief to those who knew they were soon to hang, or at least their conversion rate was higher to Catholicism than to other faiths.

The phenomenon noted earlier of whites murdering multiple victims continued between 1900 and 1907. Apart from one black who killed a neighbor couple in a dispute over a fence in New Madrid County, all perpetrators who cut down children and/or more than one person were white. Clevenger's Clay County homicides caused the death of two persons; Church's in Warren County involved two victims, and two prison guards died at the hands of Raymond, Ryan, and Vaughan. Two white men in separate and unrelated crimes each killed five persons, many of them children.

In Dunklin County near the town of Malden on April 25, 1899, John Tettalon murdered his stepmother, Mrs. Mary J. Tettalon, and her four children, George, Ben, Ada, and Ida, or the perpetrator's half-brothers and half-sisters. He then set their residence on fire; the five bodies taken from the home were burned beyond recognition. Earlier she had sued her stepson and won a judgment against him arising from the death of her husband and his father. The perpetrator wished to put an end to the court action against him. He was tried and found guilty of the first degree murder of George, the oldest child, and the Missouri Supreme Court affirmed. The sheriff hanged John Tettalon in Kennett on February 19, 1901.[119] On October 12, 1906, Joseph ("Jodia") Hamilton shot Carnie Parsons and clubbed his wife, Minnie, and their three sons, ages one, three, and five, to death in order to gain possession of the family's personal property. Earlier, the killer had purchased his victim's crop. Hamilton confessed; he was tried and found guilty. There was no appeal, and the sheriff of Texas County hanged him in Houston on December 21, 1906.[120]

The luridities associated with earlier executions continued in the first years of twentieth century. Always the threat of a lynching remained in rural areas. In 1903 in the city of St. Louis, a four-month-old baby, women, and teenagers witnessed the 6:35 a.m. execution of Charles Gurley.[121] In 1905 in St. Charles, 500 persons filed into a funeral home to gaze upon the corpse of the hanged young man, Allen Henderson.[122] In 1906 in Houston, an audience of 3,000 was on hand for Jodia Hamilton's gallows death.[123] As the photograph of the triple hanging in Jefferson City in 1907 clarifies, spectators, lots of them, sat on any and all elevated places to watch the deadly proceedings. Nothing was new in any of these circus-atmosphere events associated with the county sheriff executing a death warrant.

The law, however, was about to change. After the Civil War, all juries in Missouri death penalty cases received this instruction: "You have nothing to do with the punishment. That is fixed by law."[124] To be sure, a body of 12 white men often had the choice to find the defendant guilty of second degree murder, or of manslaughter, or to acquit him. However, if it found the accused guilty of the first degree murder, there was only one penalty available, that of death. Effective March 18, 1907, the Missouri General Assembly finally amended the statute. After this date, in all capital cases, the trial judge was required to give the jury an instruction which allowed its members to decide which punishment should be inflicted when it found the defendant guilty of first degree murder, either death or life imprisonment in the Missouri State Penitentiary.[125] As the next chapter makes clear, this change in the law was one of several indications that this state's love affair with the death penalty was waning.

6

Reform Attempts and the Continuation of Hangings, 1908–1937

The movement to permit juries to choose life imprisonment for men whom they found guilty of first degree murder began at least as early as 1900. That year a state representative from Kansas City introduced a bill to allow it. A newspaper quoted him to this effect, "There is such a strong prejudice against capital punishment that it is difficult to get a verdict [of first degree murder] although the evidence of guilt is conclusive."[1] The numbers of the executed slowed to a crawl after this legislation took effect in March 1907. Thirteen men were hanged between 1908 and 1916; nine were black and four were white. Of the nine African-Americans, three were convicted of rape, a crime discussed in Chapter 9.

The capital cases of the six black men put to death for murder during this time period arose in Jackson, Jasper, and St. Charles counties. Three of these homicides took place in Kansas City, and in two of them, the motive was robbery. On January 12, 1908, 21-year-old Claude Brooks hit his white crippled employer, Sidney Herndon, in the head with a hammer, thereby causing his death, and he took $150 from him. Brooks was tried and found guilty; the Missouri Supreme Court affirmed. According to the newspaper, attempts were made "to persuade the governor to commute the sentence on the grounds that Brooks was of a low mentality and insane at the time of the murder." They did not succeed. The county marshal hanged him at the jail in Kansas City on July 30, 1909.[2] On November 14, 1908, 22-year-old Robert Davis used a large rock to crush the skull of another young black man, his friend, 17-year-old Harry Evans, thereby causing his death. Davis' personal gain was $5 and a watch he pawned for $2. He was tried and convicted; the Missouri Supreme Court affirmed, and the county marshal hanged Robert Davis in the Kansas City jail on June 10, 1910.[3]

The third black put to death in Kansas City was illiterate Wesley Robinson. On April 11, 1913, he choked his wife, Mary Robinson, to death and eliminated the witness against him by killing 11-year-Alma Felton, his wife's daughter by a previous marriage. He subsequently dismembered their bodies, buried them, and burned most of his victims' amputated limbs in the stove in his home. His motive was a familiar one, jealousy. A month later his crime was detected. After he was apprehended, Kansas City police officers prevented a mob of black men from lynching him.[4] He was tried and convicted; the Missouri Supreme Court affirmed. The week before Robinson's scheduled execution, the prosecuting attorney of Jackson County traveled to Jefferson City to request that the governor commute Robinson's death sentence to life imprisonment on grounds that, as the newspaper reported, he "has an undeveloped mind and is tubercular. He will probably not live long in confinement."[5] The governor refused. While waiting to die for his murders in Kansas City, he admitted that some years earlier he had strangled his common-law wife in St. Louis and served 11 years and three months of a 15-year sentence at MSP for his first homicide. The county marshal hanged Wesley Robinson in the jail in Kansas City on February 15, 1915.[6]

Another death-sentenced black perpetrator was William Wilson, an illiterate 24-year-old. On July 12, 1908, at Carl Junction, he struck 25-year-old Mrs. Millie Plum, a white woman, on the head and killed her. His motive was her refusal to have sex with him. Both the perpetrator and the victim were employees of a traveling carnival company. She was a cook, and he worked at the merry-go-round. When the murder was discovered, he was taken to the jail in Carthage to prevent his being lynched. The accused was tried and found guilty; the Missouri Supreme Court affirmed, and the sheriff of Jasper County hanged William Wilson in Carthage at 5:58 a.m. at the county jail on March 4, 1910.[7]

The last execution of blacks during this time period took place in St. Charles County. On December 6, 1913, two brothers, Andrew and Harry Black, and a third Negro, the Blacks' cousin, Tom Allen, purchased cartridges and shot their pistols several times prior to their intended travel to their homes in St. Louis. They had come to St. Charles in order to gamble, and they were about to board the train for their return trip. Two white policemen, John Blair and James Lamb, attempted to arrest the three black men for the felony of carrying concealed weapons. In the ensuing fight, both the policemen and Tom Allen were killed. The police shot and killed Allen, who, according to a prosecution witness, fired first. When the Black brothers were arrested, they were taken to the jail in St. Louis City to prevent their being lynched. Afterwards they were returned to St. Charles, tried, and found guilty of the murder of two policemen. The Missouri Supreme Court affirmed, and the sheriff of St. Charles County hanged them 25 minutes apart in the county jail in St. Charles on August 18, 1916. He began with Harry at 5:26 a.m.[8]

In four of the six death penalty cases involving African-Americans between 1909 and 1916, the Missouri Supreme Court's review of their convictions was at best perfunctory. Brooks, Davis, and the Black brothers were not represented by an attorney on their appeal. In the Blacks' case, no brief was filed, and the decision which upholds their death sentences is less than one page. With the effective assistance of counsel, on appeal, if not at trial, the likely outcome would have been even fewer black men being put to death here between 1908 and 1916.

Four white men were executed during these years; two murdered one person each. The first Caucasian was tried before the March 18, 1907 law took effect. In December 1905, the prosecuting attorney of St. Charles County filed an information charging William Jeffries with the first degree murder of William Wussler on March 3, 1905. The perpetrator's motive was personal gain. According to the Missouri Supreme Court decision, the defendant told his victim, "Money or your life." The prosecution witnesses included the wife and eight-year-old daughter of the deceased. The jury was surely touched by both identifying him, especially the child. In addition, a great deal of physical evidence tied the accused to the crime. The jury found him guilty of first degree murder; the verdict was affirmed on appeal, and the sheriff hanged him in St. Charles on June 4, 1908.[9] The other, William Sprouse, killed his wife on October 31, 1914, in St. Louis County by striking her with brass knuckles and a hammer. Counting heavily against him was the testimony of their children, including nine-year-old Dessie, 11-year-old Era, and 14-year-old Roy, that he was in an adulterous relationship with a Mrs. Scott. Given such a motive to commit the crime, the jury found him guilty; the Missouri Supreme Court affirmed, and the sheriff of St. Louis County hanged William Sprouse at Clayton on July 16, 1915.[10]

The two other white men put to death here between 1908 and 1916 were mass murderers. Each killed three or more persons in a rural area. During the night of December 21, 1907, in Caldwell County, Albert Filley killed his wife, Fanny, their nine-year-old daughter, Dollie, and his brother, Clay Filley, and seriously wounded his brother's wife, Elsia Filley. She and her husband, parents of five children, were in the Albert Filley residence to care for Fanny. She had sustained a head injury on December 13, allegedly caused by a horse, but her husband, not a black mare, had attacked her. Elsia Filley survived, and at her brother in-law's trial in June 1908, on a charge of first degree murder, she was the chief prosecution witness against him. At the time of his crimes, Albert Filley had a painful abscess, and it was alleged to have clouded his reason. His defense was insanity; it did not succeed. The jury found him guilty; there was no appeal, and the sheriff hanged him in Kingston on September 21, 1908.[11] On November 20, 1910, near Guilford, Nodaway County, Hezekiah Rasco killed the four members of the Hubbell family: Oda, the husband, his wife, Clara, and their children, six-year-old Jessie and four-year-old Welton. He then set fire to their home to conceal his crime. His motive was money. He had sustained heavy losses in an all-night poker game with Oda Hubbell, and he was recouping the $300 to $400 he had lost. The defendant had an extensive criminal record prior to the Hubbell family murders. When he was 16, he had served a term at MSP for an earlier killing of a 36-year-old woman. At his trial for the Hubbell family killings, he applied for but was denied a change of venue. He was prosecuted for one count of first degree murder, that of Oda Hubbell. The jury found him guilty, and while his case was on appeal, he was kept safe from the mob in the Buchanan County jail in St. Joseph. The Missouri Supreme Court affirmed, and he was returned to the Nodaway County jail in Marysville. There, shortly before his execution, 31-year-old Hezekiah Rasco converted to Catholicism. The sheriff of Nodaway County hanged him on March 26, 1912, in Maryville. Among those in attendance was the husband of Rasco's first victim whom he had murdered in 1896.[12]

No time in Missouri's history, including the decade prior to statehood, shows the execution of fewer whites than between 1908 and 1916. In all, there was a smaller number of gallows deaths in Missouri in these years than during any decade since the 1820s. Then the state's population was about two percent of what it became by 1920. Approximately 67,000 persons lived in Missouri in 1820; by 1920 there were 3,404,055 residents here. For the only time in Missouri's history, the number of known lynchings, 13 between 1908 and 1920, exceeded the numbers legally hanged. Equally indicative of Missouri's hostility to capital punishment was the absence of executions in the city of St. Louis. According to a newspaper account, 33 policemen and numerous civilians were murdered in this city between 1907 and 1924.[13] Nonetheless, no hanging took place there after John King's on June 27, 1907, and before a dual execution on July 18, 1924, a period of slightly more than 17 years. In earlier times, this metropolis was the premier locale of capital punishment in Missouri. It had been the scene of at least 82 men being put to death, and it remained the largest city in the state. In 1920, its population was 772,897; Kansas City was second with 324,410, or less than half.

The death penalty in Missouri was going, going, and then it was gone. On April 13, 1917, the 49th General Assembly abolished capital punishment.[14] I have no better idea why the state officially stopped putting men and boys to death at this time than I know why, apart from the Civil War years, the 1890s was the most violent time in this state's history. Presumably, two factors led to the brief abolition of the death penalty during World War I: the excesses of the late nineteenth century and the idealism of the era. A week before the legislature acted here to end state-sanctioned killing, the United States entered World War I under the leadership of Woodrow Wilson, the President who sought to make the world safe for democracy. The abolition was indeed brief; the 50th General Assembly repealed the repeal. It reinstated the death penalty on July 8, 1919.[15] No one who confines his reading to the decennial revision of Missouri's laws would know that this state ever lacked a death penalty. The abolition appears only in the session laws. *The Revised Statues Missouri 1909* and the *Revised Statutes Missouri 1919* contain identical capital punishment measures.

The legislators may have been concerned that the absence of a death penalty encouraged lynchings, and such practices would give the state a bad name. It is fact that a white man, Jay Lynch, killed the sheriff of Barton County, John Harlow, and his son, Walter Harlow, on March 3, 1919. He was arrested in Colorado, and kept in the Bates County jail in Butler. On May 28, 1919, Lynch pled guilty to these killings and did so without any attorney in his behalf in a hearing in the circuit court of Barton County. The judge accepted his plea and sentenced him to life imprisonment, the only penalty then available for first degree murder. Immediately thereafter, a mob entered the courtroom, took the defendant to the courtyard, and in the presence of 500–1,000 spectators, including cheering women and children, Jay Lynch was lynched. No one was able to identify any of the men who strung up the prisoner. An elderly viewer of this courtyard extravaganza gave as his opinion that five or six of the legislators who voted to abolish capital punishment should meet the same fate. The local newspaper with tongue in cheek rhetorically commented, "Why five or six should be hanged, the remainder spared, he didn't say."[16] The Missouri General Assembly appears to have gotten the message. With all deliberate speed it called an extra session and during it reinstated the death penalty less than two months after the murder of Jay Lynch. Among its motives was punishing capitally killers of law enforcement officers.

The 1920s saw no increase in executions here. In all, between March 26, 1920, and February 1, 1929, the known legally hanged numbered 13. Of these three were for rape, discussed in Chapter 9, and 10 for murder; four were black and six were white. Lynchings here also decreased; there are seven known during this decade. What is striking about Missouri's executions for murder in the 1920s is the complete absence of women and children as victims. No men were put to death because they killed their sweethearts, mistresses, former mistresses, wives, a rival for their beloved, or their offspring. Likewise absent as victims were in-laws, quarrelling neighbors, and other persons who knew each other prior to the homicide. The great majority of cases which swelled the numbers of those capitally punished here from the immediate post–Civil War period through 1907 did not result in hangings between 1920 and 1929. It is not possible that during this 10-year-period all was sweetness and light in romance, marriage, family life, and neighborly love in Missouri. The truth is that domestic killings did not result in carried-out death sentences. Those perpetrators were all funneled out of the system by prosecutors not seeking death sentences, juries not returning them if sought, courts reversing them if obtained, and finally governors commuting them, if they had not earlier been removed from the system.

Another difference between Missouri's uses of capital punishment in the 1920s and earlier was the frequency with which two men were hanged together. What this meant was just how unusual was either a lynching or an execution here during the second decade of the twentieth century. The sheriff hanged men sentenced to death for murder in only six locales: Franklin, Jackson, Jasper, Montgomery, the city of St. Louis, and St. Louis County.

For the first time in the state's history, all known men put to death because they were con-victed of first degree murder had their cases reviewed by the Missouri Supreme Court. It would seem that extreme care was taken that no one innocent of first degree murder die on the county gallows. This care was more apparent than actual.

All murdered persons whose killers were capitally punished here between 1920 and 1929, so far as we know, were law enforcement officers and victims of attempted robbery or robbery. The slain were all white, and this is another first in Missouri's use of the death penalty. In all previous decades under state law, at least one black person who killed a black was put to death.

Three of the four hanged black men killed their victims in routine hold-ups. One case took place in the city of St. Louis when Leon Williams shot Harry Leonard in an attempted robbery of a saloon on December 30, 1923. He was tried and convicted; the Missouri Supreme Court affirmed his death sentence, and the sheriff of the city of St. Louis hanged Williams in the jail at 6:17 a.m. on July 17, 1925.[17] Two other black men, Sterling Jackson and Ralph Long, murdered George Babcock, a Carthage grocer, in an attempted robbery on April 8, 1922. Both were ex-convicts who had earlier served prison terms for robbery. The pair was arrested the day after their capital crime in Joplin. Shortly and in order to avoid their deaths at the hands of a mob, they were rushed to Miami, Oklahoma, and later lodged in the Greene County jail in Springfield. They were returned to Carthage for their trial which began on May 3, 1923, or less than a month after their crime. They were tried for first degree murder and found guilty. The Missouri Supreme Court affirmed. The day before their hanging, a newspaper reporter told them of the death of President Warren Harding. Jackson responded, "The black people sure lost a good friend."[18] Ralph Long prob-ably converted to Catholicism as his scheduled death neared. He was accompanied to the gallows by Reverend Father Francis Gulath of St. Ann's Church. The condemned men were hanged at the Jasper County jail in Carthage at an early hour, 4:56 a.m. on August 3, 1923.

The local Elks Club stayed open all night to accommodate the many out-of-town vis-itors for the county seat's big event. Two hundred persons were inside the stockade when the sheriff sprung the trap, and many persons, including women and children, were per-mitted inside the enclosure after the dual hanging to view the dead bodies. Members of the crowd cut up the ropes to retain pieces as souvenirs. Such a scenario might have happened outside the major cities of Missouri any time after the 1887 law required the building of a stockade higher than the gallows for the actual execution(s). Up to this time, as far as we know, all executions in Jasper County involved the death of only *one* man. Viewing the dead bodies of *two* was a novel experience for most spectators. The only dual deaths of alleged black criminals in Jasper County occurred on July 30, 1853. On that date, a lynch mob took two slaves, charged with robbery, rape, and murder, from law enforcement officers and burned them to death. Slightly more than 80 years later, another generation of view-ers had an opportunity to see two freshly hanged black men.[19]

The fourth and last African-American executed in Missouri in the 1920s was James Crump. He and the sheriff of Audrain County got into a gun battle at night near railroad tracks in Mexico on February 10, 1924. During it, Chal Blum, the white law enforcement officer, shot at Crump five times, hitting him in the leg with one bullet. Crump returned his fire, thereby killing the sheriff. At Crump's trial for first degree murder, his defense was self-defense. According to the Missouri Supreme Court decision, the accused claimed he was unaware the person shooting at him was the sheriff: "I never had any ill feeling toward him nor he toward me that I know of. He had never arrested me.... I am moon-eyed and can't see well in the darkness or by night light." At his first trial, the all-white male jury found him guilty and opted for a death sentence. The Missouri Supreme Court reversed because the trial judge had failed to give a jury instruction on second degree murder. On a change of venue to Montgomery County, Crump was retried and found guilty; another all-white male jury sentenced him to death. After his February 10, 1924 shoot-out, Crump spent most of the time, when he was not in a courtroom in one of two rural counties, safe from the wrath of the mob in the jail in the city of St. Louis. There he met Father John Devilbiss, a Catholic priest, who converted him to Catholicism. This priest was with the condemned black man when the sheriff of Montgomery County hanged him at 8:05 a.m. in Montgomery City on July 17, 1925. Had the victim not been a white law enforcement officer, it is unlikely that the prosecutor would have filed any charges against Crump, let alone first degree murder. This case should never have resulted in an execution.[20]

The white persons put to death between 1920 and 1929 include Charles Jacoy and John Carroll. On November 20, 1920, they killed Benjamin Schobe, a garage owner, near Berger, when he asked them for payment for repairs of $42.80 on a car they had stolen. Their victim offered to give them tires and his own car if they would spare his life. They did not. They were tried and convicted; the Missouri Supreme Court affirmed, and the sheriff of Franklin County hanged Jacoy on August 12[21] and Carroll a month later on September 12, 1921. Both executions took place in Union. Like many other condemned men, Jacoy converted to Catholicism. Rev. Father John Devilbiss accompanied him to the gallows. He was the first veteran of World War I whom the state of Missouri executed. His co-defendant, John Carroll, was the second; both had been wounded at the battle of Meuse-Argonne. Initially, Carroll had been sentenced to hang on the same day as Jacoy, but the governor gave him a reprieve of 30 days at the request of the American Legion. This organization made the request in order to allow an insanity commission to ascertain Carroll's mental state at the time of the crime. It pronounced him sane. In a failed attempted to save his life, Carroll wrote a barely literate letter to Warren Harding, then President, in which he declared his innocence. He mistakenly believed that this man had the authority to commute a death sentence which the state of Missouri imposed.[22]

The other four executions of white men in the 1920s took place in the city of St. Louis jail, and both were dual hangings. On April 22, 1922, two ex-convicts, Charles Merrell and Hugh Pinkley, shot and killed two city of St. Louis police officers, Michael O'Connor and Bernard Mengel, in the course of the officers responding to Merrell's and Pinkley's payroll robbery at the Morris Packing Company. The perpetrators were tried and convicted of the first degree murder of Patrolman O'Connor, a man survived by his wife and two children. The Missouri Supreme Court affirmed. Initially they were scheduled to hang at 6:00 a.m. on July 18, 1924. At the request of the condemned men, Father John Regan, a Catholic priest associated with St. Louis University, went to the sheriff's home at 2:00 a.m. on that date and by 4:15 a.m., he had persuaded the sheriff to delay the hanging until 4:00 p.m. that day. The priest successfully argued that the men needed the extra time to prepare themselves for death. They were accompanied to the gallows by both Father Regan and Father John Devilbiss. Father Regan supplied the information on Merrell's death certificate and admonished the crowd of 1500 outside the jail, "Be silent... Have respect for the dying." Both men received Catholic funerals and burials. Theirs were the city of St. Louis' first hangings in over 17 years.[23]

The remaining white men hanged together here in the 1920s committed separate and unrelated crimes. On September 25, 1926, Thomas Lowry shot and killed Patrolman Eugene Lovely and slightly wounded Patrolman Thomas Jones, both city of St. Louis police officers. They attempted to arrest him because Lowry had been speeding and left the scene of an accident. He was tried and convicted of the first degree murder of Officer Lovely, and the Missouri Supreme Court affirmed. He was one of two men whom the sheriff of the city of St. Louis put to death at 6:12 a.m. on February 1, 1929.[24] The other was Leonard Yeager. On November 17, 1926, he held up a soft drink parlor in the city of St. Louis and in the course of it shot and killed Gunnerious Schou, an elderly and hearing-impaired tailor who failed to stop when ordered to. Yeager was tried and convicted; the Missouri Supreme Court affirmed, and the sheriff hanged him at the same time and place he hanged Thomas Lowry.[25]

We know from a newspaper editorial that as early as 1893 a bill "to make electricity the means for capital punishment"[26] was introduced in the Missouri legislature. Obviously it failed to become law. At this time and later, electrocution was considered a more humane method of executing than hanging. There may have been other electric chair bills prior to the late 1920s, but as the few capital cases in Missouri of the time were making their way through the criminal justice system, attempts were made to change the law. In 1927 and 1929, identical bills were introduced in the Missouri house and the senate to take any death-sentenced person to the state penitentiary immediately following his capital sentence. He was to be held in this facility until his appointed date, and to be put to death in the prison by electrocution. This was to be done by placing him in an apparatus called an electric chair and turning on the necessary power. Neither bill became law. The first passed both houses, but the governor vetoed it because, as he stated, "I can see no good reason why any one community should bear the burden of all executions in the State.... Let the different counties bear the burden of such executions as the courts compel."[27] Besides avoid the expense of building, using and safely maintaining a new-fangled killing machine at MSP, the governor was pleasing residents of Jefferson City by his veto. They did not want all of the state's executions to take place where they lived. Equally important, only 26 men were executed here between 1908 and 1929, or less than one-half the number hanged between 1890 and 1899. Officials who were opposed to an electric chair may have believed the death penalty might wither of its own accord, and there was simply no need to tinker with the machinery of death. Moreover, the danger of lynchings was decreasing; seven are known in Missouri in the 1920s and two in the 1930s. There seemed little reason to execute those sentenced to death at the central location of the prison simply to save them from the wrath of the mob.

The motive of Missouri's legislators who wished to end hangings in the county of the crime and to electrocute at MSP was to be as up-to-date as were a number of other states. By 1927, no fewer than 21 American jurisdictions, many of them former members of the Confederacy, conducted their executions in the central location of the penitentiary in an electric chair.[28] This state in the 1930s continued to hang its death-sentenced prisoner at the county of the conviction of the crime. In so doing, it was in a small minority of states who left the county sheriff in charge of executing death warrants. Most had moved indoors behind prison walls, whatever their methods of implementing their death penalties, and the warden was in charge.

Between January 31, 1930, and May 21, 1937, sheriffs hanged 25 known persons here. Of these, one was a juvenile and four were rapists; their cases are discussed in chapters eight and nine respectively. The remaining 20 were adult killers. Just as the numbers were greater than during the 1920s, so too the executions took place in more counties than the 1920s; counting the juvenile and the rapists, there were uses of capital punishment in 14 counties. Including only executions for adult murderers, hangings occurred in 11: Callaway, Dunklin, Gasconade, Greene, Jackson, New Madrid, St. Charles, St. Louis City, St. Louis County, Ste. Genevieve, and Stone.

During this time period, members of the smaller group of perpetrators, two blacks and one white, killed the woman they loved or had loved at one time. The first black-on-black was William Mosley's crime. It is unlikely that his murder of his common-law wife, Mildred White, mother of his four children, would ever have been a capital case had he only killed *her* in the course of his murderous rampage on September 10, 1927. She had gone to a city of St. Louis grocery store, and according to the Missouri Supreme Court decision which affirmed his death sentence, Mosley believed, in addition to her bad habits of coming home late from work and "trifling with him.... She was also gone very long when she went to the store." He went after her, and in a jealous frenzy, he not only killed his spouse, he also killed the white owners of the grocery store, Becky and Marcus Bass. Among other activities in their business, Mosley stabbed his wife 13 times with a cheese knife he happened to pick up. At trial his defense was insanity; it did not succeed. The jury found him guilty, and on appeal its verdict was upheld. The sheriff of the city of St. Louis hanged William Mosley on January 31, 1930.[29]

The other love-gone-astray capital case involving a black perpetrator and victim was the ex-convict Frank McDaniel's shooting and killing his girlfriend, Savilla "Billie" Scott, because she told him she was leaving him. On March 28, 1933, in Greene County, McDaniel had a passenger in his car when he shot his victim five times and killed her. According to the Missouri Supreme Court decision, his earlier abuse of her was exaggerated: "I didn't black her eye; I smacked her." He told her before he began pumping bullets into her, "You did me dirty." The perpetrator's passenger testified for the prosecution. Other of the state's witnesses traced McDaniel's movements the evening of the homicide. The jury found him guilty of first degree murder; the verdict was upheld on appeal, and the sheriff of Greene County hanged Frank McDaniel at the county jail in Springfield on April 12, 1935.[30]

The rejected white would-be boyfriend, Hurt Hardy, Jr., lay in wait for 20-year-old Ethel Fahnestock in Ste. Genevieve County for three consecutive mornings before he shot her to death while she milked a cow. She had refused to attend dances and parties with her admirer, and he determined, according to the local newspaper, what other murderous suitors had resolved: "if he could not have her, no other boy would."[31] Hardy gave himself up and attempted to plead guilty to first degree murder. The judge refused his plea; at trial his defense was insanity. It did not succeed, and on appeal the Missouri Supreme Court affirmed.[32] The sheriff of Ste. Genevieve County put Hardy to death at a gallows at the poor farm near the town of Ste. Genevieve on February 26, 1937; according to the local paper, his was the county's first hanging in more than 100 years. The newspaper quoted this love-struck killer's last words, "I am prepared to meet my Master on the other side and my golden-haired darling."[33]

All other homicides which resulted in the accused being hanged here during the 1930s were committed in the perpetration of or attempt to perpetrate rape, burglary, and robbery. Whether the killing was premeditated or spontaneous was irrelevant. The necessary element of malice was implied from the defendant's intent to a commit a crime inherently dangerous to human life. If a death occurred during the perpetrator's commission of the underlying felony, the prosecutor properly filed first degree murder charges.

Only one man's underlying felony was rape or attempted rape. Paul Kaufman, a white World War I veteran, placed an ad in a Kansas City newspaper for a teenage white girl to care for a child in a good home, some time prior to August 17, 1930. On that date, 17-year-old Avis Woolery arrived in Kansas City by train from Webb City, Missouri, in response to the ad. Kaufman met her at Union Station, took her to Swope Park, and according to his confession, after he unsuccessfully solicited her consent to sexual intercourse, in the words of the Missouri Supreme Court, he "attacked" her. She resisted, and in the course of the struggle, he strangled her to death. Afterwards, he removed all of her clothing, scattered her personal effects, and buried her. Next, he sent a telegram to the young girl's mother in Webb City: "Arrived safe, satisfied, write later."[34] When his victim's body was found on October 12 and identified by October 16, 1930, Kaufman, an ex-convict, was in the Jackson County jail on a conviction of seduction. He shortly confessed to the killing of Avis Woolery. His first trial began on October 22, 1930, or less than two weeks after she was identified. His first conviction was reversed because his application for a continuance was denied. At both trials, his defense was insanity brought on by being shell-shocked during World War I; it did not succeed. The Missouri Supreme Court affirmed his second conviction, and the sheriff of Jackson County hanged Paul Kaufman on June 29, 1934, in the presence of 500 witnesses, including the brother and father of the victim.[35]

The remainder of the perpetrators hanged here for murder killed in the course of a burglary, a holdup, or in order to avoid detection or capture after committing these crimes. Six were black. On June 26, 1931, in Kansas City, Jefferson March, Sam Gordon, and a younger brother, Henry Gordon, robbed two white grocers, 62-year-old Morris Kross and his friend, Sam Slotnick, who was visiting Kross' grocery at the time of the holdup. The robbers used a piece of gas pipe to bludgeon Slotnick and Kross; the latter died six days later. Mrs. Kross was so shocked by the murder of her husband that she expired five weeks later. Their proceeds were $25; $7 from Kross and $18 from Slotnick. The three was arrested that same evening, and they confessed. Slotnick recovered and became a witness for the prosecution. They were tried and found guilty; Henry Gordon, the young brother, received a life sentence. The jury sentenced Sam Gordon and Jefferson March to death. The verdict was upheld on appeal, and the sheriff of Jackson County hanged them at the jail in Kansas City on December 15, 1933.[36]

Two crimes with black perpetrators took place in the city of St. Louis. On January 1, 1930, Emmerson White, a janitor, used a hatchet to inflict 15 to 20 blows and thereby killed 70-year-old Pinckney Hollis, a black man, in the course of robbing him. He wore his victim's clothing to an unrelated funeral, and other mourners recognized his attire. He also sold his victim's watch. White was tried and sentenced to death; the Missouri Supreme Court affirmed, and the sheriff of the city of St. Louis hanged him at the city jail on August 12, 1932.[37] On June 1, 1931, Eugene Copeland and a companion shot dead Jacob Davis, a white proprietor of Avenue Furniture Company, in the course of robbing him of $68. Copeland's accomplice was killed as he fled the scene. Three months later, he was arrested in an 85-cent holdup and identified as a participant in the furniture store robbery. He confessed, and he refused the prosecutor's offer of a life sentence if he pled guilty to the murder of Davis. Copeland was tried, and the jury opted for a death sentence. The Missouri Supreme Court affirmed, and the sheriff of the city of St. Louis hanged Eugene Copeland on June 29, 1934 in the city jail.[38]

On April 17, 1934, another black perpetrator, William Roland, killed two white Rock Island Railroad detectives, J.W. Whitted and E.C. Shane, at Bland, in the course of burglarizing a freight train. Roland was captured, and he confessed. At trial the jury found him guilty of the killing he was charged with, that of E.C. Shane. The Missouri Supreme Court affirmed, and the sheriff of Gasconade County hanged William Roland on April 12, 1935 at the county jail in Hermann.[39]

Eleven white men were executed here between 1930 and 1937. The case which received the greatest press coverage involved three bank robbers, and it took place in Kansas City on June 14, 1928. On that date, Antonio "Lollypop" Mangiaracina, John Messino, and Carl

Nasello robbed between $7,000 and $10,000 from the Home Trust Company Bank at 1119 Walnut at approximately 9:20 a.m. In the course of making their getaway at 9:30 a.m., the holdup men shot and killed James Smith, a Kansas City police officer who regularly conducted traffic at the intersection of 11th and Walnut streets. Smith was married and the father of five minor children. This robbery and all the confusion it created coincided with the opening session of the Republican National Convention, which nominated Herbert Hoover for President. The soon-to-be nominee was about to step out for lunch a few blocks away when police were still descending on the crime scene. As the bank robbers in a car passed 10th and Walnut streets, their vehicle sideswiped a traffic signal standard, and a door handle came off. It was recovered, and the police used the handle to tie the crime to a particular car and its occupants. The three were captured; they applied for but were denied a change of venue. They were put on trial on first degree murder charges in Kansas City. Their defense was alibi; it did not succeed. The jury found all three guilty of the murder of the policeman, James Smith, and it sentenced them to death. From one of three Missouri Supreme Court decisions, all of which upheld their death sentences, we know that the prosecutor referred to these defendants in closing arguments as "a bunch of Italian gangsters."[40] On July 25, 1930, and for the fourth time in Missouri's history, three men were simultaneously hanged under state authority when the sheriff of Jackson County put three Italians (the older two were born in Italy) to death in the jail at 219 E. Missouri Avenue, in the city of their crime. Well in advance of their hangings, carefully measured nooses had been prepared to accommodate their different heights and weights as they stood on prearranged parts of the gallows. Unlike the crime of three African-Americans in Kansas City — Gordon's, Gordon's, and Jefferson's robbery and killing of the grocer, Morris Kross, on June 26, 1931, wherein the youngest received a life sentence — Carl Nasello, aged 20 years at the time of the bank robbery, was also executed. Perhaps nativism or anti-foreign sentiment was

WHERE CAREERS OF CRIME END

Photograph of carefully measured nooses. These ropes accommodated the differing heights and weights of Antonio "Lollypop" Mangiaracina, John Messino, and Carl Nasello, at their hanging at the Kansas City, Jackson County, jail on July 25, 1930. They were sentenced to death for killing James Smith, a Kansas City police officer, on June 14, 1928, as they escaped from their robbery of the Home Trust Co. Bank, Kansas City. No photographs of this execution were permitted. (*Kansas City Journal-Post*, July 25, 1930. Used by permission, State Historical Society of Missouri, Columbia. All rights reserved.)

once more a factor in a jury making a death decision as it had in 1876 when three other Italians were simultaneously hanged in the city of St. Louis. As of this writing, the only additional execution of three persons sentenced to die in Missouri for the killing of one victim was carried out by the U.S. Army. The case is discussed in Chapter 11.

Another white person put to death during this time is of interest because of his religion. He is the only known Jew ever executed in Missouri's history. In Kansas City, on December 2, 1929, and in the course of making his getaway after robbing Estel Cashion, owner of a drug store at 25th and Brooklyn streets, of $18, Joe Hershon shot and killed Charles Dingman, a Kansas City police officer. He was soon arrested and soon confessed. His confession was put in writing, and it was subsequently introduced in evidence at his trial on first degree murder charges. He was found guilty and sentenced to death; the Missouri Supreme Court affirmed. We know from his death certificate that he was born in Russia, and we also know from it that no one, including the condemned, knew the day, month, or year of his birth. In the space for this information is marked "unknown." A prominent Kansas City rabbi, Samuel Mayerberg of Congregation B'Nai Jehudah, took great interest in this case. He traveled to Jefferson City in an unsuccessful attempt to get the governor to commute the death sentence. He was with the condemned at the jail on East Missouri Avenue, reciting prayers in Hebrew with him immediately before his execution, and he was at his side when the sheriff of Jackson County hanged Joe Hershon in the jail in Kansas City on January 15, 1932. Mayerberg later wrote a book which contains seven pages about this case. From them, we know that Joe Hershon was retarded. Mayerberg quotes an unnamed psychiatrist who examined Hershon and told his rabbi that "he barely reached the I.Q. of a low grade moron." As other retarded persons whom the state of Missouri earlier hanged, according to Mayerberg, Hershon "seemed to have no fear of death." The condemned man's rabbi wrote of this hanging, "When I heard the trap door this morning, [I] saw a hopeless moron blasted into eternity."[41]

On the other side of the state, two white perpetrators killed white women in the course of robbing them. On August 22, 1929, in St. Charles County, David Miller and Norman Tanner burglarized the home of Pauline Duehbert, a reclusive 46-year-old spinster, whom they believed had immense wealth hidden in cash in her home because she had no faith in banks. Miller initially became acquainted with her because he was hired to cut walnut logs on her farm. The burglars shot their victim to death, but they were frightened by noise and left without any proceeds. When they were apprehended, Tanner turned state's evidence, and in return for a life sentence; he testified against his accomplice. A jury found Miller guilty, and he was sentenced to death. The Missouri Supreme Court affirmed, and the sheriff of St. Charles County hanged him in the jail in the town of St. Charles on February 10, 1933. The local paper reported that the victim's assets were far less than the large sums her killers believed she kept in her home; what money she had, she put in banks.[42]

On January 4, 1932, in Maplewood, St. Louis County, James Kellar, a former employee of Mr. Saver in a machine shop, beat Mrs. Etta Saver to death at her home by striking and beating her about the head with an iron pipe. He obtained $22 from his victim. Her children found her body when they returned from school. Kellar became a suspect when he purchased a new hat and paid his board bill. When questioned by the police, he confessed. He pled guilty to first degree murder in the hope of leniency. He got none; the judge sentenced him to death, and on appeal the Missouri Supreme Court upheld the refusal of the circuit court judge to allow Kellar to withdraw his guilty plea and go to trial before a jury. It wrote that the defendant's "sole complaint is that had he anticipated the severity of the consequent punishment, he would not have pleaded guilty.... The court was under no obligation or duty to inform defendant in advance what sentence would be imposed." On January 20, 1933, the sheriff of St. Louis County hanged James Kellar at the jail in Clayton.[43] Other death sentences on guilty pleas to murder followed Kellar's. This was the Depression, and in such cases, the state was spared the expense of a trial.

On December 24, 1933, in New Madrid County, two white perpetrators, Edward Gayman, an ex-convict, and Roy Hamilton, shot and killed Arthur Cashion, a white filling station attendant, during an attempted robbery. They were arrested less than two weeks later on January 3. On January 15, 1934, without an attorney, they pled guilty; the trial judge sentenced both men to death. On appeal the Missouri Supreme Court dismissed their contention that they waived their right to a trial because they feared they would be lynched. It held that their fear of mob violence was without foundation, and it affirmed their death sentences. On August 30, 1935, the sheriff of New Madrid County hanged them at the jail in the town of New Madrid.[44]

In other cases, white perpetrators killed white law enforcement officers. On March 28, 1934, in Dunklin County, Fred Adams and two other men shot to death Clarence Green, night marshal of the town of Campbell, during the robbery of a White Eagle filling station. City of St. Louis police officers shot and killed one of the three, Doyne Vinyard, when they tried to arrest him. Another, Raymond Young, obtained a life sentence. When Adams was arrested in Paragould, Arkansas, he confessed and signed a statement. At his trial, the prosecutor introduced Adams' confession. The jury found him guilty of first degree murder and sentenced him to death. On appeal the Missouri Supreme Court affirmed, and the sheriff of Dunklin County hanged Fred Adams near the county jail in Kennett on April 2, 1937.[45]

The last white perpetrator hanged in Missouri who killed a law enforcement officer was George McKeever. On June 14, 1933, he and his accomplice, Francis McNeiley, were stopped in their car by Sergeant Ben Booth of the Missouri Highway Patrol and Roger Wilson, sheriff of Boone County, on suspicion that they might be Pretty Boy Floyd and Adam Richetti, suspects in a bank robbery that had occurred within the half-hour in Mexico, the seat of nearby Audrain County. When the officers approached the suspects' Ford Coupe at the junction of Highways 40 and 63, the men in the car opened fire. They shot and killed both officers. Eighteen months elapsed between the crime and their arrest. They were taken into custody in a foiled bank robbery in Iowa. McNeiley turned state's evidence and admitted to killing Sheriff Roger Wilson. He received a life sentence and was paroled in 1947. His partner, George McKeever, applied for and received a change of venue from Boone to Callaway County. There he was tried and found guilty of the first degree murder of Sergeant Ben Booth, and the jury sentenced him to death. The state put on ballistics evidence to tie the bullet which killed Booth to McKeever's .45 automatic, and a witness' partial recall of a license plate was additional evidence which helped convict McKeever. On appeal, the Missouri Supreme Court affirmed. On December 18, 1936, the sheriff of Callaway County hanged George McKeever in the loft of an old barn near the jail in Fulton. The local paper described the execution as the first in the county since 1856. The paper never mentioned that Slave Celia's hanging on December 21, 1855, was Callaway County's last gallows death prior to McKeever's.[46]

The grandson and namesake of the slain sheriff, Roger Wilson, was prominent in Missouri politics. He was elected to the Missouri Senate in 1979, elected twice as lieutenant governor, beginning in 1992, and following the untimely death of Governor Mel Carnahan on October 16, 2000, Wilson became Acting Governor of Missouri. Soon thereafter, he left public office; at present, he is a senior executive at a St. Louis area bond investment firm.

The official manuals of his years as lieutenant governor contain of him" "His grandfather, Roger Isaac Wilson, was Boone County sheriff when he and Missouri state trooper Ben Booth were killed by bank robbers in 1933."[47]

The remaining perpetrators, one black and the other white, whom the state of Missouri hanged in the 1930s, committed their crimes on different dates in different sections of the state. On December 14, 1932, in Kansas City, Dudley "Hardface" Barr, a black man, killed Walter Milton, another African-American, who happened to be in a business Barr was robbing. He feared Milton would recognize him, and he shot him dead. At Barr's first trial the jury gave him a life sentence; he appealed, and the appellate court reversed. At his second trial, the jury sentenced him to death, and the Missouri Supreme Court affirmed. The sheriff of Jackson County hanged Barr at 6:00 a.m. on May 21, 1937. Many miles south, the sheriff of Stone County hanged the man who killed Pearl Bozarth, Roscoe "Red" Jackson. On August 2, 1934, Bozarth, a white traveling salesman, picked up a hitch-hiker, Jackson, in Taney County. His passenger killed him and took his car and money. Jackson was arrested in possession of his victim's car. He obtained a change of venue from Taney to Stone County, where he was tried and found guilty of first degree murder. The Missouri Supreme Court affirmed, and after the last hanging occurred in Kansas City, the only one in Stone County took place three minutes later at 6:03 a.m. on May 21, 1937.[48]

For the most part Missouri's gallows deaths in the 1930s happened at extremely early hours. Those in Kansas City, the city of St. Louis, and St. Louis and St. Charles counties all appear to have occurred at approximately 6:00 a.m. When the sheriff of New Madrid put two men to death, he hanged Hamilton at 5:39 a.m. and Gayman at 6:05 a.m. Frank McDaniel was hanged at 5:20 a.m.; David Miller at 6:03 a.m.; George McKeever at 7:34 a.m.; Fred Adams at 8:05 a.m. The only known afternoon execution of the 1930s here was Ste. Genevieve's execution of Hurt Hardy, Jr. at 1:56 p.m. Officials selected these early hours to minimize the crowds. Nonetheless, there were never too few witnesses. Sheriffs continued to issue passes to their hangings as they had in the 1890s; they were numbered, allowed the bearer to witness the execution of a named individual between certain hours on a set date, and were signed by the sheriff.[49]

Several inexperienced officers received expert assistance in their execution duties from a professional hangman, who traveled about the South and the Midwest in the 1920s and 1930s in order to lend his expertise to the task at hand. His name was Phil Hanna, and his residence Epworth, White County, Illinois. He may have helped other Missouri sheriffs, but we know from newspaper accounts that he assisted when Hardy Jr. was hanged in Ste. Genevieve and Hamilton and Gayman in New Madrid. A report for the local newspaper in Ste. Genevieve wrote of him, "Mr. Hanna, famed throughout the Middle West for participating in over 100 executions, does not ask any compensation for his services other than his traveling expenses. It is said his motive is prompted purely from a humanitarian standpoint."[50]

Prisoners condemned to die in either Kansas City or the city of St. Louis stayed put in the jails which housed them from their initial arrest through their deaths. However, this fixity did not characterize death-sentenced rural prisoners. Several were confined at MSP in Jefferson City; George McKeever, eventually hanged in Fulton, spent 18 months in the penitentiary. Roscoe Jackson, hanged in Stone County, spent 29 months at MSP. Gay and Hamilton, who died in New Madrid, were kept in the Butler County jail in Poplar Bluff. Hardy, hanged in Ste. Genevieve, was moved three times: from Perryville to St. Louis, to Farmington. Roland, hanged at Hermann, was kept in the Franklin County jail in Union. As a result of all this moving about of death-sentenced prisoners, law enforcement officers made certain that the mob never lynched any of the men destined to die on county seat gallows.

In rural areas, the custom of viewing the dead body of the hanged, which began in the 1890s, continued in the 1930s. The local newspaper estimated that 4,000 persons looked at the corpse of Fred Adams in Kennett in 1937. The funeral home had a steady stream of viewers from 10:00 a.m. until 10:00 p.m. Its proprietor assured the reporter covering this big story that no charge was made to see the body.[51] Other older practices continued here. The sheriff's deputies cut up pieces of the rope which hanged Frank McDaniel in Springfield. The witnesses took them home as souvenirs. Newspaper photographers were busy shooting pictures at both McDaniel's hanging in Springfield and Jackson's in Galena. The sheriff of Stone County, I.H. Coin, was unable to prevent a Fox Movietone cameraman from making a motion picture of the hanging of Roscoe Jackson. According to Sheriff Coin's family he never recovered from the only hanging at which he officiated; he committed suicide within a few months of it.[52]

By the twentieth century in Kansas City and even earlier in St. Louis, no stiff-viewing for thousands of spectators, ropes as souvenirs, movie-making and photography of hanging corpses were allowed. At the execution of three Italians in Kansas City in 1930, the sheriff's orders were to break any cameras and confiscate film. No known photographs exist of twentieth century executions in Missouri's big cities. To be sure, there is a photograph of the nooses used in the mass execution in Kansas City in 1930, but the hard-core photographs of the dying and dead men all derive from small towns.

Earlier, death-sentenced men were already Catholics or converted to this religion as their remaining days dwindled. The popularity of Catholicism among the condemned continued. Kansas City's three Italians were Catholic, received Catholic funerals, and are buried at St. Mary's Cemetery at 22nd Street and Cleveland Avenue, Kansas City. In the city of St. Louis, Father John Devilbiss was with William Moseley at his death in 1930, Emmerson White in 1932, and Eugene Copeland in 1934. Rev. Charles Weinig administered the sacraments to David Miller at St. Charles in 1933. Father Hubert of Union was with Roland on the gallows in Hermann in 1935. Father Francis Berry of Hannibal and Father W.H. Baudendistel of Fulton were with McKeever in Fulton in 1936. Father Arthur Tighe stood with Dudley Barr in the Jackson County Courthouse when the prisoner was hanged there in 1937. Roscoe Jackson became a Catholic while an inmate at MSP and recited prayers with a Catholic priest immediately before his death. However, Jackson's father claimed his son's body and made certain that he had a Protestant funeral and burial in Ozark County.[53]

There were three jails, two of them long torn down, at which hangings were conducted in Kansas City. The first was the Second Street jail, on the northeast corner of the intersection of Second and Main streets; it was used between 1872 and 1892. On the spot was once the Kansas City Water Department; its main occupant now is a law firm. The second was the jail at 219 E. Missouri Avenue, in use between 1893 and 1935. The great majority of executions in Kansas City occurred within this Jackson County jail. On the site now stands a fire station, on the southeast corner of the intersection of East Missouri Avenue and Oak Street. The third was the present Jackson County Courthouse at 12th and Oak streets; its topmost floors housed the jail and many inmates over many years. Only one man was hanged there, Dudley Barr. The building was not completed at the time; its dedication would not take place for more than six months, but we know from newspaper accounts that Barr's cell was on the 11th floor; the gallows was on the 15th, and his body dropped from the 15th to the unfinished 14th. Spectators stood on the mezzanine on the 14th floor. Trial judges who presently conduct court in this building on lower floors are aware that something truly memorable took place there well above their heads. The last night of Barr's life, he requested and was allowed a companion, another-death-sentenced prisoner of the Jackson County jail, William Wright.[54] Barr's dinner guest was not hanged in the courthouse. He was one of the first persons put to death in the gas chamber in Jefferson City.

7

The Gas Chamber, 1938–1965

The movement to end semi-public hangings in Missouri started and stopped several times before the actual demise of these huge rural events. In April 1937, the town of Kennett, the seat of Dunklin County, had been the scene of 4,000 persons viewing the hanged body of Fred Adams in a local funeral parlor. The process had taken 12 continuous hours, and its carnival atmosphere shocked the responsible members of the community. Soon thereafter, an appalled and determined state senator from Kennett, Paul Jones, introduced legislation to avoid any repetition of such disgraceful behavior at any future execution in this state. His new measure required that all death-sentenced persons die in an electric chair at the prison in Jefferson City; it also limited those present to necessary officers and witnesses. His bill had considerable opposition. Both the State Prison Board and residents of the town containing the Missouri State Penitentiary were against it. The state representative from Jefferson City argued that the legislation would, as the newspaper later reported, "make the capital city the 'slaughter house' of the state."[1] Members of the Board believed that executions at the penitentiary would have a harmful effect on the convicts and perhaps lead to prison riots. At hearings on this legislation, local residents insisted that they did not want all the executions to take place within the city limits of *their* town. In the process of considerable debate, legislative supporters struck the electric chair provision and substituted the gas chamber as the means of death.

In support of his legislation, Senator Jones stated that more than 40 states had centralized their executions.[2] In addition to the supposedly greater humanity of death by lethal gas over both the noose and the electric chair, another selling point for lethal gas was its cost. According to Senator Jones, the construction of the gas chamber would cost the state about $2,500.[3] Actually it spent $4,000 on it, including the death cells.[4] It was cheap in 1937, and it would be cheap today, perhaps 12 times as much as when it was built, or approximately $50,000. The reason the gas chamber was put in place so inexpensively was not complicated. It was not built by members of various labor unions; the workers were prison inmates. One of them was later executed in the facility he helped construct.

Finally, the bill passed both houses, and Governor Lloyd Stark signed the legislation on June 4, 1937. The days of state-sanctioned hangings here, public or semi-private, had ended. Missouri joined Arizona, California, Colorado, Nevada, North Carolina, and Wyoming as lethal gas jurisdictions. Oregon (1939), Mississippi (1955), Maryland (1956), and New Mexico (1960) also chose the gas chamber. Once Missouri adopted this method of death, only Kansas, Louisiana, and Mississippi continued to execute at the county of the conviction of the crime; all other capital punishment states and the District of Columbia put their condemned to death in their prisons.[5] At long last, the warden of the state penitentiary in Missouri, not the county sheriff, was in charge, and the prison official made certain that death was inflicted in conformity with relevant state statutes.

The sheriff still had a role to play. It was his job to deliver the death-sentenced inmate to the custody of the warden of MSP in Jefferson City. The warden was, as the new law explained, "authorized and directed to provide a suitable and efficient room or place, enclosed from public view, within the walls of the penitentiary, and the necessary appliances for carrying into execution the death penalty by means of the administration of lethal gas." During any execution, the presence of the warden, deputy warden, or a representative was required. Among others, the prison official asked one or two physicians to be present. The doctors stood outside the gas chamber listening for the cessation of the prisoner's heartbeat. Their stethoscopes were attached by sound-conducting tubes to his skin near his heart. Other persons invited to the execution included the attorney general and at least 12 reputable citizens; always among these 12 citizens were members of the press, both radio and newspaper reporters. The condemned was allowed to invite one or two "ministers of the gospel ... and any person, relatives or friends, not to exceed five, ... but no person under twenty-one years of age shall be allowed to witness the execution."[6]

The priest(s) and the minister(s) continued to play an important role in most of these gas chamber deaths. In the first two, William Wright's and John Brown's, the men were held in jails in Kansas City, which were near St. Patrick's Church at 8th and Cherry streets. Father Arthur Tighe, the parish priest at this church, met Wright while he was a prisoner at the 219 E. Missouri Avenue facility, and he continued to minister to him when Wright was moved to the jail at the Jackson County Courthouse at 12th and Oak streets. Tighe and his assistant, Reverend Edward Taney, spent the last hours of both prisoners' lives with them at the MSP death house; as the condemned were being buckled into their gas chamber seats, the men recited the act of contrition which they had learned from the priests.[7] When the third death row inmate, Raymond Boyer, was executed at MSP, he was attended by three priests, Fathers Tighe and Taney, and Rev. Feldt, chaplain at the prison.[8] When Adam Ricchetti was put to death in 1938, a Catholic chaplain was with him until he was placed in the gas chamber.[9] George Bell spent his last hours with a priest before his gassing in 1949.[10] Likewise, before Arthur Brown's execution in 1956, he was attended by two priests, Reverend Rodney Crewse of Kansas City and Reverend Robert Dyer, the prison chaplain. They administered the last rites to him in the gas chamber itself.[11] Other death-sentenced men embraced Protestant religions. Charles Tiedt in 1950, Claude McGee in 1951, and Thomas Moore in 1957 all died comforted by Baptist ministers. Few men met their gassing without the consolation of some belief in the hereafter.[12]

No contemporary accounts of the deaths by lethal gas explained exactly what happened. We do know from newspapers that the condemned was led into the death chamber scantily clad and blindfolded. He was then seated and strapped into one of two chairs in the chamber. Instead of wearing a new suit, which a number of men did to their own hangings, those who died in the gas chamber wore only what was described as shorts or swimming trunks, and at times the paper specified that these garments were made of silk, a material which must have dispelled the cyanide gas far more readily than a cheaper fabric such as cotton. The blindfold shielded the bulging eyes of the dead from all present. The reason for the absence of most clothing was the danger of the gas adhering to the attire of the corpse and harming those later required to handle it. An expert described the process of death by cyanide gas, one of its many names, and its difficulties:

Breathing in cyanide gas paralyzes the heart and lungs. The victim becomes giddy. Panic gives way to severe headache, followed by chest pains. Respiration becomes impossible, so that the victim struggles vainly for breath, eyes popping, tongue hanging thick and swollen from a drooling mouth. His face turns purple.... The most dangerous part of a gas execution ... is removing the body from the chamber. For fifteen to twenty minutes after death is pronounced, the chamber is vented to dispel as much of the gas as possible. Then it has to be sprayed with ammonia to neutralize the remaining gas.... The inmate has to be completely washed down with chlorine bleach or with ammonia. The poison exudes right out through his skin. And if you gave that body to an undertaker, you'd kill the undertaker. You've got to ... completely wash the body.... [Afterwards] the execution team removes the dead inmate's clothing, which is taken away and burned. After that, the inmate is placed in a body bag ... for removal.... The gas chamber only becomes safe after every inch of it has been washed down with bleach.[13]

Such distasteful detail was never available to the general public when the gas chamber legislature was either debated or in effect. This information was printed in the 1990s, or more than 25 years after the last death by lethal gas in Missouri.

In all, there were 39 executions in this state's gas chamber between 1938 and 1965; unlike all earlier chapters in this book, these numbers are firm. For the first time in Missouri's history, records were kept. They were almost certainly kept by other prison inmates, and there are minor inaccuracies in both the age at execution and its date. However, the names, the crimes, and the counties of their convictions are correct. The demographics of the condemned and their victims are available from other sources. Of the 39 executions, six were for rape; these and the one woman and her accomplice are discussed in other chapters. The remaining 31 are described herein.

All murderers put to death at MSP in the 1930s committed their offenses, received their trials, and were sentenced to hang before the gas chamber legislation became law. As a result, before even one death could be carried out inside the prison, there were court challenges. The first three executed by lethal gas were sentenced to hang by the neck until dead because Jackson County juries found them guilty of first degree murder and assessed their punishment as death. Two were black and one was white; two of their victims were white, one black.

William Wright, Hardface Barr's last supper companion, committed his crime in the course of an attempted holdup on March 15, 1933, when he shot and killed a beloved African-American druggist, Dr. John McCampbell, at a drugstore which the victim owned at the corner of Vine and Howard streets in Kansas City. Wright confessed, was quickly brought to trial, and sentenced to hang on May 5, 1933. On appeal, the Missouri Supreme Court reversed because the trial judge had failed to give his jury a second degree murder instruction. On his retrial, the jury found him guilty and once more sentenced him to death. This time the Missouri Supreme Court affirmed, and it required the trial court to cause the defendant to be brought before it and to sentence him to death by lethal gas. Wright's oldest sister wrote the governor an undated letter requesting that he commute the sentence: "Pise [sic] give my poor Brother a chance. It was not a white man that he killed it was his owne race that he is charged with killing." The governor did not intervene, and William Wright was one of the first two men put to death at MSP.[14]

The other, another black man, was John Brown. On April 7, 1936, he shot and killed an off-duty Kansas City Police Department detective, William Cavanaugh, in an attempt to rob the Irish Tavern at 921 E. 21st Street, Kansas City. Shortly, the perpetrator was arrested at Council Grove, Kansas, and returned to the city of his capital crime. Brown confessed, and all four still living persons at the tavern at the time of the shooting identified him. At trial the jury found him guilty, and it sentenced him to death. On appeal, the Missouri

Supreme Court affirmed, and it made clear that in the legislation providing for a new manner of inflicting death, there was no violation of the ex post facto prohibition of the U.S. Constitution. It wrote that "the place of execution, when the punishment is death, within the limits of the state, is of no practical consequence to the criminal.... [The lethal gas law] did not create a new offense.... [It] provide[d] a method of inflicting the death penalty in the most humane manner known to modern science." Like Wright, Brown was brought before a Jackson County judge who set aside his sentence of death by hanging and substituted death by lethal gas. At 6:21 a.m. on March 4, 1938, William Wright and John Brown were executed at the prison in Jefferson City. A newspaper account described their clothing and obfuscated the reason for it: "When the men are led into the gas chamber they will be attired only in sports trunks as the gas which gathers in clothing may linger there to cause an accident."[15] Another newspaper reported of their executions that "an unnamed expert who has assisted in asphyxiation executions in other states will be on hand." This paper also noted that only about 25 persons, including officials, guards, and newspapermen, will witness the deaths as opposed to "thousands who flocked to public hangings."[16] The next day, a Jefferson City newspaper wrote in an editorial: "Whether or not the gas chamber will hold the same deterring influence upon the criminal as that of the noose remains to be seen. It may be such an easy way of quitting the game of life that it may hold but little dread for the man who thinks of committing a capital offense."[17]

By the next day, March 5, 1938, a third man had been put to death at MSP He was Raymond Boyer, a white man, who killed Walter Sandford, also white, a graduate of Kansas State University, and a U.S. Army reserve officer. The two met in a tavern in Kansas City, and the victim volunteered to drive his killer to St. Louis. The perpetrator shot him near Oak Grove and robbed him of his car, clothing, and personal effects. Boyer was arrested in St. Louis with the car and other possessions of his victim. He gave a detailed confession, was subsequently tried and convicted of first degree murder in Jackson County, and was sentenced to hang. On appeal, the Missouri Supreme Court affirmed, and Boyer was brought back into court and sentenced to die by lethal gas. He also was put to death at a typical hour for executing persons in the 1930s, 6:21 a.m.[18]

By the fourth death by lethal gas, that of Raymond Batson, a black man, the condemned was no longer asphyxiated at or near sunrise. Instead, he was put to death soon after midnight, perhaps in the hope that most of the other prisoners would be asleep and unaware of the unusual activity. The prison records of death in the gas chamber are at their most inaccurate in this fourth death. They state that Batson was executed on *March* 30, 1938; it was *June* 30, 1938 at 12:01 a.m.

He committed his capital offense in Kirkwood on December 28, 1934, when Batson, an unemployed chauffeur and self-styled lawyer, shot and killed two white men, Phillip Rabenau, a justice of the peace, and William Poole, a dentist who happened to be in Rabenau's office when the enraged gunman appeared. Batson's target was the JP, not the dentist. Several weeks earlier, Rabenau had found his killer's wife and aunt guilty of disturbing the peace and sentenced them to 30 days in jail. Batson had represented them and become agitated that his name had been forged on a recognizance concerning his client-relatives. Immediately before he opened fire, shot, and killed two men, and wounded a third on December 28, he shouted at his victim, "You forged my name at Clayton."[19] Batson then fled the scene, but he was eventually arrested. At trial, he was charged and convicted of the first degree murder of his accidental victim, the dentist, William Poole. On appeal the Missouri Supreme Court reversed; the trial judge had failed to instruct the jury that the state was required to "prove beyond a reasonable doubt that he committed the homicide willfully, deliberately, premeditatedly, and of his malice aforethought."[20] At Batson's second trial his defense was insanity and self-defense. The jury received the proper instructions, and it found him guilty and sentenced him to death by hanging. The Missouri Supreme Court affirmed, and it required Batson's reappearance in court for purposes of sentencing him to death by lethal gas. He was led into the gas chamber handcuffed, blindfolded, and attired only in shorts. Once the gas was released, prison physicians pronounced him dead in two and one-half minutes.[21]

Three lethal gas executions of the 1930s were of men convicted of first degree murder in the course of crimes for personal gain. Their offenses took place in the city of St. Louis and Jackson and Ste. Genevieve counties. Two of the perpetrators were white, one black, and all of their victims were white. In the city of St. Louis on January 17, 1936, Byron King, a white ex-convict with a burglary conviction, shot George Speer, a cab driver and chauffeur, aged 68 years, in a holdup. The proceeds of the robbery were $9. The victim lived until the next day, long enough to identify his murderer. King confessed; his defenses at his June 1936 trial were alibi and the coercion of his confession. The jury found him guilty and sentenced him to death by hanging; the Missouri Supreme Court affirmed with the now standard requirement that he be brought into court and resentenced to die by lethal gas. King was put to death at MSP on November 4, 1938 at 1:35 a.m., and at that latter hour because stone jars containing the deadly pellets had broken and had to be replaced.[22]

In Kansas City on October 20, 1936, Granville Allen, a black man who had earlier served time in the boys' reform school at Boonville for burglary, shot and killed Howard Preston, a white man, in the course of burglarizing his victim's apartment. Bud Preston, his son, shot at and wounded the intruder. Granville was soon apprehended, and he confessed. He was tried and found guilty of Howard Preston's murder and sentenced to hang. Once more, when the Missouri Supreme Court affirmed, it required that the prisoner be brought back into court and resentenced to death by lethal gas. At 12:08 a.m. on October 28, 1938, Granville Allen's execution began at MSP. The assistant prison physician pronounced him dead two and one-half minutes later.[23]

On August 10, 1935, in Ste. Genevieve County, John Williamson shot and killed George Williams, a recluse who lived alone in a wooded area. His motive was robbing his victim of a few hogs and other items. The perpetrator was a 59-year-old ex-convict who had already served in excess of 20 years of a prison term in Illinois for murder. The Missouri Supreme Court reversed his first conviction on grounds that Williamson's confession had been obtained by promises that the sheriff would recommend that he be returned to prison in Chester, Illinois. At his second trial, the prosecutor made a more selective use of the defendant's statements; on appeal, the court affirmed with the usual requirement that his sentence of death by hanging be changed to death by lethal gas. John Williamson, aged 62 years, was sentenced to death in the gas chamber. He died at 12:12 a.m. on February 15, 1939.[24]

Two other executions at MSP for murder occurred in the 1930s. On January 26, 1937, Robert Kenyon, a 21-year-old white farm hand who lived with his parents, Mr. and Mrs. Daniel Kenyon, in Howell County, lured Dr. J.C.B. Davis, aged 65 to 70 years, from his office in his victim's car. The murdered man was the most prominent physician in the town of Willow Springs, population 1,500; 1,800 persons attended his funeral. The ruse Kenyon used was telling the doctor that the young man's wife was ill. Kenyon's purpose in kidnapping this eminent person was money. He hoped to obtain a ransom of $5,000. At his trial on charges of first degree murder, expert witnesses tied ransom notes, which the victim's wife received, to both the perpetrator's handwriting and paper in his possession when he was arrested. Kenyon shot and killed Dr. Davis because he did not know what to do with his victim if he kept him alive. A week after his murder, he led the arresting officers to the bullet-riddled body of his victim who was found face down, with his glasses still on, and a checkbook in his hand. Kenyon had earlier attempted to abduct the coroner of St. Louis County by telling this official that there were two injured men at a tourist camp. Once taken into custody, Kenyon readily admitted to his crime and stated that he planned to plead guilty to get it over with. Once his presence in Howell County was no longer needed to make a case against him, he was taken for safe-keeping to the Jackson County jail at 12th and Oak streets, Kansas City. On a change of venue to Oregon County, Kenyon was tried in Alton; the jury found him guilty of first degree murder, and he was sentenced to death by hanging. The Missouri Supreme Court affirmed with the requirement that he be brought back into court and resentenced to death in the gas chamber. At 12:06 a.m. on April 28, 1939, 23-year-old Robert Kenyon was put to death at MSP.

Neither the Missouri Supreme Court decision nor the extensive coverage in the local paper, *The Willow Springs News*, ever hints that the perpetrator was retarded. His crime, a completely hare-brained scheme, does not indicate the capacity for what we ordinarily call thinking. His wish to get the matter over with quickly also suggests retardation. The amazement of his respectable farmer-parents that their son had committed this heinous crime also points to their son's mental deficiency. Today his attorneys would request that their client receive extensive mental tests, including the evaluation of his I.Q. Nothing in the record indicates that Kenyon's likely retardation was even considered.[25]

The remaining death by lethal gas during the 1930s at MSP was that of Adam Ricchetti on October 7, 1938. A Jackson County jury believed the perjured testimony it heard regarding his role in Kansas City's Union Station shooting and killing of five persons, four of them law enforcement officers, on June 17, 1933, at 7:15 a.m. The dead included the gangster, Frank "Jelly" Nash, arrested in Hot Springs, Arkansas, on June 16, and the lawmen who took him by train to Kansas City, with an intended transfer by car to a nearby federal penitentiary in Leavenworth, Kansas. The officers who died with Nash were Raymond Caffrey, an agent of the then new Federal Bureau of Investigation; Otto Reed, chief of police, McAlester, Oklahoma; and two Kansas City police officers, W.J. Grooms and Frank Hermanson. Excluding the deaths of members of the Union Army here during the Civil War, when much of Missouri was under martial law, this was then the second largest loss of life of law enforcement officers in the history of the state.[26] The shootings occurred in the parking lot immediately outside the train station, and 30 seconds later, five men, four of them cops, were dead. Someone had to pay; the crime could not remain unsolved.

The day before this massive shooting spree, Pretty Boy Floyd and his alcoholic sidekick, Adam Ricchetti, kidnapped Jack Killingsworth, the newly elected sheriff of Polk County, in Bolivar at a garage, where Joe Ricchetti, Adam's brother, worked. They drove with the sheriff to the Kansas City area where they eventually released him unharmed. One newspaper later quoted Killingsworth who described the incident as "13 exciting hours spent in the company of Pretty Boy Floyd and his companion, Adam Ricchetti." Another paper quoted this lawman's description of Ricchetti as "drinking too heavily ... [and being] pretty drunk."[27] At this time, Floyd and Ricchetti were believed to have killed Sergeant Ben Booth and Sheriff Roger Wilson near Columbia on June 14, 1933, after robbing a bank in Mexico, the seat of Audrain County. As Floyd's biographer phrases it, "The name Pretty Boy Floyd continually surfaced as the prime suspect in bank robberies across the country."[28] Floyd and, by extension, a besotted Adam Ricchetti were quickly blamed for the Union Station murders. Floyd immediately denied any part in them, presumably for reasons other than saving his skin. He knew that lawmen believed he was good for a number of capital crimes. He mailed a postcard to the chief of detectives of the Kansas City police department in which he denied participating "in the massacre of officers at Kansas City."[29] Within a few months, J. Edgar Hoover had settled on three culprits, Floyd, Ricchetti, and Vernon Miller, an ex-sheriff turned gangster, as the killers of five at Union Station. Had Floyd and Miller been captured alive, the odds favor that a Jackson County jury would have found them guilty of the Union Station massacre and sentenced them to death. However, the murdered body of Vernon Miller was found outside Detroit, Michigan, on November 29, 1933. Likewise, law enforcement officers shot and killed Floyd near East Liverpool, Ohio, on October 22, 1934. By the process of elimination the only one left alive to prosecute was Richetti. He had been captured alive with Pretty Boy at the same time and place Floyd died.

In June 1935, Ricchetti was brought to trial in Jackson County Circuit Court for one murder, that of a Kansas City police officer, Frank Hermanson. In his book entirely devoted to this case, Robert Unger labels the testimony of most prosecution witnesses as lies. Those who placed Miller, Floyd, and Ricchetti at Union Station on the morning of June 17, 1933, did not tell the truth. According to Unger, both the ballistics and fingerprint evidence were at best highly suspicious. The jury believed the prosecutor's witnesses; it convicted Ricchetti, and it sentenced him to hang. His defense lawyers neither had experts of their own to counter the prosecutor's ballistics and fingerprint witnesses nor access to the 89-volume Union Station Massacre file in possession of the FBI. Years later, under the Freedom of Information Act, Unger obtained the file and based his book on it. Ricchetti's lawyers were able to demolish the testimony of one supposed eye-witness, Lottie West, the woman who ran the Travelers Aid Society desk at Union Station. She claimed to have seen Floyd at her desk the morning of the crime and everything else worth seeing, including six Benedictine Sisters in their habits, a group no other witnesses had seen at the railroad station the day of the shooting. However, the demolition of one prosecution witness was not enough for the jury or the judges. Those who sit on appeals courts have no way of discovering perjury, especially when it comes from expert witnesses. Attorneys must bring these matters to their attention. In order to do so, defense lawyers must have access to far more information than Ricchetti's attorneys had managed to obtain when they argued in vain to save their client's life. Despite his lawyers' best efforts at trial and on appeal, they did not succeed. With Judge Ellison writing for the Missouri Supreme Court, it affirmed Ricchetti's death sentence with the usual requirement that he be brought back into court and resentenced to death by lethal gas. He was put to death at 12:19 a.m. at MSP on October 7, 1938. Among the headlines about his execution, one Missouri newspaper's included: "What Have I Done to Deserve This? He Asks—Observers Hear Him Scream as Fumes Rise."[30] He is buried in Greenwood Cemetery in Bolivar, the home of his mother and brother. I have visited his grave, seen his tombstone, and talked with residents who remember his case. They do not believe that he played any part in the Union Station massacre.

In the 1940s slightly more men, 15 in all, were put to death by lethal gas than during any other decade of the gas chamber's use here. More significant than the numbers of the executed was their race. Of the 15 men, two were convicted of rape, a crime discussed in Chapter 9. Thirteen of the 15 men who died at MSP's gas chamber were black. Only the first gassing of this decade and the next to the last were of white men. Such demographics mean that a higher known percentage of African-Americans was executed here in the 1940s than in any earlier decade in Missouri's history. To be sure, there may be legal executions of blacks here which I never located and documents regarding them of which I know nothing, but there may also be undiscovered instances of the capital punishment of whites in earlier times here of which I am equally ignorant. It should be mentioned that lynchings in Missouri had almost vanished by the 1940s; there is only one known. However, the fact remains that 87% of those put to death in Missouri's gas chamber between 1940 and 1949 were African-Americans.

The first man executed in this decade committed his capital crime, as did all others put to death in the 1940s, *after* the gas chamber bill became law. As a result, none of these perpetrators were ever sentenced to hang by the neck until dead and brought back into court and resentenced to death by lethal gas. All were originally sentenced to die in the gas chamber.

On June 8, 1938, in St. Louis County, Robert West, a white ex-convict, aged 22 years, shot and killed Mrs. Vivian Davidson, aged 20 years, as she sat in a car near the home of relatives. She had earlier been his sweetheart, but she married another man while her first love, West, was serving a term at MSP for robbery. She only lived with her husband three weeks because he failed to provide for her. West killed her because, as he stated both orally and in his written confession, he was jealous of her. Immediately after he shot her dead, he tried to kill himself, but instead he surrendered at the sheriff's office. At his trial, his defense was insanity; both the prosecution's and the defense's experts on mental illness took the stand. The jury believed the state's doctors who testified that, in their opinion, the defendant was sane at the time of his crime. On appeal, the Missouri Supreme Court affirmed, and the ex-convict who had earlier quarried rock for the death house at MSP died in it just after midnight on September 20, 1940.[31]

The other white who was put to death in this same facility in the 1940s was Afton Scott. On March 29, 1948, in Douglas County, he killed a circuit court judge, Charles Jackson, and Scott's wife, Verla Scott, the mother of his 10 children. The perpetrator blamed the judge for his domestic difficulties, telling him before he shot and killed him, "I have got you where I want you. You have broke up my home." Scott murdered his wife at her mother's residence; she had gone there with all the children after quarreling with her husband. When he first saw her at her mother's, she was holding the baby. He persuaded her to give the infant to one of their daughters and come outside. He shot her dead and shortly surrendered to law enforcement officers. On a change of venue to Wright County, Scott was tried in Hartville for the murder of his wife. His defense was insanity; it did not succeed. The jury found him guilty; the Missouri Supreme Court affirmed, and he was executed on November 4, 1949.[32]

The remaining 11 men who died at MSP in the 1940s were black. In two of these cases, the victims were black youngsters. On September 27, 1940, in Butler County, Wilburn Johnson used a shotgun to kill 15-year-old Willis Mitchell and his sister, 13-year-old Sarah Mitchell, over $5, which they or the girl stole from him. On the advice of his two court-appointed lawyers, Johnson pled guilty to both homicides on November 14, 1940. His judge sentenced him to 99 years for the murder of Sarah and death for the murder of Willis Mitchell. Without a trial and without an appeal, Wilburn Johnson was put to death on January 3, 1941.[33] On July 16, 1943, in Mississippi County, 72-year-old Allen Lambus attempted to rape 14-year-old Juanita Harris and swung a hay hook which caught her in the throat. She was employed as a water carrier for a group of cotton choppers. The next day her father found her in a field; she died later in the day in a hospital in Cairo, Illinois. Lambus, an ex-convict, had served time for manslaughter and attempted rape in a prison in Mississippi. On August 16, 1943, one month after his crime, he also pled guilty to first degree murder and was sentenced to death in Charleston in Mississippi County Circuit Court. After seven reprieves, beginning with his original death sentence of October 1, 1943, 73-

year-old Allen Lambus was put to death at 12:05 a.m. on June 16, 1944.[34] He remains the oldest known person executed in this state. In both his case and that of Wilburn Johnson, the brevity of the time lapse between crime and punishment is reminiscent of slavery here. However, there is one difference; slaves usually received a trial before the sheriff took them out and hanged them by the neck until dead.

Only one of the black-on-black capital crimes of this decade involved the killing of the beloved. On August 3, 1938, Chester Jackson killed Daisy Esmond in Carthage. They had lived together; she left him and refused to return. He was tried and found guilty of first degree murder in Jasper County Circuit Court in Carthage. The Missouri Supreme Court reversed his first death sentence because his newly appointed attorneys had insufficient time to prepare for his trial after his original lawyer withdrew from the case. Thus far nothing in this case distinguishes it from many others. What was new at the time Jackson was tried were his lawyers' attempts to introduce evidence of their client's retardation. We know from the Missouri Supreme Court's second decision that Jackson could do dock work, but he could neither check freight nor properly load it; he had the mind of a child; he was a man of a low grade of intelligence; and he did not have the mental age of more than a 10-year-old. His attorneys tried to put all this information before the jury to show that their client killed because he did not have the intelligence to resist the impulse to destroy the woman who left him. This so-called *irresistible impulse defense* allows that the accused may have been sane at the time he committed the crime and knew the difference between right and wrong; nonetheless he was unable to control his actions. This defense was never recognized in Missouri. The trial judge excluded evidence of Jackson's retardation, and the Missouri Supreme Court upheld the exclusion. Presiding Judge Ellison wrote, "Where it is not contended that the accused is an idiot, lunatic or insane person, evidence of feeble intellect and weak intelligence is not admissible.... Whichever age his mind may have been makes no difference." This was the law in Missouri, and it would remain the law for a number of years. The Missouri Supreme Court upheld Chester Jackson's death sentence, and he and Robert West (the white killer of his beloved) were simultaneously executed on September 20, 1940.[35]

In one other capital case, the executed African-American may have been retarded. On May 1, 1945, in St. Louis City, Van Ramsey held up Lena Davidson and killed her in the process. He had gone through the fifth grade and could read and write. The Missouri Supreme Court quoted him of his first degree murder conviction, "I didn't aim to kill that girl ... I was trying to get some money." Today, Ramsey's intelligence would be evaluated. Apparently it was not at the time, and even if it had been, any discovered retardation would not have been admissible at trial. He was convicted, and his appeal was based on the exclusion of Negroes from the city of St. Louis grand jury and the petit jury which found him guilty and sentenced him to death. The Missouri Supreme Court upheld the death sentence which the all-white jury imposed; the exclusion, this court opined, must be shown to be deliberate. Ramsey was put to death at MSP in the gas chamber on January 10, 1947.[36]

In another case, that of Floyd Cochran, the retardation is certain. On February 5, 1946, he raped and murdered 20-year-old Marylou Jenkins in Columbia. She was a recent graduate of Stephens College and home alone because her mother, a nurse, was needed to spend the night at a nearby elderly couple's home. Cochran gained admittance to the Jenkins' residence on the pretense of collecting 80 cents for garbage hauling. Once inside, he raped and strangled his victim; two and one-half weeks later, he murdered his wife. When apprehended he told the arresting officers that he could show them how he committed his crimes better than he could tell them. At his trial, his defenses were alibi and insanity. They did not succeed. The Boone County jury, from which African-Americans were excluded, found him guilty of first degree murder and sentenced him to death. We know from the Missouri Supreme Court decision that Cochran went only to the third grade and was "mentally disqualified for military service by reason of mental age less than 10 years." His attorney argued that his confession was involuntary because, in the words of the Missouri Supreme Court, defendant "was a person of low mental caliber, held incommunicado and without the advice of counsel." We also know from the newspaper account of his execution in the MSP gas chamber that immediately before his death he was unable to recite the Lord's Prayer by himself. Getting through it required coaching from his two spiritual advisers, the prison chaplains, one Protestant and the other Catholic. Floyd Cochran was put to death on September 26, 1947.[37]

Two 1940s cases took place in Kansas City. The first involved Ernest Tyler, an ex-convict who had previously served two terms at MSP for burglary. On August 16, 1940, he shot Mr. and Mrs. Erwin Schwarenholz at their home during a burglary. The wife survived; the husband, an installation and repair man with the Kansas City Gas Company, died and left his widow with children aged six and 12. Tyler was arrested later that morning and signed a confession. A Jackson County jury found him guilty of first degree murder and sentenced him to death. Instead of being kept at the jail in the Jackson County Courthouse at 12th and Oak streets, Tyler was sent to the prison at Jefferson City immediately after his trial and was in residence at MSP by December 17, 1940. The Missouri Supreme Court affirmed his conviction, and on April 24, 1942, 36-year-old Ernest Tyler died in the gas chamber. The prison record of his death is incorrect in two respects. He was not *37* years old when executed, and the date of his death was not *June* 24, 1942.[38]

The second Jackson County capital case began at 1334 Paseo Boulevard, Kansas City, on September 20, 1948, some time after 11:00 p.m. Within 30 minutes, seven persons had been shot, and five of them were Kansas City police officers. One patrolman, Kieffer Burris, was wounded and recovered. However, four of the five officers were either dead at the scene or would soon die in a hospital. Kansas City had not been the scene of such loss of law enforcement officers since the Union Station massacre more than 15 years earlier. The start of this carnage was routine. Police were attempting to arrest William Bell for disturbing the peace. The whole matter went so badly that the board of police commissioners met in emergency session the next day to devise new strategies for dealing with such matters. The officers had made the mistake of allowing him to go into another room, allegedly to retrieve his coat; he came out with a gun and killed two policemen, a black officer, 27-year-old Sandy Washington, and a white, 45-year-old Charles Perrine, and perhaps another white officer, 34-year old William Wells. William Bell was in turn shot dead by police officers, and in the immense confusion which the gun battle created on the street at the intersection of 14th and Paseo, a patrolman accidentally but fatally shot a passerby, 27-year-old Edwin Warren. Meanwhile, according to three eyewitnesses, George Bell, William Bell's brother, shot and killed a 30-year-old black officer, Charles Neaves, a former Kansas City heavyweight Golden Gloves boxing champion. Paraffin tests performed on George Bell shortly after he was taken into custody showed that he had fired a weapon. At his trial for the murder of Neaves, testimony about the extensive loss of life, including three other dead policemen George Bell was not charged with killing, was admitted into evidence. His defense was that his dead brother, William Bell, had shot and killed Officer Neaves. The jury found him guilty of first degree murder in the death of Neaves and sentenced him to death. On appeal, the Missouri Supreme Court affirmed. On December 2, 1949, at 12:12 a.m. George Bell died at MSP in the gas chamber.[39]

Two executions of co-perpetrator black men, four gas chamber deaths in all, took place at MSP during this decade. On September 30, 1941, four black males were in a stolen car in St. Louis County. The driver was going too fast, and he turned over the vehicle. The four got out of the wrecked automobile and accosted a farmer, Marvin Twillman, who had driven his truck to this particular locale in order to feed his livestock. The four kidnapped Marvin in his truck. Shortly, they met their victim's cousin, Martin Twillman, and Martin's mother in a car. For no reason ever susceptible to proof, one of the four car thieves and kidnappers of Marvin ordered his cousin Martin out of his car and shot and killed him. Eventually each of the four confessed and accused one or more of the three others of Martin Twillman's murder. Albert Butler and Willie Clayton received life sentences. In separate trials, Leo Lyles and William Talbert were both found guilty of the first degree murder of Martin Twillman and sentenced to death. Each received two trials. The Missouri Supreme Court reversed Lyles' first conviction because of faulty jury instructions, and it affirmed his second death sentence. Talbert's first death sentence was also reversed, and his second affirmed. Lyles was put to death at MSP in the gas chamber on May 25, 1945, at 12:51 a.m., and Talbert on November 16, 1945, at 12:24 a.m.[40]

On December 12, 1943, two black men, Fred Ellis and Jesse Sanford, obtained entrance to the home of a white woman, 56-year-old Mary Santo, on a farm in Franklin County on the pretext of needing a drink of water. Once inside, they killed her and split the contents of her purse, $2, or $1 each. The culprits were arrested and detained in excess of 20 hours before they confessed. Their detention was a violation of a state statute which required that the arrestee be held no longer than 20 hours before being taken before a magistrate. Sanford, an illiterate with a first grade education, was detained in two different counties before finally being taken before a judge. Their confessions were used at their March 1944 trials in Union to convict them of the first degree murder of Mary Santo; their jury assessed death sentences against them. On appeal, the issue was the admissibility of their confession. The majority affirmed their convictions; in dissent one judge wrote of their interrogation, "Brutality is substituted for brains as an instrument of crime detection." Both Ellis and Sanford were put to death in the MSP gas chamber on August 16, 1946.[41]

During the 1950s, nine men and one woman died in the gas chamber at MSP. One execution was for rape; it is discussed in Chapter 9. Three of these death sentences were for the crime of kidnapping. The woman's kidnapping conviction and that of her co-defendant are discussed in Chapter 10. The discussion of six death sentences for murder and one for kidnapping follows.

Four gas chamber deaths for murder were of black men. Two crimes took place in Jackson County. On May 19, 1951, 50-year-old Ulas Quilling killed his girlfriend, 40-year-old Lauvenia Webb, because she had tired of him and did not wish to continue their relationship. Had this perpetrator not shot and killed two others at the same time, Irene Braggs and Carl Dobbs, most likely his crime would have not resulted in a death sentence. Quilling readily confessed; at trial his defense was insanity. Today it would be retardation. According to the Missouri Supreme Court decision which affirmed his death sentence, a psychiatrist testified for the defense that he had examined the accused and "defendant was of the mental age between 6 and 9 years." On May 29, 1953, 52-year-old Ulas Quilling was put to death within three minutes at the MSP gas chamber, starting at 12:05 a.m. The Associated Press reporter wrote that the gassed man "died calmly early today, his gray head bowed."[42] On May 5, 1955, 40-year-old Thomas Moore shot and killed his wife, Opal Moore, a 36-year-old mother of three by a previous marriage, because she did not want to live with him any longer. Then he shot himself, but not fatally. According to her 18-year-old son, Moore and his mother had quarreled about Moore's drinking. At trial, the perpetrator's defense was insanity; it did not succeed. The jury found him guilty of first degree murder, assessed his punishment at death, and on appeal, the Missouri Supreme Court affirmed. On September 13, 1957, Thomas Moore, a man who had never been in criminal difficulty before, died in the MSP gas chamber shortly after midnight.[43]

On January 13, 1951, a 20-year black, Kenneth Boyd, a fugitive from a psychiatric ward at the time of his crime, killed 54-year-old Sam Barenfeld in his victim's grocery store in St. Louis City in the course of a holdup. It netted the perpetrator $30. At his trial his defense was insanity; it did not succeed. The jury found him guilty and imposed a death sentence. On appeal, the Missouri Supreme Court affirmed. On July 10, 1953, 23-year-old Kenneth Boyd died in the gas chamber at MSP shortly after midnight.[44] On August 15, 1953, in St. Louis City, Dock Booker shot his friend, Earl Harrison, in a dispute over who was the better baseball player. Harrison died four days later. Both the perpetrator and the victim were black men aged between 40 and 45 years. At his trial, Booker's defense was that the shooting was either accidental or self defense. The jury found the defendant guilty of first degree murder and assessed his punishment as death. On appeal, the Missouri Supreme Court affirmed. On April 1, 1955, Dock Booker died in the MSP gas chamber.[45]

The remaining chamber deaths at MSP during the 1950s were of white persons. Those discussed in this chapter include two for murder and one for kidnapping. On November 25, 1945, in the early morning hours, in St. Joseph, 51-year-old Charles Tiedt telephoned neighbors with whom he had earlier quarreled and asked them to come outside. Once they were, he began shooting and killed three persons, Mr. and Mrs. Delbert Machette, his neighbors, and Fred Machette, a visiting brother whom the perpetrator had never met. Tiedt was married, the father of seven children, and a veteran of World War I. His first conviction was reversed because of the prosecutor's inflammatory language. Specifically he had asked the jury for a death sentence with this question: "What have the good people of the county done that they should be continually under the hazard of having him alive?" On retrial, the jury found the defendant guilty of first degree murder and sentenced him to death a second time. On appeal, the Missouri Supreme Court affirmed. After spending 44 months at MSP as a death row inmate, Charles Tiedt was put to death in the gas chamber shortly after midnight on May 19, 1950.[46]

The other execution of a white man for murder at MSP in the 1950s was the execution of Claude McGee, an inmate at the prison, who killed another inmate and his friend, 47-year-old John Manor, in a quarrel about a debt of $20. McGee's weapon was a claw hammer with sharpened points which he used to strike his victim in the head. Both men were serving life sentences for the murder of W.T. Carlton, which they committed in the course of the burglary and robbery of their victim's home in Scott County in the 1930s. Manor was tried in the county of the crime, and his jury gave him a life sentence. He was received at MSP on August 12, 1938. McGee obtained a change of venue from Scott to Mississippi County, and his jury found him guilty of first degree murder and assessed his punishment at death. McGee was originally sentenced to hang, but the governor commuted his death sentence to life imprisonment. Now faced with another charge of first degree murder, the Cole County jury found him guilty and sentenced him to death. As far as we know, for the first time a prisoner-on-prisoner killing at MSP resulted in an execution at its gas chamber when 38-year-old Claude McGee was put to death on January 5, 1951.[47]

Three persons were executed at MSP in the 1950s for the crime of kidnapping. In 1901, this activity became a potentially capital crime under Missouri law; its punishment range was five years to death.[48] No known person was ever executed under state law for this offense. All persons convicted of kidnapping who died in the MSP gas chamber were found guilty in a federal courtroom of a crime against the United States. The first federal statue concerning this offense was passed in reaction to the March 1932 abduction of the Lindbergh baby and the May 1932 confirmation of his death. In June of that same year, the 72nd Congress made kidnapping and transporting in interstate or foreign commerce any abducted person a federal offense. In May 1934, the 73rd Congress amended the law by added an allowable death sentence if the victim has not been liberated unharmed.[49] The federal law only comes into play when the abductor crosses either a state line or goes to a foreign country with his victim. If the kidnapped person is moved from one point to another entirely within the boundaries of any one state, there is no federal offense; the crime must be prosecuted under state law. Even if the victim is taken out of state, it may still be tried under state law.

The reason the authorities usually try a kidnapper under federal law who might also be tried under state law is not complicated. The financial resources of the federal government guarantee virtually unlimited funds for the investigation and prosecution of any alleged criminal activity. Moreover, jurors are more impressed when the prosecutor is a U.S. attorney, one whom the President appointed, rather than a locally elected prosecutor. The criminal cases tried before federal judges in federal courtrooms with federal prosecutors and federal investigators are much more likely to be slam dunks for the government than those tried in state courts.[50] Even though the death sentence was obtained in a federal courtroom, from the start of the United States until long after the last federal execution in a state prison on March 15, 1963, in Iowa, there was no federal death house. Whenever the federal government executed the condemned, it borrowed the facilities and used the state's method of inflicting capital punishment. The particular one whose facilities were used was always the one in which the federal court sat wherein the death sentence was obtained. As a result, the United States hanged John McDaniel and Joseph Brown in the jail in the city of St. Louis in 1845 because they were found guilty of murder in Indian Country, and the law gave the judicial district of Missouri jurisdiction over crimes committed therein. It sat in the city of St. Louis; as a result, a murder which occurred in present day Rice County, Kansas, was tried many miles east of the homicide. Now there is a federal death house at the federal prison in Terre Haute, Indiana; it was first used in 2001 when Timothy McVeigh was put to death for his role in the 1995 bombing of the federal building in Oklahoma City. After 1963 and before 2001, there were no federal executions. During these years, all that occurred took place under the authority of various states.

The confessed crimes of Arthur Brown made him death-eligible under Missouri, Kansas, and federal law. On August 4, 1955, he left his residence at 3210 Jefferson, Kansas City, where he lived with his wife and child, and he rode a streetcar to 40th and Main streets, where a large Katz drugstore was located. At it he searched for a prosperous-looking person to rob. Finding no one who precisely fit the bill, he reboarded a street car and rode to the Brookside area. At the intersection of 63rd and Brookside, he spied 34-year-old Wilma Allen, mother of two sons and the wife of a well-known car dealer, William R. Allen, Jr. Mrs. Allen had just completed a beauty shop appointment, and at gunpoint, Brown abducted her in her car and made her drive southwest and cross the state line into Kansas. Once in rural Kansas, he robbed her, raped her, and shot her in the head, thereby causing her death. He disposed of her car by driving it to Union Station, where he left it in a parking lot. His victim's empty purse was found first, approximately six miles from her body; later her nude body was found nearly eight miles southwest of Stanley, Johnson County, Kansas. The distance between her abduction in the Brookside area of Kansas City, Missouri, and the place where her dumped body was found was approximately 23 miles.

Despite a 200-person manhunt for the victim and the perpetrator, no clue uncovered Arthur Brown. A farmer and his son who were looking for a stray cow found Mrs. Allen's remains.

On November 10, 1955, or three months after his murder of Wilma Allen, Brown kidnapped and threatened to kill his wife in Kansas City. She jumped from the car and ran to the safety of her apartment. He returned to California, where his mother lived and where he had earlier served time in San Quentin for burglary and other crimes. Eventually he was arrested in San Francisco, and while FBI agents were questioning him about his wife, he volunteered that he had killed Wilma Allen on August 4, 1955.

In January 1956, the U.S. attorney for the Western District of Missouri introduced Brown's signed confession in evidence in the federal courtroom with Judge Charles Whitaker presiding. The defendant admitted the crime, and the only issue in controversy was the punishment, life imprisonment or death. Before an all-male jury, the U.S. Attorney put on 35 exhibits and seven witnesses to bolster the veracity of Brown's confession. The jury was out about 15 minutes before it unanimously agreed on death. On January 26, 1956, Judge Whitaker sentenced Arthur Brown to die in the MSP gas chamber on February 24, 1956. There was no appeal. This judge remarked at the time that he had never previously handed down a death sentence. Following Whitaker's elevation to the Eighth Circuit Court of Appeals, President Eisenhower appointed him as an associate justice on the U.S. Supreme Court, where he served from 1957 until 1962. Presiding at the punishment phase of a capital case is not the usual experience of future U.S. Supreme Court justices, at least not in modern times.

Once sentenced to death, Brown was a model prisoner. He declined any special food for his last meal and ate what the other prisoners had. He expressed a desire to die because he could not live in prison with his crimes against Wilma Allen on his mind. Instead of the warden at MSP reading the state court order of the death sentence to Brown, the U.S. Marshal read this federal court order to him. Shortly after midnight on February 24, 1956, Arthur Brown died in the gas chamber at MSP.[51]

The 1960s was a decade of diminished use of the death penalty nationwide. In Missouri there were only two executions for murder, one white and the other black. The first was of Sammy Tucker, a white ex-convict who with two others escaped from a jail in California. They stole a car there and committed robberies in New Mexico and Kansas. On March 10, 1961, at 9:30 p.m., one of the three was casing a Kroger's Grocery Store with the intent to rob it while the other two remained in the car in Cape Girardeau, Cape Girardeau County. Police officers became suspicious and gave chase. Tucker, the driver, sped from the scene without his on-foot accomplice and shot two officers, one of whom, Herbert Goss, died at the scene, and the other, Donald Crittendon, on March 31. In addition, Tucker wounded a Wayne County sheriff, assaulted a Madison County farmer, and was finally captured when spotted by a helicopter and shot three times before being arrested in Bolinger County. One of Tucker's accomplices, Douglas Wayne Thompson, was also sentenced to death, but he managed, as did a large number of other death row inmates throughout the United States during the 1960s and 1970s, to avoid execution.

Tucker was charged with the first degree murder of a 24-year-old police officer, Donald Crittendon, in Cape Girardeau Circuit Court. The jury found him guilty and assessed his punishment at death. On appeal, the Missouri Supreme Court affirmed. On July 26, 1963, shortly after midnight, Sammy Tucker was put to death in the aging gas chamber at MSP. Unlike a number of earlier uses of the facility, contemporary newspaper coverage of Tucker's gassing contains this detail, "So powerful are the fumes that two towers on the prison wall near the death house are unmanned during an execution for fear that the guards might be overcome when the gas is blown from the chamber and dissipated into the air."[52]

The last gas chamber death at MSP was of Lloyd Anderson, a black who was 18 years old at the time of his crime on May 18, 1961. With an accomplice, Clewiston Jones, Anderson held up Speckart Drug Store in St. Louis City. They obtained $300. The store's owner, Paul Speckart, was shot and wounded, and Anderson shot and killed a delivery boy, 15-year-old Thomas Grupe, without any provocation. In another holdup, Jones was shot and killed by police while resisting arrest; Anderson was captured alive. He gave a statement to the police in which he admitted killing young Grupe in the Speckart Drug Store robbery. At trial, he was found guilty of first degree murder, and the jury assessed his punishment at death. On appeal, the Missouri Supreme Court affirmed. As the time neared for Anderson's execution, the Missouri legislature debated abolishing the death penalty. The governor stated that, if the bill to end capital punishment in Missouri passed, he would commute now 22-year-old Lloyd Anderson's death sentence. By a vote of 112–45, the bill was defeated in the Missouri house, and the governor allowed the execution to proceed. Anderson was put to death on February 26, 1965. The prison record of his execution is inaccurate. It states that he died on *January 26, 1965.*[53]

The next chapter concerns the abolition of the death penalty for juveniles and juveniles who were put to death in Missouri from the earliest records through 1993.

8

Juveniles, 1838–1993

In 2005, the U.S. Supreme Court declared in a 5–4 vote that the death penalty for persons aged less than 18 years at the time of their crime(s) is unconstitutional. It violates the 8th and 14th Amendments' prohibition against cruel and unusual punishments. The High Court used a Missouri case, Christopher Simmons,' to end capital punishment for juveniles nationwide. He is a white male, born April 26, 1976, and he was 17 on September 9, 1993, when he and his co-defendant, Charles Benjamin, a 15-year-old white male, burglarized the Jefferson County mobile home of Shirley Crook, a 46-year-old white female, who was home alone. They drove her in her own van to a trestle and murdered her by throwing her alive into the Meramec River, 40 feet below, in St. Louis County. Her body was recovered 12 hours later. A jury was selected in Cape Girardeau County which tried the case in Hillsboro, Jefferson County. Both defendants were convicted of burglary, kidnapping, and capital murder. In July 1994, Benjamin was sentenced to life imprisonment without possibility of parole, and in August 1994, Simmons was sentenced to death. Subsequently, in 2003, the Missouri Supreme Court ruled that it was cruel and unusual punishment to execute him because he was a juvenile, vacated his death sentence, and substituted life imprisonment for him.[1] Missouri's attorney general took an appeal from this decision to the U.S. Supreme Court.

For the majority, Justice Kennedy wrote that "juveniles' susceptibility to immature and irresponsible behavior means 'their irresponsible conduct is not as morally reprehensible as that of an adult.'"[2] His quotation is from a 1988 U.S. Supreme Court decision, which barred the execution of persons less than 16 years old at the time of their crimes.[3] In a 1989 decision concerning the constitutionality of the state's putting to death persons who were 16 years old at the time of their crime(s) (a Missouri case), and 17 years old at the time of their crime(s) (a Kentucky case), Justice Kennedy joined the majority of five which rejected the argument that the 8th and 14th Amendments' prohibition against cruel and unusual punishment forbids the execution of juveniles.[4] In dissent in this case were Justices Blackmun, Brennan, Marshall, and Stevens. Sixteen years later, Justice Kennedy joined Justices Breyer, Ginsburg, Souter, and Stevens to end capital punishment for persons under the age of 18 at the time they committed their crimes(s).

In 2005, in addition to noting the impulsivity of young persons, the Court also observed that "the overwhelming weight of international opinion against the juvenile death penalty is not controlling here, but provides respected and significant confirmation that the penalty is disproportionate punishment for offenders under 18. The United States is the only country in the world that continues to give official sanction to the juvenile death penalty."[5] The majority includes several appendices to its decision. Among these is a list of state statutes establishing a minimum age to vote; all deny the right to vote to any person aged less than 18 years; state statutes establishing a minimum age for jury service; all prohibit jury service by any person aged less than 18 years, and in Missouri 21; and establishing a minimum age to marry without parental or judicial consent; Missouri's is 18. These appendices reinforce the majority's decision.

In a concurrence to Kennedy's majority opinion, Justice Stevens writes, "If the meaning of that Amendment [the Eighth] had been frozen when it was originally drafted, it would impose no impediment to the execution of 7-year-old children today. The evolving standards of decency that have driven our construction of this critically important part of the Bill of Rights foreclose any such reading of the Amendment."[6] When writing as he did, Justice Stevens was well aware that English common law and its adoption in the American colonies did not prevent the execution of juveniles.

The great eighteenth century commentator on British law, William Blackstone, wrote that an eight-year-old child was capable of committing a felony. He clarified, "Thus a girl of thirteen has been burnt [to death] for killing her mistress: and one boy of ten, and another of nine years old, who had killed their companions have been sentenced to death, and he of ten years actually hanged."[7] We cannot be entirely certain what happened in Missouri. Records have surely been lost, and those we have may be incomplete.[8] As a result, all ages cannot be verified, but this much we know. This state put to death a minimum of 14 and a maximum of 18 known juveniles, that is persons less than 18-years-of-age at the time of their crimes, between 1838 and 1993.[9] As Chapter 2 made clear, the youngest known person executed in Missouri was Slave Mary, aged 12 or 13 at the time of her crime, and probably the youngest known person sentenced to death here was Slave Mat, aged 10, 11, or 12, when he killed his young victim. At least one other juvenile slave, Henry, was aged 16 years when he killed his owner in Moniteau County and was executed in 1863. Perhaps Slave Isaac, who shot and killed his mistress in Warren County in 1851, and Slave Joe, who axed and killed his leasor in Boone County in 1857, may have been aged 17 years and some months old when they committed the murders for which the state hanged them. Contemporary newspapers describe both Isaac and Joe as "about 18 years of age"[10] at the time of their crime. Since the birth dates of bondbabies were usually not recorded, fixing their precise ages is not possible.

White children of young ages who committed capital offenses were not executed here prior to the Civil War. The MSP records clarify that on at least two occasions the governor commuted the death sentence of a white boy or boys, and they were sent to prison. On December 24, 1842, in Cape Girardeau County, Amos Byrd, aged 14 or 15 years, was sentenced to hang because the jury found him guilty of having murdered John Byrd, his father, because his parent had earlier whipped him. Though the young man's attorneys asked the Missouri Supreme Court to review his case, it did not. The governor commuted the death sentence to a life prison term. Bird was received at MSP aged 15 years on February 1, 1843, and the record termed him a "boy of bad countenance" and recorded that he died on May 13, 1845.[11] At the November term, 1858, of the criminal court of St. Louis County, three young men were found guilty of the murder of Hugh Downie in St. Louis Circuit Court; they were sentenced to hang. On February 3, 1859, the governor commuted the sentence of the two younger boys to a life prison term, and the third, Theodore Debold, pled to being an accessory to the crime and was also sent to prison. The Register of Inmates records that Nicholas Trauturne, aged 15 years, Antoine Seite, aged 17 years, and Theodore Debold, aged

18 years, were received at MSP on April 6, 1859, from St. Louis County, on a charge of first degree murder. Though the prison record is a blank regarding the final outcome of Seite's and Debold's stay at MSP, it clarifies that Trauturne escaped over the wall on May 27, 1861.[12] Probably other white youths who committed capital crimes in Missouri were not executed in the antebellum period.

As Chapter 4 explained, the Union Army put to death two or three white juveniles of whom we have knowledge. In 1864 in Moniteau County, a firing squad of Union troops shot, among others, 17-year-old Paddy Mullins, for his bushwhacking activities. In 1865 in St. Louis County, the Union Army hanged 16-year-old Abraham Purvis and 17- or 18-year old Ephraim Richardson for murder. Following the war, the execution of both white and black males aged less than 18 years at the time of their crime began under state law.

The first known post–Civil War legal hanging of a white juvenile took place in Bethany, the seat of Harrison County, on October 30, 1874. A reporter from a St. Louis newspaper was sent to cover the execution, and it is from the full front page story in his paper that we know the relevant details, including the fact that the condemned was born on December 14, 1853. Joseph Hamilton shot and killed 48-year-old Elisha Hallock in Mercer County on July 14, 1871, and at that time the perpetrator was 17. He was his victim's farmhand, and at the invitation of his victim's wife, Mrs. Caroline Hallock, aged 28 years, he became her lover at age 16. He killed her husband at her request, and initially both were arrested. She received a change of venue and was tried for the first degree murder of her husband in Putnam County, where she was acquitted in December 1873. Hamilton also received a change of venue; his case was sent to Harrison County, and there a jury found him guilty of first degree murder. No mention is made of his age in the Missouri Supreme Court decision affirming his death sentence, and neither is there any emphasis given it in the lengthy St. Louis newspaper account of his hanging. That he was aged 17 years at the time of his crime was not an issue.[13]

However, by the post–Civil War period there were lower limits on the ages of the perpetrators which had not applied to black youth in the antebellum period. On August 1, 1882, in Morgan County, Tom Adams, an illiterate black male, aged 12 at the time of his trial on October 21, 1882, stabbed to death a 17-year-old white male named Henry Ostermann. The youthful perpetrator called the victim a liar, and the victim hit the perpetrator with the handle of a pitchfork, and the perpetrator, Adams, stabbed the victim, Ostermann, causing his death. At Adams' trial, the jury deliberated three hours before finding the defendant guilty of first degree murder. When returning its verdict, it requested executive clemency because of Adams' age and illiteracy. At the time Missouri law provided juries with only one penalty in first degree murder convictions, death. Accordingly, the trial judge sentenced 12-year-old Tom Adams to hang December 22, 1882. Adams' appointed attorneys argued their client's appeal before the Supreme Court of Missouri, and they secured a reversal on grounds of jury instructions which ignored the defendant's age. It reversed and remanded Tom Adams' case to the Morgan County Circuit Court. A few years earlier in 1879, the General Assembly had passed legislation prohibiting the imprisonment in the penitentiary of persons who committed any felony while aged less than 18 years. Instead, they were to be confined in a county jail, not exceeding one year. Accordingly, on April 21, 1883, 12- or 13-year-old Adams pled guilty to manslaughter in the third degree in the killing of Henry Ostermann, and the judge sentenced him to pay the costs of the prosecution and to serve twelve months in the Morgan County jail.[14]

Another youth, a white boy, also escaped the noose. On April 12, 1885, 15-year-old James Payton or his older brother, William Payton, in Christian County, fired a shot that passed through the head of a small child. Though it could not be shown which of the brothers fired the shot that ended the life of the young victim, their trials were severed. The older brother, William, was acquitted on the same evidence used to try and convict the young brother, James, of first degree murder. On appeal, the Supreme Court of Missouri affirmed. Almost immediately, the Springfield and the Missouri Bar Association and the Christian County prosecutor supported executive clemency for young Payton. The legislature apparently acted in response to the Payton case. It passed legislation which gave the governor power to commute the death sentence of any minor under the age of 18 years to a prison term of no less than two years; the act took effect immediately on March 16, 1887. From extant prison records, we know that 16-year-old James Payton entered MSP on December 23, 1887. His record contains this important notation: "Original sentence to be hanged. Commuted by Governor John Marmaduke to imprisonment in the penitentiary for life." Under the "discharged column" of Payton's entry is "Pardoned by Gov. Stone Jan. 14th, 1895."[15] James Payton, aged 15 years when he committed his crime, was released from prison when he was either 24 or 25.

Before discussing the cases wherein the Supreme Court of Missouri either did not review or upheld death sentences of juveniles, mention should be made of two cases wherein the appellate court reversed the conviction. In neither was the age of the defendant an issue; rather, his mental state at the time of the crime was the reviewing court's concern. One concerned insanity. On November 25, 1867, Max Klingler, a German youth, aged either 16 or 17 years, committed his capital offense of first degree murder. The judge of St. Louis Criminal Court sentenced him to death. The appellate court held that requiring the defendant to prove beyond a reasonable doubt that he was insane at the time of the crime is too heavy a burden; he was allowed to prove his madness by the preponderance of the evidence, a standard which required the condemned to prove his mental incapacity was more likely than not. Prison records clarify that Klinger was received at MSP on May 9, 1872, aged 22 years, to serve a 10-year sentence for murder, presumably second degree. He was discharged on April 17, 1882 after he served his full sentence.[16] In the second case, William Coats, a 17-year-old black, born on May 25, 1885, choked his mother to death on June 21, 1902, in Buchanan County. He confessed; the jury found him guilty of first degree murder, and the judge sentenced him to death. In 1903, the appellate court reversed his conviction. Its basis was the trial judge's failure to allow the accused to impeach a hostile witness. However, the actual concern of the judges was the defendant's illiteracy, youth, and retardation.[17]

As long as black youths were not convicted of the rape of white females, by the early years of the twentieth century, the Missouri Supreme Court was willing to reverse a death sentence of a mentally impaired juvenile. However, judicial review prevented few executions of juveniles. Beginning in 1880 and continuing through early 1907, there were more legal executions and lynchings here than during any other time periods. It was during these 27 years that the state of Missouri put to death most persons who can be identified as under age 18 at the time of their crime(s). In all, various county sheriffs hanged nine certain or probable juveniles between 1880 and 1906.

The first in the 1880s of whom we have knowledge was William Barton. He was one of three out-of-wedlock children of the slaves, Mary and Frank Barton, born in Corinth, Mississippi, on June 9, 1863. A few weeks earlier his father had enlisted in Company F of the 55th Colored Infantry. On February 15, 1879, young Barton, aged 15 years, killed James Clatterbuck in St. Charles County. His victim, a 26-year-old white farmhand who supervised the black teenager, was murdered after he reprimanded Barton for being lazy and doing his work improperly. Barton's motion for a change of venue, based on extensive St.

Charles County newspaper coverage of the crime, was overruled. He was tried for first degree murder in St. Charles on June 4, 1879. The jury deliberated approximately 30 minutes before bringing in its guilty verdict. On appeal, the Supreme Court of Missouri observed that "the defendant was at the time of committing the murder under 16 years old" as relevant to the issue of Barton's alleged statutory entitlement to imprisonment in a county jail instead of the penitentiary. However, the court ruled that "a felony punishable by death is not within the letter or meaning of the statute." On March 26, 1880, recent convert to Catholicism, William Barton, aged 16 years, with two priests in attendance, was hanged before 3,000 witnesses in St. Charles.[18] If Missouri put to death any person *less* than 16 years of age at the time of his crime after it hanged Barton in 1880, I have not located any documentation concerning his/her execution(s).

One other known juvenile execution occurred in the 1880s, that of William Walker, aged 16 years at the time of his crime, in Christian County, on March 11, 1887. On that date, he, his father, David Walker, John Matthews, Wiley Matthews, and a number of others stormed the cabin of James Edens, a man who had earlier made disparaging remarks about the Bald Knobbers, a vigilante organization, whose members included the Walkers and the Matthews. In the melee which followed, two young and recently married men, William Edens, the son of James Edens, and Charles Green, James Edens' son-in-law, were killed. In March and April 1888, the prosecutor tried both Walkers and Matthews individually for the Edens-Green killings. The juries found each guilty of first degree murder; all four were sentenced to hang, and the Missouri Supreme Court affirmed all four death sentences in separate decisions. On January 23, 1889, the Matthews escaped from the Christian County jail in Ozark; John was recaptured, but Wiley's escape was successful, and he lived until his natural death in 1937. In January 1889, and prior to Wiley Mathews' escape, the Christian County sheriff had contracted with a professional hangman, Daniel Binkley of Kansas City, to furnish the material for the scaffold, build it, and hang the four condemned prisoners for $350. David Walker persuaded the sheriff, as a last favor, to hang the prisoners himself. He was inexperienced at putting people to death, and he bungled the job of executing the three in Ozark on May 10, 1889. This Christian County hanging was one of four instances in Missouri's history wherein three males were sentenced to death for the same crime and the sentence was carried out. William Walker's feet touched the ground; his noose came untied; he had to be hanged twice; and he regained consciousness between his hangings. In all, his death took 34 minutes. The documentation for his age as 16 on March 11, 1887, the date of the Eden-Green murders, comes from, among other sources, his birth date of March 25, 1870.[19]

The other juvenile hanging in the 1880s is a part of one of the most famous murders and executions in Missouri history. It concerns the Talbott family of Nodaway County. The father, Perry Talbott, was a physician; he had served both in the Missouri House of Representatives in the 1856–57 term and as a surgeon in the Union Army in the 25th Missouri regiment. He was a 53-year-old highly respected medical doctor in and around Maryville at the time of his murder. He was shot through a window of his own home on September 18, 1880, after returning from a call on a sick child. The shooting occurred about 11:00 p.m., and the victim survived until the following afternoon. An inquest was held, and the initial verdict was that Dr. Talbott had come to his death at the hand of some unknown person. However, from the start, the victim's family was suspected. Dr. Talbott was known as an abusive husband and father; his home was an arsenal of weapons, and his children were familiar with their use. A Kansas City detective, posing as a bank robber, gained the confidence of the oldest Talbott son, Albert, age 21, and Charles, age 16, and they confided to him that they had murdered their father with Charles doing the actual shooting. Charles, Albert, their mother Belle Talbott, and a hired man, Henry Wyatt, were arrested, but only Charles and Albert were indicted. Their trial for first degree murder began January 13, 1881, and it lasted ten days. The defense was represented by three attorneys and the prosecution by two. After two hours of deliberating the jury returned a guilty verdict, and the judge sentenced them to be executed March 25, 1881.

On appeal, the Supreme Court of Missouri upheld the sentence without any issue, fact, or reasoning in its decision mentioning the age of either Talbott son. After their convictions were affirmed, they were resentenced to be executed on June 24, 1881. At the eleventh hour on this date, the governor granted them a stay until July 22, 1881. On that later date and in the presence of 8,000 to 10,000 witnesses at Maryville, the Talbott sons, Charles and Albert, were hanged from a public scaffold at 2:17 p.m. Their mother, Belle Talbott, buried four of her family together. Her oldest sons of her eight children, her youngest daughter, Ella Rosa, who died on June 27, 1880, at age "3 years, 8 months, and 13 days," and her murdered husband are interred on private property (once the Talbott farm) in a common plot north of Arkoe. Their gravestones have inscribed upon them their ages at death. The brothers share a common stone. On its west side is engraved: "We died innocent." Its south side states that Albert was "22 years, 5 months and 6 days old," and its north side that Charles was "17 years, 2 months, and 4 days old."[20]

During the 1890s, the first juvenile hanging was of a white youth, Charles Seaton. He was 16 years old when he shot 17-year-old Lewis Channell on June 5, 1889, at the deceased's place of employment in Joplin, Jasper County. The perpetrator wanted a ladies' gold watch in Channell's possession that belonged to his victim's mother. Seaton was arrested in possession of it in Barry County shortly after his young sister inadvertently remarked, "Charley

Inscriptions on the west side, "We Died Innocent," and the north of the Talbott sons' tombstone near Arkoe, Missouri. They were hanged on July 22, 1881, in Maryville, Nodaway County, for killing their father. The mother and wife buried her perpetrator sons, her murdered husband, and her three-year-old daughter who died a natural death together. (Photographs by the author.)

has a little gold watch that is ever so pretty." His story that he won it playing marbles quickly changed to his confession that he killed Channel for his watch. The Supreme Court of Missouri's decision affirming the defendant's first degree murder conviction and his death sentence contains the following:

> The defendant ... testified that it was represented to defendant that it would be much better for him to make confession; that he was under age, and they could not hang him or send him to the penitentiary; all they could do was send him to reform school and that there was danger of him ... being mobbed [lynched] if he did not make a statement. This testimony was contradicted by witnesses called on the part of the state, who testified that no promise or threats were made, and that the confession was made voluntarily by the defendant.

His story is probably true. Threats of lynch mobs played important roles in later juvenile cases, and Seaton's partial knowledge of Missouri law pertaining to juveniles sound much like the half-truths he might have been fed in order to obtain his confession. At his trial in Lawrence County on a change of venue from Jasper, his only jury instructions on the degree of his crime were murder in the first degree and not guilty. Seaton was hanged in Mount Vernon on December 4, 1891 at 10:25 a.m. Because of his own and his family's poverty, he wore a suit to his execution that the sheriff of Lawrence County supplied him.[21]

Seaton was one of three or four juveniles executed in Missouri in the 1890s, the decade of the greatest use of the death penalty in the state's history. The other three were Phillip Martin, aged 17 or 18 years when he committed his crime, and Peter Schmidt and James Reed, both aged 16 or 17 years, at the time of their crimes. Martin, a black youth, and one of his friends encountered two white drunks, Eli Stillwell and his brother-in-law, on a Kansas City street about 11:00 p.m. on July 4, 1893. In an argument over who had the right of way on the sidewalk, Martin, as the jury at his trial later determined, stabbed Eli Stillwell in the heart. The victim died July 5, 1893, shortly after Martin and his friend were arrested for the assault on Stillwell. The jury found Martin guilty of first degree murder, and the judge sentenced him to death. On appeal, the Missouri Supreme Court affirmed. Phillip Martin was either still 17 years old or recently turned 18 on July 4, 1893, when he committed the crime which resulted in the death of his victim and his own subsequent execution at age 19 on February 15, 1895.[22]

Peter Schmidt, his cousin John Schmidt, and Sam Foster robbed and murdered a Chicago artist, Bertram Atwater, who had come to Webster Groves, St. Louis County, by train on the night of January 23, 1896. The victim defended himself by shooting and severely wounding John Schmidt before he was gunned down by John Schmidt and Sam Foster. John Schmidt, believing he was mortally wounded, made a full confession which implicated his accomplices, who corroborated his statements about their crime. The three were tried and found guilty; the Missouri Supreme Court decision which affirmed their death sentences incorrectly identified them as "three negroes." Only Sam Foster was an African-American. The fate of John Schmidt is unknown. Foster and Peter Schmidt, a Danish youth, aged 17 years at the time of the crime, were hanged together at 7:30 a.m. on February 16, 1897 at Clayton.[23]

On December 27, 1897, 16- or 17-year-old James Reed shot and killed the woman he loved, 26-year-old Susie Blakely, at 610 E. 12th Street, Kansas City. She had moved to Kansas City from Sedalia several months prior to her murder. Shortly after she met Jim Reed, he loved her, and she had no interest in him. He shot her at her boarding house twice through the heart. He was soon captured and soon confessed. He told an assistant prosecutor at the Kansas City police station a familiar refrain, if she wouldn't have him, she shouldn't have anyone else. The jury rejected his defense of insanity, and after five minutes of deliberating, it found James Reed guilty of first degree murder. The Missouri Supreme Court affirmed, and James Reed was hanged at the jail on E. Missouri Avenue on March 30, 1899.[24] He had been eight years old and playing in a nearby room on September 16, 1890, the date upon which his father, Martin Reed, murdered his mother, Hester Reed, because, after 25 years of marriage, seven children, and many years of his abuse of her, she had filed for divorce. Martin Reed was hanged at the E. Missouri Avenue jail on January 5, 1894. Five years and less than four months later, his son, James, was put to death on the same scaffold in the same facility for a remarkably similar crime: inability to handle his woman's rejection of him.

During the first decade of the twentieth century, the state of Missouri executed two black youths at different times and places for the crime of rape. All other known persons legally put to death for this offense are discussed in the next chapter; the juveniles are described herein.

The first twentieth century case involving a juvenile death sentence for rape is especially disturbing. The defendant, an illiterate 16-year-old, named General Armstrong,[25] did not commit a capital offense. On the morning of July 12, 1900, 16-year-old Ivy Turney, a white girl, was driving her buggy on a public highway approximately seven miles northeast of Plattsburg, near Perrin, Clinton County, as she delivered baking powder at various farm houses. According to her testimony, she was approached by a young black male on a grayish-white horse who demanded a dollar from her. When she refused, he hit her over the head with a piece of wood and knocked her unconscious. When she came to, her clothing was disarranged and a sanitary napkin she had been wearing was lying on the ground. If one believes the victim's story, the defendant was, at best, guilty of attempted robbery or robbery and/or first degree assault, and at worst, attempted rape. None of these offenses have ever been capital under Missouri law. Had the youthful perpetrator been charged with and convicted of what he was arguably guilty of, his punishment would have been either imprisonment at MSP in Jefferson City or commitment to the state reform school for boys in Boonville. Under legislation amended in 1889, boys who were at least 16 years old at the time of their crime but under 18 could be sentenced to either the prison at Jefferson City or reform school in Boonville.[26]

Among so much else amiss in this sordid case, the prosecutor misrepresented the defendant's age as less than 16 at the time of his crime, and he argued to the jury that because of his youth, he could not be sent to the penitentiary, only to reform school. Therefore, the prosecution argued, the jury should return a death sentence for young Armstrong. No doubt in an effort to save his life, the defendant's father, but not his mother, testified that their son, General, had turned 15 the preceding February. Since Missouri began requiring birth certificates statewide only in 1910, apparently there was no written record of the defendant's birth. The most reliable source for the ages of General Armstrong and Ivy Turney is the 1900 census, which enumerated both them and their families: his on June 16 and hers on June 20. Probably, their mothers, at home during the day when the census taker appeared, provided all information concerning them. No statements in the census were given for trial purposes; it first became available 72 years later or in 1972. According to it, General Armstrong was born in February 1884 and was aged 16 years and four months on July 12, 1900, the date upon which he committed one or more non-capital crimes. Ivy Turney was born in April 1884 and was aged 16 years and two months on July 12, 1900. In addition, this census states that her family rented their home; his owned theirs. His father, Andrew Armstrong, a former slave, testified that he owned 20 acres, perhaps an enviable amount in the eyes of white farm laborers such as Thomas Turney, Ivy Turney's father.

General Armstrong was not charged with any offense he might have committed. Instead, rape's hue and cry was quickly raised shortly after Miss Turney regained consciousness and made her way to the nearby farmhouse of Mr. and Mrs. John Boone. A short time thereafter, young Armstrong, who lived in the vicinity with his parents and several sisters, was taken into custody. Because Ms. Turney was in the midst of her monthly menstruation, almost immediately four responsible citizens, including Dr. John Sturgis, a physician of 35 years' experience, and Mr. Cook, the former owner of the defendant's father, examined the defendant's clothing and genitals for blood, and they found no indication that he had had sexual intercourse. Though Miss Turney could and did identify the defendant as the person who accosted her, because she had been knocked unconscious, she was never able to testify that his penis had penetrated her vagina. Likewise, the attending physician, Dr. Sturgis, who was called to examine Ms. Turney at the residence of the Boones and treated her for the next seven days, found only that her hymen was entirely absent. He testified that among the causes of the absence of the hymen were "romping, jumping, sudden jars, and dancing." In answer to the question, "Is absence of the hymen proof of penetration or lack of virginity?" Dr. Sturgiss answered, "No Sir."[27]

Without any eyewitnesses, including the putative victim herself and lacking medical testimony that Ivy Turney had ever had sexual intercourse, the prosecution relied on the testimony of two men as witnesses to the defendant's alleged confession. One of these was the companion of a Plattsburg city marshal whom the lynch mob had paid $100 for procuring the defendant for it, and the prosecution was careful not to use the Plattsburg city marshal as one of its witnesses. The state's second witness was a Clay County deputy sheriff, Ed Cave, who appears to have been the law enforcement liaison with the mob. As one of the state's witnesses to Armstrong's confession, Deputy Cave was asked:

Q. You knew that there was a mob at Kearney to catch him [Armstrong] for his crime?
A. Yes sir.
Q. And he nodded his head when you asked him if he did it?
A. Yes sir.[28]

Both the city marshal's companion and Deputy Cave testified that the defendant agreed, while with them at Kearney, Clay County, on July 14, 1900, and with a mob of 30 men nearby, that he had raped Ivy Turney. Armstrong later denied that he had ever confessed, and the sheriff of Clinton County, who had earlier spent more than 48 continuous hours with young Armstrong, never obtained a confession from him.

It is to the credit of the courageous sheriff of Clinton County, John Wiser, that the defendant ever lived to stand trial. By the evening of July 12, 1900, or the same day rumors swept Clinton County that a black male had raped a white female, 100 enraged white men were ready to lynch young Armstrong. Alerted to the extreme danger of the situation, the Clinton County sheriff secretly removed his prisoner from the Clinton County jail in Plattsburg and hid both himself and his prisoner in a field of tall corn. Both the hiding boy and his keeper were without water for 24 hours and without food or sleep for 48 hours. At Mecca, Clinton County, and with the assistance of a black citizen from Bainbridge, Clinton County, the sheriff and his prisoner boarded a train for Kansas City, where Sheriff Wiser lodged General Armstrong in the jail at 219 E. Missouri Avenue, with the intention that the prisoner remain there for safe-keeping until his trial. His residence in this facility was quickly interrupted.

At the behest of the lynch mob and without Sheriff Wiser's knowledge or permission, the Plattsburg city marshal, himself in the hire of the lynch mob, obtained a state warrant for Armstrong. With his companion, one of the state's witnesses to the defendant's alleged confession, he removed the defendant from the jail in Kansas City on Saturday, July 14, 1900, and they all boarded a train. When they reached Kearney with their youthful, slow-witted, and uneducated prisoner, who should never have been in their custody, the mob was nearby and ready for action. Under these extraordinary circumstances, 16-year-old Armstrong is supposed to have confessed the rape to one of the two men who removed him from the Jackson County jail in Kansas City. After his alleged confession in Kearney, Armstrong spent the night of July 14-15 in the Clay County jail in Liberty. On July 15, the marshal and his companion returned Armstrong to the safe haven of the same Jackson County jail from which he had been removed. Under a front page headline, "Twice Escaped. The Negro Armstrong Narrowly Escapes Lynching at Kearney," the Plattsburg newspaper stated, "The confession as reported amounts to nothing under the circumstances in which it was made. It was made to one of the deputies who told him he would be protected if he told."[29]

That there survives the considerable evidence of the wrongful conviction of General Armstrong, including a typewritten trial transcript, is to the credit of his attorneys, E.C. Hall and Guy B. Park; the latter was governor of Missouri, 1932–1936. The defendant's lawyers secured a change of venue from Clinton to Platte County. Armstrong's change of venue remains a rarity; it is the one of two known changes of venue in a rape case which resulted in an execution in Missouri's history. Armstrong's lawyers so vigorously cross-examined the state's witnesses that instead of the usual speed of the return of a guilty verdict in similar cases, the jury deliberated 24 hours before finding the defendant guilty and assessing his punishment at death. Armstrong's case was appealed to the Supreme Court of Missouri, where, among many other grounds, his attorneys argued that their client's death sentence was cruel and unusual punishment and violative of the Missouri and the U.S. Constitution.[30] Nonetheless, after his trial in Platte City in December 1900, the appellate court affirmed his conviction and death sentence. After several reprieves, the sheriff of Platte County, Joseph Elgin, hanged 18-year-old General Armstrong in Platte City on April 25, 1902.[31] His case illustrates the blurry distinction of this time that separated the illegal lynching from the legal hanging. He died a victim of virulent racial prejudice, and were it not for the courage of the Clinton County sheriff who saved him from the lynch mob and Armstrong's lawyers who made the proper record in his case more than a century ago, we would know little of the particulars of his wrongful conviction and death.

The second and only other known juvenile executed for rape in Missouri was 16-year-old Curtis Jackson, a black male, born May 1, 1889, who also confessed to his crime to avoid being lynched. He was convicted of the rape on February 2, 1906, of an adult white woman, Mrs. Dan Norman, in Butler County. Jackson was kept in the St. Louis City jail for safekeeping, and he appears to have been there, not in the courtroom, during his preliminary hearing on February 15, 1906, in Poplar Bluff. He was arraigned February 19, tried February 20, and the defense put on no evidence for a defendant who may either have been completely illiterate or read at a second grade level. Jackson's jury deliberated 32 minutes before returning a guilty verdict to deafening applause in the Butler County Courtroom in which his trial was held. There was no appeal taken from his conviction, and the sheriff of Butler County hanged 16-year-old Curtis Jackson on March 22, 1906. The victim's husband, Dan Norman, appears to have assisted the sheriff in this hanging. Because of the combination of the absence of any appellate review as well as a tornado striking the Butler County Courthouse in 1927, thereby rendering circuit court records earlier than this date unavailable, it is impossible to state more than the barest facts of this case. Local and contemporary newspaper accounts are the only sources of information regarding it.[32]

Following Jackson's hanging in 1906, there were no known additional juvenile executions for more than 23 years. Beginning in 1907, juries were allowed in first degree murder convictions to assess life imprisonment instead of death. In post–Civil War rape prosecutions, juries always had a wide range of punishment options. Death sentences here were never common for teenagers, and they truly became a rarity after Jackson's Butler County execution. In the last 100 years, the state of Missouri has put to death only two known juveniles.

One was Lawrence Mabry. On Saturday evening about 7:10 p.m. on February 4, 1928, on a residential Sedalia street in the midst of a snowstorm, Lawrence Mabry shot William Busch in an attempted robbery. Because his wounded victim, a 23-year-old house painter then studying law at home, was able to make his way more than a block to the home of a friend who called a doctor, neither Mabry nor his 17-year-old accomplice, Ellis Collins, realized any bullet had hit the person they unsuccessfully sought to rob. (Ellis Collins later received a life sentence for his role in Busch's shooting; MSP records document that the governor paroled him on September 27, 1940.)[33] The young men learned from the next day's newspaper (Sunday's) that Mabry's bullet had wounded Busch. He and Ellis left Sedalia that same day, February 5, and drove to Kansas City in a stolen car.

Mabry's death certificate lists his date of birth as February 8, 1910, as does one newspaper reporter who covered his execution.[34] As such, he was 17 years, 11 months, and 27 days old when he shot Busch. By February 16, he and Collins were being held on automobile theft charges in Warrensburg. While incarcerated in the Johnson County jail for stealing a car, their third theft of a motor vehicle within the week, the boys learned from a newspaper account that Busch had died. Shortly, both Ellis and Mabry confessed to Busch's murder to the Johnson County sheriff. Their confessions received front page coverage in both the Warrensburg and Sedalia newspapers. The perpetrators agreed that Mabry fired the fatal shot.

Mabry was detained in the Johnson County jail in Warrensburg until his trial on a change of venue to Cooper County in Boonville. He was tried for attempted robbery and murder after his attorney refused to plead him guilty to second degree murder in exchange for a 40-year sentence. At trial, Mabry's defense was alibi. His attorneys used both their client and his family member as witnesses. Mabry took the stand and denied that he had shot William Busch. He stated that he was at home when the shooting took place on Saturday evening, February 4, 1928, and that he did not leave home the next day, Sunday, February 5, 1928. He claimed that he had confessed to Busch's murder to the Johnson County sheriff because he was coerced, harassed, and threatened with death. According to the trial transcript, Mabry testified, "They told me if I didn't write out a confession they was going to kill me."[35] Mabry's father, mother, and younger brother each took the stand and supported his alibi. The lateness of supper on Saturday, February 4, 1928, that it was eaten at 7:00 p.m. instead of the usual 6:00 p.m., was the litany of his family-member alibi witnesses. The jury believed neither the defendant nor his family; it convicted him of first degree murder on June 20, 1928, and it assessed his punishment at death. The judge sentenced him to be executed on July 30, 1928. An appeal was made to the Supreme Court of Missouri, and without any fact, issue, or reasoning suggestive of either Mabry's youthful age or his poor learning ability, the Court upheld his conviction and ordered his execution on January 31, 1930.

Despite the pleas of Mabry's former prosecutor, among others, Governor Caulfield refused to intervene. Mabry was kept at MSP in Jefferson City, and on January 28, 1930, Sheriff Clay Groom transferred his prisoner under heavy guard to the Cooper County jail in Boonville. At this time, Groom had been sheriff of Cooper County approximately a year. He and his family, consisting of his wife, two daughters, one aged 22 and the other aged

16, and their German shepherd, Chief, lived in the Cooper County jail with its prisoners. Sheriff Groom made arrangements for the services of a professional hangman, unnamed in all Cooper County court records and newspaper coverage. However, the likelihood is great that Phil Hanna of Epworth, White County, Illinois, was Mabry's actual hangman. In an interview, the anonymous executioner told a reporter, "I have followed the business quite awhile. I work mainly in three states: This is my 52nd execution, some by electrocution, some by hanging, hanging is best."[36] This sounds like Phil Hanna, the man who helped the sheriffs of Butler, New Madrid, and Ste. Genevieve counties in their execution duties during this same time period; in these counties, the newspapers identified him.

On January 31, 1930, 19-year-old Lawrence Mabry was put to death in Boonville in a barn-garage behind the Cooper County jail. Because of his conversion to Catholicism on the last morning of his life, a Catholic priest, Father Schroeger, accompanied him to the gallows. As the executioner, probably Hangman Hanna, drew the black hood over Mabry's face, he motioned for Sheriff Groom to get back. Then he pulled the lever. Mabry's body hurtled through a sawed-out hole in the loft floor at 9:17 a.m. Simultaneously, the Grooms' dog, Chief, in his pen near the barn-garage place of execution, began howling and continued howling for the next five minutes.

Mabry's body was claimed by his family, but as Sheriff Groom's daughter, then 16 and 77 when I interviewed her, remembered this day, the Mabry family had neither a hearse nor a cloth in which to wrap him prior to transporting him. She recalled that her father came into their jail living quarters and found a white sheet which he gave the Mabrys. They covered the freshly hanged body of their son and brother with it before they took it to Sedalia. His funeral was held February 2, 1930, at St. Patrick's Catholic Church in Sedalia. His gravestone in Sedalia's Memorial Park Cemetery bears testimony to his conversion to Catholicism. Its engraving includes the name *Lawrence Mabry*, the dates, 1910–1930, two crosses, and a heart with the initials "I.H.S.," inside the heart. This is a standard abbreviation for Jesus, Savior of Men, a conventional inscription for a Catholic grave as long as mass continued to be said in Latin.[37]

Lawrence Mabry was retarded. He quit school when he was in the fourth grade. A document he signed on April 6, 1928 — an affidavit for a change of venue — illustrates his difficulty in forming the letters of his name. Writing, reading, and reading comprehension remained lifelong problems for him. He hoped to read the Bible while in jail awaiting his hanging; doing so was far too difficult a task for him. He said immediately before his death, "God is at my right elbow," and he surely intended to say, "God is at my right hand." More than 50 years later, I taught Mabry's great-nephew at Central Missouri State University and through him met Lawrence Mabry's sister Blanche. In 1993 this 87-year-old woman told me of her family's attempts to get her retarded brother's death sentence commuted. Today, his retardation could be confirmed, and it and his age, not alibi, would make him ineligible for a death sentence.

No known executions of juveniles took place in this state for the next 63 and one-half years. None died in the gas chamber at Jefferson City. The youngest persons put to death in this facility were Leo Lyles in 1945 and Lloyd Anderson in 1965. According to Lyles' death certificate, he was born on June 19, 1923; he committed his capital crime on September 30, 1941. He was then aged 18 years and three months. According to Anderson's death certificate, he was born October 17, 1942; he committed his capital crime on May 18, 1961. He was then aged 19 years and 10 months.[38]

The death penalty for juveniles would seem to have been a thing of the past in Missouri. All this changed in 1993. During this year, the state put to death by lethal injection at Potosi Correctional Center, Washington County, 29-year-old Frederick Lashley. He was born on March 10, 1964, and he was aged 17 years when, in St. Louis City, he killed his handicapped 55-year-old second cousin and foster mother, Janie Tracy, while robbing her of $15 and her car. He drove off in his victim's automobile; he was apprehended while driving this stolen vehicle shortly after midnight. Soon he waived his rights; he admitted his crimes to police, orally, in writing, and in a video. At this time his victim was still alive, and he confessed to burglary, robbery, and assault. She died the next day, and the assault charge was changed to capital murder.

At his trial on capital charges in January 1982, his dress was inappropriate; he wore tennis shoes, far too casual footwear for such a formal and important occasion. He must have looked far older than his years. When I met him in March 1986 at the prison in Jefferson City, he had just turned 22. With his very bushy hair, heavy beard, mustache, and ringed fingers he looked at least mid–30s. Because he never testified at his trial, all his jury perceived of him was his very mature and menacing appearance.

The penalty phase of his trial was a proceeding in ineptitude on the part of the defense. The public defender who presented his evidence in mitigation remarked that she had a load of 80 cases.[39] She put on four witnesses: a professor of criminal justice who explained that the death penalty is not a deterrence; a psychologist in the city of St. Louis jail who had met the defendant and believed he could be rehabilitated; Juanita Morgan, the common-law wife of Lashley's father who had cared for the defendant when he was an infant; and 19-year-old Wardell Morgan, Juanita Morgan's son, who played with the defendant when they were younger children. Nothing in the testimony of these witnesses reached the heart of any of Lashley's jurors. They were given no reason to pity him, to show compassion, in a word to allow him to live. The prosecutor had already told them, "chronologically he is 17 years old but in terms of viciousness you don't get any older or meaner" (T.T., 681). They believed him because the defense never gave them any reason to think otherwise.

Lashley's attorneys appear never to have subpoenaed his records from the Division of Family Services. This agency is responsible for investigating child abuse/neglect, foster care placement, and the like. We know from the trial transcript that Lashley's parents were alive at the time of his trial because both the defense and the prosecutor refer to various letters he wrote to "Mommy" and "Daddy," presumably while he was being held in a jail on capital charges. The contents of these letters are not in the trial transcript. However, it is obvious that there is a big problem in family life when no closer relative than a second cousin is available to raise a child. Frederick Lashley's background was badly in need of an investigation, and there was none. A family history and mitigation evidence report, dated April 2, 1993, contains in relevant part:

> His birth mother was married to Fred's dad for a short time, until Frederick Sr. caught her stealing from him. Frederick Sr. moved out and took Fred with him. Fred's first memory of his childhood is the fact he did not have a mother. He was only two years old when his parents separated, and has only seen her twice since.... After being taken from his mother, Fred lived with Janie Tracy. He tried living with his father for a few years, from ages eight to twelve, but his father was strict with discipline, short tempered, and violent. He routinely whipped Fred with extension cords. While living with his father, Fred was so depressed he was undergoing psychiatric care through the Division of Family Services. He had been drinking heavily since the age of ten.... At the time he turned 17 he was homeless. He relied on friends for an occasional meal and a place to sleep.[40]

The jury which sentenced him to death never heard about the horror of Lashley's childhood; his attorneys asking him was not the way to learn about it. Usually, abused children are protective of their abusing parents. This information concerning Lashley's abuse was available through the records of relevant county or state services; it was never obtained and never presented to his jury. Once it assessed his punishment at death, the appellate courts, including the U.S. Supreme Court, affirmed his sentence. Despite the efforts of several very good lawyers who got his case *after* his trial, Frederick Lashley was executed at Potosi on July 28, 1993.[41]

In addition to Christopher Simmons, two other juveniles in Missouri have been sentenced to death in recent years. On July 27, 1985, 16-year-old Heath Wilkins, a white child born January 6, 1969, killed Nancy Allen, a 26-year-old mother of two small children, during the course of robbing her and her husband's convenience store in Avondale, Clay County. At age 17 and mentally ill, Wilkins represented himself, pled guilty to first degree murder, requested a death sentence of his judge, and received one. The courts, including the U.S. Supreme Court, upheld his punishment.[42] Wilkins' attorney then filed for habeas corpus relief in the federal court for the Western District of Missouri. Judge Scott Wright ruled that Wilkins' guilty plea and wavier of his right to present mitigating evidence were not made knowingly, intelligently, and voluntarily. On appeal, the Eighth Circuit Federal Court of Appeals upheld Judge Wright.[43] Afterwards, in Clay County Circuit Court before Judge David Russell, Heath Wilkins pled guilty to first degree robbery and second degree murder in the death of Nancy Allen and agreed to a life sentence. In return the prosecuting attorney dismissed the earlier case in which the juvenile pled guilty to first degree murder and was sentenced to death.[44]

In St. Louis City, on April 4, 1991, 16-year-old Antonio Richardson, a black child born September 3, 1974, with several co-defendants, including Marlin Gray, raped two white sisters, Julie Kerry, aged 21 years, and Robin Kerry, aged 19 years, and then murdered them by pushing them off the abandoned Chain of Rocks Bridge into the Mississippi River. Defense psychologists testified that Richardson had an I.Q. of 70, was mildly retarded, and functioned at less than a third grade level. At his trial, Richardson's jury was deadlocked on the punishment phase; the judge sentenced him to death. After various courts upheld his death sentence, on October 28, 2003, the chief justice of the Missouri Supreme Court, Ronnie L. White, ordered that Richardson's death sentence be set aside and that he be resentenced to life imprisonment. His authority for doing so was a retroactively applied 2002 U.S. Supreme Court decision which holds that when a jury hears a case only it, not the judge, can sentence the defendant to death.[45] On October 26, 2005, at the Eastern Reception Diagnostic and Correctional Center in Bonne Terre, the state of Missouri put to death one of Richardson's co-defendants in the Chain of Rocks Bridge case, Marlin Gray, aged 23 years at the time of his crime on April 4, 1991 and 38 when executed. Considerable doubt lingers about Gray's guilty of first degree murder. He was convicted of two counts of first degree murder as an accomplice.[46]

No juvenile other than Simmons was under sentence of death in Missouri when the U.S. Supreme Court's decision rid the death rows of various states of those under age 18 at the time of their crimes. It is no accident that 13 of the 20 jurisdictions which allowed a death sentence for juveniles in 2005 were former slave states: Alabama, Arkansas, Delaware, Florida, Georgia, Kentucky, Louisiana, Mississippi, Missouri, North Carolina, South Carolina, Texas, and Virginia.[47]

The next chapter concerns another aspect of Missouri's death penalty, execution for rape. Its use here was shared by the other former slave states. This practice was also ended by a United States Supreme Court decision.

9

Rape, 1891–1964

During the examination of jurors in Frederick Lashley's 1982 trial for murder, one responded when asked her views on the death penalty: "I cannot state flatly [that] I am opposed or in favor. Depending on the situation. If it was rape, the death penalty. I think it definitely should be considered" (T.T., 241). She came to her jury duties too late to assess capital punishment for rape. Missouri executed its last man convicted of this crime in 1964. More importantly, in 1977, the U.S. Supreme Court ruled by a 7–2 vote that the death penalty for the rape of an adult woman violates the 8th and the 14th Amendments' stricture against cruel and unusual punishments.[1] This decision ended a shameful practice of American law, the execution of black males for the criminal assault of white females. The statutes allowing such dire punishments have their origins in an abomination, slavery.

Missouri is unique among American places of bondage on the eve of the Civil War. All other slave states and the District of Columbia had a mandatory death penalty for any slave convicted of the rape of a white woman.[2] So nearly universal was the bondboys' and -men's execution for sex offenses against white girls and women that at least one current authority on slavery in the United States assumes that all slave jurisdictions punished a slave's rape of a white woman with death.[3] This state did not. Neither the District of Louisiana (1804–1805), the Territory of Louisiana (1805–1812), the Territory of Missouri (1812–1821), nor the antebellum state of Missouri (1821–1861) ever hanged for this crime. Initially the prescribed punishment here was castration, and the early Missouri statutes did not distinguish between slave and free, black and white, and young and old.

Then came statehood and with it an important document which governed the laws the legislature could enact, the 1820 Missouri Constitution. As noted in Chapter 2, it contained, among other slave rights in criminal trials, this provision: "A slave convicted of a capital offense shall suffer the same degree of punishment, and no other, that would be inflicted on a free white person for a like offence."[4] Since this constitution lasted throughout slavery, its durability barred a death penalty for a slave's violation of a white female unless *all* convicted rapists were put to death. Such equality never became law. Instead, in 1835 the Missouri General Assembly provided a prison term for rape, and on April 25, 1837, MSP received its first convict rapist. He was a 25-year-old Irishman, Brian Johnston, and he served nearly three years.[5] Both the early imprisoned rapists and their victims were white. If any male of color, slave or free, attempted to or actually raped a white female, his punishment remained castration. Despite a diligent search, I never located a single instance of this punishment being carried out. If the female victim of a slave was white, the likelihood is great that the charge was reduced to assault and the defendant bondboy or -man sold. In 1836, Missouri law required that the owner post a bond of $500 to insure that his convicted-felon slave be taken from the state within 60 days and not returned to Missouri for at least 20 years "if [the felony] be of such a nature, in the opinion of the court, that it is not safe that such slave should stay in the State."[6] Almost certainly, rapist slaves were not mutilated; rather they were sold down the river intact. As such they remained valuable properties, and they fetched far higher prices than had their purchasers known the actual nature of their crimes. When a slave sexually attacked either a female slave of his owner's or a white member of his owner's family, his crime was probably not referred to a court. His master was required to pay all court costs in any rape or attempted rape convictions, and the court-ordered punishment severely reduced the value of the castrated slave. Moreover, the owner of any raped slave who gave birth owned any child born of the assault. The owner decided the attacker's punishment, if any, and it was surely limited to a whipping, a sale, or both. As for sexually assaulted free women of color, there are no known antebellum records from Missouri. Slave women who were attacked by their owners were not victims of crime in the eyes of the law. She was his property, and he could do unto her as he wished.

Once slavery perished here, the legislature repealed the castration statutes. Following the Civil War all convicted rapists, black and white, lucky enough to escape mob violence, were punished with a term of years at MSP in Jefferson City. In 1879 the General Assembly added the sentence of death as a punishment option in rape convictions. Perhaps it did so in order to reduce extralegal activity to punish this crime. During the 1870s, in separate incidents in different Missouri counties, at least six black boys and men accused of sex crimes against white women died at the hands of white mobs. Despite the legal hanging of persons convicted of this crime, a punishment which began in 1891, the lynchings of black males for this real or imagined offense continued here as late as 1942. The mob and the law both played important roles in meting out justice for blacks accused of ravishing white women.

We can look at executions for rape in other states and the District of Columbia through a combination of the annual lists in the *Chicago Tribune* (1881–1918) and Bowers' *Legal Homicide, 1864–1982*. In chronological order and over a 38 year period, the paper listed the date, name, race, crime, town, and state of each known execution in the United States. Bowers' book contains an alphabetical list by state of all executions. He too lists the name, race, crime, and county of conviction. A perusal of both sources is necessary. Bowers' book contains only executions at penal institutions, and each state went to the central location of a prison for carrying out its executions at a different date. His District of Columbia records of executions begin in 1853; that for the state of Louisiana in 1957. An examination of the enumerations in both the newspaper and Bowers makes clear that, with two exceptions, *all* executions for rape from the 1880s until the last for this offense in the 1960s occurred in jurisdictions that were places of slavery on the eve of the Civil War. In all there were 15 states and the District of Columbia: Alabama, Arkansas, Delaware, Florida, Georgia, Louisiana, Kentucky, Maryland, Mississippi, Missouri, North Carolina, South Carolina, Tennessee, Texas, and Virginia. The two exceptions were West Virginia and Oklahoma. West Virginia was a part of Virginia until it became a separate state in 1863, and Oklahoma was settled by former residents of slave states. Even if a death sentence for rape were on the books elsewhere in the U.S., between 1881 and 1964, I could not locate a single execution under state authority for it outside the above-mentioned jurisdictions. Neither 38 years of the *Chicago Tribune*'s annual list of the names, dates, crimes, and places of executions, nor

Bowers' 125-page appendix uncovered one place outside the specified 18 which executed for this crime. Death for convicted rapists was not a nationwide practice.

To be sure, colonial America had repressive laws concerning sexual matters. Louis Crompton demonstrates that homosexual acts carried a death penalty in all 13 colonies.[7] Daniel Hearn documents executions for a variety of sexual offenses in seventeenth and eighteenth century New England and New York: adultery, incest, pederasty, and rape in Connecticut; adultery, bestiality, rape, and sodomy in Massachusetts; attempted rape, pederasty, and rape in New York; and rape in New Hampshire and Rhode Island. He lists only five executions, all for rape, in Connecticut and Massachusetts, between 1803 and 1825, and none thereafter in either New England or New York.[8] Only the 1825 execution took place after Missouri became a state. Clearly, these startling penalties had either fallen into desuetude or were repealed long before Missouri gave jurors a death penalty option in rape cases.

All versions of the Missouri statute containing an allowable death sentence for this crime were racially neutral. The Equal Protection Clause of the 14th Amendment, which became a part of the U.S. Constitution in 1868, would never have tolerated the explicit racism of the antebellum statutes, specifically a death sentence when a slave was the perpetrator and a white female the victim. The statute covered both statutory and forcible rape. In the former the victim's consent was irrelevant because she was under the age to give it, and the age was specified in the law itself. In 1879, consent was required of females under the age of 12. Subsequent lawmakers slowly increased that age: in 1889 it was under 14, and in 1919 it was under 15. The allowable punishment was five years to death between 1879 and 1920. In 1921 the age of consent was increased to under 16 and the permissible punishment ranged from two years to death.[9] A term of two years was the minimum under Missouri law for any felony punishable by imprisonment at MSP. The 1921 age of under 16 and its extraordinarily wide punishment options remained on Missouri law books until the 1970s,[10] that is until the U.S. Supreme Court decision required this state's lawmakers to remove the death penalty portion of it.

Despite the facial neutrality of the law, judges and juries understood their duties. If the victim was an African-American female, the convicted rapist's punishment was *never* assessed as death. Boys and men who raped respectable black females were found guilty to be sure, but these perpetrators were sentenced to a prison term, not to be hanged and not to be gassed. For almost the first 40 years of the law's use, all known males sentenced to death were black. This changed during the Depression, but customarily, death-sentenced perpetrators were black; their victims were *always* white.

Once an allowable death penalty for rape was put on the books in 1879, it sat unused for the next 12 years. Among the first 11 persons put to death for rape in Missouri between 1891 and 1927, there were no white boys or men. The only juveniles executed for this crime were black; their hangings took place in 1902 and 1906, and they are discussed in Chapter 8. Unlike the crime of murder wherein most capital cases were the subject of Missouri Supreme Court decisions as early as the 1880s, many of Missouri's death sentences for rape were not reviewed by an appellate court. Of the 21 known executions for this crime, in 12, or 57%, there was no appeal. Between 1895 and 1927, a period of 32 years of profound racism in the United States, the Missouri Supreme Court reviewed nine death sentences for rape: eight were of Negroes and one of a white man. It reversed the white man's conviction, and it affirmed death by hanging for all eight blacks. In these years in which Missouri's highest court affirmed the death sentences for rape of all African-Americans it reviewed, its members were elected, not appointed.

The first execution for this crime in Missouri took place in Marshall, the seat of Saline

County, in 1891. My confidence that this was the first is based on headlines in Kansas City newspapers which identified it as "Missouri's First Hanging for the Terrible Offense" and "The First Legal Instance in the State." Newspaper coverage included both the perpetrator's and the victim's names; this dual identification in the press continued for many years. One newspaper explained the crime scene. On November 18, 1890, 19-year-old Alice Ninas and her 19- or 20-year-old cousin, Amelia Ninas, were walking from an academy in Sweet Springs to their home when a black man began chasing them. The reporter wrote, "The monster held the girl [Alice] firmly, his powerful hands closed upon her slender neck, and slowly her struggles became feebler, until she finally sunk into insensibility. She had fought as only woman thus assaulted can fight, but it was a hopeless struggle."[11] Once the perpetrator, William Price, was captured and the young women identified him, law enforcement officers secretly removed him from the jail in Marshall, concealed him in a hotel there, and afterwards brought him by train to the jail in Kansas City, all this to avoid their prisoner being lynched.

Meanwhile, Alice Ninas, who had been engaged for several years, wed her young man in late 1890 or early 1891. She was not a happy bride. She brooded over both the crime and the necessity of her appearance at a preliminary hearing. On March 15, 1891, she told her family that she had taken poison, and she had. A large dose of arsenic caused her death; she had been married about six weeks. Price was indicted for rape within a week of his victim's suicide. His trial took less than a full day. In the twinkling of an eye, he was found guilty and sentenced to death. One newspaper commented, "Until the sentencing of the brute Price, ... Missouri juries had found apparently no necessity for the infliction of the death sentence. The more aggravated cases of the kind — those in which hanging was most clearly the only just punishment — have seldom been brought before formal courts of justice."[12] At 11:45 a.m. on May 8, 1891, the sheriff of Saline County hanged 23-year-old William Price on a scaffold in the jail yard in Marshall. We will never know what punishment his jury might have assessed had his victim not committed suicide shortly before his trial.[13]

The second execution for rape took place in the seat of Buchanan County, St. Joseph, on May 11, 1895. The odds are that it was a wrongful conviction because the death-sentenced black man, Joseph Burries or Burrus, was not guilty of rape. This crime requires that the penis of the attacker penetrate the vagina of the victim, and in Burries' case this appears not to have occurred. On July 30, 1894, he sexually assaulted a white child, 7-year-old Bertha Potter, but he lacerated the young girl with his hands. Her mother was a prostitute and Burries a regular customer of the child's mother. According to the local newspaper, Mrs. Potter, "at one time ... agreed to make an affidavit that Burries was not guilty and that she and the girl had testified falsely at the trial, but she became alarmed at the consequence of committing perjury and the affidavit was not forthcoming."[14] Another newspaper wrote of Burries' execution, "This was the first legal hanging for attempted outrage ever held in the state."[15] Attempted rape was never a capital offense under Missouri law. Among the headlines in a St. Joseph newspaper's detailed account of his crime and punishment was, "In the Presence of Death He [Burries] Maintains His Innocence." However, the man soon to be hanged thanked the people for the fact that he had been tried by law, not lynched. Shortly before his death, Burries became a Catholic, and Father Dominick Wagner of St. Mary's Church, St. Joseph, was with him on the scaffold. He was hanged at 10:52 a.m., and his body laid out at undertaking rooms and viewed by hundreds of people.[16] The Missouri Supreme Court affirmed Burries' death sentence in a decision of one-half of one page.[17]

It affirmed one other death sentence for this crime in the early years of the twentieth century. It arose in Aurora, Lawrence County, on March 1, 1905, when Myrtle Digby, a 20-year-old white female, claimed that Edward Bateman, a 22-year-old black male, had raped her. Both the alleged perpetrator and victim were employees at the Aurora Hotel, he as a day porter, she as a waitress and chambermaid. Prior to his trial, the prosecuting attorney offered the accused a life sentence in return for a guilty plea, but he rejected it. His defense was consent. He took the stand in his own behalf, and he told the jury that Myrtle Digby had made overtures to him. A newspaper reported of his testimony that no one believed him. The paper termed the proceedings against Bateman "the quickest trial of a capital offense ever held in Lawrence County." The jury found him guilty and sentenced him to death. On appeal the Missouri Supreme Court also found incredible Bateman's testimony "that he had sexual intercourse with her in her room on two different occasions prior to the night of the particular assault." It affirmed his conviction, and on August 7, 1906, the sheriff of Lawrence County hanged 23-year-old Edward Bateman in Mt Vernon at 10:40 a.m. Shortly thereafter, his body was placed in a coffin, carried to the basement of the courthouse, and viewed by all who wished to gaze upon it. The newspaper reported that his execution was the first legal hanging of a Negro in Lawrence County.[18]

Death sentences for rape from which there were no appeals were carried out in Clark, Jackson, Mississippi, and Butler counties. In Clark County on July 25, 1903, 22-year-old biracial Frank Clark met 17-year-old Ollie Hess, a white girl, on a road and raped her. He escaped and was finally captured in Galesburg, Illinois, on September 15. The local newspaper in Kahoka gave this case detailed coverage. Its first story appeared on July 29. Its headline included, "A crime near home. A white girl seventeen years old brutally assaulted. The fiend half Negro and half Italian." Among many other details, this account quoted the sheriff's description of Clark as "dark mulatto and might be taken for a Dago."[19] As the time neared for the defendant's trial, the paper described the mood of the people as calm; but, it added, "After the jury will have rendered a verdict in the case and the sentence passed does not come up to the expectation of the people and is deemed in sufficient there is no telling what may happen."[20] In the paper's next issue its front page printed Clark's confession, a statement which ended, "This affidavit was made of my own free will without coercion on the part of anybody. I only ask that I be treated fair. They have all talked nicely and treated me nice. I appreciate their talking to me and giving me a show. I have not been taken advantage of in anyway." The illiterate, Frank Clark, signed his confession with his mark, an "X."[21] Following his trial and death sentence, the next issue of the paper quoted some of the arguments of the prosecution and of the defense. The prosecutor told the all-white-male jury that rape "is even worse than cold-blooded murder, because the agonies of the victim of murder are soon over. But the victim of a ravisher suffers all her life." The defense told this same body, "We admit Clark's guilt, but we do not believe that he is justly entitled to the maximum penalty.... Most rapes are worse than this one."[22] In its last story dealing with this case, that of Clark's execution, it quoted him as admitting that he ought to be put to death but expressing a horror of a mob or "being burned at a stake." The newspaper printed his picture and mentioned his conversion to Catholicism one week before his death. The morning of his hanging, he was taken to the Clark County Courthouse where mass was celebrated by Father H.J. Muckerman. The sheriff of Clark County hanged Frank Clark in Kahoka on November 25, 1903, and his unclaimed body was given to a medical college.[23]

Between 1910 and 1927, Missouri put to death six black men for the rape of five white women. In the earliest of these cases, there were two perpetrators and one victim. The crime took place on December 23, 1909, when 24-year-old Mrs. W.H. Jackson, who lived with her husband at 2312 Park Street, Kansas City, alighted from a streetcar in this same city at 24th and Brooklyn streets some time after 9:00 p.m. She was a violinist and returning from a performance at the Florence Crittenton home. She was accosted by two nicely-dressed black males and at their mercy for approximately an hour. They both raped her. It was a moonlit night so their victim got a good look at them; she recalled that one was wearing a gray overcoat. This coat had been stolen from a residence the two men, George Reynolds and John Williams, had burglarized earlier that same evening. When they were arrested two hours after their attack on Mrs. Jackson, they were in possession of stolen property, including the coat. Mrs. Jackson went to police headquarters the next morning and identified the men and the gray overcoat. After the police, in the language of the day, had "sweated" the black men for six hours, they signed written confessions. The first account of this case in the newspaper carried a detailed sketch of the victim, but as was the policy of the newspapers in Kansas City, no sketches or photographs of the black defendants appeared. Within a week of their arrest and lodging in the jail at 219 E. Missouri Avenue, a newspaper reported that a man had been overheard by police to say he would bring a mob of 400: "We'll lynch the niggers if we have to dynamite the jail."[24] It was well-fortified, and no lynching was attempted.

When the trial of Mrs. Jackson's attackers began in early January 1910, a newspaper noted that "Each person admitted to the criminal court building was subjected to the most searching scrutiny, for fear he might intend summary vengeance upon the black brutes."[25] This same paper's story the next day was headlined, "Negroes' Victim Physical Wreck." It began, "Carried into the courtroom in a chair in which she had been tied by her husband and her physician, so she could maintain a sitting position, Mrs. W.F. Jackson gave her testimony this morning in the trial of the Negroes who assaulted her." The story continued, "She cried, gasped, and screamed out the details"; once, she fainted. The defendants' appointed black attorneys were so moved by the testimony of both the victim and her physician that they waived cross-examination of these prosecution witnesses.[26] The all-white-male jury's names, addresses, martial status, and occupations were printed in several newspapers during the trial. Once it got the case, its deliberations and death penalty assessment for both men took five minutes and 30 seconds.[27] The defense of mistaken identity had clearly not succeeded. One newspaper assured its readers that, "There will be no appeal to the supreme court in their cases, as there is nothing from which to appeal."[28]

As soon after their sentences were pronounced as the law permitted, they were hanged in the Jackson County jail; the date was February 8, 1910. One newspaper reported that 20,000 applications had been made to see the hangings, many hundreds from Kansas, Missouri, and Oklahoma. After all, this was a hanging involving two men, the first dual execution for rape in Missouri. Most would-be attendees, including all women applicants, were rejected. Approximately 200 men witnessed their deaths. Prominent among them was Mr. W.H. Jackson, husband of the victim; as one newspaper reported, he had a place served for him, "near the ropes."[29] From this vantage point he had a good view of the deaths by neck-breaking of his wife's assailants.[30]

Mention has already been made of the appeal of Catholicism for men sentenced to death in Missouri. Nowhere is the attractiveness of this religion more apparent than for black men about to be hanged for the crime of rape. On the last afternoon of their lives, February 7, 1910, two priests, Fathers O'Reilly and Shipley from nearby St. Patrick's Church, visited John Williams and George Reynolds in the cells. They baptized both men. Following their visit, Reynolds wore both a crucifix and a scapular about his neck.[31] Presumably one or both of these Catholic clergy were on the scaffold with the men as they died. Other priests converted other black men sentenced to death for rape. Reverend Father Petri of St. Henry's Catholic Church, Charleston, was on the scaffold with George Jackson on June 10, 1910.[32] Father O'Flaherty helped Adam Jackson die in Poplar Bluff on March 26, 1920. This condemned rapist converted to Catholicism a week before he was hanged. At the end, according to the newspaper, "He looked at the priest who told him to make any statement that he cared to. He said, 'I am guilty and sorry,'" and they recited the Lord's Prayer.[33] In Clayton on February 27, 1927, the man who was to hang the next morning, Robert Johnson, spent his last night in prayer with his spiritual adviser, Rev. Walter Riske, of All Saints Catholic Church, University City.[34] In Kansas City, Walker Lee joined two churches shortly before he was executed: the Second Negro Christian Church and the Catholic. Asked by a reporter why he had joined both churches, he explained that "he didn't want to make no mistakes." However, Father McGowan, from Kansas City's Catholic Cathedral, was on the scaffold with Lee when he was put to death.[35] The priests recited prayers to these men about to die such as "May the Lord who frees you from sin save you and raise you up."[36] They also heard their confession, gave them communion, and anointed them with the oil of extreme unction. Apparently, the salvation offered by the Protestant clergy did not comfort the condemned as did the vision of life everlasting which Catholic priests presented.

Adam Jackson was executed in Butler County because, on February 9, 1920, he raped Mrs. Emma Mann, the daughter of Ben Purdon, a Civil War veteran and much-respected citizen. Jackson's hanging took place about six weeks after his crime, or on March 26, 1920. It was the first execution in Missouri after the restoration of capital punishment. A familiar figure was on the scaffold to lend a helping hand. The humane hangman, Phil Hanna, of Epworth, Illinois, put the rope around Jackson's neck but it broke, and the prisoner had to be hanged twice. The local paper quoted this Illinois farmer, the supposed friend of the condemned, as saying he had helped put to death 19 other men. Hanna appears to have pulled these figures out of thin air; the numbers varied every time he was interviewed in another town about another execution at which he assisted.[37]

On October 28, 1909, George Jackson said that he was looking for a stray dog when he crawled out from under the house of 60-year-old Mrs. Isophrenia Henderson near Bird's Point. He caught, beat, and raped her. Because she had known him since he was an infant, she easily identified him after his capture. Once he was in custody, the authorities placed him in the jail in Poplar Bluff to avoid his being lynched. On June 10, 1910, the sheriff of Mississippi County hanged George Jackson in Charleston.[38]

In two similar cases, both of them appealed, other black men went to their deaths. In the earlier, the perpetrator, Walker Lee, a member of a railroad gang, on June 28, 1910, used the pretext of wanting matches to get into the home of Mrs. Elizabeth Dahm, two miles east of Independence. Once inside her dwelling, he struck her a violent blow, and in the words of the Missouri Supreme Court when she regained consciousness, he was having "sexual connection with her."[39] Lee was arrested in Glasgow, Lafayette County. His victim identified him, and he pled guilty to the chief of the Independence police department. In order to avoid a lynching, he was lodged in the jail in Kansas City. One newspaper described the 50-year-old victim as "aged."[40] On August 17, 1921, at 6:15 a.m., the perpetrator was hanged wearing new clothes, where he had lived for more than a year after his arrest. The husband, Mr. Dahm, viewed Lee's hanging. The Missouri Supreme Court when affirming his death sentence congratulated the authorities, "It is to the credit of the state that a case of this character has been tried within its limits, and punishment administered to a person found guilty of the detestable crime of rape, under the orderly administration of legal procedure, rather than by a resort to mob law."[41] The newspaper headline about his execution contained, "Negro goes to gallows with prayer on lips; Walker Lee pays penalty for assault on white woman."[42]

In another case, Robert Johnson, a World War I veteran, assaulted Mrs. Mabel Faenger on March 9, 1926, at her home in St. Louis County, when she let him in to give him something to eat. He was arrested four days later, and on the appeal of his death sentence, the Missouri Supreme Court rejected his contention that the threat of mob violence induced his confession. It wrote, "The statements were made by defendant of his own volition, and that being so it matters not how much excitement prevailed in the community."[43] Predictably, the newspaper headlines about his execution included, "Johnson, Negro Rapist, Dies on Clayton Gallows; Perpetrator of Dastardly Crime Against White Woman Pays Extreme Penalty" and "Negro Hanged in Clayton Jail Year After Assault, ... Victim's Husband a Witness— She Says She Will View Body and Declare Justice Has Been Done."[44] As with Lee Walker in Kansas City, so too with Robert Johnson in Clayton, the sheriff complied with his wish to be hanged and buried in a new suit.[45]

The 1930s brought a new dimension to Missouri's death penalty for rape; two *white* men were separately put to death in Jasper County for the same crime, a rape during the course of a robbery on November 15, 1931. The victim was 15-year-old Bettie Hefley; and the perpetrators, 34-year-old Lew Worden and his brother, 26-year-old Harry Worden. These men and a third, Pete Stevenson, were suspects in three recent highway robberies, the murder of a Joplin grocer, and several sexual assaults of young women. Lew Worden was the first to be arrested; he was taken into custody on November 25, 1932, in Mountain View, Howell County. His brother, Harry, and Stevenson were arrested in Carthage, Illinois, on December 5, 1932. Stevenson obtained a change of venue from Jasper to Lawrence County, and there received a 99-year prison sentence at MSP.[46] Lew Worden was too poor to afford his own lawyer, and on the advice of his court-appointed attorney, on January 27, 1932, this illiterate man pled guilty to the rape of the young girl. The judge sentenced him to death. Unlike the black men who were hanged for this crime, this white perpetrator chose Protestant clergy as spiritual advisers. On March 3, 1932, in Carthage, the sheriff of Jasper County hanged Lew Worden at 6:01 a.m., in the presence of 100 witnesses, including the father of the victim. Pieces of the rope used to hang him were carried off as souvenirs. Despite his military service in World War I, the American Legion refused to give him a military burial.[47]

His brother, Harry, was convicted of rape in a separate trial in Jasper County; he too was sentenced to death. In his case, an appeal was taken to the Missouri Supreme Court; the only mention of the victim's name appears in this court's affirmation of Harry Worden's death sentence.[48] None of the newspaper accounts of the Wordens' crime and punishment I inspected contain it. The sheriff of Jasper County hanged Harry Worden at 5:59 a.m. at the county jail in Carthage on February 10, 1933.[49] Afterwards, his body was taken to Galena, Kansas, for his funeral and burial. Among those who viewed his remains was an eight-year-old girl. She recalls that "Porter Clark's funeral home had the service for Harry. My parents thought it was a good object lesson for me to see his body after he was hanged for his crime. I remember standing beside the open casket and seeing the purplish red marks of the hangman's noose." She further explains, "Many Galena parents took their children to see him and to remind us to stay on the 'good side' of the law."[50]

What is not clear about the execution of the first white men for rape in Missouri is the lingering suspicion that the authorities saw these men as bandits on a crime spree when they happened to assault a teenage girl. Had they not been involved in several holdups and suspects in an unrelated murder, perhaps their juries would have sentenced them to a term of years at MSP. As far as we know, all white persons earlier convicted of rape here had been sentenced to the penitentiary, not to hang by the neck until dead. The only other white men sentenced to capital punishment for this crime here died in the gas chamber in the 1960s. Otherwise those executed for this crime in Missouri continued to be black men.

Following the separate hangings of the Worden brothers, the next six executions for rape here were those of African-American men. Two men in separate proceedings pled guilty, waived their right, among others, to a jury trial, and the judge sentenced them to death. In these cases, the time lapse between their crimes and punishments was approximately 10 weeks. On August 11, 1933, John Boyd raped a white woman in St. Louis County. When he was arrested on August 13 in Granite City, Illinois, he was in possession of jewelry taken from his victim's home in Osage Hills. Boyd was an ex-convict, and he had received a dishonorable discharge from the navy. By late September he admitted that he had attacked 15 white and four black women between May and August 1933; seven of these women had identified him. On September 30, he pled guilty to the rape of one white woman, and the judge sentenced him to death. John Boyd was hanged at Clayton on November 2, 1933 at 6:00 a.m.[51] On August 9, 1952, Willie Porter, a convict trusty, serving a term for robbery at MSP, purchased some beer and wine. Shortly, he raped Mrs. Belle Agee, a 70-year-old white woman. He was captured that same day and drunk at the time; a pint of whiskey broke in his pocket during the skirmish with the police who took him into custody. On August 31, he pled guilty, and the judge sentenced him to death. Porter's attorneys sought a commutation of their client's death sentence, and they pointed out to the governor that it was unusual for a death sentence to result on a plea of guilty. Governor Forest Smith refused to intervene. Shortly before he was executed, Willie Porter converted to Catholicism; he spent his last hours with Reverend A. J. Stephens, the Catholic chaplain at the prison. Porter died in the gas chamber at MSP early on October 28, 1952.[52]

On February 5, 1938, in New Madrid County, Johnnie Jones, a cotton picker from East St. Louis, Illinois, raped Mrs. G.W. Warren and tied up her husband. They were a farm couple who lived near Matthews. Once Jones was captured, both Mr. and Mrs. Warren identified him. He was an ex-convict who had previously served two terms at MSP, one for attempted rape and the other for burglary and larceny. Within a week of his rape, he signed a confession. Afterwards he was taken to the Pemiscot County jail in Caruthersville for safe-keeping. When he was tried in New Madrid in May 1938, the proceedings against him lasted five hours. His jury deliberated less than an hour; all of his jurors' names were printed in the local newspaper. His attorney had no defense to his client's crime, but he asked the jury for a term of years for him. It came in with a death sentence. Despite a petition being filed by a former state senator with the Missouri Supreme Court to grant a writ of habeas corpus to the defendant, it refused to intervene. At 12:03 a.m. on July 15, 1938, Johnnie Jones, clad only in white shorts, died in the gas chamber.[53] In Boyd's, Porter's and Jones's case, there was no appellate review.

All other executions for rape were appealed. On May 28, 1933 in Malden, Dunklin County, a black male, C.D. Ward, raped two white females as they were returning from services at the Nazarene Church. In the Missouri Supreme Court decision which affirmed his death sentence, his victims are referred to as "Emma S. _____" and "Frances S. _____." The perpetrator was arrested in Helena, Arkansas, and the girls went there to identify him. Prior to his court appearance, he signed a written confession in which he admitted that he had raped two white girls. Instead of being tried on two counts of rape, the New Madrid prosecutor tried Ward twice. At his first trial for the criminal assault on one sister, the jury returned a sentence of 99 years. At his second for the attack on the other, the jury was out

20 hours and deadlocked. The trial judge, James V. Billings, who later unsuccessfully ran on the Democratic ticket for a seat on the Missouri Supreme Court, sentenced the defendant to death. On appeal, Ward's attorneys urged the appellate court to declare that the prosecutor's argument was reversible error. He had told the jury, "This copper _____, this saddle colored defendant, this brute in man's form violated not only God's law." It did not; instead, it upheld Ward's death sentence. At 8:01 a.m. on August 16, 1935, the sheriff of Dunklin County hanged C.D. Ward.[54]

In 1970 in a case involving two separate trials for the robbery of different men at a poker party in Lee's Summit, Missouri, the U.S. Supreme Court reversed the defendant's conviction when it enunciated the doctrine of collateral estoppel. It held that the Double Jeopardy Clause of the 5th and the 14th Amendments requires the prosecutor to join at one trial all the charges against a defendant which grow out of a single criminal act or transaction. It ruled that the prosecutor cannot use the first trial as a dress rehearsal for the second.[55] In numerous cases earlier discussed, Missouri prosecutors had tried a defendant for one murder where there were several victims. In these murder prosecutions, the jurors returned a death sentence at the first trial, thus obviating any need for a second trial. However, at C.D. Ward's first trial, the jury did not return with a death sentence. Under the 1970 case, Ward could not be retried for the rape of the second sister. Under a 2002 U.S. Supreme Court decision, no judge can sentence the accused to death when the jury is hung. Doing so violates the defendant's 6th and the 14th Amendments right to a jury trial.[56] In addition to a violation under current law of the 8th and 14th Amendments' prohibition against cruel and unusual punishments in capitally punishing Ward's rape of two young women with death, the proceedings against him also violated the 5th and 6th Amendments to the U.S. Constitution.

Two other black rapists were put to death in the gas chamber at MSP. On January 10, 1943, in St. Louis County, 20-year-old James Thomas raped and robbed a 22-year-old white woman. She was married to a soldier and had a four-month-old baby. Thomas was tried in Clayton, and the jury assessed his punishment as death. Judge Ellison wrote for the Missouri Supreme Court when it affirmed his death sentence. The victim was named neither in the newspaper nor in the appellate decision. He was put to death in the gas chamber on October 20, 1944.[57] On June 2, 1945, Marshall Perkins, a janitor with three years of education, raped 13-year-old Gladys Jeffries, as she with other children was returning home from a movie in Kansas City. He was arrested and confessed two days later. Perkins was an ex-convict who had done time in Kansas, Michigan, and Illinois as well as two terms at MSP. He was tried; the jury found him guilty and assessed his punishment at death. On appeal, the Missouri Supreme Court affirmed. Perkins, aged 59 years, died in the gas chamber on January 24, 1947.[58]

The last two men put to death in Missouri for rape were white. If capital punishment had only been used for sexual assault in cases such as Charles Odom's treatment of 13-year-old Lisa Schuh, the U.S. Supreme Court would never have held that the death penalty for rape is cruel and unusual punishment. On July 23, 1961, Odom, an ex-convict from Wellington, Kansas, was driving a car when he spied Lisa Shuh, a resident of Wichita, Kansas, walking her dog near her grandmother's house in Joplin. At gunpoint he forced her and her dog into his car, and he drove them to a deserted area where he raped the child. He then used a rock to bludgeon her about the head. A painter saw the abduction, and he took down both the car's description and its license plate number. Odom was arrested within one and one-half hours of his kidnapping the child. She remained unconscious for six weeks, underwent three brain surgeries, and had to relearn walking, talking, dressing herself, and the like. Afterward, she walked with a brace and did not have the use of her right hand. Had she died, Odom would have been charged with first degree murder. She lived, and her speech was plain but slow and halting.

After speaking with a minister, Odom confessed to the crime; he was tried in Jasper County Circuit Court in Carthage. His court-appointed attorneys were distinguished, a state senator, Richard Webster, and a former state representative, Edward Farmer. They represented their client at trial and before the Missouri Supreme Court. Odom's jury deliberated about 40 minutes before finding him guilty and assessing his punishment at death. On appeal, his lawyers argued that the trial judge committed reversible error in denying their client's request for a change of venue from Jasper to Lawrence County. When the appellate court affirmed his conviction, it ruled that his denial of a change of venue was irrelevant because newspapers, radio, and television reported his crime statewide. Immediately before Odom's execution, Supreme Court Justice Byron White denied a stay. On March 6, 1964, Charles Odom was put to death in the gas chamber at MSP. At the end of his life, he rejected any religious consolation.[59]

In Missouri's last execution for rape, the defendant, Ronald Wolfe, a homeless drifter and ex-convict, had three days earlier been released from a federal prison in Atlanta, Georgia. On October 18, 1959, he was driving his third stolen car in Lincoln County, when he attempted to lure several children into his car by offering them candy bars. He succeeded in enticing an eight-year-old to enter his vehicle; she was attending Sacred Heart Catholic Church's fall festival in Troy. He raped her. He was captured in Hannibal the next day, and he admitted to various city, state, and federal officers the abduction and sexual assault of the child. In the vehicle he had used to kidnap the young girl were items such as cartons of cigarettes and candy. Subsequently, he was identified by other children whom he attempted to abduct. He applied for and was granted a change of venue from Lincoln to Pike County, only the second instance of a change in a rape case which resulted in a death sentence here; General Armstrong's from Clinton to Platte in 1900 was the first. The prosecutor charged Wolfe with statutory rape; the medical testimony and the blood type evidence which the state used to prove the crime eliminated the necessity of the young girl's coherent statement of exactly what had happened to her at the hands of the defendant. The jury found him guilty. However, under a Habitual Criminal Act, assessing his punishment was reserved for the judge, not the jury, and he sentenced Wolfe to death. Today, this law would be declared unconstitutional in a death penalty case because it deprives the accused of his 6th and 14th Amendments right to a trial and assessment of a death sentence by a jury. Yet another likely impediment to a death sentence would be the jury's *not* hearing victim-impact testimony.[60] One newspaper reported that the mother of the young victim thought that Ronald Wolfe should not be executed. Today the jury would be required to hear what the mother had to say before determining his punishment. The Missouri Supreme Court affirmed Ronald Wolfe's conviction and death sentence. On May 8, 1964, with a few picketers protesting outside the prison, Missouri gassed to death at MSP its last convicted rapist.[61]

This is not the end of the story. In later chapters, I discuss commutations, pardons and reversals of death sentences, primarily for murder. What happened to men sentenced to death for rape who were not executed is told herein. Between 1911 and 1928, three black males were sentenced to hang for the rape of three white females in unrelated cases in different locales. In each the governor commuted the death sentence to a life prison term. In the first two, the defendant was innocent, and in the third, he was guilty and retarded.

The first commutation in a rape conviction arose in a case which reads much like a novel. On March 9, 1909, in Pike County, a 14-year-old white girl, Cora Flowers, went from her farm home to a nearby woodpile at dusk to obtain firewood. While there, either by pre-arrangement or happenstance, she met two black males, Mert Holman and Marcellus Butler. Holman was 19, and Butler somewhat older, perhaps 22.[62] She was friendly with both, and off she went with the young men to a straw stack about two or three miles from her home, where they spent the night. In all, Cora was gone from early evening March 9 until 3:00 or 4:00 p.m. on March 10, approximately 18 hours. Before she went home, she visited the Riggs, a neighboring white farm family. She asked Mrs. Riggs if she would say that she spent the night there. She refused; she told Cora that her father had been by the Riggs residence looking for her, and she would not lie for her, that Cora must tell the truth. Once the 14-year-old knew that Mrs. Riggs would not support her falsehood about having spent the night at their residence, she invented a far more lethal fabrication: Holman's and Butler's kidnapping and rape of her. She embellished it by having these young black males drag her from the woodpile the two or three miles to the straw stack, hold her at bay with a razor, and forcibly restrain her while Holman raped her once and Cell twice. She only managed to escape when momentarily left unguarded. No medical doctor testified for either side in this case.

Had these fateful events taken place after the Missouri legislature raised the age for statutory rape to under 15 years in 1919, the consensual sex which Cell Butler had with 14-year-old Cora would have rendered him death-eligible. One can reasonably assume that his knowledge of the law was inadequate; however, it is probable others told him that he would hang if he went to trial. This much we know. The sheriff of Pike County did not consider the county jail in Bowling Green sufficiently secure to resist an determined effort to lynch his prisoners. Once the young men were arrested, he and his deputy took them to the woods and kept them there all night on Thursday, March 12. In June 1909, Marcellus Butler entered a guilty plea to a crime he did not commit, rape, and the judge sentenced him to MSP for 99 years. The records clarify that he was received at the prison on July 28, 1909, and on December 23, 1939, more than 30 years later, he was discharged.[63]

Holman did not plead; he went to trial, and it is from the extant transcript of the proceedings against him that we know about the life of Cora Flowers. She was the state's chief witness. She lived in three rooms with her parents and eight other children. Her mother, Louisa Flowers, was illiterate, and Cora's formal education defective. She had attended school only a few terms and those sporadically. Her father, Charles Flowers, testified to the reason she had so little schooling: "We was poor folks and wasn't fixed to send her."[64] In addition to bringing in firewood from the woodpile, her chores also involved going after her family's cows. When looking for them, she often passed the residence of a black family whose property adjoined the Flowers' farm. It consisted of Frank Adams, his wife, Mag Adams, her son and her husband's stepson, Mert Holman, and Mert's friend, Marcellus or Cell Butler. Cora Flowers stopped at the Adams residence on a number of occasions. She had known the Adams' family about a year prior to the happenings in the straw stack. Testimony developed at Holman's trial made clear that Cora had been in the habit of meeting Cell in the woods, and on various occasions she had hugged and kissed him. On her cross-examination she was asked if she planned to go to Illinois with Cell Butler and marry him. Predictably she answered, "No Sir I never I didn't want to marry Niggers" (T.T., 6–10). Almost certainly, she and Cell had had voluntary sexual relations during her 18-hour absence from home. She testified, "Cell pulled up my dress and forced my legs open and unbuttoned his pants and put his thing in me... Pushed it in and kept raising up and down." (T.T., 6–10). While this activity was going on with Cell, Mert was allegedly forcefully holding her hand. According to Cora, Holman also, "Got down on his knees, got down between my legs and unbuttoned his pants and put his thing in me" (T.T., 11) Then, as she further testified, "In about an hour Cell done it again" (T.T., 11).

To bolster the perjury of his chief witness, Cora Flowers, the prosecutor put on his second witness, Louis Campbell, the acting deputy constable who arrested Holman. Campbell's perjured testimony involved stating that Holman told him of Cora Flowers, "I screwed her once" (T.T., 38). At General Armstrong's trial, a low-level law enforcement officer testified that Armstrong admitted that he had raped Ivy Turney. It would seem that such made-up testimony was standard at rape prosecutions when the prosecutor's case consisted only of otherwise flimsy evidence.

The attorney appointed to defend Holman put on a number of witnesses to disprove that his client had assaulted Cora Flowers. Chief among them was the defendant. Holman testified that he slept on the west side of the straw stack and Cell and Cora slept on the east side, He also stated that he left at 7:00 a.m., returned to the Adams' place, and went for groceries on horseback. Holman testified that he went by the straw stack, picked up Cell, and left Cora on foot the morning of March 10, 1909. On direct examination, Holman stated that he never had sex with Cora Flowers. On cross, the prosecutor asked, "How many times did you have sexual intercourse with that girl that night?" He answered, "I didn't have none at all" (T.T., 101). The defense witnesses also included Mag and Frank Adams, Holman's mother and stepfather. Their testimony emphasized the longstanding interest that Cora had in Cell. He stated that he had seen them talking seven or eight times, seen Cora hug and kiss Cell, and had asked the girl to leave his farm. The defense attorney asked him, "Why did you drive her away from there?" Adams answered, "Because I seen her and Cell had too much talk to suit me" (T.T., 113). Mag Adams testified that Cora had been to her house a good many times, and she too had seen Cora Flowers hug and kiss Cell Butler.

The most important witness for the defense, Mrs. Riggs, never took the stand. Her husband, Alex Riggs, was a prosecution witness who testified that he, among others, had joined the search party for Cora during her 18-hour outing. The prosecutor recalled this witness for the following Q. and A.

Q. You said you live how far from the Flowers home?
A. I live a quarter and about half a quarter.
Q. Where is your wife?
A. She is at home.
Q. What is her condition?
A. She has got rheumatism in her right knee, so she can't hardly get around.
Q. She cannot travel?
A. No Sir (T.T., 79).

There was no more important witness for the defense than Mrs. Riggs. On cross-examination, Holman's attorney asked Cora Flowers if she had stopped at anyone's house before going home, and she admitted that she had stopped at Mrs. Riggs.' The defense lawyer then asked her, "I will ask you if you didn't ask Mrs. Riggs to tell your mother and father that you staid all night there and Mrs. Riggs said to you, 'no child, cant do that, your father has been here hunting you'?" Cora answered, "If I did, I don't remember nothing about it." (T.T., 30). We know that in a criminal trial for rape in Kansas City, the same year that Holman was tried for this offense in Pike County, the chief prosecution witness, a woman so distraught that she was unable to walk, was carried into the courtroom in a chair. Mrs. Riggs did not appear as a witness in Mert Holman's trial, and it is not credible that her rheumatism wholly explains her absence. The court-appointed attorney, E. H. Wright, surely feared his complete ostracism in the community in which he earned his living if he called a woman who would tell the truth and cast more than reasonable doubt on Cora Flowers' trumped-up story of kidnapping, false imprisonment, and rape at the hands of two young African-Americans. The defense attorney was not ineffective per se in defending his client, but he never subpoenaed a crucial witness, Mrs. Riggs.

The trial transcript does not include closing arguments of either the prosecution or the defense. Therefore, we can only guess what either attorney told the jury in this all-important phase of any trial. It is too much to expect that E.H. Wright spoke to the jury as did the attorney Atticus Finch in Harper Lee's fictional account of a poor white girl falsely accusing a black man of rape in a trial in an Alabama town in the 1930s:

> I have nothing but pity in my heart for the chief witness for the state, but my pity does not extend so far as to her putting a man's life at stake, which she has done in an effort to get rid of her own guilt.... She has committed no crime, she has merely broken a rigid and time-honored code of our society.... She is the victim of cruel poverty and ignorance, but I cannot pity her: she is white.... She tempted a Negro. She did something that in our society is unspeakable.... No code mattered to her before she broke it, but it came crashing down on her afterwards.[65]

The jury in the imaginary case and the real one in Pike County returned a guilty verdict and a death sentence. Mert Holman's attorney took an appeal from it, and the Missouri Supreme Court affirmed his capital conviction in less than one page. Afterwards, Governor Hadley commuted Holman's death sentence to life, a move approved in the community because his and Butler's sentence were the same. The Register of Inmates, MSP, clarifies that Mert Holman was received at the penitentiary on January 11, 1911. He was finally released from confinement on Dec. 23, 1939, and Governor Dalton restored his citizenship on October 27, 1961.[66] He served almost 29 years for a crime he never committed.[67]

The second case in which the governor commuted a death sentence for rape involves an even greater injustice than Holman's. It arose in the city of St. Louis on January 14, 1920, when a 20-year-old white female, Marcia Herbold, was raped as she alighted from a street-car at approximately 6:45 p.m. There is no question that she was sexually assaulted, but the black man who was tried for this offense and sentenced to death was not guilty of this crime or any other. He was a 26-year-old black male, named Woodville Thurston, and he was employed as a houseboy by a prominent white couple. Between the crime and his arrest, there was a delay of three weeks. The victim identified him, and a saloon keeper whose establishment was near the crime scene placed him in his business shortly before the rape. It could be shown that the saloon keeper heard of the attack much after the event. The girl was certain that her assailant was black and wearing a soldier's coat and cap, common attire in the years immediately after World War I. A St. Louis police officer took the stand and bolstered the victim's identification of Thurston. He testified that the lighting at the crime scene was good because there was a gas lamp 10 feet from where the attack occurred.

The defense seems persuasion itself. Had this been an ordinary crime, such as a purse-snatching, and involved only one race as perpetrator and victim, almost certainly the prosecutor would have dropped charges against Thurston after he talked to the arrested black man's white employers, Mr. and Mrs. James Dowling. He knew this prominent and wealthy couple. They were certain that on the night of January 14, 1920, Thurston was at their home until at least 6:30 p.m., perhaps even later, and they lived more than four miles from the crime scene. The accused could not be in two places at the same time. However, this was not a usual case. A white woman had identified a black man as her rapist; it had to be prosecuted.

It now seems obvious that the shaken victim was mistaken in her identification of Woodville Thurston. His employers were not. At his trial, they testified that in the six weeks he had worked for them he had never missed work, arrived late, or left early. The jury did not believe them; it found the accused guilty and assessed his punishment at death. The Missouri Supreme Court affirmed. Its opinion placed the Dowling residence "several blocks from the place of the assault," and its decision which sustained the trial judge's overruling a motion for a new trial, placed their residence "some 10 blocks distant." It set an execution date of July 21, 1922.[68]

The defense motion for a new trial was based on its discovery that the police officer who testified about the well-lighted crime scene had lied. We can know about such matters because 46 pages of correspondence regarding this case are extant among the papers of Governor Arthur Hyde. The defense attorney wrote the governor that after the trial, "the scene of the crime was photographed, and it was conclusively shown that there was no light of any kind nearer than 110 feet.... This newly discovered evidence ... showed this evident perjury on the part of the officer." James Dowling also wrote the governor, in relevant part, "Our house is more than four miles from the scene of the crime.... He could not possibly have left our home before 6:30 p.m. or even 6:45 p.m. and as we understand this crime took place at 6:45, we are positive that Thurston is innocent." The Archbishop of St. Louis, John Glennon, once a parish priest at St. Patrick's in Kansas City who stood on the scaffold with men about to be hanged, wrote the governor that only once before had he ever requested executive clemency, but he did for Woodville Thurston. He vouched for the integrity of the Dowlings: "I know them to be responsible and reliable people." Rev. John DeVilbiss, also an attendee at several executions in St. Louis, also wrote the governor of Thurston, "This will be the first time I must stand on the scaffold with a man whom I know is innocent." A physician, Dr. Charles Phillips Jr., personally went to the crime scene and measured the distance between the place of the attack and the light. He too wrote the governor in relevant part, "We measured and the nearest light to this point was 110 feet away.... On this perjured testimony Thurston was convicted and sentenced to the gallows." Perhaps most amazing of all, Thomas O'Brien, the attorney who prosecuted the case and put the police officer on who testified falsely about the nearness of the light, also wrote the governor, "Later I learned that the only light was not nearer than 110 feet ... I know this to be a fact for I measured it myself." His letter ended, "I should regret to see a man hanged if there is any doubt about his guilt."

Armed with a thick packet of material which clearly demonstrated Thurston's innocence, the proper course on the governor's part would have been an outright pardon. He did not pardon Thurston and restore him to his liberty. Instead, he commuted his death sentence to life imprisonment on July 14, 1922.[69] The Register of Inmates at MSP clarifies that this innocent man was received at the prison on September 27, 1922, and he was paroled on Dec. 24, 1941. His civil rights were finally restored in 1961.[70] Today, DNA test results once obtained would require his immediate release from confinement.

The third and last commutation for rape involved a 19-year-old African-American named Cleo Williams. In Kansas City, on June 28, 1927, he attacked a 14-year-old, named Alta, and the next day, a young married woman, named Beulah. When taken into custody, he and his 17-year-old co-defendant, Zanie Russie, readily confessed. Because of his youthful age, Russie was sentenced to life. The records clarify that he was received at MSP on October 18, 1927, and he was released on January 11, 1949.[71]

Despite the judge telling Williams that he could expect no leniency, he pled guilty, and the judge sentenced him to death. In addition to Williams being ignorant and illiterate, he was also retarded. He had no idea what words such as *leniency* meant or any other aspect of court proceedings. His judge set his hanging for August 17, 1927, the sixth anniversary of the execution of the convicted rapist Walker Lee, as the newspapers noted. This date came and went without Williams' death sentence being carried out because his attorneys took an appeal to the Missouri Supreme Court. It affirmed his death sentence and ordered his hanging on July 6, 1928. On July 5, 1928, Governor Baker commuted his death sentence to life imprisonment. Kansas City's black newspaper, *The Call*, gave Williams' case good coverage. It mentioned his "evident mental deficiency," described him as having "the mind of a child." According to this paper, when Williams was told that he would not be hanged, he exclaimed, "I knew I was going to get some good news because a white pigeon flew in my widow and flapped his wings three times."[72] The governor stated, as the newspaper reported, "that Williams had the mind of a 13-year-old child and it would be wrong to hang him."[73] Records clarify that he was received at MSP on July 5, 1928, and he was paroled on November 18, 1949.[74]

In three unrelated cases involving white men sentenced to death for rape in different counties between 1915 and 1960, the Missouri Supreme Court did what it had not done even once in any of the cases it reviewed of the death sentences of African-Americans convicted of rape. It reversed, and following subsequent court proceedings, none were capitally punished. All three became inmates at MSP.

We know the most about the earliest of these cases. On March 9, 1914, between 5:15 and 6:00 p.m. in Kansas City, six men, among them 32-year-old Victor Gueringer, allegedly raped and sodomized a 28-year-old nurse, Gertrude Shidler. (Others of the supposed six were separately tried; one was sentenced to 99 years and another to 24. The Missouri Supreme Court affirmed their convictions.)[75] Immediately before Gueringer's trial began, a photograph of Mrs. Gertrude Shidler appeared on the front page of a newspaper under the caption, "Picture of Gang Victim Taken Just Before She Told Story."[76] Unlike any other known prosecution for rape in Missouri in which the jury assessed the punishment at death, the defense attorney told the jury, "I want you to bear this always in mind, that the only witness who testifies against this man and offers testimony that may take his life is Gertrude Shidler, a woman who twice before has made similar charges."[77] Her previously alleged attackers included her former father-in law, from whom she had collected between $400 and $600. She had charged another man with attempting to rape her while a resident of Terre Haute, Indiana, and he went to jail. While still in Indiana, she twice married and twice divorced Clyde Shidler and in the intervals between her marriages and divorces from him became the mother of his three children. Afterwards, she moved to Kansas City and lived with a man during two different time periods; she was not married to either.[78] Clearly, Gertrude Shidler carried a great deal of baggage with her into the courtroom.

Gueringer's defense was that he was elsewhere at the time of the crime; witnesses for him, both proprietors and patrons, placed him in the Green Duck pool room and a barber shop between 5:00 and 6:00 p.m. The jury believed Mrs. Shidler, and it assessed his punishment at death. Upon hearing the verdict, as one paper noted, the victim "collapsed completely and a police motor car was summoned to take her to General Hospital." While there she remarked to a night watchman who asked about the trial, "Oh he is to hang. Isn't it too bad?" Later that same day she told a reporter, "I do not believe in capital punishment."[79] On appeal, the Missouri Supreme Court reversed Gueringer's conviction on grounds that if he did sexually assault what the court termed "a self-confessed adulteress," he may only have been guilty of sodomy, and it is not a capital crime. It remanded his case for a new trial.[80] On his retrial, he was again convicted of rape and sentenced to 75 years; subsequently, he dropped a second appeal of his conviction for lack of funds. Immediately before his departure from Kansas City to begin serving his sentence, he wrote his judge a letter, which a newspaper printed. It stated in relevant part, "I am not admitting that I am guilty, because I am not, and the day will come when that woman will be called to meet her Maker, and she can't lie to him."[81] The MSP records state that Victor Gueringer was received at the prison on December 21, 1915, and discharged on July 7, 1926, or after serving 11 and one-half years.[82]

Far less is known about the last two death sentences for rape which the Missouri Supreme Court reversed. One had its beginnings in St. Louis County on May 30, 1957, when Carl Swinburne, a married man and the father of two children, began drinking at a tavern. Afterwards he raped and sodomized an unnamed 13-year-old girl who was babysitting three children. His defense was insanity; it did not succeed. On February 21, 1958, the jury found him guilty and assessed his punishment at death. On appeal, the court reversed because of faulty jury instructions.[83] Swinburne was received at MSP on February 24, 1958. His prison record contains multiple reports about his psychological state. In the other case, the details are even sketchier. In St. Francois County, on a date unmentioned in the Missouri Supreme Court decision, James Williams raped an unnamed 68-year-old woman. He was granted a change of venue to Perry County, and on October 13, 1961, he pled guilty, and the judge sentenced him to death by lethal gas. On appeal, the Missouri Supreme Court allowed him to withdraw his guilty plea because the trial judge had neither sufficiently questioned nor cautioned him prior to accepting it.[84] Another thick prison file exists on James Williams. He was received at MSP on October 14, 1962. He obtained a trial before another judge in Perry County, which was to have begun on November 25, 1963. The record of what subsequently occurred in Perry County Circuit Court is not a part of the prison record. Suffice it to say that Williams was returned to the prison in Jefferson City. Records of the Missouri Department of Corrections state that both Carl Swinburne and James Williams were released from MSP on September 3, 1983.[85]

In the mob-dominated atmosphere in which a black male was tried for the rape of a white female, it is not surprising that justice miscarried with the frequency that it did. On several occasions which we know about sheriffs were courageous protectors of their prisoners charged with this crime. However, all too frequently, trial or circuit court judges bypassed legal niceties when dealing with men accused of rape. They accepted a guilty plea without properly establishing a factual basis for it and advising the defendant of the many rights he waived by such an action. They presided over a far greater percentage of trials which resulted in wrongful convictions of black boys and men charged with rape than those charged with murder. The Missouri Supreme Court never reversed the death sentence of even one African-American when he was condemned to death for rape. No Missouri governor issued a timely pardon for this crime, even when presented with overwhelming evidence of the black man's innocence. It is fitting and proper that this state no longer executes for this crime.

The next chapter concerns a demographic group whose members were often enough sentenced to die but who were rarely put to death: women.

10

Women, 1834–1953

Missouri's known execution of females is a slender record. It is relatively swollen during the pre–Civil War period because slavery never favored women. Males in their prime brought top dollars on the market; the other sex did not. As a result, there was a willingness to put bondgirls and -women to death, an attitude which never applied to their free counterparts. For example, when on March 20, 1843, five slaves of a Boone County owner, Hiram Beasley, ended his life with an ax, two males, Simon and David, were found guilty of second degree murder. They were sentenced to 39 lashes and transported out of state for 20 years. In effect, the estate of their owner was allowed to sell them. In contrast, Henry and his wife, America, were found guilty of the first degree murder of Beasley in May, and the sheriff hanged them in Columbia on June 10, 1843. We can be certain that at least three other Missouri sheriffs each executed one female slave. Always, she killed within the family: two murdered their owner (Boone and Callaway counties), one, her leasor's child (Crawford County), and one, five of her owner's slave children, two hers and all her master's property (Clay County). Two other bondwomen were probably hanged; one because she set fire to her owner's property (St. Louis County) and the other because she killed her new mistress (Callaway County).[1] Another slave woman, Jane, was sentenced to death in Callaway County, because in December 1830, she killed her infant daughter, Angeline. On appeal, the Missouri Supreme Court reversed; it found error in the indictment.[2] Jane's fate is unknown. The records are incomplete; four, not seven, can be confirmed. To be certain, whether four, five, six, or seven, this number is small, but it is far larger than the total number of known white women put to death in Missouri's history. There are only two, and as for Negro women, there are no known free black females ever executed here.

In the nineteenth century in this state, the only white woman whose execution is confirmed was known as Mary Andrews. She had the additional surnames of Tromley, Trumley, Treenberg, and Trumberg. She was the common-law wife of Leland Tromley, and the sheriff of Lafayette County hanged him on April 4, 1834, for the murder of a blacksmith, James Stephens. The story has it that she claimed the marital privilege and refused to testify against him; as a result she was held in contempt of court and put in jail. At that time her child, Sara, was 10 months old, and her mother kept her in the cell with her. A contemporary news account states that she choked her young daughter to death, and she gave as her reason, "that her mother had turned her out of doors, ... her sisters would not speak to her, and Tromley the father of the child was about to be hung, and she had no means of taking care of it."[3] She was kept in the Ray County jail prior to her trial; at it, she was prosecuted for the death of her daughter, found guilty of murder, and the sheriff of Lafayette County hanged her in Lexington on a public scaffold on April 30, 1834; his fee was $10.[4]

We know that Mary Andrews was not the only distraught white mother in this state who killed her child. In Scott County in 1836, another, Parmelia Yarber, was indicted for the murder of her infant daughter. However, according to the county history, she failed to appear, and the judge declared her "outlawed and convicted of the crime whereof she stands charged in the indictment. It is therefore ordered and adjudged that Parmelia Yarber be hung by the neck until she is dead."[5] There is no record of either her arrest or her hanging.

A curiosity survives among the papers of Governor John Edwards (1844–1848), a request for a pardon of Nelly, a slave girl aged approximately 15 years. She was then in the Warren County jail in Warrenton awaiting her trial on murder charges in the death of her newborn, of unspecified sex. Over 100 white male citizens signed the request for her exoneration. They advanced several reasons. These included: "She is ignorant ... & there is reason to doubt whether at the time of the act the little mind that she has was in a state to make her responsible to the law." Others included sparing the court appearance of "very respectable ladies who will have to be examined as to the facts" and "the trial will be troublesome & expensive & exceeding unpleasant to the sensibilities & delicate feelings of the whole community." Nelly's owner, Henry Edwards, had died, and she was now the property of his widow and their 10 children. It is likely that the young slave's defense attorneys intended to put Nelly on the witness stand so she could explain the sexual actions of her owner toward her. She would have told the jury that Mr. Edwards had raped her and she became pregnant. These facts would become a part of the court record if there were an evidentiary hearing. However, there was no trial. On October 15, 1846, Governor Edwards issued a full pardon to Nelly before she either pled guilty or was tried.[6] It is the only known pretrial pardon of its kind in Missouri's history.

After the Civil War, we see additional softening of attitudes toward those who ended the lives of their offspring. In 1869, the Missouri legislature added a crime which only applied to mothers. If she drowned, secretly buried, or in any other way concealed the birth so that whether it was alive or stillborn was unknown, she "shall be deemed guilty of a felony, and shall upon conviction, be imprisoned in the penitentiary not more than seven years."[7] As a result, the state did not charge young girls and women who killed their babies with murder. Rather, they were prosecuted for crimes such as "concealing a birth," "secretly burying a child," and "infanticide." In at least three instances in the early 1870s, they were kept at MSP for a short stay, one for eight, another for 12 and ½, and a third for 18 months.[8] In 1887, another mother, Julia McAltee, was found guilty of infanticide in Crawford County circuit court in Steelville and sentenced to two years at MSP.[9] After slavery ended, there are no known records of any female being sentenced to death here because she killed her infant.

The state of Missouri prosecuted four known white women for murder prior to the conclusion of the Civil War. In 1841, on a change of venue from Jackson to Van Buren County (renamed Cass County in 1849), Rebecca Hawkins was tried, convicted of putting poison in the food and drink of her husband, and sentenced to prison . She had been arrested at her husband's funeral. However, he did not die because he was poisoned; rather, his wife hired a hit man, George Goster, who shot to death Williamson Hawkins as he sat by his fireplace. As noted in Chapter 1, Goster was hanged in Independence on May 10, 1839. There is no appeal in his case, but one exists in hers. The Missouri Supreme Court affirmed the trial court;[10] however, a number of Jackson County citizens petitioned the governor that he set Mrs. Hawkins free. She was the mother of eight children, and a long-suffering abused wife. As a result, Governor Reynolds pardoned Mrs. Hawkins prior to her arrival at MSP.[11]

In Bolinger County in 1855, Sarah Buckner and her daughter by her first marriage, a teenager, Susan Leabaugh, were implicated in the murder of Whiston Buckner, Sarah's second husband. She had married him after the death of her first husband, Mr. Leabaugh. When Sarah discovered that her daughter was pregnant, the young girl named her stepfather as her impregnator. Together, the mother and daughter killed Whiston Buckner. One newspaper account states, that "his wife caught him and held him, while her daughter killed him with an ax."[12] Both were tried for his murder. Prison records clarify that 14-year-old Susan Leabaugh was received at MSP on June 15, 1855, after being convicted of second degree murder. Had she served her full sentence she would have been released on June 15, 1865. However, she died in prison, and the record keeper wrote of her, "an ignorant child."[13] Susan's mother, Sarah Buckner, received a change of venue from Bolinger to Stoddard County, and there the jury found her guilty of first degree murder, a sentence which was then automatically a death sentence. On appeal, the Missouri Supreme Court reversed on a technicality; its decision contains no facts of the crime. In 1859 the legislature passed a special law which authorized the state auditor to pay the clerk of Stoddard County Circuit Court $920.65 for fees in Sarah's case. The legislation states that since Sarah Buckner's appeal, she had broken jail and made her escape. At this time, the state, not the county, paid costs in capital cases when the accused was indigent, as she must have been. In her appeal, the Missouri Supreme Court observed that her case was "presented without any brief or without the appearance of counsel."[14] It is unlikely that this impoverished woman successfully escaped from custody without the help of one or more persons who thought she should not be retried for the first degree murder of the man who either seduced or raped her daughter.

Two other trials took place in St. Louis County, one in the mid–1850s and the other during the Civil War, in which a jury found a white woman guilty of first degree murder. The Missouri Supreme Court either refused to hear her case or upheld the trial court. In both the governor commuted the death sentence to a prison term. On December 11, 1855, Sarah Haycraft stabbed to death her lover, Samuel Hudson. When arrested she admitted the killing and gave as her reason that he had beaten her and called her a bitch. A newspaper described her as the proprietor of a St. Louis "female livery stable" and "notorious for infamy of conduct and reputation above all others of her class."[15] She was tried and found guilty of first degree murder. The judge sentenced her to hang on April 11, 1856. The Missouri Supreme Court refused to stay her execution. Shortly before her date with death, the governor commuted her sentence to 25 years at MSP. She spent precious little time at the prison. On February 27, 1858, Governor Stewart pardoned her on condition that she leave the state and not return.[16] Since at this time, the Upper Ferry crossed the Mississippi River from the city of St. Louis to Alton in Madison County, Illinois, and the Madison County, Illinois Ferry Company was licensed to keep a ferry across the Mississippi River at the North Point of the City of St. Louis,[17] Sarah Haycraft may have reopened her whorehouse in either Alton or Belleville. Her former clientele could take their buggies on the ferry and easily reach her new location in Illinois.[18]

In another case, Catharine McCoy killed a young girl, who appears not to have been her daughter, on April 20, 1863, by chopping her to pieces with a hatchet and hiding various body parts under furniture. She was tried for first degree murder, and her defense was insanity. The jury rejected it, and on appeal, the Missouri Supreme Court affirmed. This court customarily refused to second-guess a jury's assessment of the defendant's mental state, and it usually continued to affirm death sentences when the jury who saw, and perhaps heard, the live witness had judged her or him sane. Governor Hall commuted Catherine McCoy's death sentence, and she was received at MSP on June 17, 1864. As the record makes clear, her prison stay was less than a year; in March 1865 she was transferred to the lunatic asylum in Fulton.[19]

In another group of cases from the 1870s and 1880s, a woman was a co-defendant of one or more men whom a jury found guilty of first degree murder. In each, the male(s) sentenced to death were executed, but their wives or companions, and in one case, a daughter, were not. In Webster County, Charles Waller was hanged on May 17, 1872, for the 1867 murder of the William Newlon family. The motive was robbery. His co-defendant and wife, Hannah Waller, pled guilty to manslaughter, and the judge sentenced her to three years at MSP.[20] In Mercer County, on July 14, 1871, at the request of Mrs. Carolina Hallock, Joseph Hamilton, aged 17 years, shot and killed her husband, Elisha Hallock. As noted in Chapter 8, both the faithless wife and her young lover received changes of venue. He was tried, found guilty, and hanged in Harrison County on October 30, 1874. She was tried and found not guilty in Putnam County. In Gasconade County, Anna and Henry Hallenschied and their daughter, Wilhelmina Alband, killed Christ Alband, their daughter's husband, on June 16, 1875. At their trial, the jury found both Hallenschieds guilty of first degree murder, and the judge sentenced both to death. Their daughter was found guilty of second degree murder, and the judge sentenced her to 10 years at MSP. There was no appeal in any of the three defendants' cases. On December 16, Governor Hardin commuted Anna Hallenschied's death sentence to life imprisonment. The next day, December 17, 1875, the sheriff of Gasconade County hanged her husband in Hermann.[21] The governor gave as his reason for commuting the wife's death sentence to life imprisonment, "In consideration of her sex, and grave doubts of her being guilty of murder in the first degree."[22] According to a later newspaper account, Wilhelmina Albands died soon after she arrived at the prison, but her mother lived to become the oldest inmate in the prison. Anna Hallenschied died in 1891.[23]

In Audrain County, two former slaves, Joseph Muldrow and Nathan Faucett, were found guilty of the first degree murder on September 30, 1879, of Octave Inlow, a white man. The sheriff hanged them on April 16, 1880. They had an accomplice, a white female, Emma Prilley, who asked Muldrow and Faucett to kill Inlow because he had slapped her. According to the county history, the judge charged the jury that they could only find her guilty of first degree murder or acquit her. It refused to convict her, and she was asked to leave town. She did so, but she returned. She confessed her role in the murder of Inlow. She was tried and found guilty of second degree murder. The jury assessed her punishment at 12 years, and she began serving her sentence on April 20, 1880. She was discharged when she had served nine years or 3/4ths of her sentence.[24] Likewise, in Vernon County, Henry Stair and his wife or companion, Nannettie, or Nannetta Osborne, were charged with the August 5, 1885 murder of Jacob Sewell and his 17-year-old son, Mack, for purposes of robbing them. The jury found both guilty of first degree murder, and the judge sentenced both to death. On appeal, the Missouri Supreme Court affirmed Henry Stair's conviction. However, it reversed Nannettie's, and it remanded her case for a new trial. According to the county history, she pled guilty to manslaughter and was sentenced to five years at MSP.[25] In all four cases, the jury, the governor, or the Missouri Supreme Court made certain that the female defendants were not executed. This pattern continued.

One black woman was sentenced to death because she shot and killed a police officer, Sergeant Peletiah M. Jenks, as he attempted to break up a fight between her and another black woman on October 8, 1883, in an alley between Eighth and Ninth streets in the city of St. Louis. Her name was Sadie Hill, alias Hayes. Because she suffered from epileptic fits, her defenses involved both insanity and that the shooting had been accidental. They did not succeed. The jury found her guilty of the first degree murder of Officer Jenks, and the judge sentenced her to hang on January 15, 1886. Two courts reviewed her case. The first, the St. Louis Court of Appeals, affirmed her conviction, but the Missouri Supreme Court reversed on grounds of faulty jury instructions.[26] Prison records clarify that her original sentence was 99 years. She was received at MSP on January 29, 1887, and Governor Stephens pardoned her on November 24, 1898.[27]

During the 1890s, a period of more executions under state authority in Missouri than any other decade, three known women were put on trial here on first degree murder charges. One was white, and the other two black. The white homicide involved Lavinia and her husband, John Nelson. They were tried in New London for the August 5, 1893 murder of their neighbors, John Stull and his invalid mother, Mrs. Hughes. During Mrs. Nelson's stay in the Ralls County jail, she gave birth, and during her mother's trial, the child ran about the courtroom; the jury acquitted her. Her husband obtained a change of venue to Marion County, and the sheriff hanged him in Palmyra on February 28, 1896.[28]

One of the black women's cases took place in Kansas City. On May 15, 1891, Amanda Umble stabbed to death another black woman, Effie Jackson, at 5th and Holmes streets because her victim had attracted the attention of Will Jackson, a Negro whom Miss Umble considered her man. Miss Jackson died from peritonitis or infection the week following the perpetrator's knifing her six or eight times. At trial, Umble was found guilty of first degree murder, and the judge sentenced her to hang. On appeal, the Missouri Supreme Court affirmed. It wrote, "When we consider that her victim was unarmed and powerless in her hands, her conduct can only be denominated as atrocious.... The evidence justified the verdict, and the law must be permitted to take its course." Prior to her scheduled hanging, two members of the Colored Woman's League visited the governor in Jefferson City and asked that he commute the death sentence because she was a woman. In June 1893, Governor Stone signed papers which sentenced Amanda Umble to MSP for 50 years. Governor Dockery pardoned her on July 4, 1901[29]; she spent slightly more than seven years as a prison inmate.

Pearl Waters, a black woman, aged 19 or 20 years, killed Lillian Waddell, a 23-year-old black female, on February 1, 1897, at 12th and Morgan streets in the city of St. Louis in a dispute over a dime. At her trial, she was found guilty of first degree murder and sentenced to hang. She had earlier been an inmate at MSP. She was initially received at the prison on June 29, 1895 on a conviction of "assault to do great bodily harm;" she was released on December 15, 1896.[30] Six weeks later, she killed her victim. She was either retried or resentenced for her homicide because her conviction was for second degree murder. She was received at MSP on June 13, 1897, to serve a life sentence. Slightly over two years later, Governor Stephens pardoned her on July 6, 1899.[31] She is the last known African-American female sentenced to death in this state. All subsequent death-sentenced women in Missouri were white.

In the first decade of the twentieth century, juries here assessed the punishment of two women as death. The earlier case took place in Marion County. A woman named Alice who had multiple spellings of her surname, Nesenhener, Nessenhener, Nesenheur, and Nessenheimer, was charged with the July 13, 1900 poisoning of her husband Frank, who died July 14, 1900. At her trial in Hannibal, the prosecutor proved that she had purchased a quantity of morphine the day preceding his death. Moreover his life was insured, and she was his beneficiary. Two of her children had earlier died under suspicious circumstances. One was insured for $105 and the other for $85; presumably their mother was the beneficiary of her children's life insurance policies. The jury found her guilty of first degree murder, and early in 1901, the judge sentenced her to hang on April 12. A request was made to Governor Dockery for a commutation of her death sentence, but he did not act on it. On appeal, on November 12, 1901, the Missouri Supreme Court reversed her conviction and ordered her release from custody It ruled that the prosecution had not proven its case: It wrote, "There is no direct proof of the fact of poisoning, or substantial evidence that deceased in fact died of morphine poisoning." Subsequent news coverage indicates that the poisonings in the discharged prisoner's home continued. In June 1903, another child, Howard Nessenhener, died as a result of carbolic acid poisoning. The jury thought his death resulted from his mother's carelessness. Following the death of a fourth Nessenhener, the authorities sought to send Mrs. Alice Nessenhener to an asylum for the insane.[32]

The other turn of the century case took place in Kansas City. On May 11, 1904, at 12:45 a.m., at 2313 Terrace Street, 22-year-old Agnes Myers and her 20-year-old lover, Frank Hottman, killed Clarence Myers, Agnes or Aggie Myers' husband. According to Hottman's confession, their murder of her husband had been planned for several weeks. He held the victim, and Aggie stabbed him with a razor and scissors. Her first story to the police was that two black men had committed the crime for the purpose of robbing them. However, property that she said had been stolen was found concealed. They were both arrested for his murder, but they were not tried together. He was prosecuted in Jackson County, and the jury found him guilty of first degree murder in February 1905. On a change of venue, she was tried in Clay County. Hottman testified against her, and after a week-long trial in June 1905, a jury in Liberty found her guilty of the same charge. The judge sentenced her to hang on August 11, 1905. The Missouri Supreme Court wrote separate decisions in their cases, and it affirmed death sentences for both.[33] They were resentenced to hang on June 29, 1906, in different counties, she in Liberty and he in Kansas City. Their executions were postponed when her attorneys took an appeal, first to a federal court in Missouri and then to the United States Supreme Court. As her case was pending before the High Court, Governor Folk commuted both Agnes Myers' and Frank Hottman's death sentences to life imprisonment. The governor gave as his reason that "public morals would be benefited more by a life sentence than a death sentence in this case."[34] Contemporary news coverage stated of his action, "It will receive the approval of the general public ... because of the unacknowledged though keenly felt objection to hanging a woman for any cause."[35] Following the governor's commutation of her death sentence, Myers' appeal to the U.S. Supreme Court was dismissed. Both Aggie Myers and Frank Hottman were imprisoned at MSP, beginning in April 1907. Throughout the time period of her crime, trial, appeals, and commutation of her death sentence, her case received extensive publicity.[36] A newspaper story about them more than 20 years later explains that he died in prison in 1923 and she was paroled on January 9, 1925. She later married a druggist and moved to Colorado. The news account concludes that throughout the 25 years which intervened between her husband's murder when she was 22, and the story about her when she was 47, she never confessed to having had any part in Clarence Myers' death.[37]

Two Missouri wives were prosecuted in the 1930s for the murder of their husbands. In Wayne County, 42-year-old Louise Myers poisoned her husband by giving him tomato wine laced with arsenic, and after consuming several of these drinks, he died on April 15, 1939. Initially Mrs. Myers pled not guilty at a court proceeding, which began on August 14, 1939, but after a jury was selected, she pled guilty, and the judge sentenced her to MSP for life. The Missouri Department of Corrections records clarify that Louise Myers (Inmate No. 52798) was found guilty of first degree murder, and she was paroled on March 10, 1952.[38]

The better known case is that of 34-year-old Mrs. Myrtle Bennett, who shot and killed her 36-year-old husband, John G. Bennett, on September 29, 1929, at their Park Manor apartment at 902 Ward Parkway, Kansas City. The Bennetts and another couple, Mayme and Charles Hofman, were playing bridge. The same day as the homicide, a local newspaper announced that it would offer lessons in this most demanding of all card games. It wrote, "Nearly everyone wants to learn to play good bridge. Many are playing already without any particular knowledge of the rules of the game, the standard conventions, and without real knowledge of how to bid or play the hand."[39] Among those who might have profited from lessons was John Bennett. At the bridge party at his and his wife's apartment that same evening, he bid one spade, and his partner-wife raised him to four spades, or game. One of the opponents doubled, and the victim did not make his bid. He went set two tricks. Mrs. Bennett let her husband know that she considered him a poor player; he should have made four spades. He in turn slapped her, folded the bridge table, and the Hofmans left the Bennetts' apartment. About 20 minutes later, John Bennett was dead. His wife, Myrtle Bennett, had gone into a bedroom, returned with a revolver, and fired it four times. Two of the bullets hit and killed her husband. She was charged with first degree murder. Her case finally went to trial 18 months later. She chose her defense team well. Her lead attorney was James Reed, a former U.S. Senator from Missouri. After 10 days of testimony by both sides, the all-white-male jury deliberated eight hours and found the defendant not guilty. It believed that the shooting of her husband was justifiable homicide, the result of an accident, and in self-defense.[40]

The next known first degree murder prosecution here of a female was a wholly different matter. On September 28, 1953, a well-dressed 41-year-old woman, Bonnie Brown Heady, appeared at Notre Dame de Sion School, a private Catholic school, located at 3823 Locust Street, Kansas City, where six-year-old Robert C. (Bobby) Greenlease was a student. The woman told the nun that she was Bobby's aunt and had been shopping with Bobby's mother, Mrs. Virginia Greenlease, on the Plaza, a fashionable shopping center a mile or so from the school. The visitor told the sister that Mrs. Greenlease had had a heart attack and been taken to a hospital and his mother wanted her young son at her bedside. The sister suggested that while she was obtaining Bobby from his classroom, the aunt go into the school chapel to pray for Mrs. Greenlease. The visitor went into the sanctuary, kneeled, and afterwards said, "I'm not a Catholic ... but it did me good to pray."[41] Perhaps had Notre Mere Marie Irene de Sion, the mother superior of the school, been present, the results would have differed. However, she was at a teachers' meeting in Columbia. The nun released the child to the impostor-aunt. Afterwards, the sister phoned the Greenlease residence, and Mrs. Virginia Greenlease answered. Bobby's mother assured her caller she had not had a heart attack. Immediately the nun phoned the police.

Meanwhile, Bonnie Brown Heady and the boy left the school as the impostor had arrived at it, in a cab. The driver deposited them a few blocks away at Katz Drug Store, 40th and Main streets. There they left the cab and got in a late model blue Ford with a Kansas license plate. Its driver was Carl Austin Hall. He was the son of a prominent attorney in Pleasanton, Kansas, who died in 1932. His son served in the Marines during World War II. Following his mother's death in 1944, Hall squandered a $200,000 inheritance in two years. By April 1953, he was both an ex-convict and a severe alcoholic.

On September 28, 1953, Hall and his passengers, Bonnie Brown Heady and Bobby

Greenlease, drove west on Westport Road from Missouri into Kansas. When they reached a field (at what is now 95th Street and Metcalf Avenue), Hall first tried to strangle the child, and then shot and killed him. His accomplice left her hat at the crime scene. They put the dead child back in the car and drove with him to St. Joseph. In this city, Hall had already dug their victim's grave in the garden of Bonnie Brown Heady's home at 1201 South 38th Street. The same day the two kidnapped the child, they buried him beneath her chrysanthemums. They then began their request for ransom from the child's wealthy 71-year-old father, Robert C. Greenlease, an automobile dealer. They asked for and received $600,000 in 10- and 20-dollar bills. They assured the Greenlease parents that "If [you] do exactly as we say and try no tricks, your boy will be back safe within 24 hrs. after we check money."[42] Hall and Heady were arrested in St. Louis on October 6, 1953, when the two, awash in alcohol and vast quantities of money, attracted the attention of an alert cab driver. By November 1953, both had confessed their crime, a federal offense, the violation of the Lindbergh kidnapping statute, which carried a possible death sentence if the victim was transported from one state to another and not returned unharmed. At their arraignment, they both pled guilty.

The only remaining issue for their all-white-male jury at the federal court house in Kansas City was their punishment. The jury was chosen from many of the rural counties which make up the jurisdiction of the federal court of the Western District of Missouri. No member was a resident of Kansas City, or even of Jackson County. The proceedings began on November 16 with its selection, and on November 19, the jury recommended death for both. Judge Albert L. Reeves, aged 79 years, sentenced them to die on December 18, 1953, in the gas chamber at MSP in Jefferson City. This was the first use the federal government made of this state-operated killing machine. It would be used a second time when Arthur Brown was gassed to death in 1956 for the kidnapping and murder of Wilma Allen, the wife of an automobile dealer, who was also abducted in Missouri, driven to Kansas, and murdered there. There was no appeal for Hall and Heady. Eighty-one days after they kidnapped and murdered Bobby Greenlease, they died wearing bathing suits in the MSP gas chamber, on December 18, 1953.[43]

They wished to be interred together. They were not. On the morning of December 19, 1953, she was buried in a Maryville, Missouri cemetery beside her parents, French P. Brown (1878–1949) and Mabel E. Brown (1881–1914), with highway patrolmen in attendance. About this same time, Carl Austin Hall was consigned to the grave in a small Kansas town about 175 miles away.[44] It seems likely that had alcoholic Bonnie Brown Heady not met alcoholic Carl Austin Hall, she would never have been a part of the kidnapping and murder of six-year-old Bobby Greenlease. In April 1953, Hall had been paroled from MSP after serving 15 months of his five-year sentence for robbing taxicab drivers in Kansas City. Approximately a month later, this divorced and childless woman—one without brothers, sisters, and living parents—met ex-convict Hall in May 1953 at the Pony Express Bar in St. Joseph. Almost immediately they began living together in her home in this same town. Four and ½ months later, she walked into Notre Dame de Sion School pretending to be her victim's aunt. A trusting nun, who saw no evil where no evil seemed, allowed the child to leave the school. Before the year 1953 had ended, the second free woman in Missouri's history was executed. She died in the MSP gas chamber under a federal, not a state, death warrant.

No other known woman in Missouri was sentenced to die until after the method of execution had changed from the gas chamber to lethal injection. In recent times, on five occasions a jury has found a woman guilty of first degree murder here and assessed her punishment at death. None have been executed. Their crimes all took place in the late 1980s in five different counties. In two cases, the defendants are now deceased; in the other three they are serving a life sentence in a Missouri prison without possibility of parole.

On August 28, 1987, George Wacaser took a phone message for his wife, Nyla Jean Wacaser, from the attorney who had represented her in her custody battle over her two sons with her ex-husband, Bobby Lee Williams, of St. Joseph. The attorney left word that the judge had awarded custody of 11-year-old Jeremy and eight-year-old Eric to their father. The lawyer neither spoke directly to their mother nor stated that an appeal could be taken from the judge's decision. The husband told his wife what the attorney had told him. That same evening, Nyla Jean Wacaser bought her sons Happy Meals at McDonalds' and took them to a Motel 6 near N.W. Barry Road and Interstate 29, a locale in Platte County. She registered under a false name, and there she stabbed both her children to death, Eric 15 times and Jeremy 39. Initially she was charged with two counts of first degree murder, but the prosecutor proceeded only on the charge relating to Eric. Her jury found her guilty, but it could not agree on her punishment. Her trial judge sentenced her to death; under current law he could only return a life sentence. On appeal, the Missouri Supreme Court reversed because a juror, Mr. Beavers, had stated that he would tend to impose a death sentence in a case in which a child was murdered. The appellate court ruled that Beavers should have been dismissed for cause. It reversed and remanded for a new trial.

Wacaser's second trial began in April 1992 in Platte City. The jury rejected the defense's explanation of the children's murder: long-standing depression and a sleeping pill, Halcion, which their mother was taking at the time of her crime, caused her to kill her boys. The prosecutor argued that she acted out of anger and vengeance against her ex-husband. On May 8, 1992, the jury found her guilty of first degree murder. The punishment phase was set for May 9, but the jury never deliberated. Wacaser, aged 43 years, was found dead in her cell in the Platte County jail of a drug overdose early that same morning. She had attempted suicide as a teenager, and her father had killed himself. The defense attorney who went to the Platte County courthouse to argue for her life attended her funeral in St. Louis.[45]

The most widely covered of the women's death sentences was Faye Copeland's in Livingston County. She and her husband, Ray, were charged with the first degree murder of five homeless transients, Paul Cowart, John Freeman, Jimmie Harvey, Dennis Murphy, and Wayne Warner, between 1986 and 1989. The prosecutor's theory of the case was that the husband and wife were both involved in a fraudulent check and cattle buying and selling scheme. Ray recruited his victims at various homeless shelters throughout the state. From his and his wife's home in Mooreville, Ray would take the drifter to a nearby town where the homeless man would open a post office box and a checking account, using Copeland funds. Later, Ray's new employee bought cattle at various stock auctions and paid for them with a check on the account, which had insufficient funds. Immediately afterwards Ray sold the cattle and killed his employee before authorities could investigate the fraud involving cattle purchases and bad checks. This plan worked well enough five times, and then it unraveled. A sixth man, Jack McCormick, a recovering alcoholic whom Ray Copeland recruited from the Victory Mission in Springfield, lived to call a crime-stoppers hot line.

With a backhoe, other body-exhuming equipment, and various search warrants, workers acting at the behest of law enforcement officers dug up dead bodies where Ray had been a handyman. Among other evidence recovered in the Copeland home was a handwritten list of names; three of them were victims who had an X beside their names. The list was in Faye's handwriting. Other evidence tied Faye to the scheme, such as a bank starter-check and a signed bank check found in her purse. Clothing of the dead men was recovered from the closet of the Copelands' guest bedroom. Both the husband and wife were arrested, tried separately on five counts of first degree murder, and separately sentenced to death. On appeal, the Missouri Supreme Court affirmed both death sentences. It wrote of Faye Copeland's case that there was overwhelming evidence of the "defendant's involvement in the deliberate murder of five victims, including more than two hundred exhibits, testimony by sixty witnesses, and a trial that extended over six days."[46] At her trial the defense had offered to prove through the testimony of a Kansas City psychologist that Faye was suffering from battered spouse syndrome. The lower court barred this evidence, and when affirming her death sentence, the Missouri Supreme Court upheld the trial judge's exclusion. It noted that neither at common law nor under Missouri statutes was duress or coercion by a husband a defense to the wife's murder of a third party or parties.

The unusual feature of the Copelands' death sentences was their age. By the time of their first court appearances, he was 76 and she was 69. Given the length of the appellate review in modern capital cases, the odds were seen as overwhelming that neither would live long enough to be executed. Critics argued that politics was at work, and the $200,000 which Livingston County was spending on seeking death sentences in this elderly couple's cases could better be spent on more worthy projects. Ray Copeland had agreed to a plea bargain in exchange for life imprisonment for him and his wife, but the judge removed the prosecutor who negotiated the agreement.[47] Neither Ray nor Faye lived to be executed. He died a natural death at Potosi Correctional Center on October 19, 1993, aged 78 years. In 1999 a federal district court in Kansas City overturned her death sentence because the jury had not heard evidence of the battered woman syndrome. The state appealed this decision, and the Eighth Circuit federal court of appeals upheld the district court's decision. It noted, among other matters, the impropriety of the prosecutor's closing arguments. Assistant Attorney General Kenny Hulshof had told Faye Copeland's jury during the penalty phase, among other matters, that she used the clothing of the dead men to make quilts. Was there physical evidence of such quilt-making on Faye's part or did Hulshof invent the story? The federal appeals court specifically objected to his wildly hyperbolic statement to her jury: "There has never, ever been a more complete and utter disregard for the sanctity of human life as in [Faye Copeland's] case."[48] This court required that the state either hold a new sentencing hearing or commute Faye Copeland's punishment to life imprisonment without possibility of parole.[49]

At the time her death sentence was overturned, she was 78 years old; reputedly, she had been the oldest woman on any death row in the United States. Certainly, she was older than any known person put to death in the history of Missouri. In 2002 she suffered a stroke that left her partially paralyzed and unable to speak. She had become imprisoned within her own body. At this point, she became eligible for a medical parole. It is available to a prisoner in Missouri with a terminal illness or one in need of long-term nursing care.[50] Shortly, she was moved to Morning Center Nursing home in Chillicothe. On December 30, 2003, Faye Copeland, aged 82 years, mother of six, grandmother of 12 or more, and great-grandmother of five or more, died a natural death in this facility. The announcement of her passing was made by the Missouri Department of Corrections.[51]

Three other women sentenced to death here in the 1990s committed their crimes within 18 months of each other. One of their cases also involved a husband and wife acting together, but the proof of this crime was not the circumstantial case which ensnared the Copelands. On November 6, 1989, in the city of St. Louis, 46-year-old Maria Isa and her husband, 57-year-old Zein Isa, stabbed to death their youngest daughter, 16-year-old Palestina, or Tina, because she was dating an African-American and had gotten a job at a Wendy's restaurant. Next, the parents phoned various relatives that Tina had attacked them in an attempt to obtain $5,000 from them and they had killed her in self-defense. Their daughter was a person of great promise. She spoke fluent Arabic, Portuguese, Spanish, and English; she also excelled as a student at Roosevelt High School, where she played on the school's soccer and tennis teams. Although Tina was an immensely successful young American, her parents saw her as breaking their rules and escaping from their control. Her Father was a Palestinian Muslim, and her mother a Brazilian Catholic.

Unknown to the family, the U.S. government suspected that Zein Isa was a potential terrorist. Prior to the murder of their daughter and with the approval of a federal court, the FBI had placed audio surveillance equipment in the Isa apartment and tapped their phone lines. In effect, the entire conversation between Tina and her parents as the mother held her daughter while her husband stabbed the child, and their subsequent phone calls to establish their defense, were tape recorded. At their trial their lawyers sought to exclude this explosive evidence, but a federal appeals court upheld the surveillance and the admissibility of its results at the state trial of Tina's parents for her murder.[52] As a result, the main portions of the prosecutor's case were tape recordings.

The transcript of the tapes contained in the Missouri Supreme Court decision is chilling reading, and the jury was surely horrified as it listened to them. It found both parents guilty of first degree murder, and it assessed their punishment as death. On appeal, the appellate court affirmed Maria Isa's conviction, but it held that permitting "the jury to consider Zein Isa's conduct when assessing Maria Isa's punishment" was prejudicial error.[53] On February 17, 1997, Zein Isa, aged 65 years, died a natural death while a resident of Missouri's death row at Potosi. At a subsequent hearing in May 1997, Maria Isa was sentenced to life imprisonment without possibility of parole.[54] She is currently an inmate at the Women's Eastern Reception, Diagnostic, and Correction Center in Vandalia.

Two other women were sentenced to death here in the 1990s when separate juries found them guilty of first degree murder. One of their crimes took place in Pettis County, when, on May 4, 1988, 26-year-old Virginia Twenter shot and killed her father, J.D. Wells, and her stepmother, Marilyn Wells. Her motive was financial. She was badly in debt. Her father was demanding repayment of a loan; her car had been repossessed, and she was behind in her house payments. Five days before the murders, Twenter bought a new car with a $4,400 bad check. The dealer called her and insisted the check be made good. The same day the victim's bodies were discovered, the perpetrator gave the car dealer a check for $4,400 and one to a bank for $4,000, signed by her stepmother, Marilyn Wells, on the account of a restaurant, the Coffee Pot Café, which J.D. Wells, her father, owned. When interrogated by the police and at trial, Twenter stated that her parents had loaned her $8,400 during the early evening of May 4, 1988, and at that time both were alive and well. The state's evidence, among much else, showed that she did not have a good relationship with her father. In addition, the police found the murder weapon, and a ballistics expert linked the bullets which killed the victims to a pistol owned by Hugo Twenter, the perpetrator's ex-husband. He had noticed his gun was not in his truck as he left his ex-wife's residence in April 1988. He had reported that it was missing to law enforcement officers prior to the murders. The defendant could not verify her whereabouts on the night of the crime. At her trial on two counts of first degree murder, the jury found Virginia Twenter guilty. It assessed her punishment at life imprisonment without possibility of parole for 50 years for the murder of her father and death for the murder of her stepmother. On appeal, the Missouri Supreme Court affirmed her conviction, but it remanded for a new hearing on the penalty phase.[55] She was subsequently sentenced to life imprisonment without possibility of parole. She is currently housed at Chillicothe Correctional Center.

The final woman sentenced to death here as of this writing was 55-year-old Shirley Jo Phillips. In February 1992 she was found guilty of the first degree murder of 66-year-old Wilma Plaster of Hollister, on what the authorities believe was October 3, 1989. The women had been friends about a year prior to Phillips' cashing a check for $4,050 written to her on Plaster's account. According to a handwriting expert who testified at Phillips' trial on murder charges, the victim's signature was forged. Soon after this check was cashed, Plaster was murdered. Her dismembered remains were found on October 6, 1989, strewn on a country road in Greene County. Shortly, Phillips was arrested. The evidence of her guilt included large amounts of blood in the perpetrator's car and trunk, her bloody boots, the murder weapon, and the victim's cancelled checks, among other items, in a trash bag with Phillips' fingerprints on it. Among the aggravating factors the jury found when sentencing her to death was the dismemberment of her victim's body. The defense blamed Phillips' son, 32-year-old Glenn "Buddy" Minster, for both killing and dismembering Plaster.[56] On appeal, the Missouri Supreme Court affirmed Phillips' conviction, but it ordered a new penalty hearing because the trial judge excluded the statement of a witness who said that Buddy had told her that he, not his mother, had cut up Wilma Plaster's body. The appellate decision mentions that Buddy was employed both as a butcher and in the euthanasia room of the Humane Society. In addition, he had a criminal record, and he had earlier abused both drugs and alcohol. At a subsequent hearing, Shirley Jo Phillips was sentenced to life imprisonment.[57] She also is an inmate at Chillicothe Correctional Center.

Whether or not the reluctance to execute women in Missouri will continue is an open question. As of this writing, there are no women among the 53 inmates on Missouri's death row. Only six females in the history of the state can be confirmed, and none more recently than 1953. Under current law, no judge can sentence anyone, including a woman, to death if the jury cannot agree that the defendant shall die by lethal injection. As of 2005, an appellate court, either state or federal, has, at a minimum, required either a new trial or another penalty phase hearing. None of the five who committed their crimes in the 1980s will be executed; two are dead, and the other three are in prison for the remainder of their natural lives.

No Missouri governor has commuted a woman's death sentence in the past 100 years. The next chapter describes the history of commutations and pardons in this state. It extends over a period of 196 years.

11

Pardons and Commutations, 1803–1999

Over a period of more than 200 years, the executive authority has issued at least 128 commutations and/or pardons of death sentences for crimes committed on the land which now comprises the state of Missouri. The word *commutation* has a legal meaning of a change of sentence to one that is less severe. The legal meaning of the word *pardon* is the release of the person from additional punishment. The word *reprieve* has an older meaning of commutation of a capital sentence. Under the U.S. Constitution, the President has the power to grant "Reprieves and Pardons for Offenses against the United States."[1] The framers of the original Missouri Constitution of 1820 adopted identical language; they gave the governor the power to grant reprieves and pardons for offenses against the state of Missouri.[2] All subsequent Missouri constitutions retain the same gubernatorial powers pertaining to crimes under state law. Some acts of the governors' clemency have been discussed in the previous three chapters; most have not. The majority took place in the nineteenth century and early decades of the twentieth, or at a time when the federal courts usually did not review state court convictions. Even more rarely did the courts of the United States grant relief to persons sentenced to death under state law.

As mentioned in Chapter 1, the first known pardon for a capital crime committed in Missouri was under Spanish authority. The governor-general, headquartered in New Orleans, determined that only one of the five Indians found guilty in the capital city of the January 28, 1802, murder of David Trotter in Upper Louisiana should be put to death. At approximately the same time that a firing squad shot to death the ringleader, Tewanaye, in New Madrid District, the other four braves who participated in Trotter's murder were pardoned by being released to their chiefs on a pledge of good behavior.

The Spanish exonerated these Creek warriors for the same reason that President Jefferson adopted the policy of never allowing the execution of more than two Indians for the murder of one white man. Alliances could be formed with these tribes against various European powers. As noted in Chapter 1, Jefferson's appointee as governor of Louisiana Territory, James Wilkinson, followed his commander-in-chief's wishes, and he pardoned the Kickapoo Indian, Hononquise, at the same time two other Kickapoos were hanged on June 10, 1806, in St. Louis, for the December 30, 1805 murder of a white man near the Osage River.[3] In 1808 in *U.S. v Little Crow*, a St. Louis jury found the defendant, a Sac, guilty of the murder of Antoine Le Page, a white man, in St. Charles County. The judges set the date for his hanging two days later. Initially, Governor Lewis reprieved Little Crow because there then was no resolution of an unrelated case against two Ioways, Mera Naute and White Cloud. In 1808, the same year Little Crow was found guilty, another St. Louis jury found the two Ioways guilty of the murder of Marechal and Thibault, also white. The Ioway Indians were confined in the St. Louis jail with the Sac, and the Ioways managed to escape. Acting Governor Frederick Bates decided against recapturing them because, it had been determined in subsequent proceedings, the American government lacked jurisdiction to try them. Knowing the importance to American interests of avoiding favoring one tribe over another, the U.S. Indian agent, William Clark, recommended that the President pardon Little Crow. On February 25, 1810, President Madison granted him a "full free and entire pardon ... in consideration of the promise of the said Sac Tribe to behave well in the future."[4] As noted in Chapter 1, both Spanish and American officials treated Indians with fairness, if not leniency. As a result, the recipients of the first six known pardons for capital offenses in Missouri were Indians. The Spanish governor-general granted the first four, President Jefferson the fifth, and President Madison the sixth. All were awarded for sound political reasons. Nonetheless, when William Clark stood for election as governor of Missouri in 1820, as his recent biographer, Foley, explains, "Clark's critics cited the pardon [of Little Crow] as an example of his pro–Indian leanings."[5] His opponent, Alexander McNair, not the famous explorer, William Clark, of the Corps of Discovery, won 61 percent of the vote.

Other U.S. Presidents issued pardons and/or commutations for men found guilty of capital offenses against the United States in courts-martial, military commissions, and civilian trials held in Missouri. In 1829, President Andrew Jackson allowed three men to live who were condemned to death. A Missouri newspaper carried mention of the President's pardon of William Hustoff, alias William Hart, in April of that year, and in September, of James Richardson and Robert Furguson; all three had been sentenced to death for desertion. Their courts-martial took place in Jefferson Barracks in St. Louis. The President directed that these men be set free and never again permitted to join the army.[6] The following year, 1830, the U.S. Congress exempted deserters in time of peace from the punishment of death.[7] A Missouri newspaper carried an account of how soldiers who deserted in peacetime from the U.S. Army were punished immediately prior to the commencement of war with Mexico; they received 50 lashes with a rawhide whip, were branded on a cheek with the Letter D, and drummed out of the service.[8]

In a case discussed in Chapter 1, that of the murder of the Mexican merchant, Antonio Chavez, in what is now Rice County, Kansas, the capital case against the offenders was tried in St. Louis. In 1844, Supreme Court Justice John Catron, then riding circuit, sentenced four men to hang: John McDaniel, David McDaniel (John's younger brother), Joseph Brown, and Thomas Towson. Pleas for executive clemency began shortly. In June 1844, President John Tyler pardoned David McDaniel and Towson.[9] Fourteen months later, on August 16, 1845, John McDaniel and Brown were hanged in St. Louis.

During the Civil War, President Lincoln issued three known pardons to men sentenced to death in Missouri, and General Rosecrans rescinded a death sentence of a Missourian, which the President had earlier approved; his rescission was as a result of a subsequent order. There were probably more than these four; those that can be identified all occurred in 1864. On November 2, 1863, a military commission in Jefferson City found James Johnson guilty of being a guerrilla outlaw, robber, violating his oath of allegiance, and other charges. It ordered that he be put to death. On February 10, 1864, President Lincoln approved. On May 13, 1864, Rosecrans rescinded the sentence of death in the case of James Johnson.[10] On November 13, 1863, in Jefferson City, a military commission found

Francis Norvell, a citizen of Missouri, guilty of being a guerrilla and sentenced him to be shot to death with musketry at such time and place as the General Command might direct. Shortly thereafter, several Union Army generals had second thoughts. The prisoner was young, aged 21 years, and he had voluntarily surrendered. The generals recommended that Norvell be released upon taking the oath of allegiance and giving satisfactory bond. General Rosecrans forwarded his high-ranking subordinates' recommendations in *U.S. v Norvell* for the action of the President. On April 27, 1864, A. Lincoln signed his approval.[11] During 1863, another military commission in St. Joseph tried Henry Ogle of Andrew County, found him guilty of being connected with a shooting in his county, and sentenced him to be shot. In June 1864, a St. Joseph newspaper carried stories on different dates that "after a thorough examination of the evidence in the case, Mr. Lincoln directed the sentence of the Commission to be set aside." It added editorially, "Honest Old Abe has set him all right."[12] Mention was made in Chapter 3 of General Rosecrans' intention to even the score for the murder of James Wilson, a major in the Union Army, with one of equivalent rank from the other side. When Enoch Wolf, a major in the Confederate Army, was captured, the general ordered his execution to take place in St. Louis on November 11, 1864. Some concerned citizens of this city contacted Lincoln, and the President wired Rosecrans to suspend putting Wolf to death. This Confederate officer was never executed.

After the Union Army's last use of capital punishment here in June 1865, there were no known military death sentences in Missouri until 1951. In October of that year, three soldiers, stationed at Fort Leonard Wood in Pulaski County, were tried at this army post. All three were found guilty of the murder near the base during the course of a robbery of a Waynesville taxicab driver, Harry Langley, on September 21. The driver was found beaten beside his cab; he died the next day. The victim was white; and the perpetrators were all Negroes and privates: James Riggins, 24, Tallahassee, Florida; Louis Suttles, 24, Chattanooga, Tennessee; and Chastine Beverly, 22, Balty, Virginia. Today, these men would be tried in a civilian court, but this was not the law in 1951.[13] The local newspaper congratulated the citizens on avoiding a race riot.[14] The court-martial was open to the public, and it averaged about 30 civilians and military personnel during six days of testimony.[15] Shortly after their convictions and death sentences, they were taken from Fort Leonard Wood, Missouri, to the disciplinary barracks at Fort Leavenworth, Kansas, where they remained until their deaths.

Requests for clemency were initially made to Harry Truman, President, when the three were sentenced; letters to him from the mothers of each of the condemned soldiers are extant and dated October 13, 1951, August 11, 1952, and September 15, 1952.[16] On October 31, 1953, the federal court for the District of Kansas denied the habeas corpus pleas of the three death-sentenced African-Americans.[17] In September 1954, the Tenth Circuit Court of Appeals upheld the district court, and in December 1954 and January 1955, the U.S. Supreme Court denied a request for a hearing and a rehearing.[18]

Appeals for executive clemency from the mothers of the three soldiers and others to President Eisenhower date from June 8, 1953 to early 1955. They did not succeed; he approved the sentences of these men.[19] On March 1, 1955, each of the three was separately executed by hanging on a gallows constructed in a warehouse of the Kansas state penitentiary in Lansing. At this time, an army regulation barred the use of Missouri's gas chamber. It required that a military death sentence be carried into effect by shooting or hanging.[20] A newspaper account lists Chastine Beverly, 25, Balty, Virginia; James Riggins, 28, Birmingham, Alabama; and Louis Suttles, 26, Chattanooga, Tennessee, as being individually brought in a motor car from the disciplinary barracks at Fort Leavenworth. The men were dressed in an army uniform without decoration or insignia. Each was led to the gallows by a deputy warden, two prison guards, and three military guards. The first hanging, Beverly's, began a few minutes after midnight, and the last, that of Suttles, had concluded by 1:17 a.m. The spectators included three official witnesses.[21]

This dead of night execution of three black men for the murder of one white must be seen as a product of political timidity. Both the Truman and the Eisenhower administrations correctly anticipated the immense white rage of the early and mid–1950s certain to erupt if any mercy were shown these African-Americans. Race relations during these years were on the boil. Truman had integrated the Armed Forces in 1948; Eisenhower's appointee as Chief Justice of the United States, Earl Warren, in May 1954, had written a unanimous decision for the High Court which desegregated public schools, *Brown* v. *Board*. The murder of Emmett Till, the subsequent acquittal of the men charged with his murder in state court in Mississippi, and the failure of the U.S. Department of Justice to proceed against these self-confessed white killers of a black child were all just around the corner when the warehouse hangings occurred. Excluding the Civil War era and its decimal system of executions, or the 10 for one plan, there are only two other known instances in Missouri's history wherein three men were put to death for the murder of one. In the earlier executions, the three perpetrators were Italian; one trio was hanged in St. Louis in 1876 and the other in Kansas City in 1930. The third triple hanging for the murder of one man in Missouri took place in another state. The length of time between the killing of the white cabdriver in or near Waynesville, Missouri, and the execution of the black perpetrators in a warehouse in the Kansas state penitentiary three and one-half years later suggests that the Democratic President, Harry Truman, and the Republican, Dwight Eisenhower, considered granting some form of executive clemency, but the advisers of both men feared political ramifications if any lessening of these black soldiers' punishment took place. None did.

The remainder of the known pardons and all known commutations of death sentences in this state were either the acts of the governors or, in a few instances, an acting governor or a lieutenant governor. Pardons and commutations discussed in early chapters are not included herein. Overwhelmingly, the beneficiaries of executive clemency were found guilty of murder. In the earliest instances of sparing men sentenced to hang, the governor usually pardoned the offender. The first of which we have knowledge was in 1824;[22] the Missouri State Penitentiary had not yet been built. Often the surviving documents of executive clemency from the nineteenth century are sparse. Each of these governors either commuted one or more death sentences to prison terms and/or pardoned the criminal once he had spent time at MSP: Governors Boggs (1836–1840),[23] Reynolds (1840–1844),[24] King (1848–1853),[25] Price (1853–1857),[26] Stewart (1857–1861),[27] Gamble (1861–1864),[28] Hall (1864–1865),[29] Fletcher (1865–1869),[30] Brown (1871–1873),[31] Hardin (1875–1877),[32] and Phelps (1877–1881).[33] In none of these 11 governors' acts of executive clemency does the psychosis or the innocence of the defendant appear to have been a factor.

The insanity of the condemned prompted a number of Missouri's chief executive officers to commute a death sentence. The earliest such defendant was Hartford Mitchell. He was sentenced to hang in St. Louis in 1833 for the murder of Mr. Graves. Governor Dunklin (1832–1836) pardoned him and allowed the crazy man to leave by steamboat with relatives for Kentucky. An uncle of Hartford vouched for his safety; he assured the governor that if there was no improvement in the deranged young man's condition, he would be sent to a lunatic asylum. Nonetheless, the citizens were so outraged by Dunklin's pardon that 1,000 of them assembled in St. Louis and burned Daniel Dunklin in effigy to protest it. The governor wrote the editor of the *Jeffersonian Republican* that the Missouri Constitution provided for exceptions to the general rule that culprits convicted of capital crimes should be publicly executed. The editor also printed in this same issue a number of letters supportive of Dunklin's action; writers included a minister, a physician, and others knowledgeable about the mental aberrations of the pardoned man. As for Mitchell Hartford, he died less than a year later in Bowling Green, Kentucky.[34]

More than 160 years later, Governor Mel Carnahan commuted Bobby Shaw's death sentence to life imprisonment without possibility of parole. Shaw was already a prison inmate in Missouri when he committed his capital offense of killing a guard, Walter Farrow. He was sentenced to death, and the Missouri Supreme Court upheld his death sentence. His attorney, Sean O'Brien, convinced the governor that the condemned was not a fit subject for lethal injection; Shaw expected to eat breakfast after he had been put to death. According to O'Brien, the governor waited to announce his decision regarding Shaw until Carnahan's political rival, William Webster, was on the stand in a federal courtroom in Kansas City pleading guilty to two felony counts of public corruption. The governor knew that Webster's guilty plea would appear, in the parlance of newspapers, above-the-fold and his sparing a man's life would be printed in a less conspicuous location in the newspapers, or below-the-fold. As with Mitchell who died soon after his pardon, so too with Bobby Shaw; he died a natural death in prison on January 26, 2000.[35]

Between one governor's pardon of a murderer in 1833 on grounds of insanity and another's commutation for this same reason, of one capitally convicted of murder more than 150 years later, Missouri's governors have believed the condemned was crazy in a sizeable number of cases. As a result, they have pardoned him or commuted his death sentence to a prison term. Almost invariably the juries before whom these cases were tried disbelieved that the accused was insane. Its members collectively thought that any manifestation of madness on the part of the defendant was a pretense. Accordingly, the jury found an insane man guilty of murder, and he was sentenced to hang. The Missouri Supreme Court affirmed his conviction; it was usually not willing to substitute its judgment for the jurors who both observed the defendant and heard the testimony about his mental state. Governor King in 1849[36] and 1850[37]; Price in 1854[38]; Morehouse in 1888[39]; Francis in 1889 or 1890[40]; Stone in 1893[41] and 1895[42]; Stephens in 1897 or 1898[43]; Folk in 1907[44]; Hyde in 1924[45]; and Park in 1935[46] spared the lives of men sentenced to death. They became convinced that, either because of insanity, senility, or retardation, a person about to be put to death was mentally unfit to be executed. Almost certainly there are other cases wherein the mental state of the defendant was the reason he was spared the noose. Generally, the governors have been correct. The beneficiary of executive clemency was not pretending to be of unsound mind; he had serious mental problems.

Innocence, grave doubts about the guilt of the condemned, ineffective assistance of counsel, and perjury on the part of the state's witnesses were other reasons that Missouri's governors commuted death sentences and/or pardoned the condemned. Cases involving one or more of these reasons for the governor preventing an execution survive from 1865, Fletcher[47]; 1886, Marmaduke[48]; 1895[49] and 1896, Stone[50]; 1900, Stephens[51], and 1905, Folk[52]. Today, attorneys for the accused would take such issues to a federal court on a writ of habeas corpus, but all of these cases occurred well before those sentenced to death obtained relief in a court of the United States.

Only one governor is now remembered as an infamous pardoner. Chapter 3 mentioned that Lt. Colonel Thomas Crittenden, an officer in the Union Army, had presided at a drumhead court-martial, of which no written record survives. At it, he found two men, Dr. Zimmerman and Frederick Hamilton, guilty of stealing horses, and on Crittenden's orders these men were shot to death two days later at 5:00 a.m. at Tipton, Moniteau County, on September 25, 1863. Less than 20 years later, Thomas Crittenden was elected governor of Missouri; he served from 1881–1885. A bland directory of governors of the United States says of him, "Crittenden was persistent in his efforts to suppress outlawry in the state, and during his term the Jesse James Gang was broken up."[53] No details are supplied as to his precise methods of combating Missouri's most famous outlaw. This is what happened. Crittenden hired two gunmen, Robert and Charles or Charley Ford, to win the trust of Jesse James. They moved in with him, his wife and child, in St. Joseph, and at 9:30 a.m. on April 3, 1882, Robert fired the fatal shot as James, with his back to his assassin, dusted a picture on a wall in his parlor. Charles was charged with complicity in his brother's first degree murder of his victim. According to a contemporary news account, immediately after the shooting he sent a telegram to his benefactor, Governor Crittenden, and then he and his brother surrendered without any resistance.[54] Once they were taken into custody, they were placed in the Buchanan County jail in St. Joseph. On April 14, a newspaper reporter asked Charley, "Do you expect that you will be convicted of murder? He answered, "Oh probably so, but it will be all right one way or another. I expect to get pardoned."[55] This gunman knew what he was talking about. Three days later, on the morning of April 17, 1882, the Ford brothers pled guilty to first degree murder in Buchanan County Circuit Court, and the judge sentenced them to hang on May 19, 1882. According to Triplett, Governor Crittenden issued full and unconditional pardons to both the Fords at 3:45 p.m., or two hours and 15 minutes after they were sentenced to death.[56] Someone distorted the official record of Governor Crittenden's pardons. March 1882 was listed as the date of the Ford brothers' sentence; their victim, Jesse James, was alive and well the month prior to his murder. The reason for the Fords' pardon is explained as "Considerations of public policy."[57] Almost certainly, money which the railroads paid the governor and which he offered as a reward for the arrest of Jesse James wound up in the hands of these murderers. The criticism of Crittenden's unseemly speed began immediately. A few days after the Ford brothers were exonerated, the editor of the St. Joseph newspaper wrote, "We heartily wish the governor had been less hasty.... We wish he had seen in the dignity of his high office that a governor should move with calmness and composure in the exercise of the pardoning power.... We fear also that the governor has been too ostentatious of his disposition to grant this pardon. It smacks of politics to come."[58] The good life that the Ford brothers hoped to enjoy was brief. Slightly more than two years after his pardon, Charles Ford committed suicide at his father's home in Ray County; in 1892 Robert Ford was killed in Colorado by a James partisan.

At one time, a newspaper reporter asked me, "Who was the most recent person sentenced to death in Missouri who was pardoned? Who got lucky after the killers of Jesse James received their pardon?" I could not then and cannot now answer that question. The prison records which date from approximately the mid–1950s through the mid–1970s are not in possession of the Missouri State Archives. Rather, they are housed at the Fulton Reception-Diagnostic Center. Stephanie Shepherd, an employee in records at this facility, made a search of records which are neither in perfect chronological nor alphabetical order. Thanks to her efforts, we know what happened to four inmates whose death sentences various governors earlier commuted: Oscar Ashworth, Paul Barbata, Amos Carroll, and Rollie Laster. In 1968 Governor Warren Hearnes discharged from prison and restored the citizenship of Paul Barbata. This inmate may have been the most recent person death-sentenced person who legally left prison in Missouri as a result of the governor's act of executive clemency. However, either of two other inmates, Buford Cole and Marcus Goodwin, may have been released at a later date. Information regarding the discharge of Cole and Goodwin is not available.

Once the penitentiary began receiving inmates, few governors granted outright pardons to anyone. Those we know about were insane, and they were quickly gotten out of the state, if not the country. The vast majority of persons who, as a result of executive clemency, were not hanged or gassed to death spent a longer or shorter time at MSP. When the inmate was released, the press coverage of his departure from prison was not sensational, and the governor who effected the inmate's release from prison received little or no adverse publicity. Until the legislature changed the sentence for capital murder in the 1970s to death or life without possibility of parole, typically, one governor commuted a death sentence to term of years or life at MSP, and a few years or decades later another governor released that inmate from confinement. When the process begins, the word *pardon* regularly appeared in the prison records as an explanation of the inmate's discharge; eventually one governor *commuted* an earlier governor's commutation in order to allow the inmate's release. Then came the release of persons earlier sentenced to hang whose time in prison was cut short because they behaved themselves while they served 3/4ths of their sentence. Still later, the current governor *paroled* what an earlier chief executive commuted, and eventually a parole board appears to have been in charge of the inmate's release. However, no board of probation and parole has ever had the right to commute death sentences; the Missouri Constitution of 1820 gave that authority as well as the pardoning power to the governor, and they remain his exclusive prerogatives.

Following Crittenden's notorious pardon of Robert and Charles Ford in 1882, the sheer numbers of the death-sentenced here whose lives governors saved became a comment on capital punishment. As the numbers sentenced to death in Missouri increased in the 1880s, peaked during 1890s, and remained high through June 1908. Missouri's chief executives engaged in multiple acts of executive clemency. When the numbers of those sentenced to death subsided, so likewise did the commutations of death sentences. There is little to suggest that the governors were acting contrary to the wishes of their constituents when they stopped the tolling of the death knell. On the whole, the citizens seemed to approve the acts of mercy shown the condemned.

During the 1880s, in addition to the exoneration of Jesse James' killers, there were at least 11 other commutations and pardons. Only one of these was the action of a lieutenant governor, Robert Campbell. According to a biennial report, he became "satisfied from the evidence that [Joseph Degonia] was being unjustly punished," and Campbell pardoned him on April 14, 1882, see note 33. Perhaps Crittenden's lieutenant governor's pardon of an obscure convict whose death sentence Governor Phelps had earlier commuted was intended to distract attention from Crittenden's sensational pardon three days later of the Ford brothers. At any rate, the Buchanan County pardon was in the pipeline when Degonia left MSP a free man.

A new feature of executive clemency in the 1880s was the commutation of a black man's death sentence. If there were any earlier African-Americans sentenced to die in Missouri who escaped the sheriff's noose because the governor intervened, I have not discovered them. On March 16, 1885, Governor Marmaduke commuted Samuel Cook's death sentence. In a jealous rage which was exacerbated by his drinking problem, Cook killed Emma Shore, his lady friend, who was in the company of another man. Cook said of his deadly deed, "If that girl don't do me any good, she shall never do any other man any good." The county history, the appellate decision in the case, and the governor's report all state that Cook's victim was also black.[59]

Marmaduke commuted a total of eight known death sentences; one was a juvenile, noted in Chapter 8, another discussed in this chapter, note 48, and Samuel Cook, the first death-sentenced Negro shown executive clemency. The remaining five who were sent to MSP instead of being executed were white male murderers of a single white adult male victim. In four of these death sentences, two men were found guilt of the murder of one. The Missouri Supreme Court affirmed all five death sentences, and Marmaduke was motivated to allow these men to live because there were numerous citizen petitions in their behalf.[60] The first governor who followed Marmaduke, Albert Morehouse (1887–1889) commuted only one known death sentence, a mentally unstable person's, discussed in note 39. The next governor, David Francis (1889–1993), commuted two known death sentences, one of a mentally deranged person, discussed in note 40, and an abusive passenger on a train.[61] In four known cases, Governor Dockery (1901–1905) was merciful to those sentenced to death.[62]

Three of Missouri's governors, Joel Stone (1893–1897), Lawrence Stephens (1897–1901) and Joseph Folk (1905–1909), exercised executive clemency toward persons sentenced to death more frequently than any other men that ever served as this state's chief executive officer. Stone was an attorney, and as a young man he had been a prosecutor in Vernon County. He did not find the work to his liking. He preferred other employment. On at least one occasion he represented a man charged with murder in a jury trial, and he secured an acquittal for his client. It seems safe to assume that Stone had no particular enthusiasm for the death penalty, and he served as governor during the decade in which its use in Missouri was more frequent than during any other period. We know that he pardoned Thomas Brownfield, discussed in note 60, and James Payton, a juvenile discussed in Chapter 8. Probably Stone effected the release from MSP of other persons whom an earlier Missouri governor had spared the noose by commuting their death sentences. Stone's known commutations of death sentences include those of five black persons of color who killed other black persons,[63] and among his seven additional commutations were men whose sanity[64] or guilt[65] he doubted. In addition, Stone spared the lives of two other white men sentenced to death.[66]

Stone's successor in office, Lawrence "Lon" Stephens, commuted at least 10 death sentences to prison terms at MSP. An indication of the disfavor with which many Missourians now viewed capital punishment was that three of the men whose lives this governor spared were blacks who were convicted of the murder of white persons.[67] If any commutation or pardon had earlier issued in such a racial mix, I never located it. As discussed in chapter 10, Stephens pardoned two black women. The first was Sadie Hayes, a St. Louis City black woman who killed a white police officer while he was attempting to break up a fight between her and another black woman in 1883. The Missouri Supreme Court's reversal of her death sentence spared her life. She was sentenced to 99 years at MSP, and Stephens pardoned her in 1898. The other was Pearl Walters; she killed another black woman, and slightly over two years after Stephens commuted her death sentence to a term at MSP, he pardoned her. He also commuted the death sentences of two men who murdered their wives (one a gypsy[68] and the other a black),[69] and he spared the lives of four other death-sentenced male murderers: one from Boone[70]; another from Texas, tried on a change of venue in Greene[71]; one from St. Louis City,[72] and another from Holt County.[73]

Joseph Folk (1905–1909), governor when three men were hanged on June 27, 1907, for the killing of two prison guards, was the commuter of death sentences *par excellence*. During his administration, he released three men from MSP whom Governor Stephens had sent there rather than allowing them to hang.[74] Of equal, if not greater importance, between

March 1905 and May 1908, a period of 38 months, Folk commuted 14 known death sentences, including a man who killed a sheriff who attempted to arrest him. This is a greater number in a shorter time than during any period in Missouri's history. It will be remembered that in March 1907, jurors were given the choice in a first degree murder conviction of assessing the penalty at life imprisonment or death. Earlier, the trial judge instructed them that the penalty was not their concern. Without any exceptions, the 14 whose death sentences Folk commuted were all tried before jurors began assessing the penalty in first degree murder trials. Once members of the jury had a choice, Folk's commutation of death sentences ceased. None are known from his last six months in office. However, only two known men were hanged in the second half of 1908, and one of them killed five members of a family. Between 1905 and 1908, the times were right for the governor to commute death sentences and to do so with a frequency never seen in Missouri before or since. Some of Folk's commutations are discussed earlier, Fred Williams, note 52, and Agnes Myers and Frank Hottman, Chapter 10. The others are of men who killed a single victim, 11 in all. In one of Folk's commutations of death sentences, two men killed another. These cases occurred in nine counties: Jackson,[75] Dunklin,[76] Pemiscot,[77] Boone,[78] Iron,[79] Reynolds,[80] St. Louis,[81] city of St. Louis,[82] and De Kalb.[83]

In slightly more than the first 100 years of the death penalty in Missouri, or between 1803 and 1908, more than 80% of the known presidential and gubernatorial commutations and pardons were issued here. To be sure, the political career of William Clark was adversely affected by his recommendation that President Madison pardon the Indian, Little Crow. A St. Louis mob burned Governor Dunklin in effigy when it learned that he had pardoned an insane killer in 1833. When we look for the political ramifications of the flurry of commutations and pardons during the administrations of Stone, Stephens, and Folk, there were none. That they each served a single term has no significance; they, as well as the majority of Missouri's earlier governors, were limited by law to one term. We know that Missourians were growing increasingly dissatisfied with capital punishment. When George Vest, U.S. senator from Missouri (1879–1903), left office, the Missouri legislature replaced him with former governor Joel Stone. In 1908, Stone's challenger for his U.S. Senate seat was former governor Joseph Folk. It is not possible that either Stone or Folk accused the other of being soft on crime. Both men had made extensive use of the governor's power to commute and pardon, among others, those sentenced to death. Stone won his second term as a U.S. senator in the Missouri legislature. When he ran the last time, the 17th Amendment to the U.S. Constitution (1913) allowed the direct election of U.S. senators, and the people elected him to a third term. When Stone, by now chairman of the U.S. Senate Committee on Foreign Affairs, died in office on April 14, 1918,[84] capital punishment in Missouri had been abolished.

The build-up to the abolition of the death penalty began at least as early as Stone's election in 1892, and anti–capital punishment sentiment continued throughout the governorships of Stone, Stephens, Dockery, Folk, Hadley, Major, and Gardner. Governor Hadley (1909–1913) commuted two known death sentences, one from Greene County[85] and the other from Pike[86]; Governor Major (1913–1917) three, all from Jackson County[87]; and Governor Gardner (1917–1921) one, Ora Lewis,' from St. Louis City in 1918. In April 1917, the legislature had abolished capital punishment, but the Missouri Supreme Court ruled that the new law did not apply in his case. The governor believed, as a newspaper reported, that his execution would be "contrary to the will of the people as expressed in the new law." As a result, he commuted Ora Lewis' death sentence.[88] With Stone, Stephens, and Folk taking decisive leads, the seven men who served as governor of Missouri between 1893 and 1918, a period of 25 years, spared the lives of at least 43 known persons sentenced to death.

In contrast, between 1921 and 1999, a period of 78 years, 10 governors commuted 17 known death sentences. To be sure, fewer persons were put to death after the legislature restored capital punishment in 1919 than had been hanged in the previous 40 years. Nonetheless, once the county gallows returned, Missouri's governors were sparing in their use of executive clemency regarding those sentenced to death. During the 1920s, Governor Hyde (1921–1925) commuted the sentence of three men scheduled to hang[89]; his lieutenant governor, Lloyd, one,[90] and Governor Baker (1925–1929) one. Two were convicted of rape, one of Hyde's and the only one of Baker's; they are discussed in Chapter 9. During the 1930s and 1940s, the combined commutations of four governors saved the lives of eight men sentenced to death. Governor Caulfield (1929–1933) commuted one, an arsonist whose deliberate setting of a blaze killed a woman in a hotel fire in St. Louis[91]; Governor Park (1933–1937) spared three men. One of Park's commutations, an insane man's, is discussed in note 46; a second was a kidnapper, and the third was Amos Carroll.[92] Governor Stark (1937–1941) commuted the death sentences of three men, one of these was also a kidnapper and another killed another inmate and was subsequently put to death in the gas chamber.[93] In his first term, Governor Donnelly (1945–1949, 1953–1957) used executive clemency in one death penalty case,[94] and Governor Blair (1957–1961)[95] and Governor Dalton (1961–1965)[96] each commuted one death sentence.

Walter McGee's and Oscar Ashworth's commutations involve the only known men, two of them, in separate and unrelated cases, sentenced to death for kidnapping under Missouri law. In 1901, this crime became a potentially capital offense under state law. As mentioned in Chapter 7, its punishment range was five years to death. No one was sentenced to die for this crime until a sensational case took place in Jackson County. On May 27, 1933, four men, one never captured, Clarence Stevens, two brothers, George and Walter McGee, and Clarence Click, kidnapped Mary McElroy, the 24-year-old daughter of Henry McElroy, city manager of Kansas City during the tenure of Tom Pendergast as boss of the town. Most Missouri victims became newsworthy after someone committed a crime against them. As her father's daughter, Mary McElroy was already in the limelight before she was abducted from the family home at 21 West 57th Street, Kansas City. After a $30,000 ransom was paid, she was released unharmed within 48 hours. Meanwhile, three of her kidnappers were arrested, Walter McGee in Amarillo, Texas, on June 2, 1933. They were put on trial; George McGee and Clarence Click received prison terms. The jury sentenced Walter McGee to death, and he was taken to a death cell in the new Jackson County Courthouse at 12th and Oak streets. The Missouri Supreme Court affirmed his sentence, and he was scheduled to hang in the courthouse on May 31, 1935. In April 1935, Henry McElroy and his daughter traveled to Jefferson City, where they met with Governor Park. They asked that he commute Walter McGee's death sentence. By February 1935, she had already visited George McGee at MSP several times. Now Mary was her former abductors' most ardent advocate. She could not bear the thought of Walter being put to death; at her and her father's urging, Governor Park commuted his death sentence to life imprisonment on May 27, 1935; on February 8, 1949, the parole board discharged him from MSP. In pleading for Walter McGee's life, Mary McElroy told the governor, "I am pleading for my own peace of mind." In April 1939, her father resigned his position as city manager after 13 years on the job. Only his death in September of that year prevented his federal trial on corruption charges of embezzling public funds. Approximately five months later, on January 20, 1940, Mary McElroy, his daughter, committed suicide by shooting herself with a pistol in the family home. She left a note, and in part it contained, "My four kidnappers are probably the only people on earth who don't consider me an utter fool. You have your death penalty now — so — please — give them a chance."[97]

The other case of an abductor being sentenced to death under state law occurred in Buchanan County when Oscar Ashworth pled guilty in St. Joseph to the kidnapping of a young girl, aged approximately seven years, for sexual purposes. He probably sodomized her; she was the daughter of an acquaintance. The trial judge accepted Ashworth's guilty plea and sentenced him to death; the Missouri Supreme Court affirmed. After several reprieves, Governor Stark commuted Ashworth's scheduled gas chamber death to a prison term. During the course of his subsequent imprisonment at MSP, he was made a trusty. On June 6, 1953, he simply wandered away from the prison, and he was never recaptured.[98]

The remaining commutations of death sentences were those of Governor Mel Carnahan (1993–2000). His first, Bobby Shaw's, was uneventful; it is discussed earlier in this chapter. The second was Darrell Mease's. On May 15, 1988, in Taney County, Mease lay in wait for his former drug partner, Lloyd Lawrence, and he shot and killed him, his wife, Frankie Lawrence, and their 19-year-old paraplegic grandson, William "Willie" Lawrence. On a change of venue to Greene County, the jury found him guilty of capital murder and sentenced him to death. He had confessed, and his former girlfriend testified against him. The Missouri Supreme Court affirmed Mease's death sentence,[99] and every other court which looked at the case upheld the Missouri Supreme Court.

It initially scheduled his death by lethal injection for January 27, 1999, and without any explanation to the condemned prisoner himself, his death date was changed to the 10th of February. An extraordinary event was about to occur in Missouri; for the first time in the state's history, a pope was visiting St. Louis. Pope John Paul II, a forceful opponent of capital punishment and a superstar in his own right, was due in town on the very day, January 27, 1999, that Mease was scheduled for his lethal injection. On that day, Governor and Mrs. Carnahan, sat in the front pew with Al and Tipper Gore at an interfaith prayer service at the Cathedral Basilica in St. Louis, at which the pope officiated. Afterwards, John Paul II left his wooden throne, walked toward the Carnahans, and made his personal plea, "Governor, will you please have mercy on Mr. Mease?" The governor was relieved that the pope had not asked him to commute the sentences of all the inmates on Missouri's death row. The next day and after a meeting with his staff in Jefferson City, Carnahan, a Baptist, commuted Darrell Mease's death sentence to life without possibility of parole.

Unlike Carnahan's sparing Bobby Shaw in 1993, this time there was no bigger story to capture headlines and above-the-fold stories in the state's daily newspapers. The *Kansas City Star*'s headline proclaimed, "Pope Plea Saves Inmate on Death Row. Carnahan Changes Killer's Sentence to Life without Parole." The *New York Times*' front page and above-the-fold story was headlined, "Governor Grants Pope's Plea for Life of a Missouri Inmate." *U.S.A. Today*'s front page contained, "Pope's Plea Cancels Execution." A faculty member at Fordham University began his research about the prisoner, Pope John Paul II, and Governor Mel Carnahan; it is the only book-length study of a Missouri governor's commutation of a death sentence.[100] Not only were newspapers spreading the word, television and radio stations blanketed the state with news of the commutation. Although Carnahan's staff was able to contact some of the relatives of Mease's victims prior to the announcement, it was unable to reach all of them. Among others who learned from a TV report that Mease would not be executed was a daughter-in-law of two of his victims, and she voiced her displeasure that she had not been notified before this startling news was made public.

John Ashcroft, Mel Carnahan's Republican opponent for a U.S. senate seat, initially had no response to Mease's good fortune. However, by late March 1999, he was calling for a constitutional amendment which would require that governors notify surviving relatives of victims prior to any commutation of a death sentence. That a sizeable portion of Missourians were displeased by Carnahan's decision and welcomed Ashcroft's response to it can be seen by a sampling of the letters the governor received protesting his action regarding Darrell Mease. One letter concluded, "You whimped out and are a disgrace to the State of Missouri!" It is signed "Disappointed" and its author drew a down turned face. A self-styled "Presbyterian taxpayer" wrote the governor that he was "disgusted by your pardon of a killer of three people." A Baptist minister who used his church's stationery ended his letter, "I shall remember your grievous mistake in this matter in any future attempts by you to seek public office and shall bring it to the remembrance of all with whom I come in contact." In other letters, the governor was reminded, "Please be advised that I will not be a supporter of your candidacy for any future office"; "I will never again support you, vote for you or express confidence in your ability to run this state"; and "You will not receive my vote in the future."[101] Obviously, Ashcroft was picking up support as a result of the commutation. Whether or not he would have defeated his opponent for the U.S. senate seat in the November 2000 election became an unanswerable question when, on Oct. 16, 2000, Governor Mel Carnahan, his son, and an aide were killed in a plane crash. On April 2, 2005, Pope John Paul II died. How strange it seems that the governor who commuted Mease's death sentence and the pope who influenced his commutation are now dead, and the man originally scheduled for lethal injection on January 27, 1999, is alive.

As this chapter demonstrated, four U.S. Presidents and most of Missouri's 54 governors commuted and/or pardoned one or more persons sentenced to death in this state. The political repercussions were minor to non-existent in the vast majority of cases. As the courts, especially the federal, have played an increasingly important role in death penalty matters, Missouri's governors have granted few commutations and no pardons of death row inmates. This trend should continue.

The next chapter looks at the role of the judiciary in sparing the death-sentenced in Missouri.

12

Appellate Court Reversals, 1818–2005

At present, the federal courts play vital roles in death penalty litigation in this state and every other American jurisdiction which puts persons to death as punishment for crime. In 1972, a U.S. Supreme Court decision, decided by a 5–4 vote, in cases from Georgia and Texas, *Furman* v. *Georgia*, *Jackson* v. *Georgia*, and *Branch* v. *Texas*, emptied all death rows in America of their prisoners. The High Court held that the capital punishment laws throughout the United States gave too much discretion to the judge and jury; as a result, the death penalty was arbitrary and irrational. Its use violated the due process clause of the 14th Amendment.[1] Following this decision, approximately 600 death row inmates nationwide, including at least 10 men sentenced to die and waiting to be put to death in the gas chamber at MSP, were not executed. In American history, nothing so sweeping concerning capital punishment had ever come from the nation's highest court. Within another four years, the state legislatures rewrote their death penalty statutes. With only Justices Brennan and Marshall dissenting, in 1976, the U.S. Supreme Court ruled by a 7–2 vote, in *Gregg* v. *Georgia*, *Proffitt* v. *Florida*, and *Jurek* v. *Texas*, that the rewritten death penalty statutes did not violate the 8th and 14th Amendments ban on cruel and unusual punishments.[2] As a result, capital punishment was alive and well here and in every other state with rewritten capital punishment statutes. One aspect was clear; the appellate courts were permanently involved in approving or disapproving death sentences. Earlier, the Missouri Supreme Court was not required to review every death sentence which a judge or jury decided. As a result of *Gregg* and its companion cases, appellate review was mandatory. The state of Missouri vested it only in its supreme court. The Missouri Court of Appeals, or the Eastern, Western, and Southern Districts, were bypassed in all death penalty cases.

Excluding the one known territorial case, all reversals of this state's death sentences by any Missouri or federal appellate court are in print; there is never a requirement that handwritten records be first located and then deciphered in order to understand them. Moreover, the reporters which contain the appellate reversals of Missouri's death sentences can be found in the library of any accredited law school in the United States. For these reasons, the majority are not discussed herein.

Judicial review of capital punishment cases in Missouri began slowly. Only one is known from the territorial period; in *U.S.* v *Slave Elijah* (1818), the Superior Court reversed the slave's death sentence and spared his life. Between Missouri's admission to the Union in 1821 and throughout the Civil War years, only 12 instances are known in which a decision of the Missouri Supreme Court probably prevented an execution. Three bondfemales' and one -male's death sentences were reversed on appeal. Only the outcome of 13- or 14-year-old Slave Mary's case is known; she was retried and sentenced to death a second time, and the sheriff of Crawford County hanged her in Steelville on August 11, 1838. After reversing Mary's first trial in 1837, the Missouri Supreme Court issued no additional decision in any slave capital case. Stated another way, at least 92% of the bondpersons whom Missouri sheriffs hanged never had their sentences reviewed.

Of the remaining eight antebellum capital cases which this court reversed, one was of a white woman, Sarah Buchner; it is discussed in Chapter 10. As far as we know, all other reversals of death sentences involved white men. For the most part, their final resolution is lost. In a few cases, we know the outcome. In the 1840s, James McLean was repeatedly tried in St. Louis County for the murder of Major Floyd. The Missouri Supreme Court granted him another trial after his first death sentence; the fourth time he was tried, he was acquitted.[3] After this court reversed Nelson Cross' death sentence, he pled guilty to second degree murder in Franklin County Circuit Court. The judge sentenced him to 25 years at MSP. He was received at the prison on April 25, 1859, and Governor Fletcher pardoned him on March 11, 1865.[4]

Between 1868 and 1907, the Missouri Supreme Court reversed approximately 50 death sentences. Some involve insanity. Usually, the appellate court did not concern itself with the mental state of the defendant. Now and then it did. In 1878, in a murder case from Howell County because its degree is not specified, we do not know whether or not it was capital, the Missouri Supreme Court faulted the conviction because the trial judge disallowed all but direct evidence of insanity. As a result the jury never learned, in the words of the court, that the defendant's "aunt had died in a mad-house, and two of [his] sisters were maniacs."[5] On his retrial, the defense could put on evidence of their client's unfortunate lineage. In one Jackson County case, the reversal was based on the trial court's refusal to allow experts to testify that the accused was insane as a result of his masturbatory habits. It wrote that one of the physicians would have testified that the mind of the accused "had been seriously impaired, if indeed, he had not been rendered insane, by the practice of that vice.... The other that he was a mental wreck."[6] In its boldest statement on mental illness as a defense, the appellate court reviewed another Jackson County conviction of first degree murder. It concerned a father, John Speyer, who killed his six-year-old son by cutting his throat as the child slept. The case was tried three times, and three times the Missouri Supreme Court reversed. In its third decision, it wrote, "That his act in taking the life of his son, under the circumstances disclosed by the record, was that of an insane man, hardly admits of a doubt.... With due deference to the men who composed these juries, we must say that we are not satisfied with their verdict ... and feel constrained to say that we do not think it ought to be permitted to stand."[7] These words were written in December 1907, and they reflect more than appellate judges' dislike of the death penalty. Most Missourians viewed capital punishment with considerable animosity during this time period.

Another curiosity about Missouri Supreme Court reversals between 1868 and 1907 concerns Chinese men being sentenced to death. To be sure, the Asian population of the state would have been small in the nineteenth century. Nonetheless, the almost complete absence of Asians in the history of this state's death penalty is surely a comment on just how few ever got into difficulty with the law in Missouri. On June 1, 1885, in the city of St. Louis, someone murdered Lon Johnson, a Chinese person, by knifing him. The state tried Chyo Chiagk, among other Chinese men, for Johnson's murder; the jury found him guilty of first degree murder, and he was sentenced to death. The appellate court's decision is a strong one; it believed in the innocence of the accused, and among other grounds, it reversed his conviction because the jury had not been instructed to acquit if accomplice testimony was not corroborated. In a companion case, the court reversed the conviction of Chyo Goom, another Chinese convicted of the murder of Lon Johnson.[8] Otherwise, Asians do not appear in death penalty cases in Missouri.

In 1882, the Missouri Supreme Court reversed its first known death sentences of Negroes. One was an illiterate 12-year-old, discussed in Chapter 8. The other was George Grant, charged with and convicted of the first degree murder of Patrick Jones, a Kansas City police officer, on April 3, 1882, the same day the Ford brothers killed Jesse James in St. Joseph. The state contended that Grant had stolen two pails of butter, and he shot the policeman to death to avoid arrest. Although the judge sentenced him to hang, this was not an open and shut case. Grant was tried at least three times, perhaps four, and on appeal, his case was reversed twice.[9] Obviously there was considerable doubt about his guilt. The appellate judges appear to have prevented Grant's execution. Eighteen months after their second reversal of his death sentence, Governor Marmaduke commuted Sam Cook's death sentence; Cook was a Negro. It is the first known commutation given to any African-American in a capital case in the history of Missouri. Apart from Slave Nelly, as far as we know, this state's governors never prevented one slave's from being executed. In contrast, the judiciary may have prevented three slaves from being put to death. Likewise, in the 1880s, the Missouri Supreme Court acted slightly earlier than the governor to spare the lives of persons of color.

In 1901, the appellate judges reversed the death sentence of a 19-year-old white, Elijah Moore, who, on November 16, 1899, in Stoddard County, shot to death his father, an abusive minister, as his victim slept at 3:30 a.m. That evening in this same county, a mob took a white man, William Huff, charged with the murder of another white man, from the jail in Bloomfield and lynched him. The sheriff used the threat, in the words of the court, of "the Huff matter" to extract a confession from the young man. According to the appellate decision, the sheriff told the prisoner, "There is a mob on the streets, and one in your county, and by God I can't save you unless you do what I say." The appellate court ruled that a confession "made under threats, either express or implied, of mob violence in case defendant failed to confess to the crime charged ... is wholly inadmissible."[10] The next year the Missouri Supreme court lacked the moral courage to use its own recent precedent to reverse the conviction and death sentence of 16-year-old General Armstrong for rape. As emphasized in Chapter 9, this state's highest court never found the confession of a black who admitted to the rape of a white female involuntary or forced. It approved every scaffold and gas chamber death of the few that it reviewed when a black was sentenced to death for the rape of a white female.

Between 1908 and the last gas chamber death at MSP in 1965, the Missouri Supreme Court reversed at least 21 death sentences, far fewer than it had earlier. However, under state authority between 1868 and 1907, a period of 39 years, 183 known persons were put to death here. Between 1908 and 1965, a period of 57 years, 93 known persons, who were sentenced to die under state, federal, and U.S. Army authority in Missouri, were executed. The machinery of capital punishment dramatically slowed between one time period of 39 years and another of 57. Moreover, because there are no official collected records of legal hangings by the state's county sheriffs, any investigator, no matter how careful, can miss executions here prior to 1938. Gas chamber deaths at MSP are officially recorded; they cannot be missed. There may be more than 183 executions between 1868 and 1907; this figure represents the number which can be confirmed. Hence it is not surprising that the state's highest court reversed fewer death sentences in the later time period than in the earlier.

Among this court's reversals between 1908 and 1965 were several which concern African-American defendants. In Henry County, on October 18, 1930, two black males, Emmett Gallie and Eual Richardson, killed a 60-year-old white female, Mrs. Elizabeth Neiman, for purposes of robbing her. Her body was discovered several days later, and the perpetrators were arrested on October 24. In order to avoid their being lynched, one was held in the Johnson County jail in Warrensburg and the other in the Jackson County jail in Kansas City. Their trial began with breath-taking speed on October 31, 1930. At it, according to one account, the courthouse in Clinton was surrounded by a mob of 2,000 persons, and their attorney, Frederick Wesner of Sedalia, had no opportunity to consult with his clients until 20 minutes before proceedings against them began.[11] Their lawyer asked for a change of venue and a continuance; the judge refused both his requests. Their jury deliberated about 25 minutes before finding Gallie and Richardson guilty and assessing their punishment at death. On appeal in 1932, the Missouri Supreme Court reversed their convictions for the same reason the U.S. Supreme Court later that same year reversed the death sentences of the Scottsboro defendants. In both, the attorney had no opportunity to consult with his clients, investigate their case, and prepare their defense.[12] At the second trial in the Missouri case, the defendants received a change of venue. A St. Clair County jury found them guilty, and they received life sentences.[13]

In Boone County, Anderson Logan was charged with the January 3, 1935 murder of his wife, Angela Logan. Both the perpetrator and his victim were Negroes. On a change of venue, he was tried for her murder in Callaway County before an all-white-male jury; its members sentenced him to death. His lawyer based his attack on his client's conviction on the intentional and systematic exclusion of African-Americans from jury service. He argued that the exclusion of blacks violated the 5th and the 14th Amendments to the U.S. Constitution, the Missouri Constitution, and the holding in the U.S. Supreme Court's second reversal of the Scottsboro trial, *Norris* v. *Alabama* (1935). The Missouri Supreme Court agreed. Its decision includes the answers the defense attorney received to his questions about Negroes serving on juries. The official court reporter of 26 years' service, as the decision noted, "testified that during all the time he had never seen or known of a Negro being called for jury service in [Callaway] county." Likewise the decision also includes the sheriff's answer when Logan's attorney asked if he had ever selected a Negro for jury service, "I could answer you better out of the courtroom. We haven't been raised that way, now, to be plain with you."[14] At Logan's second trial, six Negroes were called for jury service, but the prosecutor eliminated all of them, one for cause because the prospective black juror would never vote in favor of capital punishment and the others through the state's peremptory strikes of jurors. This time the all-white-male jury returned a life sentence, and Logan's conviction was affirmed on appeal.[15]

One of the last men spared execution in the gas chamber at MSP by direct appeal to the Missouri Supreme Court was Earl Nickens. On March 4, 1963, he shot and killed a St. Louis policeman, Donald Sparks, as the officer sought to apprehend him for the robbery of a grocery store. The jury sentenced the perpetrator to death. At trial, his defense had been that he suffered from a mental disease or defect, which excluded his responsibility for the charged crimes. Psychiatrists testified both for the defendant and the state. The reversal of Nickens' death sentence is based on the testimony of the expert for the state. Judge Henley wrote that the doctor's "function as an expert does not extend to expressing an opinion that an accused should be restrained or imprisoned even for the offense with which he is charged. That determination is the exclusive function and province of the jury.... This expert should not be permitted to express an opinion ... that [Nickens's] 'undoubtedly' will commit similar crimes in the future 'if unrestrained.'"[16] No expert, no matter how learned, was permitted to testify to the future dangerousness of the defendant. The *Nickens* decision was written in June 1966, or more than 17 months after the state of Missouri put to death its last prisoner in January 1965 in the gas chamber at MSP. There would be no additional executions in this state for the next 24 years.

Once the use of the death penalty returned with its first use here in 1989, a small percentage of the condemned was spared being put to death as a result of appellate action. A study of reversal rates in capital cases for the years 1973–1995 ranks Missouri next to the bottom of 26 states at 17% reversed on direct appeal and 20% including all appeals in state court. The national average was 41% on direct appeal and 47%, including all appeals in the respective state courts. At the federal habeas corpus stage, the national average was 40% and for Missouri 15%. In this study only Virginia had a lower reversal rate.[17] This does not mean that Missouri is average in its reversal rate in capital cases. Twenty four states either ban capital punishment by state statute or state constitution, or had not put any person to death in the post–Furman era by 1995.

The reversal percentage in capital cases remains approximately the same between 1996 and 2005 as in earlier years of lethal injection. It does not appear to be any higher than between 1989 and 1995. In 2002, the High Court held in *Adkins* v. *Virginia* that it was cruel and unusual punishment to put to death the retarded; that same year, the Missouri General Assembly by statute prohibited their execution. The next year, the Missouri Supreme Court revisited the case of Ernest Johnson, a man who committed a triple murder in 1994 in Boone County. He was tried and sentenced to death, and the Missouri Supreme Court affirmed his guilt, but remanded it for a new penalty hearing. Johnson was again sentenced to death. When his case came before the Missouri Supreme Court in 2003, Judge Ronnie White wrote for the majority: "Taken together, the United States Supreme Court's *Atkins* case, the General Assembly's enactment of a statute prohibiting the death penalty for mentally retarded individuals, and the contradictory evidence of appellant's mental abilities, this case requires remand."[18] Among other evidence presented to this court was Johnson's inability to live alone, his poor awareness of social mores, which included his belief that no one should pay taxes, and his inability to complete a test written for a person with a sixth-grade reading level. As a result of subsequent proceedings, Ernest Johnson is now serving a life sentence without possibility of parole.

In 2002, the U.S. Supreme Court also ruled in *Ring* v. *Arizona* that a judge cannot sentence the defendant to death when members of the jury cannot agree in the penalty phase of the trial; only they can return a death sentence when the defendant has elected trial by jury. However, nothing in the high court decision bars the accused from pleading guilty before a judge and that judge sentencing him to death. As a result of *Ring*, four persons, Antonio Richardson, Joseph Whitfield, Andrew Morrow, and James Ervin, sentenced to death in Missouri, left its death row, and they are now serving life sentences without possibility of parole. The *Ring* decision does not affect the guilty plea of Roderick Nunley; he elected a bench trial and pled guilty to first degree murder before a Jackson County judge.

In 2005, the U.S. Supreme Court ended the death penalty for juveniles; as a result, Christopher Simmons left death row and is now serving life without possibility of parole. In another case, also decided in 2005, the high court required a new penalty phase hearing for Carmen Deck in Jefferson County Circuit Court. At his earlier court appearance, he was required to wear leg irons, handcuffs, and a belly chain during the penalty phase of his capital case in the presence of the jury. Writing for the majority of 7–2, Justice Breyer held that shackling a convicted offender during the penalty phase of a capital case violates the Federal Constitution's 5th and 14th Amendments due process requirements unless that use is "justified by an essential state interest — such as the interest in courtroom security — specific to the defendant on trial."[19] The High Court reversed the Missouri Supreme Court which had initially ordered a new penalty phase hearing for Deck, and when the jury again sentenced him to die by lethal injection, the Missouri appellate court upheld his death sentence.[20] The outcome of the third penalty phase hearing for Carmen Deck and another penalty phase hearing for Donald Hall, also displayed in chains before a jury in Greene County and sentenced to death, are pending as of this writing.

When we turn to other reversals in recent years of Missouri's death sentences, federal courts have played vital roles in removing persons from this state's death row. One juvenile, Heath Wilkins, and two women, Faye Copeland and Maria Isa, were spared execution because the U.S. Courts for both the Western and the Eastern Districts of Missouri as well as the Eighth Circuit Court of Appeals reached favorable habeas corpus decisions regarding their cases. Four unrelated cases involve prison inmates sentenced to death for first degree murder. As of this writing, two remain incarcerated and two have been released. Federal court action helped keep all four alive a sufficiently long period of time for each to establish that he was not guilty of a capital crime.

The state has several build-in advantages when it seeks a death sentence against a prison inmate. One is statutory. Under aggravating circumstances is No.9 "The murder in the first degree was committed by a person in ... [a] place of lawful confinement." The other concerns the credibility of her witnesses. Jurors tend to believe the state's witnesses, not the defense's, even when both sides rely on inmate testimony. Corrections officers, or guards, are usually prosecution witnesses, and jurors find them more believable than inmates. Corrections officers may or may not be more truthful.

On February 23, 1984, Lloyd Schlup, an inmate at MSP, was charged with the first degree murder of another inmate, Arthur Dade. The state's theory of the case was that Schlup held Dade while another inmate, Robert O'Neal, stabbed Dade to death. O'Neal is discussed in the next chapter. Schlup's defense was that he had nothing to do with Dade's murder; rather, he was in a food line when the homicide occurred well behind him. He was not out of breath, and there was no blood on his clothing. As Justice Stevens, writing for the majority of the U.S. Supreme Court, noted, "The State produced no physical evidence connecting Schlup to the killing, and no witnesses other than Flowers and Maylee [prison guards] testified to Schlup's involvement in the murder."[21] In Schlup's case, a guard, Robert Faherty, who testified at his trial, was never asked how long Lloyd and he were together in the hall at the time of the murder. In an affidavit, dated October 26, 1993, Faherty states, "I saw Lloyd Schlup coming down the corridor toward me. He was walking at a leisurely pace with his hands in his pockets.... Lloyd was not perspiring or breathing hard, and he was not nervous.... Lloyd could not be guilty of this crime."[22]

Lloyd Schlup was tried for the murder of Arthur Dade, and his jurors believed neither him nor his witnesses. They sentenced him to death for the murder of Arthur Dade. Over a period of 14 years he managed to stay alive. The Missouri Supreme Court set death dates for him on March 12, 1992, and November 19, 1993. According to Schlup's attorney, Sean O'Brien, Ida B. Dade, the victim's mother, called Governor Mel Carnahan and told him that she did not believe that Lloyd Schlup had played any part in the murder of her son. The governor issued a last minute stay on November 18, 1993. Finally, in 1995, the U.S.

Supreme Court ordered a new trial for him because of the ineffectiveness of his trial attorney. Just before he was ready for a new trial, the attorney general's office offered him a second degree murder charge with a life sentence. He accepted. He told another inmate, Robert Driscoll, that he feared the jury would not believe either him or his witnesses on a retrial, and he could not put his mother through the very real likelihood that he would once more be sentenced to death.[23] At present, he is an inmate at the Southeast Correctional Center in Charleston. He is eligible for parole in September 2007.[24]

Another killing at MSP involved Eric Clemmons. He was charged with the August 7, 1985 murder of another inmate, Henry Johnson. An officer, Thomas Steigerwald, saw two inmates and chased Clemmons; Steigerwald became a witness against Clemmons at trial. The defendant stated that the guard saw the victim run into him after another inmate, Fred Bagby, had already fatally stabbed Johnson. On a change of venue to Greene County, the jury found Clemmons guilty of the murder of Henry Johnson, and it sentenced him to death. The Missouri Supreme Court affirmed his conviction and death sentence.[25] The 8th Circuit Federal Court of Appeals granted Clemmons a new trial. It was based both on ineffective assistance of counsel and a failure of the state to turn over to the defense exculpatory evidence, or that which would tend to free the accused from blame. Although Bagby had died by the time of Clemmons trial, he was alive when another inmate, Dwight Clark, identified Bagby as the killer within one hour of the crime. Moreover, Clark's statement was written up in memo form, but Clemmons was not given a copy of it.[26] At his second trial in Greene County, among much else, an expert testified that the blood on Clemmon's sweatshirt and hat was not the splatter pattern of a stabbing, but it was consistent with a blood-drenched man running into him. The jury deliberated three hours, and on February 18, 2000, it found Clemmons not guilty. Although he remains in prison on another first murder conviction, he is no longer a death row inmate.[27]

In two other cases Missouri prison inmates were sentenced to death, one at MSP and the other at Moberly Correctional Center, the federal courts' actions kept them alive a sufficiently long period of time for them to establish that they were not guilty of a capital crime. Both left prison alive and did so legally.

Robert Driscoll, then serving a prison term for robbery at the Missouri Training Center for Men in Moberly, was charged with the stabbing death of a guard, Officer Tom Jackson, on July 3, 1983. On that date, Driscoll and his cellmate, Jimmie Jenkins, spent the day and the evening drinking alcoholic beverages, some of it made in the prison and some illegally brought to them from a liquor store. By 9:45 p.m. Jenkins had become unruly, and the victim-officer asked him to leave his cell. According to the state's theory of the case, while Officer Jackson waited for assistance in handling Jenkins, Driscoll stabbed Jackson three times, thereby causing his death. Jackson's mortal wounds were inflicted at the same time a prison riot involving out-of-control fighting between prisoners and guards was taking place. Driscoll was tried for Jackson's murder, and the jury recommended that he be sentenced to death. On direct appeal, the Missouri Supreme Court affirmed the prisoner's death sentence; it subsequently denied post-conviction relief. Driscoll unsuccessfully appealed both decisions of Missouri's highest court to the U.S. Supreme Court. It denied review.[28] He then petitioned the U.S. District Court for the Eastern District of Missouri for habeas corpus relief. This court granted it on three independent grounds, and the 8th Circuit Federal Court of Appeals upheld the district court's order. Both federal courts concluded that Driscoll's trial lawyer was ineffective because his counsel did not make clear that the victim's blood was not on Driscoll's knife; his lawyer failed to impeach a state eyewitness with his prior inconsistent statement, and the prosecutor's improper argument to the jury diminished its awareness that it was responsible for Driscoll's death sentence, an 8th Amendment violation.[29] When Driscoll was retried, the state used Driscoll's membership in a white racist hate group, the Aryan Brotherhood, to bolster its theory that he stabbed a prison guard to death. It put on evidence that he had several tattoos on his chest, "Wis Mach," German for white power, and the initials "AB" for Aryan Brotherhood. A second jury sentenced Driscoll to death. On appeal, the Missouri Supreme Court reversed on several grounds, one of which was the Aryan Brotherhood evidence. Since the victim was also white, the defendant's membership in a group to enhance white power was not legally relevant. Equally important, this decision summarizes the holes in the state's case: (1) three guards other than Jackson were stabbed during the prison melee, and Driscoll, who admitted stabbing an officer, but which one he did not know, may not have been the prisoner who stabbed the guard who died; (2) the prison guard who testified that he saw the defendant stab Jackson had earlier testified that he had not seen Driscoll stab Jackson; (3) two other prison guards made written statements shortly after the riot that they had seen another inmate, Rodney Carr, stab Jackson; (4) two inmates who testified that Driscoll stabbed Jackson had not mentioned Driscoll's role in Jackson's death in written statements they gave prison officials shortly after the riot; and (5) the knife identified as Driscoll's had no stains of the victim's blood on it. For all these reasons, the Missouri Supreme Court granted Driscoll a third trial.[30]

At his third trial in 2004, the state was barred from mentioning the Aryan Brotherhood material, and the jury heard that Jackson's blood was never found on Driscoll's knife. His new defense attorneys, David Bruins and Brad Kessler, realized that their best witness was the defendant himself. He had spent 21 years studying every aspect of his capital case. Because of his emphysema, atrophied legs, and other health problems, Driscoll's physical health was so poor that he had to be assisted to the witness stand in his wheelchair; nonetheless, his mind was clear. His testimony persuaded the jury that he was guilty of no higher offense than manslaughter, a crime for which no more than 10 years can be imposed. Because he had already spent 21 years on death row, he had more than served his time for manslaughter. His Phelps County trial judge sent him back to the Missouri Department of Corrections, and after a short stay in the Fulton Reception and Diagnostic Center, he was released on March 31, 2004. His Native American wife, Linda, whom he married in 1989, picked him up, and drove him to St. Louis. Robert Driscoll now works for Brad Kessler, one of the attorneys who represented him at his third trial.[31] The murder of Tom Jackson, the corrections guard, is not an unsolved or cold case. Inmates Rodney Carr and Roy "Hog" Roberts were also charged and convicted of his murder. The odds are that neither was guilty of the murder of Jackson. Carr was sentenced to life imprisonment, and Roy Roberts was sentenced to death for holding Tom Jackson as Robert Driscoll stabbed him, Roberts was executed on March 10, 1999.[32]

In 2003, Joe Amrine, a man who spent 16 years on death row at Potosi Correctional Center, walked out of prison a free man. Unlike almost every other person discussed in this book, he was freed because a court finally determined that he had not committed the crime for which he was sentenced to death. It was not that the state had failed to prove every element of the capital offense charged beyond a reasonable doubt. He was released because he plain didn't do it.

Amrine was already an inmate, serving time at MSP for robbery and forgery, when a killing occurred on Oct. 18, 1985, in a prison auditorium, which at the time of the homicide contained approximately 200 persons, including Amrine, Terry Russell, the inmate-perpetrator of the crime, Gary Barber, the inmate-victim of the crime, and Gary Noble, the corrections officer who identified Russell as Barber's assailant. In the words of the Missouri Supreme Court decision almost 18 years after this killing:

> While being questioned about Barber's murder, Russell claimed that Amrine admitted that he had stabbed Barber. Amrine was charged with Barber's murder. The state's case against Amrine rested on the testimony of inmate witnesses Terry Russell, Randy Ferguson, and Jerry Poe. Russell testified that Amrine admitted to the murder. Ferguson testified that Amrine was walking next to Barber for several minutes before pulling a knife out of his waistband and stabbing Barber. Poe was not asked to describe the murder and testified only that he witnessed Amrine stab Barber. There was no physical evidence linking Amrine to the murder.
>
> Amrine introduced evidence showing that he was not the killer and that Terry Russell was. Officer Noble testified that he saw Barber chase Russell across the recreation room before Barber pulled the knife from his back, collapsed, and died. Six inmates testified that Amrine was playing poker at the time of the stabbing. Three of those inmates identified Terry Russell as the person that Barber was chasing. None of them named Amrine. The jury found Amrine guilty of Barber's murder, and he was sentenced to death.[33]

Over the course of the many years that Joe Amrine sat on death row awaiting his death by lethal injection, each of the jailbird witnesses against him admitted that he had lied. The reasons for their perjury included threats of being accused of Barber's murder themselves, threats of being termed a snitch by prison officials so that they would be murdered by other inmates, protective custody for one of the state's prisoner-witnesses who was then being repeatedly raped by other inmates, and favorable comment about their cases to the parole board.[34] In the course of the protracted legal proceedings involving this case, the Western Missouri Coalition to Abolish the Death Penalty received a grant for $5,000 to make 800 copies of a documentary video in which the false-swearing witnesses against Joe Amrine admitted to their lies and gave their reasons for them. This movie was shown to theatre, church, and community hall audiences statewide, and it built grassroots support for the release of a condemned and innocent man.

Amrine's appeal of his wrongful conviction began so early that when the U.S. Supreme Court first denied review of his case in 1988, Justices Brennan and Marshall were still on the court. They wrote of the denial of certiorari in Amrine's and nine other capital cases nationwide, "Adhering to our views that the death penalty is in all circumstances cruel and unusual punishment prohibited by the Eighth and Fourteenth Amendments, ... we would grant certiorari and vacate the death sentences in these cases."[35] Between this denied appeal and others which followed before the federal court for the Western District of Missouri, the United States Court of Appeals for the Eighth Circuit, and the Missouri Supreme Court,[36] it was essential that Amrine not be given a lethal injection; otherwise, his appeal would have been mooted by his death. Fortunately, truth has a long fuse, and it would eventually be known despite the mistakes of the trial, including the perjury, which put Joe Amrine on death row. On April 29, 2003, the Supreme Court of Missouri ordered Amrine's release unless the state elected to file new charges against him within 45 days. Initially the Cole County prosecutor refused to drop charges on grounds that he wanted to compare blood from Amrine's clothes to the victim's DNA. On July 27, he announced that in the 17 years of storage at MSP, the evidence on the clothing had so degraded that it could not be matched to DNA. The prosecutor's announcement cleared the way for Amrine's release; at 8:00 a.m. the next day, Joe Amrine was free, after 26 years in prison, 18 of them on death row. He had survived four different execution dates, and he had known the 62 men who were executed in Missouri during his time in their company. His joyous reunion with his sisters outside a relative's home in Kansas City was the subject of a front page photograph

Photograph of Joe Amrine embracing one sister, Marva Amrine, while another, Renee Amrine McDaniel, left, joyfully waits her turn in Kansas City, Missouri. Joe spent 18 years on Missouri's death row for a crime he did not commit. (*Kansas City Star*, July 29, 2003. Used by permission, *Kansas City Star*. All rights reserved.)

with an accompanying story in the *Kansas City Star* on July 29, 2003. The next day in an excellent commentary, Barbara Shelly wrote a poignant piece about Amrine's release, entitled, "Missouri Should Be Ashamed." She concluded it, "People who watched Amrine walk out of prison said it was like seeing a rebirth. But the state showed little urgency in releasing him from the shadow of death."[37] At present, Joe Amrine is both an employee of the Public Interest Litigation Clinic in Kansas City, Missouri, and a frequent and effective public speaker against the death penalty.

Unlike Joe Amrine' case, another death penalty case was reversed before the federal courts became involved. According to the statement of Clarence Dexter, the husband of 22 years of Carol Dexter, on November 18, 1990, he left their home in Clay County for the grocery store at approximately 7:30 on November 18, 1990, and when he returned at 8:30 p.m. he found the dead body of his wife. The prosecutor charged him with her murder; at the first proceeding against him there was a mistrial. At the second, the jury could not agree on the penalty, and the judge sentenced him to death. This is a clear violation of *Ring* v. *Arizona*, a subsequent decision of the U.S. Supreme Court. The Missouri Supreme Court reversed and remanded Dexter's case. It did so because the state violated the defendant's 5th Amendment right against self-incrimination with repeated references in the presence of the jury to Dexter's silence after he had been given his Miranda warnings.[38] The law is clear; the accused has the right to remain silent, and his failure to speak cannot be used against him. At his second trial, the prosecutors had misplaced so much evidence that the state was required to drop the charges against him in the death of his wife, and he left the Clay County Courthouse a free man.[39]

Clarence Dexter is the exception to the rule that most of the persons sentenced to death in Missouri who have not been executed owe much of the fact that they are still alive to the lower federal courts. It is not that the judges on these courts have necessarily found in their favor. Rather, the right of federal habeas corpus, a right guaranteed in the U.S. Constitution, has allowed the death row inmate to bring an appeal and during its pendency to avoid death by lethal injection. In Schlup's, Clemmons,' Driscoll's and Amrine's cases, these men survived because the present system of appeals kept them alive until they could reach an agreement with the prosecutor, be acquitted by a jury, or establish that they were innocence of a capital crime.

All of this may soon change. Virtually identical bills have been introduced in both houses of the U.S. Congress which would severely restrict the scope of federal judicial review. These bills go by a very appealing name: the Streamlined Procedures Act. If the pending legislation becomes law, instead of various members of the federal judiciary determining the constitutionality of a death sentence obtained in state court, a member of the executive, specifically, the attorney general of the United States will make that determination.[40] In an editorial, *The New York Times* denounced this would-be law, which would transfer most review power away from judges and give it to the attorney general. It writes, "That's right: The chief prosecutor of the United States would become the judge of whether state courts behave fairly enough toward defendants appealing capital convictions.... Repeatedly federal court scrutiny has laid bare the shoddy state of capital justice in the states.... This oppressive bill ... would make the execution of the innocent even more likely than it already is."[41]

It is the claim of death penalty enthusiasts that in modern times there has not been an execution of an innocent person. Obviously, one cannot discuss Robert Driscoll's and Joe Amrine's cases because these men were not executed. Larry Griffin, a black male, was put to death in 1995 at the Potosi Correctional Center, Mineral Point, Missouri, for the June 26, 1980 drive-by shooting of another black male, Quintin Moss, a St. Louis drug dealer. Among those who have long believed that Griffin was innocent is Joe Amrine, a man who spent a number of years with Griffin on death row. Others include Cathleen Burnett, an expert on Missouri's current death penalty, who terms the eye-witnesses testimony against Griffin perjury. Evidence which the Kansas City attorneys, Sean O'Brien and Kent Gipson, the lawyers who handled Griffin's appeals, located a decade ago now forms the basis of a report by the NAACP Legal Defense and Education Fund. Samuel Gross, a law professor at the University of Michigan, oversaw the NAACP investigation. It was released to the press in July 2005.

The principal evidence against Larry Griffin was the eye-witness testimony of Robert Fitzgerald, a white man, who, so he testified, happened to be at the crime scene in a largely black neighborhood because his car had broken down. A decision of the Missouri Supreme Court, which upheld Griffin's death sentence in 1984, summarizes the testimony of the state's chief witness:

> Fitzgerald saw the defendant [Larry Griffin] firing a pistol through the open window of the passenger side of the front seat of [a faded 1967 or 1968 Chevrolet].... A passerby, Wallace Conners, was struck in the buttocks by one of the bullets. Fitzgerald had an unobstructed view of the defendant throughout the shooting and as the Chevrolet drove away, Fitzgerald saw the license plate on the rear of the car and memorized the number. He provided this information to the police and accompanied the officers to the police station where he identified defendant from a group of photographs as being the person firing the pistol from the front seat of the Chevrolet.[42]

This decision omits a great deal about Robert Fitzgerald. He was a career criminal, an admitted drug addict, a professional snitch who had been convicted of heroin possession, auto theft, armed robbery, and possession of burglary tools. Equally important, he was in St. Louis because he had been relocated there from Boston, Massachusetts, by the Federal Witness Protection Program, whose charge he was. At the time Fitzgerald testified against Griffin he was in jail on four felony counts of credit card fraud. Once the conviction against Griffin was secured, Fitzgerald was released for time served. According to Cathleen Burnett and Sean O'Brien, Fitzgerald admitted some 12 years later that he committed perjury in Larry Griffin's trial.

Although Fitzgerald has since died, another important witness is still alive. The year-long investigation by the NAACP Legal Defense and Education Fund has located Wallace Conners, a black male, aged 52 years, formerly of St. Louis. On the day Moss was shot dead while selling drugs, Conners was there to buy them; the Missouri Supreme Court decision places him at the crime scene as the man hit in the buttock by one of the bullets. This man left St. Louis, and he was never called as a witness at the court proceedings involving Griffin. He was shocked to learn that Larry Griffin had been executed; Conners knew Griffin, and Conners says Griffin was not there. Neither, adds Conners, was any white man present, including Robert Fitzgerald, or any broken-down car. Otherwise, he would have gotten behind it to avoid being hit when the shooting started. The victim's sister, Patricia Moss Mason, told investigators that she had seen the shooting, and she had not seen any white man in the vicinity. According to police reports, when officers visited Conners in the hospital and showed him a photo of Larry Griffin, he did not identify Griffin as being present. Further, the police officer, Michael Ruggeri, now retired, who testified that Fitzgerald was at the crime scene, now says Fitzgerald was not there when he arrived and, if Fitzgerald had reported a license plate number, he would have noted it in his report. In summary, copious material points to Missouri having executed the wrong man when it put Larry Griffin to death.

In an attempt to give federal legislators pause before they enact the Streamlined Procedures Act, the NAACP Legal Defense and Educational Fund has persuaded the top prosecutor in the city of St. Louis, Jennifer Joyce, to reopen Griffin's case. Her report is currently pending.[43] Even if she concludes that the evidence of his guilt or innocence is inconclusive because 25 years have lapsed between the crime and her investigation, her decision will not be a shining moment for this state. After all, the burden of proof in a criminal case is guilt beyond a reasonable doubt; no one who looks at all the evidence in Griffin's case can conclude that the state met its burden. I have discussed his case in this chapter because an appellate court, either state or federal, should have written a decision which reversed his conviction and death sentence. Any jury informed of the sordid facts of the prosecutor's case would have acquitted Larry Griffin of the murder of Quinton Moss.

Over a period of 187 years as of this writing, appellate courts, initially federal, for many years state, and then both state and federal, have reversed death sentences in Missouri. It is vital to the administration of justice in capital cases that all courts which currently review this state's capital cases continue to scrutinize the convictions of those sentenced to death here. Passage of the Streamlined Procedures Act can only worsen an already badly flawed system.

The next and final chapter concerns the executions by lethal injection in Missouri which have taken place between 1989 and 2005.

13

Lethal Injection, 1989–2005

On July 2, 1976, the U.S. Supreme Court upheld the state of Georgia's rewritten capital punishment statutes in *Gregg* v. *Georgia*. The approved laws require a two-part or bifurcated trial. These separate proceedings are termed the guilt phase and the penalty phase. If it is determined that the accused has committed first degree murder, the penalty phase comes into play. During it in Missouri, either the judge in a bench trial or 12 citizens in a jury trial must determine whether the defendant shall be sentenced to death or life imprisonment without eligibility for probation, parole, or release except by act of the governor. When pondering death as a punishment option, the fact-finder is required to consider evidence of both the aggravating and the mitigating circumstances of the crime(s). If a death sentence is returned, appellate review of it is mandatory. In *Gregg*, the court observed that at least 35 states and the U.S. Congress had enacted death penalty laws since its 1972 decision, *Furman* v. *Georgia*, had determined all then existing American capital punishment laws were unconstitutional. In its 1976 decision, most of the justices asserted that the majority of the American people approved of the death penalty, and members of our highest court assumed that the rewritten laws would end the arbitrary and capricious aspects of the old capital punishment laws. In dissent in *Gregg*, Justice Marshall correctly stated that "the American people know little about the death penalty, and ... the opinions of an informed public would differ significantly from those of a public unaware of the consequences and effects of the death penalty."[1] On February 2, 1994, Justice Blackmun decided as Justices Marshall and Brennan did earlier, that no human power can make the death penalty fair. In a Texas case, Blackmun, wrote, "From this day forward, I no longer shall tinker with the machinery of death.... The problem is that the inevitability of factual, legal, and moral error gives us a system that we know must wrongly kill some defendants, a system that fails to deliver the fair, consistent, and reliable sentences of death required by the constitution."[2]

Apart from the Union Army's terrible excesses during the Civil War years in this state, the 1880s and 1890s remain the decades during which Missouri executed the most people. The next greatest use of this state's death penalty is now. Although capital punishment laws took effect here in May 1977, nearly 12 years passed before this state's first execution by lethal injection occurred. Despite the lateness of its first use in 1989, a later date than many other states, she has more than made up for its slow start. In the past 16 years Missouri has executed 66 persons. Our present rank order among 54 American jurisdictions, that is 50 states, Puerto Rico, the District of Columbia, the U.S. Government, and the U.S. Military, is fourth. Stated another way, 50 other U.S. legal authorities have put fewer, if any, persons to death since 1972. Only Texas with 355 uses of lethal injection, Virginia with 94, and Oklahoma with 79 have executed more persons in the post–*Furman* era than this state.[3] Missouri's enthusiastic use of the death penalty has not made this state a safer place than other American jurisdictions wherein few or no executions have taken place in the past 25 years. On the contrary, the most recent figures, those from 2002, rank order Missouri 12th among the 50 states with 6.6 homicides per 100,000 population, ahead of both California (6.4), New York (5.0), and significantly ahead of Massachusetts (2.3) in its murder and non-negligent manslaughter rates.[4] In the post–*Furman* era or since 1972, California has executed 12 persons and New York and Massachusetts none. No fewer than 38 states have lower homicide rates than the Show Me State. How could this be? Are murderous Missourians and outsiders who come here to commit first degree murder not getting the message? Justice Brandeis explained it well in his famous dissent in a 1928 case in which he termed the government a lawbreaker. In the particular case the violation was an unreasonable search and seizure, but what he wrote applies to any other official activity: "Our Government is the potent, the omnipresent teacher. For good or for ill, it teaches the whole people by its example."[5] If the state deals with that slimy son-of-a-bitch by taking him out, the private citizen may well be encouraged to do the same with his real or imagined enemies, with those who are weaker than he is, and with those who have material possessions which he covets. "Thou shalt not kill," Exodus 20 reminds us, but both this state and many lawbreakers here have ignored this Commandment.

In anticipation that Missouri would remain a death penalty jurisdiction, the legislature enacted the necessary and proper laws to insure a smooth transition between the old and new ways of trying defendants in capital cases and executing them. The lawmakers added a penalty phase provision to the old first degree murder statute. This law now lists no fewer than 17 aggravating circumstances, including No. 7: "The murder in the first degree was outrageously or wantonly vile, horrible or inhuman in that it involved torture, or depravity of mind." However, a 1980 U.S. Supreme Court requires that this linguistic vagueness be narrowly construed and the jury instructed on its narrow construction. The prosecutor must put on evidence of serious physical abuse before death. Too broad a interpretation of this nebulous language violates the 8th and 14th Amendments' prohibitions regarding cruel and unusual punishments.[6] There are significantly fewer mitigating than aggravating circumstances, only seven. They include: (No. 1) "The defendant has no significant history of prior criminal activity" and (No. 7) "The age of the defendant at the time of the crime." Another statute requires the Missouri Supreme Court to review all death sentences.[7]

Other laws lay out the specifics of how the state may put persons to death. In 1988, the legislature passed a statute which allows death to be inflicted either by the administration of lethal gas or lethal injection. Because it permits two means of death, no person initially sentenced to die in the gas chamber was required to be brought back to court and to be resentenced to die by lethal injection. It will be remembered that when the gas chamber replaced the noose in 1938, all persons sentenced to death by hanging were required to appear before a judge in a separate proceeding in order to be resentenced to death in the gas chamber.

Missouri had only one gas chamber, and it was never mobile. It was located at MSP in Jefferson City. Death by lethal injection is not limited to a single prison; it may be carried out in any correctional center of the department of corrections, or in any prison run by the state as opposed to a county or city jail.[8] Thus far, executions by lethal injection have taken place in three different facilities in three different counties: MSP in Cole County; Potosi Correctional Center, Mineral Point, Washington County; and the Eastern Reception Diagnostic and Correctional Center, Bonne Terre, St. Francois County. Only the first occurred at MSP, an aging facility, one which began receiving inmates in 1836. MSP was never intended to be a lethal injection center. The designated killing center was Potosi Correctional Center. When it began receiving inmates in February 1989, the death row population at MSP was moved there. This maximum security prison was the locale of all executions here between January 18, 1990 and March 16, 2005. It remains home for the state's death row prisoners, but it is no longer the correctional facility where they will be executed. The strain of helping to put people to death whom the guards at Potosi have gotten to know well over the years of their confinement has proven psychologically debilitating for the prison personnel involved.[9] Under the new plan, the death-sentenced are transferred to another prison for the last month of their lives. That way the guards and other prison personnel where death by lethal injection will take place will be far less acquainted with those who must die. The new place of death is the Eastern Reception Diagnostic and Correctional Center in Bonne Terre. It opened in November 2002, and its first use of lethal injection took place on April 27, 2005.

When prison officials were getting ready for their first execution in 24 years in 1989, there was a novel approach regarding the other inmates. The newspaper reported, "A brief religious service was held for top corrections officials about 7 p.m. in the prison chapel. The two prison employees who operated the lethal injection machine were also at the service." The news story continued that "the approximately 1,900 prisoners ... were returned to their cells, to be locked in for the night. They were to resume normal activities about 5:30 a.m."[10] What no newspaper reported was the entertainment, for at least the death row prisoners, that evening. They were shown a pornographic movie, *Confessions of an American Housewife.* When the next execution occurred, the first at Potosi, the death rowers were shown another obscene film, *Double Penetration*; it concerns a sexual relationship between an inmate and a guard. After the second smutty flick was shown, a female corrections officer complained, and prison officials discontinued their showing those under death sentences porn the night of an execution.[11]

Unlike my earlier chapters wherein there is little or no collected information available either in print or through any use of a computer, in the post–*Furman* era, websites, such as the Death Penalty Information Center[12] and Missouri's Death Row: Executions: 1989–2005,[13] contain a wealth of information. I have heavily relied on both sources for the names of the executed and demographic material such as the race and age of the perpetrator(s) and the race and age of the victim(s). Through most of Missouri's history, the racism of the courts and newspapers made it easy to determine the race or races involved in any crime. One could safely assume that the participants, both perpetrator(s) and victim(s), were white people; otherwise the newspaper account or the appellate decision would state otherwise. This is no longer true. For the most part, neither court decisions nor newspapers specify the race of the perpetrator(s) and the victim(s) of crime(s). Although newspapers usually carry photographs of the executed, as a general rule there are no photographs of the victim(s) on the date of the perpetrator's execution. The date of the crime, its place(s), and the names of the victims are usually available in the Missouri Supreme Court decision.

I make extensive use of these appellate decisions for the circumstances of the homicide(s), their perpetrator(s), and other related criminal behavior, if any, of the cases which I discuss. As in Chapter 12, I do not describe each crime. My tabular summary includes sufficient detail for anyone to locate in an accredited law school library the numerous court decisions pertaining to all persons whom Missouri has executed by lethal injection. In addition, Cathleen Burnett's *Justice Denied* discusses every Missouri execution between 1989 and 2000. It is a handy book to consult for readers who do not have access to legal materials.

In the late 1980s, the U.S. Supreme Court upheld the execution of juveniles and the mentally retarded; in separate cases, the majority ruled that putting members of either group to death did not violate the 8th and the 14th Amendments' ban on cruel and unusual punishment. In 2002 this same court ruled that the mentally retarded could not be executed. Also in 2002, it prohibited a judge from imposing a death sentence when the jury could not agree; doing so, it held, violates the defendant's 6th and 14th Amendments' right to a jury trial. Finally in 2005, it banned any state from putting to death a juvenile, that is, anyone aged less than 18 years at the time of the crime. Had these U.S. Supreme Court decisions, two in 2002 and one in 2005, been in place when Missouri resumed executions in 1989, at least six persons would have been spared execution.

Frederick Lashley, aged 17 at the time of his crime, was executed in 1993. No execution of a juvenile had then occurred in Missouri since Lawrence Mabry was hanged in 1930, a period of 63 years. Three would likely have avoided death by lethal injection because they were retarded. Ricky Grubbs was executed in 1992 because, following a drinking session with an acquaintance, he robbed and killed him in St. Francois County in 1984. Burnett considers Grubbs retarded. She writes of him, "Psychological testing throughout his childhood found Mr. Grubbs had IQ scores in the low 70s. He received failing grades all his life."[14] Roy Ramsey robbed and murdered a couple in Jackson County in 1988. He was executed in 1999. In his case the Missouri Supreme court wrote that "low average intelligence is not a basis for refusing to impose the death penalty."[15] In 1986 in St. Louis City, Reginald Powell robbed and murdered two brothers. He was executed in 1998. In Powell's case, the Missouri Supreme Court ruled that his retardation was only a mitigating factor.[16]

Retarded Reginald Powell, aged 18 years at the time of his crime, Andrew Six, aged 21 at the time of his crime, executed in 1997, and Milton Griffin-El, aged 25 at the time of his crime, were all sentenced to death by a judge when members of their juries could not agree on their penalties. In 1986, Griffin-El, with other participants who avoided execution, robbed and murdered a St. Louis City couple who were parents of a four-month old baby.[17] He was executed in 1998. These U.S. Supreme Court decisions dealing with age, retardation, and judge-overrides in 2002 and 2005 have removed living persons from Missouri's death row. However these subsequent U.S. Supreme Court decisions cannot bring back to life the nine percent (6 out of 66) of the lethally injected who could not be put to death under current law.

The largest group of the post–*Furman* executed here killed in the course of robbing one or more persons. Leonard Laws was executed in May 1990, and his co-defendant, George Gilmore, in August of that same year. Between them they killed five victims, all of whom were either elderly and/or disabled. Their youngest victim was aged 65, and he had no legs and one arm. These homicides took place in 1979 and 1980. Laws received a change of venue from St. Louis County to Greene, and Gilmore one to Osage from Franklin County. That Laws was a Vietnam veteran and perhaps suffering from post–traumatic stress disorder when he committed his crimes did not dissuade his jury from sentencing him to death.[18] In two other cases which involved two participants in the criminal activity, both persons were sentenced to death. Bert Hunter and Tomas Ervin killed and robbed a man and his mother in Cole County in 1988. Hunter pled guilty, gave up his appeals, and is classified as a volunteer; he was executed in June 2000. His accomplice, Ervin, was put to death in March 2001.[19] In April 1987, Andrew Six and his uncle, Donald Petary, terrorized a family, the Allens, who lived in Ottumwa, Iowa. Had the state of Iowa tried them, the maximum punishment they might have received was life without parole. Iowa has no death penalty, and she never tried these men. Instead, the federal government prosecuted them on kidnapping charges, and Schuyler County on first degree murder charges. Six and Petary took Mr. Allen's wallet, assaulted his wife, raped their 17-year-old daughter, and murdered their 12-year-old daughter, a special education student. Her body was found in Schuyler County. The jury assessed Six's Uncle Donald's punishment at death; he was aged 50 years old at the time of his crimes. As mentioned earlier, the judge imposed a death sentence for 21-year-old Andrew Six when his jury could not agree. The year after Six was executed, Donald Petary died of natural causes in prison on May 12, 1998.[20]

Laws and Gilmore, Hunter and Ervin, and Six and Petary received equal treatment. Their cases are exceptions, not the rule. However, none of these co-defendants were simultaneously executed. The last time three men were sentenced to death in Missouri they were hanged in a warehouse in a Kansas prison in 1955. It has been more than 50 years since a Missouri prison was the locale of the simultaneous execution of two persons, Bonnie Brown Heady and Carl Austin in 1953. Perhaps in order to avoid any use of capital punishment likely to attract large numbers of protestors and receive extensive media coverage, thus far Missouri has lethally injected no more than one person on any given date. The shortest interval between executions has been six days, and most have had far wider spacing. Single executions and the timing between them could always change. These aspects of capital punishment here may or may not be factors in the very unequal treatment of the participants in most burglaries, robberies, and capital murders in the post–*Furman* era.

Robert Murray and his brother, William Murray, robbed and murdered two men in a St. Louis City apartment in 1985.[21] Robert was executed in 1995, and his brother, who may have been the trigger man, received a life sentence.[22] Robert Walls had two helpers when he killed an 88-year-old man in 1985 in St. Louis County and placed his body in a freezer. He and his co-defendants were residents of a half-way house when they burglarized, robbed, and murdered their elderly victim. Walls was executed in 1999, and his co-defendants, Terry Wilson and Tommy Thomas, are serving either life or life without parole.[23] Bruce Kilgore and Willie Luckett kidnapped, robbed, and murdered a female restaurant employee as she left work in 1986 in the city of St. Louis.[24] Kilgore was executed in 1999, and Luckett is currently an inmate at Southeast Correctional Center in Charleston, serving life without parole and lesser sentences for robbery and kidnapping. He was convicted of these felonies in 1987 in St. Louis City. Roll was sentenced to death for the 1993 Boone County murder and robbery of three members of a family.[25] He was executed in 2000 for the 1993 Boone County murder and robbery of three members of a family. One of Roll's co defendants, David Rhodes, currently housed at MSP (now termed Jefferson City Correctional Center), is serving three life sentences to run consecutively for three counts of second degree murder and one count of robbery. Roll's other co-defendant, John Browne, is currently an inmate at Northeast Correctional Center in Bowling Green and serving a life sentence for second degree murder. Stephen Johns was executed in 2001 for the 1982 murder of a 17-year-old customer in the robbery of a gas station in St. Louis City.[26] Three of his co-defendants, Linda Klund, David Smith, and Shawn Wishon, testified for the state, and they all avoided death sentences. Stanley Hall was put to death in 2005 for the 1994 murder in St. Louis County of a woman whose car he and his co-defendant, Rance Burton, stole.[27] Burton, currently house at Boonville Correctional Center, is serving 10 years for tampering with a motor vehicle and possession of a controlled substance. He was convicted on the tampering charge in 1996 and the possession charge in 1998, both in St. Louis County. Eric Schneider was executed in 1997 for the 1985 murder of a Jefferson County gay couple. His co-defendants pled guilty and received 30 years. In dissent, Supreme Court Judge Blackmar would have granted Schneider a new trial because the trial judge refused to grant a change of venue and the jury who sentenced Schneider to death never knew about the lenient treatment of the equally responsible partners in the robbery and murder of what the perpetrators termed "a couple of faggots."[28]

Three men put to death were hired killers. Walter Blair was executed in 1993 for the 1979 murder of Kathy Allen, a rape victim, in Jackson County.[29] Larry Jackson paid Blair $6,000 for the killing. Alan Bannister was put to death in 1997 for the 1983 killing in Jasper County of the man living with Linda McCormick. Her husband, Richard McCormick, paid Bannister for the murder.[30] Daniel Basile was executed in 2002 for the 1992 murder in St. Charles County of Elizabeth DeCaro. Her husband, Richard DeCaro, had purchased a $100,000 life insurance policy on his wife, and he hired Basile to kill her while he took their children and the family dog to the Ozarks. He checked into a Holiday Inn at 2:59 p.m. on the day his wife's body was found face down on the kitchen floor.[31] Richard DeCaro is not an inmate in the Missouri Department of Corrections; he may be in the federal system. Richard McCormick cannot be located in the Missouri prison system. Larry Jackson, if it is the correct Larry Jackson, was convicted of first degree murder and other charges in Jackson County in 1980. He has had two parole hearings, one in 1995 and the other in 2000; he is scheduled for another parole hearing in October 2005.[32] I can make neither a moral nor a legal distinction between a hirer and a hiree of murder. To be sure, the hirer has more money than the hired killer; the hirer may also not like the sight of blood, but it is unacceptable that all three boss men who paid another to do their dirty work have been punished far less severely than their employee.

A number of other men who acted alone when they killed their victim(s) in the course of a burglary and/or a robbery have been executed at Potosi. Some cases involved crime sprees. In November 1983, Emmett Nave killed the owner or manager of an apartment building where he lived in Cole County. He also took four women hostage at an alcohol abuse treatment center; he required oral sex of three of them. On a change of venue he was sentenced to death in St. Charles County.[33] Nave was executed in 1996. In January 1984 in Poplar Bluff, Kenneth Kenley robbed, murdered, attempted to kidnap, and required oral sex of the owner of a tavern who escaped from him. He was captured in Corning, Arkansas, and returned to Poplar Bluff. At his trial in Butler County, he was sentenced to death.[34] Kenley was executed in 2003. In December 1991, in Moniteau County, James Johnson, a Vietnam veteran, who had argued with his wife and her 19-year-old daughter, began shooting. He shot at and killed the wife of the Moniteau County sheriff, the sheriff and a deputy sheriff of Cooper County, and a deputy sheriff of Miller County. He wounded another Moniteau County deputy sheriff who survived. On a change of venue to Laclede County, his defense of post traumatic stress disorder did not succeed.[35] Johnson was executed in 2002.

Two men were tried and executed because in unrelated cases each killed a highway patrolman and did so in order to avoid arrest. In 1987 in Greene County, Glennon Sweet murdered one to avoid arrest for an outstanding warrant. On a change of venue to Clay County, he was sentenced to death by a jury.[36] Sweet was executed in 1998. In Perry County in March 1985, Jerome Mallett killed another highway patrolman, James Froemsdorf. Mallett had robbed a jewelry store in Plano, Texas, the previous month and was thought to be heading toward Missouri. In an extraordinary change of venue from Perry to Schuyler County, a jury sentenced him to death.[37] Mallett was executed in 2001.

Two men who were put to death killed their grandmothers in the process of robbing them. One was Robert Sidebottom in Jackson County in 1985;[38] he was executed in 1995, and the other, Donald Jones, in St. Louis City in 1993. Despite the fact that the family did not want Jones executed, the jury returned a death sentence.[39] Jones was the first inmate to die at Bonne Terre. He was executed in 2005. A 19-year-old, Jeffrey Sloan, in 1985 in Clinton County killed his entire family, which consisted of his parents and two younger brothers. On a change of venue to Clay County, a jury sentenced him to death.[40] Sloan was executed in 1996. In all three of these family member killings, the perpetrators were illegal drug users. In no case did their drug habits spare their lives.

Other lethally injected men first committed sex crimes and then murdered their victims. All received changes of venue. In 1978 in Jackson County, George "Tiny" Mercer raped and murdered Karen Keeton, a 22-year-old waitress; his friends had given her to him as a birthday gift. He was tried in Greene County, and the jury sentenced him to death.[41] He was executed in 1989. Mercer's was the first use of capital punishment under the authority of the state of Missouri in 24 years; his death by lethal injection is the only execution in the post–Furman era which took place at MSP; it received extensive press coverage. In 1992 in Pike County, Paul Kreutzer sexually assaulted and murdered a 36-year-old woman. Her young daughters found her nude body. He was tried in Callaway County; the jury sentenced him to death.[42] Kreutzer was executed in 2002. In Ripley County in 1985, Stanley Lingar and his co-defendant, David Smith, picked up in their car a 17-year-old boy who had run out of gas. The boy was sexually assaulted and murdered. On a change of venue to St. Francois County, Lingar's jury sentenced him to death.[43] Lingar was executed in 2001. Because the Missouri Department of Corrections currently houses almost 200 inmates named David Smith, it is not possible to locate Lingar's co-defendant through prison records.[44]

Wife-murder is not the capital crime it was in the 1890s, a decade during which at least 11 men were hanged because they murdered their spouses. Thus far only two wife-murderers have been put to death by lethal injection. Ralph Davis killed his wife, Susan, in Boone County in 1985. Her body was never recovered, but her car, a red Ford Escort, was the crime scene. Her husband put it in storage with air fresheners in Jefferson City, and 20 months after Susan's disappearance, law enforcement officer retrieved it. A Boone County jury sentenced him to death,[45] and Davis was executed in 1999. In St. Louis City in 1989, Timothy Johnson beat his wife, Susan, to death, in the presence of their 11-year-old daughter. A St, Louis City jury sentenced him to death,[46] and Johnson was executed at Bonne Terre in 2005.

Death sentences for killing in a Missouri prison are the most significant departure from earlier capital offenses. In the entire history of MSP in Jefferson City, I never located an execution of one prisoner for the killing of another until Claude McGee died in the gas chamber in 1951 for the murder of a fellow inmate. In 1839, a guard was executed for the murder of an inmate. In 1842 and 1894, crimes spaced more than 50 years apart, one prisoner was hanged for the murder of one guard. In 1902, the sheriff of Cole County hanged a prisoner who in escaping from MSP had killed a deputized prison guard. In 1907, three inmates were executed for killing two guards as the prisoners attempted to escape. In 1924, Governor Hyde commuted the sentence of John Lee, a prisoner who was sentenced to death for killing another inmate. In 1941, Governor Stark paroled Lee. In 1957, Governor Blair commuted the death sentence of Rollie Laster, an inmate at MSP, for the murder in 1954 of another inmate. I might always have missed a case, but the Jefferson City newspapers ran several retrospectives on executions in Cole County. In none of these known cases in which an MSP inmate was the perpetrator was there any change of venue. All were tried in Cole County. Prior to Lee's death sentence in the 1920s, one inmate's murder of another in the state's only penitentiary, MSP in Jefferson City, does not appear to have been prosecuted as a death penalty crime. Between 1836, the year prisoners began arriving at MSP, and 1922, the year Lee stabbed one of his cellmates to death, there are no known capital crimes involving one inmate's murder of another, a period of 86 years. Surely, at least one inmate murdered another during the first eight and one-half decades of MSP housing persons convicted of felonies here.

Then came the new death penalty laws in the post–Furman era and their rigorous application to prison homicides. During the 1980s, the state of Missouri obtained at least 13 death sentences for murders in the various correctional facilities throughout the state. Many of these prison homicide cases involved changes of venue. Their numbers are unprecedented. Some of these prisoners were guilty as charged. Martsay Bolder, an African-American, was already serving a life sentence at MSP for a Jackson County killing when, on March 14, 1979, he stabbed to death another black inmate, Thereon King. The victim had called the perpetrator "a pussy-assed nigger," a reference to 21-year-old Bolder's status as a prison sex object. On a change of venue to Randolph County, he was sentenced to death.[47] Bolder was executed in 1993. On January 25, 1981, at MSP, Frank Guinam and Richard Zeitvogel stabbed their fellow inmate, John McBroom, to death. On a change of venue from Cole to Franklin County, Guinam was sentenced to death.[48] He was executed in 1993. On a change of venue from Cole to Randolph County, Zeitvogel was sentenced to life without parole in the killing of John McBroom. On March 25, 1984, Zeitvogel strangled to death his cellmate, Gary Wayne Dew, called a corrections officer, and told him, "I killed my cellie."[49] Burnett makes a convincing case that Zeitvogel and Dew should never have been placed in the same cell. Zeitvogel had been a witness to an earlier attempted murder in the basement of the prison chapel, and he had identified Dew as one of the perpetrators. Dew's attorney told him who had pointed him out to prison authorities; Dew may have wished to get even with a man who had snitched on him and been the initial aggressor.[50] Zeitvogel may also have wished to share a cell with Frank Guinam, then on death row for the murder of John McBroom. Zeitvogel was executed in 1996.

Meanwhile, Gerald Smith and Frank Guinam killed Robert Baker at MSP on November 29, 1985. The unusual aspect of this crime was that both the perpetrators and the victim were all already under death sentences for unrelated crimes. Nonetheless, Smith and Guinam were prosecuted for Baker's murder. The state obtained additional death sentences for both, presumably as back-up if for some reason their initial death sentences were overturned on appeal. Gerald Smith was the first prison put to death at Potosi, for the 1980 St. Louis County murder of a former girlfriend, but at the time he was executed in 1990, he also faced another death sentence for his death row killing in 1985.[51] Guinam was executed in 1993 for the murder of one inmate, John McBroom, in 1981, but he was also under sentence of death for the murder of another, Robert Baker, in 1985.[52]

On February 23, 1984, according to the state's theory, Robert O'Neal, a white inmate, stabbed Arthur Dade, a black inmate, while Lloyd Schlup, another white inmate held Dade. (Schlup's case is discussed in Chapter 12.) On a change of venue to Butler County, nine inmate witnesses said the victim attacked the perpetrator, and the killing was in self defense. The jury did not believe these defense witnesses. Its members sentenced O'Neal to death. In affirming the Missouri Supreme Court abandoned its usual silence on the race of the perpetrator and the victim; it specified that a white man killed a black.[53] O'Neal was put to death in 1995. The last time a white man was executed in Missouri for the murder of a black was 1876 in Warren County, or 119 years earlier. It is unlikely that the state could obtain a death sentence for a white man's murder of a black outside a prison setting.

Other prison inmates sentenced to death for the murder of another inmate include Sam Smith and Michael Taylor. Sam Smith was a prisoner at MSP when he stabbed Marlin Mays to death on January 15, 1897. On a change of venue from Cole to Callaway County, the jury sentenced him to death.[54] Sam Smith was executed in 2001. Michael Taylor was a prisoner at Potosi when on October 3, 1999, he strangled his cellmate, Shackrein Thomas, to death in their cell shortly after they appear to have had consensual sex. On a change of venue from Washington to St. Charles County, the jury rejected Taylor's insanity defense; it sentenced him to death. The Missouri Supreme Court affirmed his sentence.[55] He is currently an inmate on death row at Potosi. Taylor may not be competent. Rather he may resemble two other inmates sentenced to death for prison killings.

On July 15, 1979, Bobby Shaw, a retarded, brain-damaged, and mentally ill prisoner, stabbed a guard, Walter Farrow, to death at MSP. He was sentenced to death; Governor Carnahan commuted Shaw's death sentence to life imprisonment shortly before his scheduled execution. Shaw has subsequently died a natural death in prison. On November 24, 1985, Steven Parkus, an inmate at MSP, strangled Mark Steffenhagen to death after these inmates, like Taylor and his victim, had had consensual sex. On a change of venue from Cole to Cape Girardeau County, Parkus was sentenced to death, and the Missouri Supreme Court affirmed. Judge Blackmar concurred in the guilt of Parkus, but he dissented on the punishment. He wrote,

> The record shows that the defendant has lived his life from a very young age in some form of custody in a Missouri institution. He has been unable to adapt to any environment in which he finds himself. The easiest course of action might be to execute him as a means of extermination or euthanasia, but there should be a limit to the process of burying our mistakes.... I would exercise our statutory authority by mitigating the death sentence to life imprisonment.[56]

In a case in which a federal court remanded Parkus' death sentence for a hearing on the ineffectiveness of his counsel, one of the judges wrote of Parkus:

> Steven Parkus suffered physical abuse, sexual abuse and neglect throughout his childhood. At age three, his parents abandoned him to the custody of an alcoholic uncle, who brutalized and sexually abused him.... Some records describe Parkus as mentally defective, borderline mentally retarded, borderline psychotic, or schizophrenic. Other medical opinions state his condition less severely, or place more emphasis on Parkus' sociopathic nature. Parkus' IQ generally tested at a little over 70, which indicates borderline mental retardation.[57]

By executive order in September 1999, Governor Carnahan stayed the execution of Parkus in order for experts to make a determination of his mental fitness for being put to death. As of this writing, Steven Parkus remains on death row; he has been there longer than all but four of the current residents.

One of the inmates executed for the murder of another inmate was Roy "Hog" Roberts. He was charged as an accomplice of Robert Driscoll in the July 3, 1983 killing of a prison guard at Moberly. On a change of venue from Randolph to Marion County, the jury did not believe the eight inmate witnesses who testified that "Hog" was not involved in the murder of Officer Jackson. Its members sentenced him to death. He had always admitted to striking a guard during the riot in which 30 to 60 persons were present. In 1986, the Missouri Supreme Court affirmed Roberts' death sentence. This court always presents the version of events most favorable to the prosecution when it upholds the conviction. Its decision includes the following:

> It appeared momentarily that Jackson might escape but he was stopped short of the control center door by appellant [Roy "Hog" Roberts] who seized him by the arm and hair, twisting his head "completely around" and pinning him against the door casing. With Jackson held in this position by appellant, inmate Driscoll stabbed him three times in the chest, two of which penetrated the heart.... After appellant had released Jackson and struck the would-be rescuer, he resumed his grip on the stabbed and bleeding Jackson and inmate Rodney Carr then stabbed Jackson in the abdomen. Jackson was also stabbed near his left eye, possibly by Driscoll.... Five guards and approximately thirty inmates required treatment for injuries.[58]

I mailed Robert Driscoll this portion of the decision at his place of employment and asked him to contact me. He phoned me in response. He scoffed at the official explanation of Officer Jackson's death. He said neither Roberts nor Carr was involved. He emphasized that Roberts' cell was never searched, no bloody clothes of his were found, and Roberts never confessed. Initially he had been written up for striking a guard in the face. Had Roberts actually been seen holding Officer Jackson as first Robert Driscoll and next Rodney Carr stabbed him, the initial write-up should have included Roberts' participation in Jackson's murder. According to Driscoll, it did not. Driscoll has carefully read the transcripts of all the trials pertaining to the July 3, 1983, events at Moberly Correctional Center; he maintains there are major inconsistencies in the testimony of the state's witnesses. Whatever one may conclude about who caused the death of Officer Jackson, one cannot be confident that "Hog," the man sentenced to death for his murder, was guilty as charged. There was surely a miscarriage of justice when he was executed in 1999 for allegedly holding the victim guard as the current employee of a St. Louis law firm, Robert Driscoll, stabbed him. As of this writing that employee has cherished his freedom since his release from prison in 2003. He told me that he had not so much as jay-walked.

Thanks largely to the federal courts, of the 13 men sentenced to death for prison killings in the 1980s, six or 46%— Joe Amrine, Eric Clemmons, Robert Driscoll, Steven Parkus, Bobby Shaw, and Lloyd Schlup — were not, for one reason or another, death-eligible. No other crime scene has yielded such uncertain results. The extensive number of changes

Photograph of Cathleen Burnett at a vigil on November 29, 2005, held at the J.C. Nichols Fountain on the Plaza, Kansas City. She was protesting the upcoming 1000th execution in the United States since the reinstatement of the death penalty in 1976. On December 2, 2005, the state of North Carolina executed Kenneth Boyd; he was the 1000th person put to death in the United States since 1976. (Photograph by the author.)

of venue out of the county containing the various prisons in which either guards or inmates were killed has cured very little. For the most part the jurors have believed the state's witnesses, not the defendants. Without the availability of extensive appellate remedies, more than one person innocent of a prison murder would have been executed.

Because Missouri's death row currently houses many inmates and its capital punishment statutes are alive and well, this book ends in the middle of things. This may not be a satisfactory conclusion, but it is the only one possible when one writes about a state which now is rank-ordered fourth in the nation in her use of execution by lethal injection. There is always the hope that Missourians will sicken of capital punishment as they did early in the twentieth century. During the 1890s, more boys and men were hanged under the authority of the state of Missouri than in any other decade. The excesses of this time period eventually gave way to the dwindling use of the death penalty and finally to its abolition. Perhaps history will repeat itself.

Appendix 1: Executions of Death Sentences in Missouri, 1803–2005

Abbreviations: I=Indian; W=White; B=Black; M=Male; F=Female; A=Adult; C=Child; and "=same crime as above.

Note: In column 1, the 39 Gas Chamber executions are noted as (GC); and (LI) indicates execution by Lethal Injection. As of October 26, 2005, there have been 66 Lethal Injection executions.

In the name column, the entries marked with an asterisk (*) indicate information located independent of Watt Espy.

A note on the "County" column: Missouri was divided into districts until 1812, when the territorial governor changed the chief unit of government from district to county. Only five executions which took place in Missouri's districts can be documented. One, the earliest, occurred under Spanish rule in New Madrid District; the other four were under American rule, three in St. Louis District and one in Ste. Genevieve District. All other known death sentences in Missouri were obtained in counties.

Effective August 22, 1876, St. Louis County was divided into St. Louis City County and St. Louis County, with Clayton the seat of the latter.

Name, Race, Sex, and Age	Race, Sex, and Age of Victim(s)	Date of Execution	Executing Offense	County	Authority	Appealed
1. *Tewanye, IMA	WM48	Jan. 3, 1803	Murder	New Madrid	Spain	No
2. *Quabesca, IMA	WMA	June 10, 1806	Murder	St. Louis	U.S.	No
3. *Ouifumcaka, IMA	"	June 10, 1806	Murder	St. Louis	U.S.	No
4. Long, John Jr., WMA	WM51	Sept. 16, 1809	Murder	St. Louis	U.S.	No
5. Johnston, Peter, WMA	WMA	Aug. 3, 1810	Murder	Ste. Genevieve	U.S.	No
6. Heath, Charles, WMA	WMA	March 9, 1812	Murder	Ste. Genevieve	U.S.	No
7. Gordon, William, WMA	Unknown	1820	Murder	New Madrid	U.S.	No
8. Duncan, John, WM19	W Family 4	April 5, 1821	Murder	Madison	MO	No
9. Short, William, WMA	WMA	April 17, 1824	Murder	Howard	MO	No
10. *Slave Luke, BMA	WMA	Sept. 2, 1826	Murder	Cooper	MO	No
11. King, Hugh, WMA	WMA	May 19, 1827	Murder	St. Louis	MO	Yes
12. Morris, Pressly, WMA	WMA	May 26, 1828	Murder	Cape Girardeau	MO	No
13. *Slave Annice, BFA	5 slave children	Aug. 23, 1828	Murder	Clay	MO	No
14. Slave Moses, BMA	WMA	Spring 1829	Murder	Montgomery	MO	No
15. *Cogland, Michael, WMA	WMA	Sept. 26, 1829	Murder	St. Louis	MO	Yes
16. *Stewart, Jacob, WMA	WMA	April 13, 1830	Murder	Howard	MO	No
17. *Slave Jack, BMA	WMA	1830	Murder	Cooper	MO	No
18. *Jenkins, James, WMA	WFA	Sept. 29, 1830	Murder	St. Louis	MO	No
19. Earls, Samuel, WM60	WMA	Dec. 13, 1831	Murder	Boone	MO	Yes
20. Slave Hampton, BMA	WMA	March 23, 1832	Murder	Howard	MO	No
21. Whitson, Isaac, WMA	WMA	Jan. 30, 1833	Murder	Cape Girardeau	MO	No
22. Hubbard, James, WMA	WMA	Jan. 1834	Murder	St. Louis	MO	No
23. Trumley, Leland, WMA	WMA	April 4, 1834	Murder	Lafayette	MO	No
24. Trumley, Mary, WFA	W Infant	April 30, 1834	Murder	Lafayette	MO	No
25. *Slave Archie, BMA	WMA	1835	Murder	Boone	MO	No
26. *Slave Conway, BMA	WMA	April 8, 1836	Murder	Callaway	MO	No
27. *Slave Jake, BMA	"	June 20, 1836	Murder	Callaway	MO	No
28. *Slave Washington Hill, BMA	WMA (blind)	1837	Murder	Howard	MO	No
29. *Slave David Gates, BMA	"	1837	Murder	Howard	MO	No
30. Slave Henry, BMA	WFA	Aug. 11, 1837	Murder	Ray	MO	No
31. Slave Ish, BMA	"	Aug. 11, 1837	Murder	Ray	MO	No
32. Slave Mary, BF13/14	WF2	Aug. 11, 1838	Murder	Crawford	MO	Yes
33. *Goster, George, WMA	WMA	May 10, 1839	Murder	Jackson	MO	No
34. Lane, Henry, WMA	WM21	Oct. 14, 1839	Murder	Cole	MO	No
35. Buchanan, James, WMA	WMA	Jan. 3, 1840	Murder	St. Louis	MO	No

36. *Brown, Charles, BM26/27	2 WM22	July 9, 1841	Murder	St. Louis	MO	No
37. Sewell, James, BM27/28	"	July 9, 1841	Murder	St. Louis	MO	No
38. Warrick, Amos, BM26	"	July 9, 1841	Murder	St. Louis	MO	No
39. Slave Madison Henderson, BM34/35	"	July 9, 1841	Murder	St Louis	MO	No
40. Slave Lewis, BMA	WMA	Aug. 7, 1841	Murder	Pike	MO	No
41. *Howard, [last name only], WMA	Unknown	Aug. 13, 1841	Murder	Cooper	MO	No
42. White, Ben, WMA	WMA	Aug. 13, 1841	Murder	Ray	MO	No
43. Savilia, Joseph, WMA	WMA	Jan. 28, 1842	Murder	Lafayette	MO	No
44. Berry, William, WMA	WMA	Feb. 10, 1842	Murder	Cole	MO	No
45. Burr, Dedimus, WMA	WFA	July 8, 1842	Murder	Cole	MO	No
46. Johnson, [last name only], WMA	WMA	March 3, 1843	Murder	St. Louis	MO	No
47. Slave America, BFA	WMA	June 10, 1843	Murder	Boone	MO	No
48. Slave Henry, BMA	"	June 10, 1843	Murder	Boone	MO	No
49. Freeman, John, WMA	WMA	1844	Murder	Montgomery	MO	No
50. Myers, Conrad, WMA	WMA	May 24, 1844	Murder	Crawford	MO	No
51. McDaniel, John,WMA	WMA	Aug. 16, 1845	Murder	St. Louis	U.S.	No
52. Brown, Joseph, WMA	"	Aug. 16, 1845	Murder	St. Louis	U.S.	No
53. Lester, John, WMA	WM20	July 31, 1846	Murder	Henry	MO	Yes
54. *Slave Nathan, BMA	BMA	Feb. 20, 1847	Murder	Cape Girardeau	MO	No
55. Slave Peter Douglas, BMA	WFA and 3 slave children	1848	Murder	Dade	MO	No
56. Slave Ben, BMA	WM10 and WF12	Jan. 11, 1850	Murder	Marion	MO	No
57. Gallagher, Hugh, WMA	WFA	Dec. 13, 1850	Murder	St. Louis	MO	No
58. Thomas, John, WMA	WMA	Feb. 14, 1851	Murder	St. Louis	MO	No
59. Slave Isaac, BM18	WFA	Nov. 14, 1851	Murder	Warren	MO	No
60. Elliott, Joel, WMA	WMA	Sept. 10, 1852	Murder	Lafayette	MO	No
61. Slave Abe, BMA	BMA	June 24, 1853	Murder	Platte	MO	No
62. Dodge [last name only], WMA	Unknown	July 22, 1853	Murder	St. Louis	MO	No
63. Schoen, [last name only], WMA	Unknown	July 22, 1853	Murder	St. Louis	MO	No
64. Jennings, Augustus, WMA	WMA	Sept. 2, 1853	Murder	Buchanan	MO	Yes
65. Washam, Willis, WMA	WM14	Aug. 25, 1854	Murder	Greene	MO	No
66. Huting, John, WMA	WF21	Aug. 31, 1855	Murder	Montgomery	MO	Yes
67. Nottingham, William, WMA	WFA	Nov. 23, 1855	Murder	Bates	MO	No
68. Slave Celia, BF19	WM70	Dec. 21, 1855	Murder	Callaway	MO	No
69. Slave Henry, BMA	WMA	July 11, 1856	Murder	Lafayette	MO	No
70. *Nichols, James, WMA	WMA	June 5, 1857	Murder	Johnson	MO	No
71. Neuslein, Jacob, WMA	WFA	June 19, 1857	Murder	St. Louis	Mo	Yes
72. LaPointe, John, WMA	WMA	June 19, 1857	Murder	St. Louis	MO	No
73. Shoultz, Israel, WM18–20	WMA	June 19, 1857	Murder	St. Louis	MO	Yes
74. Worrell, Edward, WM27/28	WM30	June 27, 1857	Murder	Franklin	MO	Yes

Name, Race, Sex, and Age on date of crime	Race, Sex, and Age of Victim(s)	Date of Execution	Executing Offense	County	Authority	Appealed
75. *Slave Joe, BM18	WMA	Nov. 13, 1857	Murder	Boone	MO	No
76. Shehane, Robert, WMA	WMA	Aug. 7, 1858	Murder	Oregon	MO	Yes
77. *Chapman, John, WM34	WMA	July 16, 1858	Murder	Howard	Mo	No
78. Slave John, BMA	WMA	Dec. 31, 1858	Murder	Lafayette	MO	No
79. Slave Larrell, BMA	"	Dec. 31, 1858	Murder	Lafayette	MO	No
80. Owens, John, BMA	Unknown	1859	Murder	Randolph	MO	No
81. *Slave George Bruce, BMA	WMA	Jan. 7, 1859	Murder	Randolph	MO	No
82. Lamb, George, WMA	WFA	June 17, 1859	Murder	St. Louis	MO	Yes
83. Thorton, Joseph, WM38	WMA	Nov. 11, 1859	Murder	St. Louis	MO	No
84. Slave Green, BM18/19	WMA	Dec. 2, 1859	Murder	Buchanan	MO	No
85. Brust, Samuel, WMA	WMA	Aug. 31, 1860	Murder	St. Louis	MO	No
86. Baird, Joseph, WM40	WM52	May 10, 1861	Murder	Lewis	MO	No
87. *Cole, John, WMA	WMA	July 25, 1861	Murder	Greene	Union Army	No
88. *Owens, John, WMA		June 8, 1862	Bushwhacking	Monroe	Union Army	No
89. *Unnamed, WMU		"	Bushwhacking	Lafayette	Union Army	No
90. *Unnamed, WMU		"	Bushwhacking	Lafayette	Union Army	No
91. *Unnamed, WMU		"	Bushwhacking	Lafayette	Union Army	No
92. *Unnamed, WMU		"	Bushwhacking	Lafayette	Union Army	No
93. *Unnamed, WMU		"	Bushwhacking	Lafayette	Union Army	No
94. *Unnamed, WMU		"	Bushwhacking	Lafayette	Union Army	No
95. *Unnamed, WMU		"	Bushwhacking	Lafayette	Union Army	No
96. *Unnamed, WMU		"	"	"	Union Army	No
97. Wilson, William, WMA	WMA	June 8, 1862	Murder	St. Louis	MO	No
98. *Ballee, William, WMA		June 27, 1862	Parole Violation	Adair	Union Army	No
99. *Bates, William, WMA		Aug. 7, 1862	Parole Violation	Adair	Union Army	No
100. *Brannon, Hamilton, WMA		"	Parole Violation	Adair	Union Army	No
101. *Christian, James, WMA		"	Parole Violation	Adair	Union Army	No
102. *Galbreath, R.M., WMA		"	Parole Violation	Adair	Union Army	No
103. *Green, Reuben, WMA		"	Parole Violation	Adair	Union Army	No
104. *Harris, Columbus, WMA		"	Parole Violation	Adair	Union Army	No
105. *Hayden, Bennett, WMA		"	Parole Violation	Adair	Union Army	No
106. *Kent, John, WMA		"	Parole Violation	Adair	Union Army	No
107. *Rollins, Lewis, WMA		"	Parole Violation	Adair	Union Army	No
108. *Thomas, Reuben, WMA		"	Parole Violation	Adair	Union Army	No
109. *Webb, Thomas, WMA		"	Parole Violation	Adair	Union Army	No
110. *Wilson, William, WMA		"	Parole Violation	Adair	Union Army	No

#	Name	Code	Date	Crime	County	Force	
111.	*Wood, David, WMA		"	Parole Violation	Adair	Union Army	No
112.	*Wood, Jesse, WMA		"	Parole Violation	Adair	Union Army	No
113.	*M.C. Cullough, Frisby, WM32		Aug. 8, 1862	Bushwhacking and Guerrilla Activity	Adair	Union Army	No
114.	Sartain, Calvin, WMA Lt. (Price's Army)	WMA	Aug. 15, 1862	Murder of the pilot of the *White Cloud*	Linn	Union Army	No
115.	*Richardson, John, WMA		Sept. 4, 1862	Counterfeiting Confederate treasury notes	Clay	Union Army	No
116.	*Slave, unknown, BMA	WFA WF12	Sept. 6, 1862	Attempted Rape	Ray	Union Army	No
117.	*Bell, David, WMA		Sept. 26, 1862	Treason, Perjury, and Murder	Macon	Union Army	No
118.	*Drake, Frank, WMA		"	Treason, Perjury and Murder	Macon	Union Army	No
119.	*Fox, J.H., WMA		"	Treason, Perjury and Murder	Macon	Union Army	No
120.	*Hall, James, WMA		"	Treason, Perjury and Murder	Macon	Union Army	No
121.	*Hamilton, Elbert, WMA		"	Treason, Perjury, and Murder	Macon	Union Army	No
122.	*Oldham, John, WMA		"	Treason, Perjury, and Murder	Macon	Union Army	No
123.	*Riggs, Edward, WMA		"	Treason, Perjury, and Murder	Macon	Union Army	No
124.	*Rowe, A.C M.D., WMA		"	Treason, Perjury, and Murder	Macon	Union Army	No
125.	*Searcy, William, WMA		"	Treason, Perjury, and Murder	Macon	Union Army	No
126.	*Wysong, J.A., WM20/21		"	Treason, Perjury, and Murder	Macon	Union Army	No
127.	*Washburne, D.S., WMA		"	Unknown	Randolph	Union Army	No
128.	*Baker, Willis, WMA	WMA	Oct. 18, 1862	Abduction and probable murder	Marion	Union Army	No
129.	*Bixler, Morgan, WMA	"		Abduction and probable murder	Marion	Union Army	No
130.	*Hudson, Herbert, WMA	"		Abduction and probable murder	Marion	Union Army	No
131.	*Humston, Thomas, WMA	"		Abduction and probable murder	Marion	Union Army	No
132.	*Lair, Francis, WMA	"		Abduction and probable murder	Marion	Union Army	No

Name, Race, Sex, and Age on date of crime	Race, Sex, and Age of Victim(s)	Date of Execution	Executing Offense	County	Authority	Appealed
			probable murder			
133. *Lear, Eleazer, WMA	"	"	Abduction and probable murder	Marion	Union Army	No
134. *McPheeters, John, WMA		"	Abduction and probable murder	Marion	Union Army	No
135. *Smith, Hiram, WM17		"	Abduction and probable murder	Marion	Union Army	No
136. *Sidenor, Thomas, WMA		"	Abduction and probable murder	Marion	Union Army	No
137. *Wade, John, WMA		"	Abduction and probable murder	Marion	Union Army	No
138. Kearns, Michael, WMA	WMA	Jan. 23, 1863	Murder	St. Louis	MO	No
139. Edmonds, James, WMA	WMA	March 6, 1863	Murder	Jefferson	MO	No
140. Burns, Joseph, WMA	WMA	May 8, 1863	Murder	St. Louis	MO	Yes
141. Dale, Samuel, WMA	WMA	May 26, 1863	Bushwhacking and murder	Clark	Union Army	No
142. Standiford, Aquilla, WMA	"	May 26, 1863	Bushwhacking and murder	Clark	Union Army,	No
143. *Snelling, Benjamin, WMA		Aug. 15, 1863	Bushwhacking and terrorizing Johnson and Henry Counties	Henry	Union Army	No
144. Slave Henry, BM16	WM63	Aug. 28, 1863	Murder	Moniteau	MO	No
145. *Carlyle, [last name only], WMA		Sept. 9, 1863	Bushwhacking	Lafayette	Union Army	No
146. *Hamilton, Frederick, WMA		Sept. 25, 1863	Horse stealing	Moniteau	Union Army	No
147. *Zimmerman, M.D., WMA [last name only]	"	"	Horse stealing	Moniteau	Union Army	No
148. *Nichols, John, WM22	BMA	Oct. 30, 1863	Guerrilla activity and killing a Negro	Cole	Union Army	No
149. Linville, William, WM19	WMA	Nov. 6, 1863	Murder	Buchanan	MO	No
150. Kingston, Paul, Corporal, WM34	WMA	Nov. 27, 1863	Murder	Cape Girardeau	Union Army	No
151. Hansen, Valentine, WM35	WMA	April 16, 1864	Murder	St. Louis	MO	No
152. Mullins, Paddy, WM17		April 23, 1864	Bushwhacking	Moniteau	Union Army	No

	Date	Crime	County	Military	
153. *Reily, John, Private, WMA	April 29, 1864	Murder	Johnson	Union Army	No
154. *Snyder, Andrew, WMA	May 6, 1864	Guerrilla activity	Macon	Union Army	No
155. *Hadley, Willard, WM22	May 20, 1864	Guerrilla activity	Johnson	Union Army	No
156. Lanier, Joseph, WMA	June 10, 1864	Aiding rebellion against U.S.	Andrew	Union Army	No
157. *Fielding, [last name only], WMA	June 12, 1864	Guerrilla activity	Platte	Union Army	No
158. *Oldham, Lt. (Confederate), WMA	June 12, 1864	Guerrilla Activity	Platte	Union Army	No
159. *Gibbons, Barney, Private, WM27	Aug. 12, 1864	Desertion	St. Louis	Union Army	No
160. *Wilcox, John, WMA	Aug. 12, 1864	Bushwhacking	Cole	Union Army	No
161. *Livingston, William, WM46/47	Aug. 19, 1864	Spying	St. Louis	Union Army	No
162. Bowyer, A.J., WM21/22	Sept. 9, 1864	Guerrilla activity and robbery	Buchanan	Union Army	No
163. *Smith, Stephen, WM37	Sept. 9, 1864	Guerrilla activity and spying	St. Louis	Union Army	No
164. *Moore, William, WM22	Sept. 9, 1864	Guerrilla activity and spying	St. Louis	Union Army	No
165. Griffith, Henry, WMA	Sept. 23, 1864	Guerrilla activity and robbery	Buchanan	Union Army	No
166. *Gallup, William, WM21	Oct. 10, 1864	Bushwhacking	Lewis	Union Army	No
167. *Abshire, John, WM20/21	Oct. 17, 1864	Violation of the laws of war & murder	St. Louis	Union Army	No
168. Jefferson, Jackson, Private, WMA	Oct. 28, 1864	Murder	Buchanan	Union Army	No
169. *Blackburn, Harvey, WMA	Oct. 29, 1864	Retaliation for murder of Union Army Major and 6 others	St. Louis	Union Army	No
170. *Bunch, George, WM22	"	"	St. Louis	Union Army	No
171. *Gates, James, WM21	"	"	St. Louis.	Union Army	No
172. *Ladd, Asa, WM34	"	"	St. Louis	Union Army	No
173. *Minniken, Charles, WM22	"	"	St. Louis	Union Army	No
174. *Nichols, John, WM21		"	St. Louis	Union Army	No
175. *Eastman, Edward, Private, WM19/20	Nov. 25, 1864	Article 52 Violation	Phelps	Union Army	No
176. *Utz, James, WM26	Dec. 26, 1864	Spying and recruiting for the Rebel Army	St. Louis	Union Army	No

Name, Race, Sex, and Age on date of crime	Race, Sex, and Age of Victim(s)	Date of Execution	Executing Offense	County	Authority	Appealed
177. Purvis, Abraham, Private, WM16	WMA	Jan. 13, 1865	Murder	St. Louis	Union Army	No
178. Richardson, Ephraim, Private, WM 17/18	"	"	Murder	St. Louis	Union Army	No
179. *Hamilton, James, WMA		March 3, 1865	Guerrilla activity	Macon	Union Army	No
180. Harris, William, WMA		March 24, 1865	Guerrilla activity	St. Louis	Union Army	No
181. *Thorpe, Thomas, WM29	WMA	May 1, 1865	Murder and guerrilla activity	St. Louis	Union Army	No
182. *Wright, G.P., WMA		June 2, 1865	Guerrilla Activity	Johnson	Union Army	No
183. Willis, Green, WMA	WMA	March 1, 1866	Murder	Buchanan	MO	No
184. Hart, Zeke, WMA	WMA	Oct. 19, 1866	Murder	Morgan	MO	No
185. Blue, Thomas, BMA	WFA & WMA	June 21, 1867	Murder	Monroe	MO	No
186. Christman, Peter, WM19/20	WMA & WMC	Dec. 6, 1867	Murder	St. Louis	MO	No
187. Hughes, Alfred, BMA	WMA	July 24, 1868	Murder	Clinton	MO	No
188. Edwards, William, BM31/32	BMA	July 23, 1869	Murder	St. Louis	MO	No
189. Skaggs, John, WMA	WMA	Aug. 6, 1870	Murder	Stoddard	MO	No
190. Grable, John, WM33	WM46	Sept. 9, 1870	Murder	Buchanan	MO	Yes
191. Bailey, Jeremiah, WM20	WM24	Dec. 13, 1870	Murder	New Madrid	MO	No
192. Jolly, Charles, WM32	W Family (5)	Jan. 27, 1871	Murder	Washington	MO	No
193. Armstrong, John, WM32	"	"	"	"	"	"
194. Waller, Charles, WMA	W Family (3)	May 17, 1872	Murder	Webster	MO	No
195. Champion, Robert, BMA	BFA	Feb. 21, 1873	Murder	Howard	MO	No
196. *Walker, Samuel, BMA	BFA	May 15, 1874	Murder	Clay	MO	No
197. *Carlisle, John, WM19/20	WMA	July 24, 1874	Murder	Saline	MO	Yes
198. Hamilton, Joseph, WM17/19	WMA	Oct. 30, 1874	Murder	Harrison	MO	Yes
199. O'Shea, Patrick, WMA	WFA	April 9, 1875	Murder	St. Louis	MO	No
200. Travis, Harris, WM34/35	WM65	April 16, 1875	Murder	Scott	MO	Yes
201. Brown, Henry, BM25	WM52	Oct. 22, 1875	Murder	St. Louis	MO	Yes
202. Hallenscheid, Henry, WM54	WM28	Dec. 17, 1875	Murder	Gasconade	MO	No
203. Catalano, Antonio, WMA	WM25	Feb. 18, 1876	Murder	St. Louis	MO	No
204. Damina, Dominico, WMA	"	"	"	"	"	
205. Lombardo, Bastiano, WM21	"	"	"	"	"	
206. Foster, William, WM26	BMA	June 19, 1876	Murder	Warren	MO	Yes
207. Price, Daniel, BMA	WMA	Jan. 18, 1877	Murder	Warren	MO	Yes
208. Pints, William, WM30	WF9	April 27, 1877	Murder	Bolinger	MO	Yes
209. Edmundson, Poindexter, WMA	WMA	July 13, 1877	Murder	Stoddard	MO	Yes

No.	Name	Code	Date	Crime	County	State	
210.	Orr, Samuel, WM21/22	WMA	May 18, 1877	Murder	Lawrence	MO	Yes
211.	Wieners, William, WM21	WMA	Feb. 1, 1878	Murder	St. Louis City	MO	Yes
212.	Ables, John, WM60+	WMA	Feb. 15, 1878	Murder	Jasper	MO	Yes
213.	Green, Richard, WM27	WMA	March 1, 1878	Murder	Jackson	MO	Yes
214.	Daniels, John, WMA	WMA	March 1, 1878	Murder	Johnson	MO	Yes
215.	Isaacs, Richard, WMA	WM30	Oct. 25, 1878	Murder	Cass	MO	No
216.	West, John, WM23	WM28	May 16, 1879	Murder	Cooper	MO	Yes
217.	Blan, John, WM21/22	WMA	June 6, 1879	Murder	St. Charles	MO	Yes
218.	Guy, Monroe, BM21	BMA	June 6, 1879	Murder	Jefferson	MO	Yes
219.	Davidson, Frank, WM24	WMA	July 10, 1879	Murder	Johnson	MO	Yes
220.	Hardin, Charles, WMA	WMA	Jan. 23, 1880	Murder	St. Francois	MO	No
221.	Kilgore, John, WM22	WMA	March 5, 1880	Murder	Audrain	MO	No
222.	Core, Joseph, WMA	WMA	March 5, 1880	Murder	Laclede	MO	Yes
223.	Barton, William, BM15	WM26	March 26, 1880	Murder	St. Charles	MO	No
224.	Muldrow, Joseph, BM19	WMA	April 16, 1880	Murder	Audrain	MO	No
225.	Faucett, Nathan, BM35	"	"	"	"	"	"
226.	Nugent, Edward, WM46	WFA	April 23, 1880	Murder	St. Louis City	MO	Yes
227.	Redemeier, Henry, WM31	WMA	April 23, 1880	Murder	St. Louis City	MO	Yes
228.	Cropp, John, BMA	WMA	June 11, 1880	Murder	Chariton	MO	No
229.	*Hopper, Thomas, WMA	WMA	June 25, 1880	Murder	Dade	MO	Yes
230.	Brown, James, WMA	WMA	June 25, 1881	Murder	Randolph	MO	Yes
231.	Meyers, Jesse, WMA	WMA	July 15, 1881	Murder	New Madrid	MO	No
232.	Brown, Frank, WMA	"	"	"	"	"	"
233.	*Patterson, John, WMA	WMA	July 22, 1881	Murder	Henry	MO	Yes
234.	Talbott, Charles, WM16	WM53	July 22, 1881	Murder	Nodaway	MO	Yes
235.	Talbott, Albert, WM21	"	"	"	"	"	"
236.	Erb, William, WMA	WFA	Dec. 30, 1881	Murder	St. Louis City	MO	Yes
237.	Ellis, Charles, BMA	BMA	Jan. 6, 1882	Murder	St. Louis City	MO	Yes
238.	Kotovsky, Joseph, WMA	WFA	Jan. 6, 1882	Murder	St. Louis City	MO	Yes
239.	Phelps, John, WMA	WMA	Jan. 6, 1882	Murder	Saline	MO	Yes
240.	Baber, Thaddeus, WM31	2 WFA	Jan. 13, 1882	Murder	St. Louis City	MO	Yes
241.	Ward, William, BM27	BFA	Jan. 13, 1882	Murder	St. Louis City	MO	No
242.	Bohanan, George, WM19	WM21	April 21, 1882	Murder	Phelps	MO	No
243.	Sanders, Alfred, BMA	BFA	April 6, 1883	Murder	Mississippi	MO	No
244.	Underwood, Howard, BM60	BFA	Dec. 8, 1882	Murder	Mississippi	MO	Yes
245.	Fox, William, WMA	WMA	Dec. 28, 1883	Murder	Vernon	MO	No
246.	Lewis, Matthew, BM38	BFA	March 14, 1884	Murder	St. Louis City	MO	Yes
247.	Dickson, Thomas, WMA	WMA	May 2, 1884	Murder	Stoddard	MO	Yes
248.	Hamilton, Charley, WMA	WMA	July 11, 1884	Murder	Johnson	MO	No
249.	Hamilton, Billy, WMA	"	"	"	"	"	"

Name, Race, Sex, and Age on date of crime	Race, Sex, and Age of Victim(s)	Date of Execution	Executing Offense	County	Authority	Appealed
250. Bateman, Oliver, WM22	WF7 & WF9	Nov. 21, 1884	Murder	Andrew	MO	No
251. Collins, Samuel, WMA	WMA	Aug. 28, 1885	Murder	Pike	MO	Yes
252. Stair, Henry, WM35	WM16/17 & WM55	Jan. 15, 1886	Murder	Vernon	MO	Yes
253. Wilson, Charles, BM24	WM27	Jan. 15, 1886	Murder	St. Louis City	MO	Yes
254. Wilson, Jeff, BMA	BFA	April 2, 1886	Murder	Lafayette	MO	Yes
255. Jump, Joseph, WM20	WMA	July 23, 1886	Murder	Daviess	MO	No
256. Smith, John, WM22	"	Aug. 6, 1886	"	"	"	"
257. Graynor, Robert, BM25	BMA	Dec. 10, 1886	Murder	St. Louis City	MO	Yes
258. Clum, Edward, WM42	WF17 &WM47	April 15, 1887	Murder	Barry	MO	Yes
259. Jewell, Daniel, BM24	BFl7	April 15, 1887	Murder	St. Louis City	MO	Yes
260. Blunt, Alfred, BM32	BFA	June 24, 1887	Murder	St. Louis City	MO	Yes
261. Sneed, Edwarrd, WMA	WMA	June 24, 1887	Murder	Jackson (Independence)	MO	Yes
262. Hronek, Peter, WM32	WFA	June 29, 1888	Murder	Buchanan	MO	Yes
263. Rider, George, WMA	WMA	July 13, 1888	Murder	Saline	MO	Yes
264. Brooks, Hugh, alias Maxwell, Walter, WM27	WM27	Aug. 10, 1888	Murder	St. Louis City	MO	Yes
265. Langraf, alias Langford Henry, WM30	WF21	Aug. 10, 1888	Murder	St. Louis City	MO	Yes
266. Matthews, John, WM41	2 WMA	May 10, 1889	Murder	Christian	MO	Yes
267. Walker, David, WM44	"	"	"	"	"	"
268. Walker, William, WM16/18	"	"	"	"	"	"
269. Turlington, John, alias West, William, WM27	WMA	March 6, 1891	Murder	Cooper	MO	Yes
270. Jackson, Webster, WMA	WMA	April 25, 1891	Murder	Gasconade	MO	Yes
271. Price, William, BM23	WF19	May 8, 1891	Rape	Saline	MO	No
272. Henson, Henry, WM36	WFA	Aug. 13, 1891	Murder	St. Louis City	MO	Yes
273. Young, Chris, WM29	WMA	Aug. 13, 1891	Murder	Lafayette	MO	Yes
274. Bulling, Louis, WMA	WFA	Sept. 4, 1891	Murder	Andrew	MO	Yes
275. Williamson, Thomas, WM56	WM29 &WM58	Oct. 31, 1891	Murder	Pettis	MO	Yes
276. Seaton, Charles, WM16	WM17	Dec. 4, 1891	Murder	Lawrence	MO	Yes
277. Harben, William, WMA	WMA	Jan. 15, 1892	Murder	Butler	MO	Yes
278. McCoy, William, BM35	BF38	Feb. 16, 1893	Murder	Lafayette	MO	Yes
279. Avery, Amos, WM19	WM21	May 24, 1893	Murder	Barton	MO	Yes
280. Howell, Joseph, WM24	WFA, WM9, WF7, WF5, WM2	Aug. 4, 1893	Murder	Grundy	MO	Yes
281. Robinson, Dick, BMA	WFA	Dec. 15, 1893	Murder	Pettis	MO	Yes

No.	Name		Date	Crime	County	State	
282.	Banks, Charles, BMA	BMA	Dec. 29, 1893	Murder	Johnson	MO	Yes
283.	Reed, Martin, BM65	BF51	Jan. 5, 1894	Murder	Jackson	MO	Yes
284.	Welsor, Samuel, WM46	WFA	Jan. 12, 1894	Murder	St. Louis City	MO	Yes
285.	Howard, Wilson, WM31	WMA	Jan. 19, 1894	Murder	Laclede	MO	Yes
286.	*Wisdom, Charles, BM25	WM40	April 13, 1894	Murder	St. Louis City	MO	Yes
287.	Brown, Jake, alias John Coleman, BMA	WMA	May 4, 1894	Murder	Cole	MO	Yes
288.	Jones, Harry, WM30	WFA	June 29, 1894	Murder	Jackson	MO	No
289.	Clark, John, alias Ricksher, William, WM37	"	"	Murder	"	"	Yes
290.	Wilson, Charles, BM29	BMA	July 26, 1894	Murder	St. Louis City	MO	Yes
291.	Duncan, Harry, alias Harrison, William, BMA	WMA	July 27, 1894	Murder	St. Louis (Clayton)	MO	Yes
292.	Martin, Phillip, BM17-18/19	WM34	Feb. 15, 1895	Murder	Jackson	MO	Yes
293.	Burries or Burrus, Joseph, BM20	WF7	May 11, 1895	Rape	Buchanan	MO	Yes
294.	Murray, James, BMA	WMA	May 11, 1895	Murder	St. Louis (Clayton)	MO	Yes
295.	Murray, Edward, BMA	"	"	"	Gasconade	MO	Yes
296.	David, Emile, WMA	WMA	Feb. 15, 1896	Murder	Osage	MO	Yes
297.	Fitzgerald, James, WM29	WFA	Feb. 20, 1896	Murder	St. Louis City	MO	Yes
298.	Nelson, John, WMA	WF56 & WMA	Feb. 28, 1896	Murder	Marion	MO	Yes
299.	Taylor, William, WM34	WM33, WF30, WF4, WF1	April 30, 1896	Murder	Carroll	MO	Yes
300.	Wright, William, BM40	BFA	Aug. 10, 1896	Murder	Vernon	MO	Yes
301.	Anderson, George, WMA	WFA	Aug. 21, 1896	Murder	Macon	MO	No
302.	Inks, James, WMA	WMA	Jan. 30, 1897	Murder	Holt	MO	Yes
303.	Perry, Edward, WM24	2 WMA & WFA	Jan. 30, 1897	Murder	Douglas	MO	Yes
304.	Schmidt, Peter, WM17	WMA	Feb. 16, 1897	Murder	St. Louis (Clayton)	MO	Yes
305.	Foster, Samuel, BMA	"	"	"	"	"	"
306.	Duestrow, Arthur, WM29	WFA & WM2	Feb. 17, 1897	Murder	Franklin	MO	Yes
307.	Pollard, James, BMA	BMA	June 25, 1897	Murder	Buchanan	MO	No
308.	Johnson, Thomas, BMA	WM18	Nov. 18, 1897	Murder	St. Louis City	MO	No
309.	Carr, William, WMA	WF3	Dec. 17, 1897	Murder	Clay	MO	No
310.	Lanahan, Tobe, BMA	BF12	June 22, 1898	Rape and Murder	Cole	MO	Yes
311.	McKenzie, Ed, BMA	WMA	June 22, 1898	Murder	Cole	MO	Yes
312.	Tomasitz, John, WM27	WFA	June 22, 1898	Murder	St. Louis City	MO	Yes
313.	Albright, James, WMA	WMA	July 9, 1898	Murder	Mississippi	MO	Yes
314.	Thompson, George, BMA	WMA	Aug. 1, 1898	Murder	St. Louis City	MO	Yes
315.	Brown, James, BM31	BM28	Dec. 28, 1898	Murder	Jackson	MO	Yes
316.	Sexton, Ira, WM23	WM36	Dec. 28, 1898	Murder	Mercer	MO	Yes
317.	Baker, Oscar, WM45	WFA	Jan. 10, 1899	Murder	Shannon	MO	Yes

Name, Race, Sex, and Age on date of crime	Race, Sex, and Age of Victim(s)	Date of Execution	Executing Offense	County	Authority	Appealed
318. Reed, James, BM16	BF26	March 30, 1899	Murder	Jackson	MO	Yes
319. Soper, Bates, WMA	WFA, WF6, & WM3	March 30, 1899	Murder	Cass	MO	Yes
320. Hancock, Matthew, BM25	WMA	April 8, 1899	Murder	St. Louis City	MO	Yes
321. Bronstine, Fred, WMA	WFA	May 8, 1899	Murder	Clark	MO	Yes
322. Burns, Will, BMA	BFA	May 29, 1899	Murder	Scott	MO	Yes
323. Cochran, Freeman, WMA	WMA	June 7, 1899	Murder	Harrison	MO	Yes
324. Kindred, Peter, WM22	WMA	June 7, 1899	Murder	Mercer	MO	Yes
325. Headrick, John, WM19	WMA	June 15, 1899	Murder	Cape Girardeau	MO	Yes
326. Rice, Carroll, WMA	WF20	June 15, 1899	Murder	Oregon	MO	Yes
327. McAfee, James, WMA	WM24	July 7, 1899	Murder	Jasper	MO	Yes
328. Nettles, James, BM29	WMA	May 7, 1900	Murder	St. Louis City	MO	Yes
329. Clevenger, Ernest, WM25	WMA &WFA	June 15, 1900	Murder	Clay	MO	Yes
330. *Holloway, John, WM31	WMA	June 15, 1900	Murder	Osage	MO	Yes
331. Waters, Samuel, BMA	BMA & BFA	June 15, 1900	Murder	New Madrid	MO	Yes
332. *McGinnis, Noah, WMA	WMA	Dec. 30, 1900	Murder	Bates	MO	Yes
333. Tettalon, James, WMA	WFA, 2 WMC, & 2 WFC	Feb. 19, 1901	Murder	Dunklin	MO	Yes
334. Milo, Gregory, WM26	WMA	March 21, 1901	Murder	Dunklin	MO	Yes
335. Evans, Ellsworth, BMA	WMA	April 12, 1901	Murder	Cooper	MO	Yes
336. *Reid, alias Reed, Ernest, BMA	BFA	July 5, 1901	Murder	Jasper	MO	Yes
337. Garth, Albert, BM26	BFA	Jan. 21, 1902	Murder	Jackson	MO	Yes
338. Craft, Joshua, WM27	WMA	Jan. 21, 1902	Murder	Cole	MO	Yes
339. Jackson, James, BM26	BM24	April 11, 1902	Murder	Jackson	MO	Yes
340. Flutcher, Henry, BM27	WMA	April 11, 1902	Murder	St. Louis City	MO	Yes
341. Armstrong, General, BM16/18	WF16	April 25, 1902	Rape	Platte	MO	No
342. Reeves, Charles, BMA	BFA	May 23, 1902	Murder	Cooper	MO	Yes
343. Brown, Sam, WMA	WMA	June 27, 1902	Murder	Wayne	MO	Yes
344. Johnson, Jesse, BMA	WMA	Sept. 12, 1902	Murder	Ralls	MO	No
345. Dunn, Thomas, BM29	BMA	Jan. 2, 1903	Murder	St. Louis City	MO	Yes
346. Gurley, Charles, BM28	BF20	Feb. 3, 1903	Murder	St. Louis City	MO	Yes
347. Clark, Steve, WMA	WFA	Feb. 6, 1903	Murder	Butler	MO	Yes
348. Gatlin, Will, BMA	BMA	Feb. 6, 1903	Murder	Butler	MO	Yes
349. Taylor, John, WM28	WF18	April 17, 1903	Murder	Jackson	MO	Yes
350. May, Charles, WM29	WMA	April 17, 1903	Murder	Buchanan	MO	Yes
351. Gartrell, James, WM68	WMA	April 17, 1903	Murder	Bates	MO	Yes

#	Name	Victim	Date	Crime	County	State	
352.	Gray, Sampson, BM23	BMA	May 8, 1903	Murder	St. Louis City	MO	Yes
353.	Wilson, Henry, BM23	WMA	May 8, 1903	Murder	St. Louis City	MO	Yes
354.	Clark, Frank, BM22	WF17	Nov. 25, 1903	Rape	Clark	MO	No
355.	Robertson, John, WMA	WM65	Jan. 15, 1904	Murder	Adair	MO	Yes
356.	Dunn, Mark, WM36	WMA	March 11, 1904	Murder	Buchanan	MO	Yes
357.	Collins, George, alias Lewis, Fred, WMA	WMA	March 26, 1904	Murder	Franklin	MO	Yes
358.	Smith, Elias, WMA	WMA	April 21, 1905	Murder	Pulaski	MO	No
359.	Rudolph, Bill, WMA	WMA	May 8, 1905	Murder	Franklin	MO	Yes
360.	Henderson, Allen, BM18	BMA	June 15, 1905	Murder	St. Charles	MO	Yes
361.	Heusack, Henry, WM55	WM77	Aug. 21, 1905	Murder	St. Louis City	MO	Yes
362.	Jackson, Curtis, BM16	WFA	March 22, 1906	Rape	Butler	MO	No
363.	Bateman, Edward, BM23	WF20	Aug. 7, 1906	Rape	Lawrence	MO	Yes
364.	Hamilton, Joseph, WM20	5 family members	Dec. 21, 1906	Murder	Texas	MO	No
365.	Church, William, WM25	WMA & WFA	Jan. 10, 1907	Murder	Warren	MO	Yes
366.	King, John, BM21	BF20	June 27, 1907	Murder	St. Louis City	MO	Yes
367.	Raymond, Edward, WMA	2 WMA	June 27, 1907	Murder	Cole	MO	Yes
368.	Ryan, George, WMA	"	"	"	"	"	"
369.	Vaughn, Harry H., WMA	"	"	"	"	"	"
370.	Jeffries, William, WM28	WMA	June 4, 1908	Murder	St. Charles	MO	Yes
371.	Filley, Albert, WM32	4 W family members	Sept. 21, 1908	Murder	Caldwell	MO	No
372.	Brooks, Claud, BM22	WM46	July 30, 1909	Murder	Jackson	MO	Yes
373.	Williams, John, BMA	WF24	Feb. 8, 1910	Rape	Jackson	MO	No
374.	Reynolds, George, BM24	"	"	"	"	"	"
375.	Wilson, William, BM26	WF25	March 4, 1910	Murder	Jasper	MO	Yes
376.	Davis, Robert, BM24	BM17	June 10, 1910	Murder	Jackson	MO	Yes
377.	Jackson, George, BM19	WF60	June 10, 1910	Rape	Mississippi	MO	No
378.	Rasco, Hezekiah, WM31	4 W family members	March 26, 1912	Murder	Nodaway	MO	Yes
379.	*Robinson, Wesley, BMA	BFA & BFI1	Feb. 15, 1915	Murder	Jackson	MO	Yes
380.	Sprouse, William, WMA	WFA	July 16, 1915	Murder	St. Louis (Clayton)	MO	Yes
381.	Black, Andrew, BM27	WM45 & WM46	Aug. 18, 1916	Murder	St. Charles	MO	Yes
382.	Black, Harry, BM29	"	"	"	"	"	"
383.	Jackson, Adam, alias Johnson, James, BM39	WFA	March 26, 1920	Rape	Butler	MO	No
384.	Jacoy, Charles, WM23	WMA	Aug. 12, 1921	Murder	Franklin	MO	Yes
385.	*Lee, Walker, BM38	WF50	Aug. 17, 1921	Rape	Jackson (Kansas City)	MO	Yes
386.	Carroll, John, WMA	WMA	Sept. 12, 1921	Murder	Franklin	MO	Yes
387.	*Jackson, Sterling, BM23	WM66	Aug. 3, 1923	Murder	Jasper	MO	Yes

Name, Race, Sex, and Age on date of crime	Race, Sex, and Age of Victim(s)	Date of Execution	Executing Offense	County	Authority	Appealed
388. *Long, Ralph, BM26	"	"	"	"	"	"
389. Merrell, Charles, WM23	WM43 & WM52	July 18, 1924	Murder	St. Louis City	MO	Yes
390. Pinkley, Hugh, WM35	"	"	"	"	"	"
391. Williams, Leon, BM26	WM43	July 17, 1925	Murder	St. Louis City	MO	Yes
392. Crump, James, BM25	WMA	July 17, 1925	Murder	Montgomery	MO	Yes
393. *Johnson, Robert, BM29	WFA	Feb. 28, 1927	Rape	St. Louis (Clayton)	MO	Yes
394. Lowry, Thomas, WM24	WMA	Feb. 1, 1929	Murder	St. Louis City	MO	Yes
395. Yeager, Leonard, WM31	WMA	Feb. 1, 1929	Murder	St. Louis City	MO	Yes
396. Mabry, Lawrence, WM17/19	WMA	Jan. 31, 1930	Murder	Cooper	MO	Yes
397. *Mosley, William, BM54	BF42, WMA, & WFA	Jan. 31, 1930	Murder	St. Louis City	MO	Yes
398. Mangiaracina, Antonio, WM30	WMA	July 25, 1930	Murder	Jackson (Kansas City)	MO	Yes
399. Messino, John, WM29	"	"	"	"	"	"
400. Nasello, Carl, WM22	"	"	"	"	"	"
401. Hershon, Joe, WM26	WMA	Jan. 15, 1932	Murder	Jackson (Kansas City)	MO	Yes
402. Worden, Lew, WM34	WF16	March 3, 1932	Rape	Jasper	MO	No
403. *White, Emmerson, BM32	BM70	Aug. 12, 1932	Murder	St. Louis City	MO	Yes
404. Kellar, James, WM30	WF25	Jan. 20, 1933	Murder	St. Louis (Clayton)	MO	Yes
405. Worden, Harry, WM27	WF15	Feb. 10, 1933	Rape	Jasper	MO	Yes
406. Miller, David, WM48	WF46	Feb. 10, 1933	Murder	St. Charles	MO	Yes
407. Boyd, John, BM32	WFA	Nov. 2, 1933	Rape	St. Louis (Clayton)	MO	No
408. Gordon, Sam, BM22	WM62	Dec. 15, 1933	Murder	Jackson (Kansas City)	MO	Yes
409. Jefferson, March, BM28	"	"	"	"	"	"
410. *Copeland, Eugene, BMA	WMA	June 29, 1934	Murder	St. Louis City	MO	Yes
411. Kaufman, Paul, WM36	WF17	June 29, 1934	Murder	Jackson (Kansas City)	MO	Yes
412. McDaniel, Frank, BM30	BFA	April 12, 1935	Murder	Greene	MO	Yes
413. Roland, William, BM45	2 WMA	April 12, 1935	Murder	Gasconade	MO	Yes
414. *Ward, C.D., BM25	WF27	Aug. 16, 1935	Rape	Dunklin	MO	Yes
415. Gayman, Edward, WM43	WMA	Aug. 30, 1935	Murder	New Madrid	MO	Yes
416. Hamilton, Roy, WM25	"	"	"	"	"	"
417. McKeever, George, WM36	2 WMA	Dec. 18, 1936	Murder	Callaway	MO	Yes
418. Hardy, Hurt, WM32	WF20	Feb. 26, 1937	Murder	Ste. Genevieve	MO	Yes
419. Adams, Fred, WM22	WM26	April 2, 1937	Murder	Dunklin	MO	Yes
420. Barr, Dudley, BM29	BMA	May 21, 1937	Murder	Jackson (Kansas City)	MO	Yes
421. Jackson, Roscoe, WM36	WMA	May 21, 1937	Murder	Stone	MO	Yes
422. Brown, John (GC), BM35	WMA	March 4, 1938	Murder	Jackson at MSP	MO	Yes

423. Wright, William (GC), BM32	BMA	March 4, 1938	Murder	Jackson at MSP	MO	Yes
424. Boyer, Raymond (GC), WM35	WM30	March 5, 1938	Murder	Jackson at MSP	MO	Yes
425. Batson, Raymond (GC), BM32	WM45	June 30, 1938	Murder	St. Louis at MSP	MO	Yes
426. Jones, Johnnie (GC), BM34	WF45	July 15, 1938	Rape	New Madrid at MSP	MO	No
427. Ricchetti, Adam (GC), WM28	5 WMA	Oct. 7, 1938	Murder	Jackson at MSP	MO	Yes
428. Allen, Granville (GC), BMA	WM47	Oct. 28, 1938	Murder	Jackson at MSP	MO	Yes
429. King, Byron (GC), WM27	WM68	Nov. 4, 1938	Murder	St. Louis City at MSP	MO	Yes
430. Williamson, John (GC), WM62	WMA	Feb. 15, 1939	Murder	Ste. Genevieve at MSP	MO	Yes
431. Kenyon, Robert (GC), WM23	WMA	April 28, 1939	Murder	Oregon at MSP	MO	Yes
432. West, Robert (GC), WM24	WF20	Sept. 20, 1940	Murder	St. Louis at MSP	MO	Yes
433. Jackson, Chester (GC), BM31	BFA	Sept. 20, 1940	Murder	Jasper at MSP	MO	Yes
434. Johnson, Wilburn (GC), BM39	BF13 & BM15	Jan. 3, 1941	Murder	Butler at MSP	MO	No
435. Tyler, Ernest (GC), BM36	WM40	April 24, 1942	Murder	Jackson at MSP	MO	Yes
436. Lambus, Allen (GC), BM73	BF14	June 16, 1944	Rape and Murder	Mississippi at MSP	MO	No
437. Thomas, James (GC), BM20	WF22	Oct. 20, 1944	Rape	St. Louis at MSP	MO	Yes
438. Lyles, Leo (GC), BM21	WM23	May 25, 1945	Murder	St. Louis at MSP	MO	Yes
439. Talbert, William (GC), BM24	WMA	Nov. 16, 1945	Murder	St. Louis at MSP	MO	Yes
440. Ellis, Fred (GC), BMA	WF56	Aug. 16, 1946	Murder	Franklin at MSP	MO	Yes
441. Sanford, Jesse (GC), BMA	"	"	"	"	"	"
442. Ramsey, Van (GC), BM36	WF19	Jan. 10, 1947	Murder	St. Louis City at MSP	MO	Yes
443. Perkins, Marshall (GC), BM59	WF13	Jan. 24, 1947	Rape	Jackson at MSP	MO	Yes
444. Cochran, Floyd (GC), BM35	WF20	Sept. 26, 1947	Rape and Murder	Boone at MSP	MO	Yes
445. Scott, Afton (GC), WM48	WFA & WMA	Nov. 4, 1949	Murder	Wright at MSP	MO	Yes
446. Bell, George (GC), BM35	BM30	Dec. 2, 1949	Murder	Jackson at MSP	MO	Yes
447. Tiedt, Charles (GC), WM55	2 WMA & WFA	May 19, 1950	Murder	Buchanan at MSP	MO	Yes
448. McGee, Claude (GC), WM38	WM47	Jan. 5, 1951	Murder	Cole at MSP	MO	Yes
449. Porter, Willie (GC), BM29	WF70	Oct. 28, 1952	Rape	Cole at MSP	MO	No
450. Quilling, Ulas (GC), BM50	2 BF40 & BMA	May 29, 1953	Murder	Jackson at MSP	MO	Yes
451. Boyd, Kenneth (GC), BM23	WM54	July 10, 1953	Murder	St. Louis City at MSP	MO	Yes
452. Heady, Bonnie (GC), WF41	WM6	Dec. 18, 1953	Kidnapping and Murder	Jackson at MSP	U.S.	No
453. Hall, Carl 32 (GC), WM34	"	"	"	"	"	"
454. Beverly, Chastine, Private, BM25	WM52	March 1, 1955	Murder	Pulaski at Lansing, KS Prison	U.S. Army	Yes
455. Riggins, James, Private, BM28	"	"	"	"	"	"
456. Suttles, Louis, Private, BM26	"	"	"	"	"	"
457. Booker, Dock (GC), BM46	BMA	April 1, 1955	Murder	St. Louis City at MSP	MO	Yes
458. Brown, Arthur (GC), WM31	WF34	Feb. 24, 1956	Kidnapping	Jackson at MSP	U.S.	No
459. Moore, Thomas (GC), BM42	BF36	Sept. 13, 1957	Murder	Jackson	MO	Yes

Name, Race, Sex, and Age on date of crime	Race, Sex, and Age of Victim(s)	Date of Execution	Executing Offense	County	Authority	Appealed
460. Tucker, Sammy (GC), WM26	WM67 & WM24	July 26, 1963	Murder	Cape Girardeau at MSP	MO	Yes
461. Odom, Charles (GC), WM32	WF13	March 6, 1964	Rape	Jasper at MSP	MO	Yes
462. Wolfe, Ronald (GC), WM34	WF8	May 8, 1964	Rape	Pike at MSP	MO	Yes
463. Anderson, Lloyd (GC), BM22	WM15	Feb 26, 1965	Murder	St. Louis City at MSP	MO	Yes
464. Mercer, George (LI), WM34/44	WF22	Jan. 6, 1989	Murder	Greene at MSP	MO	Yes
465. Smith, Gerald (LI), WMA	WF20	Jan. 18, 1990	Murder	St. Louis City at Potosi	MO	Yes
466. Stokes, Winford (LI), BM26/39	WF33	May 11, 1990	Murder	St. Louis at Potosi	MO	Yes
467. Laws, Leonard (LI), WM31/40	WM83 WF81 WF72	May 17, 1990	Murder	St. Louis at Potosi	MO	Yes
468. Gilmore, George (LI), WM33/44	"	Aug. 31, 1990	Murder	St. Louis at Potosi	MO	Yes
469. Byrd, Maurice (LI), BM25/36	WM51 WF51 WF68 WF37	Aug. 23, 1991	Murder	St. Louis at Potosi	MO	Yes
470. Grubbs, Ricky (LI), WM25/33	WM36	Oct. 21, 1992	Murder	St. Francois at Potosi	MO	Yes
471. Bolder, Martsay (LI), BM21/35	BMA	Jan. 27, 1993	Murder	Randolph at Potosi	MO	Yes
472. Blair, Walter (LI), BM18/32	WF21	July 21, 1993	Murder	Jackson at Potosi	MO	Yes
473. Lashley, Frederick (LI), BM17/29	BF54	July 28, 1993	Murder	St. Louis City at Potosi	MO	Yes
474. Guinan, Frank (LI), WM35/47	WM30	Oct. 6, 1993	Murder	Franklin at Potosi	MO	Yes
475. Foster, Emmitt (LI), BM32/44	BM26	May 3, 1995	Murder	St. Louis at Potosi	MO	Yes
476. Griffin, Larry (LI), BM25/40	BM19	June 21, 1995	Murder	St. Louis City at Potosi	MO	Yes
477. Murray, Robert (LI), BM22/32	2 BMA	July 26, 1995	Murder	St. Louis City at Potosi	MO	Yes
478. Sidebottom, Robert (LI), WM23/33	WF74	Nov. 15, 1995	Murder	Jackson at Potosi	MO	Yes
479. Larette, Anthony (LI), WM28/44	WF18	Nov. 29, 1995	Murder	Warren at Potosi	MO	Yes
480. O'Neal, Robert (LI), WM23/34	BM32	Dec. 6, 1995	Murder	Butler at Potosi	MO	Yes
481. Sloan, Jeffrey (LI), WM19/29	WMA WFA WM18 WM8	Feb. 21, 1996	Murder	Clay at Potosi	MO	Yes
482. Williams, Doyle (LI), WM33/48	WMA	April 10, 1996	Murder	Clay at Potosi	MO	Yes
483. Nave, Emmett (LI), BM43/55	WFA	July 31, 1996	Murder	St. Charles at Potosi	MO	Yes
484. Battle, Thomas (LI), BM18/34	BF80	Aug. 7, 1996	Murder	St. Louis City at Potosi	MO	Yes
485. Oxford, Richard (LI), WM30/39	WMA WFA	Aug. 21, 1996	Murder	Platte at Potosi	MO	Yes
486. Zeitvogel, Richard (LI), WM27/40	WMA	Dec. 11, 1996	Murder	Cole at Potosi	MO	Yes
487. Schneider, Eric (LI), WM23/35	2 WMA	Jan. 29, 1997	Murder	Jefferson at Potosi	MO	Yes
488. Feltrop, Ralph (LI), WM32/42	WFA	Aug. 6, 1997	Murder	Jefferson at Potosi	MO	Yes
489. Reese, Donald (LI), WM43/54	2 WMA	Aug. 13, 1997	Murder	Jefferson at Potosi	MO	Yes
490. Six, Andrew (LI), WM21/32	WF12	Aug. 20, 1997	Murder	Schuyler at Potosi	MO	Yes
491. McDonald, Samuel (LI), BM32/48	WMA	Sept. 24, 1997	Murder	St. Louis City at Potosi	MO	Yes
492. Bannister, Alan (LI), WM24/39	WMA	Oct. 22, 1997	Murder	McDonald at Potosi	MO	Yes
493. Powell, Reginald (LI), BM18/29	2 BMA	Feb. 25, 1998	Murder	St. Louis City at Potosi	MO	Yes

#	Name	Victim	Crime	Date	Location	State	
494.	Griffin-El, Milton (LI), BM25/37	BFA BMA	Murder	March 25, 1998	St. Louis City at Potosi	MO	Yes
495.	Sweet, Glennon (LI), WM21/33	WMA	Murder	April 22, 1998	Clay at Potosi	MO	Yes
496.	Malone, Kelvin (LI), BM20/38	WM62	Murder	Jan. 13, 1999	St. Louis at Potosi	MO	Yes
497.	Rodden, James (LI), WM23/38	WFA	Murder	Feb. 24, 1999	Clay at Potosi	MO	Yes
498.	Roberts, Roy (LI), WM30/46	WM62	Murder	March 10, 1999	Marion at Potosi	MO	Yes
499.	Ramsey, Roy (LI), BM35/45	WFA WM65	Murder	April 14, 1999	Jackson at Potosi	MO	Yes
500.	Davis, Ralph (LI), BM48/61	WFA	Murder	April 28, 1999	Boone at Potosi	MO	Yes
501.	Wise, Jessie (LI), BM35/46	BFA	Murder	May 26, 1999	St. Louis at Potosi	MO	Yes
502.	Kilgore, Bruce (LI), BM26/38	WF54	Murder	June 16, 1999	St. Louis City at Potosi	MO	Yes
503.	Walls, Robert (LI), WM20/33	WM88	Murder	June 30, 1999	St. Louis at Potosi	MO	Yes
504.	Leisure, David (LI), WM30/49	WMA	Murder	Sept. 1, 1999	St. Louis City at Potosi	MO	Yes
505.	Hampton, James (LI), WM54	WFA	Murder	March 22, 2000	Callaway at Potosi	MO	Yes
506.	Hunter, Bert (LI), WM41/53	WM49 WF75	Murder	June 28, 2000	Cole at Potosi	MO	Yes
507.	Roll, Gary (LI), WM/48	2 WMA WFA	Murder	Aug. 30, 2000	Boone at Potosi	MO	Yes
508.	Harris, George (LI), BM30/41	BMA	Murder	Sept. 13, 2000	Jackson at Potosi	MO	Yes
509.	Chambers, James (LI), WM30/48	WMA	Murder	Nov. 15, 2000	Jefferson at Potosi	MO	Yes
510.	Lingar, Stanley (LI), WM22/37	WM17	Murder	Feb. 7, 2001	St. Francois at Potosi	MO	Yes
511.	Ervin, Tomas (LI), WM50	WM49 WF75	Murder	March 28, 2001	Callaway at Potosi	MO	Yes
512.	Young, Mose (LI), BM27/46	3 BMA	Murder	April 25, 2001.	St. Louis City at Potosi	MO	Yes
513.	Smith, Sam (LI), BM26/40	BMA	Murder	May 23, 2001	Callaway at Potosi	MO	Yes
514.	Mallett, Jerome (LI), BM26/42	WMA	Murder	July 11, 2001	Schuyler at Potosi	MO	Yes
515.	Roberts, Michael (LI), WM19/27	WF56	Murder	Oct. 3, 2001	St. Louis at Potosi	MO	Yes
516.	Johns, Stephen (LI), WM35/55	WM17	Murder	Oct. 24, 2001	St. Louis City at Potosi	MO	Yes
517.	Johnson, James (LI), WM42/52	2 WFA 2 WMA	Murder	Jan. 9, 2002	Laclede at Potosi	MO	Yes
518.	Owsley, Michael (LI), BM31/40	BMA	Murder	Feb. 6, 2002	Jackson at Potosi	MO	Yes
519.	Tokar, Jeffrey (LI), WM27/37	WMA	Murder	March 6, 2002	Warren at Potosi	MO	Yes
520.	Kreutzer, Paul (LI), WM20/30	WF36	Murder	April 10, 2002	Callaway at Potosi	MO	Yes
521.	Basile, Daniel (LI), WM25/35	WFA	Murder	Aug. 14, 2002	St. Charles at Potosi	MO	Yes
522.	Jones, William (LI), WM21/37	WMA	Murder	Oct. 29, 2002	Jackson at Potosi	MO	Yes
523.	Kenley, Kenneth (LI), WM23/42	WMA	Murder	Feb. 5, 2003	Butler at Potosi	MO	Yes
524.	Smith, John (LI), BM35/41	WFA WMA	Murder	Oct. 29, 2003	Audrain at Potosi	MO	Yes
525.	Hall, Stanley (LI), BM26/37	WFA	Murder	March 16, 2005	St. Louis at Potosi	MO	Yes
526.	Jones, Donald (LI), BM26/38	BFA	Murder	April 27, 2005	St. Louis City at Bonne Terre	MO	Yes
527.	Brown, Vernon (LI), BM31/51	BFA	Murder	May 18, 2005	St. Louis City at Bonne Terre	MO	Yes
528.	Johnson, Timothy (LI), WM28/44	WFA	Murder	Aug. 31, 2005	St. Louis City at Bonne Terre	MO	Yes
529.	Gray, Marlin, BM23/38	WF19 WF21	Murder	Oct. 26, 2005	St. Louis City at Bonne Terre	MO	Yes

Appendix 2: Pardons and Commutations in Death Sentences in Missouri, 1803–1999

Abbreviations: I=Indian; W=White; B=Black; M=Male; F=Female; A=Adult; C=Child; and "=same crime as above.

Name	Race and Age of Perpetrator	Race and Age of Victim(s)	Date of Commutation/ Pardon	Offense	County/ District	Commuting/ Pardoning Authority
1. Unknown Creek Indian	IMA	WM48	Jan. 3, 1803	Murder	New Madrid	Spain P
2. Unknown Creek Indian	IMA	"	Jan. 3, 1803	Murder	New Madrid	Spain P
3. Unknown Creek Indian	IMA	"	Jan. 3, 1803	Murder	New Madrid	Spain P
4. Unknown Creek Indian	IMA	"	Jan. 3, 1803	Murder	New Madrid	Spain P
5. Hononquise	IMA	WMA	June 10, 1806	Murder	St. Louis	U.S. Jefferson P
6. Little Crow	IMA	WMA	Feb. 25, 1810	Murder	St. Louis	U.S. Madison P
7. Hall, Reuben	WMA	WMA	Dec. 6, 1824	Murder	Cole	MO Bates P
8. Hustoff, William	WMA		April 1829	Desertion	St. Louis	U.S. Jackson P
9. Furguson, Robert	WMA		Sept. 29, 1829	Desertion	St. Louis	U.S. Jackson P
10. Richardson, James	WMA		Sept. 29, 1829	Desertion	St. Louis	U.S. Jackson P
11. Mitchell, Hartford	WMA	WMA	Nov. 1833	Murder	St. Louis	MO Dunklin P
12. Hawkins, Alfred	WMA	WMA	May 1838	Murder	Carroll	MO Boggs C; died at MSP 1840
13. Hunting, Edward	WMA	WMA	May 1838	Murder	St. Charles	MO Boggs C
14. Grizzle, William	WMA	WMA	June 1840	Murder	Benton	Mo Boggs C; died at MSP 1845
15. Bird, Amos	WM15	WMA	Jan. 1843	Murder	Cape Girardeau	MO Reynolds C; died at MSP May 13, 1845
16. McDaniel, David	WMA	WMA	June 1844	Murder	St. Louis	U.S. Tyler P
17. Towson, Thomas	WMA	"	"	"	"	U.S. Tyler P
18. Slave Nelly	BF15	B Infant	Oct. 15, 1846	Murder	Warren	MO Edwards P
19. Baldwin, Elisha	WMA	WMA	July 2, 1849	Murder	St. Louis	MO King P
20. Montesquious, Gonzales	WMA	2 WMA	Oct. 1850	Murder	St. Louis	MO King P
21. Montesquious, Rignard	WMA	"	Oct. 1850	Murder	St. Louis	MO King P
22. Roberts, John, alias Ward	WM29	WMA	Feb. 22, 1852	Murder	St. Louis	MO King C; MSP record blankon when or if released
23. Conner, Michael	WM27	Unknown	March 22, 1854– March 21, 1860	Murder	St. Louis	MO Price C & Stewart P
24. Shoots, Benjamin	WM23	WFA	Oct. 26, 1854–Nov. 23, 1854	Murder	Monroe	MO Price C & P
25. Hays, Ethelred	WMA	WMA	July 12, 1855–Feb. 4, 1857	Murder	Randolph	MO Price C & Stewart P
26. Haycraft, Sarah	WFA	WMA	June 1856–Feb. 27, 1858	Murder	St. Louis	MO Price C & Stewart P

#	Name	Code	Date	Crime	County	Notes
27.	Trauturne, Nicholas	WM15	Feb. 3, 1859	Murder	St. Louis	MO Stewart C; escaped May 27, 1861
28.	Seite, Antoine	WM17	"	Murder	St. Louis	MO Stewart C.; record blank on when or if released
29.	Houser, Stephen	WMA	Oct. 7, 1859–May 15, 1861	Murder	St. Louis	MO Stewart C & Clairborne Jackson P
30.	Brady, King	WM21	April 18, 1860–Aug. 1, 1866	Murder	Carroll	MO Stewart C & Fletcher P
31.	Schoenwald, Henry	WM23	Dec. 22, 1860–April 3, 1871	Murder	St. Louis	MO Stewart C & Brown P
32.	Wisdom, Jack	WM45	July 15, 1862–March 4, 1865	Murder	Washington	MO Gamble C & Fletcher P
33.	Walter, William	WM35	Nov. 28, 1862–Nov. 28, 1877	Murder	St. Louis	Mo Gamble C; served full sentence
34.	Norvell, Francis	WMA	April 27, 1864	Being a Guerrilla	Cole	U.S. Lincoln P
35.	Ogle, Henry	WMA	Spring 1864	Involved in a shooting	Andrew	U.S. Lincoln P
36.	Johnson, James	WMA	May 13, 1864	Being a Guerrilla	Cole	U.S. Lincoln P
37.	McCoy, Catherine	WFA	June 17, 1864–March 1865	Murder	St. Louis .	MO Hall C & transfer to lunatic asylum
38.	Wolf, Enoch	WMA	Nov. 1864	Retaliation for murder of Union Army major	St. Louis	U.S. Lincoln P
39.	Shoemaker, James	WM27	Oct. 5, 1865–July 1, 1870	Murder	Franklin	MO Fletcher C & McClurg P
40.	Starr, George	WM42	June 9, 1866–Nov. 23, 1867	Murder	St. Louis	MO Fletcher C & P
41.	Marshall, Richard	WM27	Nov. 27, 1866–July 20, 1867	Murder	Washington	MO Hall C & Fletcher P
42.	Beck, George	WM46	Jan. 7, 1867	Murder	Texas	MO Fletcher C; died at MSP July 31, 1869
43.	Everman [last name only]	WMA	1867–68	Murder	Marion	MO Fletcher P
44.	Estill, William	WMA	Jan. 23, 1871–Feb. 16, 1880	Murder	Howard	MO Brown C & Phelps P
45.	Duffy, Patrick	WM31	Aug. 2, 1871	Murder	St. Louis	MO Brown C; died Oct. 2, 1878 at MSP
46.	Burns, Patrick	WM25	Aug. 3, 1871–Sept. 2, 1874	Murder	St. Louis	MO Brown C & Act. Gov. Johnson P
47.	Watson, John	WM20	Feb. 15, 1872–Jan. 12, 1875	Murder	Grundy	Mo Brown C & Woodson P

Name	Race and Age of Perpetrator	Race and Age of Victim(s)	Date of Commutation/ Pardon	Offense	County/ District	Commuting/ Pardoning Authority
48. Scanlan, Michael	WMA	WFA	Feb. 3, 1875	Murder	St. Louis	MO Hardin C
49. Hallenschied, Anna	WFA	WMA	Dec. 16, 1875	Murder	Gasconade	MO Hardin C; died Sept. 1891 MSP
50. Brown, Frank	WMA	WMA	1876	Murder	Buchanan	MO Phelps C
51. Lawrence, John	WM26	WMA	1877–Dec. 25, 1891	Murder	Buchanan	MO Phelps C & Francis P
52. Miller, Frank	WMA	WMA	1878	Murder	Jackson	MO Phelps C
53. Degonia, Joseph	WMA	WMA	Summer 1879–April 14, 1882	Murder	Washington	MO Phelps C & Lt. Gov. Campbell P
54. Ford, Charles	WMA	WM34	April 17, 1882	Murder	Buchanan	MO Crittenden P
55. Ford, Robert	WM21	"	"	"	"	"
56. Cook, Samuel	BMA	BFA	March 16, 1885	Murder	Washington	MO Marmaduke C
57. Hopkirk, James	WMA	WMA	March 16, 1885	Murder	Henry	MO Marmaduke C
58. Brownfield, Thomas	WMA	"	March 17, 1885	"	"	MO Marmaduke C & Stone P
59. Wisdom, James	WMA	WMA	March 17, 1885–Oct. 8, 1887	Murder	McDonald	MO Marmaduke C & Morehouse P
60. Anderson, Joel	WMA	WMA	July 7, 1886	Murder	Carroll	MO Marmaduke C; died at MSP Jan. 29, 1890
61. Baugh, Laurel	WMA	"	July 7, 1886–Nov. 25, 1897	"	"	MO Marmaduke C & Stephens P
62. Leabo, John	WMA	WFA	July 30, 1886	Murder	Bates	MO Marmaduke C
63. Payton, James	WM15	WMC	Dec. 23, 1887–Jan. 14, 1895	Murder	Christian	MO Marmaduke C & Stone P
64. Bryant, John	WMA	WMA	Early 1888–July 4, 1898	Murder	Clark	MO Morehouse C & Stephens P
65. Mitchell, William	WMA	WMA	1889–1890	Murder	Jackson	MO Francis C & died at MSP March 5, 1891
66. Blunt, Newt	WMA	WMA	Sept. 15, 1892	Murder	McDonald	MO Francis C
67. Smith, Thomas	BMA	BMA	May 23, 1893	Murder	Jackson	MO Stone C
68. Umble, Amanda	BFA	BFA	June 1893–July 4, 1901	Murder	Jackson	MO Stone C & Dockery P
69. Schaeffer, George	WM20	WM21	July 14, 1893	Murder	St. Louis City	MO Stone C to lunatic asylum

70. Mosely, John	WMS	WMA	Fall 1893–July 4, 1904	Murder	Pemiscot	MO Stone C
71. Henze, Jacob	WMA	WMA	May 8, 1895	Murder	St. Louis City	MO Stone C
72. Kaiser, Henry	WM27	"	"	"	"	"
73. Taylor, William	BM40/42	BMA	May 8, 1895	Murder	St. Louis City	MO Stone C
74. Crisp, John	WMA	WMA	Oct. 1895	Murder	Webster	MO Stone C to lunatic asylum in Nevada, MO
75. Donnelly, John	WMA	WMA	1896–Nov. 29, 1900	Murder	Audrain	MO Stone C & Stephens P
76. Punshon, Thomas	WMA	WFA	May 4, 1896–Dec. 25, 1902	Murder	Buchanan	MO Stone C & Dockery P
77. Pollard, Foster	BMA	BMA	June 17, 1896–Dec. 21, 1911	Murder	Jackson	MO Stone C & Hadley C
78. Harris, Frank	BMA	"	June 17, 1896–Dec. 23, 1911	"	"	MO Stone C & Hadley C
79. Waters, Pearl	BFA	BFA	June 1897–July 1899	Murder	St. Louis City	MO Stephens C & P
80. Worton, Andrew	WMA (Gypsy)	WFA (Gypsy)	July 1897	Murder	St. Louis City	MO Stephens C
81. Williams, William	BMA	WMA	Nov.–Dec. 1897	Murder	Jackson	MO Stephens C & P
82. Hunt, John	WM71/73	WFA	1897 1898	Murder	Boone	MO Stephens C
83. Black, Walter	BMA	WMA	April 1898–June 26, 1900	Murder	St. Louis	MO Stephens C & P
84. Renfrow, Peter	WMA	WMA	May 4, 1898–May 13, 1905	Murder	Greene	MO Stephens & Folk Commute
85. Shackelford, Thomas	BM18/19	BM30	June 6, 1899–April 23, 1906	Murder	St. Louis City	MO Stephens C & Folk C
86. Grant, Charles	BMA	BFA	Jan. 1900–May 27, 1904	Murder	Platte	MO Stephens C & Folk C
87. Miller, David	WMA	WMA	June 1900	Murder	Holt	MO Stephens C
88. Cushenberry, Robert	BMA	WMA	July 10, 1900–Aug. 15, 1910	Murder	Clinton	MO Stephens C & Hadley C
89. Furgerson, William	WM36	WMA	June 20, 1901–July 3, 1916	Murder	Grundy	MO Dockery C & Major Discharge
90. Vinso, John	WMA	WM24	May 1903–Nov. 27, 1912	Murder	Lawrence	MO Dockery C & Hadley C
91. Williams, Fred	BMA	BMA	March 9, 1905–Oct. 12 1907	Murder	St. Louis City	MO Folk C & Discharge under 3/4s law
92. Bailey, Edgar	WMA	WMA	Oct. 20, 1905–July 3, 1915	Murder	Jackson	MO Folk C & Major C
93. Eaton, Louis	WM22/24	WMA	Feb. 10, 1906	Murder	Dunklin	MO Folk C; died in MSP hospital

Name	Race and Age of Perpetrator	Date of Commutation/Pardon	Race and Age of Victim(s)	Offense	County/District	Commuting/Pardoning Authority
94. Crane, John	WMA	After March 1907	WFA	Murder	Jackson	Feb. 3, 1908 MO Folk C & 3/4ths law
95. Myers, Agnes	WF22/25	April 8, 1907–1925	WMA	Murder	Clay	MO Folk C & Hyde Parole
96. Hottman, Frank	WM20/23	April 8, 1907	WMA	Murder	Jackson	MO Folk C; died in MSP hospital Sept. 15, 1923
97. Long, Dave	WM48	June 15, 1907	WMA	Murder	Pemiscot	MO Folk C; died in MSP hospital May 29, 1913
98. Clay, Tom	BM26/28	July 19, 1907–Feb. 17, 1918	BMA	Murder	Boone	MO Folk C & 3/4ths law
99. Brooks, John	WMA	July 1907	WMA	Murder	Iron	MO Folk C
100. Brooks, Ameleck	WMA	"	"	Murder	"	MO Folk C
101. Spaugh, William	WMA	July 1907	WMA	Murder	Reynolds	MO Folk C; died at MSP Aug. 25, 1913
102. Barrington, Frederick	WM43	Aug. 28, 1907–Dec. 24, 1918	WMA	Murder	St. Louis	MO Folk C & Gardner C
103. Paulsgrove, Martin	WM27	Dec. 16, 1907–	WFA	Murder	De Kalb	MO Folk C; transfer to lunatic asylum March 16, 1918; died in MSP hospital Jan. 31, 1939
104. Baker, John	BM21	April 7, 1908–Nov. 27, 1918	BMA	Murder	Boone	MO Folk C & Gardner C
105. Daly, Frank, alias A.C. Biles	WM28	May 23, 1908–Jan. 2, 1913	WMA	Murder	St. Louis City	MO Folk C & Hadley C
106. Holman, Mert	BM18/19	Jan. 17, 1911–Dec. 23, 1939	WF14	Rape	Pike	MO Hadley C & Stark Parole
107. Tucker, Eugene	WM37	March 15, 1911–March 15, 1919	WMA	Murder	Greene	MO Hadley C & Gardner C
108. Bonner, George	BM25/28	Sept. 1, 1914	WMA	Murder	Jackson	MO Major C; died at MSP Oct. 8, 1917.
109. Sherman, Samuel	WM21/24	April 2, 1915–July 2, 1928	WMA	Murder	Jackson	MO Major C & Baker

No. Name	Offender	Victim(s)	Date	Crime	County	Action
110. Tatman, John	WM25/27		April 2, 1915–Dec. 24, 1926		"	Parole; MO Major C & Baker Parole
111. Lewis, Ora	WMA	2 WMA	April 1918	Murder	St. Louis City	MO Gardner & unspecified when discharged
112. Moore, John	WMA	2 WMA	Dec. 24, 1921	Murder	Jackson	MO Hyde C
113. Thurston, Woodville	BM26	WF20	July 14, 1922–Dec. 24, 1941	Rape	St. Louis City	MO Hyde C; Donnell parole & Dalton citizenship restoration Oct. 27, 1961
114. Seward, James	WMA	WMA	Aug. 1923–Oct. 11, 1939	Murder	Jefferson	MO Lt. Gov. Lloyd C & Stark Parole
115. Lee, John	BMA	BMA	May 2, 1924–Feb. 26, 1941	Murder	Cole	MO Hyde C & Stark Parole
116. Williams, Cleo	BM19	WF14 & WFA	July 5, 1928–Nov. 18, 1949	Rape	Jackson	MO Baker C & Blair C
117. Meadows, Andrew	WM56	WFA in hotel fire	1932	Murder by Arson	St. Louis City	MO Caulfield C; died at MSP Jan. 31, 1958
118. Carroll, Amos	BM48	BMA	Oct. 19, 1933	Murder	St. Louis City	MO Park C; died at MSP Sept. 26, 1934
119. Barbata, Paul	WM32	WF18	Feb. 26, 1935–March 25, 1968	Murder	St. Louis City	MO Park C; Hearnes discharge & restoration of citizenship
120. McGee, Walter	WM29	WF24	May 27, 1935–Feb. 8, 1949	Kidnapping	Jackson	MO Park C & Parole Board
121. Richardson, James E.	WMA	WMA	May 15, 1937–March 29, 1955	Murder	Grundy	MO Stark C & Parole Board Discharge
122. McGee, Claude	WMA	WMA	Nov. 5, 1937–Jan. 5, 1951	Murder	Mississippi	MO Stark C & executed Jan. 5, 1951 for an inmate murder at MSP
123. Ashworth, Oscar	WMA	WFC	Oct. 1940–June 6, 1953	Kidnapping	Buchanan	MO Stark C; escaped
124. Cole, Buford	BM29	BF7	Aug. 1945	Murder	St. Louis City	MO Donnelly C
125. Laster, Rollie	WM21	WMA	Jan. 15, 1957	Murder	Cole	MO Blair C; died MSP May 14, 1977
126. Goodwin, Marcus	WMA	WFA	Jan. 1962	Murder	Jackson	MO Dalton C
127. Shaw, Bobby	BMA	WMA	June 3, 1993	Murder	Franklin	MO Carnahan C; died at Potosi hospital Jan. 26, 2000
128. Mease, Darrell	WMA	WMA, WFA & WM18	Jan. 28, 1999	Murder	Greene	MO Carnahan C

Chapter Notes

Abbreviations: CT *Chicago Tribune*; DMB *Dictionary of Missouri Biography*; EHSL *Encyclopedia of the History of St. Louis*; FHC Family History Center, Church of Jesus Christ of Latter-Day Saints, 703 Walnut St., Independence, MO; Joint Collection: Western Historical Manuscript Collection, State Historical Society of Missouri Manuscripts Kansas City and the University of Missouri–Kansas City Archives; KCS *Kansas City Star*; KCT *Kansas City Times*; KNG *Knob Noster Gem*; LT *Liberty Tribune*; MHS Missouri Historical Society, 5700 Lindell Blvd., St. Louis, MO; MORE *Missouri Republican* (St. Louis); MSA Missouri State Archives, 600 W. Main St., P.O. Box 1747, Jefferson City, MO; MSHS Missouri State Historical Society, 1020 Lowry Street, Columbia, MO; NA National Archives, 700 Pennsylvania Ave., NW, Washington, D.C.; RC *Randolph Citizen* (Huntsville); RG Record Group (National Archives); SLCP St. Louis Courthouse Papers, MHS; *SLPD St. Louis Post-Dispatch*; T.T. Trial Transcript; WHMC Western Historical Manuscript Collection, Ellis Library, University of Missouri, Columbia, MO.

1. Indians and Whites, 1803–1864

1. John B. Dillon, *A History of Indiana*, 31–43, contains an English translation of the Black Code in its entirety. All textual references are to its specific articles.

2. Gustavus Schmidt, ed. *Louisiana Law Journal*, Aug. 1841, 1–65, contains an English translation of O'Reilly, "Ordinances and Instructions." All textual references are to its sections.

3. *Laws of a Public and General Nature of the District of Louisiana, of the Territory of Louisiana, of the Territory of Missouri, and of the State of Missouri Up to the Year 1824*, chap. 3, 30–31. Hereafter cited as *Laws*.

4. A Law Respecting Crimes and Punishments," in *Laws of Northwest Territory, 1788–1800*, 322–24.

5. 1 Stat. 113.

6. Derek N. Kerr, *Petty Felony*, 98.

7. "Inquest: Slave Belonging to Jean Baptiste Datchurut," November 16, 1783, trans. Sylvia L. Richards. F421, Collection, WHMC.

8. Carl J. Ekberg, *Colonial Ste. Genevieve*, 372–73.

9. *Ibid.*, 371–72.

10. Kerr, *Petty Felony*, 130.

11. Louis Houck, *History of Missouri*, 3:37; David March, *History of Missouri*, 1:216; Ekberg, *Colonial Ste. Genevieve*, 122–23; William E. Foley, *Genesis of Missouri*, 92–93; Jacqueline Brelsford Baker Humphrey, "The 1802 Murder of David Trotter in Missouri," 198–203.

12. 1 Stat. 119.

13. *Laws* (1808), Chap. 65. sec. 2, 210.

14. Mo. Rev. Stat., art. 8, secs.11–14 (1835).

15. 1 Stat. 118–19.

16. *Laws*, (1807) Chap. 38, sec. 13, 111.

17. Pierre Chouteau to Henry Dearborn, March 11, 1805, Pierre Chouteau Letterbook, MHS.

18. *Journals of the Lewis & Clark Expedition*, Gary E. Moulton, ed., vol. 8, 347–48, citing the research of William Foley, Dec. 1991.

19. *Ibid.*

20. *Louisiana Gazette* (St. Louis), Aug. 10, 1808, 3:2.

21. Cited in William E. Foley, "Different Notions of Justice," 12.

22. *Ibid.*, 12.

23. *Missouri Gazette* (St. Louis), May 28, 1814, 3:3.

24. *Ibid.*, June 4, 1814, 3:3–4.

25. Francis Paul Prucha, *The Great Father*, 43.

26. *Ibid.*, 44.

27. Prucha, *Broadax and Bayonet*, 85.

28. Foley, *The Genesis of Missouri*, 234.

29. See *U.S.* v. *Joseph Leblond*, Nov. 16 and 20, 1813, John B.C. Lucas Collection, MHS and Harrison Trexler, *Slavery in Missouri*, 68–69.

30. *U.S.* v. *Long*, Box 7, F 13:32, SLCP, MHS.

31. *Missouri Gazette* (St. Louis), Sept. 20, 1809, 3:3.

32. *Ibid.*, June 7, 1810, 3:3.

33. *History of Southeast Missouri*, 311.

34. *Missouri Gazette* (St. Louis), Feb. 29, 1812, 3:3.

35. *History of Southeast Missouri*, 311–12.

36. *Ibid.*, 330.

37. *Ibid.*, 753.

38. See *Missourian* (St. Charles), May 9, 1821, 1:1 and *Missouri Gazette*, May 9, 3:1.

39. *Enquirer* (St. Louis), May 5, 1821, 3:1.

40. 1849 Mo. 4.

41. *King v. State*, 1 Mo. 387, 388 (1827).

42. *Samuels v. State*, 3 Mo. 69 (1831).

43. *Ford, Sheriff v. Circuit Court of Howard County*, 3 Mo. 167 (1834).

44. *MORE*, Aug. 24, 1830, 3:1 and Sept. 5, 1830, 3:1, and *St. Louis Beacon*, Sept. 30, 1830, 3:5.

45. *Missouri Intelligencer* (Fayette), May 31, 1827, 2:4.

46. *King v. State*, 1 Mo. 387 (1827).

47. 2 Stat. 364, art. 33; 12 Stat. 736, art., 30. 18 Stat., Pt 1, 235, art. 58.

48. *MORE*, Sept. 1, 1829, 3:1.

49. Mo. Rev. Stat., art 2, secs. 1–2, 187 (1835).

50. *Missouri Intelligencer* (Columbia), Dec. 11, 1830, 3:1 and *Jefferson Republican* (Jefferson City), June 16, 1833, 2:1.

51. On June 17, 1843 in Farmington (St. Francois County), a crowd of 3,000 persons assembled to watch the hanging of James Layton, convicted on a change of venue from Perry County for the murder of his wife. The mob did not understand that the governor's reprieve of the condemned until the first of September would not cheat justice. It burst open the county jail, obtained Layton, built its own gallows, and its members hanged him, and went their separate ways. See *Missouri Statesman* (Columbia) June 30, 1843, 2:3 and *History of Southeast Missouri*, 846.

52. 1856 Mo. 69–70.

53. William Hyde and Howard L. Conard, *EHSL*, 2: 711.

54. *Ibid.*, 711 and *MORE*, Dec. 14, 1850, 2:2.

55. *MORE*, Aug. 13, 1841, 2:2.

56. *St. Joseph Gazette*, Oct. 6, 1852, 1:7.

57. *Kansas City Enterprise*, July 4, 1857, 1:7.

58. *State v. Jennings*, 18 Mo. 436 (1853) and *State v. Neuslein*, 25 Mo. 111 (1857).

59. *State v. Huting*, 21 Mo. 464 (1855).

60. *Jeffersonian* (Jefferson City), Aug.12, 2:1, Sept. 7, 2:2, and Oct. 19, 1839, 2:3 and Register of Inmates, MSP, Vol. A, 9.

61. *Salt River Journal* (Bowling Green), June 20, 1841, 2:3.

62. George Thompson, *Prison Life and Reflections*, 175 and *Jefferson Inquirer*, Feb. 10, 1842, 2:1.

63. *History of Franklin, Jefferson, Washington, Crawford, and Gasconade Counties*, 559.

64. See *MORE*, May 9, 1863, 3:5 and *State v. Burns*, 33 Mo. 483 (1863).

65. 4 Stat. 733.

66. Most of my information about this case derives from Larry D. Ball's excellent article, "Federal Justice on the Santa Fe Trail: The Murder of Antonio Jose Chavez."

67. *History of Jackson County, Missouri*, 641.

68. *Missouri Statesman* (Columbia), March 10, 1843, 3:2.

69. *Ibid.* Aug. 14, 1846, 1:4 and *Lester v. State*, 9 Mo. 666 (1846).

70. *MORE*, Feb. 15, 1851, 2:1.

71. *State v. Worrell*, 25 Mo. 205, 238 (1857).

72. *Ibid.*, 213.

73. *RC* (Huntsville), July 9, 1857, 3:2.

74. *State v. Shehane*, 25 Mo. 565 (1857).

75. *History of Montgomery County, Missouri*, 589–90.

76. *EHSL*, 2:712.

77. *History of Cole, Moniteau, Morgan, Benton, Miller, Maries and Osage Counties, Missouri*, 237.

78. *State v. Lamb*, 28 Mo. 218 (1859) and *Missouri Democrat* (St. Louis), June 18, 1859, 2:3.

79. *History of Greene County, Missouri*, 231.

80. The handwritten Oregon County record, dated Aug. 7, 1858, confirms that Shehane was not executed June 11, 1858, as Lewis A.W. Simpson in *Oregon County's Three Flags*, 26–27, states when discussing this case. The circuit court of this county sentenced him to die on the earlier date, but he was reprieved until the latter.

81. *MORE*, Oct. 22, 1863, 3:3.

82. *Morning Herald* (St. Joseph), Nov. 7, 1863, 2:1. See also Chris L. Rutt, ed., *History of Buchanan County and the City of St. Joseph*, 215–16.

83. *Missouri Intelligencer* (Columbia), July 9, 1831, 2:3.

84. *MORE* (St. Louis), Dec. 14, 1850, 2:2.

85. *Ibid.* Feb. 15, 1851, 2:1.

86. *Ibid.* July 23, 1853, 2:3.

87. *Ibid.* April 16, 1864, 3:4.

2. Slaves and Free Blacks, 1826–1863

1. Houck, *History of Missouri*, 1:282.

2. Houck, ed. *Spanish Regime in Missouri*, 2: unnumbered foldout page in appendix.

3. *Negro Population, 1790–1915*, 57.

4. Derek Kerr, *Petty Felony*, 138.

5. *U.S. v. Elijah*, Box T 11/13, MSA.

6. Floyd Shoemaker, *Missouri's Struggle for Statehood, 1804–1821*, 96–97.

7. *Ibid.* reprints this document in its entirety. All references to it are cited to the Mo. Const.

8. *Missouri Gazette* (St. Louis), April 5, 1820, 1:5; *Missouri Herald* (Jackson), April 8, 1820, 1:3.

9. The *MORE* story was reprinted in the *Sun* (Baltimore), June 15, 1837, 3:3 and the *Liberator* (Boston), June 16, 1837, 3:4.

10. *Jefferson Republican* (Jefferson City), Sept. 30, 1837, 2:3.

11. *State v. Mary, a Slave*, Crawford County Circuit Court Records, 1837.

12. *State v. Mat, a Slave*, Callaway County Circuit Court Records, July–Oct., 1855 (Italics and capitalization in the original.)

13. *Thompson v. Oklahoma*, 487 U.S. 815 (1988).

14. *Missouri Statesman*, Nov. 23, 1855, 2:5.

15. Eleanor Roosevelt's great-uncle, Daniel Stewart Elliott, killed his bondchild in a fit of pique on a Georgia plantation in the 1850's. Elliott, approximately Slave Mat's age at the time he murdered a child known as his little black shadow, was sent to Europe for a year as punishment. Blanch Wiesen Cook, *Eleanor Roosevelt*, 1:28.

16. *California News*, July 18, 1:2 and August 1, 1863, 2:1.

17. James E. Ford, *History of Moniteau County*, 47.

18. *History of St. Charles, Montgomery, and Warren Counties*, 1003–04.

19. *History of Boone County, Missouri*, 388.

20. *Missouri Intelligencer* (Columbia), March 24, 1832, 2:4.

21. *History of Callaway County, Missouri*, 283–86.

22. *RC*, Dec. 16, 1859, 2:2.

23. *Ibid.*, Nov. 26, 1858, 2:2; Jan. 7, 1859, 3:6.

24. Mo. Const., art 13, sec. 9 (1820).

25. *Fanny, a Slave* v. *State*, 6 Mo. 122 (1839).
26. *Jane, a Slave* v. *State*, 3 Mo. 61 (1831).
27. *History of St. Charles, Montgomery and Warren Counties, Missouri*, 578. There are no extant Montgomery County court records from this period.
28. North Todd Gentry, *The Bench and Bar of Boone County, Missouri*, 114–15.
29. *Ewing* v. *Thompson*, 13 Mo. 132, 137–39 (1850); *Jennings* v. *Kavanaugh*, 5 Mo. 25 (1837)
30. 1836 Mo. Laws 60.
31. *History of St. Charles, Montgomery and Warren Counties, Missouri*, 1004.
32. *State* v. *Annice, a Slave*, Clay County Circuit Court Records, 1828.
33. *State* v. *Susan*, Callaway County Circuit Court Records, 1844.
34. *Boonville Observer*, March 25, 1845, 1:2 and *Missouri Statesman* (Columbia) March 7, 1845, 2:1.
35. Robert W. Duffner, "Slavery in Missouri River Counties," 63
36. *History of Franklin, Jefferson, Washington, Crawford and Gasconade Counties, Missouri*, 405.
37. *Missouri Statesman* (Columbia), March 24, 2:3, May 12, 2:1, May 19, 2:1, and June 16, 1843, 2:1.
38. The particulars of this case are taken from Mary E. Seematter's "Trials and Confessions: Race and Justice in Antebellum St. Louis," 36–47, a fabulous piece of far-ranging and thorough scholarship. All capitalization is in the original in the handbill.
39. *State* v. *Slave Ben, Marion County Circuit Court Records*, Oct. 31, 1849–Jan. 11, 1850; *Missouri Courier* (Hannibal) Dec. 6, 1849, 1:1–5
40. Pardon Papers, Box 4, F 27, MSA
41. Pardon Papers, Box 6, F 29, MSA.
42. *State* v. *Anderson*, 19 Mo. 241 (1953).
43. *Jefferson Republican*, Dec. 17, 1836, 3:2–6. No state censuses are extant. These figures are only available in contemporary newspapers.
44. *Brunswicker*, Feb. 27, 1857, 1:6
45. *MORE*, June 30, 1834, 3:3.
46. Robert [surname illegible] to William Selby Harney, July 4, 1834; James Clemens Jr. to WSH, Aug 2, 4, 13, 1834, Mary C. Clemens Collection, MHS
47. Journals and Diaries, James Kennerly Collection, March 27, 1835, MHS.
48. William G. Eliot, *The Story of Archer Alexander*, 91–93.
49. Correspondence, William E. Lind and David H. Wallace, Old Military and Civil Records, NA.
50. *Street Directory of the Principal Cities of the United States, 1908*, 340.
51. *State* v. *Celia, a Slave*, Callaway County Circuit Court Records, June–Dec., 1855. This material consists of over 60 unnumbered and handwritten pages.
52. *New York Times*, Jan. 16, 1856, 2:6 and *Sun* (Baltimore), Jan. 17, 1856, 1:5.
53. Hugh P. Williamson, "Document: The State against Celia, A Slave," 408–20.
54. Melton A. McLauren, *Celia, a Slave*.
55. Antonia Fraser, *Marie Antoinette: The Journey*, 444–46.

3. *Union Army Executions, 1861–1865*

1. 2 Stat. 364
2. Abraham Lincoln, *Collected Works*, ed. Roy P. Basler, 5:436–37.
3. 12 Stat. 755

4. *LT*, July 21, 1865, 3:3.
5. James M. Bean, editor of the *Paris Mercury*, was lucky. After time spent in custody in Mexico, Missouri, he was released, and the military allowed his newspaper to resume publication, *California News*, May 31, 1862, 2:1.
6. See my chapters eight and nine, *Runaway and Freed Missouri Slaves and Those Who Helped Them*, 117–41.
7. *Lawrence Republican* (Lawrence, KS), July 25, 1861, 2:1.
8. *Warrensburg Standard*, June 17, 1865, 3:1.
9. Charles Fairman, *The Law of Martial Rule*, 41.
10. 12 U.S. 281.
11. *Weekly Herald* (St. Joseph), Sept. 18, 1862, 3:1.
12. Bruce Nichols, *Guerrilla Warfare in Civil War Missouri, 1862*, 25.
13. *Missouri Democrat* (St. Louis), June 14, 1862, 2:1.
14. Cited in Joseph A. Mudd, *With Porter in North Missouri*, 264.
15. E.M. Violette, *History of Adair County*, 103 (emphasis mine).
16. Mudd, *With Porter in North Missouri*, 280.
17. *KCS*, Aug. 11, 1993, F1:2.
18. *California News*, June 21, 1862, 3:1. See also *Morning Herald* (St. Joseph) June 12, 1862, 2:2.
19. *LT*, Aug. 29, 1862, 2:2. The newspaper does not name the executed man. Nichols, *Guerrilla Warfare in Civil War Missouri, 1862*, 140, identifies him.
20. *Encyclopedia of the American Civil War*, 3:1562–63.
21. Frederick Way Jr., compiler, *Way's Packet Directory, 1848–1994*, 485.
22. *LT*, September 5, 1862, 3:1.
23. *Northwest Conservator* (Richmond), Sept. 11, 1862, 2:2. Article reprinted in *LT*, Sept. 19, 1862, 3:2.
24. Mudd, *With Porter in North Missouri*, 70.
25. *General History of Macon County, Missouri*, 179.
26. W.F. Switzler, *History of Missouri*, 418.
27. Mudd, *With Porter in North Missouri*, 70–71.
28. Cited in Switzler, *History of Missouri*, 418.
29. *Ibid.*, 418.
30. *History of Marion County, Missouri*, 493–94.
31. The coverage goes on. Beginning on Nov. 21, 1990 and continuing through Jan. 30, 1991, the *Palmyra Spectator* ran a detailed nine-part series on the Palmyra Massacre.
32. *Herald* (Quincy, IL), Oct. 20, 1862, 2:1.
33. The *California News* ran an account which reads in part, "Gen. McNeil, commanding in the Northeast, had ten prisoners taken from the jail in Palmyra, a few days since, and shot, in retaliation for the carrying off of a prisoner named Allsman, by Porter's men, when they made their raid into Palmyra," Nov. 1, 1862, 2:1.
34. *London Star's* comments on Palmyra Massacre reprinted in *New York Times*. Dec. 1. 1862, 8:5.
35. Mudd, *With Porter in North Missouri*, 304.
36. The *St. Louis Globe-Democrat*, June 8, 1891, 4:5 was apparently still fighting the Union cause. It buried McNeil's role at Palmyra in its obituary of him: "General McNeil, while in command at Palmyra, restored to several [severe?] measures to quell these robbers and murderers." The *New York Times*, June 9, 1891, 4:7 termed him "The Butcher of Palmyra." His infamy survives; a Google search under "John McNeil Civil War" puts "the Butcher of Palmyra" on one's computer screen in large letters.
37. *History of Marion County*, 512 (emphasis in the original).
38. *Ibid.*, 513.
39. *California News*, Sep. 12, 1863, 2:1.

40. Cited in *Marion County History*, 513–14.

41. *New York Times*, Aug. 1, 1864, 8:5.

42. *Democrat* (St. Louis), Oct. 29, 1864, 4:1.

43. *MORE* (St. Louis) Oct. 31, 1864, 1:4.

44. Thomas Scharf, *History of Saint Louis City and County*, 1: 444. See also a biography of General Rosecrans, William M. Lamers, *The Edge of Glory*, 435.

45. John W. Carty, convicted of feeding and harboring guerrillas in Reynolds County at Pilot Knob, Oct. 28, 1863, Alton prison term, "during the war," Case LL 1238, RG 153, NA. Charles Tatum, convicted of robbery in Lawrence County on May 15, 1864, in Springfield, July 26, 1864, Alton term, "during the war," Case LL 2616, RG 153, NA. Reese Gott, found guilty of being a guerrilla in Dade and Lawrence Counties on or about May 20, 1864, in Springfield, Aug. 10, 1864, Alton term, three years, Case LL 2674, RG 153, NA. John Estes, convicted of being a guerrilla [in or near Clay County] in 1862 and 1863 at St. Louis, Oct. 23, 1864, Alton term, five years, Case NN 2672, RG 153, NA. Oscar Davis, convicted of oath violation at or near Prairie du Rocher, IL [near Ste. Genevieve] on Sept. 28, 1864, at St. Louis on Dec. 29, 1864, Alton term, "during the war," Case NN 3334, RG 153, NA.

46. Charles Wells, found guilty of being a guerrilla in Dunklin County in 1862 and 1863 at St. Louis after Aug. 1863, Alton term, "during the war" and a $500 fine, Case NN 1237, RG 153, NA, and James Blaketon, found guilty of being a guerrilla at or near St. Louis in 1862 at St. Louis on Dec. 28, 1863, Alton term, six months or until $1,200 fine paid but not more than two years, Case NN 1252, RG 153, NA.

47. *MORE*, May 20, 1863, 3:4.

48. Aaron Alderman, found guilty of robbery and being a guerrilla in Buchanan County on or about July 11, 1864, at St. Joseph, Nov. 3, 1864, MSP term, 20 years, Case NN 3356, RG 153, NA, and Charles White, found guilty of being a guerrilla, locale unspecified, on Aug. 29, 1864, at St. Louis, Dec. 21, 1864, MSP term, three years, Case 3245, RG 153, NA.

49. *Weekly Herald* (St. Joseph) Sept. 29, 1864, 4:1.

50. Lafayette Carty, found guilty of harboring and feeding guerrillas in Reynolds County during 1862 and 1863 at Pilot Knob, Oct. 28, 1863, Case LL 1302, RG 153, NA.

51. In Clark County, Aquilla Standiford and Samuel Dale were arrested, tried, and found guilty of, as the county history phrased it "being with the party that bushwhacked [killed] Staples," a Union Army lieutenant. They were executed on May 26, 1863, at Fairmont, *History of Lewis, Clark, Knox, and Scotland Counties*, 389. A drumhead court-martial passed a death sentence against Andrew Snyder on April 22 on charges of his guerrilla activity; he was shot on May 6, 1864, at the city of Macon, Macon County, *Missouri Telegraph* (Fulton) May 13, 1864, 1:5. In Monticello, Lewis County, William Gallup was found guilty of being a member of a bushwhacking gang and stealing horses. He was shot October 10, 1864, *History of Lewis, Clark, Knox, and Scotland Counties, Missouri*, 99–100. James Hamilton, convicted by a military commission of robbery and bushwhacking, was hanged at the city of Macon, Macon County, on March 3, 1865, *Weekly Mercury* (Paris) March 10, 1865, and cited in Fellman, *Inside War*, 274, Hamilton's extant court-martial, Macon, Jan. 30, 1865, Case 00 303, Record Group, 153, NA.

52. *California News*, Sept. 26, 3:3 and Oct. 16, 1863, 1:2 and Frank Triplett, "The Drum Head Court-Martial," *The Life, Times, and Treacherous Death of Jesse James*, 269–77.

53. These are Benjamin Snelling, shot at Clinton, Henry County, Aug. 15,1863, *Weekly Union*, Lexington, Aug. 15, 1863, 3:1; Carlyle (last name only), executed on Sept. 9, 1863, at Lexington, Lafayette County, *Young's History of Lafayette County, Missouri*, 131; Willard Francis Hadley, shot on May 20, 1864, at Warrensburg, Johnson County. His last words included, "I went into the war to be a terror to the feds.... I thought the South had her rights trampled upon," *Morning Herald* (St. Joseph), June 19, 1864, 2:4; and G. P. Wright in Warrensburg on June 2, 1865, reference, note 8, this chapter.

54. *California News*, April 23, 1:6, April 30, 1864, 2:3, and *History of Moniteau County*, 46.

55. *California News*, Oct. 31, 2:1 and Nov. 7, 1863, 2:1 and cited in Fellman, *Inside War*, 276, Nichols' extant court-martial, Jefferson City, June 1863, Case MM 746, RG 153, NA.

56. *California News*, Nov. 21, 1863, 1:2.

57. Joseph Lanier, bushwhacker, was tried by a military commission in St. Joseph, Buchanan County, and shot in nearby Savannah, Andrew County, on June 10, 1864, *Morning Herald*, June 16, 1864, 1:6, *LT*, June 17, 1864, 2:2, and *History of Buchanan County and St. Joseph*, Rutt, ed., 216–17. On June 12, 1864, Fielding (last name only) was tried at Ridgely, Platte County, by a drumhead court-martial and shot the same day, *MORE*, June 16, 1864, 1:1. Also at Ridgely and on June 12, 1864, the Confederate, Lt. Oldham (last name only) was executed by shooting after being wounded, James J. Fisher, *KCS*, March 21, 1993, G1. In late August 1864, a military commission in St. Joseph tried A. J. Bowyer for his guerrilla activity, found him guilty, sentenced him to hang, and General Rosecrans approved the sentence. On Sept. 9, 1864, Bowyer was hanged in St. Joseph in the presence of 2,000 persons, *Morning Herald*, Sept. 16, 1864, 2:6 and *History of Buchanan County and St. Joseph*, Rutt, ed. 217. Two weeks later, Henry A. Griffith, bushwhacker, as the local newspaper termed him, was hanged on the same St. Joseph scaffold upon which Bowyer died, *Morning Herald*, Sept. 22, 3:1 and 24, 3:1: 1864, and cited in Fellman, *Inside War*, 276, Griffith's extant court-martial, St. Joseph, Sept. 7, 1864, Case LL 2638, RG 153, NA.

58. William Jackson Livingston was tried by a military commission on charges of spying, found guilty and hanged in the St. Louis County jail on Aug. 19, 1864, *MORE*, Aug. 20, 1864, 3:4. Stephen R. Smith and William Moore, convicted of spying and guerrilla activity by military commission, were hanged together, Sept. 9, 1864, on a St. Louis scaffold near the intersection of Poplar and 11 Sts. Smith had been active in Oregon County and Moore in New Madrid, *MORE*, Sept. 10, 1864, 3:4, and cited in Fellman, *Inside War*, 290. Smith's extant court-martial, St. Louis, July 15, 1864, Case NN 2125, RG 153, NA. John F. Abshire was tried by a military commission, which convened Sept. 29, 1864, on charges of violating the laws and customs of war, or more specifically of killing William Hayes in Wayne County on Jan. 20, 1864. Abshire was hanged Oct. 17, 1864, in Gratiot St. Prison, St. Louis, *MORE*, Oct. 17, 1864, 4:4. James M. Utz was tried by a military commission, found guilty of spying, and hanged in the St. Louis County jail, on Dec. 26, 1864, Scharf, *History of St. Louis City and County*, 1: 446; Switzler, *History of Missouri*, 442, and cited in Stanley, Wilson and Wilson, *Death Records from Missouri Newspapers, The Civil War Years*, *MORE*, Dec. 28, 1864. William J. Harris was convicted of guerrilla activity by a military commission, and on March 24, 1865, he was hanged at Gratiot St. Prison, *New York Times*, April 2, 1865, 6:1. Thomas J. Thorpe was tried by a court-martial held in Pilot Knob, Iron County, and hanged in Gratiot St. Prison on May 1, 1865, *MORE*,

May 3, 1865, 2:5 and cited in Fellman, *Inside War*, 273, Thorpe's extant court-martial, Pilot Knob, April 14, 1864, Case NN 1815, RG 153, NA.

59. Fellman, *Inside War*, 5.

60. *U.S. v. McDaniels*, Case MM 671, RG 153, NA.

61. *U.S. v. Erwin*, Case 00 303, RG, 153, NA.

62. *U.S. v. Cox*, Case 138, RG 153, NA. The 1885 list does not contain Cox's name; his service record indicates that he was imprisoned in St. Louis, and there the trail ends.

63. Reprinted in Robert I. Alotta, *Civil War Justice: Union Army Executions Under Lincoln*, Appendix 1, 191–201.

64. Cited in *Kansans at Wilson Creek: Soldiers' Letters from the Campaign For Southwest Missouri*, eds. Richard W. Hatcher III and William Garrett Piston, 55. Their footnote 57, on p. 53, states that Cole is buried in the Springfield National Cemetery, Springfield, MO.

65. Service Record, John Reily, Jr., Missouri Volunteer, Co. L, 2 Artillery Regiment. Mid-Continent Library, Independence, MO, houses the service records of all Missouri volunteers first by regiment and then alphabetically by name. The 1885 list contains, among other information, the name of the executed, the state from which he was a volunteer, and his regiment.

66. 3 Stat. 418.

67. 12 Stat. 733.

68. Alotta, *Civil War Justice*, 123, places Gibbons' desertion "while his unit was on duty at Jacksonville, Florida." This is a mistake; both his court-martial transcript and St. Louis newspaper coverage of his execution identify Gibbons' Union Army service as occurring in Utah Territory, New Mexico Territory, and Texas.

69. *U.S. v. Barney Gibbons*, Proceedings of U.S. Court Martial, St. Louis, MO, July 13, 1864, FHC, Independence, MO.

70. *MORE*, Aug. 13, 1864, 3:1.

71. Mark Twain, "The Private History of a Campaign that Failed," *The Century*, 195.

72. Margaret Sanborn, *Mark Twain: The Bachelor Years*, 150–51.

73. Unless otherwise indication all quoted material is from *U.S. v. Eastman*, Proceedings of U.S. Court Martial, Rolla, MO, Sept. 16, 1864, FHC, Independence, MO.

74. *California News*, Oct. 1, 1864, 1:4.

75. Service Record, Private Edward Eastman, Co. B, 2nd Artillery, Missouri Volunteers.

76. Alotta, *Civil War, Justice*, 132, writes that Eastman's execution occurred on Sept. 25, 1864. He is mistaken.

77. *U.S. v. Paul Kingston*, Proceedings of U.S. Court Martial, Cape Girardeau, MO, Sept. 21, 1863, FHC, Independence, MO.

78. *Perryville Union*, Sept. 11, 1863, 2:1.

79. Service Record, Corporal Paul Kingston, Co. M, 1st Calvary, Missouri Volunteers.

80. Alotta, *Civil War Justice*, 89, writes, "Corporal Kingston was tried by general court-martial, found guilty of desertion and the 'theft of a pistol,' and sentenced to be hanged.... Nowhere in his records is there any mention of, or allusion to, murder." Oh yes there is.

81. *U.S. v. Purvis* and *U.S. v. Richardson*, Proceedings of U.S. Court Martial, St. Louis, MO, Dec. 7, 1864, FHC, Independence, MO.

82. Service Record, Private Abraham Purvis, Co. C, 21st Infantry, Missouri Volunteers.

83. Service Record, Private Ephraim Richardson, Co. C, 21 Infantry, Missouri Volunteers.

84. *Democrat* (St. Louis), Jan. 14, 1865, 4:1.

85. *MORE*, Jan. 14, 1865, 2:7. Alotta, *Civil War Justice*, 153–54, confuses their ages. He lists Richardson as 16 and Purvis as 18. The author also writes that, "The two ... in an undescribed incident, murdered a civilian." Their crime is fully described in the transcript of their court-martial and in contemporary newspaper coverage.

86. William Blackstone, *Commentaries on the Laws of England*, 4:190–91.

87. Alotta, *Civil War Justice*, 134, writes, "Jefferson Jackson's service record indicates he was in arrest since 27 August 1864, so the crime he committed — murder probably of a civilian — had to take place shortly before that time.... The local newspapers suggested that he [Jackson] had committed other murders and was actually a member of the Confederate Army." Alotta's comments are complete nonsense.

88. *U.S. v. Jefferson Jackson*, Proceedings of U.S. Court Martial, St. Joseph, MO, Sept. 6, 1864, FHC, Independence, MO.

89. *Weekly Herald* (St. Joseph), Oct. 20, 1864, 3:2.

90. *Ibid.*, Oct. 27, 1864, 4:2.

91. *Ibid.*, Oct. 29, 1864, 2:2.

4. Black and White, 1866–1889

1. Frederick H. Dyer, *A Compendium of the War of the Rebellion*, 15.

2. Fellman, *Inside War: The Guerrilla Conflict in Missouri During the American Civil War* and Nichols, *Guerrilla Warfare in Civil War Missouri*, 1862.

3. Mudd, *With Porter in North Missouri*, 285–86.

4. J.M. Da Costa, "On Irritable Heart," 25.

5. I.S. Parrish, *Military Veterans PTSD Reference Manual*, 19.

6 . *Diagnostic and Statistical Manual of Mental Disorders*, 4th ed., 467.

7. David McCullough, *Truman*, 28.

8. James R. McGovern, *Anatomy of a Lynching*, x.

9. *Morning Herald* (St. Joseph), March 2, 1866, 2:2 and Chris L. Rutt, ed., *History of Buchanan County and St. Joseph*, 218.

10. *History of Cole, Moniteau, Morgan, Benton, Miller, Maries and Osage Counties*, 416–17.

11. *Weekly Patriot* (Springfield) Jan. 17, 1867, 4:2; *Louisiana Journal*, May 17, 1867, 3:2; *Palmyra Spectator*, June 28, 1867, 2:3, and *History of Monroe and Shelby Counties, Missouri*, 215.

12. *Joplin Standard*, Aug. 27, 1889, 2:5.

13. Register of Inmates, MSP, Vol. C, Reel S 213, p. 221 and Pardon Papers, Box 31, F 14, MSA.

14. *St. Louis Democrat*, story carried in *Weekly Patriot* (Springfield), Oct. 24, 1867, 1:6.

15. *MORE* (St. Louis), Dec. 7, 1867, 3:3.

16. *Penry v. Lynbaugh*, 492 U.S. 302.

17. *Atkins v. Virginia*, 563 U.S. 304.

18. Mo. Rev. Stat. 565.030(4) (Supp. 2002).

19. *History of Clay and Platte Counties, Missouri*, 740.

20. *History of Clinton County, Missouri*, 423–26 and *Missouri Democrat* (St. Louis), Aug. 5, 1868, 2:3.

21. *MORE* (St. Louis), July 24, 1869, 2:4.

22. *Missouri Democrat* (St. Louis) cited in *EHSL*, 2:713.

23. *List of Pardons, Commutations and Reprieves Granted by the Governor from January 1, 1869, to December 31, 1870, Inclusive*, 26.

24. DMB, *s.v.* McClurg, Joseph W.

25. *EHSL*, 2:713.

26. *Dispatch* (Commerce), Sept. 3, 1870, 2:2.

27. *State v. Orr*, 64 Mo. 339, 342 (1876).

28. *Springfield Patriot-Advertiser*, May 24, 1877, 1:5. In

The Death Penalty for Juveniles, Victor Streib lists Samuel Orr's race as unknown and his age as 12 at the time of the crime and 15 when executed. Watt Espy gave Streib a newspaper article about this case which contained a faint impression of the number 2: "Orr was a young man, not more than 25 years old." The "2" was mistaken for a "1," *Constitution* (Atlanta, GA), May 20, 1877, 1:2. The 1870 census of Greene County, Missouri, enumerated July 25, 1870, lists Samuel as white, aged 17 years, in a household headed by James Orr, his father.

29. *State v. Able* [*sic*], 65 Mo. 37 and 65 Mo. 357 (1877).

30. *Carthage Press,* Aug. 3, 1923, 11 reprints its Feb. 15, 1878 four column coverage of Ables' case.

31. *Johnson County Star,* Dec. 30, 1890 and *State v. Daniels,* 66 Mo. 192 (1877).

32. *State v. Foster,* 1 Mo. App. 1 and 61 Mo. 549 (1876); *St. Louis Globe-Democrat,* June 20, 1876, 1:3; and *History of St. Charles, Montgomery and Warren Counties,* 997–1000.

33. The name *Nancy Thompson* may be only a coincidence, but this is also the name of the African-American woman whom William Edwards stabbed his rival to death about at a ball in St. Louis in 1868 and was hanged the next year. However, St. Louis and Jefferson Counties are contiguous, and the *femme fatale* at the dance may be the same alluring woman at the church revival ten years later.

34. *SLPD,* June 6, 1879, 1:6; *State v. Guy,* 69 Mo. 430 (1879); and *History of Franklin, Jefferson, Washington, Crawford and Gasconade Counties, Missouri,* 409–10. Newspaper coverage indicates that the threat to lynch Guy came primarily from African-Americans in Jefferson County.

35. *Weekly Herald* (St. Joseph), Jan. 13, 2:4 and Sept. 9, 1870, 4:3; State v. *Grable,* 46 Mo. 350 (1870); and Rutt. *History of Buchanan County and the City of St. Joseph,* 218–20.

36. *SLPD,* April 16, 1875, 1:1; *MORE,* April 17, 1875, 1:3; *KCT,* April 17, 1875, 1:4; *State v. Harris,* 59 Mo. 550 (1875); and *History of Southeast Missouri,* 355.

37. *SLPD,* June 6, 1879, 1:4; *State v. Blan,* 7 Mo. App. 580 and 69 Mo. 317 (1879).

38. *SLPD,* May 16, 1879, 1:4; *State v. West,* 69 Mo. 401 (1879); and *History of Howard and Cooper Counties, Missouri,* 783.

39. *KCT,* March 2, 1918, 14:6 and *State v. Green,* 66 Mo. 631 (1877).

40. *EHSL,* 2:714 and *State v. Wieners,* 66 Mo. 11 (1877).

41. *Johnson County Star,* Dec. 30, 1893, 1:1 and *State v. Davidson,* 69 Mo. 509 (1879).

42. *Saline County Progress* (Marshall), July 24, 1874, 3:2; *State v. Carlisle,* 57 Mo. 102 (1874); and *History of Saline County,* 383.

43. *History of Southeast Missouri,* 361 and *State v. Edmundson,* 64 MO. 398 (1877).

44. Mary Hahn, *Bits of History,* 71.

45. *Ibid.,* 69 and *State v. Pints,* 64 Mo. 317 (1876).

46. *MORE.* Dec. 15, 1870, 3:6.

47. James J. Fisher column, *KCS,* March 29, 1989, sec. B, 1:6.

48. Champion: *Boonville Weekly Eagle,* Feb. 28, 1873, 2:5; Walker: *LT,* May 22, 1874, 2:2.

49. *Dispatch* (St. Louis), May 28, 1875, 4:2.

50. *State v. Brown,* 1 Mo. App. 449 (1876). See also *SLPD,* Oct. 22, 1875, 1:1 and *St. Louis Globe-Democrat,* Sept. 8, 1875, 4:4 and Oct. 22, 1875, 1:1.

51. *History of St. Charles, Montgomery and Warren County,* 1000–02 and *State v. Price,* 3 Mo. App. 586 (1876).

52. See generally John Higham, *Strangers in the Land: Patterns of American Nativism, 1860–1925.*

53. *EHSL,* 2:713–14.

54. *Herman Advertiser,* Nov. 5, 4:1; Nov. 12, 4:1; and Dec. 17, 1875, 5:1 and *History of Franklin, Jefferson, Washington, Crawford, and Gasconade Counties,* 651.

55. *MORE,* Feb. 16, 1876, 8:1.

56. *Ibid.,* Feb. 17, 1876, 8:2.

57. *Ibid.,* Feb. 19, 1876, 3:1.

58. *EHSL,* 2: 714.

59. *Washington County Journal* (Potosi), Nov. 24, 1870, 2:5.

60. *History of Franklin, Jefferson, Washington, Crawford and Gasconade Counties, Missouri,* 502–03.

61. Norma Peterson, *Freedom and Franchise: The Political Career of B. Gratz Brown,* 193.

62. *History of Laclede, Camden, Dallas, Webster, Wright, Texas, Pulaski, Phelps and Dent Counties, Missouri,* 201 and *Springfield News & Leader,* Oct. 4, 1953, D10:1.

63. Thomas Hopper murdered Samuel Ham in Cedar County in the course of an attempted robbery. On a change of venue he was tried and hanged in Greenfield, Dade County, on June 25, 1880, *History of Hickory, Polk, Cedar, Dade and Barton Counties,* 454 and *State v. Hopper,* 71 Mo. 425 (1880). John Patterson killed James Clark in Henry County in late Nov.–early Dec. 1868 for purposes of robbing him. Patterson received a change of venue to Morgan County, where, after he was tried, he escaped from jail and remained a free man for the next 12 years. He was rearrested after his father's death when the estate's administrator found a letter from him from Illinois. He was taken into custody in Livingstone County, Illinois, under the name of John Williams, in August 1880, returned to Henry County, retried, found guilty, and hanged in Clinton, Henry County, on July 22, 1881, *History of Henry and St. Clair Counties, Missouri,* 209–16 and *State v. Patterson,* 73 Mo. 695 (1881).

64. History of Audrain County, 254–56.

65. *History of Howard and Chariton Counties, Missouri,* 620–25.

66. *EHSL,* 2:715, *State v. Charles Wilson,* 86 Mo. 520 (1885), *KCS,* Jan. 15, 1886, 1:1 and *KCT,* Jan. 16, 1886, 1:1.

67. Charles Ellis killed Mack Sanders in St. Louis, as the newspaper phrased it, "in a colored gambling house ... during a general row" on May 9, 1880. He was tried, convicted; his conviction was upheld on appeal, 74 Mo. 207 (1881), and he was hanged in St. Louis on Jan. 6, 1882, *KCS,* Jan. 6, 1882, 1:3.

68. In St. Louis and in the course of squabbling with his roommate and fellow employee, Berry Evans, at a stables about their work, Robert Grayor clubbed him to death on May 6, 1883, was tried, found guilty, and the St. Louis Court of Appeals and the Mo. Supreme Court affirmed, 16 Mo. App. 558 and 1 SW 365 (1886). Grayor was hanged in St. Louis on Dec. 10, 1886, *EHSL,* 2: 715 and *St. Louis Globe-Democrat,* Dec. 10, 1886, 8:1

69. Alfred Sanders killed Moses Wing by cutting his throat on November 19, 1881, in Mississippi County. The perpetrator was tried, found guilty, and hanged Dec. 8, 1882 in Charleston, *History of Southeast Missouri,* 365. There was no appeal.

70. Three capital wife homicides arose in St. Louis. In a fit of jealousy, Matthew Lewis murdered his wife, Mary Ann Lewis, on October 13, 1876, by slitting her throat ear to ear. After four trials, four appeals, and seven years in the city jail, he was hanged on March 14, 1884, *EHSL,* 2:715 and 69 Mo. 92 (1878), 9 Mo. App. 321 (1880), 74 Mo. 222 (1881), and 80 Mo. 110 (1883). Daniel Jewell killed his 17-year-old wife, Eliza, because she refused to live with him. He attacked her with a knife on Dec. 30, 1884, and she lingered until her death on April 27, 1885. He was

tried and found guilty; the Mo. Supreme Court affirmed, 3 SW 77 (1887), and he was hanged on April 15, 1887, *EHSL*, 2:715. Alfred Blunt, a hunchback, slit the throat of his wife, Mary Blunt, with a razor on May 21, 1886. She had earlier complained that he did nothing to support her and their two children and he that she was intimate with other men. At his trial for her murder he testified that she despised him because of his deformity. He was found guilty, the Mo. Supreme Court affirmed, 4 SW 394 (1887), and he was hanged on June 24, 1887, *EHSL*, 2:715, *St. Louis Globe-Democrat*, Dec. 10, 1886, 12:4.

71. William Ward murdered Annie Lewis because she refused to marry him. He was tried, found guilty, and hanged in St. Louis on Jan. 13, 1882, *St. Louis Globe-Democrat*, Jan. 13, 1882, 3:1. There was no appeal.

72. In Mississippi County on Aug. 6, 1881, Howard Underwood, aged late fifties and a good provider for his wife and children, first shot and then split the skull of his long-term mistress, Belle Lucas, because of her newfound interest in another man. He escaped to Illinois and was caught a year later. He was tried, found guilty, the Mo. Supreme Court affirmed, 76 Mo. 630 (1882), and he was hanged in Charleston on April 6, 1883, *History of Southeast Missouri*, 365 and *Kansas City Journal*, April 7, 1883, 1:5.

73. *State v. Wilson*, 88 Mo. 13, 17 (1885).

74. Jeff Wilson was tried twice; the first trial was reversed on appeal, 85 Mo. 134 (1884), and the second affirmed, 88 Mo. 13 (1885). He was hanged in Lexington, Lafayette County, on April 2, 1886, *KCT*, April 3, 1886, 5:1.

75. *KCS*, Nov. 21, 1884, 1:3.

76. *Ibid.*, 1:2.

77. *Kansas City Journal*, Sept. 9, 1884, 1:7.

78. *Nodaway Democrat* (Maryville), Nov. 27, 1884, 2:5.

79. *History of Andrew County and De Kalb Counties, Missouri*, 132.

80. *KCS*, Nov. 21, 1884, 1:3.

81. *History of Andrew and De Kalb Counties, Missouri*, 134–35.

82. *Nodaway Democrat*, Nov. 27, 1884, 2:5.

83. *KCT*, July 12, 1884, 5:1. There was no appeal in their cases.

84. Joe Snyder, "The Hanging of Joe Jump," 135–44 and *Gallatin Democrat*, "Life, Trial and Conviction of Joe Jump and John Smith," 1–21.

85. Retrospective, *Evening Press* (Farmington), Feb. 7, 1975, 1:3.

86. State v. Dickson, 78 Mo. 438 (1883); *Callaway Gazette* (Fulton), May 9, 1884, 2:2, *Linn County News* (Linneus), May 15, 1884, 1:4 and *History of Southeast Missouri*, 361.

87. *State v. Stair*, 87 Mo. 268 (1885) and *KCS*, Jan. 16, 1886, 1:1.

88. *History of Southeast Missouri*, 331–33.

89. Walker Kilgore killed Lorenzo Willingham on Jan. 27, 1879, in Audrain County, over the disposal of corn fodder. He was tried, found guilty, the Mo. Supreme Court affirmed, 70 Mo. 546 (1879), and he was hanged in Mexico on March 5, 1880. The perpetrator was probably retarded. The county history states, "Kilgore was a person dwarfed in intellect ... entirely uneducated and not capable of understanding moral obligations," *History of Audrain County*, 256–58. Expectedly, the appellate court decision contains no mention of Kilgore's likely mental retardation.

90. Joseph Core fatally shot his neighbor, George King, over burnt wheat stacks, was indicted in Laclede County Circuit Court in Feb. 1879, and found guilty; on appeal, the Mo. Supreme Court affirmed, 70 Mo. 491 (1879). He was hanged at Lebanon on March 5, 1880, *History of La-*

clede, Camden, Dallas, Webster, Wright, Texas, Pulaski, Phelps and Dent Counties, 59–60.

91. On Aug. 15, 1881, in Phelps County, George Bohanan killed William Light at a picnic over an earlier disputed land sale. He was tried, found guilty, and on appeal the Mo. Supreme Court reversed, 76 Mo. 562 (1882). He was retried and hanged at Rolla on April 21, 1882, *CT*, Jan. 1, 1883, 6:4.

92. After their drinking stopped, in Vernon County on May 19, 1883, William Fox shot his companion, Thomas Howard, after he lured him to a deserted part of town. He was tried, found guilty, no appeal was taken, and Fox was hanged on Dec. 28, 1883 in Nevada, *History of Vernon County*, 334 and *CT*, Dec. 29, 1883, 5:3. In Kansas City on July 27, 1884, Edward Sneed shot and killed Orleans Loomis after they finished imbibing together and left the Blue Front Saloon. After three trials and two reversals, Sneed was hanged at Independence, Jackson County, on June 24, 1887, 88 Mo. 138 (1885) and 4 SW 411 (1887), *CT*, Jan. 1, 1888, 2:3.

93. On Sept. 24, 1883, in Pike County; Samuel Collins killed Owen Utterback because he believed his victim had slander the perpetrator's wife. He was tried, found guilty, and the appellate court reversed, 81 Mo. 652 (1884). Two more trials followed, and the Mo. Supreme Court sustained the verdict, 86 Mo. 245 (1885). Collins was hanged at Bowling Green on Aug. 28, 1885, *SLPD*, Aug. 28, 1885, 2:2.

94. Henry Redemeier killed a stone mason, Franz Vosz, while Vosz and six others were placing a large stone at a work site in St. Louis. When asked why he had committed the act, the perpetrator replied that he had "had it in" for his victim about two years. Redemeier was tried and found guilty; both the St. Louis Court of Appeals and the Mo. Supreme Court affirmed, 8 Mo. App.3 and 71 Mo. 173 (1879). He was hanged in St. Louis on April 23, 1880, *EHSL*, 2:714.

95. On Aug. 20, Edward Nugent shot his wife to death because she refused to serve him a meal which he demanded. After 11 continuances, he was convicted of her murder; his case was affirmed on appeal, 8 Mo. App. 563 and 71 Mo. 136 (1879), and he was hanged April 23, 1880 in the city of St. Louis, *EHSL*, 2:714–15. On April 17, 1886, Peter Hronek, a drunken Bohemian, shot and killed his wife. He was convicted; an appeal was taken, and the Mo. Supreme Court affirmed, 8 SW 227 (1888). Hronek was hanged in St. Joseph on June 29, 1888, *History of Buchanan County and the City of St. Joseph*, 220.

96. On June 19, 1879, William Erb, a German alcoholic, killed his divorced wife, Rose Mion, alias Aglae Rosalie Erb, by stabbing her to death because, after a lengthy divorce from him, she planned to remarry. Erb was tried, convicted, and on appeal, the St. Louis Court of Appeals reversed, 9 Mo. App. 588 (1881). The state appealed the reversal, and the Mo. Supreme Court reinstated the conviction, 74 Mo. 199 (1881). Erb was hanged in St. Louis on Dec. 30, 1881, *CT*, Jan. 1, 1882, 9:4.

97. On Oct. 10, 1878, Joseph Kotovsky, a Bohemian, shot Augusta Simon on a St. Louis street as she returned to the residence of her employment with a pitcher of beer. She had rejected his offer of marriage. After several trials, he was convicted, and his conviction affirmed on appeal, 11 Mo. App 584 and 74 Mo. 247 (1881). Kotovsky was hanged Jan. 6, 1882 in St. Louis, *KCS*, Jan. 16, 1882, 1:3. Henry Landgraf, alias Langford, first accused his 21-year-old girlfriend, Annie Fisch, a servant in a house where Langraf boarded, of unacceptable familiarity with other men because she spoke to them. He asked her to avoid talking to other male boarders; she refused to obey him, and on March 5, 1885, he shot her in the head on a St.

Louis street. She died 10 days later. He was tried, convicted, and the Mo. Supreme Court affirmed, 8 SW 237 (1888). He was hanged in St. Louis Aug. 10, 1888, *EHSL*, 2:715–16 and *St. Louis Globe-Democrat*, Aug. 10, 1888, 2:6.

98. On Aug. 14, 1878, Thaddeus Baber killed two women, Lizzie Schuendler, his mistress, and her mother, Frederika Schuendler. Because of his jealousy, Lizzie left him after six years and returned to her mother. Baber was tried, convicted, and the appeals courts affirmed, 11 Mo. App. 585 and 74 Mo 292 (1881). Baber was hanged on Jan. 13, 1882 in St. Louis, *St. Louis Globe-Democrat*, Jan. 13, 1882, 3:1.

99. In Randolph County on July 23, 1878, James Brown shot and killed his mother-in-law, Mrs. Parrish, and wounded his physician father-in-law, Dr. J.C. Parrish, after their daughter, Brown's wife, returned to her parents' home because her husband beat her. After three trials and an appeal to the Mo. Supreme Court, which affirmed the defendant's conviction, Brown, who had been boarded in the Jackson County jail in Kansas City, was returned to Huntsville and hanged there on June 25, 1880. On that same day, his wife, Sue Parrish Brown, shot herself to death in her Kansas City boardinghouse. Perhaps the couple had a suicide agreement, 71 Mo. 454 (1880), *History of Randolph and Macon Counties*, 250–51, and James J. Fisher column, *KCT*, Dec. 6, 1989, C1:6.

100. Near Miami, Saline County on July 23, 1885, George Rider ambushed R. P. Tallent in the belief that his victim was intimate with Rider's putative wife. Following his first trial, the Mo. Supreme Court reversed on grounds of inadmissible hearsay, such as the wife of the deceased testifying that Mrs. Rider said, "She was afraid Mart Rider would kill her, that he had beat her up with a club, and she was bloody as a hog," 1 SW 825, 826 (1886). Rider was retried, found guilty, and the trial court was upheld on appeal, 8 SW 723 (1888). He was hanged in Marshall on July 13, 1888, *KCT*, July 14, 1888, 2:2.

101. On April 23, 1881, in Saline Co., John Phelps killed Elijah Keyton, a wealthy farmer whose daugher the perpetrator loved. He was tried, found guilty, and his conviction was affirmed, 74 Mo. 128 (1881). On Jan. 6, 1882, the sheriff hanged Phelps in Marshall, *KCT*, Jan. 7, 1882, 1:1.

102. This case is the subject of a small book, which I have heavily relied on in describing these complicated relations, Emory Melton, *Hanged by the Neck Until Dead*. See also James J. Fisher column, *KCT*, March 2, 1988, B1:5; Robert K. Gilmore, *Ozark Baptizings, Hangings, and Other Diversions*, 160–61; and *State v. Clum*, 3 SW 200 (1887).

103. Thomas Duke, *Celebrated Criminal Cases of America*, 486.

104. *Brooks v. Missouri*, 124 U.S, 394 (1888).

105. In *Illinois v. Perkins*, 496 U.S. 292 (1990), the U.S. Supreme Court upheld placing an undercover government agent in a cell with a suspect in order to obtain information about a crime unrelated to the inmate's incarceration. It ruled that *Miranda* warnings are unnecessary when the prisoner is unaware that he is speaking to a law enforcement officer and talks voluntarily.

106. Duke, *Celebrated Criminal Cases of America*, 486–95; *St. Louis Globe-Democrat*, Aug. 10, 1888, 1:3; *EHSL*, 2:716; *State v. Brooks*, 5 SW 257 (1887) and 124 U.S. 394 (1888).

107. *History of Clay and Platte Counties, Missouri*, 423.

108. *Springfield Patriot-Advertiser*, May 24, 1877, 1:6.

109. *SLPD*, June 6, 1879, 1:6.

110. *KCS*, Nov. 21, 1884, 1:1.

111. Snyder, "The Hanging of Joe Jump," 136.

5. The Nineties and Beyond, 1890–1907

1. RMoS. sec. 1856 (1879).

2. *State v. Jackson*, 8 SW 749, 762 (1888).

3. J.E. Curry, *A Reminiscent History of Douglas County, Missouri*, 64.

4. *State v. McKenzie*, 45 SW 1117, 1118 (1898).

5. Undated newspaper retrospective, provided by Cole County Historical Society, Lanahan file.

6. *State v. Headrick*, 51 SW 99 (1899).

7. George Thompson, *Prison Life and Reflections*, 91.

8. In 1923 the U.S. Supreme Court finally ruled in a capital case from Arkansas that mob domination of the atmosphere of a trial denied the defendant his right to a fair trial guaranteed by the Sixth Amendment, *Moore v. Dempsey*, 260 U.S. 377. There were surely many mobs which influenced the outcome of cases in rural areas where lynchings flourished between the end of the Civil War and 1923.

9. Charles Wisdom killed Edward Drexler on April 24, 1892. He was tried, sentenced to death, the Supreme Court of Missouri affirmed, and Wisdom was hanged in the city of St. Louis on April 13, 1894, *State v. Wisdom*, 24 SW 1047 (1894) and *SLPD*, April 13, 1894, 1:5.

10. Ed McKenzie, farm laborer, clubbed Nicholas Linhardt, a farmer, to death the night of April 30, 1896. After his arrest, he escaped; he was recaptured in Sept. 1897 and tried in Jan. 1898; the Mo. Supreme Court affirmed, and he was hanged in Jefferson City on June 22, 1898, *State v. McKenzie*, 45 SW 1117 (1898) and *CT*, Dec. 31, 1898, 20:1.

11. The Murray brothers, James and Edward, shot Edward Fitzwilliams on Sept. 23, 1893. They were subsequently identified by a streetcar passenger. James was tried and convicted; the Mo. Supreme Court affirmed, and he was hanged in Clayton at 6 a.m. on May 11, 1895. On a change of venue, Edward was tried and convicted in Gasconade County; the Missouri Supreme Court affirmed, and he was hanged in Hermann, at 8:00 a.m., two hours later, that same day, *State v. James Murray*, 29 SW 700 (1895) and *State v. Edward Murray*, 29 SW 590 (1895) and *KNG*, May 24, 1895, 7:1.

12. Webster Jackson was hanged in Hermann, Gasconade County, on April 25, 1891, for the Oct. 22, 1886 murder of Alexander McVickers in Franklin County. He was arrested in Hamilton, Ohio, on a charge of horse stealing and returned to Missouri. He was first tried in Union, and when the Mo. Supreme Court reversed his conviction, he was granted a change of venue and retried in Gasconade County. After three appeals, he was hanged in Hermann on April 25, 1891, *State v. Jackson*, 8 SW 749 (1888), 12 SW 367 (1889), and 15 SW 333 (1891); *History of Franklin, Jefferson, Washington, Crawford & Gasconade Counties, Missouri*, 282–83; and *CT*, Jan. 1, 1892, 12:5.

13. On July 31, 1897, James McAfee shot William Brewer, aged approximately 24 years, in Joplin because, as McAfee stated, "I want what you've got." His victim died on Aug. 5, 1897. He was tried and found guilty in Carthage; the Mo. Supreme Court affirmed, and the sheriff of Jasper County hanged him on July 7, 1899, *State v. McAfee*, 50 SW 82, 83 (1899); *Carthage Press*, July 6, 1899, 1:3; and *KNG*, July 13, 1899, 2:1.

14. *State v. Williamson*, 17 SW 172 (1891) and *KNG*, Nov. 30, 1891, 6:4

15. *KCT*, March 12, 1892, 8:3.

16. *State v. Avery*, 21 SW 193 (1893); *Lamar Democrat*, May 25, 1893, 2:2; *SLPD*, May 24, 1893, 1:5; and *KCT*, May 25, 1893, 1:6.

17. On May 21, 1896, Edward Perry killed Lafayette Sawyer, his wife, and son Ernest by bludgeoning them to death with a gas pipe. The perpetrator, a neighbor, had earlier done odd jobs for the family, and he killed them in order to rob them of $156. Perry disposed of the bodies by piling them under the bed. He was suspected, confessed, tried, his conviction was upheld on appeal, and the sheriff of Douglas County hanged him in Ava on Jan. 30, 1897, *State* v. *Perry*, 37 SW 804 (1896); *Douglas County Herald* (Ava), Feb. 4, 1897, 2:1; James J. Fisher column, *KCS*, Oct. 30, 1991, I 1:2; Gilmore, *Ozark Baptizings, Hangings, and Other Diversions*, 158–60; and Curry, *A Reminiscent History of Douglas County, Missouri*, 51–79.

18. On April 27, 1889, Wilson Howard murdered Thomas McMichael(s), a deaf mute, in Dixon, Pulaski County, in order to rob him of $50. Wilson was located serving a term for robbery in California at San Quentin Penitentiary under the name of Charles Brown. Once his identity was discovered and the necessary extradition paperwork completed, a Missouri sheriff went to the California prison and brought Howard back. On a change of venue, he was tried in Laclede County and found guilty; the Mo. Supreme Court affirmed, and Howard was hanged in Lebanon on Jan. 19, 1894, *State* v. *Howard*, 24 SW 41 (1893); *Fountain and Journal* (Mt. Vernon), Jan. 25, 1894, 2:3; and *CT*, Jan. 1, 1895, 9:7.

19. On Oct. 28, 1897, Ira Sexton shot Nathaniel Stark in an attempted robbery near Mercer, Mercer County. His victim died the next day, and he gave a lengthy dying declaration in which he quoted the perpetrator as saying, "'It's your money I want.' Nath says, 'I haven't got any.' 'Yes you have damm you; it's your money I want.'" *State* v. *Sexton*, 48 SW 452, 454 (1898). Sexton was tried and convicted; the Mo. Supreme Court affirmed, and he was hanged in Princeton on Dec. 28, 1898, *KNG*, Jan. 6, 1899, 2:4.

20. *KCS*, June 29, 1894, 1:6; *Kansas City Journal*, June 29, 3:1 and 30, 1894, 3:1; *KCT*, June 30, 1894, 8:1; and *State* v. *Clark*, 26 SW 562 (1894).

21. *State* v. *Banks*, 23 SW 1079 (1893) and *Standard-Herald* (Warrensburg), Dec. 29, 1893, 1:1. The newspaper also contains a retrospective on the four earlier post–Civil War executions in Warrensburg.

22. Thomas Johnson, alias Henry Clay, shot and killed a newsboy, 18-year-old William Amend, in August 1896, in the belief that his victim was cheating at a crap game he was only watching. One-legged Johnson was tried and convicted. He was hanged in the city of St. Louis on Nov. 18, 1897. There was no appeal, *St. Louis Globe-Democrat*, Nov. 17, 1:4 and 11:4, Nov. 18, 9:4, and Nov. 19, 1897, 7:1.

23. On July 25, 1897, Matthew Hancock shot a ticket broker, George Horton, in front of Union Station when the stranger asked, "Where do you live?," and the victim refused to answer. He died on July 29, 1897. The perpetrator was tried and convicted; the Mo. Supreme Court affirmed, and Hancock was hanged in the city of St. Louis jail yard on April 8, 1899, *State* v. *Hancock*, 50 SW 112 (1899) and *CT*, Dec. 31, 1899, 43:2.

24. On September 29, 1894, George Thompson murdered Joseph Cunningham by poisoning him. The perpetrator invited the victim to eat a lunch heavily laced with strychnine. He was tried and convicted; the Mo. Supreme Court reversed, *State* v. *Thompson*, 34 SW 31 (1896). Thompson was retried, found guilty, and hanged on Aug. 1, 1898 in the city of St. Louis, *EHSL*, 2:717.

25. *Brown* v. *State*, 24 SW 1027 (1894) and *KNG*, May 11, 1894, 3:1.

26. *State* v. *Duncan*, 27 SW 699 (1893); *Duncan* v. *State*, 152 U.S. 377 (1894); Lorenzo Greene, Gary R. Kre-

mer, and Anthony Holland, *Missouri's Black Heritage*, 96; and *CT*, Jan. 1, 1895, 9:7.

27. *KNG*, March 23, 1894, 7:1.

28. William F. Johnson, *History of Cooper County, Missouri*, 350–51; *Historical Listing of the Missouri Legislature*, 28; *State* v. *Turlington*, 15 SW 141 (1891); and *KNG*, March 13, 1891, 4:1.

29. Correspondence, Mississippi County Historical Society; *State* v. *Albright*, 46 SW 620 (1898); *KNG*, July 15, 1898, 2:4; and *CT*, Dec. 31, 1898, 29:1.

30. On Aug. 5, 1893, in Ralls Co. John Nelson and his wife, Lavinia, killed their neighbors, John Stull and his feeble and nearly blind mother, Mrs. Hughes. The victims had cared for Mr. Nelson's ill mother whom he and his wife neglected. Both of the Nelson parents were arrested. Mrs. Nelson had given birth to a daughter in Nov. 1893 in the Ralls Co. jail, and during her mother's trial in New London, the young child ran about the courtroom; the jury acquitted her. Mr. Nelson obtained a change of venue to Marion County; he was found guilty of first degree murder; the Mo. Supreme Court affirmed, and he was hanged in Palmyra on Feb. 28, 1896. The couple may have been retarded; at any rate, he was illiterate, Goldena Roland Howard, *Ralls County Missouri*. 103; State v. *Nelson*, 33 SW 809 (1896); and *KNG*, March 6, 1896, 6:4.

31. On Aug. 17, 1897, in Harrison Co., Freeman Cochran shot his neighbor and in-law, George Stanbrough, after an earlier argument following which they ostensibly made up. The perpetrator shot the victim in the back of the head, and the couple at whose home the shooting occurred, Mr. and Mrs. Briant, testified for the prosecution. Cochran was tried in Bethany, found guilty, the Mo. Supreme Court affirmed, and the sheriff of Harrison Co. hanged him on June 7, 1899, *State* v. *Cochran*, 49 SW 558 (1899) and *CT*, Dec. 31, 1899, 43:1.

32. On Dec. 10, 1897, at Corder and after drinking together, illiterate Chris Young assaulted Stephen Ferguson with a knife and killed him. He was tried for murder in Lexington, and the Mo. Supreme Court reversed on the basis of the prosecutor's offensive remarks, Among other obnoxious names, he termed the defendant "a mean, low-down, wicked dirty devil," *State* v. *Young*, 12 SW 879, 884 (1891). He was retried; the Missouri Supreme Court affirmed, and the sheriff of Lafayette Co. hanged Chris Young in Lexington on Aug 13, 1891, *State* v. *Young*, 16 SW 408 (1891) and *Lexington News Supplement*, Aug. 13, 1891, 1:1.

33. In Mound City on May 15, 1895, James B. Inks, the evicted tenant, shot and killed his landlord, John Patterson. Earlier the victim had successfully sued the perpetrator over his failure to pay rent. Inks's defense at trial was that Patterson was too attentive to Mrs. Inks. However, prosecution witnesses testified that after the shooting, Inks made statements such as, "I am the man that done the killing ... I am not sorry for it," and "I killed the man. If I hadn't, I wouldn't have done what I intended to do," *State* v. *Inks*, 37 SW 942, 943 (1896). The jury believed that Patterson's earlier eviction for Inks's failure to pay rent explained the killing. It found him guilty; the Court affirmed, and on Jan. 30, 1897, the sheriff of Holt Co. hanged Inks in Oregon, MO, *CT*, Jan. 1, 1898, 20:5.

34. On Feb. 5, 1898, Peter Kindred killed Andrew Alley and dangerous wounded his cousin, Joseph Alley, in Mercer Co. in an argument over extended credit. The victim, a storekeeper, had earlier obtained a judgment against the perpetrator, and when he came into his hardware store, the victim said, "You don't pay your debts," *State* v. *Kindred*, 49 SW 845, 846 (1899). The perpetrator preferred to fight it out, and he drew a revolver and shot two

unarmed men, one of whom died. Kindred applied for but was denied a change of venue; the jury found him guilty of first degree murder, the Mo. Supreme Court affirmed, and the sheriff of Mercer Co. hanged him in Princeton on June 7, 1899, *CT*, Dec. 31, 1899, 43:2.

35. On July 4, 1888, William Harben shot and killed A.L. Smith in Butler Co.; the perpetrator owed the victim money. The defense was self-defense, but the jury did not believe it and found Harben guilty of first degree murder; the Mo. Supreme Court affirmed in a 17-line, one column decision, and the sheriff of Butler Co. hanged Harben on Jan. 15, 1892, *State v. Harben*, 16 SW 938 (1891), *Poplar Bluff Republican*, Jan. 14, [*sic*] 1892, 4:3 and *SLPD*, Jan. 15, 1892, 1:7.

36. Charles Wilson shot Moses Hodges on Nov. 8; he died on Dec. 18, 1892. Their woman was Lydia Nichols, and the victim was at her house when the perpetrator arrived and exclaimed, "I've got you now." Wilson was tried and found guilty, the Mo. Supreme Court affirmed, and he was hanged July 26, 1894, in the city of St. Louis, *State v. Wilson*, 26 SW 357 (1894) and *EHSL*, 2:716.

37. On July 30, 1895, James Pollard intended to kill David Irwin because they had quarreled about a young black woman teaching school near De Kalb. His aim was bad, and he killed Joseph Irwin, the brother of his intended victim. The state transferred the perpetrator's intent from one brother to the other; the defendant was tried and found guilty; the Mo. Supreme Court affirmed. Pollard was hanged in St. Joseph on June 25, 1897, *State v. Pollard*, 40 SW 949 (1897); Rutt, *History of Buchanan County and St. Joseph*, 220; and *St. Joseph Weekly Herald*, July 1, 1897, 1:1.

38. In Kansas City on April 1, 1896, James Brown shot and killed Henry Prather over a Mrs. Williams. Brown was captured in Quincy, IL, because another rival for his new lady love knew of Brown's killing Prather and notified the authorities. He was tried and found guilty; the Mo. Supreme Court affirmed, and he was hanged at the jail in Kansas City on Dec. 28, 1898, *State v. Brown* 47 SW 789 (1898) and *KCT*, Dec. 28, 1898, 5:1.

39. *KCT*, April 8, 1891, 8:5.

40. *Ibid.*, Feb. 16, 1893, 2:6.

41. *State v. McCoy*, 20 SW 240 (1892) and *KCT*, Feb.16, 1893, 3:2.

42. *Lexington News*, Feb. 23, 1893, 1:4.

43. *State v. Robinson*, 23 SW 1066, 1068 (1893).

44. *KNG*, June 9, 1893, 4:4.

45. *CT*, Dec. 31, 1893, 26:5.

46. *State v. Lanahan*, 45 SW 1090 (1898) and *CT*, Dec. 31, 1898, 20:1.

47. *KCS*, Oct. 25, 1:2, Oct. 26, 1:5, and Oct. 27, 1:3, 1897 and *KCT*, Dec. 18, 1897, 1:7.

48. *Kansas City Journal*, Jan. 21, 1889, 1:3; *Joplin Daily Standard*, July 30, 1889, 2:2; *Trenton Daily Evening Republican*, Aug. 4, 1893, 2:1; *St. Joseph Herald*, Aug. 5, 1893, 1:6; *SLPD*, Aug. 4, 1893, 1:4; and *State v. Howell*, 14 SW 4 (1890) and 23 SW 263, 264 (1893).

49. Roy Blunt, *Historical Listing of the Missouri Legislature*, 120.

50. *State v. Taylor*, 35 SW 92 (1896); *KNG*, May 8, 1896, 7:2; *Maryville Republican*, May 7, 1896, 1:1; Olive Woolley Burt, ed. *American Murder Ballads and Their Stories*, 232–36.

51. *State v. Soper*, 49 SW 1007 (1899) and *Kansas City Mail*, March 31, 1899, 1:4.

52. *State v. Duestrow*, 38 SW 554 and 39 SW 266 (1897) and *St. Louis Globe-Democrat*, Feb. 17, 1897, 1:7.

53. On July 1, 1898, in Cape Girardeau County, John Headrick lay in wait for his former employer, a farmer, James Lail, who had earlier fired him because he was arrested for taking a horse and buggy belonging to someone else. Headrick had also formed an attachment to Jessie, the Lails' daughter. This dismissed farmhand killed Mr. Lail and wounded his wife. He was tried and found guilty; the Mo. Supreme Court affirmed, and the sheriff of Cape Girardeau County hanged him in Jackson on June 15, 1899, *State v. Headrick*, 51 SW 99 (1899) and *CT*, Dec. 31, 1899, 43:2.

54. On Jan. 8, 1894, Emile David poisoned Frank Henderson in Osage County by putting strychnine in a drink of whiskey. The case is chiefly of interest because the victim's stomach was removed, placed in a sealed jar, and delivered to a chemistry professor in St. Louis who testified for the prosecution that the victim was poisoned. The state put on no motive, but it showed the perpetrator's intent. The jury found the defendant guilty; the Mo. Supreme Court affirmed, and the sheriff of Osage County hanged Emile David in Linn on Feb. 15, 1896, *State v. David*, 33 SW 28 (1895) and *KNG*, Feb. 21, 1896, 4:4.

55. On Nov. 24, 1893, James Fitzgerald killed 18-year-old Annie Naessens, then shot himself but not fatally, and blamed his crime on a third person. She was depressed, weary of life, and wished herself dead. She asked him to shoot her, and he obliged. Fitzgerald was tried for her first degree murder and found guilty. The Mo. Supreme Court affirmed, and he was hanged on Feb. 20, 1896, *State v. Fitzgerald*, 32 SW 1113 (1895); *EHSL*, 2:717, and *KNG*, Feb. 28, 1896, 5:1.

56. On April 6, 1897, John Tomasitz, a Bohemian, shot Anna Rausch because she refused to marry him. She died a month later, on May 7. At his trial his defense was insanity. The jury rejected it and found him guilty; the Mo. Supreme Court affirmed. Tomasitz was hanged on June 22, 1898, *State v. Tomasitz*, 45 SW 1106 (1898) and *EHSL*, 2:717

57. Samuel Welsor shot Clementine Manning on Aug. 4, 1890; he was tried and found guilty of first degree murder; the Mo. Supreme Court affirmed, and he was put to death in the city of St. Louis on Jan. 12, 1894, *State v. Welsor*, 21 SW 443, 444 (1893) and *EHSL*, 2:716.

58. *State v. Wright*, 35 SW 1145, 1148 (1896) and *KNG*, Aug. 21, 1895, 4:4.

59. Hester Reed had left her husband, and she had filed for divorce, *Kansas City Star*, Sept. 16, 1890, 1:3; *KCT*, Jan. 6, 1894, 8:1, and *State v. Reed*, 23 SW 886 (1893).

60. *Benton Record*, June 2, 1899, 8:1.

61. *State v. Burns*, 49 SW 1005, 1007 (1899).

62. Bulling was first tried in Buchanan Co., but the appellate court reversed on grounds that the trial judge was not qualified. On a change of venue to Andrew Co., he was retried; his insanity defense did not succeed. He was found guilty; the Mo. Supreme Court affirmed, and the sheriff of Andrew Co. hanged Louis Bulling in Savannah on Sept. 4, 1891, *State v. Bulling*, 12 SW 356 (1889) and 15 SW 367, 369 (1891) and *KNG*, Sept. 11, 1891, 4:2.

63. At his trial, Henson's defense was that his shooting his wife was an accident. The jury found him guilty; the Mo. Supreme Court affirmed, and Henson, a native of Denmark, was hanged in the exercise yard of the city of St. Louis jail on Aug. 13, 1891, *State v. Henson*, 16 SW 285 (1891) and *EHSL*, 2:716.

64. At Anderson's first trial, the jury was hung; at his second he was found guilty, and the sheriff of Macon Co. hanged George Anderson in the city of Macon on Aug. 21, 1896, *General History of Macon County, Missouri*, 209–11.

65. Bronstine's defense was insanity; it did not succeed. The jury found him guilty; the Mo. Supreme Court affirmed, and the sheriff of Clark Co. hanged him in Ka-

hoka on May 8, 1899, *State* v. *Bronstine*, 49 SW 512 (1899) and *Clark County Courier* (Kahoka), May 12, 1899, 8:1.

66. At his trial Baker's defense was, in the words of the appellate decision, "that he had merely struck his wife one blow with his fist, in a heat of passion, because she gave him a swat with a wash rag she had in her hand." The jury found him guilty of first degree murder; the Mo. Supreme Court affirmed, and the sheriff of Shannon Co. hanged Oscar Baker at Eminence on Jan. 10, 1899, *State* v. *Baker*, 48 SW 475, 78 (1898) and *Current Wave* (Eminence) Jan. 12, 1899, 1:1.

67. Rice's defense was self-defense. It did not succeed. According to the Mo. Supreme Court decision in his case, he had repeatedly threatened to kill his wife if she did not return to live with him. The jury found him guilty of first degree murder; the appellate court affirmed, and the sheriff of Oregon Co. hanged Carroll Rice at Alton on June 15, 1899, *State* v. *Rice*, 51 SW 78 (1899) and Lewis A.W. Simpson, *Oregon County's Three Flags*, 61.

68. RMoS 1889, art. 8, sec. 4258.

69. *KNG*, Jan. 3, 1906, 6:6.

70. This listing derives from Bowers, *Legal Homicide*, 399–523.

71. *KCS*, Dec. 18, 1897, 1:1 and *KNG*, Dec. 31, 1897.

72. *Kansas City World*, March 30, 1899, 1:4.

73. Feb. 5, 1895 news story provided by Johnson Co. Historical Society, Banks file.

74. On June 19, 1900, in Jasper Co., Ernest Reid, alias Reed, shot his wife, Amanda Gertrude; she died the next day. He gambled her wages, and she refused to live with him. He preferred to kill her rather than have her live with someone else. He was tried and found guilty; the Mo. Supreme Court affirmed his death sentence, and the sheriff hanged him at Carthage on July 5, 1901, *State* v. *Reed*, 62 SW 982 (1901) and *Carthage Press*, July 5, 1901, 1:1.

75. On Feb 24, 1902, in Cooper Co., Charles Reeves shot and killed his wife, from whom he was separated, when they met at a dance, and she called him a liar. The local newspaper quoted him as stating of her remark, "This made my blood boil; I couldn't stand it any longer. I just pulled out my gun and began shooting." He was tried and convicted of first degree murder within a week of his crime, and his legal counsel did not appeal his client's conviction. The sheriff hanged him on May 23, 1902, in Boonville, *Missouri Democrat* (Boonville), May 23, 1902, 1:1.

76. On May 1, 1901, in the city of St. Louis, Charles Gurley stabbed to death Rosie Higgins. They had lived together; she left him, kept company with another man, and refused to return to Gurley. After his crime he escaped on a steamboat and was captured in Arkansas. Upon his return to St. Louis he was tried and convicted, and the Mo. Supreme Court affirmed, *State* v. *Gurley*, 70 SW 875 (1902). Immediately before his hanging on Feb. 3, 1903, he stated, "I am getting just what I deserve. But ... I am saved by grace," *SLPD*, Feb. 3, 1903, 8:2. On Nov. 28, 1905, John King repeatedly shot Hallie Douglas outside a grocery store on a St. Louis street. According to the Mo. Supreme Court decision which affirmed King's death sentence, he and Hallie had been sweethearts and quarreled. Her last words to him were, "Nobody can make me have anybody if I don't want to," *State* v. *King*, 102 SW 315, 317 (1907). After killing her, he turned himself in at the police station. He was tried and convicted; the Mo. Supreme Court affirmed. King was hanged on June 27, 1907 in the city of St. Louis, *State* v. *King*. 102 SW 315 (1907); *SLPD*, June 27, 3:2 and *St. Louis Globe-Democrat*, June 28, 1907, 4:3.

77. On Dec. 23, 1899, in Kansas City, Albert Garth, a brickyard employee who had a wife and children elsewhere, beat and stabbed Minnie Woods, his former mistress. She died Jan. 1, 1900. According to the Mo. Supreme Court decision which affirmed his death sentence, Garth stated of the deceased prior to his murderous attack on her that he would "kill the damm whore that night," *State* v. *Garth*, 65 SW 275 (1901). After his trial, conviction, and appeal, the sheriff of Jackson Co. hanged Garth in Kansas City on Jan. 21, 1902, *Kansas City Journal*, Jan. 22, 1902, 3:3.

78. On Sept. 10, 1901, in Butler Co., Will Gatlin was the accomplice of Zeb Crite, who shot and killed Thomas Graham, Crite's rival for Carrie Bryant. Crite was also tried and sentenced to death, but he committed suicide while in jail by eating soap. After Gatlin's trial and conviction on first degree murder charges, the Mo. Supreme Court affirmed, and the sheriff hanged him in Poplar Bluff on Feb. 6, 1903, *State* v. *Gatlin*, 70 SW 885 (1902); *SLPD*, Feb. 6, 1903, 16:3, and *St. Louis Globe-Democrat*, Feb. 7, 1903, 2:4.

79. On April 14, 1899, in New Madrid Co., Samuel Waters killed Frank Holmes and his wife, Millie, in a dispute over a fence which separated their two- and three-acre properties. Waters was tried and convicted, and the Mo. Supreme Court affirmed in a one page decision. The sheriff hanged him at New Madrid on June 15, 1900, *State* v. *Waters*, 56 SW 734 (1900) and *Southeast Missourian* (New Madrid), June 21, 1900, 1:1.

80. On Dec. 22, 1900, James Jackson followed, shot, and killed Prophet Everett in one saloon in Kansas City after a disagreement about a card game with him in another drinking establishment two blocks away. Jackson was tried and convicted; the Mo. Supreme Court affirmed, and the sheriff hanged him in Kansas City on April 11, 1902, *State* v. *Jackson*, 66 SW 938 (1902) and *KCS*, April 11, 1902, 1:1.

81. On Oct. 29, 1900, in the city of St. Louis, Thomas Dunn shot Peter Jackson, who died the next day. The victim owed the perpetrator four dollars. The debtor became angry when the creditor asked for his money, and Dunn, the lender, began shooting his pistol at Jackson, the borrower. He was tried and convicted; the Mo. Supreme Court affirmed, and Dunn was hanged in St. Louis on Jan. 2, 1903, *State* v. *Dunn*, 70 SW 118 (1902) and *St. Louis Globe-Democrat*, Jan. 3, 1903, 16:3.

82. On June 9, 1901, in the city of St. Louis, Sampson Gray shot George Jones in a robbery of one dollar and the victim's watch. The wife of the deceased identified the pawned watch, and this led to the perpetrator's arrest. Gray was tried and convicted; the Mo. Supreme Court affirmed, and he was hanged in St. Louis on May 8, 1903, *State* v. *Gray*, 72, SW 698 (1903) and *SLPD*, May 8, 1903, 2:3.

83. *State* v. *Henderson*, 85 SW 576, 578 (1905).

84. *St. Charles Cosmos-Monitor*, May 3, 1905, 7:3.

85. *Ibid.*, June 2, 1905, 8:4.

86. *St. Charles Banner-News*, Feb. 22, 1905. 1:2.

87. *CT*, Dec. 31, 1905, sec. 7, 5:3 and *St. Charles Cosmos-Monitor*, June 21, 1905, 2:1.

88. *State* v. *Nettles*, 55 SW 70 (1900) and *CT*, Jan.1, 1901, 25:2.

89. *State* v. *Flutcher*, 66 SW 429 (1902) and *KCS*, April 11, 1902, 1:7.

90. *State* v. *Wilson*, 72 SW 696 (1903) and *SLPD*, May 8, 1903, 2:3.

91. *State* v. *Evans*, 61 SW 590 (1901) and *KNG*, April 19, 1901, 2:3.

92. *Ralls County Times* (New London), Sept. 12, 1902,

1:1 and *Ralls County Record* (New London), Sept. 19, 1902, 3:3.

93. *State v. Clevenger*, 56 SW 1078 (1900) and *KCT*, June 16, 1900, 4:6.

94. *State v. Taylor*, 71 SW 1005, 1006 (1903) and *Kansas City Journal*, April 18, 1903, 3:3.

95. *State v. Clark*, 70 SW 1117 (1902); *KNG*, Oct. 25, 1901, 4:1, and *St. Louis Globe-Democrat*, Feb. 7, 1903, 2:4.

96. In Bates Co. on April 16, 1899, Noah "Bunk" McGinnis shot Frederick Borcherding, a German farmer, in an attempted robbery. The victim died three days later. His wife, who testified through an interpreter, identified the perpetrator a few days after the shooting of her husband. McGinnis was tried and convicted; the Mo. Supreme Court affirmed, and the sheriff of Bates County hanged him at Butler on Dec. 30, 1900, *State v. McGinnis*, 59 SW 83 (1900) and William O. Atkeson, *History of Bates County, Missouri*, 239. In this same county on March 19, 1901, James Gartrell axed to death D.B. Donegan, a miner from Colorado, for his $260 in cash and his watch. The perpetrator freely spent the proceeds of his robbery in the saloons of Kansas City. When he was apprehended he confessed that he wanted his victim's money. Gartrell was tried and convicted; the Mo. Supreme Court affirmed, and the sheriff of Bates Co. hanged this 68-year-old criminal at Butler on April 17, 1903, *State v. Gartrell*, 71 SW 1045 (1903) and *KCS*, April 17, 1903, 7:1.

97. On March 20, 1900, in Wayne Co. and with his co-defendant, William Grant, who turned state's evidence and escaped the gallows, Sam Brown shot and killed George Richardson, a prosperous railroad tie-cutter for his money. The victim carried $700 on his person in a leather belt. Brown was tried and convicted; the Mo. Supreme Court affirmed, and the sheriff of Wayne Co. hanged Sam Brown in Greenville on June 27, 1902, *State v. Brown*, 68 SW 568 (1902) and Rose Fulton Cramer, *Wayne County, Missouri*, 244.

98. On Nov. 7, 1904, Elias Smith bludgeoned to death James Smith in Pulaski County. The perpetrator was not a relative of the victim; he was hired to help James Smith clear his land. Elias Smith confessed that he committed the crime in order to obtain possession of some of his employer's personal property and money. He was tried and found guilty in mid–March 1905; no appeal was taken, and the sheriff of Pulaski County hanged Elias Smith in Waynesville on April 21, 1905, *Pulaski County Democrat* (Waynesville), Nov. 18, 1904, 1:4 and April 21, 1905. 1:4.

99. On Feb. 20, 1899, in Dunklin Co. Gregory Milo shot and killed the storekeeper, Joseph Covert. According to the Mo. Supreme Court decision which affirmed his death sentence, Milo stated before the shooting, "I'm going to get that watch, and if Mr. Covert kicks, I aim to shoot him like shooting a ... rabbit." Milo was tried and convicted, and the sheriff of Dunklin Co. hanged him at Kennett on March 21, 1901, *State v. Milo*, 59 SW 89, 90 (1900) and *CT*, Jan. 1, 1902, 21:5.

100. On Dec. 27, 1900, at a dance near De Kalb, Charles May shot and killed John Martin. Earlier May had killed a farmer, James Burdette, and he served time in MSP for his first homicide. He was tried and found guilty of first degree murder in the killing of John Martin. The Mo. Supreme Court affirmed, and the sheriff of Buchanan County hanged May on April 17, 1903, *State v. May*, 67 SW 566 (1903) and *KCS*, April 17, 1903, 7:1.

101. On July 20, 1902, in Rushville, Mark Dunn shot and killed Alfred Fenton. According to the Mo. Supreme Court decision affirming his death sentence, the perpetrator had earlier stated, "I am hunting Luther Moberly or Jeff Fenton. I don't give a damm which one it is.... I have got it in for them." When the brother of one of his intended victims drove up in a buggy, Dunn opened fire. He was a house painter, and his defense of "lead insanity" did not succeed. He was tried and convicted, and his case was affirmed on appeal. The sheriff of Buchanan Co. hanged Mark Dunn on March 11, 1904, *State v. Dunn*, 77 SW 848, 849 (1903) and Rutt, *History of Buchanan County and St. Joseph*, 221.

102. In Aud, Osage Co., on December 24, 1898, John Holloway shot and killed Julius Boillot; the victim's family had earlier purchased the perpetrator's family's land. The sale had been necessitated by Holloway's father's death, and the son remained angry about the sale. Approximately six months before he killed his victim, Holloway purchased and wore an 18-pound bullet proof vest at all times. According to the Mo. Supreme Court decision affirming his death sentence, when he gunned down his victim, he stated, "I am the Reverend John Holloway, and I have killed Jul Boillot." The defense was insanity; it did not convince the jury who found Holloway guilty of first degree murder. The Mo. Supreme Court affirmed, and the sheriff of Osage Co. hanged John Holloway in Linn on June 15, 1900, *State v. Holloway*, 56 SW 734, 735 (1900); James J. Fisher column, *KCS*, Feb. 10, 1991, sec I, 1:l., and *Kansas City Journal*, June 16, 1900, 8:2.

103. In the city of St. Louis on March 10, 1904, Henry Heusack fractured the skull of his father-in-law, August Raphael; and the victim's hemorrhage into his brain caused his death. The perpetrator, a thriftless alcoholic, blamed his wife's father for her refusal to give him money. According to the Mo. Supreme Court decision which affirmed his death sentence, Heusack had earlier remarked of his victim, "I am going to kill the old son of a bitch one of these days." The perpetrator was tried and found guilty; the Mo. Supreme Court affirmed, and he was hanged in the city of St. Louis on Aug. 21, 1905, *State v. Heusack*, 88 SW 21, 22 (1905) and *CT*, Dec. 31, 1905, sec. 7, 5:4.

104. In Adair Co. on Nov. 13, 1902, John Robertson killed his father-in-law, George Conkle, when the victim refused to sign a note which would have given the perpetrator $150 in connection with the sale of land. He was tried and found guilty; the Mo. Supreme Court affirmed, and the sheriff hanged John Robertson in Kirksville on Jan. 15, 1904, *State v. Robertson*, 77 SW 528 (1903) and *CT*, Dec. 31, 1904, 16:4.

105. *State v. Church*, 98 SW 16, 19 (1906).

106. See Arthur N. Gilbert, "Doctor, Patient, and Onanist Diseases in the Nineteenth Century," 217–234.

107. *State v. Church*, 98 SW 16, 19 (1906).

108. *CT*, Jan. 10, 1907, 20:2.

109. On Dec, 26, 1902, Fred Lewis, alias George Collins, and Bill Rudolph burglarized a bank in Union. They used explosives to blow the vault open, thereby taking and carrying away $10,000 in cash and $80,000 in notes and securities. The bank in Union notified the American Bankers Association., and it in turn contacted the St. Louis office of the Pinkerton Detective Agency. By Jan. 24, 1903, a posse surrounded the home of Rudolph's parents in Stanton, MO. Lewis and Rudolph came out firing, and they shot and killed a Pinkerton operative, Charles Schumacher. The culprits were arrested in Hartford, CT, about a month later; they were then returned to St. Louis and locked up in the city jail. Rudolph managed to escape. Collins was returned to Union, tried, and convicted of the first degree murder of Schumacher. The Mo. Supreme Court affirmed, and he was hanged in Union on March 26, 1904. Rudolph was located at the KS state prison at

Leavenworth under the name of Charles Gorney. He was brought back to Union, tried, and convicted of Schumacher's murder. The Mo. Supreme Court affirmed his conviction, and Rudolph was hanged in Union on May 8, 1905. He also became a Catholic shortly before his execution; James D. Horan, *The Pinkertons*, 403–16; *State v. Lewis*, 79 SW 671 (1904); *KNG*, April 1, 1904, 7:2; *State v. Rudolph*, 85 SW 584 (1905); and *St. Charles Cosmos-Monitor*, May 10, 1905, 8:5.

110. On Dec. 9, 1899, Joshua Craft, an MSP inmate, convicted of train robbery in Lawrence Co., while making his escape from the penitentiary, shot and killed Henry Spieker, earlier deputized by a prison guard to capture Craft. The prisoner was tried and convicted; the Mo. Supreme Court affirmed, and Craft was hanged in the Cole Co. jail in Jefferson City on Jan. 21, 1902, *State v. Craft*, 65 SW 280 (1901) and *Kansas City Journal*, Jan. 22, 1902, 2:4.

111. *SLPD*, Nov. 25, 1905, 1:6.

112. *Ibid.*, 1:1.

113. *State v. Vaughan*, 98 SW 2, 6 (1906).

114. *KCS*, Feb. 10, 1906, 4:3; *State v. Vaughan*, 102 SW 644 (1907); and *St. Louis Globe-Democrat*, June 27, 1907, 1:3.

115. Correspondence from Rev. Robert Kurwicki, Secretary to the Bishop, Diocese of Jefferson City, MO.

116. *KCS*, April 17, 1903, 1:2.

117. XII, 567–68.

118. *Pastoral Care of the Sick*, 80. My conversations with Father Michael Coleman, archivist, and John Schmiedeler, retired superintendent of schools, Diocese of Kansas City and St. Joseph, form the background of my discussion of Catholicism and capital punishment. This church's current opposition to capital punishment is a teaching of the religion, not a dogma. Such teachings mean different things to different members of this faith. As a result, Catholic prosecutors remain free to seek death sentences and simultaneously remain in good standing with the Catholic Church.

119. *State v. Tettalon*, 60 SW 743 (1900) and *KCT*, Feb. 20, 1901, 2:1.

120. *Houston Herald*, Oct. 18, 1:3 and Dec. 27, 1906, 2:1 and *KNG*, Dec. 28, 1906, 2:3.

121. *St. Louis Globe-Democrat*, Feb. 4, 1903, 14:2.

122. *St. Charles Cosmos-Monitor*, May 17, 1905, 6:4.

123. Gilmore, *Ozark Baptizings, Hangings, and Other Diversions*, 160.

124. *State v. Garth*, 65 SW 275, 277 (1901).

125. 1907 Mo. Laws 236.

6. Reform Attempts and the Continuation of Hangings, 1908–1937

1. *KNG*, Nov. 16, 1900, 7:2.

2. *State v. Brooks*, 119 SW 353 (1909) and *KCT*, July 30, 1909, 1:1.

3. *State v. Davis*, 126 SW 470 (1910) and *KCS*, June 10, 1910, 1:1.

4. *KNG*, May 29, 1913, 2:1,

5. *Kansas City Post*, Feb. 8, 1915, 1:1.

6. *State v. Robinson*, 172 SW 598 (1915) and *Kansas City Journal*, Feb. 15, 1915, 1:1.

7. *State v. Wilson*, 122 SW 671 (1909); *KNG*, July 17, 1908, 6:1; and *Evening Press* (Carthage), March 4, 1910, 1:1.

8. *State v. Black*, 186 SW 1047 (1916) and *St. Charles Daily Cosmos-Monitor*, Aug. 18, 1916, 1:1.

9. *State v. Jeffries*, 109 SW 614, 617 (1908) and *CT*, Jan. 1, 1909, 22:6.

10. *State v. Sprouse*, 177 SW 338 (1915) and *CT*, Dec. 31, 1915, 14 R: 6.

11. *KCS*, Sept. 21, 1908, 1:3 and typed transcript of Elsia Filley's direct testimony, Filley file.

12. This perpetrator was extensively covered in Missouri newspapers. In *The Trials of Hez Rasco*, Janet Hawley, P.O. Box 66, Barnard, MO 64423, circa 1991, compiled 306 pages of news stories and a name index ; *State v. Rasco*, 144 SW 449 (1912) and *Maryville Tribune*, March 21, 1912, 1:4.

13. *SLPD*, July 19, 1924, 2:1.

14. 1917 Mo. 246.

15. 1919 Mo. 778–81.

16. *Lamar Democrat*, May 29, 1919, 7:4 and June 5, 1919, front page, and *New York Times*, May 29, 1919, 1:3.

17. *State v. Williams*, 274 SW 427 (1925) and death certificate of Leon Williams.

18. *Carthage Evening Press*, Aug. 3, 1923, 4:3.

19. *State v. Long*, 253 SW 729 (1923); *State v. Jackson*, 253 S.W. 734 (1923): and Carthage Evening Press, Aug. 3, 1923, 1:5.

20. *State v. Crump*, 267 SW 822 (1924) and 274 SW 62, 66 (1925) and *Montgomery Standard* (Montgomery City), July 17 and 24, 1925, 1:1.

21. The *Kansas City Post*, Aug. 12, 1921, 1:2, gave Jacoy's age as 18 when he was hanged. This is an error. According to his death certificate, he was born July 1, 1898. As a result, he was 22 years old on Nov. 20, 1920, and 23 years old when he was hanged. Professor Streib lists Jacoy as aged 17 years when he committed his crime and 18 when executed. He also lists both Jacoy's and Schobe's race as unknown. Both were white, *The Death Penalty for Juveniles*, 199.

22. *State v. Carroll* and *Jocoy* [sic], 232 SW 699 (1921); Hyde Collection, C-7, f. 369; *SLPD*, Aug. 12, 1921, 1:2 and *KCS*, 1:4.

23. *State v. Merrell et al.*, 263 SW 118 (1924); *SLPD*, April 22, 1922, 1:4 and July 19, 1924, 2:1.

24. *State v. Lowry*, 12 SW 2d 469 (1929) and death certificate of Thomas Lowry.

25. *State v. Yeager*, 12 SW 2d 30 (1928) and *SLPD*, Feb. 1, 1929, 1:8.

26. *Springfield Leader*, Feb. 24, 1893, 6:2.

27. *Messages and Proclamations of the Governors of the State of Missouri*, eds. Sarah Guitar and Floyd C. Shoemaker, Vol. 12. Columbia: State Historical Society of Missouri, 1930.

28. Electric chair bills were introduced in the 54th and 55th General Assemblies. Senate Bill No. 87, introduced by Senator Ford, was first read Jan. 20, 1927; House Bill No. 253, introduced by Mr. Roberts, was first read Jan. 24, 1927. On Jan. 15, 1929, House Bill No. 95 was introduced by Mr. Hastings and on Jan. 16, 1929, Senate Bill No. 9 was introduced by Senator Haymes; see also *Daily Capital News* (Jefferson City), Jan. 17, 1929, 2:2. The 21 jurisdictions, according to Bowers, *Legal Homicide*, 399–523, with electric chairs were, in order of their adoption of this new method of capital punishment: New York (1890), Ohio (1897), Massachusetts (1901), New Jersey (1907), Virginia (1908), North Carolina (1910), Kentucky for murderers (1911), South Carolina (1912), Arkansas (1913), Indiana (1914), Oklahoma (1915), Pennsylvania (1915), Tennessee (1916), Vermont (1919), Nebraska (1920), Texas (1924), Florida (1924), Georgia (1924), Alabama (1927), District of Columbia (1928), and Illinois (1928).

29. *State v. Mosley*, 22 SW2d 784, 785 (1929); *KCS*, Jan. 31, 1930, 2:1; and *SLPD*, Jan. 31, 1930, 1:3.

30. *State v. McDaniel*, 80 SW 2d 185, 186–87 (1935) and *Springfield Leader and Press*, April 12, 1935, 1:8. On its 10th page, this newspaper ran four photographs of McDaniel's hanging.

31. *Fairplay* (Ste. Genevieve), Feb. 27, 1937, 1:1.

32. *State v. Hardy*, 98 SW2d 593 (1936).

33. *Fairplay* (Ste. Genevieve), March 6, 1937, 1:5. See also this paper's Feb. 20, 1937, 1:6 story about this case.

34. *State v. Kaufman*, 46 SW2d 843, 844 (1932).

35. *KCS*, Oct. 15, 1930, 1:6; *State v. Kaufman*, 73 SW2d 217 (1934); *SLPD*, June 29, 1934, 1B:1; and *KCS*, June 29, 1934.

36. *State v. Jefferson, et al.*, 64 SW2d 929 (1933) and *KCS*, Dec. 15, 1933, 1:3.

37. *State v. White*, 51 SW2d 109 (1932) and *SLPD*, Aug. 12, 1934, A1:5.

38. *State v. Copeland*, 71 SW2d 746 (1934) and *SLPD*, June 29, 1934, 1:1.

39. *State v. Roland*, 79 SW2d 1050 (1935) and *Advertiser-Courier* (Hermann), April 12, 1935, 1:1.

40. *State v. Mangercino* [*sic*], 30 SW2d 763, 766 (1930); *State v. Messino* 30 SW2d 750 (1930); *State v. Nasello*, 30 SW2d 132 (1930); *Kansas City Journal-Post*, July 25, 1930, front page; and *New York Times*, July 26, 1930, 15:8.

41. *State v. Hershon*, 45 SW2d 60 (1931); Samuel S. Mayerberg, *Chronicle of an American Crusader*, 51–57, and death certificate of Joe Hershon.

42. *State v. Miller*, 56 SW2d 92 (1932) and *St. Charles Cosmos-Monitor*, Feb. 15, 1933, front page.

43. *State v. Kellar*, 55 SW2d 969, 972–74 (1932); *St. Louis Globe-Democrat*, Jan. 20, 1933, 1:5; and *SLPD*, Jan. 20, 1933, 1:1.

44. *State v. Hamilton et al.*, 85 SW2d 35 (1935) and *Weekly Record* (New Madrid), Aug. 9, 1:1; Aug. 16, 1:4; Aug. 30, 1935, 1:3.

45. *State v. Adams*, 98 SW2d 632 (1936) and *Dunklin Democrat* (Kennett), April 6, 1937, 1:1.

46. *State v. McKeever*, 101 SW2d 22 (1936) and *Fulton Daily Sun-Gazette*. Dec. 18, 1936, 1:1.

47. *Official Manual State of Missouri, 1999–2000*. 65.

48. *State v. Jackson*, 102 SW2d 612 (1937) and *Stone County News-Oracle* (Galena), May 26, 1937, 1:1.

49. I have a photocopy of one for the hanging of Roscoe "Red" Jackson. It was issued to the grandfather of a student who was in my classes at Central MO State in the early 1990s. She knew of my interest in the subject matter, and she brought me for copying, not keeping, what had become a family heirloom.

50. *Fairplay* (Ste. Genevieve), Feb. 20, 1937, 1:6.

51. *Dunklin Democrat* (Kennett), April 6, 1937, 1:1.

52. Retrospective, *KCS*, June 8, 2001, 1:7

53. *Stone County News-Oracle* (Galena), May 26, 1937, 1:1.

54. *State v. Barr*, 78 SW2d 104 (1935) and 102 SW2d 629 (1937); *KCS*, May 21, 1937, 1:4; *Call* (Kansas City), May 21, 1937, 1:2; and *Kansas City Journal-Post*, May 21, 1937, 1:6.

7. The Gas Chamber, 1938–1965

1. *News and Tribune* (Jefferson City), March 6, 1938, 2:7.

2. *New York Times*, May 30, 1937, IV, 10:1

3. *Stone County News Oracle* (Galena), April 21, 1937, 1:4.

4. *Kansas City Journal-Post*, March 4, 1938, 2:1.

5. Bowers, *Legal Homicide*, 399–523.

6. 1937 Mo. 221–23 and Mo. Rev. Stat., secs. 4111–4115 (1939).

7. *Call* (Kansas City) March 11, 1938, 1:7 and *Kansas City Journal-Post*, March 4, 1938, 2:1.

8. *Kansas City Journal-Post*, March 5, 1938, 1:1.

9. *SLPD*, Oct. 7, 1938, 1:1.

10. *Call*, Dec. 9, 1949, 4:3.

11. *KCT*, Feb. 24, 1956, 1:8.

12. My discussion of the influence of religion, especially Catholicism, immediately preceding death is based almost entirely on contemporary newspaper coverage of the execution(s). Once death by lethal injection began in this state in 1989, the press was no longer printing any information concerning the religion of the executed; presumably such matters had become strictly private.

13. Stephen Trombley, *The Execution Protocol*, 12 and 98.

14. *State v. Wright*, 85 SW2d 7 (1935) and 112 SW2d 571 (1937); Park, Guy B. Papers, Box 8, F 556; and *Call* (Kansas City) March 4, 1938, 1:1,

15. *State v. Brown*, 112 SW 2d 568, 570 (1937) and *KCT*, March 4, 1938, 8:5.

16. *Daily Capital News* (Jefferson City), March 4, 1938, 1:5.

17. *Ibid.*, March, 5, 1938, 4:1.

18. *State v. Boyer*, 112 SW2d 575 (1937) and *Kansas City Journal-Post*, March 5, 1938, 1:1.

19. *SLPD*, Dec. 29, 1934, 1:4.

20. *State v. Batson*, 96 SW2d 384, 391 (1936).

21. *State v. Batson*, 116 SW2d 35 (1938); *SLPD*, June 30, 1938, 1:4, and death certificate of Raymond Batson.

22. *State v. King*, 119 SW2d 322 (1938) and *SLPD*, Nov. 4, 1938, 1:4.

23. *State v. Allen*, 119 SW2d 304 (1938); *Kansas City Journal-Post*, Oct. 28, 1935; and death certificate of Granville Allen.

24. *State v. Williamson*, 99 SW2d 76 (1936) and 123 SW2d 42 (1938); *Fair Play* (Ste. Genevieve), Feb. 18, 1939, 1:5, misdates this execution as occurring on Wed., Feb. 14, 1939. That year Wed. was Feb. 15. See also death certificate of John Williamson.

25. *State v. Kenyon*, 126 SW2d 245 (1938); death certificate of Robert Kenyon, and *Willow Springs News*, Jan. 28, Feb. 4, Feb. 11, Feb. 18, and Feb. 25, 1937, front and back page stories in their original size, were provided by John Taylor, then one of my students at Central MO State U. His grandfather, Ted Taylor, was a member of the state highway patrol who arrested the perpetrator. When Kenyon led officers to his victim's body, he was chained to this officer. Ted Taylor's photograph appeared in the local paper, Feb. 4, 1937, 6:3.

26. The Young brothers, Harry and Jennings, shot and killed six policemen on Jan. 2, 1932, near Springfield, MO. Soon thereafter, the perpetrators died in Houston, TX, in a double suicide. See *Barnett & Barnett, Young Brothers Massacre*.

27. *Bolivar Free Press*, June 22, 1933, 1:1 and *SLPD*, June 17, 1933, 3A:1.

28. Michael Wallis, *The Life and Times of Charles Arthur Floyd*, 291.

29. *Bolivar Free Press*, June 22, 1933, 1:1.

30. *SLPD*, Oct. 7, 1938, 1:1; *State v. Richetti* [*sic*], 119 SW 330 (1938); and Robert Unger, *The Union Station Massacre*, 1–244.

31. *State v. West*, 112 SW2d 468 (1940) and death certificate of Robert West.

32. *State v. Scott*, 233 SW2d 453, 454 (1949) and *Wright County Republican* (Hartville), April 1, 1948, 1:1 and Oct. 27, 1949, 1:2 and MSP prison record.

33. Certified copy of Circuit Court Record, Butler Co.

MO, *State v. Wilburn Johnson*, No. 451, Nov. 14, 1940; *American Republic* (Poplar Bluff), Sept. 27, 1:1, Nov. 12, 8:5, Nov. 14, 1940,1:1, and Jan 2, 1941, 8:6; *Citizen-Democrat* (Poplar Bluff). Nov. 14, 1940, 4:4; and *Jefferson City Post-Tribune*, Jan. 3, 1941, 1:2.

34. *Charleston Enterprise-Courier*, July 22, 1:6, Aug. 19, 1943, 1:6, and June 22, 1944, 1:5.

35. *State v. Jackson*, 130 SW2d 595 (1939) and 142 SW2d 45, 49–50 (1940); and *SLPD*, Sept. 20, 1940, 4E: 1.

36. *State v. Ramsey*, 197 SW2d 949, 955 (1946); *SLPD*, Jan. 9, 1947, 3:5, and MSP prison record.

37. *State v. Cochran*, 203 SW2d 707, 708 and 710 (1947); *Columbia Missourian*, Feb. 6, 1946, 1:7 and Sept. 26, 1947, 1:2.

38. *State v. Tyler*, 159 SW2d 777 (1942); *KCS*, Aug. 16, 1940, 1:4; *KCT*, Aug. 17, 1940, 1:2; April 24, 1942, 12:2; and death certificate of Ernest Tyler.

39. *State v. Bell*, 223 SW2d 469 (1949); *KCS*, Sept. 21, 1948, 1:1–8; *KCT*, Sept. 21, 1:6; Sept. 22, 1:5, 1948, and Dec. 2, 1949, 3:1; *Call*, Dec. 9, 1949, 4:3.

40. *State v. Lyles*, 175 SW2d 587 (1943) and 185 SW2d 642 (1945); *State v. Talbert*, 174 SW2d 144 (1943) and 189 SW2d 555 (1945); *SLPD*, Oct. 1, 1941, 1:1; May 25, 1945, 2B:2; and Nov. 16, 1945, 7A:3; and death certificates of Leo Lyles and William Talbert.

41. *State v. Ellis*, 193 SW2d 31 (1946); *State v. Sanford*, 193 SW3d 35 and 193 SW2d 37, 39 (1946); *Franklin County Tribune* (Union) Aug. 23, 1946, 1:6.

42. *State v. Quilling*, 256 SW2d 751, 752 (1953) and *KCT*, May 29, 1953, 1:3.

43. *KCT*, Sept. 13, 1951, 19:1; *KCS*, May 5, 1955, 1:4; and *State v. Moore*, 303 SW2d 60 (1957).

44. *State v. Boyd*, 256 SW2d 765 (1953); *SLPD*, July 10, 1953, 5A:3; and death certificate of Kenneth Boyd.

45. *State v. Booker*, 276 SW2d 104 (1955) and *SLPD*, April 1, 1955, 7A:3.

46. *State v. Tiedt*, 206 SW2d 524, 527 (1947) and 229 SW2d 582 (1950) and *St. Joseph News-Press*, May 17, 1:4; May 18, 1:6; and May 19, 1950, 1:6

47. *Post-Tribune* (Jefferson City), Jan. 11, 1948, 1:8; *State v. McGee*, 234 SW2d 587 (1950); and *Daily Tribune* (Columbia), Jan. 5, 1951, 3:6.

48. 1901 Mo. Laws 133. See also Mo. Rev. Stat. art. 2, sec. 1854 (1906).

49. See 47 Stat. 326 and 48 Stat. 781.

50. Lisa Montgomery's case is now in a federal court in Kansas City, MO. On December 16, 2004, she is alleged to have kidnapped an unborn fetus in Nodaway County, MO after killing the mother, Bobbie Jo Stinnett, and then taken the infant across a state line to Melvern, Kansas. The baby girl was found alive, taken to a Topeka, KS hospital, and has since been returned to the victim's family. Montgomery is charged under the Lindbergh law with kidnapping resulting in death.

51. *KCS*, Aug. 7, 1955, 1:7 and Jan. 24, 1956, 1:8; *KCT*, Aug. 8, front page; Nov. 15, 1955, front page; Jan. 24, 1:1; Jan. 25, 1:1; and Feb. 24, 1956, 1:8.

52. *Southeast Missourian* (Cape Girardeau), July 26, 1963, 1:8. See also this same newspaper, March 11, 1961, front page and *State v. Tucker*, 362 SW2d 509 (1962).

53. *SLPD*, May 19, 1961, 1:3 and Feb. 26, 1965, front page; *State v. Anderson*, 386 SW3d 225 (1965); and death certificate of Lloyd Anderson.

8. Juveniles, 1838–1993

1. *State ex rel. Simmons v. Roper*, 112 SW3d 397 (2003).

2. *Roper v. Simmons*, 125 S. Ct. 1183, 1184 (2005).

3. *Thompson v. Oklahoma*, 487 U.S. 815 (1988).

4. *Stanford v. Kentucky*, 492 U.S. 361 (1989).

5. *Roper v. Simmons*, 125 S. Ct. 1183, 1187–88 (2005).

6. *Ibid.*, 1205.

7. William Blackstone, *Commentaries on the Laws of England*, 4: 23.

8. In Dec. 1990 and Jan.-Feb, 1991, the *J. of the Missouri Bar* published my two-part article, "The Execution of Juveniles in Missouri." In it I discussed the 10 persons executed here that were then identified as juveniles at the time of their crime(s). Since this article appeared I have corrected Slave Mary's age—she was younger than the county history described her as being—and I have located somewhere between three and seven other juveniles executed here between 1865 and 1902.

9. As clarified earlier, ch. 4, note 28 (Samuel Orr) and ch. 6, note 21 (Charles Jacoy), two of the six persons executed in Missouri whom Victor Streib identified as juveniles at the time of their crime were adults. Of the remaining four, only the demographics concerning William Barton are entirely correct. At the time Streib's *Death Penalty for Juveniles* was published, 1987, Frederick Lashley was alive on Missouri's death row and the author was a professor at Cleveland-Marshall College of Law, Cleveland, Ohio. He missed somewhere between nine and 13 other juveniles legally executed here between 1863 and 1930.

10. *LT*, June 6, 1851, 2:1 and *RC*, Oct, 8, 1857, 3:2.

11. *State v. Amos Byrd*, Cape Girardeau Circuit Court Records, Bk. G, 709, Microfilm No. 0925689; *Tarboro Press* (Tarboro, NC), Jan. 14, 1843; and Register of Inmates, Reel I, n.p. no. The court record spells the name *Byrd;* the prison record *Bird.*

12. *Missouri Democrat* (St. Louis), April 1, 1859, 2:5; *Messages and Proclamations of the Governors of the State of Missouri*, III, 286; and Register of Inmates, Reel 1, Series 2, 174.

13. *State v. Hamilton*, 55 Mo. 520 (1874) and *St. Louis Daily Globe*, Nov. 9, 1874, front page.

14. *Weekly Gazette* (Versailles), Oct. 26, 1882, 3:8 and April 26, 1883, 3:6; *State v. Adams*, 76 Mo. 355 (1882); Mo. Rev. Stat., art. 9, ch. 24, sec. 1666 (1879); and Docket Book, April 21, 1883 entry, Morgan County Circuit Court.

15. *State v. Payton*, 2 SW 394 (1886); *St. Louis Globe-Democrat*, Dec. 11, 1886, 3:1; 1887 Mo. 166; and Register of Inmates, Vol. N, 43, entry 6256, Microfilm Roll 8.

16. *State v. Max Klinger*, 43 Mo. 127 (1868) and Register of Inmates, Reel 3, 80.

17. *State v. Coats*, 74 SW 864 (1903) and *St. Joseph Gazette Herald*, June 28, 1902, 1:7.

18. *Barton v. State*, 71 Mo. 288, 290 (1879) and *St. Louis Daily Globe-Democrat* (March 27, 1880, 2:3.

19. *State v. William Walker*, 9 SW 646 (1888); *State v. David Walker*, 11 SW 727 (1889); *State v. John Mathews*, 10 SW 30 (1889); *State v. Wiley Mathews*, 10 SW 144 (1888); Mary Hartman and Elmo Ingenthron, *Bald Knobbers: Vigilantes on the Ozarks Frontier*, 234–240; *KCS*, May 10, 1889, 1:1; and *Kansas City Daily Journal*, May 11, 1889, 1:8.

20. *State v. Albert and Charles Talbott*, 73 Mo. 347 (1881); Janet Hawley, *The Murder of Dr. Talbott* (a compilation of newspaper material on this case, 221 pages including surname index); *Evening News* (St. Joseph), July 22, 1881, front page; and *KCT*, July 23, 1881, front page. The inspection and photographing of the Talbott graves were made possible by Mrs. Joan Eitel of Maryville who accompanied me to them.

21. *Joplin Daily Herald*, June 25, 1889, 1:5; *State v. Seaton*, 17 SW 169, 170 (1891), and *Joplin Herald*, Dec. 6, 1891, 1:1.

22. *State v. Martin*, 28 SW 12 (1894); *KCT*, July 6, 1893, 5:4 and Feb. 15, 1895, 1:4; *Kansas City World*, Feb. 18, 1895, 2:1. Father Glennon converted Martin to Catholicism while the teenager was in jail, and the priest was on the scaffold with him at his death, *KCS*, Feb. 15, 1895, 1:1.

23. *State v. Schmidt*, 38 SW 719, 720 (1897); *State v. Foster*, 38 SW 721 (1897); *Republic* (St. Louis) Feb. 16, 3:3 and Feb. 17, 1897, 2:1; *St. Louis Globe-Democrat*, Feb. 17, 12:2 and Feb. 18, 12:1.

24. *State v. Reid* [sic], 49 SW 1116 (1899); *KCT*, March 31, 1899, 8:1; *Kansas City World*, March 30, 1899, 1:4; and *KCS*, March 30, 1899, 2:3.

25. He was probably named for General George Armstrong Custer, the youngest Union Army general in the Civil War and later the immensely popular slain hero of the battle of Little Bighorn, Montana, in June 1876. After his death, Custer's faithful widow kept his memory alive with books, articles, and speeches.

26. Mo. Rev. Stat., art. 9, ch. 47, sec. 3961.

27. *State v. Armstrong*, T.T., 38.

28. *Ibid.*, 52.

29. *Democrat Lever* (Plattsburg), July 20, 1900, front page.

30. *State v. Armstrong*, 66 SW 961 (1902).

31. *Kansas City Journal*, April 25, 1902, 1:4 and *KCS*, April 25, 1902, 1:4.

32. *Poplar Bluff Citizen*, Feb. 8, front page and 5:3; Feb. 22, front page; and March 22, 1906, front page.

33. Index to Register of Inmates, Vol. 3, Box 18, 56.

34. *Boonville Daily News*, Jan. 31, 1930, 2:2.

35. *State v. Mabry*, T.T., 132.

36. *Boonville Republican*, Jan. 31, 1930, 1:3.

37. *State v. Mabry*, 22 SW2d 639 (1930); *KCT*, Jan. 31, 1930, 7:5; *Boonville Daily News*, Jan. 31, 1930, 1:7; and conversation with Dorothy McKinley.

38. In a dissent in the case of a teenager sentenced to death, then Chief Justice of the Mo. Supreme Court Charles Blackmar wrote that both Lyles and Anderson were aged less than 18 years at the time of their crimes. He was mistaken, *State v. Battle*, 661 SW2d 487, 496.

39. *State v. Frederick Lashley*, T.T., 771. A subsequent quotation from this document follows the quoted material.

40. Cedric Brown, then an attorney with the Missouri Capital Punishment Resource Center, supplied me with a document entitled "Family History and Mitigation Evidence Regarding Frederick Lashley," dated April 2, 1993.

41. *State v. Lashley*, 667 SW2d 712 (1984); *Delo v. Lashley*, 507 U.S. 272 (1993); and *KCS*, July 29, 1993, C3:2.

42. *Wilkins v. Missouri* and *Stanford v. Kentucky*, 492 U.S. 262 (1989).

43. *Wilkins v. Bowersox*, 933 F. Supp. 1496 (1996) and 145 F.3rd 1006 (1998).

44. *State v. Wilkins*, Case No. CR 199–1686, Clay County Circuit Court, May 20, 1999. Sean O'Brien represented Wilkins in these habeas appeals and before Clay County Circuit Court judge, David Russell.

45. *Ring v. Arizona*, 536 U.S. 584 (2002); *State v. Richardson*, 923 SW3d 301 (1996); MO. St. Ct. order of Oct. 28, 2003, and *KCS*, Oct. 29, 2003, B1:6.

46. *State v. Gray*, 887 SW2d 369 (1994); Gray's last words before he was executed were, "I go with a peace of mind that comes from never having taken a human life." *St. Louis Post-Dispatch*, Oct. 27, 2005, B1:2. Earlier, U.S. Congressman William Clay wrote the governor, Matt Blunt, asking for clemency for Marlin Gray. Clay likened

Gray's execution to Larry Griffin's as "another wrongful execution in Missouri," *KCS*, Oct. 27, 2005, B8:1. Griffin's case is discussed in Chapter 12.

47. *Roper v. Simmons*, Appendix A, 1200.

9. Rape, 1891–1964

1. *Coker v. Georgia*, 433 U.S. 584 (1977).

2. The follow citations document the death penalty for the slave's attempted rape and/or rape of a white woman: *Lewis, a Slave v. State*, 35 Ala. 380 (1860); *Dennis, a Slave v. State*, 5 Ark. 230 (1843); Laws of Delaware, ch. 162, 711 (1826); D.C. Code, ch. 138, sec. 6 (1835); *Cato, a Slave v. State*, 9 Fla. 163 (1860); *Stephen, a Slave v. State*, 11 Ga. 225 (1852); Ky. Rev. Stat., Vol. 2, sec. 4 (1860); *State v. Peter*, 14 La. Ann. 521 (1859); "Under the act of Assembly of Maryland 1751, an attempt by a slave, to ravish a white woman is punishable by death," *U.S. v. Patrick*, 27 F. Cas. 460 (D.C. Cir. 1812) (No. 16,006); *Wash a Slave v. Mississippi*, 22 Miss. (14 S & M 120); *State v. Jim, a Negro Slave*, 12 N.C. 142 (1826); *State v. Lewis, a Slave*, S.C. (1849) cited in *2 Helen Catterall, Judicial Cases Concerning Slavery and the Negro*, 413; *Sydney v. State*, 22 Tenn. (3 Hum.) 478 (1842); Laws of Texas, tit. 3, ch. 1, art. 819 (1858); and *Thompson v. Commonwealth*, Va. (1833) cited in 1 Catterall 174.

3. Peter Kolchin, *American Slavery: 1619–1877*, 125.

4. Mo. Consti., art. 3, sec. 27 (1820).

5. Register of Inmates, Vol. A, 4, entry 7.

6. 1836 Mo. Laws 60.

7. Louis Crompton, "Homosexuals and the Death Penalty in Colonial America," *J. of Homosexuality* 1 (1976): 277–93.

8. Daniel Allen Hearn, *Legal Executions in New York State, 1639–1963* and *Legal Executions in New England, 1623–1960*, passim.

9. 1921 Mo. Law 284a.

10. Mo. Rev. Stat., sec. 559.260 (1972).

11. *KCT*, May 9, 1891, 1:1. See also *Kansas City Journal*, May 9, 1891, 1:1 and *KCS*, May 8, 1891, 1:5.

12. *KCT*, May 9, 1891, 1:1.

13. *Kansas City Journal*, May 9, 1891, 1:1 and *KCS*, May 8, 1891, 1:5.

14. *St. Joseph Herald*, May 11, 1895, 3:4.

15. *KCS*, May 11, 1895, 1:3.

16. *St. Joseph Herald*, May 12, 1895, 3:1.

17. *State v. Burries*, 29 SW 842 (1895).

18. *Lawrence Chieftain* (Mt. Vernon), March 30, 1: 5; April 6, 1905; and Aug. 9, 1906, 8:1; and *State v. Bateman*, 94 SW 843, 845 (1906).

19. *Kahoka Weekly Review*, July 29, 1903, 3:4.

20. *Ibid.*, Oct. 7, 1903, 3:3.

21. *Ibid.*, Oct. 16, 1903, front page.

22. *Ibid.*, Oct. 21, 1903, front page.

23. *Ibid.*, Nov. 25, 1903, 3:3.

24. *Kansas City Journal*, Jan. 2, 1910, 1:4.

25. *Kansas City Post*, Jan. 3, 1910, 1:6.

26. *Ibid.*, Jan. 4, 1910, 9:1.

27. *KCT*, Jan. 5, 1910, 1:7.

28. *Kansas City Post*, Jan. 5, 1910, 2:6.

29. *Kansas City Journal*, Feb. 7, 1910, 1:2.

30. *KCS*, Feb. 8, 1910, 1:4.

31. *Kansas City Journal*, Feb. 8, 1910, 1:1.

32. *Charleston Republican*, June 16, 1910, 1:1.

33. *Poplar Bluff Republican*, April 1, 1920, 1:1.

34. *Watchman Advocate* (St. Louis) March 1, 1927, 1:1.

35. *KCS*, Aug. 17, 1921, 2:4.

36. *The Pastoral Care of the Sick*, 80.

37. *Poplar Bluff Republican*, April 1, 1920, 1:1. See also David Deem, *A History of Butler County*, 22.

38. *Charleston Republican*, April 7, 1:3 and June 16, 1910, 1:1, and death certificate of George Jackson.

39. *State v. Lee*, 231 SW 619, 620 (1921).

40. *Kansas City Journal*, July 2, 1920, 1:6.

41. *State v. Lee*, 231 SW 619, 622 (1921).

42. *Kansas City Journal*, Aug. 18, 1921, 2:7.

43. State v. *Johnson*, 289 SW 847, 850 (1926).

44. *Watchman Advocate* (St. Louis), March 1, 1927, 1:1 and *SLPD*, Feb. 28, 1927, 1:1

45. *Watchman Advocate*, Feb. 25, 1927, 1:3.

46. Pete Stevenson began serving his sentence on May 11, 1932, and he died in the prison hospital on May 25, 1934, *State Pen Records by County*, Vol. 5, (1932–1942), 314.

47. *Carthage Evening Press*, March 3, 1932, 1:6; *Kansas City Journal-Post*, March 3, 1932, 1:2; and death certificate of Lew Worden.

48. *State v. Worden*, 56 SW2d 595 (1932).

49. *Carthage Evening Press*, Feb. 10, 1933, 1:7 and death certificate of Harry Worden.

50. Correspondence, Joanna E. Green.

51. *St. Louis Globe-Democrat*, Oct. 1, 6A:2; Nov. 2, 1:7; and Nov. 3, 1933, 2A:2; *SLPD*, Sept. 30, 1:3 and Nov. 2, 1933, 1:1, and death certificate of John Winston Boyd.

52. *Jefferson City Post-Tribune*, Oct. 27, 1:7 and Oct., 28, 1952, 2:1.

53. *Weekly Record* (New Madrid), Feb. 11, 1:6; May 20, 1:1, and June 3, 1938, 1:6; *Daily Capital-News* (Jefferson City), July 15, 1938, 1:6; *Call* (Kansas City), July 15, 1938, 2:1, and sheriff's return of death warrant, filed July 23, 1938, Criminal Record, Circuit Court, New Madrid Co., 133.

54. *Dunklin Democrat* (Kennett) Aug. 16, 1:7 and Aug. 20, 1935, 3:1 and *State v. Ward*, 85 SW2d 1, 7 (1935).

55. *Ashe v. Swenson*, 397 U.S. 436 (1970).

56. *Ring v. Arizona*, 536 U.S. 584 (2002).

57. *SLPD*, Oct. 19, 7C:3 and Oct. 20, 1944, 3B:3, and *State. v. Thomas*, 182 SW2nd 534 (1944).

58. *Jefferson City Post-Tribune*, Jan. 24, 1947, 10:5 and *State v. Perkins*, 198 SW2d 704 (1947).

59. *Joplin Globe*, July 24, 1A:3, July 27, 1961, 1A:1; March 5, 1A:5 and March 6, 1:1, 1964; *State v. Odom*, 369 SW2d 173 (1963); *Jefferson City Post-Tribune*, March 5, 2:4 and March 6, 1964, 2:6.

60. In *Booth v. Maryland*, 482 U.S. 496 (1987), the U.S. Supreme Court prohibited victim-impact testimony in death penalty cases; it overruled *Booth* in *Payne v. Tennessee*, 501 U.S. 808 (1991), and juries now regularly listen to family members of the victim in the penalty phrase of any capital trial.

61. *Troy Free Press*, Oct. 23, 1959, 1:4; *Bowling Green Times*, Oct. 23, 1:6, 1959; March 3, 1:7 and March 10, 1:1, 1960, and May 13, 1964, 6:3; *Hannibal Courier-Post*, Oct. 19, 1959, 1:4; *State v. Wolfe*, 343 SW2d 10 (1961); and *Jefferson City Post-Tribune*, May 8, 1964, 2:6.

62. The prison record gives Marcellus Butler's age as 34. This is totally at odds with all contemporary newspaper coverage which describes him as "young" or no more than 22.

63. *State Pen Register, 1907–1910*, Reel 228, 273 A & B.

64. *State v. Mert Holman*, T.T., 64. The page number(s) other quoted material from this source follows the quotation.

65. Harper Lee, *To Kill a Mockingbird*, 232.

66. *State Pen Register, 1922–1924*, Reel S 234, 87A & B.

67. My sources for Holman's case also include *Clarksville Piker*, March 18, 1909, 1:5; *Pike County News* (Loui-

siana), March 18, 5:3 and July 8, 1909. 5:1; *Quincy Daily Democrat*, March 12, 1909, 1:1; *Hannibal Courier-Post*, March 12, 1:2 and July 2, 1909, 1:4, and *State v. Holman*, 132 SW 695 (1910).

68. *State v. Thurston*, 242 SW 908, 909–10, (1922).

69. Hyde Collection, Box 7, F. 382.

70. *State Pen Register*, 1922–1924, Reel S 234, 87 A & B.

71. *State Pen Register*, 1926–1927, Reel S 237, 233 A & B.

72. *Call* (Kansas City), July 6, 1928, 1:4.

73. *Call* (Kansas City) June 29, 10:1. See also *State v. Williams*, 6 SW2d 915 (1928); *Kansas City Journal*, July 14, 1927, 14:1; *Kansas City Post*, July 13, 1927, 1:1; and *KCS*, July 13, 1927, 1:5.

74. *State Pen Register*, 1927–1929, Reel S 238, 165 A & B.

75. *State v. Lewkowitz*, 178 SW 58 (1915) and *State v. Harrison*, 174 SW 57 (1915).

76. *Kansas City Post*, April 3, 1914, front page.

77. *Kansas City Journal*, April 5, 1914, 1:6.

78. See the scathing account about Mrs. Gertrude Shidler in *State v. Lewkowitz*, 178 SW 58, 59–60 (1915).

79. *Kansas City Journal*, April 5, 1914, front page.

80. *State v. Gueringer*, 178 SW 65, 68 (1915).

81. *Kansas City Journal*, Dec. 17, 1915, 1:6.

82. Register of Inmates, RG 213, Reg. No. 17832, Dec. 21, 1915.

83. *State v. Swinburne*, 324 SW2d 746 (1959).

84. *State v. Williams*, 361 SW2d 772 (1962).

85. MO State Archives has voluminous prison files on both men; however, their records end in the mid–1960s. They contain the dates of these men's birth, and by using them, Jennie Waymeier, Office of Public Information, MO Dept. of Corrections, was able to give me the date of their release from prison.

10. Women, 1834–1953

1. See my *Slavery and Crime in Missouri, 1773–1865*, 167–194, for details of all known slave girls and women sentenced to death.

2. *Jane, a Slave v. State*, 3 Mo. 61 (1831).

3. *Missouri Intelligencer* (Columbia), March 22, 1834, 2:5.

4. Lafayette County Circuit Court Record, Book 3, 114, April 1–2 and 30, 1834.

5. *History of Southeast Missouri*, 355.

6. Pardon Papers, Box 3, F. 16, MSA.

7. Mo. Rev. Stat. art 2, sec. 22 (1869).

8. Register of Inmates, under names of Malinda King, Luticia Banister, and Harriet Alexander, Reel 3, 53, 58, and 71.

9. *History of Franklin, Jefferson, Washington, Crawford & Gasconade Counties, Missouri*, 565.

10. *Hawkins v. State*, 7 Mo. 190 (1841).

11. Gary Kremer, "Strangers to Domestic Virtues: Nineteenth-Century Women in the Missouri Prison," 294–95.

12. *LT*, Feb. 16, 1855, 2:6.

13. Register of Inmates, Reel 1, 2nd Series, 75.

14. 1858–59 Laws 39 and *State v. Buckner*, 25 Mo. 167, 169 (1857).

15. *RC*, Dec. 20, 1855, 2:5.

16. *RC*, Feb. 7, 2:5, Feb. 28, 3:2, April 10, 1:4, and April 17, 1856, 3:1; *LT*, Feb. 29, 1856, 2:4; and Register of Inmates, B, 99.

17. See two County Court of St. Louis licenses, both for Nathaniel Buckermaster's companies to cross the Mississippi River to the Illinois side. One, dated June 16, 1848, was to keep a ferry at the Upper Ferry in the city of St.

Louis, and the other, dated August 13, 1849, for the Madison County Ferry Company to keep a ferry at the North Point of the city of St. Louis, Tiffany Collection, MHS.

18. Register of Inmates, Reel S 212, Vol. B, 99, Reel S 212.

19. *LT*, May 27, 1864, 2:4; *State v. Catharine McCoy*, 34 Mo. 531 (1864); and Register of Inmates, Reel 2, Register B, 331.

20. *History of Laclede, Camden, Dallas, Webster, Wright, Texas, Pulaski, Phelps and Dent Counties, Missouri*, 201.

21. *History of Franklin, Jefferson, Washington, Crawford, & Gasconade Counties, Missouri*, 651.

22. *List of Commutations Granted by Governor Hardin, from January 12, 1875, to January 5, 1876.*

23. *KNG*, Sept. 25, 1891, 2:4.

24. *History of Audrain County*, 254–56 and Register of Inmates, Reel S 216, Vol. H, 78.

25. *State v. Stair et al.*, 87 Mo. 268 (1885) and *History of Vernon County, Missouri*, I, 334–337.

26. *St. Louis Globe-Democrat*, Oct. 9, 1883, 4:1; *State v. Hayes*, 16 Mo. App. 560 (1885) and *State v. Hays* [sic] 89 Mo. 262 (1886).

27. Register of Inmates, Reel S 218, Vol. N, 26.

28. See Chapter 5, note 30.

29. *Kansas City Journal*, June 14, 1893, 3:4; *KCS*, June 14, 1893. 1:1; *State v. Umble*, 22 SW 378, 381 (1893); and *KNG*, July 12, 1891. 3:1.

30. *St. Louis Globe-Democrat*, May 22, 1897, 13:4 and Register of Inmates, Reel ll, Vol. U, 12906.

31. Register of Inmates, Reel S 223, Vol. V, 132.

32. *KNG*, Feb, 8, 2:4, Feb. 15, 7:2. Aug. 30, 1901, 6:1, and June 5, 1903, 7:4. and *State v. Nesenhener*, 65 SW 230, 232 (1901).

33. *State v. Hottman*, 94 SW 237 (1906) and *State v. Myers*, 94 SW 242 (1906).

34. Report of Governor Joseph W. Folk to the 45 General Assembly concerning Reprieves, Commutations, and Pardons, 1909.

35. *Kansas City Post*, April 9, 1907, 6:3.

36. Among other new stories, there are two regarding her in the *New York Times*, June 12, 6:2 and June 25, 1905, 5:2.

37. Register of Inmates, Index, 147 and *KCS*, Dec. 8, 1929, 1:6.

38. Rose Fulton Cramer, *Wayne County Missouri*, 244–45 and e-mail, John Fougere.

39. *Kansas City Journal-Post*, Sept. 29, 1929, 1:7.

40. *KCT*, Sept. 30, 1929, front page; *New York Times*, Oct. 1, 1929, 5:2; *KCS*, Feb. 23, 1:1 and Feb. 26, 1931, 1:1; and *Journal-Post* (Kansas City), March 2, 1931, and March 6, 1931, front pages.

41. *KCS*, Sept. 28, 1953, 1:6.

42. *KCT*, Nov. 17, 1953, front page.

43. This is a much-written about and well-remembered case in Kansas City. James Deakin's *A Grave For Bobby: The Greenlease Slaying* is a detailed account of this crime and the sidebar of the likely theft of $300,000 of the ransom money by two St. Louis, MO police officers. My friend, Rosemary Schmiedeler, taught Bobby Greenlease as a kindergarten student at Notre Dame de Sion during the 1952–53 year. She well remembers that her husband, later superintendent of schools for the Diocese of Kansas City–St. Joseph, was not permitted to step inside the school with various teaching supplies he brought his wife. The sister who released the child to Bonnie Brown Heady never recovered her mental faculties. The Greenlease Library and the Greenlease Gallery at Rockhurst University, 1100 Rockhurst Road, Kansas City are named for the young victim. In 1962, Robert C. Greenlease donated one million dollars in his murdered son's memory to begin the building of Rockhurst High School at a separate location at 9301 State Line Road, Kansas City. The entire campus of this facility is called the Greenlease Memorial Campus. The *KCT* and the *KCS* gave the crime, the capture of the culprits, their court appearance, and their execution front page coverage, as did a number of other newspapers nationwide.

44. James J. Fisher, *KCT*, Nov. 20, 1987, B: 1:6.

45. *State v. Wacaser*, 794 SW2d 190 (1990) and *KCS*, April 19, 1:2, May 9, 1:4, and May 10, 1992, 1:5.

46. *State v. Faye Copeland*, 928 SW2d 828, 844 (1996).

47. *KCS*, Feb. 22, 1991, 1:4.

48. *Washington v. Copeland*, 232 F3rd 969, 972 (8 Cir., 2000).

49. *Ibid.*, 977.

50. Rev. Mo. Stat., 217.250 (2004).

51. *KCS*, Dec. 31, 2003, B1:5.

52. *U.S. v. Isa*, 923 F2d 1300 (1991).

53. *State v. Maria Isa*, 850 SW2d 876, 903 (1993).

54. *SLPD*, May 17, 10:3 and June 21, 1997, 11:6.

55. *State v. Twenter*, 818 SW2d 628 (1991).

56. The Missouri Dept. of Corrections' records show that Glenn Minster is not currently an inmate in a MO prison, but he was convicted in Greene and Lawrence Counties of various crimes, and he was a MO prison inmate between Aug. 8, 1991, and Aug. 31, 1994, e-mail, John Fougere.

57. *State v. Phillips*, 940 SW2d 512 (1997).

11. Pardons and Commutations, 1803–1999

1. U.S. Const., art. 2, sec 2 [1].

2. Mo. Const., art. 4, sec. 6 (1820).

3. See note 18, Chapter 1.

4. My entire discussion of the American cases against these three Indians derives from William E. Foley, "Different Notions of Justice: The Case of the 1808 St. Louis Murder Trials," 2–13.

5. William E. Foley, *Wilderness Journey: The Life of William Clark*, 170.

6. *MORE* (St. Louis) April 21, 1829, 2:6 and *Monitor* (Fayette) Dec. 5, 1829. 3:2.

7. 3 Stat. 418

8. *Missouri Statesman* (Columbia), Nov. 12, 1847, 1:5.

9. *Ibid.*, June 21, 1844, 2:1.

10. *U.S. v. Johnson*, Case MM 1021, Box 967, RG 153, NA.

11. *U.S. v. Norvell*, Case 00303, RG 153, NA.

12. *Morning Herald* (St. Joseph), June 9, 3:2 and June 16, 1864, 4:1.

13. In 1969, the U.S. Supreme Court held that when a member of the armed forces is charged with a crime against a civilian and it takes place off his military base, he is entitled to a trial in a civilian court, *O'Callahan v. Parker*, 395 U.S. 258.

14. *Pulaski County Democrat* (Waynesville), Sept., 27, 1951, 7:2.

15. *Sentinel* (Iberia), October 18, 1951, 1:1.

16. Correspondence from Laurel Boechman, Sr. Reference Specialist, State Historical Society of Missouri, regarding information received from Sam Rusahy, Archivist, Harry S. Truman Presidential Library, Independence, MO.

17. *New York Times*, Nov. 1, 1953, 47:5.

18. *Suttles et al. v. Davis*, 215 F2d 760 (1954), 348 U.S. 903 (1954), and 348 U.S. 932 (1955).

19. Correspondence from David J. Haight, Archivist, Eisenhower Library, Abilene, KS.

20. Dept. of Army Pamphlet 27–4, Procedure for Military Executions, June 24, 1953.

21. *KCT*, March 1, 1955, 8:3. I was able to locate any mention of these hangings only because, at my request, Janet Wray, Public Information Officer, Ft. Leavenworth, verified the information and passed it on to me, including the base's vertical file of newspaper coverage about this case in the *Leavenworth Times* and the *Topeka State Journal*, and the Dept. of the Army Pamphlet 27–4.

22. Gov. Frederick Bates pardoned Reuben Hall, convicted in Cole Co. of the murder of Stephen Ray on July 10 and sentenced to hang on Sept. 4, 1824, *Intelligencer* (Franklin), Aug. 14, 1824, 2:3 and *History of Cole, Moniteau, Benton, Miller, Maries and Osage Counties, Missouri*, 235.

23. In Carroll Co., Alfred Hawkins was scheduled to hang for the murder of James Dunbar. Citizens petitioned Boggs, and he commuted Hawkins' death sentence in May 1838; Hawkins died at the prison two years later, S.K. Turner and S.A. Clark, *Twentieth Century History of Carroll County, Missouri*, Vol. 1, 450. In St. Charles Co. in May 1838, this same governor commuted the death sentence of Edward Hunting, murderer of an unnamed victim, to 20 years at MSP upon the petition of a large number of persons in the county of the crime and elsewhere, *Jefferson Republican*, April 28, 2:5 and May 26, 1838, 2:5. On a change of venue from Pulaski to Benton Co., William Grizzle was sentenced to hang for the murder of a man who had improper relations with the perpetrator's wife. Boggs commuted Grizzle's sentence to a prison term in June 1840, *History of Cole, Moniteau, Morgan, Benton, Miller, Maries, and Osage Counties, Missouri*, 480 and Register of Inmates, S 212, 22.

24. Gov. Reynolds commuted the death sentence of a juvenile, Amos Bird. It is discussed in Chapter 8.

25. King commuted the death sentence of John Roberts, alias Ward, to a life sentence at MSP. He killed a St. Louis police officer, Ephraim Hibler, when the officer attempted to arrest him for vagrancy. The Mo. Supreme Court reversed his first trial, *Roberts, alias Ward v. State*, 14 Mo. 138 (1851) and affirmed his second, 15 Mo. 28 (1851). Roberts was received at MSP on Feb. 22, 1852, but the record is blank regarding his discharge, Register of Inmates, Reel 1, 153.

26. On March 22, 1854, Price commuted the death sentence of Michael Conner, sentenced to hang in St. Louis Co. for murder, to 20 years at MSP, and Stewart pardoned Conner on March 21, 1860, *Brunswicker*, April 8, 1854, 2:3 and Register of Inmates, Reel 1, 2nd Series, 54. On a change of venue to Randolph from Howard Co., Ethelred Hayes was found guilty of the March 1854 murder of a book peddler and merchant in Glasgow. He was sentenced to hang. Price commuted his death sentence; Hays was received at MSP on July 12, 1855, and because he materially assisted in preventing a prison revolt, Stewart pardoned him on Feb. 4, 1857, *History of Howard and Chariton Counties, Missouri*, 256; *RC*, May 31, 1855, 2:2 and Feb. 18, 1857, 3:1, and Register of Inmates, Reel 1, 2nd Series, 75.

27. On a change of venue from Gasconade to St. Louis Co., Stephen Houser was found guilty of murder and sentenced to hang. On the petition of citizens from Benton Co., where Houser was born and raised, Stewart commuted his sentence to life. He was received at MSP on Oct. 7, 1859, and Clairborne Jackson pardoned Houser on May 15, 1861, *California News*, June 25, 4:1 and July 2, 1859, 2:4, and Register of Inmates, B, 190. In Carroll Co

on Nov. 6, 1858, King Brady killed Thomas Nash with a knife. The perpetrator was tried and sentenced to hang on May 18, 1860. Stewart commuted his sentence to life at MSP. Brady was received at the prison on April 18, 1860, and Fletcher pardoned him on Aug. 1, 1866, Turner and Clark, *Twentieth Century History of Carroll County, Missouri*, Vol 1, 450–1 and Register of Inmates, Reel 2, Series 2, 217. In St. Louis Co., Henry Schoenwald was convicted of the murder of John Acres, sentenced to hang, the Mo. Supreme Court affirmed, *State v. Schoenwald*, 31 Mo. 147 (1860), and Stewart commuted his sentenced to life at MSP. He was received at the prison on Dec. 22, 1860, and Brown pardoned him on April 3, 1871, *California News*, Dec. 22, 1860, 2:3 and Register of Inmates, Reel 2, 246 and 313.

28. In Washington Co. in Dec. 1861, Jack Wisdom killed Joseph Huff; he was tried and sentenced to hang on July 18, 1862. Gamble commuted his sentence to life imprisonment. Wisdom was received at MSP on July 15, 1862, and Fletcher pardoned him on March 4, 1865, *History of Franklin, Jefferson, Washington, Crawford, & Gasconade Counties, Missouri*, 501 and Register of Inmates, Reel 2, 286. In Jan 1861, in St. Louis, William Walter killed a soldier, was tried, and sentenced to hang on Oct. 31, 1862. Gamble commuted his sentence to 15 years at MSP; he was received on Nov. 28, 1862, and he was released on Nov. 28, 1877, *MORE*, Sept. 19, 1862, 3:7 and Register of Inmates, Reel, 2, 293.

29. In Washington Co in 1863, Richard Marshall killed Moses Miller. He was tried, found guilty, sentenced to hang, and the Mo. Supreme Court affirmed. Hall commuted his death sentence, and Marshall was received at MSP on Nov. 27, 1866. Fletcher pardoned him on July 20, 1867, *State v. Marshall* 36 Mo. 400 (1865); *History of Franklin, Jefferson, Washington, Crawford & Gasconade Counties, Missouri*, 501, and Register of Inmates, Reel 2, 135.

30. In 1864, George Starr murdered William Smith in St. Louis. He was tried, found guilty, and sentenced to hang, and the Mo. Supreme Court affirmed. Fletcher commuted his death sentence; Starr was received at MSP on June 9, 1866, and this same governor pardoned him on Nov. 23, 1867, *State v. Starr*, 38 Mo. 270 (1866) and Register of Inmates, Reel 1, 2nd Series, 105. In Texas Co., George Beck was indicted for murder about 1866, tried, and sentenced to hang. Fletcher commuted his sentence to life imprisonment; Beck was received at MSP on Jan. 7, 1867, and he died there on July 31, 1869, *History of Laclede, Camden, Dallas, Webster, Wright, Texas, Pulaski, Phelps and Dent Counties, Missouri*, 447 and Register of Inmates, Reel 2, 2nd Series, 200. In Knox Co. in June 1867, a man known only by his surname, Everman, killed a Dr. Taylor over an argument about raising the U.S. flag or no flag at all at a tournament in Newark. Everman had fought on the Confederate side, and his victim for the Union. On a change of venue to Marion Co., Everman was tried and found guilty; Fletcher pardoned him before his sentence was pronounced but after he was tried and convicted of first degree murder, *History of Lewis, Clark, Knox and Scotland Counties, Missouri*, 626.

31. Brown commuted the death sentences of William Estill; he was found guilty of murder and sentenced to hang in Howard Co. Estill was received at MSP on Jan. 23, 1871, and Phelps pardoned him on Feb. 16, 1880, Register of Inmates, Reel 2, 384. In St. Louis, Patrick Duffy and Patrick Burns were found guilty of the murder of Mary Ostermeyer, and they were both sentenced to hang. The Mo. Supreme Court affirmed. Gov. Brown commuted their death sentences. Duffy was received at MSP

on Aug. 2, and Burns on Aug. 3, 1871. Duffy died in the prison hospital on Oct. 2, 1878, and Acting Gov. Johnson pardoned Burns on Sept. 2, 1874, *State v. Duffy*, 48 Mo. 440 (1871) and *State v. Burns*, 48 Mo. 438 (1871). Duffy's entry is Register of Inmates Reel 3, 22 and Burns's is Reel, 3, 23. John Watson was found guilty of murder in Grundy Co. and sentenced to hang. Brown commuted Watson's death sentence to 20 years; he was received at MSP on Feb. 15, 1872, and Woodson pardoned him on Jan. 12, 1875, Register of Inmates, Reel 3, 65.

32. Hardin commuted Michael Scanlan's death sentence. He murdered his wife in St. Louis; the Mo. Supreme Court affirmed, and he was received at MSP on Feb. 3, 1875, *State v. Scanlan*, 58 Mo 204 (1874) and *Biennial Report of the Board of Inspectors of the Missouri Penitentiary to the Regular Session of the 29th General Assembly, 1875 & 1876*, 60.

33. Phelps commuted the death sentence of John Lawrence who, on Jan. 9, 1876, murdered his father, Hiram Lawrence, in Holt Co. On a change of venue to Buchanan Co., he was tried and found guilty of first degree murder. Lawrence was received at MSP in 1877, and Gov. Francis pardoned him on Dec. 25, 1891; *History of Holt and Atchison Counties, Missouri*, 493–500 and *Report of Commutations and Pardons Granted by Governor David R. Francis During the Years 1891 and 1892*, 8. Phelps also commuted the death sentences of Frank Brown to imprisonment for life. Brown was found guilty of the murder of James Spratt in Buchanan County Circuit Court at the July term, 1875, and the Mo. Supreme Court affirmed, *State v. Brown*, 63 Mo. 439 (1876) and MSA, Pardon Papers, Reel S 117. This governor also commuted the death sentence of Frank Miller to 10 years at MSP in approximately 1878. Miller was a co-defendant of Richard Green; Green was hanged for the Feb. 10, 1877 murder of Deputy Marshal, Henry Hughes, near Independence in 1878. Phelps' fourth commutation of a death sentence was that of Joseph Degonia, found guilty of the murder of Jules Polite, in Washington Co. and sentenced to hang in Potosi on June 27, 1879. On April 14, 1882, Lt. Gov. Campbell pardoned Degonia, *State v. Degonia*, 69 Mo. 485 (1879); *History of Franklin, Jefferson, Washington, Crawford & Gasconade Counties, Missouri*, 505 and *Report of the Board of Inspectors of the Missouri Penitentiary*, 222.

34. *Mitchell v. State*, 3 Mo. 283 (1833); *Missouri Intelligencer* (Columbia), Nov. 30, 1833, 2:4 and Sept. 13, 1834, 3:2; *Jefferson Republican*, Dec. 14, 1833, 1:1 and Aug. 30, 1834, 2:4.

35. *State v. Shaw*, 636 SW2d 667 (1982); *KCS*, June 3, 1993, front page; and information about Shaw's death supplied me by the MO Dept. of Corrections.

36. In Jan. 1848, Elisha Baldwin killed his brother-in-law, Victor Matthews, in St. Louis. The perpetrator was under an insane delusion that his victim had abused Baldwin's sister. He was tried, sentenced to hang, and the Mo. Supreme Court affirmed. Baldwin arrived at MSP on June 3, and Gov. King pardoned him on July 2, 1849. A newspaper reported that the public generally believed his idiocy to be a pretense, *Baldwin v. State*, 12 Mo. 223 (1848), *LT*, Aug. 11, 1848, 2:4, and Register of Inmates, Reel 1, 122.

37. Two French brothers, Gonzales and Raymond Montesquious killed Albert Jones and T.K. Barnum in St. Louis in Oct. 1849. They were from a distinguished French family, which was afflicted with insanity; they had a mad father and a brother. Neither Frenchman was ever convicted of a crime; their trials on first degree murder charges in April and May 1850 resulted in hung juries.

After the second proceeding, Gov. King pardoned them, and they returned to France. According to Scharf, Gonzales "died a raving maniac," *History of St. Louis City and County*, Vol. 2, 1466–67 and *LT*, Nov. 8, 1850, 1:6.

38. On Aug. 29, 1854, in Monroe Co., Benjamin Shoots killed his wife and attempted suicide by ripping open his abdomen with a large butcher knife; physicians sewed him up. He pled guilty and was sentenced to hang. Gov. Price commuted his sentence to life imprisonment, and he was received at MSP on Oct. 26, 1854. His stay there was brief. He was sent to the lunatic asylum in Fulton; its superintendent certified to the governor that Shoots was insane, and King pardoned him on Nov. 23, 1854, *Whig* (Palmyra), Sept. 14, 2:1 and Nov. 2, 1854, 2:3; *LT*, Sept. 1, 1854, 1:1; and Register of Inmates, Reel 1, 2nd Series, 64.

39. In Clark Co., on Feb. 8, 1886, John Bryant killed Elijah "Lige" Lee in the belief that his victim had debauched the perpetrator's wife. Bryant was tried, found guilty, and sentenced to hang. The Mo. Supreme Court decision observed of the condemned man, "It was also shown that in his boyhood and early youth he had fits, and on attaining his majority had twice attempted suicide. It was also testified that his great-grandmother on his mother's side was insane, and died in an insane asylum in North Carolina; that his aunt on his mother's side was insane, and is now in the insane asylum at Fulton, Missouri, and that his grandfather on the same side, now living in Boone County, Missouri, is not right in his mind at times." Nonetheless, the appellate court affirmed Bryant's death sentence. In early 1888 Gov. Morehouse commuted Bryant's death sentence, and Gov. Stephens pardoned him on July 4, 1898; *History of Lewis, Clark, Knox, and Scotland Counties, Missouri*, 334, *State v. Bryant*, 6 SW 102, 115 (1887); *KNG*, July 15, 1898, 2:4, and Index, Register of Inmates.

40. In Aug. 1888, in Jackson Co., William Mitchell killed a waiter called Voiceless Mike in an argument about a glass of wine. He was tried, convicted, and sentenced to hang. The Mo. Supreme Court's decision mentions that at age 15 the condemned suffered a brain injury as a result of a fall from a horse and a physician, if called, would prove that Mitchell suffered "periodical mental derangement ... rendering him at times of said mental derangements morally irresponsible." Nonetheless, the appellate court affirmed his conviction. Gov. Francis commuted his death sentence late in 1889 or early 1890, and Mitchell died at MSP of consumption in 1891, *State v. Mitchell*, 12 SW 379, 380 (1889); *KNG*, March 13, 1891, 6:2, and Index, Register of Inmates.

41. On Sept. 21, 1890, in St. Louis City, George Schaeffer shot and killed Henry Graham, when the victim and another friend went to the perpetrator's house to get him to accompany them to the theatre. Schaeffer was tried, found guilty of murder, and sentenced to hang. Although the Mo. Supreme Court noted that at one time the condemned, a white man, wanted to unite all the Indians against the whites and kill the whites, it affirmed Schaeffer's death sentence. It stated that the jury is the exclusive judge of the credibility of the witnesses, and the perpetrator must prove his insanity. In July 1893, Stone commuted Schaeffer's death sentence to 50 years in prison, but the governor ordered that the young man remain in an asylum until cured of his insanity before being received at MSP, *State v. Schaeffer*, 22 SW 447, 448–451 (1893), *SLPD*, July 9, 1893, 10:2, *Palmyra Spectator*, July 13, 1893, 1:3 and *KNG*, July 14, 1893, 2:4.

42. On July 27, 1891, in Wright Co., John Crisp killed John Pruet. On a change of venue to Webster Co., Crisp

was tried, found guilty, and was sentenced to death. On appeal, the Mo. Supreme Court affirmed; it upheld the exclusion of a witness who would have testified to the defendant's mental derangement. In Oct. 1895, Gov. Stone commuted the condemned's death sentence, and ordered that he be sent to the lunatic asylum in Nevada, MO, *State v. Crisp*, 29 SW 699 (1895) and *KNG*, Oct. 11, 1895, 6:4.

43. On Aug. 29, 1896 in Boone Co., John Hunt Sr. shot and killed his daughter while quarreling with his wife about living in the country versus living in town. He was tried, found guilty, and sentenced to hang; the Mo. Supreme Court affirmed his death sentence. Late in 1897 or early in 1898, Gov. Stephens commuted Hunt's death sentence because the aged perpetrator was nearly blind, crippled by disease and dissipation, and not responsible for his actions. Today, he might be diagnosed as suffering from Alzheimer's disease, *State v. Hunt*, 43 SW 889 (1897) and *KNG*, Dec. 17, 1897, 7:1.

44. On Feb. 18, 1905, in Andrew Co., Paul Paulsgrove killed Miss Mary Newman. On a change of venue he was tried in De Kalb Co., found guilty, and sentenced to hang. His defense of insanity did not succeed. When affirmed his death sentence, the Mo. Supreme Court quoted the perpetrator's reason for his crime, "I loved her, and she threw me away. I could not stand it, and I killed her." In Dec. 1907, Gov. Folk commuted Paulsgrove's death sentence to life imprisonment. On March 16, 1918, Paulsgrove was sent to the insane asylum, and he escaped from it on March 13, 1921. He was returned to MSP on Aug. 24, 1925, and he died in the prison hospital on Jan. 31, 1939, *State v. Paulsgrove*, 101 SW 27, 28 (1907) and Register of Inmates, Reel 16, No. 9416. On July 8, 1905 in Jackson Co., John Crane murdered his ex-wife, Henriette Crane. His defense of insanity did not succeed; the jury found him guilty of first degree murder, and the judge sentenced him to hang. The Mo. Supreme Court affirmed on March 5, 1907, *State v. Crane*, 100 SW 422 (1907). Gov. Folk commuted Crane's death sentence, presumably to life imprisonment, after March 5, 1907; Crane was discharged under the ¾ths law at a date that is not legible in the Index of Prison Records.

45. On Oct. 10, 1922, in Cole Co., John Lee killed his cellmate at MSP in the presence of two other convicts. He was tried, found guilty, and sentenced to hang; the Mo. Supreme Court affirmed his death sentence. Gov. Hyde's only child, a young daughter, Carolyn, interceded in behalf of Lee. Convinced that Lee was "mentally subnormal," on May 2, 1924, Hyde commuted Lee's death sentence to 40 years at MSP. Gov. Stark paroled Lee on Feb. 26, 1941, *State v. Lee*, 259 SW 798 (1924); *KCS*, May 4, 1924, 1:2; and Index, Register of Inmates.

46. On Jan. 6, 1933, in St. Louis City, 32-year-old Paul Barbata, a married man who had a son, killed the object of his affection because her family had told him to stay away from Lillian Salamoni, aged 18 years. In addition to killing her, he killed her father, Sam Salamoni, and he tried to kill her sister and mother. He turned himself in at the police station, and according to the Mo. Supreme Court decision, he told the arresting officers, "I intended to kill the whole family and myself." Barbata's defense of insanity did not succeed. The jury assessed his punishment at death, and the Mo. Supreme Court affirmed. In 1935, Gov. Park commuted Barbata's death sentence because three physicians whom he listened to pronounced him insane, and he was sent to MSP, *State v. Barbata*, 80 SW2d 865, 868 (1935); *SLPD*, March 20, 1935, 1:7; and correspondence from MO Dept. of Corrections.

47. At the Sept. term, 1865, of Franklin Co. Circuit Court, James Shoemaker was found guilty of first degree murder and sentenced to hang. Gov. Fletcher commuted Shoemaker's death sentence to life imprisonment, and he was received at MSP on Oct. 5, 1865. Nearly five years later, Gov. McClurg pardoned him because McClurg became convinced that "Shoemaker could not have committed the murder as he was some miles distant from the scene of the crime and not an accessory," Vertical file, MSHS *"List of Pardons, Commutations and Reprieves [Granted by Governor Joseph W. McClurg]*, 67.

48. After three trials in Bates Co., John Leabo was found guilty of the Dec. 19, 1883 murder of his wife, Luella Leabo, and he was sentenced to hang. The Mo. Supreme Court reversed his first conviction because evidence of his wife's despondence had been excluded; the second proceeding against him resulted in a mistrial, and the appellate court affirmed his third jury's death sentence. In July 1886, Gov. Marmaduke commuted Leabo's death sentence to life imprisonment at MSP because he was uncertain whether Luella Leabo's death was murder or a suicide, *State v. Leabo*, 84 Mo 163 (1884) and 1 SW 288 (1886) and *Governor's Report of Pardons, Commutations and Reprieves for the Years 1885 and 1886*, 19.

49. On March 2, 1893, Edwin Brown was beaten to death and robbed by three men in St. Louis Co. Jacob Henze and Henry Kaiser were charged with the victim's murder, found guilty, and sentenced to death. The jury who heard the case did not believe the defendants' alibi witnesses. On appeal, the Mo. Supreme Court affirmed. Gov. Stone gave them six respites, and in May 1895, he commuted their death sentences to life imprisonment. The *St. Louis Globe-Democrat* quoted the governor as saying of the question of the identity of these men, "The more I've looked into the case the more doubt has grown upon me," May 9, 1895. 7:1. The robbers took a gold watch, and it was never recovered. A principal witness for the state was prosecuted for perjury. The convicted men consistently maintained their innocence, *State v. Kaiser et al.* 28 SW 182 (1894).

50. On Jan. 5, 1894, in Buchanan Co. Jennie Punshon was found dead. Her husband, Thomas, was charged with her murder. At his first trial, her prior suicide threats were excluded. The defendant maintained that his wife took a revolver out of his pocket and shot herself in a carriage. His first trial was reversed because of improper jury instructions. At his second trial, he was found guilty of first degree murder and sentenced to hang. The Mo. Supreme Court upheld his death sentence. In May 1896, Gov. Stone commuted Punshon's death sentence to 20 years at MSP because of his doubt about the circumstances of Mrs. Punshon's death; it may have been a suicide. Gov. Dockery pardoned Punshon on Dec. 25, 1902, *State v. Punshon*, 27 SW 111 (1894) and 34 SW 25 (1896); *St. Joseph Weekly News*, May 8, 1896, 7:1, and Index, Register of Inmates. In Kansas City, on Dec. 17, 1894, a deputy constable, Isaac Cahn, was murdered. Foster Pollard and Frank Harris were arrested, tried, convicted of the first degree murder of the victim, and sentenced to hang. The Mo. Supreme Court affirmed their convictions. On the basis of the perjury of Clay McDonald, the state's chief witness at their trial, in June 1896, Gov. Stone commuted their death sentences to 50 years at MSP. On Dec. 21, 1911, Gov. Hadley released Pollard from MSP by commuting his sentence to time served, and two days later he commuted Harris' sentence to time served, *State v. Pollard et. al.* 34 SW 29 (1896), *Kansas City Journal*, June 18, 1896, 5:5; *KNG*, June 27, 1896, 4:4, and Index, Register of Inmates.

51. On March 16, 1898, in Clinton Co., the marshal of Cameron, a white man, was shot and killed. Robert Cushenberry, a Negro, was tried twice; his first jury was

hung. His defense was that he was in Topeka, KS, on both the day before and the day of the murder. Nonetheless, six witnesses placed him in Cameron on March 15, 1898. At his second trial, the defendant was convicted and sentenced to hang. The Mo. Supreme Court affirmed. After several respites, Gov. Stephens commuted his death sentence on July 10, 1900. The ex–chief of police of Topeka and other residents of this city said the wrong man was convicted. Ten years after Cushenberry arrived at the prison, Gov. Hadley paroled him on Aug 15, 1910, *State v. Cushenberry*, 56 SW 737 (1900); *Democrat Lever* (Plattsburg), July 20, 1900, 1:1; *KNG*, Sept. 5, 1902, 3:1 and Aug. 26, 1910, 2:3, and Index, Register of Inmates.

52. On August 3, 1903, Fred Williams, a Negro, killed Luther Lewis, also black, in the city of St. Louis; he was tried, found guilty, and sentenced to death. The condemned was not represented by counsel before the Mo. Supreme Court, and it affirmed the trial court. On March 9, 1905, Gov. Folk commuted William's death sentence to life imprisonment. He explained his action: "I am satisfied that if Williams had been properly defended the jury would not have imposed the extreme punishment of death." *Lawrence Chieftain* (Mt. Vernon), March 16, 1905, 3:3. On Oct. 12, 1907, Williams was discharged under the ¾ths law, *State v. Williams* 84 SW 924 (1905); and Index, Register of Inmates.

53. *Biographical Directory of the Governors of the United States, 1789–1978*, Vol. 2, 853.

54. *Springfield Express*, April 14, 1882, 1:3.

55. *St. Joseph Gazette*, April 14, 1882, 4:4.

56. Frank Triplett, *Life, Times and Treacherous Death of Jesse James*, 260. The exact timing of the pardon cannot be verified with reference to the front page story about the case in the St. Joseph newspaper on April 17, 1882. It is missing.

57. Vertical file, MSHS, "Pardons Issued by the Governor," 224.

58. *St. Joseph Gazette*, April 19, 2:3.

59. *State v. Cook*, 84 Mo. 40, 42 (1884); *History of Franklin, Jefferson, Washington, Crawford & Gasconade Counties, Missouri*, 505; and *Governor's Report of Pardons, Commutations and Reprieves ... For the Years 1885 and 1886*, 33.

60. On Feb. 29, 1884, in Henry Co., Frank Hopkirk and Thomas Brownfield killed John Wells, an elderly neighbor, in order to rob him. Marmaduke commuted Hopkirk's (the younger man) death sentence on March 16, 1885, and Brownfield's on March 17, 1885. Gov. Stone pardoned Brownfield, *State v. Hopkirk*, 84 Mo. 278 (1884), *State v. Brownfield*, 83 Mo. 448 (1884), and vertical file, MSHS, "Pardons, Commutations, and Paroles," 32. On Dec. 3, 1883, in McDonald Co., James Wisdom killed William Judy in an argument over who would ride on which horse. The Mo. Supreme Court affirmed Wisdom's death sentence, and on March 17, 1885, Marmaduke commuted Wisdom's death sentence to life imprisonment at MSP; Gov. Morehouse pardoned him on Oct. 8, 1887, *History of Newton, Lawrence, Barry & McDonald Counties, Missouri*, 747; *State v. Wisdom*, 84 Mo 177 (1884); vertical file, MSHS, "Pardons, Commutations, and Paroles," 33, and Index, Register of Inmates. On April 8, 1884, in Carroll Co., Joel Anderson and Laurel Baugh killed John Rea. At their trial, the jury did not believe their defense of self defense; it found them guilty of first degree murder. The Mo. Supreme Court affirmed their death sentences. Acting on many petitions, including those from relatives of the victim, on July 7, 1886, Marmaduke commuted Anderson's and Baugh's death sentences. Joel Anderson died in the prison hospital on Jan.

29, 1890, and Gov. Stephens pardoned Laurel Baugh on Nov. 25, 1897, Turner and Clark, *Twentieth Century History of Carroll County, Missouri*, Vol. 1, 449–50, *State v. Anderson and Another*, 1 SW 135 (1886), and vertical file, MSHS, "Pardons, Commutations, and Paroles," 33.

61. On Dec. 26, 1890, Newt "Bud" Blunt killed Jack Majors, a brakeman on the Frisco Railroad in Newton Co. On a change of venue to McDonald Co., a jury in Pineville found Blunt guilty of first degree murder and sentenced him to hang. The Mo. Supreme Court affirmed. The day before he was scheduled to die on Sept. 16, Gov. Francis commuted his sentence to life imprisonment at MSP on Sept. 16, 1892; *State v. Blunt*, 19 SW 650 (1892) and *Pineville News*, Sept. 16, 1892, 3:3.

62. Dockery pardoned Amanda Umble, discussed in Chapter 10 and Thomas Punshon, discussed in note 50. He also commuted two death sentences. One was of William Furgerson, who on March 25, 1897, killed Stephen Wilson in Grundy Co. Furgerson's case went to the Mo. Supreme Court twice. It first reversed and then affirmed his conviction. He was received at MSP on June 20, 1901, and Gov Major released him by commuting his earlier commute on July 3, 1916, *State v. Furgerson*, 53 SW 427 (1899) and 63 SW 101 (1901) and Register of Inmates, No. 4038. Gov. Dockery also spared the life of John Vinso who, on Oct. 13, 1901, in Lawrence Co., killed William Ward, a stranger, by throwing at rock at him, after a senseless exchange of words as to who could whip whom. The Mo. Supreme Court affirmed Vinso's death sentence, In May 1903, Dockery commuted it to life at MSP; on Nov. 27, 1912, Gov. Hadley released Vinso by commuting his earlier commute, *State v. Vinso*, 71 SW 1034 (1903), *KNG*, May 22, 1903, 6:2, and Index, Register of Inmates.

63. Thomas Smith, a black man, shot and killed George Cameron, also black, when they got into a shouting match at a saloon. The jury did not believe Smith's defense of self defense; its members sentenced him to death, and the Mo. Supreme Court affirmed. On May 23, 1893, Gov. Stone commuted Smith's death sentence to 30 years at MSP, *State v. Smith*, 21 SW 827 (1893) and *KCT*, May 24, 1893, 5:3. In June 1893, Stone spared Amanda Umble's life. She was a black woman who killed another black woman; she is discussed in Chapter 10. On May 8, 1895, Stone commuted the death sentence of William Taylor, a black man who on March 13, 1893, in St. Louis City, killed another black man, Tobe Carlisle, to 10 years at MSP so the prisoner could benefit from the ¾ths rule. The perpetrator had warned the victim to stay away from Taylor's wife. The jury found Taylor guilty of first degree murder and sentenced him to hang. The Mo. Supreme Court affirmed, *State v. Taylor*, 29 SW 598 (1895) and *St. Louis Globe-Democrat*, May 9, 1895, 7:1. The two other black men, Foster Pollard and Frank Harris, whose death sentences Stone commuted, are discussed in note 50.

64. George Schaeffer, discussed in note 41, and John Crisp, discussed in note 42, were mentally incompetent.

65. The possible innocence of Jacob Henze and Henry Kaiser, discussed in note 49, and Thomas Punshon, discussed in note 50, prompted Stone to commute all three of their death sentences.

66. On March 17, 1892, in Pemiscot Co., John Mosley murdered Andy Seaton. After the Mo. Supreme Court affirmed Mosley's death sentence. he was scheduled to hang on July 25, 1893. Many residents of Pemiscot Co. petitioned Stone to commute this death sentence. He did so Fall 1893, *State v. Mosley*, 22 SW 804 (1893), *Palmyra Spectator*, June 22, 1893, 1:3; and *KNG*, Oct. 6, 1893, 6:4. On July 29, 1893, in Audrain Co., Joseph Donnelly killed Samuel Turner after they spent the night drinking to-

gether. The Mo. Supreme Court affirmed Donnelly's death sentence. Stone commuted it to a term at MSP, and Stephens pardoned Donnelly on Nov. 29, 1900, *State v. Donnelly*, 32 SW 1124 (1895); *KNG*, Dec. 7, 1900, 7:3; and Index, Register of Inmates.

67. On Nov. 23, 1896, William "Billy" Williams, a black man, killed Lawrence Schubel, a white Hungarian, in a chance encounter on a Kansas City street after the victim shouted a hurrah for William Jennings Bryan. The perpetrator wanted to kill a Bryan man. The Mo. Supreme Ct. affirmed Williams' death sentence. In Nov. or Dec. 1897, Stephens commuted Williams' sentence to 50 years at MSP, and in 1901 Stephens pardoned him, *State v. Williams*, 42 SW 720 (1897) and KNG, Jan. 18, 1901, 2:3. On May 5, 1897, in St. Louis Co., Walter Black, a Negro, killed Michael Prendergast, a white man, in the process of stealing corn from his victim. The Mo. Supreme Ct. affirmed Black's death sentence. In April 1898, Stephens commuted Black's death sentence to 99 years at MSP; slightly over two years later, June 26, 1900, Stephens pardoned Black, *State v. Black*, 44 SW 340 (1898), *KNG*, July 6, 1900, 5:3, and index to Register of Inmates. The third black whose death sentence Stephens commuted was Robert Cushenberry's. His case is discussed in note 51.

68. On March 5, 1896, in St. Louis City, Andrew Morton, a gypsy horse trader, killed Mrs. Louis Worton, his common-law wife, because he was jealous of her going with other men. The Mo. Supreme Court affirmed his death sentence; in July 1897, Stephens commuted it to 50 years at MSP, *State v. Worton*, 41 SW 218 (1897) and *Franklin County Tribune* (Union) July 16, 1897, 2:3.

69. On Oct. 22, 1897, in Platte Co., Charles Grant, a black man, killed his black wife, Maggie Grant. The Mo. Supreme Court affirmed his death sentence, and in Jan. 1900, Stephens commuted Grant's death sentence to 50 years at MSP. On May 27, 1904, Folk effected Grant's release from prison by commuting his death sentence, *State v. Grant*, 53, SW 432 (1899); *KNG*, Jan. 5, 1900, 6:1, and Index, Register of Inmates.

70. John Hunt was either senile or insane; his case is discussed in note 43.

71. On July 18, 1888, in Texas Co., Peter Renfrow, a white man, killed Charles Dorris, a white constable of Carroll Township. On a change of venue to Greene Co., the jury disbelieved Renfrow's defense of self defense, found him guilty of first degree murder, and he was sentenced to hang in 1891. The Mo. Supreme Court affirmed his death sentence, but he escaped with 14 other prisoners from the Greene Co. jail in Springfield. A guard was killed in their escape. Renfrow was captured near Doniphan, Ripley Co., in Feb. 1898, and he was resentenced to hang on May 21, 1898. By this time, law enforcement officers in Greene Co. favored a prison term for him. On May 4, 1898, Stephens commuted Renfrow's sentence to a term at MSP; on May 13, 1905, Gov. Folk commuted the remainder of Renfrow's sentence, and he was a free man, *History of Laclede, Camden, Dallas, Webster, Wright, Texas, Pulaski, Phelps, and Dent Counties, Missouri*, 449; *State v. Renfrow*, 20 SW 299 (1892); *KNG*, April 8, 1893, 3:3; *Leader-Democrat* (Springfield), May 5, 1898, 7:2, and Index, Register of Inmates.

72. In St. Louis City, on Nov. 20, 1897, Thomas Shackelford, age 18 or 19, put a deadly dose of arsenic in George Taylor's coffee at the request of Nettie Taylor, the victim's wife and the beneficiary of the victim's life insurance policy. She wanted her husband dead after he moved out and spent time with other women. All participants in this crime were black. The Mo. Supreme Court. affirmed Shackelford's death sentence. In June 1899, Stephens com-

muted it to 50 years at MSP, and Gov. Folk commuted the earlier commute. Shackelford regained his freedom on April 23, 1906, *State v. Shackelford*, 50 SW 105 (1899) and Register of Inmates, No. 2303.

73. On March 26, 1899, in Holt Co., David Miller, a white man, beat to death Samuel Crow, an old and feeble white man, in order to avoid an indictment for stealing. The Mo. Supreme Court affirmed Miller's death sentence, and in June 1900, Stephens commuted it to 50 years at MSP, *State v. Miller*, 56 SW 907 (1900) and *KNG*, June 22, 1900, 2:2.

74. See note 71, Peter Renfrow; note 72, Thomas Shackelford; and note 69, Charles Grant.

75. On March 19, 1904, Edgar Bailey, a union hack driver, shot to death Albert Ferguson, a non-union driver. His trial began on June 21, and it ended on July 21, 1904, with his being sentenced to death. The Mo Supreme Court affirmed. On Oct. 20, 1905, Folk commuted it to life imprisonment at MSP. On July 3, 1915, Gov. Major effected Bailey's release from MSP by commuting his sentence, *State v. Bailey*, 88 SW 733 (1905); *KCT*, Oct. 21, 1905, 1:1; and Index, Register of Inmates.

76. In Dunklin Co., on Dec. 5, 1903, Louis Eaton shot to death Frank Huff, who died the next day. The perpetrator told the victim who was with a girl and another couple walking on railroad tracks to stop. They did not, and Eaton shot Huff. The jury rejected his defense that the shooting was accidental. It found him guilty of first degree murder, and the Mo. Supreme Court affirmed his death sentence. Folk commuted it to life imprisonment; Eaton was received at MSP on Feb. 10, 1906, and he died in the prison hospital on Feb. 3, 1908, *State v. Eaton*, 89 SW 949 (1905) and Register of Inmates, Reel 16, No. 8023.

77. On Oct. 1, 1905, in Pemiscot Co., Dave Long killed his neighbor, C.C. Still, with whom he quarreled The Mo. Supreme Court affirmed Long's death sentence, and Folk commuted it to life imprisonment. Long was received at MSP on June 15, 1907, and he died in the prison hospital on May 29, 1913, *Pineville Democrat*, March 8, 1907, 1:3; *State v. Long*, 100 SW 587 (1907); and Register of Inmates, Reel 16, No. 9121.

78. On Oct. 10, 1905, in Boone Co., Tom Clay, a black man, shot and killed Warren Merideth, also black and an ex-convict, at a colored portion of a Columbia saloon, in the language of the day. The jury disbelieved Clay's defense of self defense, and it found him guilty of first degree murder. The Mo. Supreme Court affirmed Clay's death sentence. Folk commuted it to life imprisonment. Clay was received at MSP on July 19, 1907, and Gov. Gardner released him on Feb. 17, 1918, by commuting his sentence, *Pineville Democrat*, March 8, 1907, 1:3; *State v. Clay*, 100 SW 439 (1907); and Register of Inmates, Reel 16, No. 9185. On June 10 or early on June 11, 1906, in Boone Co., John Baker, a Negro, shot two men, also black, following a disagreement at a picnic. One victim recovered, and the other, Boss Hall, died. Baker was found guilty of first degree murder, and he was sentenced to hang. The Mo. Supreme Court affirmed. Folk also commuted Baker's death sentence to life imprisonment. He was received at MSP on April 7, 1908, and Gov. Gardner released him by commuting his sentence on Nov. 27, 1918, *Baker v. State*, 108 SW 6 (1908) and Register of Inmates, Reel 17, No. 9762.

79. On Aug. 12, 1905, in Graniteville, Iron Co., John Brooks, assisted and aided by his brother, Ameleck Brooks, shot to death John Clemonds, as these men and others quarreled and drank. The jury rejected their defense of self defense; it found them guilty of first degree murder; the Mo. Supreme Court affirmed their death sen-

tences. In July 1907, Folk commuted their sentences to life imprisonment at MSP, *State* v. *Brooks et al.*, 100 SW 416 (1907) and *Arcadia Valley Enterprise* (Ironton), July 25, 1907, 5:1.

80. On May 25, 1905, in Iron Co., William Spaugh, his brother, Arthur Spaugh, and their mother, Mary Spaugh, were all involved in the shooting death of the sheriff, John Polk, as he attempted to arrest William Spaugh for mayhem in putting out the eye of a 17-year-old boy. The sheriff's body was found in the Spaugh home with four bullet wounds in it. The prosecutor's theory of the case is that Mary Spaugh stepped over the body as she fixed dinner. When her sons were arrested in Madison Co., they were taken to St. Louis to avoid their being lynched. In separate trials, Mary, who was tried twice, was eventually found not guilty, and Arthur was found guilty of second degree murder and sentenced to 30 years at MSP. William received a change of venue from Iron to Reynolds Co., and in Dec. 1905, he was found guilty of first degree murder; the Mo. Supreme Court affirmed his death sentence. On a habeas proceeding, the U.S. Supreme Court affirmed the Mo. Supreme Court. In July 1907, Folk commuted William Spaugh's death sentence to life imprisonment at MSP; he died in the prison hospital on Aug. 25, 1913, *SLPD*, Nov. 27, 1905, 16:5; *State* v. *Spaugh*, 98 SW 55 (1906); *Spaugh* v. *Fitts*, 205 U.S. 540 (1907); *Acadia Valley Enterprise*, July 25, 1907, 5:1, and Index, Register of Inmates.

81. On June 18, 1903, in St. Louis Co., Frederick Barrington, alias George Barton, killed his benefactor, James McCann. The jury found the perpetrator, an English criminal who used the title "Lord," guilty of first degree murder. The Mo. Supreme Court affirmed his death sentence, and on a habeas appeal the U.S Supreme Court affirmed the Mo. Supreme Court. Folk commuted Barrington's death sentence to life imprisonment. He was received at MSP on Aug. 28, 1907, and Gov. Gardner commuted his sentence; he was released from prison on Dec. 24, 1918, *KNG*, March 2, 1906, 7:1; *State* v. *Barrington*, 95 SW 235 (1906); *Barrington* v. *Missouri*, 205 U.S. 483 (1907); and Register of Inmates, Reel 16, No. 9225.

82. In the city of St. Louis, on Nov. 9, 1906, Frank Daly, alias A.C. Biles, killed Robert Harvey, for purposes of robbing him, by administering morphine mixed in beer as the two drank together at a saloon. The jury found him guilty of first degree murder, and he was sentenced to death. The Mo. Supreme Court affirmed. In May 1908, Gov. Folk commuted Daly's sentence to 99 years; had he lived to serve it, he would have been released, as the record noted, on May 20, 2006. Gov. Hadley released Daly by commuting his sentence on Jan. 2, 1913, *State* v. *Daly*, 109 SW 53 (1908) and Register of Inmates, Reel S-228, No. 9901.

83. Paul Paulsgrove, discussed in note 44.

84. The coverage of U.S. Senator Stone's death includes the *New York Times*, April 15, 15:1; April 17, 13:4; and April 18, 1818, 13:8; *KCT*, April 15, 1918, 1:7; and *Kansas City Journal*, April 15, 1918, 1:6. It is from this last mentioned source that Stone's defense of a man on murder charges was located.

85. On Feb. 22, 1909, in Greene Co., Eugene Tucker killed his neighbor, Elizabeth Ellis, because her husband had impounded the perpetrator's cattle. At trial, he was found guilty of first degree murder, and the jury assessed his punishment at death. The Mo. Supreme Court affirmed. Gov. Hadley commuted Tucker's death sentence to life imprisonment. He was received at MSP on March 15, 1911, and Gov. Gardner released him from prison by commuting the remainder of his sentence on March 15, 1918, *State* v. *Tucker*, 133 SW 27 (1910) and Register of Inmates, Reel 18, No. 12340.

86. Mert Holman's case is discussed in Chapter 9.

87. On Dec. 1, 1911, George Bonner, a black man, killed Albert Underwood, white, in the office of a railroad co. in Kansas City in the course of a robbery. Bonner was found guilty; the jury sentenced him to death, and the Mo. Supreme Court affirmed. Gov. Major commuted Bonner's death sentence to life imprisonment. He was received at MSP on Sept. 1, 1914, and he died in the prison hospital on Oct. 8, 1917, *State* v. *Bonner*, 168 SW 591 (1914) and Register of Inmates, Reel 19, No. 16099. On April 30, 1913, in Kansas City, John Tatman and Samuel Sherman shot Patrolman John Lynch of the Kansas City police department while running from him as he sought to question them. The officer later died from his wounds. At their trial, the jury assessed their punishment at death, and the Mo. Supreme Court affirmed. They were sentenced to hang on April 9, 1915. A week prior to their scheduled execution, Gov. Major commuted their sentence to life imprisonment. He based his decision on their youth — they were in their mid–20s— and their being first offenders. Gov. Baker discharged both men by paroling them; Tatman on Dec. 24, 1926, and Sherman on July 2, 1928. Several decades later, John Barker, who as attorney general had argued both Bonner's and Tatman's cases for the state before the Mo. Supreme Court, wrote that both Bonner and Tatman were hanged. Barker was mistaken, *Missouri Lawyer*, 124–25; *State* v. *Tatman*, 175 SW 69 (1915); *State* v. *Sherman*, 175 SW 73 (1915); *Kansas City Post*, April 2, 1915, 1:3; and Index, Register of Inmates.

88. On April 7, 1916, Ora Lewis and his brother, Roy, shot and killed John McKenna and William Dillon, both police officers in the city of St. Louis. The victims were attempting to arrest the Lewis brothers as thieves; they were tried for the murder of McKenna. The jury found both men guilty of first degree murder and assessed their punishment at death. The trial judge commuted Roy's death sentence to life imprisonment at MSP. Roy was present at the shooting, but his brother, Ora, was the trigger man. The Mo. Supreme Court affirmed Ora's death sentence, and Gov. Gardner commuted Ora's death sentence to imprisonment at MSP in April 1918, *State* v. *Lewis et al.*, 201 SW 80 (1918); *SLPD*, March 24, 4:3 and April 3, 1918, 3:8.

89. One of Hyde's commutations was Woodville Thurston's death sentence; it is discussed in Chapter 9; another was John Lee's; it is discussed in note 45. On April 20, 1920, in Kansas City, John Moore killed two men, Kirk Tate, owner of a saloon, and Ula McMahan of the Kansas City police department, when admonished outside Tate's business to go home and go to bed. He was tried for the killing of the officer, and the jury assessed his punishment at death. The Mo Supreme Court affirmed. Six days before his scheduled hanging on Dec. 31, 1921, Hyde commuted Moore's death sentence to life imprisonment on Dec. 24, 1921, *State* v. *Moore*, 235 SW 1056 (1921) and *KCS*, Dec. 24, 1921, 1:4.

90. On Feb. 26, 1921, in Herculaneum, Jefferson Co., James Seward killed Andrew Deck, a prohibition informer. The perpetrator was in the hire of bootleggers. Seward confessed; his jury assessed his punishment at death. The Mo. Supreme Court affirmed. While Gov. Hyde was attending President Harding's funeral in early Aug. 1923, Lt. Gov. Lloyd commuted Seward's death sentence to a term at MSP; Gov. Stark paroled Seward, and he was discharged on Oct. 11, 1939, *State* v. *Seward*, 247 SW 150 (1922); *Jefferson County Record* (Hillsboro), Aug. 23, 1923, 4:1; and Index, Register of Inmates.

91. On Dec. 5, 1927, in the city of St. Louis, Andrew Meadows set fire to the Buckingham Hotel; May Frazier

and several other guests died in the fire. He was tried for her murder; the jury assessed his punishment at death, and the Mo. Supreme Court affirmed. In 1932, Gov. Caulfield commuted Meadows' death sentence to a term at MSP; he died in the prison hospital on Jan. 31, 1958, *State* v. *Meadows*, 51 SW2d 1033 (1932); *Kansas City Journal-Post*, July 15, 1932, 2:3; *SLPD*, Oct. 19, 1933, 3A:4; and Index, Register of Inmates.

92. On May 12, 1930, in the city of St. Louis, Amos Carroll, a black man, killed Roy Clark, also black, in an argument over $10. The jury found Carroll guilty of first degree murder; it assessed his punishment at death. The Mo. Supreme Court affirmed, and he was scheduled to hang on Oct. 20, 1933; 18 hours before his scheduled execution, Gov. Park commuted Carroll's death sentence to life imprisonment, *State* v. *Carroll*, 62 SW2d 863 (1933); *SLPD*, Oct. 19, 1933, 3A:4; and correspondence from MO Dept. of Corrections.

93. On May 30, 1935, in Grundy Co., James Richardson and two others, Ellis Nave and Gilbert Glidewell, met Elmer Davis, a farmer who lived near Laredo, MO. The victim and another man caught the three attempting to steal gas from his car; Davis became a passenger in the perpetrators' car because he intended to buy them gas. They shot him; prior to his death in a Trenton hospital on June 2, he identified the men brought into his room. Richardson was tried separately; the jury found him guilty of first degree murder, assessed his punishment at death, and the Mo. Supreme Court affirmed. On May 15, six days before his scheduled hanging on May 21, 1937, Gov. Stark commuted Richardson's death sentence to life imprisonment because nine of the 12 jurors who convicted him signed a petition for the commutation, *State* v. *Richardson*, 102, SW 653 (1937); *Gallatin Democrat*, May 20, 1937, 1:6; and Index, Register of Inmates.

94. On Dec. 19, 1941, in the city of St. Louis, Buford Cole, an illiterate black man, raped and murdered Geraldine Brookfield, a seven-year-old black child. He was tried twice; the Mo. Supreme Court reversed his first conviction, and it affirmed his second. Cole was scheduled to die in the gas chamber at MSP on July 27, 1945. Gov. Donnelly commuted his death sentence in August 1945. *State* v. *Cole*, 174 SW2d 173 (1943) and 188 SW2d 43 (1945); *St. Louis Argus*, Dec. 26, 1941, 1:4; Jan. 16, 1942, 1:1; and June 15, 1945, 1:5; and *St. Louis Globe-Democrat*, Nov. 16, 1945.

95. On Sept. 22, 1954, Rollie Laster and eight others, including Herman Trout and James Creighton, all inmates at MSP, participated in the murder of Walter Donnell, another inmate, in the course of a prison riot. Laster was tried separately, Jan. 24–27, 1955, and he was sentenced to death; the Mo. Supreme Court affirmed his death sentence. Six other inmates involved in the murder of Donnell, William Hoover, Jackie Noble, Paul Kenton, James Stidham, Don Delapp, and Joseph Vidauri, in separate proceedings received life sentences. In return for Trout and Creighton testifying for the state against Laster, Gov. Donnelly commuted their sentences to time served. Trout was received at MSP from Butler Co. on Jan. 3, 1944, for kidnapping, assault, and robbery. Creighton began serving a life sentence for murder from Barton Co. on Jan. 17, 1933. Both Trout and Creighton left MSP free men on Jan. 13, 1956. Thomas Rose, a courageous Jefferson City attorney, who estimated his time on Laster's case at 550 hours; a circuit court judge, Sam Blair, and perhaps others convinced Gov. James Blair to commute Laster's death sentence, on Jan. 15, 1957, to the same punishment the other inmates involved in Donnell's murder received, life imprisonment, *State* v. *Laster*, 293 SW2sd

300 (1956); 96 photocopied pages of documents pertaining to Laster's case, courtesy Thomas Rose; and correspondence from MO Dept. of Corrections.

96. On May 30, 1959, in Kansas City, Marcus Goodwin killed his common-law wife, Mazie Lee, the mother of his three children. He shot and stabbed her to death shortly after they separated. In a one-day trial, he was found guilty and sentenced to death. The Mo. Supreme Court affirmed. Early in 1962, Gov. Dalton commuted Goodwin's sentence to life imprisonment, *State* v. *Goodwin*, 352 SW2d 615 (1962); 359 SW2d 601 (1962); 396 SW2d 548 (1965). Mention is made in this last cited case of the governor's commutation of Goodwin's death sentence.

97. *State* v. *McGee*, 83 SW2d 98 (1935); William Reddig, *Tom's Town*, 342–53; *KCS*, May 27, 1935, 1:1; *SLPD*, 3A:5; *Kansas City Journal-Post*, May 27, 1935, 1:8, and Index, Register of Inmates

98. *State* v. *Ashworth*, 143 SW 279 (1940); *St. Joseph Gazette*, Oct. 19, 1940, 3:2; conversation with Fred Slater, *St. Joseph News-Press* columnist; and correspondence from MO Dept. of Corrections.

99. *State* v. *Mease*, 842 SW2d 98 (1992).

100. Michael W. Cuneo, *Almost Midnight: An American Story of Murder and Redemption.*

101. Constituent Correspondence, February 1999; Darrell Mease, Box 28 (unprocessed); Execution Files; Mel Carnahan 1993–2000; Office of Governor, Record Group 3.51, MSA.

12. Appellate Court Reversals, 1818–2005

1. 408 U.S. 238

2. 428 U.S. 153, 428 U.S. 242, and 428 U.S. 262 (1976).

3. *McLean* v. *State*, 8 Mo. 153 (1843) and W.V. N. Bay, *Reminiscences of the Bench and Bar of Missouri*, 71–72.

4. *State* v. *Cross*, 27 Mo. 332 (1858); *History of Franklin, Jefferson, Washington, Crawford & Gasconade Counties, Missouri*, 280; and Register of Inmates, Reel 1, 2nd Series, 176.

5. *State* v. *Simms*, 68 Mo. 306, 309 (1878).

6. *State* v. *Meyers*, 12 SW 516, 520 (1889).

7. *State* v. *Speyer*, 81 SW 430 (1904); 91 SW 1075 (1906); and 106 SW 505, 510 (1907).

8. *State* v. *Chyo Chiagk*, 4 SW 704 (1887) and *State* v. *Chyo Goom*, 4 SW 712 (1887).

9. *State* v. *Grant*, 76 Mo. 236 (1882) and 79 Mo. 113 (1883).

10. *KNG*, Dec. 1, 1899, 6:3 and March 23, 1900, 2:3 and *State* v. *Moore*, 61 SW 199, 203 and 205 (1901).

11. *New York Times*, April 21, 1931, 32:6.

12. *State* v. *Richardson et al.*, 46 SW2d 576 (1932) and *Powell* v. *Alabama*, 287 U.S. 45 (1932). The Mo. Supreme Court decision was decided on February 17, 1932 and the U.S. Supreme Court decision on Nov. 7, 1932.

13. *Clinton Eye*, Oct. 23, 1:3, Oct. 30, 1:3, Nov. 6, 1930, 1:4, Feb. 25, 1:2, and July 7, 1932, 1:3.

14. *State* v. *Logan*, 111 SW2d 110, 112–113 (1937) cites *Norris* v. *Alabama*, 294 U.S. 587 (1935) as a controlling decision. The U.S. Supreme Court held in *Norris* that the systematic exclusion of blacks from the grand and trial juries when a black defendant is on trial in state court denies the accused the equal protection of the law guaranteed by the 14th Amendment.

15. *SLPD*, March 31, 9A:2, 1938 and *State* v. *Logan*, 126 SW2d 256 (1939).

16. *State* v. *Nickens*, 403 SW2d 582, 587 (1966).

17. James Liebman, Jeffrey Faggan, and Valerie West, *A Broken System: Error Rates in Capital Cases, 1973–1995*, App. A-6–A-7.

18. *Johnson* v. *State*, 102 SW3rd 535, 539 (2003).

19. *Deck* v. *Missouri*, 125 S. Ct. 2007 (2005) and 994 SW2d 527 (1999).

20. *State* v. *Deck*, 68 SW3d 418 (2002) and 136 SW3d 481 (2004).

21. *Schlup* v. *Delo*, 513 U.S. 298, 302 (1995).

22. Affidavit of Robert Faherty, Jackson Co., State of Missouri, Oct. 26, 1993.

23. *Pitch* (Kansas City), April 27, 2000, 6 and conversation with Robert Driscoll.

24. Conversation with Records Office, Southeast Correctional Center, Charleston, MO.

25. State v. Clemmons, 753 SW2d 901 (1988) and 785 SW2d 524 (1990).

26. *Clemmons* v. *Delo*, 124 F3d 944 (8th Cir.: 1997).

27. *KCS*, Feb. 28, 2000, 1:4.

28. *State* v. *Driscoll*, 711 SW2d 512, 479 U.S. 922 (1986), 767 SW2d 5, and 492 U.S. 874 (1989).

29. *Driscoll* v. *Delo*, 71 F 3d 701 (8th Cir.: 1995).

30. *State* v. *Driscoll*, 55 SW 3d 350 (2001).

31. Conversation with David Bruns.

32. *State* v. *Carr*, 708 SW2d 313 (1986); *State* v. *Roberts*, 709 SW2d 857 (1986); and Death Row, Capital Punishment in Missouri, Executions: 1989–2005, http://www.missourideathrow.com.

33. *Amrine* v. *Roper*, 102 SW3d 541, 544 (2003).

34. Testimony of Terry Russell, Randall Ferguson, and Jerry Poe in July 1998 video, "Unreasonable Doubt: The Joe Amrine Case" (2002).

35. 486 U.S. 1017 (1988).

36. *Amrine* v. *State*, 785 SW2d 531 (1990); *Amrine* v. *Bowersox*, 128 F 3d 1222 (8th Cir.: 1997); and *Amrine* v. *Bowersox*, 238 F 3d 1023 (8th Cir.: 2001).

37. *KCS*, July 30, 2003, B1:1.

38. *State* v. *Dexter*, 954 SW2d 332 (1997).

39. *KCS*, June 8, 1:1 and June 9, 1999, B1:1 and Dec. 29, 1999, B1:1.

40. Streamlined Procedures Act of 2005, introduced in the Senate, S. 1088, and introduced in the House, H.R. 3035. Its Sec. 9 would amend Sec. 2264 of Chapter 154, title 28, U.S. Code, the federal law which specifically allows a state prisoner under capital sentence to file a petition for habeas corpus relief in federal court.

41. *New York Times*, July 16, 2005, A26:1.

42. *State* v. *Griffin*, 662 SW2d 854, 856 (1984).

43. Kathleen Burnett, *Justice Denied*, 29–38; *SLPD*, July 12, 1:1 and July 13, 1:5, 2005; *KCS*, July 15, B 7:1 and July 17, B1:1, 2005; *New York Times*, July 19, 1:1, 2005; and a conversation with Joe Amrine all contributed to my account of Larry Griffin's wrongful execution.

13. *Lethal Injection, 1989–2005*

1. *Gregg* v. *Georgia*, 428 U.S. 153, 232 (1976).

2. *Callins* v. *Collins*, 510 U.S. 1141, 1145–46 (1994).

3. These figures are derived from the Death Penalty Information Center website at http:www,deathpenalty-info.org.

4. *Sourcebook of Criminal Justice Statistics Online*, 288, www.albany.edu/sourcebook.

5. *Olmstead* v. *U.S.*, 277 U.S. 438, 485 (1928).

6. *Godfrey* v. *Georgia*, 446 U.S. 420 (1980).

7. Mo. Rev. Stat. 565.030, 565.032, and 565.035.

8. Mo. Rev. Stat. 546.720.

9. Conversation with Joe Amrine.

10. *KCT*, Jan. 6, 1989, 1:1.

11. Separation conversations with Frederick Lashley and Joe Amrine.

12. http://www.deathpenaltyinfo.org.

13. Google "MO executions, 1989–2005."

14. Cathleen Burnett, *Justice Denied*, 205.

15. *State* v. *Ramsey*, 864 SW2d 320, 327 (1993).

16. *State* v. *Powell*, 798 SW2d 709 (1990).

17. *State* v. *Griffin-El*, 756 SW2d 475 (1988).

18. *State* v. *Laws*, 699 SW2d 102 (1985) and *State* v. *Gilmore*, 661 SW2d 519 (1983).

19. *State* v. *Hunter*, 840 SW2d 850 (1992) and *State* v. *Ervin*, 835 SW2d 905 (1992).

20. John Fougere, Public Information Officer, MO Dept. of Corrections.

21. *State* v. *Robert Murray*, 744 SW2d 762 (1988).

22. Burnett, *Justice Denied*, 209.

23. *State* v. *Walls*, 744 SW2d 791 (1988) and Burnett, *Justice Denied*, 216.

24. *State* v. *Kilgore*, 771 SW2d 57 (1989).

25. *State* v. *Roll*, 942 SW2d 370 (1997).

26. *State* v. *Johns*, 679 SW2d 253 (1984).

27. *State* v. *Hall*, 955 SW2d 198 (1997).

28. *State* v. *Schneider*, 736 SW2d 392, 405–06 (1987).

29. *State* v. *Blair*, 638 SW2d 739 (1982).

30. *State* v. *Bannister*, 680 SW2d 141 (1984).

31. *State* v. *Basile*, 942 SW2d 342 (1997).

32. John Fougere, Public Information Officer, made an extensive search of Missouri prison records regarding all the inmates located in any of the state's correctional centers who were co-defendants of men who were executed by lethal injection. He could not locate Richard McCormick. The *KCS* reported that "Jackson was never convicted of raping Allen or any role in her murder," July 14, 1993, C5:2.

33. *State* v. *Nave*, 694 SW2d 729 (1985).

34. *State* v. *Kenley*, 693 SW2d 79 (1985).

35. *State* v. *Johnson*, 968 SW2d 123 (1998).

36. *State* v. *Sweet*, 796 SW2d 607 (1990).

37. *State* v. *Mallett*, 732 SW2d 527 (1987).

38. *State* v. *Sidebottom*, 753 SW2d 915 (1988).

39. *State* v. *Jones*, 979 SW2d 171 (1998).

40. *State* v. *Sloan*, 756 SW2d 503 (1988).

41. *State* v. *Mercer*, 618 SW2d 1 (1981).

42. *State* v. *Kreutzer*, 928 SW2d 854 (1996).

43. *State* v. *Lingar*, 726 SW2d 728 (1987).

44. Information courtesy of John Fougere.

45. *State* v. *Davis*, 814 SW2d 593 (1991).

46. *State* v. *Johnson*, 957 SW2d 734 (1997).

47. *State* v. *Bolder*, 635 SW2d 673, 679 (1982).

48. *State* v. *Guinam*, 665 SW2d 325 (1984).

49. *State* v. *Zeitvogel*, 707 SW2d 365, 366 (1980).

50. Burnett, *Justice Denied*, 78–86 and 211.

51. *State* v. *Smith*, 756 SW2d 493 (1988).

52. *New York Times*, Oct. 7, 1993, A16:1.

53. *State* v. *O'Neal*, 718 SW2d 498 (1986).

54. *State* v. *Smith*, 781 SW2d 761 (1990).

55. *State* v. *Taylor*, 134 SW3d 21 (2004).

56. *State* v. *Parkus*, 753 SW2d 881, 890–91 (1988).

57. *Parkus* v. *Delo*, 33 F3d 933, 935 (8 Cir.: 1994).

58. *State* v. *Roberts*, 709 SW2d 857. 860 (1986).

Bibliography

Books

Alotta, Robert I. *Civil War Justice: Union Army Executions under Lincoln.* Shippensburg, PA: White Mane Publishing Co., 1989.

Atkeson, William O. *History of Bates County, Missouri.* Topeka, KS: Cleveland Historical Publishing Co., 1918.

Bay, W.V.N. *Reminiscences of the Bench and Bar of Missouri.* St. Louis: F.H. Thomas and Co., 1878.

Binet, Alfred, and T.H. Simon. *Mentally Defective Children.* London: Edward Arnold, 1914.

Blackstone, William. *Commentaries on the Laws of England: A Facsimile of the First Edition of 1765–1769.* Vol. 4. Chicago: University of Chicago Press, 1979.

Bowers, William J. *Legal Homicide: Death as Punishment in America, 1864–1982.* Boston: Northeastern University Press, 1984.

Burnett, Cathleen. *Justice Denied: Clemency Appeals in Death Penalty Cases.* Boston: Northeastern University Press, 2002.

Burt, Olive Wooley, ed. *American Murder Ballads and Their Stories.* New York: Oxford University Press, 1958.

Catholic Encyclopedia, ed. Charles G. Herbermann et al. Vol. 12. New York: Appleton Publishing Co., 1911.

Catterall, Helen, ed. *Judicial Cases Concerning American Slavery and the Negro.* 5 vols. New York: Octagon Books, 1968.

Conard, Howard L., and William Hyde, eds. *Encyclopedia of the History of St. Louis.* 4 vols. St. Louis: Southern Historical Co., 1899.

Cramer, Rose Fulton. *Wayne County, Missouri.* Cape Girardeau: Ramfre Press, 1972.

Cuneo, Michael. *Almost Midnight: An American Story of Murder and Redemption.* New York: Broadway Books, 2004.

Curry, J.E. *A Reminiscent History of Douglas County, Missouri.* Ava: Douglas County Herald, 1957.

Deakin, James. *A Grave for Bobby: The Greenlease Slaying.* New York: William Morrow and Co., 1990.

Deem, David B. *A History of Butler County, Missouri.* N.p.: 1925.

Diagnostic and Statistical Manual of Mental Disorders, 4th ed. Washington, D.C.: American Psychiatric Association, 2000.

Dictionary of Missouri Biography, eds. Christensen, Lawrence O., William E. Foley, Gary R. Kremer, and Kenneth H. Winn. Columbia: University of Missouri Press, 1999.

Duke, Thomas. *Celebrated Criminal Cases of America.* San Francisco: James H. Barry Co., 1910.

Ekberg, Carl J. *Colonial Ste. Genevieve.* Gerald, MO: Patrice Press, 1985.

Eliot, William G. *The Story of Archer Alexander: From Slavery to Freedom.* Boston: Cupples, Upham & Co., 1885; Rpt. Westport, Ct: Negro Universities Press, 1970.

Encyclopedia of the American Civil War, David Stephen Heidler, ed. New York: W.W. Norton, 2002.

Espy, M Watt, and John Ortiz Smykla. *Executions in the United States, 1608–1987: The Espy File.* Ann Arbor: Inter-university Consortium for Political and Social Research, 1987.

Dyer, Frederick H. *A Compendium of the War of the Rebellion.* Broadfoot Publishing Co., 1908, rpt. n.p., 1994.

Fairman, Charles. *The Law of Martial Rule.* Chicago: Callaghan, 1943.

Fellman, Michael. *Inside War: The Guerrilla Conflict in Missouri during the American Civil War.* New York: Oxford University Press, 1990.

Foley, William E. *The Genesis of Missouri: From*

Wilderness Outpost to Statehood. Columbia: University of Missouri Press, 1989.

_____. *Wilderness Journey: The Life of William Clark.* Columbia: University of Missouri Press, 2004.

Ford, James E. *History of Moniteau County, Missouri.* California, MO: Marvin H. Crawford, 1936.

Fraser, Antonia. *Maria Antoinette: The Journey.* New York: Doubleday, 2001.

Frazier, Harriet C. *Runaway and Freed Missouri Slaves and Those Who Helped Them.* Jefferson, NC: McFarland & Co., 2004.

_____. *Slavery and Crime in Missouri, 1773–1865.* Jefferson, NC: McFarland & Co., 2001.

General History of Macon County, Missouri. Chicago: H. Taylor, 1910.

Gentry, North Todd. *The Bench and Bar of Boone County, Missouri.* Columbia: Published by the author, 1916.

Gilmore, Robert K. *Ozark Baptizings, Hangings, and Other Diversions: Theatrical Folkways of Rural Missouri, 1885–1910.* Norman: University of Oklahoma Press, 1984.

Greene, Lorenzo J., Gary R. Kremer, and Anthony Holland, *Missouri's Black Heritage.* St. Louis: Forum Press, 1980.

Hahn, Mary. *Bits of History.* Cape Girardeau: Ramfre Press, 1972.

Hartman, Mary, and Elmo Ingenthron. *Bald Knobbers: Vigilantes on the Ozarks Frontier.* Gretna, MO: Pelican, 1989.

Hatcher, Richard W. III, and William Garrett Piston. *Kansans at Wilson's Creek: Soldiers' Letters from the Campaign for Southwest Missouri.* Springfield, MO: Wilson's Creek National Battlefield Foundation, 1993.

Hawley, Janet, compiler. *The Murder of Dr. Talbott.* Maryville, MO: Accent Printing, n.d.

_____, compiler. *The Trials of Hez Rasco.* Barnard, MO: circa 1991.

Hearn, Daniel. *Legal Executions in New England, 1623–1960.* Jefferson, N.C.: McFarland & Co., 1999.

_____. *Legal Executions in New York State, 1639–1963.* Jefferson, N.C.: McFarland & Co., 1997.

Heidler, David S., and Jeanne T. Heidler, eds. *Encyclopedia of the American Civil War.* Vol. 3. Santa Barbara, CA: ABC-CIIO, 2000.

Higham, John. *Strangers in the Land: Patterns of American Nativism, 1860–1925.* New Brunswick: Rutgers University Press, 1994.

History of Andrew and De Kalb Counties Missouri. Chicago: Goodspeed Publishing Co., 1888.

History of Audrain County, Missouri. St. Louis: National Historical Co. 1884.

History of Clay and Platte Counties, Missouri. St. Louis: National Historical Co., 1885.

History of Clinton County, Missouri. St. Joseph: National Historical Co., 1881.

History of Cole, Moniteau, Morgan, Benton, Miller, Maries and Osage Counties, Missouri. Chicago: Goodspeed, 1889, rpt. Henry County Historical Society, Clinton, MO, 1968.

History of Franklin, Jefferson, Washington, Crawford, and Gasconade Counties, Missouri. Chicago: Goodspeed, 1888.

History of Greene County, Missouri. St. Louis: Western Historical Co., 1883.

History of Henry and St. Clair Counties, Missouri. St. Joseph, MO: National Historical Co., 1883.

History of Hickory, Polk, Cedar, Dade and Barton Counties, Missouri. Chicago: Goodspeed Publishing Co. 1889.

History of Holt and Atchison Counties, Missouri. St, Joseph: National Historical Co., 1882.

History of Howard and Chariton Counties, Missouri. St. Louis: National Historical Co., 1883.

History of Howard and Cooper Counties, Missouri. St. Louis: National Historical Co., 1883.

History of Jackson County, Missouri. 1881; rpt. Cape Girardeau: Ramfre Press, 1966.

History of Laclede, Camden, Dallas, Webster, Wright, Texas, Pulaski, Phelps and Dent Counties. Chicago: Goodspeed Publishing Co. 1889.

History of Lewis, Clark, Knox, and Scotland Counties, Missouri. Chicago: Goodspeed Publishing Co., 1887.

History of Marion County, Missouri. St. Louis: E.F. Perkins, 1884.

History of Monroe and Shelby Counties, Missouri. St. Louis: National Historical Co., 1884.

History of Montgomery County, Missouri. St. Louis: National Historical Co., 1885.

History of Newton, Lawrence, Barry and McDonald Counties, Missouri. Chicago: Goodspeed Publishing Co., 1888.

History of Nodaway County, Missouri. St. Joseph: National Historical Co. 1882.

History of Randolph and Macon Counties. St. Louis: National Historical Co., 1884.

History of Saline County, Missouri. St. Louis: Missouri Historical Co., 1881.

History of St. Charles, Montgomery and Warren Counties, Missouri. St. Louis: National Historical Co., 1885.

History of Southeast Missouri. Chicago: Goodspeed Publishing Co. 1888.

History of Vernon County. Vol. 1. Chicago: C.F. Cooper & Co., 1911.

Horan, James D. *The Pinkertons: The Detective Dynasty That Made History.* New York: Crown Publishers, 1967.

Houck, Louis. *A History of Missouri.* 3 vols. Chicago: R.R. Donnelley, 1908.

_____, ed. *The Spanish Regime in Missouri*. 2 vols. Chicago: R.R. Donnelley & Sons, 1909.

Howard, Goldena Roland. *Ralls County Missouri*. N.p., 1980.

Hyde, William, and Howard L. Conard, eds. *Encyclopedia of the History of St. Louis*. 6 vols. St. Louis: Southern History Co., 1899.

Johnson, William F. *History of Cooper County, Missouri*. Topeka, KS: Historical Publishing Co. 1919.

Kerr, Derek N. *Petty Felony, Slave Defiance, and Frontier Villainy; Crime and Criminal Justice in Spanish Louisiana, 1770–1803*. New York: Garland, 1993.

Kolchin, Peter. *American Slavery: 1619–1877*. New York: Hill and Wang, 1993.

Lamers, William M. *The Edge of Glory: A Biography of General William S. Rosecrans, U.S.A.* New York: Harcourt, Brace & World, 1961.

Lee, Harper. *To Kill a Mockingbird*. New York: HarperCollins, 1993.

Liebman, James, Jeffrey Faggan, and Valerie West. *A Broken System: Error Rates in Capital Cases, 1973–1995*. New York: Columbia University Press, 2000.

Life, Trial and Conviction of Joe Jump and John Smith, rpt., Gallatin: *Gallatin Democrat*, n.d.

Lincoln, Abraham, Collected Works of, ed. Roy P. Basler. Vol. 5. New Brunswick: Rutgers University Press, 1953.

March, David. *History of Missouri*. 4 vols. New York: Lewis Historical Publishing Co., 1967.

Mayerberg, Samuel S. *Chronicle of An American Crusader*. New York: Bloch Publishing Co., 1944.

McCullough, *Truman*. New York: Simon & Schuster, 1992.

McGovern, James R. *Anatomy of a Lynching: The Killing of Claude Neal*. Baton Rouge: Louisiana State University Press, 1982.

McLaurin, Melton. *Celia, a Slave*. Athens: University of Georgia Press, 1991.

Melton, Emory. *Hanged By the Neck Until Dead*. Cassville, MO: Litho Printers, 1985.

Moulton, Gary, ed. The Journals of the Lewis and Clark Expedition, vol. 8. Lincoln: University of Nebraska Press, 1993.

Mudd, Joseph A. *With Porter in North Missouri*. Washington, D.C.: National Publishing Co., 1909. Rpt. Press of Camp Pope Bookshop, Iowa City, IA, 1992.

Nichols, Bruce. *Guerrilla Warfare in Civil War Missouri, 1862*. Jefferson, NC: McFarland & Co., 2004.

Parrish, I.S. *Military Veterans PTSD Reference Manual*. Bryn Mawr, PA: Buy Books on the Web. com, 1999.

Pastoral Care of the Sick. Chicago: Liturgy Training Publications, 1986.

Peterson, Norma L. *Freedom and Franchise: The Po-litical Career of B. Gratz Brown*. Columbia: University of Missouri Press, 1965.

Prucha, Francis Paul. *Broadax and Bayonet: The Role of the United States Army in the Development of the Northwest, 1815–1860*. Lincoln: University of Nebraska Press, 1967.

_____. *The Great Father: The United States Government and the American Indians*, abridged ed. Lincoln: University of Nebraska Press, 1986.

Reddig, William. *Tom's Town: Kansas City and the Pendergast Legend*. Columbia: University of Missouri Press, 1986.

Rutt, Chris L., ed. *History of Buchanan County and the City of St. Joseph*. Chicago: Biographical, 1904.

Sanborn. Margaret. *Mark Twain: The Bachelor Years*. New York: Doubleday, 1990.

Scharf, J. Thomas. *History of Saint Louis City and County*. 2 vols. Philadelphia: Louis H. Everts, 1883.

Shoemaker, Floyd. *Missouri's Struggle for Statehood, 1804–1821*. New York: Russell & Russell, 1916, reissued 1969.

Simpson, Lewis A.W. *Oregon County's Three Flags*. Thayer, Missouri: Thayer News, 1971.

Sobel, Robert, and John Raimo, eds. *Biographical Directory of the Governors of the United States, 1789–1978*. Vol. 2. Westport, CT: Meckler Books, 1978.

Sourcebook of Criminal Justice Statistics Online. http:///www.albany.edu/sourcebook.

Stanley, Lois, George F. Wilson, Maryhelen Wilson. *Death Records from the Missouri Newspapers: The Civil War Years, January 1861–December 1865*. Greenville, SC: Southern Historical Press, 1990.

Streib, Victor. *The Death Penalty for Juveniles*. Bloomington: Indiana University Press, 1987.

Switzler, W.F. *History of Missouri*. St. Louis: C.R. Barnes, 1881.

Thompson, George. *Prison Life and Reflections or A Narrative of the Arrest, Trial, Conviction, Imprisonment, Treatment, Observations, Reflections and Deliverance of Work, Burr and Thompson who Suffered an Unjust and Cruel Punishment in Missouri Penitentiary for Attempting to Aid Some Slaves to Liberty*. Antioch, Ohio: James M. Fitch, printer, 1847.

Trexler, Harrison. *Slavery in Missouri, 1804–1865*. Baltimore: Johns Hopkins Press, 1914.

Triplett, Frank. *The Life, Times, and Treacherous Death of Jesse James*. Chicago: Swallow Press, 1970.

Trombley, Stephen. *The Execution Protocol*. New York: Crown Publishers, 1992.

Twentieth Century History of Carroll County, Missouri. Vol. 1. Indianapolis: B.F. Bowen & Co., 1911.

Unger, Robert. *The Union Station Massacre: The Original Sin of J. Edgar Hoover's FBI.* Kansas City: Andrews McMeel Universal Co., 1997.

United States Post Office Dept. *Street Directory of the Principal Cities of the United States.* Washington, D.C.: Postmaster General, 1908, Rpt. Gale Research Co., 1973.

Violette, E. M. *History of Adair County.* N.p: Denslow History Co., 1911.

Wallis, Michael. *The Life and Times of Charles Arthur Floyd.* New York: St. Martin's Press, 1992.

Way, Fredick Jr., compiler. *Way's Packet Directory, 1848–1994.* Athens, Ohio: Ohio University Press, 1994.

Young, William. *Young's History of Lafayette County, Missouri.* Indianapolis: B.F. Brown and Co., 1910.

Articles

Ball, Larry D. "Federal Justice on the Santa Fe Trail: The Murder of Antonio Jose Chavez." *Missouri Historical Review.* 81 (1987) 1–17.

Crompton, Louis. "Homosexuals and the Death Penalty in Colonial America." *J. of Homosexuality* 1 (1976) 277–93.

Da Costa, J. Mendez. "On Irritable Heart." *American J. of the Medical Sciences.* No. 71 (Jan. 1871), 2–53.

Foley, William E. "Different Notions of Justice: The Case of the 1808 St. Louis Murder Trials." *Gateway Heritage* 9 (Winter 1988–1989) 2–13.

Frazier, Harriet C. "The Execution of Juveniles in Missouri." *J. of the Missouri Bar.* 46 (Dec. 1990): 633–642 and 47 (Jan.-Feb. 1991): 42–52.

Gilbert, Arthur N. "Doctor, Patient, and Onanist Diseases in the Nineteenth Century." *J. of History and Medicine and Allied Sciences* 30 (July 1975) 217–234.

Humphrey, Jacqueline Brelsford Baker. "The 1802 Murder of David Trotter in Missouri." *Missouri State Genealogical Association Journal* 13 (Fall 1993): 198–205.

Kremer, Gary. "Strangers to Domestic Virtues: Nineteenth-Century Women in the Missouri Prison." *Missouri Historical Review* 89 (April 1990): 293–310.

Seemater, Mary E. "Trials and Confessions: Race and Justice in Antebellum St. Louis." *Gateway Heritage* 12 (Fall 1991):36–47.

Snyder, Joe. "The Hanging of Joe Jump," *County Seat Paper: A glimpse into the life and times of one small town, Gallatin, Missouri.* Gallatin: Joe Snyder, n.d., review James J. Fisher, *Kansas City Star*, July 20, 1992: 135–44.

Twain, Mark. "The Private History of a Campaign that Failed," *The Century: A Popular Quarterly* 31 (Dec. 1885): 193–204.

Videos

Unreasonable Doubt: The Joe Amrine Case (2002).

Dissertations

Duffner, Robert W. "Slavery in Missouri River Counties, 1820–1865," Ph.d. diss., University of Missouri–Columbia, 1974.

Newspapers

Advertiser Courier (Hermann), *American Republic* (Poplar Bluff), *Arcadia Valley Enterprise* (Ironton), *Benton Record, Bolivar Free Press, Boonville Daily News, Boonville Observer, Boonville Republican, Boonville Weekly Eagle, Bowling Green Times, Brunswicker* (Brunswick), *California News, Call* (Kansas City), *Carthage Press, Charleston Enterprise-Courier, Charleston Republican, Chicago-Tribune, Citizen Democrat* (Poplar Bluff), *Clark County Courier* (Kahoka), *Clarksville Piker, Clinton Eye, Columbia Missourian, Constitution* (Atlanta), *Current Wave* (Eminence), *Democrat* (St. Louis), *Daily Capital-News* (Jefferson City), *Daily Tribune* (Columbia), *Democratic Lever* (Plattsburg), *Dispatch* (Commerce), *Dispatch* (St. Louis), *Douglas County Herald* (Ava), *Dunklin Democrat* (Kennett), *Enquirer* (St. Louis), *Evening Press* (Carthage), *Evening Press* (Farmington), *Fair Play* (Ste. Genevieve), *Franklin County Tribune* (Union), *Fulton Daily Sun-Gazette, Gallatin Democrat, Globe-Democrat* (St. Louis), *Fountain and Journal* (Mt. Vernon), *Hannibal Courier-Post, Herman Advertiser, Herald* (Quincy, IL), *Houston Herald, Intelligencer* (Franklin), *Intelligencer* (Mexico), *Jefferson City Post-Tribune, Jefferson County Record* (Hillsboro), *Jeffersonian* (Jefferson City), *Jefferson Republican* (Jefferson City), *Johnson County Star* (Warrensburg), *Joplin Daily Herald, Joplin Standard, Joplin Globe, Joplin Herald, Kahoka Weekly Review, Kansas City Journal, Kansas City Journal-Post, Kansas City Mail, Kansas City Post, Kansas City Times, Kansas City Star, Kansas City World, Knob Noster Gem, Lamar Democrat, Lawrence Chieftain* (Mt. Vernon), *Lawrence Republican* (Lawrence, KS), *Leader-Democrat* (Springfield), *Leavenworth Times* (Leavenworth, KS), *Lexington News, Lexington News Supplement, Liberator* (Boston), *Liberty Tribune, Linn County News* (Linneus), *Louisiana Gazette* (St. Louis), *Louisiana Journal, Mercury* (Paris), *Maryville Republican, Maryville Tribune, Missouri Courier* (Hannibal), *Missouri Democrat* (Boonville), *Missouri Democrat* (St. Louis), *Missouri Gazette* (St. Louis), *Missouri Herald*

(Jackson), *Missouri Intelligencer* (Columbia and Fayette), *Missouri Republican* (St. Louis), *Missouri Statesman* (Columbia), *Missouri Telegraph* (Fulton), *Missourian* (St. Charles), *Monitor* (Fayette), *Montgomery Standard* (Montgomery City), *Morning Herald* (St. Joseph), *News and Tribune* (Jefferson City), *New York Times*, *Nodaway Democrat* (Maryville), *Northwest Conservator* (Richmond) *Palmyra Spectator, Perryville Union, Pike County News* (Louisiana), *Pineville Democrat, Pineville News, Pitch* (Kansas City), *Poplar Bluff Citizen, Poplar Bluff Republican, Post-Tribune* (Jefferson City), *Pulaski County Democrat* (Waynesville), *Quincy Daily Democrat, Ralls County Record* (New London), *Ralls County Times* (New London), *Randolph Citizen* (Huntsville), *Republic* (St. Louis), *St. Charles Banner-News, St. Charles Cosmos-Monitor, St. Joseph Gazette, St. Joseph Herald, St. Joseph News-Press, St. Joseph Weekly News, St. Louis Argus, St. Louis Beacon, St. Louis Daily Globe, St. Louis Globe-Democrat, St. Louis Post-Dispatch, Saline County Progress* (Marshall), *Salt River Journal* (Bowling Green), *Sentinel* (Iberia), *Southeastern Missourian* (New Madrid), *Springfield Express, Springfield Leader and Press, Springfield Leader, Springfield Patriot-Advertiser, Southeast Missourian* (Cape Girardeau), *Standard-Herald* (Warrensburg), *Stone County News-Oracle* (Galena), *Sun* (Baltimore), *Taraboro Press* (Taraboro, NC), *Topeka State Journal* (Topeka, KS), *Trenton Daily Evening Republican, Troy Free Press, Warrensburg Standard, Washington County Journal* (Potosi), *Watchman Advocate* (St. Louis), *Weekly Gazette* (Versailles), *Weekly Herald* (St. Joseph), *Weekly Mercury* (Paris), *Weekly Patriot* (Springfield), *Weekly Record* (New Madrid), *Weekly Union* (Lexington), *Whig* (Palmyra) *Willow Springs News, Wright County Republican* (Hartville).

Government Documents

Bureau of Vital Records, Missouri Dept. of Health, multiple death certificates of the executed.

Blunt, Roy D., *Historical Listing of the Missouri Legislature.* Jefferson City: Missouri State Archives, 1998.

List of Pardons, Commutations and Reprieves Granted by Joseph W. McClurg, Governor from ... 1869, to ... 1870.

Official Manuals, State of Missouri, 1999–2000–2003–2004. Jefferson City: Office of Secretary of State.

U.S. Post Office Dept. *Street Directory of the Principal Cities of the United States.* Washington, DC: The Postmaster General, 1908; Rpt. Detroit: Gale Research Co., 1973.

U.S. Dept. of Commerce. *Negro Population, 1790–1915.* Washington, D.C.: Government Printing Office, 1915.

Military Documents, Handwritten

Proceedings of U.S. Army Courts-martial and Military commissions of Union soldiers executed by U.S. Military Authorities, 1861–1866, Family History Center, Church of Jesus Christ of the Latter Day Saints, Independence, MO.

Service Records: Missouri Volunteers in the Civil War.

Trial Transcripts

Armstrong, State v., Mo. State Archives.

Holman, State v., Mo. State Archives.

Lashley, State v., courtesy of Robert Duncan, Esq.

Mabry, State v., Boonville Historical Society.

Archival Material

Joint Collection.
  Hyde Collection.
  Park, Guy B. Papers
Missouri Historical Society, St. Louis, MO.
  Chouteau, Pierre, Letterbook.
  Clements, Mary C. Collection.
  Kennery, James Collection.
  Lucas, John B.C. Collection.
  St. Louis Courthouse Papers.
  Tiffany Collection.
Missouri State Archives, Jefferson City, MO
  General Assembly Bills
  Governor's Veto
  Missouri State Penitentiary, Register of Inmates, 1836–1965.
  Pardon Papers, 1849–1961
Missouri State Historical Society, Columbia, MO.
  Vertical File, Governors' Commutations and Pardons.
Western Missouri Manuscript Collection, Columbia, MO.
  Ste. Genevieve District and County Court Records, Collection 3636

Statutory Law

Code Noir, 1724 in John B. Dillon, *History of Indiana.* Indianapolis: Bingham & Doughty, 1859, 31–43.

Laws of Northwest Territory (1788–1800), ed. Theodore Calvin Pease. Illinois State Historical Library. Springfield, Illinois, 1925.

Missouri, Laws of (1804–2005).

[Spanish Colonial Law] O'Reilly, Don Alejandro. "Ordinances and Instructions," trans. Gustavus Schmidt. 1 *Louisiana Law J.* (Aug. 1841), 1–65.

United States, Statutes at Large (1790–1990).

Court Records

Handwritten and typed court records: Missouri's Districts/Counties

BUTLER
Johnson, Wilburn, State v., Certified copy of Circuit Court Record, Nov. 14, 1940

CALLAWAY
Celia, State v. (1855), *Mat, State* v. (1855), *Susan, State* v. (1844).

CAPE GIRARDEAU
Byrd, Amos, State v. (1843).

CLAY
Annice, a Slave, State v. (1828).
Wilkins, State v. Case NO. CR 199–1686, May 20, 1999.

CRAWFORD
Mary, a Slave, State v. (1837).

LAFAYETTE
Andrews, Mary, alias Mary Trumberg, State v., Circuit Court Records, April 30, 1834.

MARION
Ben, a Slave, State v. (1849–50).

MORGAN
Adams, State v., Docket Book, April 21, 1883.

NEW MADRID
Jones, State v. Sheriff's return of death warrant, July 23, 1938.

STE. GENEVIEVE
Inquest: *Tacoua, Slave Belonging to Jean Baptiste Datchurut* (1783).

ST. LOUIS
Elijah, U.S. v. (1818); *Leblond, U.S.* v. (1813); *Long, U.S.* v. (1809);

Printed court records are in the Chapter Notes.

Index

Regardless of the locale of the execution, districts/counties are those of the conviction of the crime. Name(s) before the slash are perpetrators or alleged perpetrators, those following it victims or alleged victims. A "v" following names = change of venue to the county; "x" = an execution for murder; "xk" = an execution for kidnapping; "xr" = an execution for rape, forcible or statutory; "c" = clemency, and "r" = a reversal of death sentence.